Journeys Beyond the Frontier:

A Rebellious Guide to Psychosis and Other Extraordinary Experiences

Mark Ragins, MD

Based on a career's worth of true stories

Copyright © 2021 Mark Ragins, MD
All rights reserved.

Dedicated to all the people who came together to create,
sustain, and support the Village, giving me so much,
so that I can now give this book to all of you.

and

to the memories of Robbyn Panitch and Lesley Bradford

Table of Contents

Part I: Introduction: Taking a New Approach 1

    Chapter 1: Why do we need a guidebook? 2

    Chapter 2: Introducing your guide 25

    Chapter 3: What am I rebelling against? 49

    Chapter 4: Preparing for our journeys: Understanding psychosis 86

Part II: The Guide: Eight Interrelated Journeys 109

    Chapter 5: Overview of the journeys 111

    Chapter 6: Journey 1: Loss and grief 120

    Chapter 7: Journey 2: Psychotic reactions 140

    Chapter 8: Journey 3:
            Difficulties in making sense of the world 160

    Chapter 9: Journey 4: Childhood trauma 218

    Chapter 10: Journey 5: Losing balance 246

    Chapter 11: Journey 6: Drugs and alcohol 323

    Chapter 12: Journey 7: Psychiatric illnesses 384

    Chapter 13: Journey 8: Brain damage
             and other neurological and medical conditions 443

    Chapter 14: Putting together your journey 473

Part III: Creating Your Own Journey of Recovery 486

    Chapter 15: What we do matters—
             Three intertwined dimensions of recovery 487

    Chapter 16: Practical travel tips—
             Facing today's challenges 557

    Chapter 17: Bon voyage 621

Part I:

Introduction:

Taking a New Approach

Chapter 1

Why do we need a guidebook?

It was a bright, cool, crisp morning in Montana. I was sitting in a mental health clubhouse ready to begin a workshop on recovery for people with mental illnesses. The audience included a large group of the clubhouse's members, the rehabilitation staff, several who had mental illnesses, a few family members, and community members including a local judge who had recently seen more people with mental illnesses in her courtroom.

As I looked around the eager group, not knowing who was who, I began my presentation, "I know it's hard to take that first step to talk to a mental health professional, especially a psychiatrist. You face a lot of stigma and you have fears. I want you to remember that first time you reached out for help. How many of you thought it was going to work out more or less the way it does in movies, or on TV, or in commercials? For instance, you'd talk to someone, answer some questions, and probably get some therapy and some pills, and in a matter of months, you'd be treated successfully and back to your normal self."

All the clients' hands went up.

"And for how many of you is that about how it worked out?"

All the hands went down.

"And how long did it take you to figure out that it wasn't going to work that way?"

Now, they hesitated. They looked at each other. After a few moments, a young man seated on the side said, "I guess about 2 or 3 years." Heads nodded, and a murmur of agreement spread around the room.

"And then, what did you do?"

Now, the answers flowed from the clubhouse members.

"I asked around to see how other people coped with hearing voices."

"I learned how to hold a job even with my voices."

"I learned how to wait until it's been going good to tell a date that I have a mental illness." Everyone laughed a little.

"I got educated about mental illness and pills, so I could help myself."

"I helped my family learn about my illness, so they wouldn't be so frightened, and they could help me."

"I stopped waiting for the doctor to fix me and started doing things even though I wasn't back to myself, and I may never be."

"I found other people who could understand what I'm going through, so I don't have to go through this alone."

"I worked on getting over being angry for having this, so I could go on with my life."

"I learned how to pull out of it when a relapse hit me."

They stopped and looked over to me to see how I'd react to their answers.

I nodded in approval and said, "I think it's a shame you had to wait 2 or 3 years to start doing the things that really work to recover. Let's see if we can learn some more things from each other today."

If you're reading this book, the odds are that something very strange has happened to you or someone you care about, or maybe you are like me, you want to help people who are going through extraordinary experiences.

Maybe you're hearing voices talking to you or have become aware that there are people who are trying to kill you or maybe someone is communicating special information just to you or you're being monitored by an implant. Maybe those ideas sound crazy to you. They would to most people. They're certainly beyond the frontier of normal experience. But chances are, if they're happening to you, you know you're not going crazy. Well, you're pretty sure …. It would be nice to find someone with whom you can check it out. But what if they lock you up in a mental hospital or mess you up with a lot of medications? Isn't that what's happening to people who go too far? Maybe it would be better to wait and see what happens next. Maybe you can figure it out yourself. The average time in the United States between when people start experiencing something strange and when they go for help is 2 years. A lot can happen in 2 years. A life can fall apart

If you've looked around for help from mental health professionals or books or the Internet, it's likely you've found some version of the prevailing medical model. You've learned that psychiatrists diagnose many strange experiences as psychosis or schizophrenia, both of which are medical conditions. They're biological illnesses of the brain, similar to illnesses in other parts of your body. It's nothing to be ashamed of. It's no one's fault. Psychosis and schizophrenia are caused by genetics and imbalances in the chemicals that nerve cells use to send messages to each other. Medications can correct those underlying imbalances, so that the brain will function more or less normally again—if you're lucky and if you do what the psychiatrists tell you to do. All in all, it's a rather reassuring, easy-to-understand explanation and model. You haven't really gone too far to be saved.

But it just doesn't seem to fit what you're going through. How could a vision of God be caused by a chemical imbalance? How do you know it's not really God? How could being able to see the true multidimensional nature of the universe, or knowing when it's going to end, be the product of an ill brain?

> *When I was in my residency, I met a Hispanic woman in her 50s who was in the medical ward for appendicitis. The next morning, after her appendix had been removed, her*

daughter, looking very stylish, stopped to talk with me. She said, "I heard you're a psychiatry resident."

Warily, I looked up, "Yeah."

"Did my mom tell you the story of how she learned to read and write?"

"No, she didn't."

"When she was 18, illiterate, living in a small village in Mexico, her new husband, my dad, decided to leave for Los Angeles to look for work. He told her that he'd send for her when he got settled. She was heartbroken and prayed to Jesus for help. The roof of their hut opened up and a ray of beautiful blue light came through and lit up her face as she looked up. In that moment, she was given the ability to read and write, so she could send letters to her husband and be comforted. She eventually did join him here. She's always told the story that way and my older relatives in Mexico say that's what happened, but I'm not so sure. Ever since then, my mother has been very religious. She has a small alter to Jesus that she prays to daily and goes to church every week. She says that she talks with God. That's not normal, is it? Do you think that she has a mental illness and should be taking medication?"

I thought a moment and then replied, "Why would I want to give her some Haldol and find out if God stops talking to her when it's the most cherished thing about her life? What harm is this doing?"

A few months later, I went to the burn ward to meet another woman. I had to wear a mask and gown to see her because she had burn wounds all over her body that could get infected. The nurse was changing her bandages, and although she was given heavy pain medications, she was crying out in agony. It was too much for me to take, so I came back later on when they were finished.

She told me that for several years, she had been taking medications for hearing voices, and that they'd quieted the voices down. Her boyfriend didn't think she needed the medications and wanted her to smoke marijuana with him instead to "mellow out." He told her that the pills would rot her brain. When she stopped the pills, the voices got louder. She got scared and started her medications again, but the voices would trick her into thinking that she'd taken them when she really hadn't. They kept messing with her and confusing her until they got stronger and stronger, and then they talked her into setting herself on fire.

Now, in the burn ward, they were tormenting her day and night by laughing at her and saying that she was so stupid that she'd let them talk her into making herself into a human BBQ. "Why don't you just kill yourself and get it over with? No one will want you now."

How can those be stories about a chemical imbalance? Wouldn't that be more like hearing static on a poorly tuned radio? When the TV malfunctions, it doesn't turn on new programs it makes up. And why would one person have a miraculous power and another one a tragic self-immolation as a result of the same illness? How does any of this make sense? And how did those sadistic voices figure out how to fool her into making them stronger? That sure sounds more like a demon, or an unconscious death wish, or a tormentor who put an audio transmitter in her head, than an illness "just like illnesses in other parts of your body." And the other story is even stranger. You can't learn how to read from a beam of light, can you? That doesn't sound like a mental illness either. What's really going on here? Nobody could be that crazy ... or that blessed, could they?

Those people are really out there. Don't you have any tests to figure this out, doc? Maybe a brain scan?

Nope. Nobody's ever seen a voice on a brain scan, God's or otherwise.

Frightened of traveling beyond the frontier to psychosis?

> About 20 years ago, at a mental health conference, I was sitting near the back of the room next to a friend, Judy, the director of our Antelope Valley mental health program. The speaker wasn't very good, so we were whispering to each other, catching up on gossip, and flirting a little. She was proud to have just published a small book of her poetry and asked me if I'd like to see it. I said, "Sure," and started flipping through the pages, slowing down to read a few of the poems.
>
> That's when I was stunned.
>
> These poems were talking about hearing voices, being suicidal, being locked in a mental hospital, tied down, and forcibly medicated. I didn't even know that Judy had a mental illness. My brain started to freeze up. How could the person I'd known as a colleague and friend, a likable leader, and a thoughtful, funny person have been psychotic? It just didn't fit.
>
> Slowly, my brain started to move again. Maybe it didn't matter. Maybe she was still Judy, the person I liked and admired. Maybe psychosis could fit in with everything else I knew about her. Gradually, I returned to whispering, gossiping, and flirting with her.
>
> It turned out that she had come into mental health as a psychotic, locked-up patient, but that she'd gradually recovered. She moved from initially being a group leader of a self-help client group all the way to becoming a program director. She'd gotten off medications entirely. She thinks that I'm more likely to become psychotic than she is at this point because she knows how to take care of herself and I don't. Maybe she's right. I'm working on it.

Remember those old medieval maps where there were large areas of "terra incognito," unknown territory? And remember how when they got to the edge of the known world, they'd write, "Here, there be monsters" and they'd draw a ferocious, imaginary, frightening creature? Mental illness, and especially psychosis, lives in a place beyond the comfortable, civilized, known world, a place beyond the frontier of normal. Here, there be people losing their minds, suicide, violence, hallucinations, paranoia, people who think they're Christ, and lost souls. In this book, we're going to be traveling well past anyone's comfort zone. That's why there are so much fear, stigma, and avoidance of people with mental illnesses. That's why we usually assume that anyone who's psychotic needs to be "put away" somewhere. After all, monsters need to be killed or at least locked up and tied down.

If we're really going to help people with mental illness, or even get to know them enough to live and work alongside them, we're going to have to do something about our fears. We're all frightened by mental illnesses and people with mental illnesses. People with illnesses are afraid of going crazy, being locked up, being drugged, never recovering, and losing their lives. Families are afraid that it's their fault, that they'll never have their loved one back, that they'll be shamed, and that their family won't make it through this. Staff are afraid that we'll be helpless, overwhelmed, and overstressed, and that we'll lose our license and be sued. Administrators are afraid of auditors, loss of funding, bad publicity, and their supervisors. Communities are afraid of crime, homelessness, and becoming overrun. *And we're all afraid of violence.*

I want more people to see people with mental illnesses through my eyes, instead of through eyes of fear and avoidance. I believe that the best way to fight stigma is by emotionally connecting with people enough to destroy our preconceptions and stereotypes. I've included lots of stories of people with psychosis and other extraordinary experiences in this book. Most of these stories won't turn out the way you expect them to. They take unexpected turns. That's because the stories of real people with mental illnesses don't match the stereotyped stories we've all heard before. I hope I describe their stories well enough for you to be touched by them. Most of all, I want you to be able to see them as real people you'd like to have in your life.

> *I remember going to Sacramento with a large group of mental health consumers, family members, and professionals for our annual Mental Health Advocacy Day to bring attention*

to mental health issues and lobby congressmen. I was unfamiliar with lobbying, so I was assigned to go with a group of four people with mental illnesses who were experienced and could show me the ropes. One of them was Gail, who you'll meet near the end of this book, a woman I was treating for schizophrenia and worked alongside in our Homeless Assistance Program where she was a street outreach worker. We went into the congresswoman's office, and the four of them each spoke for a few minutes with their well-prepared message. I don't remember exactly what our message was, probably something about needing more money. We're always asking the government for more money. Each of them used their own story of recovery as a compelling example of what money spent on mental health services can buy.

Then, it was my turn to speak, and I didn't know what to say. My companions were clearly better than me at this and had covered everything. It popped into my head to ask the congresswoman, "When you think about people with mental illnesses, people with schizophrenia, when you're considering laws and budgets about them, are these the kind of people you visualize?"

The congresswoman and I looked back at the group of well dressed, competent, persuasive people sitting next to me and reflected for a moment. Then, she turned to me and said, "No, I really don't. Are you sure they have mental illnesses?"

"Yes, I am. I'm even prescribing one of them antipsychotic medications right now."

She looked back over the group and nodded thoughtfully.

I got her.

"The next time you evaluate proposals for people with mental illnesses, please don't just think about the stereotypes—about homelessness, violence, and craziness—think about *these four people and how you can help others recover like them."*

But, doc, let's be real here. Doesn't being psychotic mean you're at risk of being violent? All those mass murderers we hear about have mental illnesses. Maybe you should have called this book dangerous journeys.

Tommy had been hearing voices and talking to himself ever since he was a teenager. Dropping out of school and using a lot of speed didn't help. His father was a retired policeman. Even though Tommy had never done anything violent, his dad "knew" that people like his son murdered people. He'd seen it on the streets. But he loved his son so much, he let him live with him anyway. He kept his guard up all the time and carried his gun with him everywhere he went, but every night when he went to sleep, he "knew" that Tommy might stab him in his sleep, and he'd be helpless to stop him.

The tension between them was terrible. Tommy sensed there was something wrong but didn't know what it was. The voices warned him there was something wrong with his dad. The voices kept talking about his dad's gun and how his dad was going to shoot him sooner or later. Finally, Tommy left and went to live with his grandmother, but she was scared of him, too, and wouldn't let him stay with her. He didn't want to go back to his dad. The voices told him not to go.

Tommy ended up homeless and came to our program. We helped him get a room in a group home where he's lived ever since. He still won't take medications, but he's never hurt anyone. He hasn't had any contact with his father or grandmother for years. Gradually, he's gotten duller emotionally and doesn't really interact with anyone. He's learned to stay alone. He eats lots of unhealthy Board and Care food to fill his emptiness; so, he's quite obese now. He

> *looks forward to spending whatever little money he gets on speed, so he can feel alive for a day.*
>
> *He lost the people in his life he loved the most because they were too frightened of him to share his life.*

"Explaining" mass murderers by saying that they all have serious mental illnesses may be reassuring for most people. At least that way, you can tell yourself that someone should've noticed the problem and taken care of them, locking them up, if necessary, to keep us all safe; the murders were a preventable tragedy if only mental health services were vastly improved. That may even be a way for mental health to get more government money, but it isn't reassuring to me because I know better. I know that mass murder doesn't make any more sense in the world of mental illness than it does anywhere else.

Biological psychiatrists are trying to fill in more of the map of our world to decrease the areas where monsters reside and stigma reigns. Their message of reassurance is simple: These monsters are all patients with brain illnesses that are increasingly treatable if you just turn them over to us. Don't worry about the emotional or family or social or cultural issues. Don't worry about suicide or violence. We can prevent all of it. Once their "monstrous" illnesses are medicated, they'll be normal again. We'll all be safe again. We can tame their monsters just like we do with cancer and polio and all the other frightening monstrous illnesses we've conquered.

That approach might be more reassuring if people trusted psychiatrists more than they do: Aren't we the same people who ran the snake pit institutions when we did have more power to lock up people? Didn't we line the patients up and give them shock therapy and lobotomies, sticking ice picks into their brains? (In today's world, there are fewer people with horrific institutionalization stories like that. Most of today's horrific stories consist of complaining that they were given six different diagnoses by six different psychiatrists, that they were drugged, or that they were prescribed three medications by a psychiatrist who only spent 10 minutes with them. They complain that the medications badly damaged them and were extremely difficult to get off.) Aren't we the same people who hand out pills like candy in assembly lines?

The approach might be more reassuring if people trusted pharmaceutical companies more: Aren't they the same people who are fined hundreds of millions of dollars for lying about their pills and hiding negative effects? Don't they put profits ahead of health, trying to get as many people hooked on their pills as possible? Don't they pay off Congress and the Food and Drug Administration? Aren't they the people who caused the opiate epidemic and are pushing the emerging prescription stimulant epidemic?

There's more than enough suspicion to go around: Aren't those for-profit hospitals and medical insurance companies throwing people into the street if they don't have money? Isn't there institutionalized racism in these systems, locking up and drugging Black adults and taking away their kids? Don't the police shoot and kill people with mental illnesses? Don't people with mental illnesses get beaten and mysteriously die in jails and prisons?

Should we really be surprised that people often don't come in voluntarily asking for our help once they've journeyed off the edge of the map, even though neither they nor their families know what to do anymore?

We're not going to earn the world's trust by proclaiming our biological expertise or with slick medication ads on TV. We're going to have to really listen to people. We're going to have to prove we personally care about them, and they're not just a case number to us. We're going to have to show them we really understand them and aren't hiding behind confusing diagnostic labels. We're going to have to show a willingness to travel alongside people, taking risks with them, and returning safely.

These journeys will take hard work

If the medical model seems overly simplistic to you and you think there must be some other answers, keep reading.

It's strange to me that the entire psychiatric field seems content to lump together all the people with psychosis and just give them whatever the newest antipsychotic medication is … for the rest of their lives. Shouldn't we be interested enough to carefully evaluate each person to figure out what's going on with them and what they really need? Shouldn't we give people with these very complex conditions more than a 15-minute or even half-hour medication visit once every month or two? Surely, we should care enough to take the time to really understand each person's story. Our present system is more or less the equivalent of finding out that someone has cancer, not bothering to figure out what kind it is or how it's affecting them, and giving them all the same toxic chemotherapy because it will help some of them.

Why a guidebook for psychosis?

Guidebooks describe what you're likely to see and experience where you're traveling and give practical information to help make the most of your travels.

> The most notable "guidebook" for psychosis is E. Fuller Torrey's "Surviving Schizophrenia: A Family Manual." This best seller, originally published in 1983, is now in its 6th edition. Now 80 years old, Dr. Torrey has had a long, illustrious, and controversial career focused on people with schizophrenia. His older sister became psychotic when she was in college and struggled throughout her life, including lots of institutionalization. That was in the era when "schizophrenogenic mothers" and their families were blamed for creating psychosis. Dr. Torrey was part of the biological revolution in psychiatry that replaced psychoanalysts with the current medical model. He's very sympathetic to family members whose lives have been tragically impacted with schizophrenia and wrote this book to help them literally "survive" this burdensome, in his view usually hopeless, illness that he believes is caused by viral infections. He advocates heavily for more support for the victims of severe mental illnesses and their families. He also strongly advocates for more involuntary, forced medication and locked treatment, and less jailing and homelessness. I admire his long-standing passion, but, like many people, I'm not keen on reopening large psychiatric hospitals as medical asylums. Instead of going back to men in white coats taking away undesirable people, handing them over to psychiatrists with increased powers, I'm ready to move on to more collaborative, holistic approaches.

Reading that type of informational books and articles is probably how you found out about the medical model. They are written by the established experts in the field and contain the established facts. Those are the books we give to students learning to be mental health professionals. But we're at the point where there are so many cracks in the official edifice, so many things that don't fit, that we're primed for a revolution—a recovery revolution.

Here are some strange facts for you:

- People with schizophrenia in third world countries tend to have better outcomes than those in first world countries.
- People with spiritual explanations for their conditions tend to have better outcomes than people with medical explanations.
- Small "moral treatment" institutions in America in the 1800s had about a 2/3 recovery rate from psychosis in 6 months, better than any treatment program since then.
- People with schizophrenia who didn't respond to the first medication, Thorazine, but who were kicked out of the back wards of the state hospital in Vermont to save money had about a 2/3 recovery rate when they were tracked down after 20–25 years (and it wasn't because better medications were invented).
- People with schizophrenia in England who were given "befriending" for an hour once a week had a major improvement in their psychotic and depressive symptoms after 6 months without a medication change.
- In the Netherlands, after 7 years of being treated with medications following a first-break psychosis, only 17% of patients who were told to stay on their medications were going to school or working, while 40% of patients who kept trying to lower their dosage and get off their medications were going to school or working, even though only a few actually managed to stay off their medications

None of those facts fit into the "chemical imbalance—take your meds" mantra. Don't get me wrong, medications can be incredibly helpful for many people with psychosis, but it's much more complicated than that. Our brains are complex. Our minds are even more complex. And every one of us is different. If you're going to make any sense of this to understand where you're traveling, you're going to need more perspectives than the established experts give you.

You may have met some people or read some impressive autobiographies written by people who have experienced psychosis and had remarkable lives, like Elyn Saks's *The Center Cannot Hold: My Journey Through Madness*. I love people and books like that. I even love books that are collections of autobiographical recovery stories that a number of programs have put together. They're so inspiring—and they often include what they did that helped them. The problem is what helps one person may be the opposite of what helps someone else.

> *I have two colleagues who both have recovered from schizophrenia and lead very successful lives: Dan Fisher is a psychiatrist and Fred Frese was a psychologist until his recent death. Coincidentally, while in their 20s, they were both locked up in the psychiatric ward at St. Elizabeth's during the same year.*
>
> *Dan had received his PhD and was a medical student when he became psychotic. He was working in a neuropsychiatry lab trying to understand how the chemicals in our brains make us function. As he put in very long hours, mostly isolated, he began to think that he was just the product of chemicals in his head. He began to think that he had no free will. He was a biological machine. He stopped expressing himself and became quieter and quieter. He moved less and less until he was entirely mute and still. They hospitalized him repeatedly and gave him medications to try to bring him back to life. He passively waited for them to work. Unfortunately, most of the medications seemed to make things worse. After quite a long time, he decided that he was actually an emotional being, not a biological machine, and that he was in an emotional crisis caused by his isolation and that he'd lost all his will to live because he was so disconnected with everyone else. He worked hard to restart his mind and connect emotionally to other people. He recovered, returned to his studies, and graduated. Today, he is married with adult children. He's a prominent*

psychiatrist. He doesn't take any medications, but he still makes sure he has enough emotional contact with others to keep going. He invented a treatment program called PACE (Personal Assistance in Community Existence) based on his own experiences. He strongly believes in peer support—that people with lived experience of mental illnesses can share their stories and form helpful relationships to accompany and guide other people as they recover. When Dan tells other psychiatrists that he's recovered from schizophrenia and doesn't take medications, they tell him he must've been misdiagnosed in the first place because people with schizophrenia don't recover. But he wasn't misdiagnosed. He knows a lot of people with schizophrenia who have recovered. Were they all misdiagnosed, or are they the "data" that schizophrenia isn't incurable? Check out his National Empowerment Center at power2u.org.

Fred's mind tended to expand beyond his control. He liked how creative it could be and believed he has altered brain abilities, not just disabilities, but it could be difficult for him to function while he was traveling to different planets or was lost in philosophical reveries. I once heard him say that he knew that the answer he was supposed to give is, "We're sitting in the evaluation area of the psychiatric emergency room at Ohio State University" but he couldn't help himself from saying, "We're on the third planet revolving around a medium size star in a small solar system on the edge of the Milky Way galaxy" even though that answer got him hospitalized again. Over the years, he has learned to carefully take medications to keep his brain functioning within a socially acceptable range and still be creative. He said he also requires being on a "thought diet." In the same way that some people need to avoid foods that are unhealthy for them, he needs to avoid tempting expansive thoughts that are unhealthy for him. He also believes that when he is so out of control, he doesn't know what he's doing in normal reality, that he should be forcibly hospitalized and

> medicated to bring him back to self-control. Fred did complete his PhD in psychology despite being told when he was in a state hospital that becoming a psychologist was a grandiose delusion. He, too, had a distinguished career, including being an amazing writer, speaker, and advocate.

My point in describing these two very different, but both highly successful, journeys with psychosis is to insist that understanding the details of each of their conditions is essential to finding an approach that they were able to respond to effectively. What each of them needed to succeed was very different from each other. There was no one approach that would've helped both of them, and the standard approach would've helped neither of them.

As I've met more successfully adapted people, each of them illuminates some other aspect of the variety of psychosis. Patricia Deegan, an accomplished psychologist, writer, and speaker, had to learn how to advocate with her psychiatrist to use her medications more effectively and find other "personal medications" to help herself like meditation, exercise, journaling, and spending time with others. Elyn Saks used psychoanalysis and very strong medications as she obtained multiple degrees—even with severe symptoms—and, later on, receiving support from an understanding husband, she became a distinguished law professor at USC. Everyone is different.

Finding the path and the tools that are best for each person requires finding yourself within the great diversity of experiences we call psychosis. Everyone has to create their own journey, but you don't have to do it blind or invent it all by yourself. I hope this guidebook provides enough descriptions, explanations, and stories to orient you—whether you are a person going through extraordinary experiences, someone who cares about them, or a professional trying to be of help. (By the way, having all of you in my audience sometimes brings up pronoun problems: Are "we" having extraordinary experiences supported by "them," or are "we" supporting "them" as they go through their experiences, or most inclusively, are all of us helping ourselves and supporting each other?)

You may notice that, like other guidebooks, I don't have a list of references at the back of the book to justify my content. What I do have, sprinkled throughout the book, are true experiences of interesting people, books, movies, websites, TED talks, and therapeutic practices that you can explore on your own to find something uniquely valuable to you.

But does it have to be so long?

This guidebook is rather long. Unfortunately, it has to be long because there are so many different routes to psychosis, so many different ways of looking at it, so many ways to promote recovery, and so many obstacles and challenges along the way. I don't know which route you're on or how you're looking at it. If I wrote a short "My favorite approach to recovery with psychosis" book, it would be the wrong journey for most people. I've come to the point where anytime I read anything about psychosis—whether they say it's caused by a virus or trauma or is a pathway to enlightenment or a genetic brain condition or whatever—I'm most likely to think that's probably true for some people and not true for many others. Even the same destination—and some of my stories could be put in different journeys—looks different to people who got there on different paths. You can go to Paris as an art lover or a romantic or a foodie or a kid, but you'll engage with it differently and enjoy different things, depending on who you are. Similarly, if trauma isn't your thing, check out a more biological or developmental journey. Look for yourself reflected in the stories and the explanations in a way you can engage with and enjoy that part, but skim over the rest.

> *After I finished medical school in St. Louis, I wanted to return home to California for my psychiatry residency. The two major universities in Los Angeles had very different programs. UCLA's Neuropsychiatric Institute, based in a large academic center in Westwood, offered a very biological program. They were very highly regarded and produced a large number of research papers. The residents were taught about mental illnesses and their treatment by doing literature reviews and then applying what they read to their patients. NPI didn't accept patients with Medi-Cal or uninsured patients; so, most poor people were excluded. Since most people with serious mental illnesses either start out or become poor, they were excluded.*

> USC wasn't housed at the university. It was housed in a very large public hospital, "County General" in a Hispanic barrio near downtown Los Angeles. You could frequently hear gunshots in the park across the street. The hospital was overflowing with patients. Mothers delivered babies in the hallways when they ran out of space. There was a United Nations of languages being spoken in the Emergency Room where the wait was up to 14 hours. The police brought in a steady stream of disruptive, violent, confused, manic, psychotic, and worst of all, people strung out on angel dust to the psychiatric hospital. Most of the time, there were almost no professors or supervising psychiatrists available. After rounds, they left immediately to go to their private practices. It was basically a "learn by doing" hospital, where we were likely to see anything.
>
> I chose USC.

I'm just old enough to remember when doctors were supposed to learn from our patients, and just young enough to remember when we started making fun of that view of practice, calling it old-fashioned, unscientific, unreliable, and misguided. The only truths, it's now claimed, come from researchers doing controlled studies in academic settings. These experts provide whatever knowledge and guidance we need in algorithms to produce efficient, effective, proven "evidence-based practices." It seems that neither the practicing clinician nor the patients know anything worthwhile. My book is filled with knowledge and learning, but it is learning I got from sharing my life with my colleagues and my patients and from truly listening to their stories. It's "practice-based evidence."

> I worked at the Village with Erin Von Fempe for 25 years, most of the time with our desks literally side-by-side. She has a wonderful way of asking, "How are you?" that expresses far more than a greeting. She pauses to actually listen to the response, and if someone just answers, "Fine" she'll press until they tell her how they really are. She really wants to know. She had a fancy sign over her desk that read "Imago Dei". When people would ask her what it meant, she'd say, "We're made in the image of God. And since God

doesn't make garbage, we must all be valuable." She didn't have that sign because she's especially religious, but to remind all of us to approach everyone as someone who is precious.

I believe that the single most effective way to learn about how the mind is working is to ask someone what's going on inside themselves and listen to their observations of themselves. It takes a lot of time and patience to do that, time most psychiatrists don't spend. That may not be the best way to learn about kidneys or lungs, but it is the best way to learn about minds. You won't find many references to research studies in this book. What you will find is lots of stories of people teaching me about what they're experiencing and me trying to make sense of what they're telling me. Much of what I've learned runs contrary to what you've heard and what the experts have taught us, but it makes sense and connects to people's actual experiences. I don't need data to tell me when I've gotten something right when I hear people who actually live with mental illnesses tell me, "Yes, that's the way it is. Yes, that's what really helps."

This is also where my responsibilities as a psychiatrist and as a writer conflict the most. As a psychiatrist, I'm supposed to protect my patients' privacy. If I write about them, I'm supposed to change their names and their stories enough to hide them beyond recognition. As a guidebook writer, I'm supposed to make their stories as vivid and realistic as possible, building on truthful details to create an accurate portrait. I've tried to meet both responsibilities. I changed all of their names. I combined details from different people to hide their identities. I've tried to be truthful without always being accurate. Also, for the most part, I've included people who I know have shared their stories publicly, or who wanted me to write about them and wanted other people to benefit from their stories. I've tried to emphasize my experiences and learning, instead of theirs. If any of you recognize yourself, I hope you feel that I have told your stories with respect and empathy. I have been blessed to know you. I carry a part of you with me. To the many others who wanted to be included in this book, but weren't, please don't take that as meaning you're not important to me or your story isn't worthwhile. The truth is simply that I've been touched by far more people than can be included in one book, even a long one.

Like most travel guidebooks, I've divided this book into three sections:

- ➤ The first section introduces you to me and my approach to journeying with psychosis and other extraordinary experiences.
- ➤ The second section divides the landscape into eight different types of journeys, eight different formulations of how these strange journeys unfold—grief, psychotic reactions, difficulties in making sense of the world, childhood trauma, losing balance, drugs and alcohol, psychiatric illnesses, and neurological/medical conditions. I firmly believe that we need to differentiate psychosis more carefully to be able to recover. A guidebook is only useful if you're reading the chapter about the place you're in. A description of Beijing isn't very helpful In London and a description of a universal, generic city isn't particularly useful anywhere.
- ➤ The third section is designed to help as you move into recovery. I have long sections on how to promote recovery within three different dimensions—self-identity, experiencing reality, and relationships. I've also included travel tips for some key challenges you're likely to face on your own journeys as you seek out recovery, including areas like poverty, hospitals, families, and suicide. After all, what good is a guidebook if you don't use it to improve your own journey?

Do you really want to know?

Everyone in the psych hospital called John "Wolfman Jack" because he would make himself hoarse by yelling nonstop, so he sounded like the old radio DJ. Everyone knew Wolfman Jack and most of the staff liked him. He had five volumes in his chart because he was brought to the hospital every other month. He kept stopping his medications, getting very agitated, and harassing policemen, throwing traffic barricades, and pounding on their cars. They kept bringing him to us. We'd patch him up by putting him back on medications and send him out to do it all over again.

When it was my turn to take care of him, I didn't really feel like taking his history for the 20th time. I told him that I'd just copy it from the last resident's admission note, but before I did, I wanted to know something.

"What's that?" he growled.

"Why do you do this?"

"Do what?"

"Why do you keep stopping your medications, getting manic, harassing policemen, and getting thrown back in here, over and over again?" I leaned back, gestured vaguely, and waited for his reply.

That's when he asked me the key question, *"Do you really want to know?"*

Think about that for a minute because that's always the key question even when they don't ask it. Do you really want to know what it's like to have a child taken away and have a black hole in your heart where the tears flow out from forever? Do you really want to know what it's like to have voices talk you into lighting yourself on fire? Do you really want to know what it's like to be making love to your husband and have a flashback to your father's drunken friend on top of you as a child and tighten up in terror? If you don't really want to know, they'll get the message and shut down, and you'll be of very little help.

But back then, I was young and naïve and confident and didn't think about all that. I just answered, *"Sure."*

"My mother is a holocaust survivor. She's a very depressed, bitter, old woman. I live with her and take care of her and she takes out her pain on me, making me miserable, too."

Wait a minute. I knew that people who are abused sometimes abuse their kids, but I'd never thought about how that applied to holocaust survivors. I'd always thought of them as almost saintly. Now, he was making me wonder how many of them abused their kids. Talk about something I didn't really want to know. But I was already in too far to stop now.

After taking a deep breath, he went on, *"I wish I could kill myself, but since I'm also devoutly Jewish, suicide is out of the* question. So, what I do is stop my medication, get manic, and go find the police, hoping they'll eventually kill me and end my misery. It hasn't happened yet, but I read about police killing other mentally ill people; so, I know it's possible."

Did I really want to know all this? By the way, who is getting "insight" in this story, him or me?

I took a minute to absorb his story. He seemed to appreciate that. I continued, "That makes sense to me. If you don't mind, I have a couple more questions."

"Go ahead."

"First, do you think God is going to be fooled by that?" I was even more of a smart ass back then.

"What do you mean?"

"Well, it seems to me you're still committing suicide even if you get a policeman to do it for you, except that you've made it worse by making him feel guilty for the rest of his life for killing you. He might even get fired."

"I never thought about it that way." This time he paused to think about it. I appreciated that.

He continued, "What's your other question?"

"I could help you find someone from In Home Supportive Services to be with your mom sometimes. You're obviously not with her when you're here in the hospital anyway. I also know about a drop-in center near where you live where you could hang out and make some new friends. I notice you like talking to the other patients here in the hospital, trying to help them out. And I could see you in the clinic myself, so you wouldn't have to go through a lot of paperwork. Just show up and I'll see you in between other patients to give you your lithium refills. Maybe then, you wouldn't be so miserable, and you could stop figuring out how to die. Would you be willing to try that?"

That's what he ended up doing and he stayed out of the hospital for the next year for the first time and began to rebuild his life. By "really wanting to know," I had really connected with him. I hadn't learned any more about his illness than any of the other residents. I had learned more about him as a person. I hadn't figured out how to improve his medications. I figured out how to improve his life.

One last image before we leave Wolfman Jack: During that hospitalization, he had a birthday. The nurses who knew him well put together a few bucks of their own money and got him a cake and some candles. We all sang happy birthday to him, and they gave him a small wrapped present that was a package of white socks. He broke down into tears saying it was the best birthday he could remember. I wondered how empty his life must be if our small celebration on a cramped, physically run-down, county hospital ward behind a locked door could touch him like that.

Do you really want to know?

CHAPTER 2

INTRODUCING YOUR GUIDE

Here's the bio I distribute to people when I give lectures:

Mark Ragins, MD, was the Medical Director at the MHA Village Integrated Service Agency in Long Beach, California, an award-winning model of recovery-based mental health care for 27 years. Since its inception in 1990, he worked as a psychiatrist for the adult service coordination teams, the Homeless Assistance Program, the Transition Age Youth Academy, and the Welcoming Team until he departed in 2017 to work at the Counseling and Psychological Services and the Student Health Center at California State University, Long Beach. His practice and vision have been grounded in more than 30 years of ongoing clinical work with some of the most underserved and difficult-to-engage people in our community.

Over the years, he has been very active in promoting system change, focusing on integrated services, rehabilitation, and recovery for people with serious mental illnesses. Countless numbers of people have come to experience firsthand the work being done at the Village, and Mark has traveled to over 40 different counties in California since the passage of the Mental Health Services Act to train thousands of people and catalyze recovery-based transformation. He was a consultant to the Los Angeles County Department of Mental Health (DMH), one of the largest community mental health systems, working to implement recovery-based practice. He has given hundreds of presentations and lectures to diverse audiences and has spoken at numerous conferences nationally and internationally from Norway to Singapore.

His writings include a short book, "A Road to Recovery," and two textbook chapters, as well as numerous other published and unpublished articles that have been posted on a variety of websites, including official government websites, professional publications, national advocacy organizations, local mental health reference guides, self-help websites, and even in the L.A. Times and Steve Lopez's book, "The Soloist." He is a creator of Mental Health America of Los Angeles's (MHALA) Milestones of Recovery Scale and The Recovery Culture Progress Report tools. He has consulted with Entertainment Industries Council, Inc. regarding the portrayal of people with mental illnesses in the media.

Over the years, Mark has won a number of awards, including being the co-winner of the American Psychiatric Association's Arnold van Ameringen Award in Psychiatric Rehabilitation in 1995. The MHA Village was honored with the Gold Medal Award from the Institute for Psychiatric Services as the program of the year in 2000. In 2006, he was selected by the American Psychiatric Association as a distinguished fellow. In 2011, the US Psychiatric Rehabilitation Association gave him their John Beard award for his outstanding lifetime contribution to psychiatric rehabilitation. In 2013, the National Alliance on Mental Illness (NAMI) California selected him as their recovery practitioner of the year, and Mental Health Advocacy Services honored him for his lifetime of advocacy efforts onbehalf of people with severe mental illnesses.

If you're going to read this book, you'd probably like to know me better, more personally. The stories in this chapter should help you see if I'm the kind of guide that you'd like to travel with.

My name is Mark Ragins. Most people at the Village where I worked called me Dr. Mark, except those who have known me long enough to forgo that pedestal and just call me Mark. I'm a psychiatrist, a storyteller, and the kid who used to drive his parents and teachers crazy by asking incessantly "Why?" and then, being never satisfied with their answers, I looked for my own answers and returned to tell them that their answers were wrong.

I'm not the kind of psychiatrist who sees people lying on a couch. I've worked with people with severe mental illnesses like schizophrenia who would've been locked up in hospitals years ago. I've worked with drug addicts on the streets and with badly abused kids who leave foster care at age 18 with nothing, trying to help them to make it in our world. I've worked as part of a whole team intent on getting them money, housing, food, some friends, even a job, so that they can become a part of the community. Sometimes, that means getting them a Christmas tree and some presents to give to their kids.

That description usually changes people's initial reactions. That sounds like honorable work helping people who really need it. Maybe I'm not sitting there psychoanalyzing my wife's friends at PTA meetings. "That's good. We need people like you to help them." But their next comment is almost always, "That must be very difficult work." I tell them that it is hard at times, but that it's very rewarding because many people do so well. That takes them totally by surprise. "I thought people like that never get better."

Most of the people I've worked with have experienced an enormous amount of rejection in their lives—from schools, families, jobs, landlords, police, and even doctors. Everyone "normal" would walk to the other side of the street to avoid the people with whom I've spent my life. Maybe I am "abnormal in just that certain special way" that causes my heart to reach out to them instead of reject them. Maybe you are, too. By writing this book, I'm offering to be your guide into the world of people with psychosis. I'll share with you my experiences and what I've learned.

I'm a good guide because even after all these years, I'm still an enthusiastic explorer.

> *My oldest son once called me a "crazy person magnet." We had just gotten off a 4-hour public bus ride across the high desert of Peru, and I'd spent most of the time talking with*

the man next to me about his struggles with mental illness and substance abuse while he was in the army. After returning from Vietnam, he'd had a hard time, but he eventually recovered enough to be a peer–staff member helping other veterans in Massachusetts.

"Why do you talk to crazy people like that?" my son pleaded in a voice familiar to all parents who have embarrassed and somehow permanently ruined their child's reputation.

"Because I'm interested in their stories. I think that people who are different, who live on the edge, may see things that people in the middle can't see."

"No, they don't. They're just crazy."

"Besides that, it's not how I talk to people that's unusual. It's how I listen to them. They tell me stories they'd usually keep hidden."

He rolled his eyes, "So what?"

"And another thing: There are a lot fewer 'normal' people in this world than you think there are. You didn't know he was a crazy person, whatever that means, until you heard him telling me his story. You thought he was just another middle-aged American tourist far from home."

My son shook his head hopelessly and walked off. He became an ER doctor, not a psychiatrist.

Choosing psychiatry

I didn't always know I wanted to be a psychiatrist. When I was in high school, there was a TV show you might remember if you're old enough called "The 6 Million Dollar Man," and I thought I wanted to be a biomedical engineer and make bionic body parts. It turned out that I couldn't even make an electronic alarm clock that worked in physics lab; so, I moved on.

Maybe I could do research and find the cure to cancer, or something really important like that. I signed up to work in a genetics lab. Since it was

Caltech, it turned out the elderly leader of the lab, Dr. Lewis, was a Nobel Prize winner. I rarely saw him. My job was to spend hours all by myself shining a light through small glass tubes filled with small amounts of DNA and writing down columns of numbers. It was torture to me. Also, I tended to spill some of the liquid when I moved it around using a tiny glass pipette, and that angered the graduate student I was assisting. So much for research.

In the meantime, I found my psychology classes more interesting. Reading Freud courageously exploring his own mind and the minds of his patients felt more like an exciting journey of discovery than research ever did. He was asking, and making progress, answering fascinating questions like: Why do we dream, grieve, fall in love, think jokes are funny, get irrational fears, and have religion? Each book had something new in it. My abnormal psychology professor was a practicing psychologist, and he brought in videotapes of himself interviewing people with real mental illnesses. They were fascinating. How did those people get that way?

During that same time, my father was assigned to be a judge in the mental health court in Los Angeles. All of the clients in that court have mental illnesses. Sometimes, he'd pick me up at lunchtime on Fridays. I recall sitting in the gallery of his court room, often reading, doing homework, and listening to the cases. The hearings involved mental health holds and conservatorships and determining whether the clients had the mental competency to stand trial and whether they were not guilty by reason of insanity.

> *One afternoon, the client was a young woman just about the same age I was, 19 or so. Sitting next to her public defender, she looked scared and overwhelmed.*
>
> *The lawyers finished their routine legalese mumbo jumbo. I looked up from my textbook. Her psychiatrist was on the stand testifying to try to keep her in the hospital against her will. The county council began asking questions. "Have you come to any conclusion about if she has a mental illness?"*
>
> *"Yes, I have."*

"What is your conclusion?"

"That she does have a mental illness."

"And what is her diagnosis?"

"Manic depression. She shows classic signs of racing thoughts, poor sleep, increased energy, grandiosity, elevated mood, irritability, impulsiveness, and disinhibition."

Sounds like a lot of my college classmates to me.

"And is she gravely disabled because of this condition?"

"Yes, she is. She has no housing or source of income. If she was released today, she'd have nowhere to go and would end up homeless, off her medications, and more manic."

"But couldn't she go back to her parents' home?"

"No. Her parents are no longer able to take care of her in her condition. They may be able to take her home after further treatment if she improves substantially." I wondered who coached them to say that. The girl glared over at her parents sitting in the gallery near me. Her mother looked away and kept wiping her eyes with a Kleenex. Her father shook his head.

"And is she voluntarily complying with treatment?"

"We've had a lot of trouble getting her to take her medications regularly. She misses dosages. To treat her mania, we're trying lithium, which is a new medication that takes about a week to work effectively after the blood levels are stabilized. She hasn't been cooperating with having the blood tests for monitoring her lithium levels."

"Do you believe she would voluntarily comply with treatment if she was released today?"

"No, I don't."

"No further questions, Your Honor." My father looked bored. He preferred the exotic entertaining cases, like Meda Magnifico who thought she was FDR's mistress and the only six-star general, or the man who wanted to drop his pants while on the stand to show the judge that he really did have three testicles.

Now, it was time for the girl to take the stand to fight to get out. I wondered how she'd do. Let's see what she's got.

"Do you believe you have a mental illness?"

"The doctor says that I have manic depression."

"But what do you think?"

"I think I have some emotional problems I'm working through. My parents and I have a lot of arguments, but I'm not convinced I have a chemical imbalance in my brain. They didn't do any tests that found an illness." That wasn't bad, but she didn't know there aren't any tests, there's just the doctor's word for diagnosis.

The lawyer went on, "Do you think you need medications?"

"I think I need them sometimes, and I do take them when I'm having a problem, but not every day like they give them to me. They just want me on pills for the rest of my life." Also, a dead end. The doctor says when you need medications, not you.

"And how would you take care of your food, clothing, and shelter if you left the hospital today?" Here's the tough one.

"Well, I don't have any money with me; so, I'd have to stay with a friend for a few days, until I got a job, and then I'd rent my own room. I saw some cheap places in the Penny Saver."

"But what would you do today?"

"I'd have to find a friend."

"What friend?"

Her plan was falling apart. She stammered something that sounded like "I don't know."

"Excuse me. I couldn't hear you. What friend?" She fell silent.

"You'd end up homeless and starving if we let you go, wouldn't you?" Fighting back her tears, she looked over to her parents again, her eyes silently begging for help. Her parents were fighting off tears, too, but they held firm.

"So, you are gravely disabled, aren't you?" Looking back, I don't think I could've passed this test if it had been me up there. After all, my parents were paying for my tuition and college dorm. I didn't have a job or any money of my own either.

She turned away angrily and glared at her doctor and the lawyers before she gave up.

I couldn't decide if she should be locked up or not. Maybe lithium would help her. Who knows? Certainly not my father. He just believed the doctors. What was clear to me was that she'd been humiliated in court that day, and she sure needed a friend to be with her while she went through this. I know she had a public defender advocating for her, but she's just another case to him. He loses almost every case. He's used to it. I grew up around lawyers and court rooms, and I know what everyone's role is and what they were all talking about, but I doubt she did. She just looked confused, angry, and frightened to me. I bet if I could've talked with her, I could've helped her. She shouldn't have had to struggle alone.

The lawyers talked some more but it was clear the case was over. "Petition granted," *my father ruled.* "Next case."

I went on to spend a lifetime walking alongside people who are struggling with serious mental illnesses.

When I began my path to becoming a psychiatrist, I was fascinated by the array of strange experiences people could have. Some people had been contacted by God. Others thought that their body was rotting inside of them and they were emitting a terrible smell. One woman thought she had millions of admirers and a fortune, while another one thought that her husband was trying to poison her. Some people did everything incredibly rapidly, overwhelming everyone with their energy and getting irritated that no one could keep up with them, while other people had to count every word they wrote, check things over and over again, and take forever to do anything.

I kept wondering if people who lived on the edge of normalcy could see things the rest of us couldn't.

I kept wondering if people who used hallucinogenic drugs, mystics who described heightened states of reality and seemingly magical powers, and psychotics in mental hospitals had something in common.

For the most part, I was pretty sure I wouldn't get bored working with people like them; so, I went to medical school to become a psychiatrist without really knowing what a psychiatrist does.

I didn't realize that many people find mental illnesses fascinating, but don't actually like spending time with people who have mental illnesses. Most people would prefer to keep their distance from psychotic people: They're strange. They can be hard to relate to. Sometimes, they're frightening.

> *In my third year of medical school, after years of memorizing medical textbooks, learning about infections and how the kidney works, medications, and all the parts of the body, even the ones you can only see with a microscope, I finally got to go to a psychiatric hospital and meet the people I'd been studying for all these years to try to help. At Malcolm Bliss state hospital in the heart of the Black ghetto of St. Louis, I walked into a scene from "One Flew over the Cuckoo's Nest." A nurse reluctantly unlocked the door to let me in and then went back into the glass walled nursing station with the other nurses. I followed hesitantly and sat down. They were writing in charts and talking with each other. If a patient came up to the window to ask for something, they yelled at them until they shuffled away cowering. After a while, I got bored and went out to the day room where the patients were just finishing lunch and sat on one of the tables to see who would come over and talk with me. The tables had long benches like the cafeteria tables in school. Finally, I get to start learning to be a psychiatrist.*

Desperate as the patients were, many did come up. Pretty soon, a small crowd gathered, and they were all talking at once.

"Are you the new medical student?"

"What's your name?"

"Can you talk to the doctor for me? My medications don't work right. Have you ever tried taking these medications? I can't think straight on them. I think they're poisoning me."

"Can you help me call my daughter? She doesn't know where I am, and she's probably worried about me."

"Can you help me get out of here? I've been in here for 3 months and I'm better now, but they won't let me out. My rent hasn't been paid and I'm going to lose everything."

"I don't belong here. My husband put me here because he's just a little boy in a man's body."

I began to feel overwhelmed. What have I gotten myself into? This wasn't what I had imagined.

In short order, one of the nurses came up, not to rescue me, but to reprimand me, "You can't sit on the tables there talking to the patients. It's against the rules to sit on the tables and we have to enforce all the rules here to maintain control. You're setting a bad example."

"Okay. I'm sorry," I mumbled. A little disoriented, I slid down to sit on the bench seat.

"And besides that, you shouldn't be talking to the patients. You're only going to be here for 6 weeks. The patients will get attached to you, and then when you leave, they'll be upset, and we'll be left having to deal with them." This was a serious blow. I'll harm the patients by talking with them; so, I'm not allowed to. How am I going to learn anything?

I looked around to see what everyone else was doing. No one was talking to the patients!

> The nurses were sitting in their station making sure the patients didn't cross the yellow line. The doctors, all of whom were foreign medical graduates, had left the ward after the staff meeting, and I later found out they were at the library studying for their board examinations. The other medical students, who didn't want to learn psychiatry and were frightened and disgusted by mental patients, also left the ward as fast as possible and took advantage of this "easy rotation." Only the maids, the janitors, and the aids serving the meals were with the patients.

As the years have gone on, I've spent more and more time with the patients despite those nurses' objections, and they've taught me what it's like to live with a mental illness. They taught me things that aren't in any book or any research study. They shared their experiences with me. Fortunately, I like them, and I'm not frightened of them; I take enough time, and I listen well enough to have learned a great deal over the years.

> One of my most impressive and most unlikely moments as a psychiatrist involved literally unchaining a dangerous, mentally ill man. At the time, I was working as a resident on my Consult-Liaison residency rotation in the main medical hospital. The bulk of my job was to talk with people who had survived trying to kill themselves to decide what should happen next and to talk with bizarre, injured, or physically ill people who were handcuffed and brought in by the police to decide whether it was safe to let them go. The medical wards kept all of these people restrained. I carried a small key around with me to unlock them. Every time I used it, I felt like a great liberator, but I also worried. What if something bad happened?

> On this memorable day, I made my one and only visit to a very strange place, the jail ward. Men's Central Jail, where Dr. Lamb did his groundbreaking research, was just a couple miles from the hospital. The jail itself had lots of medical and psychiatric care inside it, but if there was a medical emergency or someone needed surgery, the sheriffs drove them to the county hospital where there was a heavily

guarded medical ward. Normally, there aren't psychiatric consultations on the jail ward because you don't usually call psychiatrists in the middle of medical emergencies, but that's where my beeper said they needed a psychiatrist emergently; so, up the elevator I went.

The elevator opened onto a complicated guard station. They hurried me through the process of showing my ID and having my fingerprints checked. I then entered a scene of absolute chaos.

The patient was tied to the bed with leather restraints, wearing only torn shreds of clothing, covered with blood, with shards of glass stuck in him and scattered everywhere. He was thrashing and yelling. Pieces of equipment were strewn around, and a set of extremely frustrated surgeons and a couple of sheriffs were all standing just out of his restrained arms' reach. None of them seemed confident that I could help, but nonetheless someone had called for a psychiatrist.

"He has manic depression. He stopped his medications, lost control, and shot up a K-Mart. The broken glass is from the shattered store window."

"Was anyone hurt?"

"We don't know. The police took him down and brought him directly here."

Usually in situations like this, several people would hold the patient still and someone would give him an injection of "the cocktail," a combination of Haldol, Ativan, and Cogentin, to knock him out, so that they could do whatever they needed to do. They'd worry about his mental state after he woke up back in jail. There's an entire jail building devoted to treating mentally ill inmates. They were afraid to do that with this patient, however, because there was blood everywhere and this was at the height of the AIDS epidemic and there weren't any effective treatments for AIDS yet. Another floor of the hospital was filled with patients dying of AIDS with Pneumocystis pneumonia in their lungs and large purple Kaposi's sarcomas on their skins.

I felt desperate and overwhelmed, but every medical student learns to always act like you know what you're doing, no matter what. "Let me see if I can calm him down a little."

They moved aside to let me approach his bedside.

I hesitated. Prior to our reliance on psychiatric medications, psychiatrists were trained to be able to "talk people down," but that was before my training began. I'd only ever really seen it done once with a floridly psychotic woman. She walked around the ward at the Maudsley Institute in London where I was training, holding a teacup all day and insisted that none of us were real. An elderly psychiatrist did a case conference with her demonstrating a controversial psychoanalytic technique reflecting and responding to everything she said as though it made sense, and over about 30 minutes he gradually helped her actually make more and more sense. I'd been taught not to do that because it "fed into their delusions," but by the end of that interview, she was explaining that her whole life had turned upside down and confused her, nothing seemed real, and she was trying to hold on to the daily ritual of tea time as her last anchor to her normal life. We could now understand her. By the time he finished, she was ready to work with us to get her life back.

Without any real alternatives, this seemed like the time for me to try talking down a psychotic person by myself.

I walked up to him. I started nervously and a bit too loudly, "Hi. I'm Dr. Ragins. What's your name?"

He looked over at me and yelled even louder, "I don't have a name."

"That's interesting. I've never met anyone without a name before. Why didn't your mother name you?"

He stared at me harder. "I don't have a mother."

"Really? How were you born?"

"I'm an alien."

"Better yet, I've always wanted to meet an alien. Are you from outer space?" The hovering surgeons didn't seem impressed, but I did have his attention and he wasn't flailing and screaming.

"I'm from Jupiter."

"That's coincidental. I was trying to figure out how to get a star ship to Jupiter. How's the gravity on Jupiter?"

He looked at me quizzically, "Uh, it's heavy."

"What color is the aliens' blood on Jupiter?"

"Purple."

"But yours isn't purple. Your blood looks red to me."

We went on like this for a while. Eventually he said, "I've had enough of you. It's time for me to go back to Jupiter. I'm going to hold my breath until I'm gone." Then, he took a huge breath and held it and kept holding it until he started turning blue. The room grew quiet as everyone started paying attention. Maybe something was going to happen.

I said, "I know you'd like to disappear to another planet, or anywhere else but here, after what happened at the K-Mart, but you're going to have to breathe again sooner or later and you'll still be here." When he finally let out his breath, the tears began to flow.

"You're in a terrible situation. You may have even killed someone. I don't know how it's going to work out, but let's start facing it by taking one step at a time. How about if we start by taking the glass out of you?" I pointed to the nurse holding a pair of tweezers in her gloved hands. He nodded while sniffling.

Over the next 20 minutes or so, we moved on to cleaning him up, bandaging and sewing up some of the cuts, and calling his wife and leaving a message for her. He asked me if we'd let him go to the bathroom. He probably hadn't gone for hours by this point. I looked over to the security guard who nodded. He came over and started unshackling him, leaving him in walking restraints and walked him to the bathroom.

The strange thing was that not only had he changed, becoming calmer and working with us, but all of us had changed, too. We were calmer and not frightened of him anymore. Instead of fighting with a dangerous man, we were working to help a desperately needy man on the worst day of his life. We'd reconnected to why we were working there in the first place. Looking back, I don't know if it really was my strange technique that worked, or just that I cared enough to try to really reach out to him and "meet him where he was at," regardless of how crazy and frightening that place was.

My job was done. I shook his hand as he walked to the bathroom and wished him luck. I left with the distinct feeling that I might become a good psychiatrist someday.

Coastal and "the back of the hand"

After I graduated from my residency at LA County–USC Medical Center, it was time to look for a real job. I went to work at Coastal Community Mental Health Center (CMHC) (familiar to all as "Coastal"), a quiet, small government-run clinic in Carson, a city in Los Angeles County. Typical of clinics at the time, it was hidden away in the back of an industrial park with a very small sign and no neighbors to complain. Our clients could even sneak in and park behind the building to avoid anyone noticing they were going to a mental health clinic.

I enjoyed working there and made some friends. I started my "promising career" creating a schizophrenia rehabilitation clinic and a panic disorder group and helping our outreach worker with homeless people. They gave me a lot of freedom.

Steve fit the description of what I thought a schizophrenic patient was like, and he was smart enough to be interesting to talk with.

Steve had a normal White middle-class upbringing in Torrance, where I'd bought a house to raise my family. Steve's mother was a teacher and his father was an engineer. There wasn't any obvious abuse or neglect in his family although his parents did get divorced when he was 14 and his dad left the state. Divorce can be harder on kids than we think, but I doubt it triggered his schizophrenia. He was still doing fine after his parents' divorce. He graduated from high school and went to college.

While in college, he became psychotic, hearing voices and getting paranoid. It took several hospitalizations to get him to take his medications and by then, his college career was destroyed. His mother took him back home and helped him get Social Security Income (SSI), $630 per month when I met him. Over the next 10 years, she'd helped him try to live as independently as possible. She helped him get a room of his own.

The only places to rent in Torrance under $450 per month were in the run-down area that used to be downtown. There were a few small rooms above the mostly boarded up businesses there. One day, Steve described his life using the old Paul Simon lyrics from "The Boxer"—"seeking out the poorer quarters where the ragged people go." The few homeless alcoholics and prostitutes Torrance had were his neighbors. "I do declare there were times when I was so lonesome I took some comfort there."

Steve never had enough money. One day, he said to me, "I looked it up. The federal poverty level for one person is $11,500 per year. I'm on disability and they give me $7,500 per year to live on. Who decided that people who are disabled should have to live at two thirds of the poverty level?"

"I don't know, Steve. I really don't know."

(Thirty years later, their financial situation is much worse. SSI had increased over the years from $630 per month to $950, but rents had gone up, too; so now, there are virtually no apartments under $1,200 anywhere in Los Angeles county. Torrance's old town has been fixed up and is now filled with senior housing, fancy restaurants, and bars. People on disability had to move to the poorest, most dangerous parts of the county or further out to the desert. Most of them have to rely on food banks to get food.)

Steve's mother tried to help out when she could. She gave him her old car and got him a little job driving around an older man and waiting for him. She made sure he didn't make more than $85 per month, so that his Social Security income wouldn't be cut. He spent a lot of time in that old car daydreaming about nothing in particular.

We didn't always talk about money. One day, Steve walked in and held up his right hand with his palm facing toward me. "What do you see?"

"Good afternoon, Steve. I see your hand."

"Be more specific."

What is this about? I never know what he's going to do next. I'll play along. "Okay. Let me look more closely." I stared at his hand. "I see the swirls of your fingerprints. Every one is different. I see the creases between your knuckles. And I see your life line and your love line. I don't know which one is which, but I can see them." I paused to see how he would react.

He used his left hand to point to the back of his right hand. "When you can see nails and knuckles and hair, then you'll be able to start helping me because you'll be seeing the world from my side, instead of from yours."

He stopped and looked up at me. I felt like I stopped breathing and time froze momentarily. That's really deep. I've got to remember that.

"That's very good advice, Steve. How does the world look from your side today?"

That time when he talked about his poverty and his little apartment and his driving job, I tried to imagine being him, and I felt things I hadn't felt before. I felt how ashamed he was of being poor, of being a failure, and of disappointing his mother. But I also felt how proud he was to be doing what he was doing and how much effort it took him just to get up each day. He knew people didn't want him around and they thought he was crazy. He had to continually fight the urge to go back to the hospital to get away from everyone and just give up.

Over the years, the "back of the hand" story has become my favorite story, and I tell it to almost every audience. (If you want to hear me tell the story, it's halfway through a Recovery Conference keynote speech I presented in London in 2012, which is available at vimeo.com/41980608.) I've come to understand that "compassion" comes from seeing someone from our side, whereas "empathy" (not sympathy) comes from seeing someone from their side of the hand: When we hear their story and have an emotional reaction and often a desire to help, we're being compassionate, which is a good thing. Lots of positive action and help come from compassion. Unfortunately, compassion also comes with compassion burnout. Sometimes, our emotional reactions overwhelm us over time When we hear their story and have a vicarious experience of feeling their emotions, we're being empathetic. If we're going to use client-driven services, motivational interviewing, or shared decision-making, we'll have to build it on empathetically "meeting them where they're at." And, by the way, there's no such thing as empathy burnout. Being empathetic leads to both people feeling connected, with our hearts going out to each other, and a calm connectedness, as opposed to feeling drained.

Surviving tragedy

My best friend at Coastal was Robbyn. She was about my age, just a few years out of social work school. Her first job for the county had been in the jail because there are always job openings there. More people are being treated for mental illnesses in the Los Angeles jail than in any mental hospital in the country. The conditions are truly unbelievable there, and it feels like there's suffering oozing out of the walls. The mental health staff in the jail burns out rapidly. Robbyn had been recruited to come to Coastal to fill a new position: Homeless Outreach Worker. Homelessness had been rapidly increasing in the 1980s. Most people thought the increase was due to a combination of Reagan's cuts in the social welfare system, especially in housing subsidies, the war on drugs, and a failure of the community mental health system. By the end of the 1980s, it had become clear that the majority of homeless struggled with mental illnesses or substance abuse or both. With the help of the media, we created a moral outcry argument: Since we'd closed the institutions where these people had been treated and we hadn't provided enough money and services to help them, they'd ended up on the streets and in jail. We owed them better than that. Sometimes, that argument actually got us more funds.

> *In early March, Linda brought me the news. She was one of our psychiatric emergency team workers. They went out in the field to respond to emergency calls and hospitalize people, involuntarily, if necessary. I suppose they are what's left of the "men in white coats." Linda waited until I was between patients, and she came in looking very upset and closed the door behind her—never a good sign.*
>
> *"I have bad news about Robbyn."*
>
> *A few months earlier, Robbyn had been transferred to work in a clinic in Santa Monica to shorten her drive to work since her back had been acting up. I'd missed her.*
>
> *"What is it?"*
>
> *"One of her homeless clients walked in to see her today. He was very psychotic and thought she was the Devil, and he stabbed her." Linda took a deep breath to compose herself.*

Journeys Beyond the Frontier

I began to get upset, too. Was it the man she'd talked to me about the week before who she was worried about? What had she told me about him? ... Why can't I think clearly?

Linda continued, "Robbyn was in her office all alone because her office mate was out on an interview looking for another job." *Please get to the end of this story faster, so I'll know she's all right.*

"He stabbed her 27 times before her screams drew help. By that time, she'd bled to death." *She didn't just say Robbyn's dead, did she really?*

"I wanted you to hear it from me first." By this time, Linda couldn't hold back her tears anymore.

Stunned, I thanked her and tried to pull myself together to see my next patient who was waiting for me. After all, I'm a professional. I can handle this. I really couldn't tell you what happened the rest of that day or even that week.

If you've had someone close to you die, you probably know the strange feeling that came over me. I felt as if I was detached from everyone else, almost like I was listening to them underwater, but it seemed like they were the ones who were disconnected from reality, not me. How could they be sitting, talking, and laughing at lunch, gossiping and analyzing the Laker game as though life was still going on normally? Didn't they understand that Robbyn had been killed? Nothing could be normal again. That feeling lasted for weeks.

I continued working without really noticing that I wasn't nearly as effective as I had been before Robbyn's death. By the time I went on vacation a few months later, four of my patients were in the hospital at once, although it had been unusual for more than one at a time to be that impaired before her death.

Robbyn's death seemed to embody all the losses both I and the mental health system had been going through. Hundreds more employees quit in the next few days. There was a candlelight vigil on the promenade in Santa

Monica that included the unions singing "We Will Overcome" as though a collapsed mine had killed a worker. The leaders of the system reacted powerfully out of fear. They put in metal detectors and security guards and glass walls separating the staff and clients and the receptionist talked through a microphone. No longer were the clients allowed to walk around the clinic on their own. Now, there were locked keypads on the doors of the reception areas, keeping them segregated in small waiting rooms locked away from the staff. Ironically, the staff were the ones locked in, while the frightening clients walked freely around our communities. All pretense of providing a welcoming, healing environment was sacrificed. The clinic in Santa Monica that had been a beautiful and peaceful courtyard was moved into a fortress-like building a few miles away.

I met weekly for dinner with a group of colleagues who worked closely with Robbyn as we tried to console each other. Ultimately, only one other member of the group, Randi, the Recreation Therapist, and I ended up continuing to work with psychotic people. Linda became a mental illness police educator, Susan transferred to work with patients with AIDS, and Barbara ended up doing disaster response and suicide prevention education. I lost track of the rest of the group.

I didn't realize at the time that I basically had three choices: The first alternative was that I could abandon working with psychotic people—nobody really cares about them anyway. They killed my friend. I'm a smart guy. I could start a private practice in Beverly Hills instead. The second alternative was that I could continue to work with psychotic people, but put up enough walls and protection to make sure "it would never happen again." That's the choice the system took. The problem with that choice is that no matter how many walls and barriers and protections we build, we never stop being frightened inside those walls. We get obsessed with maintaining our walls and barriers as though our safety depends on them, and we never get back to doing good work. No one else in DMH has been killed in the last 25 plus years, not because of the protections but because despite appearances, murder is a very rare event. In over 50 years covering thousands of employees and hundreds of thousands of clients, only Robbyn has been murdered. It just happened to be that she was my close friend. The third alternative was the one that we teach to rape victims, so that they can go on with their lives: We can never be totally safe. We need to accept that reality. We don't have to be reckless or thoughtless, but if we hide and stop doing what we love, we're letting the rapist, or the murderer, and our fear win. The third choice was the most appealing to me. After all, "practice what you preach." But it's easier said than done.

Accept that I, too, could be killed at work on an innocent, sunny day in March? And leave my wife and small children alone?

When we're threatened or frightened, the most natural, normal human response is to hunker down alone and hide away and build walls around us to protect us. The entire mental health field excels at hiding in little private offices, raising confidentiality to a religion, and maintaining lots of rules about appropriate boundaries to separate us from the people we're serving. The rest of the world assumes that behind all those walls and contained within our esoteric language and locked institutions, we know what we're doing and we're keeping all of you safe, too.

The problem is that being curled up in a ball isn't a safe position even though it looks like one. I still remember when they told us we'd be safe from atomic bombs hunkered under our school desks. The safest position is when we stand up and reach out our arms to hold each other's hands. It doesn't look safe, or feel safe, but it is. Remember right after September 11 or Hurricane Katrina, before the fear mongers took over? We didn't hide away. We reached out to each other. We helped each other. We thanked each other. We prayed for each other. I believe that's what a good mental health system should look like, with everyone in the community pitching in and reaching out to each other. Robbyn didn't need more metal detectors and security guards to protect her. She needed teammates and a community who can find a place for everyone. (By the way, some years later in Nevada county, a small goldrush county in California responded to the shooting of the mental health clinic receptionist, by coming together as a community, and set up the first Assisted Outpatient Treatment program in California where the local judge actively negotiated with difficult, uncooperative, potentially violent clients, helping nearly all of them to receive treatment collaboratively and safely in the community.)

At the time, however, I saw my choice as between blaming the patient and saying we need to have more power to involuntarily medicate, restrain, and lock them up and blaming the system and saying we need to find better ways to work with people than having one young social worker single-handedly working the streets trying to help some of the most disturbed and dangerous people in our community.

When I heard that the California state legislature was funding a demonstration program to show what the best community mental health could be, to show that the dream of deinstitutionalization could be a practical reality, my choice was made and I knew that was where I had to go.

A career at the Village, an "island of misfit people," exploring recovery

I spent 27 years working at the Village in Long Beach, California. Over those years, we went from being an exciting startup program to being one of the most respected and award-winning mental health programs anywhere, with an impact on the Recovery Movement and mental health programs throughout California and beyond. I was one of the leaders throughout, developing better and better recovery-based practices and spreading the word. In 2004, California voters passed Proposition 63, the Mental Health Services Act, a 1% tax on millionaires that now brings over $2 billion per year to mental health to create services like those we pioneered, helping thousands of people.

But that description doesn't really capture the essence of the Village. I think we were really the "Island of Misfit People."

Remember the Island of Misfit Toys in "Rudolph the Red-Nosed Reindeer"? Rudolph had been rejected by all the other reindeer because of his strange red nose. He couldn't hide it no matter how hard he tried, and "they wouldn't let him play in any reindeer games." After wandering in a blizzard, he ended up at the Island of Misfit Toys along with the Abominable Snowman, an elf who wanted to be a dentist, a Jack-in-the Box named Stanley, and a host of other misfit toys. There they all accepted each other as fellow rejects.

It would be a stupid story if it ended there: Rudolph with your nose so bright, won't you find a sanctuary to hide out in tonight? Instead, in that atmosphere of acceptance, they began to discover their individual gifts, and they each found unique niches and ways to contribute in the real world. The Abominable Snowman puts the star on the Christmas tree, the dentist elf fixes a toothache, Stanley finds a little girl to play with him, and most famously, Rudolph leads Santa's sleigh through the fog.

The Village wasn't a place to live. It wasn't a place to hide out. It was a place to be accepted, to find your gifts, and to participate in the community.

It was a special place not just for the people we serve but also for the staff who worked there. For 27 years, the Village was a place for the somewhat strange "Dr. Mark" to be accepted, find my gifts, and participate in the community. The Village nurtured my attraction to people with extreme experiences because I'm "abnormal in a certain special way," helping me walk alongside them sharing their lives even though my best friend was murdered. It also tolerated me asking "why" too much, so that I could keep learning what people at the edge can see that the rest of us can't see.

Chapter 3

What am I rebelling against?

The outpatient psychiatric clinic at LA County General Hospital included a "medication follow-up clinic." It ran one morning a week and the third-year residents wrote refill prescriptions for people with psychosis and other severe mental illnesses to keep them stable and out of the hospital. We saw them as rapidly as we could because they weren't going to do very well anyway, and we wanted to spend as much time as possible with the therapy patients who we thought we really could help. I worked alongside Jeannie, a kind nurse who had been there forever. She'd known many of these patients for many years. She called them her "little sickies."

But I had become a psychiatrist because I wanted to work with people with serious mental illnesses, not to push them aside. Couldn't they be helped, too? I started spending more and more time with my medication follow-up patients. They started missing fewer appointments and dropping out less. By the end of the year, there were so many of them I had a medication follow-up clinic three mornings a week, instead of just one.

One of my medication follow-up patients was Omar. Omar had paranoid schizophrenia, but like most people with paranoid schizophrenia, he didn't realize that he had it. From his point of view, the problem wasn't his perception of reality. The problem was a series of dreadful jobs where he'd been persecuted.

"I can't believe these people. They are the ones who are going into my computer when I'm not there and changing the data I've entered. They are the ones who are setting it up, so that my computer will crash and I look like I don't know what I'm doing. But when I went to the supervisor and complained, I was the one who got fired. He must have been in on it, too."

"In on what?"

"Haven't you been listening to me? They were all conspiring to get rid of me."

He was getting visibly more agitated, but I pushed forward anyway, "But why would they do that? Why wouldn't they want to help the new guy do his job? Now, they have to hire and train someone else."

"This is the way it always goes for me. They see the work I can do, and they get afraid that I'll be taking their job; so, they make me look bad from the very beginning."

"But the last job, you said you thought the other workers got jealous because one of the female coworkers was starting to be interested in you and that's why they changed your computer's programs, so that you'd look incompetent."

"That's right. People just don't want me to be happy or succeed wherever I go. They make my life miserable."

"But why would they always pick on you, people who are total strangers?"

He leaned back and sighed, "Because I'm Iranian. They're all prejudiced against Iranians here."

He has an answer for everything. If only he'd take his medications regularly, he wouldn't be so paranoid and maybe he'd hold onto a job.

"So, is there anything I can do to be helpful? What brought you in today to see me? It's been a few months since you've been here. I almost closed your case."

"Well, all the pressure from being fired again is getting to me. I keep thinking about what they did to me at the job, but I can't prove anything. I should've been smarter and collected evidence before I left. I think about it all the time, going around and around with the same things. I can't sleep. My family is tired of hearing about it. And now, I'm a financial burden on my family again. I was wondering if you could give me some medication to help me get through this hard time."

He's not exactly admitting he has a mental illness, but it's better than nothing. At least, he'll get back on meds for a while. "How about if you go back on Navane? That helped you before and it doesn't give you any side effects."

"Is that the pink pill?"

"I think so."

"That wasn't too bad. I'll take some until I'm feeling better again."

And then, you'll stop it again, and we'll go around and around some more. "Here's a new prescription. I'll see you again in a couple weeks to see how you're doing."

"Thanks, doc." *At least, he still likes me and doesn't think I'm persecuting him or poisoning him.*

I brought up Omar's case with my supervisor the next week since I was frustrated. Dr. Lamb was one of the giants in community mental health. He was the one who had the courage to go into the LA county jail, and his original research revealed the jail was "the largest mental hospital in the country." Even though he hated the psychoanalysts who had trained him, in some ways he was a caricature of them. He went through a ritual of preparing and smoking a small pipe every time we met. He spoke slowly and gently. "It's very hard to get some people to realize they have a mental illness. It's part of their illness. Try to find some way for him to accept that he has a mental illness and that he needs to take his medications even if he doesn't call it schizophrenia. Maybe talk about how he can't handle stress and that's why he needs to take medications. Also, working is just too hard for him. It keeps triggering his paranoia. Tell him that after all these bad experiences at work, he needs to go on Social Security instead of working, and then, he'll be contributing to his family, instead of being a burden. He just can't handle the pressures of life with his mental illness. He needs you and especially his parents to take care of him."

Sounds like a plan.

Over the next 6 months, I worked hard to accomplish our plan. When Omar missed appointments, I'd call him and encourage him to come in. I talked him into applying for Social Security "to help your parents" and filled out all the forms so that he received it. I used the fondness and trust he had for me to keep us moving forward. As he stayed on medications longer and longer, he still believed that the past jobs had persecuted him, but he ruminated on it less and less. He gradually became less agitated. He was less suspicious and got into fewer arguments.

It was hard work.

My supervisor was happy. Omar said his parents were very happy. Even Omar seemed to appreciate the new calm in his life. Everyone was happy except me. It seemed to me that now when I met with Omar, all the life had gone out of him. He had become compliant with his appointments and his medications, but we had nothing to talk about anymore. All of the indignant passion toward his coworkers was gone. His life was empty. He didn't really have any reason to get up each day. Sometimes, he'd stay up late watching TV and then not get up until 1 pm. He didn't shave as often and he wasn't as clean. He wasn't exactly depressed. It was more like he was lifeless.

"Do you think I've overmedicated him?" I asked Dr. Lamb.

> "No. If you decrease the medications, he'll just start to get more agitated and paranoid again. Those issues aren't side effects of medications. They're negative symptoms. Many people with schizophrenia have them. They have low-level energy and motivation. They're more emotionally distant and passive. Their sleep cycles and self-care drift away. Now that you treated his more dramatic positive symptoms, the delusions and the paranoia, you can see the negative symptoms better."

"But isn't there anything I can do about the negative symptoms?"

"The medications don't really help with those symptoms. They just have to live with them. Maybe he can handle doing something not too stressful, like taking a PE class at the community college or volunteering somewhere."

"But isn't he going to get depressed as life starts passing him by? His younger brother is working and just got engaged and Omar's not doing anything with his life."

"You can help him with his rationalizations. Tell him that his parents are getting older and appreciate having him at home with them or tell him that he's in early retirement."

Early retirement? At 32? Are you kidding me? Is this really the best we can do?

Dr. Lamb must have sensed my dissatisfaction. "Remember, Mark, he does have an incurable severe mental illness. You did a good job with him. This is the most you can really hope for in patients with paranoid schizophrenia."

It may surprise you that I started out this chapter on "What am I rebelling against?" with a story like Omar's when there are so many heartbreaking tragedies and abuses to rail against. I know that people with mental illnesses who are disruptive and break laws are sent to jail, and even prison, for the most part, because there aren't psychiatric facilities (or, probably more importantly, decent housing) to send them to, and horrendous things happen to them there. I know that our psychiatric Emergency Rooms are crowded with people, who are mostly brought by police, with no beds to send them to; so, they're heavily sedated and released. I know that, on the one hand, pharmaceutical companies distort and lie about their products and cozy up to psychiatrists to expand their markets and profits well beyond people who would actually be helped, harming many people along the way, while, on the other hand, many people suffer tragically who could be helped with medications, if only we could engage them in treatment. I know that there are profound funding shortages throughout mental health and substance abuse services, leaving most people who want treatment without anything beyond waiting lists and rushed medication checks. I know that people with mental illnesses face unwarranted fear and relentless rejection every day.

Then, why didn't you tell us a story that included those things?

You can find plenty of other angry people and books railing against all of those other things. Those books are trying to build "out-rage" to get people to push for changing things other people are doing. In my opinion, that's the easiest kind of change to promote—change someone else has to make. I want you to look deeper—and see our role in what's wrong. I want to create "in-sight," instead of "out-rage." I'm trying to promote the most difficult type of change, namely, changes in how we act given the heartbreaking realities all around us, the kind of change Gandhi was talking about when he said, "Be the change that you wish to see in the world."

Take another look at Omar's story. Do you think Omar ever felt understood by me? Did I help him come to terms with what happened to him? Did I help him pursue any goals beyond getting on medications and staying out of trouble? Did I ever meet his parents who have spent a lifetime together with him? Did I give him any hope? Did I include him in any meaningful way? Did I try to help him avoid isolation, stagnation, or lifetime poverty and poor physical health?

No. No. No. No. No. No. No.

Now, think about the stories of successful people I've told you so far. Every story and every book about recovery with psychosis (or any other mental condition, for that matter) include precisely those things I didn't do.

So, why wasn't I taught to do the things that actually help people recover? I think there are four, largely unspoken and unchallenged, premises that have led us astray:

1) We assume people with psychosis aren't worth listening to and don't have any meaningful contribution to make to their own treatments or lives.
2) We struggle to understand psychosis (or mental illnesses in general); so, instead of developing individualized formulations, we use *The Diagnostic and Statistical Manual of Mental Disorders (DSM)*, a "Psychiatry for Dummies" checklist diagnostic system, devoid of understanding, and we focus entirely on reducing their dramatic symptoms, rather than on improving their whole lives.
3) We struggle to connect to people with psychosis and we are often frightened by them; so, we don't think relationships can be important or healing to them.
4) Besides giving medications, we feel helpless; so, we assume they're hopeless.

Those four underlying premises are what I'm rebelling against, and what we all have to change within ourselves, to help people with psychosis recover.

1) **We assume people with psychosis aren't worth listening to and don't have any meaningful contribution to make to their own treatments or lives.**

    ➢ **Here is my better, rebellious approach: People with psychosis are worth listening to and have many meaningful contributions to make to their own treatments and lives.**

    One of my electives in medical school was at a famous psychoanalytic hospital, the Menninger Clinic, in Topeka, Kansas. This was a fancy, expensive place where patients came from all over the country and stayed for over a year on average. They weren't solely focused on medications there.

Their patients received psychoanalysis as part of their treatment four times a week. Families from all over the country came to attended meetings, some in private jets.

I was assigned to evaluate a young man, Martin, who believed that there were satellites from outer space talking to him. He was also kind of immature and spoiled, in my opinion.

"I don't really know much about the aliens or where they come from, but they told me they're going to take me away when the time is right. You see, I don't really belong in this hospital. They told me I have a special purpose. I just have to wait here until they call me. It's hard waiting but it'll be worth it." Now, we're getting somewhere. This is fascinating stuff. This is why I became a psychiatrist.

"How do the aliens communicate with you?"

"It's really hard. It's not exactly like talking to you. I have to really focus on listening to them. They don't really talk in words; it's more like feelings or impressions. It's easier at night when everything is quiet. Sometimes, I stay up late on purpose to try to figure out what's going on with them. Why are they taking so long to come for me?"

"But wouldn't you miss living on Earth? You have a life here."

"You call this a life? Hanging out in the hospital? Going to groups? Taking walks? Talking about my past with a therapist? None of this will matter when everything changes."

"But what if it doesn't change? What if the aliens never come to get you?"

He looked distressed, but gathered himself enough to insist, "They will come. I know they will."

My supervisors criticized me in a more sophisticated manner than the nurses at the state hospital had, "If you talk about his delusions, you'll feed into them and make them stronger. Tell him that you're here to help him reconnect to *reality and his feelings and steer him away from talking about his delusions."*

The next day when I went to see Martin, he was excited. "Last night they told me it won't be long until they come. And they said they have something very special for me to do. They need me."

"That's interesting, but I was wondering if today we could talk more about what it's going to be like for you when you go home with your family. How have the family meetings been going?"

He just stared at me for a moment. I couldn't tell if he was hurt or confused. "Didn't you hear what I said? I'm not going home with my family. The aliens are going to take me away. And it's not going to be long now."

This isn't going well. Let's try again. "I know that's what you're hoping for, but maybe you should have a backup plan in case that doesn't work out. Maybe something more realistic."

He glared at me. Oops, maybe "realistic" wasn't the right word.

"You really don't understand, do you? You're just like all the rest of them. You think you know everything and I'm just crazy." He walked away.

Wait a minute. What just happened?

I was taught, even by modern psychoanalysts, not to "feed into people's delusions" by talking about them as though they're real. It's taken me years to figure out the problem with that common strategy: What we call hallucinations and delusions are, in fact, some of the most powerful and important experiences that these people experience in their entire life. Every time we try to steer them away, it feels to them like we're not really listening and don't really care because we're not responding to what's important to them. Imagine if we were working with a battered woman whose husband was still actively beating her, and we said, "Talking so much about your husband and the beatings is upsetting to you. I want to focus the

Journeys Beyond the Frontier | 57

conversation for a while on something that will connect you to other people better." I'd expect her to think we don't know what we're doing and aren't likely to be able to help her. Now, imagine she's no longer being beaten, but is still haunted by the beatings. I still don't think it would work to steer her away from those memories. She's going to have to deal with them if she's going to heal. If no one will talk with her about them, she'll most likely feel isolated, ashamed, defensive, like she's the only one going through this, and she might never get better on her own. Now, imagine that she was never really beaten. She's imagining it. She's paranoid and delusional. But it's still real to her. How are we going to connect with her without talking about the beatings?

I now talk regularly about "delusions," while keeping one foot in my reality, to engage people by "meeting them where they're at." If I was working with Martin today, I'd try to get him to include me in his world: "What do the aliens say about me?" "How can I help you prepare for their coming?" "How would you say goodbye to everyone here before you left?" "What would you miss most?" "Is it easier or harder to communicate in feelings, instead of words?" "Have you ever tried communicating with a person with feelings, instead of words?" "What do they see in you that makes you valuable to them that most people seem to miss? I'd like to see that part of you, too." "Why do they keep putting off coming to get you? Isn't that frustrating to you?" "I wonder if you're supposed to do something here to prove yourself first." "I hate to say this, but I wonder if they're setting you up for disappointment just like your parents did." "You don't have to struggle alone." Notice that I'm not discounting his experiences by contradicting them and telling him they're not real, but I'm also not agreeing that he's reacting, or even perceiving, realistically. I'm engaging him while purposefully opening up a collaborative, problem-solving conversation where none existed previously.

A man once told me, "Being paranoid is like being in a Nazi concentration camp. It feels like people are watching you every minute, doing things to torture you and break you down, and you could be killed at any time. You learn to be on your guard and watch for signs to stay alive. But now, imagine that the camp is never liberated. The torture and the horror just go on year after year. And even worse, imagine that no one believes you that the torture exists. They tell you it's all in your own mind. You know how angry

Jews get when someone says the Holocaust never happened? That's how angry I felt when someone told me I wasn't being tortured, that I'm just being paranoid. How would you respond if the doctors told you to trust them and take your medications and you'll be fine?"

2) **We struggle to understand psychosis (or mental illnesses in general); so, instead of developing individualized formulations, we use** *The Diagnostic and Statistical Manual of Mental Disorders* **(*DSM*), a "Psychiatry for Dummies" checklist diagnostic system, devoid of understanding, and we focus entirely on reducing their dramatic symptoms, rather than on improving their whole lives.**

> ➤ Here is my better, rebellious approach: We need to work hard to understand each individual's path to psychosis, so that we can develop individualized formulations, including how they understand reality, how they hold themselves together, and how they relate to others.

Although I didn't know it at the time, the medical school I went to, Washington University in St. Louis, was one of the hot spots for the biological revolution in psychiatry that was well underway by the time I got there in 1979. The Department of Psychiatry was led by two very different people, Dr. Guze and Dr. Robins, both of whom excelled in psychiatric epidemiological research—counting people and their symptoms.

Dr. Guze, an internist turned psychiatrist, was one of the first people I met in medical school since he was the chair of the entire medical center, quite unusual for a psychiatrist. He stood proudly welcoming us in his long white coat. He was a respected medical specialist. Almost all psychiatrists his age had to undergo substantial psychoanalytic training and usually they were analyzed themselves. Many of the early biologically oriented, medical-model psychiatrists severely resented these "superstitious" "witch doctor" psychoanalysts and were determined to overthrow them. They worked on taking control of the departments of psychiatry, research funding, and journals, and most pointedly the diagnostic system to rejoin the medical establishment. Dr. Guze wasn't just accepted by his medical colleagues—he was leading them.

My memory of Dr. Robins is very different. He had severe muscular sclerosis, and he sat in a wheelchair in the front row, sometimes dozing off. But when it was his turn to interview a patient for us to learn from him, he came alive. The patient was a young lady who had some serious problems because of drug use. She said she wanted to stop doing them, but as Dr. Robins talked to her about her life—hanging out with drug dealers and their money, fast cars, sex, and all the excitement—she lit up. He said it wasn't just drugs she'd be giving up. It was almost everything that made her feel alive, and that's a lot to ask her to give up. "Just say no" wasn't going to work.

In the early 1970s, they began working on creating diagnostic criteria for psychiatry that would reliably identify objective syndromes that could be studied and treated, just like the diagnoses "real doctors" use in the rest of medicine, to replace complex psychoanalytic formulations that relied on elaborate interpretations. In 1972, they published their first set of criteria for 14 conditions with their chief resident, Dr. Feighner, as the first author in case their efforts were ridiculed by clinicians. Unlike the American Psychiatric Association's (APA's) prevailing *DSM-II* that was based on clinical expertise and consensus, these criteria were based on longitudinal and family research studies and were determined by researchers like them, instead of by experienced psychoanalysts.

As a medical student, I carried around a clipboard with the "Feighner criteria" and learned to do checkbox diagnosis. I was on the lookout to determine if the patient had hallucinations or delusions and illogical or difficult-to-understand speech (and they weren't depressed or manic) for at least 6 months, along with three of the following:

1) Single
2) Poor premorbid social adjustment or work history
3) Family history of schizophrenia
4) Absence of alcoholism or drug abuse within 1 year of onset of psychosis
5) Onset of illness prior to age 40

Statistically, I could then make the diagnosis of schizophrenia. We also had a study that showed statistically that we had to give them Haldol if their symptoms were going to improve; so, we did.

Take a moment to read that last paragraph again to really appreciate what they did. Even with the "Chinese menu" choices, these diagnostic criteria are easy to use, "reliable" (meaning multiple observers would likely come to the same diagnosis), and don't require a lengthy evaluation by a trained psychiatrist of your drives and defenses, repressions and projections, object relationships, and psychosexual developmental stages. Just like that, everyone could diagnose schizophrenia (and 13 other test diagnoses). You don't have to understand anything about what the patients are going through or why it happened. You barely need to talk with them at all.

I learned years later that "negative symptoms" weren't in the Feighner criteria because Dr. Robins thought "flat affect" was mostly an impression by some of the examiners. My guess is that he was such a good interviewer, he even connected with people with schizophrenia and brought them to life, so that they weren't flat anymore. Negative symptoms would be back by the publication of *DSM-III*, probably rediscovered by poor interviewers.

In 1973, their work got an unexpected boost. A Stanford psychologist, David Rosenhan, published an explosive article called "On Being Sane in Insane Places" in the prestigious, popular journal *Science*. He reported that he and some colleagues and students presented themselves to a dozen different psychiatric hospitals saying that they were hearing voices saying words like "empty," "hollow," or "thud," and then, they told their own stories. They were all admitted, diagnosed based on their admitting psychiatrist's clinical expertise, with a variety of conditions, usually schizophrenia; to earn release, they were forced to take medications that they threw away, and their "normal" histories were distorted into elaborate explanations of these existential hallucinations. The other patients often knew they weren't patients, mostly because they took notes while they were on the ward, but also because they didn't do anything abnormal after they were admitted, but the staff couldn't identify them as imposters. So much for clinical expertise and psychoanalytic "mumbo jumbo." They couldn't even tell normal people from those with schizophrenia.

In an effort to restore their reputation, one of the higher-regarded hospitals challenged Dr. Rosenhan to send more pseudo-patients whom they were sure that they could identify now that they were on the lookout. The hospital identified about 40 of the next 200 patients as pseudo-patients, but Rosenhan hadn't sent any more pseudo-patients. It appeared that psychiatric hospitals couldn't tell who had mental illness and who didn't, let alone what mental illnesses they had, or if they needed medications.

Clearly, the biologists claimed, psychiatry was in need of a reliable, objective, medical diagnosis.

> *A fascinating recent book, "The Great Pretender," by Susannah Calahan digs deeply into this key study, which I read as a student and is still cited in many textbooks, exposing a great deal of it as misdirection and even outright fraud. Rosenhan invented data and even excluded one test subject who later said he benefited from the insights and therapy he received in the hospital even though he was there on a pretense. Instead of criticizing the same incredibly short evaluations and lack of communication between staff and patients that I saw in St. Louis, Rosenhan focused on criticizing the validity of our diagnostic paradigms. The modernizing world wanted to hear that we needed scientific alternatives to psychoanalysis and that's what he gave them. The world didn't want to hear that neglecting and dehumanizing people was the problem; so, that message was consistently buried. We now have a more biological version of dehumanizing, instead of something more humane. Is that really progress?*

In 1980, 1 year after I entered medical school, the biological psychiatrists, mostly from New York, but including the St. Louis and Iowa groups, secured their triumph. Organized psychiatry took a massive step by adopting the radically revised *DSM-III* as our *Diagnostic and Statistical Manual* of psychiatric disorders. It applied the Feighner criteria methods to all psychiatric diagnoses. (There's a good description of their ongoing triumph by one of their most powerful proponents, Dr. Jeffrey Lieberman, in his book, *Shrinks*.) Here are the current *DSM-V* criteria for schizophrenia:

- Two or more of
    - Delusions
    - Hallucinations
    - Disorganized speech
    - Grossly disorganized or catatonic behavior
    - Negative symptoms

- Disturbed for over 6 months
- Decreased level of functioning
- Not from a mood disorder, substance abuse, medications, medical or neurologic condition

And that's how we've made psychiatric diagnoses ever since. Simple, right? Congratulations! We're just like the rest of medicine. We have reliable, objective, symptom-based diagnosable illnesses. **These criteria don't eliminate our lack of understanding, difficulty in relating, or our hopelessness—it expects them and enshrines them.**

If I'm feeling particularly nasty, I might say that if only *DSM* had a black and yellow cover, it could be renamed *Psychiatry for Dummies*.

Most people don't realize how simplistic most medical diagnoses are. Most medical diagnoses are simply repeating the person's presenting symptom, or lab abnormality, in medical words or abbreviations—hypertension, epilepsy, dementia, arthritis, anemia, alopecia, dysmenorrhea, CHF, and COPD. Many of these diagnoses don't imply any known causality or underlying pathophysiology, and they often lump several causes into one diagnosis. Similarly, treatments tend not to fix the underlying pathophysiology—they do something to relieve the symptom, regardless of the cause.

So, for example, if they find that my blood pressure is high at my annual checkup, they will likely add the diagnosis of hypertension to my problem list and begin prescribing medications to lower it, so that I'm less likely to get a heart attack or a stroke. They may, or may not, do an extensive workup to try to find the cause of the hypertension, and even things they do find are more likely known correlations with high blood pressure—like high cholesterol, being overweight, family history, and stress—rather than clearly demonstrated causes in my particular body. The blood pressure medication I get won't be matched to my personal cause. I might be started on a diuretic, for example, Lasix, to lower the blood volume my heart has to push around which will lower my blood pressure, whether or not my kidney is managing my blood volume normally. I'll be medicated to have an abnormally low blood volume because it's a useful way to lower blood pressure, not because there was anything wrong with my blood volume in the first place.

Medicine does figure out the causes behind some illnesses—like sickle cell anemia or cystic fibrosis, which are both genetic, and scurvy, which is a vitamin deficiency, and tuberculosis, which is an infection. But the more an illness is caused by an internal malfunction of some reasonably complicated organ or process, the harder it gets. By the time we get to the brain, we're in trouble. Virtually, all of the psychiatric disorders are of complex, unknown causes. The idea that they're clearly describabable as genetically predisposed chemical imbalances is a fairy tale that is good mostly for 60-second medication commercials on TV.

Think about it. Depression, mania, panic attacks, psychosis, obsessive compulsive disorder, anorexia, bulimia, ADHD, PTSD, alcohol dependency: Aren't they all just restating the presenting symptom in fancier words or abbreviations?

Psychosis originally (in the 1840s) meant psychic illnesses as contrasted with physical illnesses. Over time, they discovered more physical "organic" conditions affecting people's brains—like neurosyphilis, or vitamin deficiencies, or multiple sclerosis or Alzheimer's dementia—those conditions were split off from the psychosis because they now had known causes or at least clear physical pathology. When Freud and the psychoanalysts started understanding the psychological causes for neurosis, they were split off from the psychosis, too, which they still couldn't understand.

Think about that for a minute: By the early 20th century, psychosis literally means something is seriously wrong with your brain that we can't understand either biologically or psychologically. On this level, psychosis means an incomprehensible mental illness: The patient is very strange, and we don't know why.

If we look at it from the other person's point of view, or as Steve put it, from the back of the hand, calling what they're going through psychosis may or may not fit what they're experiencing. The more they have an explanation for what they're going through, even if it doesn't make sense to us—like the Mafia having a hit out on them or having a chip implanted in them or even that their family has been harassing them, instead of letting them chill out—the less likely they are to describe themselves as psychotic—having an incomprehensible mental illness. For the label of psychosis to fit, they have to believe they have a serious mental illness and they can't make sense of what they're going through. That does work for some people: "Sometimes when things overwhelm me, I just lose it and go psycho for a while" or "When I'm schizo, I don't know what's going on and my family has to take me to the hospital until I'm OK again." For all of the others, it feels like everyone else are the ones who aren't understanding them. That's why the title of this book includes both "psychosis and other extraordinary experiences."

The diagnostic system embodied in *DSM-III* through *DSM-V* does not provide an understandable explanation of what's causing these conditions. Instead, it lumps together a number of "signs and symptoms" that statistically tend to cluster together and gives them the name of a condition, for instance, acute psychosis if it lasts for 2 weeks, schizophreniform disorder if it lasts up to 6 months, and schizophrenia if it lasts more than 6 months.

DSM-III, *DSM-IV*, and *DSM-V* intentionally avoid speculation on possible causes unless they're certain—like being intoxicated because you were drinking alcohol. But without a cause, how can you make a plan of what to do to get better?

Most psychiatrists today talk about genetic predispositions and environmental triggers or stressors that released your underlying tendencies (seemingly whether or not you have a family member with similar symptoms and whether or not that family member may have in some way "taught" you those symptoms). It's a generic formula, "stress-diathesis," and tends to lead to a generic treatment plan, that can be conveniently summarized as: "There's nothing you can do about your genetic predispositions; so, avoid stress and take medications to suppress your symptoms." Our medications have even been marketed around which symptom cluster they are likely to relieve—antipsychotics, mood stabilizers, antidepressants, and anxiolytics. Sometimes, this formula and plan are embellished with the additional "scientific basis" that the medications are correcting an underlying chemical imbalance that causes the symptoms. There is no definitive biological evidence for that embellishment.

Let's see how this works with real people, instead of generic ones:

> *I was an award winner and a keynote speaker at a California NAMI conference some years ago. Hundreds of family members of people with serious mental illnesses were there looking for*

hope for their loved ones and for the system. I joined them for an evening session where they showed a documentary film about bipolar disorder. The film followed the lives of five different people all diagnosed with and treated with medications for bipolar disorder:

- One was a young woman who had been brutally raped a couple years ago and had been an emotional wreck ever since.

- One was a man in his 50s who had been in foster care as a kid and a speed addict most of his life. When he was using speed, he was full of energy and very creative, painting salable modern art paintings. When he was off speed, he'd end up feeling lethargic, purposeless, depressed, and also isolated, and he had attempted suicide on several occasions. He'd had a heart attack a few months ago; so, he'd stopped using speed again and was depressed, isolating, and suicidal again.

- One was a woman who had episodes that lasted a few months during which she was high—not sleeping, full of energy, hypersexual, spending lots of money, euphoric—and episodes that lasted a few months during which the opposite occurred—being depressed, sluggish, not being able to think straight or get herself out of bed. In between episodes, she was normal and worked as a radio DJ. Her mother had a similar pattern for years until her condition was stabilized with lithium.

- One was a woman who had an emotionally erratic upbringing and was very emotionally erratic as an adult. She was in and out of relationships and jobs. Her apartment was a mess, and she owed lots of money.

- The last one was the boyfriend of the emotionally erratic woman, who also became emotionally erratic trying to cope with her. He didn't believe he had bipolar disorder and wouldn't take his medications.

I became more and more frustrated and agitated watching this film. Even though the filmmaker got to know all of these people well enough to know that they all had different things wrong with them, she still was selling the medical model, fast food psychiatry paradigm: They all have bipolar disorder, a defined biological disorder, and they need to take their medications. And now, all of these family members were being "educated" in this same "Emperor's New Clothes" paradigm.

Although all of these people "meet the criteria" for bipolar disorder—meaning that they have a set of symptoms that statistically make it likely they have bipolar disorder—only one of them actually has a genetic, biological condition. All of the others are misdiagnosed (It doesn't help that "rape victim" and "childhood trauma survivor" and "girlfriend who drives you crazy" aren't choices in the DSM book.). All of them need different treatments, all of which are reasonably effective, not the generic medications for bipolar disorder.

We're efficiently mass producing meaningless diagnoses and ineffective treatments for most people.

Notice something about my brief descriptions for each of the five people above. For each one, I gave you the basis for an understandable story of how their symptoms came to be. These brief individual "formulations" are far more useful than the *DSM* diagnosis for building compelling, personalized treatment plans: The first woman needs rape counseling, the older man needs help in sustaining sobriety and finding meaning in his life probably through his art to fill the hole he's had inside him since childhood, the radio DJ needs medications targeted at her episodes, the last woman needs long-term therapy like Dialectic Behavior Therapy to build emotional stability and skills, and the last man needs a new girlfriend or at least couple's therapy.

Labeling all of them as having "bipolar disorder" and telling them to avoid stress and take medications will end up depriving them of a personalized treatment plan that would have a greater likelihood of making sense to them, engaging them, and actually working.

The middle section of this guidebook is designed to provide enough of an understanding of how psychosis and other extreme experiences emerge to inform individual "formulations," that are created collaboratively relying on a shared, respectful inquiry, and that can be used for building compelling, personalized treatment plans. The neurobiology and psychology behind each of these understandings are not by any means certain, and they never will be; our minds are just too complex, but they're all reasonable and understandable and fit with our current knowledge base and people's personal experiences. Some people's formulations follow a single path and other's follow multiple paths (like the man above who encountered childhood trauma, substance abuse, and a medical condition).

3) **We struggle to connect to people with psychosis, and we are often frightened by them; so, we don't think relationships can be important or healing to them.**
    - ➤ **Here is my better, rebellious approach: We need to work hard to connect to people with psychosis and overcome our fear of them because relationships and connectedness are crucial to their healing and recovery.**

The word "schizophrenia" was made up by Eugen Bleuler, a Swiss psychiatrist in 1908. The initial part of the word "schiz" means "split" and "phrenia" means "feelings." He apparently was a humane psychiatrist who tried hard to connect with his patients in his institution. He was describing the problems he was having connecting on a feeling level with people with schizophrenia, not an internal split within them. He went on to describe "4 A's" of schizophrenia:

- Affect—another word for the feelings he had trouble connecting to
- Associations—the connections they make between different thoughts that are hard to follow
- Ambivalence—the indecision they sometimes show probably because they're confused and have trouble relating to other people; so, it is more difficult for them to make decisions
- Autism—another word he invented to describe their retreat into their own world away from others

Notice how Bleuler's not talking about hallucinations or delusions at all. He's just saying he's having a hard time connecting with these patients. Without being able to connect and without any medications, he was helpless. His conclusion: Schizophrenia is fundamentally a physical disease process characterized by exacerbations and remissions. No one was ever completely "cured" of schizophrenia. There was always some sort of lasting cognitive weakness or defect that was manifest in their behavior.

What if schizophrenia is really a "relationship illness" with "psychosis complications," instead of a "psychotic illness" with "relationship complications"?

Today's description of schizophrenia usually includes several stages: First is the "prodromal" stage that can go on for years, when the person is increasingly disconnected, awkward, anxious, and hard to relate to, but isn't hallucinating or delusional. Then comes the "first break" when the "true psychosis" appears. There's often a sustained period of "untreated psychosis" during which the person's life collapses entirely, and they withdraw into their own reality. Then, treatment begins, usually in fits and starts, with a resistant patient being coerced into taking medications. Episodic "noncompliance" leads to more relapses, hospitalizations, and loss of function. Eventually, the person is stabilized on medications and must deal with ongoing symptoms, disability, and social disconnectedness—unless they continue to resist treatment and deteriorate. Either way they're likely to die 20–25 years early, not because of violence, suicide, or drugs, but because of unhealthy lifestyles and heart disease.

Sometimes, it strikes me as strange that we consider this a "psychotic" illness, instead of a "connectedness" illness. Why don't we count the "prodrome" as a key part of the illness itself?

Saying that someone may have trouble connecting to others but they don't have schizophrenia until they've developed hallucinations and delusions reminds me of how we describe AIDS: Someone gets infected with the HIV virus, but they don't have "AIDS" until it's killed enough of their T cells that they're likely to contract severe infections and die. Some treatments are targeted at avoiding the HIV infection, some are targeted at building the body's resistance to the effects of the HIV virus, and some are targeted at fighting the bizarre, opportunistic infections, like *Pneumocystis* pneumonia and Kaposi's sarcoma, after they emerge. Using this analogy, some schizophrenia treatments should be targeted at avoiding the disconnection itself, some treatments should be targeted at avoiding the disconnection leading to psychosis, and some treatments should be targeted at the bizarre, "opportunistic" psychotic symptoms, like hallucinations and delusions, after they emerge.

In fact, there are effective "early intervention" strategies from Australia like Dr. Patrick McGorry's Headspace centers for adolescents that focus on social skills and isolation; however, in America, medications for psychosis seem to receive all of the attention and funding.

So, what would happen if promoting relatedness was our first priority treatment for every stage of the illness?

Instead of promoting involuntary medications and hospitalizations regardless of the relationship and isolation costs (I sometimes sarcastically call this current practice "period of unengaged treatment"), we could cultivate connectedness. As it happens, we currently have two competing approaches: one that promotes medications, psychoeducation, and rehabilitation, and the other that promotes relationships and social connectedness:

First, in the biological establishment corner of the ring, we have a relatively new, exemplary program the American military is running in San Diego based on the National Institute of Mental Health (NIMH) RAISE (Recovery After Initial Schizophrenia Episode) research and model. They locate people throughout the armed forces within 6 weeks of their initial psychosis and transfer them to a residential treatment facility in San Diego across the street from the hospital where they're sent to repeatedly if they don't take their medications. Their medical discharge from the military is fast tracked, and they are given psychoeducation and rehabilitation services (personal, educational, and vocational) to reorient them to their new disabled life as they're sent home to receive ongoing care and "benefits" at their local Veterans Affairs medical center. Fewer than 20% of them ever get off medications without relapsing.

Next, in the outsider's corner of the ring, from a remote area of rural Finland, we have the "Open Dialogue" program that has been going on for about 30 years. When someone has a psychiatric crisis there, instead of removing them from their connections, hospitalizing and forcibly medicating them, they send staff with family therapy expertise into people's homes to convene groups of everyone who cares about the person, called "open dialogues," week after week, to help them stay in their community. Sometimes, they do need to use psychiatric medications and even forcibly hospitalize people, but those are rare occurrences compared to the United

States. At this point, the communities there are familiar with this approach and don't get upset that they have an ongoing role and responsibility in supporting the persons with psychosis, instead of being able to send them away somewhere to be fixed for them. They expect the staff to support them in keeping their family member at home, not to take over from them. Life continues, as supportively and as normally as possible, while the person goes through their psychotic experience. According to their published outcomes, 80% of people with "first-break" psychosis have recovered and are off medications within 6 months, including many who never required antipsychotic medications.

What is the "judge's decision"? Open dialogue is "disqualified": Those people in Finland probably didn't have schizophrenia in the first place since they got better without medications. We need more definitive studies of open dialogue in the United States (Dan Fisher—whose personal recovery received the same circular argument response—and others are currently working on this in Massachusetts, New York, and elsewhere). The status quo continues in the meantime.

My rebellious decision: That's an impressive difference in outcomes apparently from targeting disconnection and isolation as the most serious parts of the condition, instead of targeting hallucinations and delusions as the most serious parts of the condition. I'd better come up with a new model of psychosis that prominently includes relationships, and our treatment approaches need to focus on relationships, not just symptoms.

Let's revisit the two women I began this book with, the one who Christ taught to read and the one who lit herself on fire. When the first woman had a "crisis in connectedness" when her newlywed husband left her, overwhelming her rational defenses, she was, nonetheless, filled with love, and the resulting "psychosis" was constructive and loving, actually improving her life considerably. In contrast, the second woman was highly insecure, negative about herself, mired in a life she felt was a failure, with an inconsiderate boyfriend, distancing herself from her feelings and her life with drugs. Her "psychosis" was hateful and destructive, further isolating her and almost killing her. When we rely on medications alone to treat the "symptoms" of psychosis, we're missing all the underlying emotional connectedness issues that could bring understanding and true healing.

It's not that prescribing medications can't be done while supporting connectedness—it just usually isn't in our current practice. Too often, medications are accompanied with diagnoses that separate people from their identities and other people, moving them, often forcibly, away from their lives and families, to hospitals or other environments that only have people with mental illnesses and mental health staff there, and they have side effects that make them feel strange and stand out from other people. An effective approach would have to actively challenge and change all of those tendencies.

4) **Besides giving medications, we feel helpless; so, we assume they're hopeless.**

   ➢ **Here is my better, rebellious approach: There are plenty of reasons to be hopeful. The vast majority of people with psychosis can recover, especially if we believe in them and work hard to promote their recoveries.**

   When I was a medical student, I went to Topeka, Kansas, in the middle of the winter to study at the Menninger Institute, one of the last great psychoanalytic treatment centers at the time. It was very cold and my new wife was back in St. Louis; so, I had a lot of time to read. I spent a considerable amount of time learning about psychoanalytic theory and treatment, but a small, out-of-print booklet that one of my supervisors handed me was the most influential thing I read while I was there. It was a description of Moral Treatment in America in the mid-1800s. At that point, America was a very religious country, and it approached mental illness as a moral condition. There weren't many big public mental hospitals back then (although there were debtor's prisons). The hospitals tended to be small and Church run. They believed that their "psychotic" patients were lost souls and that everyone is made in God's image and has a precious soul that could be rescued with enough kindness, compassion, and prayer. These hospitals were physically attractive. Exercise and gardening were popular. The profession of Occupational Therapy was created there.

The booklet included their outcome data: Within 6 months, two thirds of the patients with psychosis had recovered and returned home from these hospitals.

I thought that was incredible. It seems like hardly anyone with psychosis recovers today. How did they do that, especially since they didn't have any medications?

Maybe kindness, compassion, and prayer are more powerful than we think they are, especially for people who have a mental condition that isolates them from "normal" people.

How did we get the idea that schizophrenia is incurable and a deteriorating condition anyway?

Before Bleuler coined the word "schizophrenia," a German psychiatrist, Emil Kraepelin divided his patients with psychosis into two groups: One group had manic depressive psychosis and had an up-and-down course. The other group had "dementia praecox" (meaning dementia before they got old) and had a chronically deteriorating course. That group was eventually diagnosed as having schizophrenia with the expectation of a negative prognosis. I should point out that during this period, patients with psychosis included a lot of patients with neurological illnesses that they couldn't diagnose or treat at the time. I've read estimates that perhaps a third of Kraepelin's patients with dementia praecox had neurosyphilis (that is, syphilis that was so severe that it got into their brains and gradually destroyed their nerve cells), which wasn't diagnosable or treatable at the time, but was quite common and it had a deteriorating course. Kraepelin lumped together all his non-manic-depressive psychosis patients and said they had the same incurable, deteriorating condition. Now more than over a hundred 100 years later, we're still doing more or less the same thing—lumping all the confusing, chronic people into the schizophrenia bucket. It's become circular reasoning: If you're chronically psychotic and we can't figure out any way to help you, then you have schizophrenia and you're going to deteriorate. If you get better, then you didn't have schizophrenia in the first place. (Remember that same argument with Dan Fisher, the psychiatrist who has recovered from schizophrenia, and with Finland's Open Dialogue?)

Journeys Beyond the Frontier | 73

Almost everyone agrees that schizophrenia encompasses many different illnesses. Yet, our *DSM* and all of our treatment studies lump them all together. Wouldn't you expect long-term psychosis that has childhood roots talking with spirits to respond differently than someone who thinks he's God since his life fell apart and he couldn't handle it and also to respond differently from someone who lost their identity in college, used a lot of drugs, heard voices telling him to burn down a building, and then ended up locked up for the last 5 years—away from society and heavily medicated?

Why can't we separate them out, so we could give more targeted effective treatments?

Because it's hard work and because it's very difficult to get everyone to agree on how to separate them out. It's easier for me to write a book like this and tell you how I separate them out, than it is to convince all the psychiatrists and researchers to do it the same way.

Hopeful research

A number of years ago, psychologist Courtney Harding, a friend of the Village director Martha Long, came to visit the Village. I was excited to meet her since she was the primary investigator on the most important study ever done on the long-term outcome of schizophrenia, the Vermont Longitudinal Study.

Back in the 1950s, the first antipsychotic medication (then called "major tranquilizers"), Thorazine, was being used successfully to treat long-term state hospital patients and release them back into the community. Many governors, including the one in Vermont, saw this as an opportunity to close these expensive, unpopular, and sometimes scandalous institutions. The psychiatrists protested, saying that not all of the patients had responded to medications and that they still needed to stay locked up indefinitely. The governor proceeded with the closures anyway, but gave them a little money for community follow-up.

Thirty-two years later, Courtney led an effort to find 269 discharged patients with schizophrenia to see how their lives had gone. In her van as a single mother, she tracked down over 90% of them, either interviewing them or someone who knew them before they had died. Ten years after their release, over 70% had stayed out of the hospital although many were socially isolated and struggling. Approximately 20 to 25 years after their release, instead of deteriorating, half to two thirds had achieved considerable improvement or recovery. What does she mean by "considerable improvement or recovery"? About 72% had slight or no symptoms, 83% hadn't been hospitalized in the previous year, 76% had close friends, 55% had slight or no impairment in function, 76% had moderately fulfilling or very full lives, and 47% were employed!

This wasn't a fringe study. Its research methodology was sound. The study was performed at Yale with an NIMH grant and was published in the most prestigious psychiatric journal, the *American Journal of Psychiatry*, in 1987. So, why did she have to fight to present the study at universities? Why isn't it in textbooks? Why isn't it taught to new psychiatrists? And, perhaps most importantly, why isn't its hopeful conclusion—over time, half to two thirds of people with schizophrenia recover in meaningful ways—what we tell our patients and our communities?

And why wasn't I taught to help Omar get back to work, socialize with friends, and lead a full life, instead of giving him Social Security disability and rationalizations?

Because these findings are unbelievable to the experts.

Courtney calls this the "clinician's illusion." If someone does well and doesn't need us anymore, we never hear about it. If someone does poorly, we have to spend more time with them. After a while, it seems like everyone is doing poorly because that's who we're spending our time on, and even more importantly, that's who we worry about and talk about in team meetings. The same thing happens in NAMI family support groups. The families who do well move on and spend their time on other activities, while the families who have unending suffering keep coming to NAMI groups and activities seeking hope and relief. After a while, it seems like all of the families are doing poorly because they are the ones who are left.

Our distorted experience tells us that the vast majority of people do poorly, and we're likely to discount any data to the contrary.

Courtney told me that the classic example of the clinician's illusion was Eugen Bleuler himself. He would visit the psychiatric hospital where he did his training when he went on skiing vacations in Switzerland, and over time, the patients he knew deteriorated. Maybe they'd get better for a little while, but over time, they deteriorated. But those were just the patients who stayed in the hospital. His grandson, Manfred Bleuler, did a long-term follow-up study of the patients who were in that hospital, including those who had been discharged. He tracked them down around Switzerland, locating more than 90% of them, and he found the same thing Courtney did—about two thirds of them recovered. But his grandfather never saw most of the people who had recovered.

> Years ago, I went scuba diving in Monterey Bay. After the dive, I helped the guide wash the equipment. He asked me where I was from and what brought me up to Monterrey. I reluctantly told him that I'm a psychiatrist and that I'd just been to a psychiatrists' convention in San Francisco.
>
> He said, "I don't tell this to many people, but when I was in my 20s, after my girlfriend left me, I went through a tough time. I started hearing voices and spent about a month in a psychiatric hospital. They told me that I had schizophrenia and would have to take Mellaril for the rest of my life, but it didn't turn out that way. About a year later, my life got better again, and I stopped the medications that were drugging me up anyway and making it hard to have sex, and I've been doing fine ever since. I've never been back to a psychiatrist since then and hope I never have to."
>
> Since his psychiatrist never saw his recovery, he doesn't know it's possible. He probably won't even try to help the next person with schizophrenia recover because he'll think it doesn't matter what he does, it's hopeless.

Virtually every long-term study on schizophrenia shows the same hopeful outcomes. Who knows how well they'd do if we really believed that what we do matters and that we can really help people recover.

> Clara was in her 60s when I met her as one of my first teammates at the Village. She was a 5-foot-tall dynamo. She was originally from Puerto Rico, but she'd moved to New York and had run a bar by the time she was 19. She'd worn out three husbands along the way and had a soft spot for her grown son to whom she was always "loaning" money. Her

formal education ended in high school, but we hired her as a "personal service coordinator" anyway because she'd done a nice job raising a developmentally disabled daughter balancing protection and independence, she was a good church organizer, and she made dances more fun. We figured all three of those traits would help members at the Village have better lives.

Clara believed that every member she had could recover and have a good life, and she worked hard to help them do just that.

Helen was one of her first members. Helen was in her 40s and had paranoid schizophrenia. Even with medications, she was still paranoid and believed that there were people in the alley plotting against her and that sometimes her food was poisoned. She had been living in a run-down Board and Care for about a decade, not doing much besides smoking and drinking coffee.

Clara began with Helen by asking her what she wanted.

"I don't want to live here anymore, I want an apartment of my own," Helen replied with determination.

Clara began working on looking for an apartment for her. With the benefit of my education, I knew that people like Helen, who are actively paranoid and psychotic even with medications, do not live in their own apartments. They need to be supervised.

Clara wanted to try anyway. Clara believed that her job was to help every single person assigned to her to have a better life, and she believed they could do that together. Fortified by that belief, she worked hard … and the vast majority of the time, she succeeded.

Helen's sister called Clara, "Please, please, don't move Helen to her own apartment. She tried that when she was younger. She'd never take her medications right, and then, she'd become more paranoid and would stop eating and bathing and would barricade herself in the apartment. You people from mental health weren't any help. It all fell on me. It took me forever to get her hospitalized and into this Board and Care. I can't go through all that again."

"Thank you for your concern, but I work for Helen, not for you," Clara forcefully replied.

That's when I decided to back off and let Clara do things her way.

Clara worked really hard alongside Helen to get her into an apartment: They went apartment hunting together, with Clara saying she was Helen's friend, instead of her mental health worker. She helped her with the applications and taught her what questions to ask. She even took Helen back in the evenings to see if the apartment was safe. She prepared the rental paperwork and offered Helen a loan to cover the security deposit.

After they rented the apartment, Clara showed Helen where the local stores and laundromat were. She didn't do her shopping and laundry for her. She coached Helen throughout the entire process. She rode the local buses with her until Helen learned the routes. She got weekly boxes of medications from me, showed Helen how to take the medications, and made sure she did. She got her some donated furniture and pots and dishes, and helped her decorate the apartment, making it a real home. We even had a housewarming party there with some staff, other Village members, and several neighbors.

Much to my surprise, it seemed to be working.

But, 3 months later, I got an urgent call from Helen. She said that her landlord was pumping poisoned gas into her apartment trying to kill her and that she had to get out of there fast.

With the benefit of my education, I knew that this was the psychotic break I'd been expecting. The pressure of taking *care of her own place was too much for her. At least, I could reassure Clara that she'd done her best, but she'd learn that people like Helen couldn't live in their own homes.*

Clara, without the benefit of my education, went over to the apartment, and smelled a leak in the gas pipes there. She paid for Helen to stay in a hotel room for a couple nights while she harassed the hell out of the landlord to get the leak fixed.

Helen lived in that apartment for the next 15 years even though I knew it was impossible.

Unfortunately, that's not the end of the story. Over the years, time passed Helen by. Her hobby, ham radios, became obsolete and she never followed through with learning new technology. She did fall in love with one of our other members and they were lovers for a while, but about 5 years later, her girlfriend died of a drug overdose. Five years later, her sister died, too. Clara retired and Helen never really connected to the new staff in the same way. Eventually, we stopped paying close attention to Helen, and she became more isolated, stopped her medications, and got more paranoid. She ended up abandoning her apartment and riding the buses all night. Eventually, she ended up hospitalized and back in a Board and Care where she died a few years later from consequences of smoking and diabetes.

I wondered if that meant we should have never taken her out of the Board and Care in the first place, but I've decided that it was worth helping Helen have the best life she could have for as long as she could, even though it didn't last forever. We had to take risks together for her to grow.

Over the years, I've seen lots more people like Helen have homes and love. Now, I know it's possible. Now that I've seen it, I can help people do it.

Working in recovery, I've faced many situations where something I was taught was impossible happened: Someone with severe paranoia could live in their own apartment. Someone who had killed their wife turned out to be the sweetest person I've ever met. Someone could go from being a homeless addict to being one of my friends and a valued coworker. When we stopped trying to prevent suicide and locking people up when they were suicidal, they became too busy living to try to kill themselves. When we helped people get a job they weren't prepared for and too ill to do, they made changes to hold the job because it was so important to them. A man with schizophrenia, who refused all treatment, became a great father. Seeing all of these things happen has made me an even more courageous explorer. What else is possible that I was taught was impossible? Maybe Omar could've been helped if I had valued his experience and listened to him, had developed a shared understanding, really connected with him, and, perhaps above all, been hopeful.

Looking back over more than 40 years of the "triumph" of biological psychiatry, it seems to me that what we've really created is "fast food psychiatry": We spend very little time with people, give them simplistic, check-box diagnoses and standardized medication regimens with automatic refill authorizations. Usually, they can't even "have it your way." We incorporate very little health or healing, focusing on efficiency and productivity, while generating pharmaceutical and healthcare corporate profits, and justify it all by telling everyone that the patients are hopeless anyway.

Putting it all together: A compass for our journeys

If we're going to journey beyond the frontier of our normal comfort zone and our normal mental health system, we're going to have to make some serious changes in how we navigate or we'll become just as lost as so many others are. Here are four key transformations that together form the cardinal points of our compass. We'll be using all of them on every journey.

There are times when I need to dig deep and really practice what I preach to restore a life and a family:

> Our case worker returned from Long Beach Community Hospital's psychiatric unit after meeting Nancy, our newest referral, and the news was grim. Nancy had tried to smother her 2-year-old son with a pillow and the Department of Children and Family Services (DCFS) had been called in. DCFS said she couldn't return home to her family (she lived with her mother, husband, and three children) or they'd take away her son to foster care to keep him safe. Nancy had no money and nowhere else to go. Her husband's salary as a grocery store cashier was barely enough to support this family in their two-bedroom apartment. They didn't have health insurance either.
>
> The probable future we'd been asked to help Nancy with—getting on disability and Medi-Cal, taking psychiatric medications, living in a Board and Care, losing her family, likely leading to lifelong heartbreak, depression, and isolation—was profoundly discouraging, but we paid for her to stay in a Board and Care and enrolled her anyway. To make matters worse, they had her on Clozaril, our strongest antipsychotic medication, with the most side effects, that required weekly blood tests I'd have to talk her into and keep track of.

When I met Nancy, she seemed to be in an emotional daze, with a pasted-on smile and very short answers to everything I asked. She said everything was fine and wanted to know when she could go home. Surprisingly, she didn't seem to have any significant mental health history until recently. Her mother had schizophrenia that was stabilized on medications, and Nancy had postpartum depression for a few months after her oldest son's birth. She didn't have any discharge paperwork from the hospital.

I stayed late the next day to meet her husband to try to get a better story of what had happened. I usually find it well worth the time and complications of meeting people's families whenever I can. He came with all three children—a 12-year-old boy focused on his smart phone, a timid 8-year-old daughter with a bow in her hair who wanted to sit with her mother, and an active 2-year-old who set out to explore everything in my office, but wasn't able to talk. They all wanted to know when Nancy could come home.

Nancy's husband, Jim, said that Nancy was essentially her normal self, except that the medications made her sleepy all day. This was her normal mood and quietness. She'd once tried working for a few months but didn't like it; so, she stayed home with the kids and her mom. The kids, including the youngest, all interacted normally with her.

"Can you tell me what happened?"

Jim gently told the story, looking over reassuringly to his wife. "A couple of months ago, Nancy started worrying more and more about Tommy—that's our youngest—thinking something was wrong or something bad was going to happen to him. She would stay up all night watching him sleep, getting more and more nervous; so, I took her to the hospital."

"I did notice that Tommy doesn't talk. Is there something wrong with him?"

"We took him to the pediatrician who told us not to worry, that he'd catch up later on, that there was nothing wrong."

"Really? Even though he's 2."

"He told us that when he turns 4, if he's still having trouble, we can get help from a preschool program, but there's nothing we can get before that without insurance."

"OK. What happened at the hospital?"

"They gave her some medication, risperidone, I think, to help her sleep and calm down, and after a few days, they sent her home, but we couldn't pay for the prescription after we got home."

"She seemed to be gradually getting worse. She'd be distracted a lot. I asked her if she was hearing voices like her mother, but she kept shaking her head no. A couple weeks later, I took her back to the hospital. This time, they gave her a shot of the same medication, so that she'd have it in her system for a couple weeks, and we made an appointment to try to get Medi-Cal before they sent her home again."

"How did that work?"

"Honestly, I think that shot made everything worse. She was restless and couldn't sit still after that, and she was constantly pacing. She was more and more frantic about something being wrong with Tommy. Then, one evening after work, we were sitting on the couch and watching TV, and she suddenly got up and put a pillow on Tommy's face, so that he couldn't breathe. I panicked and got up and grabbed her and the pillow and yelled at her, 'What are you doing?'"

I looked over to Nancy. She looked even more distant than usual. The kids were quietly listening.

"She looked startled at me and said, 'They told me I needed to save him. I'm sorry. I'm sorry. I didn't mean to hurt him.'

This time when I took her to the hospital, they put her on these new pills that make her sleepy, but they seem to have stopped the voices, too."

"I'm not hearing voices," Nancy chimed in. "I'll take my medicine. I'm fine now."

"We'll do whatever it takes to help her get home again. I got a day care to watch the kids after school until I get off work, and an all-day program for Tommy. I won't leave her alone with him again until he's old enough to protect himself. We're all doing more at home. We didn't realize how much we just left for Nancy to do."

"I'm helping, too," the daughter added quietly.

"OK. Let's see what we can do." It was both heartbreaking to see this family in crisis and heartwarming to see how much they cared about each other.

We all worked hard the next 6 months.

I saw Nancy weekly for her medications and blood tests, and I tried to get her to understand what had happened. Her side effects mounted. Not only was she sleepy, she drooled all over her pillow at night. Her menstrual periods stopped. She gained 20 pounds. I didn't want to try other, less toxic medications because if they didn't work, everything would be lost. I ordered a blood test that showed her Clozaril level was on the high side; so, I cautiously lowered her dosage until almost all of the side effects were gone and the psychosis was still controlled. Some of her emotions seemed to return, too. Nancy got good at going weekly to the lab herself and taking care of everything. She kept every appointment with me and with the DCFS worker. She even went to parenting groups since the children's dependency court ordered them. We got Nancy Social Security Income and Medi-Cal; so, there was some money to work with and we put them on a list to get a subsidized apartment for the entire family.

Every evening after work, Jim would pick up Nancy from the Board and Care. She'd make dinner and help the kids with their homework. They'd eat together and after the kids went to bed, Jim would drive her back to the Board and Care. I stayed late and met with the family together once a month to help them through this. Tommy's day care did think there was something wrong with his speech and found him a therapist. He still wasn't talking at 3. It turned out Nancy had been right.

When it came for their 6-month court hearing to decide if Nancy could return home, it seemed that against all odds, it was going to happen. The DCFS worker agreed. I wrote a letter emphasizing how cooperative she'd been and how the whole family had pulled together, recommending reunification. But, when the DCFS supervisor found out what was going on, he said no, even though he'd never met the family. He didn't want to take the risk of a dead child.

Jim didn't stop fighting. He talked to the judge himself and brought my letter to her directly. The judge hesitated and compromised. If things went well another 3 months, she'd let Nancy return home.

Three months later, they moved into a new apartment together.

At their last family meeting a few months later, I asked them if any good had come from all these struggles, if it had made them stronger. After a pause, the shy daughter spoke up, "I think we've learned how to take care of each other. We didn't used to do that before mommy got sick."

Chapter 4

Preparing for our journeys: Understanding psychosis

"Hey, Dr. Mark." Patty's yell pierced the entire basement that housed our Homeless Assistance Program.

Patty was one of our regulars. We'd known her for years. Even though pound for pound she could create more havoc than anyone else, virtually all of the staff and many of the other homeless members loved her anyway. We're strange that way. She used a lot of speed and could swear like a sailor. We knew she was really high when she started singing loudly (and badly). She prostituted herself and got thrown out of every room we helped her get. She even called herself a pain in the ass, but she was our pain in the ass. She always came back, sometimes after being beaten or jailed, sometimes after being hospitalized and tied down and forcibly medicated, and we always welcomed her back. She was houseless, but we were her home.

"What, Patty?" I yelled back just as loudly and waved at her to come over.

She walked over to me and sat down next to my messy desk. "You've known me for a long time now. What's my diagnosis?"

I thought for a moment. If I gave her the professional answer, "You have schizoaffective disorder, manic type, post-traumatic stress disorder, amphetamine dependence, a borderline personality disorder, and seizures," I could almost guarantee her response would not be, "Sounds right to me, let's make a treatment plan." She wouldn't be able to use that answer. It would be mumbo jumbo to her. It would just make her feel stupid and small. And she is asking me a real question, "What's wrong with me?" An idea came to me. I could answer her question in words she'd understand.

"You're a pain in the ass."

"What do you mean, I'm a pain in the ass?"

"Well, you never knew who your father was, and your mother was a drug addict and a prostitute. She probably used drugs while she was pregnant, making you a fussy baby and kid. She would leave you alone a lot when you were little and probably even sold you to some of her Johns. When you were 3 years old, you were taken away by DCFS and given to a foster family where they abused you, too. By the time you got to school, you were always agitated and fought with everyone just to survive. They thought you were retarded and had ADHD because you couldn't focus on learning anything even though you're not, and they put you in special classes with retarded kids and gave you Ritalin. That led to all the other kids teasing you for being a 'retard' and a 'freak,' and you had to fight even more. When you were 12, you were drinking and into older boys. By 14, you were into drugs and ditching school. You dropped out of school and ran away at 15 and became homeless and survived by prostituting. You had two kids taken away from you even though you promised yourself you'd never do to them what your mom had done to you, and you've been heartbroken ever since. Now, you're older. You can't really handle the streets anymore or drugs. You hear babies calling to you at night, 'Where are you, mommy?' You can't sleep unless you're drunk or drugged up. You're scared and worn out. Even when someone tries to help you, who you know cares about you, like we do, you still fight us because that's what you do ... and that makes you a pain in the ass."

She sat quietly for a moment thinking before she said, "Can you write that down for me?"

I wrote it down on a piece of paper and gave it to her. She carried it around the center showing it to all the other staff and members saying, "Look at this. The doctor understands me."

It's time for us to take a major conceptual step that today's psychiatry rarely takes. We need to move from thinking about our brains to thinking about our minds.

Science uses a hierarchy of complexity as we try to understand our world and ourselves: We begin at the most fundamental level with physics. As various subatomic, charged particles combine together to form atoms, a new set of properties emerge with chemistry. As atoms combine into more complex molecules, some of those molecules become self-replicating and purposeful, and "life" emerges with biology. As the biochemical processes of the body and brain develop and form complex connections both within themselves and with other living beings, our mind emerges.

(Ken Wilber describes this hierarchy of "holons" that build on each other in great detail in many of his books, including *A Brief History of Everything*. For a concise, but dense, definition of the mind that dovetails nicely with these conceptions, check out Dr. Dan Siegel's definition of the mind as "the emergent self-organizing process, both embodied and relational, that regulates energy and information flow within and among us" and his "mindsight" work.)

When we try to understand things "reductionistically," we "reduce" them to their underlying components. Today's biological psychiatry is fundamentally a reductionistic approach that tries to "reduce" the mind to computer-like brain functions to understand how it works (which is a good deal of why it often feels dehumanizing).

When we try to understand things "integrationally" or "holistically," we try to understand the properties that "emerge" from the underlying complexity and connectedness. Unlike the psychiatrists who recently announced that all mental illnesses are brain illnesses, I think that most mental conditions are mind conditions. Computers don't get mental illnesses. Even the word "illness" only really exists at the biological level, not above or below it. Atoms and molecules don't get ill, only living things do. The restrictiveness and "poor fit" of the term "mental illness" to describe the extraordinary experiences (including the suffering and altered abilities and disconnection that can often accompany them, even to the point of leading to suicide) are, in my opinion, because these experiences exist only when the mind emerges from the complexity of life. If we're going to understand mental experiences, including psychosis, we're going to have to look not just at biology and life but also at the mind.

From this perspective, the key question is: How do our minds emerge from our brains, our bodies, and our relationships?

It's our challenge to try to trace the growth and the evolution of their minds, track impacts on them, and create a formulation—like I did for Patty.

> *When I was a kid, we used to go on long family camping trips often focusing on visiting the national parks and monuments in the West. We would stop by the visitor centers to look in the museum and watch the orientation movie. We'd go on self-guided trails reading the pamphlets and the signs, so that we'd understand what we were looking at. We weren't supposed to just play around and have fun or enjoy the view. We had to learn something, too. We went to evening campfire programs and especially on ranger-led walks.*
>
> *Skilled and experienced park rangers can read the history of an area by looking at the terrain and the plants and animals living there. They can describe how there were shallow seas when there were dinosaurs; so, there are fossils in the sandstone. They can describe how the plates of the earth moved to cause the mountains to rise. They can see the impact of the ice age glaciers carving the mountains. They can also describe how the forest changes depending on beavers' damming rivers, wildfires coming*

through, and even the lack of wolves leading to an overabundance of elk eating the shrubs by the river. More recently, they've focused on the effects of man causing soil erosion, air pollution, or global warming that leads to hot dry conditions that lead to bark beetles killing thousands of stressed trees.

The landscape is literally the living record of the history of the park and its relationships.

As a skilled and experienced psychiatrist, I should be able to read the history of a person by looking at the terrain and the patterns of connections in someone's mind.

But how can you "look at" someone's mind? You said you can't see voices on a brain scan.

That's right. It turns out we can learn very little about complex psychiatric functions by observing how different parts of the brain are behaving or by taking sophisticated high-tech pictures of them, like neurologists do. We have almost no useful "tests." Nearly everything of importance is only visible to the person looking at themselves. We have to ask them what they can see about their own minds and then listen carefully to their answers.

But it seems as though most doctors hate to listen to their patients. Some have their patients fill out lengthy questionnaires in the waiting room. Some have nurses take the history first to save time. Within seconds of asking, "What brought you here today?," they interrupt to direct the patient to what they think is important. They don't believe the patients much of the time anyway (but, to be fair, if the patient doesn't trust them or have a good relationship with them, they're not likely to be forthcoming). They describe patients as poor historians, manipulative, drug-seeking, in denial, etc. Many doctors seem to have a special hatred for listening to psychiatric patients: "They're all crazy."

More specifically, we have to explore together: Staff must build trust first and along the way, share ourselves, too. We have to make it "getting to know each other," instead of a "clinical interrogation." We must have an attitude of "respectful curiosity," instead of being judgmental or shaming. We have to ask patients, "What happened to you?," not just "What's wrong with you?" We have to explore their areas of interest, not just what we want to know, so that they'll be motivated to explore their minds with us. We have to explore their strengths as well as their weaknesses. We have to "listen to the music, not just the words." We have to share what we're learning with them, so that we can learn together. Two heads are better than one. (Often times, adding more people who know them is even better.) We have to take the time to really get to know them.

And if we do, they'll have a story to tell.

Our minds are literally the record of the journey we've been on.

Before birth, the development of our brains recreates our evolution. We have "reptilian" brains first and then "mammalian brains" and then "human brains." Our family's inheritance expresses itself next, whether it's grandpa's singing voice or our aunt's high anxiety, as the structures start to fill in with cells. The prenatal environment—whether mom's drug use or the high level of stress hormones from dad's beatings or attachment hormones from mom feeling loved and loving—may all leave their marks. A difficult birth can cause damage. Early childhood emotional experiences create the templates that we interpret the world through. Childhood trauma has lasting effects. The "mirroring" we get from those around us help us form our identities. The way people around us react as our internal traits emerge—whether it's intuitive abilities, our sexual attractions, and gender identity, or heightened physical sensitivities, etc.—influence how we connect the nerves within our brains—and so do our reactions to ourselves. The process continues through adulthood as we fall in love, are disappointed and heartbroken, are sent to war, get in a car crash, etc. It's all there if you look hard enough and know what you're looking for.

Many people are frightened by this vision because everything matters. That's more responsibility and especially blame than we want to face. Facing all of our responsibilities compassionately, with acceptance and forgiveness, while doing the best we can, is hard to do. It's easier to say there's a chemical imbalance and leave it to the doctor and the medications to fix. But even doctors and medications work better if everyone is actively involved and responsible than if we say, "Can I just get my medications and leave?"

Consider these four stories:

When Maria was a small child in rural Mexico, she had the ability to sense who was sick in her village. They believed that this ability was a blessing from God and encouraged her to develop it. She learned how to use some folk remedies and perform spiritual healing. She came to Los Angeles with her husband and son illegally when she was in her 20s. She supplemented her income as a maid by selling healing potions. After several years, her husband left her, she was barely able to support herself and her son, and her son's behavior became worse and worse. The school became concerned, and he was diagnosed with ADHD and given some Social Security income. Children's services told Maria to stop her "witchcraft business" or risk losing him. She reluctantly gave it up, but had less and less to hold on to: She was a failure as a wife, mother, and healer, and she was impoverished and at risk of deportation. When she broke down in tears at her son's school, they sent her to me to treat her depression. She admitted that she was hearing negative, critical voices that she couldn't handle, and she agreed to take medication for both her depression and the voices. I carefully titrated the dosage of Abilify to quiet the voices, but not take away her sensitivity to others that she still considered a blessing from God. I told her that she still had a good mother inside of her that she needed to trust and encourage. Gradually, she began to rebuild herself.

Doug grew up in an upper-middle class family in South Carolina with very conservative, traditional values. Nonetheless, his father paid for him to go to an expensive, private liberal arts college where he increasingly questioned and rebelled against the values he'd grown up with. He also experimented with drugs. One night at a party, he tried LSD and felt he was "opened up to the true spiritual nature of the universe." He also had the best sex of his life. Somehow, that experience led to his running naked around the campus and yelling for the girl to marry him. The campus police brought him to the psychiatric hospital where, surprisingly, it took 2 weeks and antipsychotic medication to feel normal again, but even then, his world view was forever altered. When his father found out he'd been using drugs and "wasting my money," as he put it, he cut him off. Doug took off for California to broaden his world, where he discovered even more drugs, including speed, and ended up being arrested for breaking into and disrupting a Yoga class and saying he was Paul McCartney and singing loudly. When I met him, he insisted that he wanted to continue to expand his consciousness with drugs and that he was done with his father's limited world. He refused medications. He couldn't hold a job and continued to be repeatedly jailed for disruptive behavior.

R. J. emerged from a violent, fragmented, frequently incarcerated family in the black ghetto of South Central Los Angeles as both a high school dropout and a successful rap musician who had a recording contract and even toured in Asia. Hanging out with his family, he had several incidents where he was accosted by police and even beaten by them, and he ended up in jail repeatedly as a result. He became more and more paranoid of the police and started smoking marijuana daily. When tens of thousands of dollars of recording equipment was stolen, he suspected a police plot and frightened his girlfriend by leaving his apartment and hiding from the police in various run-down hotels. He couldn't really describe how he landed in jail the next time, but while he was there, he was "incoherent" and forced to take antipsychotic medications that calmed him down and made him more cooperative, but that also dulled his thinking and made it impossible for him to compose lyrics. His public defender got him conditionally released to live with his girlfriend and enrolled in the Village program. Over the next few months, with his girlfriend's support, he stayed away from marijuana and the police, and gradually I helped him taper off his medications. For about a year, his paranoia did not return, and he began working regularly as a musician again. As the pressure mounted, however, he returned to marijuana and again became more and more paranoid. He absolutely refused to believe he was mentally ill or should get back on his medications. Instead, he focused his anger on his mother who he said hadn't protected him from his stepfather's sexual abuse, and he also directed his anger at his cousin who had been arrested for murder when they were kids. His threatening and hatred-filled messages to his mother were nearly incoherent, including accusing her of having a life of rape and murder and serving Satan. His girlfriend became more and more desperate as she tried to keep from losing him forever.

And finally, Christina could always see spirits of dead people as a child and had amazing intuition to the point of seeming to be able to read minds. This wasn't surprising in her family because her aunt and grandmother had the same traits. With their support, she went to medical school and became a highly successful intuitive healer, including leading workshops and writing books. As she's explored her own consciousness, she's become involved in women's alchemy and personal transformation. She believes that her spirit came to Earth from another planet and that she's here, in this crucial moment in history, to help humankind to take the next step in our spiritual evolution. She's happily married with a family and has numerous loyal followers.

Which of these people are psychotic?

Do they have different types of psychosis? (Or maybe we should say different journeys with psychosis and other extraordinary experiences?)

Should we try to help them in different ways?

The overarching problem, in my view, is that our DSM definition of psychosis and schizophrenia is unidimensional—it only evaluates people on the basis of their symptoms. Each of their "symptoms" must be put into some context—a context of how they view themselves, their relationships, their community, and their culture. Doing that shouldn't just be an afterthought—"let's be culturally competent in our assessments"—it should be imbedded in the way we assess and treat everyone with psychosis and other extraordinary experiences.

Instead of conceptualizing psychosis as a disorder you have in your brain, I'm urging that we conceptualize psychosis as a profound experience that emerges (and resolves) as a product of multiple alterations in function acting in combination, no one of which produces psychosis on its own.

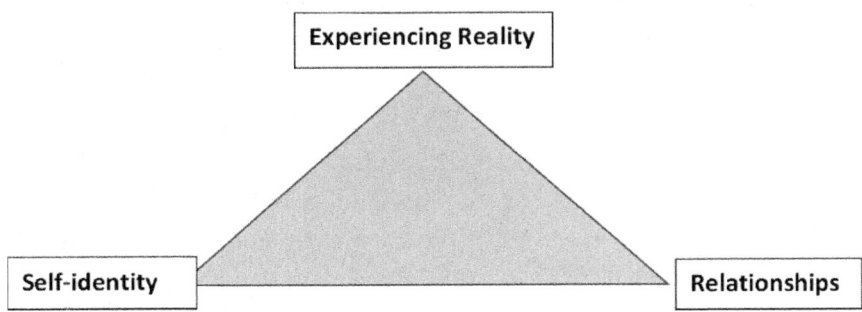

The Psychosis Triangle

The three interacting dimensions that lead to psychosis are as follows:

1) There are changes in how they are experiencing "reality"—e.g., hallucinations, delusions, paranoia, or spiritual experiences as well as changes in how they process reality like making idiosyncratic connections or relying on irrational "primary process" thinking.
2) There are changes in their internal processing and self-identity—e.g., how they hold themselves together, balancing rational and irrational portions, self-observation, or creating their own stories. It can also include "anhedonia," the inability to feel joy or pleasure in life.
3) There are changes in how they relate to other people—e.g., disconnected, missing "normal" social signals, hard to relate to, socially anxious, avoidant, or even paranoid.

None of these dimensions falling apart on its own creates psychosis. All three of them must be seriously impaired for someone to become psychotic. Any of the three can act as the initial weak point, putting its neighboring dimensions at risk. Once two dimensions are compromised, the third dimension in the triangle is under severe strain, and if it also falls, psychosis is the result—or it could be a stronghold to rebuild the other two dimensions, leading to recovery.

For example, if someone has difficulties perceiving reality, that can stress their self-identity, but they could contain the damage if they can solidify an identity as an intuitive healer or a voice-hearer. Their relationships will also be strained, but if they can find people who can relate to them and who accept those self-identities and altered reality, the damage may be contained, and their social roles can persist relatively unharmed. While this is an unusual outcome in our society for people with auditory hallucinations, it is a common outcome for blind people, even though their perception of reality is more damaged than most people who have hallucinations.

Although our current medical model conceptualizes all psychosis as beginning with difficulties perceiving reality (and often looks no further), psychosis can begin with any of the three areas of functioning. For example, if someone's relationships are highly abusive and traumatizing, that can put their self-identity and their perception of reality at risk. If the damage progresses to two dimensions, we call it a personality disorder (with impaired relationships and self-identity) or PTSD (with impaired relationships and perception of reality). But there's a strong risk that the third dimension will also fall: For example, loss of relationships and self-identity can often make it hard to perceive reality, and severe dissociations and flashbacks can make it hard to sustain a self-identity, as can an unbearable loss that is responded to with denial of the reality of the loss.

In my opinion, this is a truly mind-based, holistic, biopsychosocial model with all three dimensions interacting as equals.

Let's examine each of the three dimensions in a little more detail:

1) Experiencing and processing reality: All of us have a set of senses that bring our minds information about reality—including the usual "five senses," some intuitive/emotional senses, and even "spiritual" senses. These bring in an enormous amount of information that require rapid processing to put together a coherent perception of the world for us. That processing includes synthesizing the information, combining it with past experiences, and creating meaning. A small portion of this processing is conscious and rational. Most of it is unconscious and irrational. All

of these types of processing need to be effectively integrated to create a coherent, meaningful, and hopefully accurate experience. A process this complicated is vulnerable to errors and distortions of a variety of types. Someone may or may not be aware of their own errors and distortions. Many of the most common of these errors—for instance, hallucinations, delusions, paranoia, and changes in time perception—are included within the broad heading of psychosis. Others are included within grief, love, creativity, spirituality, brain or nerve damage, delirium, addiction, and cultural beliefs. In my opinion, it's important to take enough time to really understand how someone is perceiving and processing, instead of just labeling them as psychotic and moving on to prescribing medications.

2) We all have images of ourselves that we use to integrate our experiences. These self-identities are formed by our experiences of ourselves (and we sometimes struggle when we observe ourselves doing something that doesn't fit in with our self-identity) and, probably more importantly, by how we see ourselves though other people's perceptions of us. Other people's reactions to us hold up a mirror to enrich our self-identity. This "mirroring" begins early when adults make faces at infants responding carefully to their smiles and frowns. It moves on to our roles in our families, our peer interactions, and especially falling in love. It can even continue to seeing ourselves reflected in nature, holy texts, and spiritual awakenings. Once again, there's a lot of vulnerability in all these complexities. Some people end up feeling like they "don't fit in" or "can't connect" or "nobody understands them" or even "I didn't realize it was abnormal to hear voices until I got older and found out other people weren't like me." It can be a serious challenge to form a strong, balanced self-identity—a task many of us keep working at and developing our entire lives. A strong sense of self-identity needs to develop over time and adapt to new stressors. To other people around them, many people with psychosis may seem as though "they're not all there" or "they have split personalities that change unpredictably" or "they're lost in their own worlds." It can take a great deal of acceptance and compassion to give enough

empathetic mirroring to people who are that broken to help them grow, develop, and heal.

3) Man is both a profoundly social animal and a profoundly socially fearful animal. While very few people can thrive while living an isolated life, nearly everyone has considerable social anxiety. We evolved in small family-based groups, each one only trusting its own members, developing its own customs and languages to ease connections, and avoiding "strangers." In today's society, our relationships are heavily dependent on the roles we have—family, employment, romantic, community, spiritual, financial, etc. Making things even harder, our relationships can be seriously damaged by factors entirely out of our control. People we're close to can turn on us, reject us, or be taken away from us … and we have to adapt and go on with our lives. Once again, all that complexity leaves a lot of room for things to go wrong. Most people who have psychotic experiences had long-standing preexisting issues in their relationships, often including intense isolation. (Remember the discussion in Chapter 3 about schizophrenia being a "connectedness" illness, instead of a "psychotic" illness?) For many people, the ability to sustain relationships is crucial to the development of and recovery from psychosis.

Now, let's look back at our four people:

- Maria always had an unusual perception of reality, but she had strong relationships and self-identity; so, she was fine for most of her life. When her relationships were severely damaged—her husband left her, her son disobeyed and disrespected her, and then her healing clientele was all taken away, it put stress on both her self-identity and her reality perception. When she lost her personal roles and integrity—becoming a failure as a wife, mother, healer, wage earner, and citizen—she became more isolated, and she began hearing disturbing voices emerging from her destructive self-doubts. All three points of the triangle collapsed. Our services were designed to restore all three at the same time to help her recover: medications for the voices, propping up her self-identity as a good mother, and helping her form new positive relationships.

- Doug had a very unstable self-identity since he rebelled against his family's values. With a push from LSD, he lost touch with reality, which would likely have been temporary, if he'd had a strong self-identity and relationships, and if his treatment hadn't included taking him away from all his relationships, and trying to give him a psychotic identity that he rejected. His family abandoned him, leaving him even more adrift, and then he made things much worse by traveling to California with no identity, relationships, and more reality-impairing drugs. We tried to connect him to our "Island of Misfit People" subculture to try to strengthen his relationships and self-identity, but repeated jailing kept him isolated, demoralized, and psychotic.
- R. J. also began with an impaired self-identity, but he was holding it together until a series of events traumatized him, isolated him, and incarcerated him. Add marijuana and all three points of the triangle were damaged. We initially helped him recover and restabilize, including continuing a strong relationship with his girlfriend, returning to his musician identity, and improving his reality perception with short-term medications and staying off drugs. I didn't realize that there was substantial underlying weakness in his self-integration and relationships from his severe childhood trauma, and so, when stress increased and he restarted marijuana use and refused to restart medications, all three points fell apart again, with his girlfriend desperately holding on.
- Christina, like Maria, began with an unusual perception of reality, but she's had an amazingly strong self-identity and relationships throughout her life. Even when she's encountered more unusual perceptions, for instance, feeling like an alien, she's able to integrate them into her life without negatively impacting the other two points. She's also found that some, even if not all, of her unusual perceptions of reality are very helpful to other people; so, they're not even disabilities for her. By my multimodal model, she's never been psychotic or schizophrenic.

OK. That makes sense to me. I can see how you put those stories together using your triangle.

Notice the shifts I've made from our usual "fast food" psychiatry assessments to "make sense":

- I gave you a formulation, instead of a diagnosis, for each one.
- I described how they grew and changed, both getting better and worse, over time.
- I included their perspective and self-identity in our formulations.
- I put their symptoms into a personal relationship as well as social and cultural context.

Explaining our "strange facts"

Before we set out on our journeys, let's test this three-dimensional model of psychosis to see if it can explain the "strange facts" I began this book with:

- **People with schizophrenia in third world countries tend to have better outcomes than those in first world countries.**

This research finding is from a World Health Organization (WHO) multisite study that included India, South America, and Africa. The best outcomes were seen in the India sites, but only if the patient's family lived near the hospital. In these hospitals, there isn't funding for food or much care; so, the family has to come and be with the patient, bringing them meals throughout their stay. When that happens, the patients can sustain their relationships and self-identity and recover. Not all third world sites do well. For example, there are long-term psychiatric institutions in India, where the family has no contact with their mentally ill family member except for sending monthly checks to the facility and the patients are often mistreated and rarely recover. In Malaysia, patients could only leave the hospital if they were totally cured and didn't need any medication or supportive services and even then, skeptical families usually refused to take them home and no one would rent to them.

- **People with spiritual explanations for their conditions tend to have better outcomes than people with medical explanations.**

This is likely a result of how much easier it is to integrate a self-image based on unusual spiritual experiences than to integrate a "mentally ill" identity, assuming that the spiritual identity is positive, for example, being "touched by God," rather than "demonic" and subject to exorcism or being tied to a tree until the evil spirits leave them. Over the last several decades, in America, we've been fighting stigma by promoting a medical illness model. The result has been that people are more patient with and less rejecting and blaming of people with mental illnesses, but they are even more segregating of them. They're seen as having an illness that isn't their fault, but that separates them from normal people, and the possibility of normal life, barring curative pharmaceutic treatments. Even if the pills work to improve reality perception and processing, their self-identity and relationships are often damaged too badly along the way to really recover—thus, the large numbers of chronically medicated, chronically isolated, empty people in our system.

Think again about the contrast between the RAISE model where the young soldiers were forcibly removed from their lives and their dreams while they were medicated, given disability payments, and told they'd need to be in treatment forever and the Open Dialogue model where they worked primarily to keep the person's relationships, roles, and self-determination as strong as possible. No wonder the recovery rates are so different.

- **Small "moral treatment" institutions in America in the 1800s had about a 2/3 recovery rate from psychosis in 6 months, which is better than any treatment program since then.**

Moral treatment, like Open Dialogue, can help us focus on what strategies are likely to be most effective in strengthening relationships and self-identity. Those staff didn't see themselves as different from their patients—all of them were God's creations. They expected that they could help restore people's identities by reconnecting them to pleasurable activities, to nature, to other people, and to God. They were hopeful and empowering. They believed in what they were doing.

- **People with schizophrenia who didn't respond to the first medication, Thorazine, but who were kicked out of the back wards of the state hospital in Vermont to save money had about a 2/3 recovery rate when they were tracked down after 20–25 years (and it wasn't because better medications were invented).**

Look again at Courtney Harding's data: 72% had slight or no symptoms, 83% hadn't been in the hospital in the previous year, 76% had close friends, 55%

had slight or no impairment in function, 76% had moderately fulfilling or very full lives, and 47% were employed. What if our usual thinking, that people need to have their symptoms effectively treated before they can return to life and functioning is backward? What if their symptoms subsided because they had close friends, jobs, and full lives?

One of the key breakthroughs of Psychosocial Rehabilitation has been to reverse the common treatment approach. Instead of working hard to eliminate all of their symptoms to make them "ready" to return to their lives, we created "supported services"—supported housing, employment, education, etc.—where someone who isn't symptom free but is motivated is supported to do something with someone helping, as a "coach," learning while doing. Maybe this strategy is very effective because it emphasizes taking on the role of apartment dweller, employee, or student—as a self-identity, as an integral part of learning the needed skills—all while being supported with a personal relationship. Strengthening self-identity and relationships around new positive roles might indirectly reduce symptoms, too.

Courtney told me one other observation she had that wasn't published: Almost no one recovered who had a relapse and was rehospitalized after SSI disability income was invented. Sure, that group is a worse prognosis group since they relapsed, but we shouldn't underestimate the damage that giving people a "totally permanently disabled" identity could be causing ... and we don't have to make eligibility for social financial support and medical care destroy your identity. There are other ways to design the system, as pioneered below:

> In the 1980s, Bill Anthony and the Center for Psychiatric Rehabilitation at Boston University began focusing, not on the symptoms themselves, but on the resultant functional limitations, disabilities, and handicaps of psychiatric conditions. For physical conditions, like paralysis, people aren't expected to be symptom free, able to walk, before they can go to college or work. We help them with accommodations, adaptations, and supports to work and study alongside us, not just in special sheltered environments. Boston University conceptualized people with long-standing psychiatric disabilities the same way. They didn't have to be free of psychiatric symptoms to go to college or work.

They needed rehabilitation plans filled with accommodations, adaptations, and supports.

When they began with the premise that these people could learn and work, even with their psychiatric disabilities, they did.

By the time I met Bill Anthony, in 1991, when he came to see our new program at the Village and write an article about Martha's leadership, he was convinced that recovery was going to be "the next big thing in mental health." Since then, he and his colleagues have spread the vision of recovery as an organizing, client-centered goal around which all our services could be arrayed. "Recovery can occur even though symptoms reoccur" and "Recovery from the consequences of the illness is sometimes more difficult than recovering from the illness itself" were two of their basic assumptions. They developed detailed approaches for every part of the recovery process from coaching techniques to fighting discrimination to finding meaning and inclusion. They've described the Recovery system I believe we should have.

- **People with schizophrenia in England who were given "befriending" for an hour once a week experienced a major improvement in their psychotic and depressive symptoms after 6 months without a medication change.**

A group in England, led by Turkington and Kingdon, developed a new Cognitive Behavioral Therapy (CBT) approach to treat people with schizophrenia. Instead of telling them their psychosis wasn't real or avoiding talking about it to refrain from "feeding into their delusions," they talked with their patients at length, trying to understand what they were experiencing from their point of view, especially about how their delusions initially emerged. Collaboratively, they painstakingly uncover their patients' thought patterns, looking for ways to help them find alternatives that might work better for them. Once again, this strategy appears to be improving self-identity while supporting their patients with a personal relationship.

The outcomes were striking: With weekly 1-hour sessions for 6 months, they had a substantial reduction (about a third) in their patients' hallucinations and delusions, passivity, and depression. They said that the magnitude of this change was about the same as we would expect if we put them on Clozaril, our most powerful, dangerous medication, instead of their usual pills. This research has been replicated, and now CBT for psychosis is offered regularly in the British health service. However, despite being published in the prestigious American journal, *The Archives of General Psychiatry*, CBT for psychosis barely exists in America because, in my opinion, we're usually unwilling to really try to collaboratively understand our patients' thoughts.

When I first saw this group present their approach at an American Psychiatric Association conference, probably 15 years ago, a strange detail caught my attention: In their research, they included a control group. Half of the patients got highly formatted CBT for psychosis and the other half got "befriending" for an hour a week. They described "befriending" as a friendly visit with someone who expressed interest in and concern for the patient, talking about anything, often about cricket matches. Surprisingly, after 6 months, both groups improved similarly on all three scales. Just talking to them in a friendly, concerned way for an hour a week had a dramatic effect. It turned out that friendly "relationships," even an hour a week, have a substantial healing effect.

But there's one more thing. They checked the patients again after another 1 1/2 years. This time, the two groups were different. The "befriending" patients deteriorated somewhat without their friends, but not as bad as they started out, while the CBT patients continued to improve further even without their therapists. It appears that the CBT taught them ways of thinking that continued to improve their self-identity and their experience of reality.

Wow! All those things that didn't make sense when we started fit together when we look at it from all three dimensions. It's just hard for me to believe that those other things are as important as medications.

Wait until you see this last strange fact.

- **In the Netherlands, after 7 years of being treated with medications following a first-break psychosis, only 17% of patients who were told to stay on their medications were going to school or working, while 40% of patients who kept trying to lower their dosage and get off their medications were going to school or working, even though only a few actually managed to stay off their medications.**

First the data: This is the "Wunderink" study, published in 2013. They followed two groups of people with first-break psychosis for 7 years—an extraordinarily long time for a medication study—comparing two treatment approaches. The first group was put on "maintenance" medications for the rest of their lives. This is the standard treatment. It's built on the idea that schizophrenia is a chronic condition and that it's critical to avoid relapses, which happen more often when people stop their medications, because relapses and rehospitalizations can destroy lives and damage brains. The second group was put on a "dose reduction/discontinuation" strategy where every time the person was doing better, they tried to lower their dosage or even get off their medications. This is usually considered a high-risk strategy because the person is likely to get damaging relapses triggered by stopping their protective medications. Many prescribers (and families) refuse to do this, sometimes even threatening to hospitalize the person who is "playing with their medications."

In the first 6 months, the people who stayed on their medications, as expected, had fewer relapses than those who tried stopping them. From there, the "maintenance" group started to do somewhat worse. Whenever they did have a relapse, their medications were increased, and they ended up on more and more medications with more and more relapses. At the same time, the "dose reduction/discontinuation" group seemed to start having fewer and fewer relapses, perhaps figuring out what was causing them and learning how to deal with them. At 3 years, the two groups evened out and after that, the "dose reduction/continuation" group gradually did better than the "maintenance" group, even though very few actually were able to get off their medications permanently. But the biggest shocker were the recovery stats I quoted above—40% vs. 17%. Why would that be?

Here's a back story for the Wunderink study: Robert Whitaker has been on a crusade for several years now to publicize studies, like this one, that challenge the "medications for life to treat an underlying chemical imbalance" model. His "Mad in America" website is an impressive, wide-open forum for bloggers of all stripes, occasionally including me, to share opinions in a highly emotionally charged environment, free from the usual "professional peer review" criteria. Robert is a journalist, not a mental health professional. I'd even go so far as to call him a "muckraking journalist" in the best sense of the word. He's dug around our medication practices, turning up things we haven't wanted to look at, and he tries his hardest to make us face them. His first book, *Mad in America*, is basically a historical review of psychiatric practice in America for the last 150 years or so. His main point in that book was that in every era, there have been "scientifically approved" treatments that have been the standard of care, ranging from wrapping people in wet sheets, to spinning them rapidly in chairs, to electroshock therapy, to lobotomies, that in retrospect look somewhere between foolish and downright cruel and destructive—and that, in all likelihood, even though we're so self-assured and smug, today's practices will be similarly discredited in the future.

His second book, *Anatomy of an Epidemic*, poses the question, "If psychiatric conditions are caused by chemical imbalances and we've created medications to correct those imbalances, why does it appear that the rates, severity, and chronicity of mental illnesses and their resultant disability are going up and up?" He combs the biological psychiatry literature and notices that while there are considerable short-term data that taking pills helps the presenting symptoms, it's far less clear whether taking those same pills for extended periods of time is helpful or harmful. There aren't that many good long-term studies because they're very hard to do and lots of people drop out over time. (The usual FDA drug approval studies that all medications go through are 6 to 12 weeks and we're prescribing these pills for decades.) Interpreting these studies is hard (mostly because of the dropouts and because people's treatments change over the years). Whitaker's analysis shows that with regularity, the people who are not on medications do better (for example, they have fewer symptoms and hospitalizations, and they have more homes and jobs) than the people who take medications. I was taught, and the leading biological psychiatrists (almost all of whom receive money from pharmaceutical companies) still teach, that is not because the medications are harmful over the long term. It's because people who have more serious illnesses would be more likely to have to be on medications and the people who are functioning off medications had milder illnesses in the first place.

Whitaker instead comes to the provocative conclusion that since our brain is filled with feedback loops, when we give it a medication that creates a "new imbalance," over time, our brain responds by creating the opposite—more undesirable imbalances. He posits that when we try to get someone off medications, we're not only fighting the original illness but also the additional feedback the medications caused. Suddenly stopping medications someone has been on for a long time and having them do poorly doesn't necessarily prove they're still ill and need the medications. It might prove they've developed new problems from the brain counteracting the medications that mimic, to some degree, the original condition the medication fought to control. Whitaker concludes that not only do medications often stop working over the long run, that they likely make things worse than they would've been if the person had never been on medications or tapered off them—a challenging conclusion, to say the least.

Many people have responded to this conclusion by saying that they knew medications were bad and probably what caused their problems in the first place and they shouldn't have ever taken medications, and no one should be forced to take medications because they're harmful. Whitaker objected, saying he never said no one should take medications, but that we should think carefully about how we use medications, especially long-term medications, instead of putting almost everyone on "maintenance medication" for the rest of their lives "to prevent relapses."

He's been very disappointed, perhaps naïvely so, that the psychiatric establishment has responded to his analysis, not by trying to dig into the matter to figure out what's really happening and how we could be using medications in a more strategic and effective manner, but largely by becoming increasingly defensive and dogmatic. (Dr. Sandy Steingard and others at the Foundation for Excellence in Mental Health Care are striking counterexamples worth following.)

Now, my opinion: Imagine the medication visits in these two groups. The "maintenance" group, on the one hand, were likely told they had a permanent condition and were dependent on the medications to stay well and were urged to avoid triggers. The "dosage reduction/discontinuation" group, on the other hand, were likely taught to be more self-observant of their own state and their current need for medications. They gradually learned that they could handle their condition, reducing their relapses and rehospitalizations more and more over time. Instead of feeling helpless, this group gradually felt more and more empowered and in control of their lives. From my perspective, it's not that surprising that they had the confidence to try to go back to school and work far more often than the helpless, maintenance group.

My conclusion: What they and their psychiatrist talked about and how they internalized their conditions and how they learned to use, and not just take, their medications make a dramatic difference in how their lives turned out. Of course, the original authors weren't tracking all those conversations; so, we'll never know. I doubt that medications are hardly ever either the entire savior or destroyer for people with long-term psychosis.

Part II

The Guide:
Eight Interrelated Journeys

CHAPTER 5

OVERVIEW OF THE JOURNEYS

I was a little worried about meeting Shirley the first time. Her clinic records were quite long and filled with crises and medication changes. One particular note from the frustrated psychiatrist caught my eye, "I will not let her manipulate me into another medication change!!!"

I took my time listening to her story as we sat outside on the patio: She was originally from Pennsylvania where she'd worked as a nurse, married a doctor, and had two children. Since she couldn't lose her "baby weight," her husband started prescribing stimulant diet pills for her. They did help lose weight, but they also made her moody and irritable and unable to sleep. As the arguments increased, she began to think that he was out to get her. He responded to her growing agitation and paranoia by divorcing her and taking the kids, sending her across the state back to her father's house.

Now, with her life fallen entirely apart, Shirley was depressed all the time, crying nonstop about missing her children. When she started imagining that they were in the house and she ran round frantically looking for them, her father tied her up with a rope and drove her to the state hospital where he dropped her off on the doorstep and drove away. She never saw him again.

When she was released several months later, heavily medicated, she had no money, no family, and nowhere to go. She began wandering the country begging, trading sex for food, and using drugs and alcohol to maintain a haze. She also began having dreams and then firm beliefs that the Rapture had come and everyone else had been taken to heaven, leaving her behind.

By the time she got to Los Angeles, there was very little of the old Shirley left. They tried to stabilize her with Social Security to live on, a Board and Care, and put her back on medications. She was calmer, but she shuffled around smoking cigarettes and drinking coffee. She no longer used drugs and alcohol. However, she still felt enormous loss and guilt. She tried to find some solace in the Hari Krishna temple that welcomes anyone to free vegetarian meals and chanting, but every time she did that, she felt like she was sinning and the feeling she was missing heaven returned. Changing medications didn't seem to help with any of this.

We'd been talking for about an hour and a half at this point with several tearful breaks, when she said, "No one has asked me about most of those things in a long time. It felt good to be listened to. So, what do you think is wrong with me?"

I thought a moment, and then replied, "I think that you have three layers of issues that fed into each other: The first one was the impact of the amphetamine diet pills that made you irritable and paranoid and led to the loss of your normal life, including your husband and kids and job, years ago, leaving you lost and alone. The second one was the impact of all the drugs and living on the streets for years that has been very isolating and degrading to you. And the third one is a spiritual battle between the Christian Church that you fear has condemned and abandoned you and the Hari Krishna that is welcoming, but you suspect is sinful. To deal with all of this, you're likely to need medications to stabilize your brain's functioning and your emotions, get a new home, not just a house but a home, grieve your losses, remember who you were before all of this to find your strengths and reconnect to other people, and try to find your sacred soul, forgiveness, acceptance, and a state of grace again."

She looked at me stunned, "Well, at least, I can never again say that I never had a psychiatrist who understands me."

Fast forward to 10 years later: Shirley was living in a nice, subsidized apartment building that we ran, surrounded by other members who had become her friends. It was truly her home. She had a practical case manager, Esther, who helped her with everything from shopping to fixing her plugged toilet to going to the movies to going to the doctor's office. Esther was also flexible enough to take Shirley to either Church or the Hari Krishna temple, depending on what mood Shirley was in. She never found the acceptance and forgiveness she sought in the Church or really felt at peace at the Hari Krishna temple, but it rarely got to the point of full psychosis of missing the Rapture again. I let Shirley direct her medications, without getting frustrated or lashing out at her, even though she still changed them a lot. For a while, the building hosted Project Return's Long Beach Social Center, run by people with mental illnesses. Shirley helped out with the barbeques and holiday celebrations. She was also in a modest love triangle, competing with her best friend for the same man's attention, while he seemed to juggle both of them without getting either one too angry at him. They both helped take care of him when his health deteriorated as the years went on. After he died, she still had her friend and her cat.

Shirley felt understood and supported by all of us and knew she wouldn't have to go through life rejected and alone anymore. Maybe just as importantly, she understood and supported her friends and neighbors all around the building.

It's time for us to head out on our journeys together. Think about these journeys not so much as exploring different countries but as exploring the same countryside from different perspectives—like a nature trip, a family trip, a food trip, and a historical trip. After all, this is supposed to be your journey, not mine. I'm here to share with you what the possibilities are. The goal for each journey is to be able to put together a compelling formulation of what a person with psychosis or other extraordinary experiences (it could be you or someone you're trying to be supportive of) is going through as a foundation for shared action. To be useful, each formulation should include the three aspects we defined earlier:

1) There are changes in how you are experiencing and processing "reality."
2) There are changes in your self-identity.
3) There are changes in how you relate to other people.

Each journey will have its strong and weak points across these aspects. I'll try to point them out along the way, so that you'll be able to better choose which journey(s) you want as your foundation. At our best, we should be flexible and adaptable enough, so that different people should be able to go with us on different journeys, depending on where they're at. They may even want different journeys at different times in their lives.

Here's a map of where we'll be going.

Journey 1: Grief is a short "weekend trip" going not too far from home.

When faced with grieving a serious loss, many people, probably the majority of people if they were honest, will experience things that would usually be considered psychosis—for example, hearing the voice of the dead person calling to them or seeing them standing in their room or feeling their presence. We may believe that they had premonitions of the loss or are getting messages from the beyond. Even with "normal grief," we may feel like our internal world is falling apart, like the world doesn't make sense anymore or there's no reason to live. We may feel like time is passing strangely or like we've become detached and distanced from everyone around us as though our entire world has changed. People may relate to us differently. Our roles may change. We may be segregated from our normal lives. Society may put different demands and expectations on us. Society may even have a predetermined set of things we must do to fit in again.

All of these aspects of grief are reasonably familiar to us, so they're not that scary, and yet, they're also features of psychosis; so, they'll help us get used to what's to come. In other words, it's a good first trip to see how you like to travel and what you should pack for longer trips.

Even grief, however, doesn't always work out as a short trip where we return home fine. Grief can lead to very serious, long-term problems. We'll explore some of those problems, too, so that we'll know better what to look out for as we take longer journeys.

Journey 2: Psychotic reactions builds on a classic, "old-fashioned" journey.

It's common sense that if we're behaving very strangely, something terrible must have happened to us that we couldn't handle. As a result, we had a "nervous breakdown" or a "psychotic break" and "lost it." If we're treated well, if we could get away from stress, and if we could "get some rest," we should be able to "pull it together." This kind of thinking underlies the psychoanalytically informed first edition of *DSM* in 1952 that was filled with "reactions"—"depressive reaction," "schizophrenic reaction," and "manic reaction."

Many people, when faced with psychotic experiences, will first try to use a "psychotic reaction" formulation to make sense of what has happened to them and figure out what to do next. Many people probably recover using this approach, the majority of whom would have never contacted mental health professionals.

To understand this journey, we must be able to distinguish between PTSD where an overwhelming event is suppressed but keeps coming out anyway as nightmares, flashbacks, and hypervigilance, and a "psychotic reaction" where our normal rational and emotional adaptations are overwhelmed and our unconscious creates a psychotic adaptation.

This formulation is most common with short-term situations, when someone was "fine" until something happened, and they need help to get back to themselves soon. Since we as mental health professionals tend to spend most of our time with people who have quite long-standing problems or were "always different," we rarely use this approach ... even when it might be the best one.

Most people have a tendency to focus on the emergence of hallucinations and delusions as a "psychotic break" and the most important issues to resolve to recover, rather than seeing how the psychosis emerged from ongoing weaknesses in other areas, that need to be included in our formulations and treatments. So, the next three journeys look at how someone may be predisposed to become psychotic, one from each point of our triangle: experiencing reality, relationships, and self-identity.

Journey 3: Difficulties in making sense of the world is a neuropsychological journey.

This journey focuses on "how the brain is wired." It emphasizes "what" the challenges in processing reality are, rather than "why," and it also emphasizes how we can adapt to these challenges.

Beginning with understanding why people who are hearing voices can't tell they're not real, I'll break down this journey of how we make sense of the world into a set of steps; so, hopefully, it doesn't all blur together. I'll try to describe the steps in a way that everyone can understand them, so that it's a more collaborative journey, instead of a "follow the doctor's orders" experience.

This journey crosses the artificial borders between psychiatry and neurology and between psychosis and other conditions like autism, so that we can put experiences in a larger context and incorporate some helpful approaches that are usually not used for schizophrenia.

Journey 4: Childhood trauma is currently reemerging as an important journey, especially from the perspective of the people who are experiencing psychosis.

Despite efforts to highly medicalize psychosis, emphasizing the genetic components and attempting to decrease shaming and blaming of families, there are strong data that people who have experienced considerable trauma have a higher likelihood of becoming psychotic. This journey will explore pathways that lead from trauma to psychosis.

Trauma has been "rediscovered" and "lost again" many times. It's a territory that drives away many potential explorers because it's so emotionally difficult, but it is worth the difficult journey because of how well it matches many people's experience of what they've been through (as opposed to what's wrong with them) and can be very healing. It does require careful emotional preparation.

We'll use some of the things we learned in the grief and nervous breakdown journeys, but the focus of thsis journey is more about the impact of ongoing childhood trauma, than about single impactful events. How does long-term trauma impact us at different ages and developmental stages? What protective strengths didn't develop successfully? How does how we've learned to cope over time sometimes lead to psychosis when cracks open up?

This chapter will also include a discussion of "multiple personalities" as one of the most severe impacts of childhood trauma.

Journey 5: Losing balance is the most developmental journey and my own creation. I built it on the premise that psychosis can emerge in almost anyone if we lose our balance, but how it looks will depend on where we are when we lose our balance.

We'll begin by talking about how we normally develop—moving from having our basic needs met by others, to relying on ourselves, to sustaining ourselves using emotional connections with other people all the way to experiencing global and spiritual connectedness.

When we start losing our balance and "falling apart," psychosis can result. This can take place on any of the four levels: 1) We may not be having our basic needs met (which can lead to severe passiveness). 2) We may feel attacked by others and fighting the world on our own, struggling to survive (which can lead to paranoia). 3) We may have had our relationship balances fall apart and be experiencing our brains trying to connect in unusual ways to compensate (which can lead to ideas of reference, extrasensory perceptions, thought insertion, and withdrawal). 4) We can be "drowning in deep spiritual waters" we're not prepared to handle. Depending on where we are when we lose our balance, there are different challenges to creating and sustaining helping relationships.

Journey 6: Drugs and alcohol are the most socially divisive factors and likely the most common journey to psychosis. In addition to their life-destroying effects, there are specific intoxication, withdrawal, and long-term brain damage effects from drugs and alcohol that can lead to psychosis.

This is a very difficult journey because of the personal reactions most of us have to people who abuse substances. Substance abuse occurs within a complex, judgmental, and almost always rejecting personal, emotional, and social context. Most communities punish, rather than treat, drug and alcohol users. We're going to have to do some serious work to be able to be on this journey at all; however, the rewards, not just for the people abusing substances but also for all of us sharing their lives, can be striking. Some of the most amazing recoveries I've ever seen are on this journey.

Once we've overcome our reactions to substance use, this journey can become a very biological journey. This chapter contains a lot of practical information about how different substances impact our brains and lives.

Journey 7: **Psychiatric illnesses** is the medical model journey that dominates our current mental health system. For the last 50 years, this "illness-centered" journey has been the pervasive approach that our psychiatric establishment and much of our community applies to virtually everyone. It builds on the past successes of the medical model, especially with infectious diseases and cancer, and the future promise of genetic research to identify more and more specific illnesses lurking in our genes.

This is the journey that most mental health professionals, especially psychiatrists, are trained in and use. It is the foundation for the vast majority of today's research, medication usage, and public advocacy. This is also the journey that is most frequently used for "fast food" psychiatry, sound bites, and TV commercials.

Correctly diagnosing which psychotic illness we're fighting—schizophrenia, schizoaffective disorder, bipolar disorder with psychosis, major depression with psychosis, and borderline personality disorder with brief reactive psychosis—is the crucial foundation to a good treatment plan. The more we know about the illness, the more effectively we can treat it.

Unfortunately, by focusing so single-mindedly on the illness, the person themselves is often relegated to be the battlefield on which the illness is fought, dehumanizing and damaging them in the process. A single-minded "illness as dangerous adversary" approach sometimes seems to fit amazingly well and sometimes seems to neglect so many important other factors.

Journey 8: **Brain damage and other neurological and medical conditions** are journeys often taken in other systems of care, like our medical system or our developmental disabilities system, rather than in our mental health system. Brain damage (including developmental disorders, delirium, aging disorders, and physical brain trauma) can cause psychosis as part of being unable to function well in reality with diminished capacities. Psychosis can also be a direct symptom of specific neurological and medical conditions.

This journey has been rather rare in my practice, except when I was working in a large medical hospital. I don't know if that's because we're failing to recognize most of the people on this journey or because this journey is rare compared to the others or because most of the people on this journey aren't in the mental health system. Given the limitations of our developmental disability system and the almost total lack of a public neurology rehabilitation system, I have to wonder if there aren't a lot of people who might be best served on this journey, but we're not there for them.

I believe that we need to be more prepared to connect mind and body, and physician and healer, to move beyond "dual-diagnoses" to a more truly integrative approach to take this journey more effectively.

Let's go!

Chapter 6

Journey 1: Loss and grief

"I don't really have good words to ask you this, but has your mother been in contact with you since she died?"

Suzanne looked at me quizzically. I suspected she thought this was a trick to get her to say something that would make her sound crazy. "What do you mean?"

"Well, like I remember after my grandfather died, for a few weeks, I kept thinking I saw him."

"But that was just in your mind, wasn't it? That's not really like your grandfather was there."

"When she was about 9, my wife moved into the house where her grandfather had died, and she said she thought his ghost was in that house."

"I know what you mean, but I don't really believe in ghosts."

"What do you think happens when we die?"

"Hopefully, if we've been good, we'll go to heaven."

"So, is that where your mother is now?"

Suzanne paused. "Can I tell you something strange?"

"Sure."

"I think she's still around and hasn't gone to heaven yet. Sometimes, it feels like she's in the room with me, but when I turn around to look, all I see is a shadow that disappears."

"Can she communicate with you?"

"Like how?"

"Well, sometimes it's not in words, more like a feeling, or sometimes it's in dreams."

"I've been dreaming about my mom a lot since she died."

"What does she say in the dreams?"

"Good, reassuring stuff, like she knows I'll be OK and be able to handle things on my own. It feels good to hear that, but I'm not sure I really can make it without her. I just miss her so much."

"Maybe that's why she's sticking around, instead of going straight to heaven, to make sure you're OK."

This time, Suzanne's look was one of relief. "That's what I thought, too."

"Do you think she's in a hurry to move on to heaven, or is she OK staying with you for a while?"

"She'll stay as long as I need."

"Do you feel guilty for holding her back from moving on to heaven?"

"I didn't think of it like that. Maybe I am holding her back, but I'll let her move on when I'm a little stronger."

"Do you think she's OK with that?"

She nodded, "I do."

"Do you have anyone else to help you through this loss?"

"Besides you, you mean?"

I smiled, "Yeah, besides me."

"My sister has been spending a lot of time with me. We talk about old times together with mom, eat ice cream, and cry together. Other family members have been calling and checking on me, too. Work is taking it easy on me, since they know about mom dying and they feel bad for me."

"Sounds good to me."

This loss and grief journey may be your first steps into extraordinary experiences that are sometimes called psychotic, but fortunately, they're usually familiar steps. Many people have had experiences like Suzanne's. She hasn't gone "beyond the edge of the map." She's still in known territory; so, it's not that scary, or stigmatized. We have explanations—either that it's in our minds or about spirits, ghosts, or an afterlife—we can use to make sense of what we're experiencing. Even though she's going through one of the hardest times of her life, none of the three dimensions of psychosis are really in serious doubt:

1) She's experiencing reality the way other people do and knows which of her experiences are extraordinary and might sound crazy to someone else and which ones are more ordinary.
2) Although she has doubts, mostly she knows who she is and she knows that she'll be OK on her own after she goes through some more grief.
3) She has an array of relationships with people who understand what she's going through, so that she's not struggling alone.

Let's take another step, this time off the edge of the map.

> *The high point of Celia's life was back in her late teens. She was thin and sexy. She partied a lot and loved roller-skating and makeup. She had a fast food job that brought in enough money to meet her needs since she lived with her parents; so, dropping out of high school wasn't a big deal.*
>
> *She was also in love with a young man, Antonio, who enjoyed many of the same things she did. Even now, 20 years later, she still lights up when she talks about him. They were inseparable and she was sure they'd be together forever. He was fun to be with and made her laugh. He was exciting to be with, escaping from whatever risks he took. He was charming to be with and took away all of her worries.*
>
> *Antonio did, however, have a tendency to flirt with other girls, too, but he always told her he only loved her. He would disappear for weeks at a time, but he always*

returned to her, and she always waited for him. He never had much of a job, but he knew how to hustle; so, he always had money to spend on her.

When she was 20, her mother brought her the devastating news: Antonio had been killed in a car accident.

Celia didn't believe her. She made her mother take her to the morgue to make sure it really was him.

The body looked like him, but it couldn't really be him, could it? Antonio had always been such a trickster; maybe this was another one of his jokes. Maybe he'd show up and say, "Just fooling. Scared you, didn't I?"

And it seemed like she could see him in the days that followed, lurking in the shadows, just out of sight, grinning at her, and then disappearing again. She even thought she saw him at the funeral, watching from a distance.

As the months went on, her mother started to worry. Celia was still acting like Antonio wasn't dead and talking about seeing him. Maybe they buried someone else. Maybe he faked his death to escape from someone who was after him. He's clever enough to do something like that. Sometimes, she even said that he was coming to her room secretively, late at night, when no one could see him just to be with her. Hoping to convince Celia that he was really dead, her mother sent for his death certificate, but she said that Tony knew people in the coroner's office and that he had it faked.

She stopped going out with her friends and seemed to drift into a world of her own. She gained weight and stopped going to work. She said everything would be fine again when Antonio returned. As the years went on, she seemed stuck in time, not realizing life was passing her by.

By the time I met Celia, all three dimensions were struggling:

1) Because of her inability to face reality, she's experiencing reality more and more differently from everyone else, and she's more and more sure she's right and everyone else is wrong.

2) She's lost her sense of self. She literally can't be herself without Antonio. Her life has lost any sense of continuity or time.
3) She's become isolated and lost all her normal roles.

Serious loss and grief are the closest most people will come to experiencing psychosis, not because the sadness, even agonizing sadness, of loss and grief itself is psychotic, but because of how much difficulty most of us have dealing with severe loss, and as a result, how it can break us down in many of the same ways that other pathways to psychosis do. If we can't grieve in healthy ways, severe loss can "change our worlds forever" and challenge our self-identity, confront us with "unbelievable" realities we can't face, isolate us, alter the flow of time, and disconnect us from our emotions and our relationships.

One of the changes in *DSM-V* was to eliminate the diagnosis of "pathological grief." The logic given was that it doesn't matter if someone is grieving or not, if they're experiencing disturbing, disruptive symptoms that fit some other diagnoses, say depression or psychosis; they have the condition and deserve treatment for it to alleviate their symptoms. I strongly disagree. Disturbing, disruptive feelings aren't always symptoms that need to be eliminated; sometimes, they're part of a journey we're on. We may need our psychiatrists to act more like midwifes helping guide us through the process, than we need them to act like surgeons removing what's wrong with us and throwing it away.

If we rebel and decide that it does matter how the person got this way and why they're struggling, and if we conclude that people like Celia need help with their grief process, we have some good information that we can use to help them.

When I was a college student, I remember reading a very old article by Freud called "On Mourning and Melancholia." Despite his esoteric language, like "decathecting libidinal affect," his overall logic made sense to me: When we're really attached to someone, our mind is filled with emotional memories of them (especially memories of us together). These memories gave our relationship depth and meaning. We have a lot of ourselves invested in the relationship. When we lose the other person, we're stuck with all those emotional memories with no one left to relate to. If we just bury them and try not to think about them, we can't free up those emotions to connect to someone else. If instead we reexperience those memories, we can release the emotions to form new attachments and relationships. Healthy grief includes telling and retelling stories about the person (perhaps wearing out everyone around us), freeing up more and more feelings to be able to love again.

Emotional memories apparently are stored in our brains with an image of the other person, an image of ourselves, and the emotions between us. It seems to me that it's important to realize that sometimes it isn't just the other person who's been lost, it's also how we were when we were around them. For example, Celia's best, most confident memories of herself were with Antonio; so, if she let go of him, she'd also risk losing those parts of herself (which may have been part of why she couldn't face the loss). Do you remember Peter Cetera in the band *Chicago* worrying about losing the biggest part of himself, his very heart, in the song *If You Leave Me Now*? Sometimes, losses leave holes too big to keep going.

Many years later, Elizabeth Kubler-Ross spent a lot of time talking with people who were facing their own deaths, usually from cancer. From their stories she developed a set of five stages she felt applied more universally to loss and grief:

- Denial—We're unable to face the loss, "in shock," "this can't be happening to me."
- Anger—If this is what's really happening to me, I'm mad about it, "it's unfair," "I don't deserve this," "make it go away—do whatever it takes."
- Bargaining—When rage and threats don't work, we try to figure out a way around it, "I'll stop smoking, or pray to God or be good if you'll give me another chance," "tell me what I need to do to make this go away."
- Depression—When there's no way around it, we feel helpless and hopeless and depressed. "I can't handle this—I'm not strong enough—I give up."
- Acceptance—Giving up is an illusion, so long as we're still alive we have to face this. "I accepted my new reality and found a way to go on, day by day."

These are fluid stages; so, people can go up and back as they struggle to grieve their loss. Sometimes, people get stuck along the way. In 1969, she put these stages together in her landmark book titled *On Death and Dying*, which became the foundation for hospice and are now part of our culture.

If we look at these stages, the one we're most afraid of is usually depression. We worry that we won't be able to handle the sadness or the empty hole inside us. We'll never stop crying. Our heart will break. So, we prolong one of the earlier, "unrealistic" stages—getting stuck in denial, anger, or bargaining—to avoid depression. Normally, with the help of friends and loved ones, and time, we gradually face our loss, relive the memories, restore our emotional balance, and find a way to accept our loss and go on.

So, what did you do to help Celia?

We helped strengthen her, meeting her where she was at, until she was able to resume grieving her loss. Even though she was in her 30s, we treated her like she was still 20. We hooked her up with a young case worker who would do her makeup and braid her hair at her desk. They'd look at magazines for young women together. We'd take her with a group to happy hour and a little dancing. Some of the other members flirted with her a little. We helped her remember, and let go of, memories of her life with Antonio. She started building a new life to replace the one she had lost. We helped her get her first apartment at a Housing and Urban Development (HUD) subsidized building we owned and taught her how to take care of it. She became neighbors and best friends with Shirley, who you met at the end of Chapter 4. They'd gossip together. She worked part time making sandwiches in our Deli. We even helped her get new roller skates, and she led an outing at the roller rink. Overall, we helped her create enough new emotional memories to sustain herself that she didn't need her boyfriend (except in times of terrible stress—like when Shirley eventually died). We didn't confront her denial or "feed into it." We understood why she needed it and helped her not be too scared to move on.

That doesn't sound that different from what I would normally do with a friend going through a bad breakup.

Think about that for a minute. Even though Celia was "chronically psychotic," what she really needed was for someone to take the time to understand her story and how she got that way, and then, help her grow and adapt in different more healthy ways, just like you would for a "normal person" in a similar situation. Her situation was worse than the usual "bad breakup" and her response was stranger, but she wasn't beyond connecting to other people and rebuilding her self-identity.

But doesn't she have an illness? Didn't she need to take medications?

She had a major loss that threatened to break down her self-identity that she responded to with denial and withdrawing from reality and other people. Those experiences persisted for a long time until they were incorporated in the programming of her brain. Even with good healing and strengthening experiences, it didn't seem to restore her "programming"; so, yes, I did give her medication, and I even increased the dosage when she was in severe stress and falling apart.

Here's my point: Just because she was psychotic and could be helped with medications doesn't mean that she's off the edge of the map where monsters are. She's still a person who is going through an emotional process that we can help her with.

I know it takes longer to understand her that way, using a full formulation, than it would be to use the "fast food" approach of diagnosing her with schizophrenia, writing her off as hopeless, and medicating her indefinitely, but this way promotes actual healing and recovery. This recovery approach isn't about not using medications. It's about integrating medications into a truly holistic recovery plan.

Let's journey even further, meeting someone who has been psychotic and homeless, refusing medications and repeatedly hospitalized, to find a way to include all of that in our services.

> When I first met Betsy, a small, very pleasant, polite, middle-aged Black woman, she reminded me of a kind grandmother. She'd just gotten out of the hospital and had accepted an apartment from us after being homeless for a long time. The staff were frantic, trying to get me to put her on long-acting shots because she wasn't taking the pills they'd prescribe at the time of her hospital discharge and they knew that, without these medications, she'd fall apart again.

She didn't really have any reason not to take the shot I offered her. She seemed to like me. But she was immovable in her polite refusal.

"I'll try again next week," I said to reassure the staff.

They shook their heads, "She'll be paranoid again by then. We've seen this before."

They were right. She was looking around the room suspiciously the next time I saw her. After that, she huddled in the corner by herself afraid and became more and more disheveled. A month later, she left the apartment without saying why.

A month after that, I went to visit her with Cherokee, our outreach worker, and found her sitting on the ground in a parking lot behind a gas station, with a shopping cart of belongings and what appeared to be trash.

I had to comment on the collection of small dirty, half broken dolls she had in a semicircle around her, "Hi, Betsy. Why do you have those dolls?"

"Hi, Dr. Mark. Those are my children. I'm protecting them."

"Really? You have a lot of children there."

"God blessed me with nine children."

"Weren't they safer inside the apartment than they are out here?"

"No. Here I can see danger coming. They were sneaking up on me back there."

"Who was?"

"You don't know about them?" She rearranged the dolls in front of her.

"No."

"Then, I'll protect you, too."

"Thank you. Can I ask you about something else? You haven't had your medication in a few months. I brought a shot with me here today. Could I give it to you?"

"Thank you for thinking of me, but I don't need it. No."

"How about a sandwich, then?"

"No. Nothing." She seemed like she was drifting away again, lost in her own thoughts.

As we walked away, I asked Cherokee, "Does she have any real children?"

"I don't know. I think maybe out of state, but I've never met any."

About a month later, the police brought her to the hospital again. They got her better again with medications and were set to discharge her. But we insisted that if they wouldn't go to court to argue for the judge to put her on a conservatorship so we could continue to give her medications, we'd go. They let us go and even though the judge thought it was strange that it was me instead of the hospital psychiatrist arguing the case, he agreed that she was gravely disabled.

For the next year, she took the shots every 2 weeks and lived in the apartment. At my urging, we found out she did have children, nine, in fact, scattered around the country, including a couple in Southern California. We helped her reconnect to them one at a time. She was enthusiastically invested in the search. We expected her children to be worried about their mother, but mostly they tried to get money from her limited Social Security check for their own lives, which she happily gave them. By the time the end of the year-long conservatorship came, we didn't need to renew it because she was no longer rejecting medications or frightened. She was surrounded by her real children, either protecting them or being taking advantage of by them, depending on how you look at it, but exactly where she wanted to be. Her loss had been restored.

At the Village, we spend a fair bit of time helping people grieve. Whenever someone dies, we have a memorial service. I've released balloons off Signal Hill, thrown flowers into the ocean at Belmont Pier, and sprinkled ashes off the cliffs (word of warning—check the wind direction first). We grieve together—staff members, families, and neighbors—emphasizing how grief is a normal healthy process for all of us.

When we meet a member like Celia with unresolved grief issues, we push them to move forward, lighting candles of remembrance or writing letters to send to heaven. Sometimes, emotional conflict and trauma can complicate the grief process. For example, I've been to the cemetery looking for the grave site of a 15-year-old brother who was shot and killed by a gang member several years ago, and I've also gone to the cemetery with a 50-year-old man who hadn't forgiven his father, dead for over 30 years, for beating him when he was a child.

> Gloria had a childhood filled with abuse and neglect. She never felt she was worth anything or been able to protect herself. She needed a man to take care of her. Manny seemed to fit the bill. He was big and powerful, aggressive and strong enough to stand up to her family, marry her, and take her away. Her description made him sound like a force of nature. Unfortunately, as it seems to happen too often, he was also cruel and abusive. He convinced her that she was nothing without him and that she owed him everything. He'd get drunk and repeatedly beat and rape her. She was most distressed when she told him she was pregnant, and he beat her savagely until she had a miscarriage and then couldn't conceive after that.
>
> Over the years, he'd wander away for months at a time, when other women caught his interest, but he always returned and reclaimed her. He'd destroy whatever she'd fixed up in the apartment while he was gone. Once she'd gotten a dog, and he took it away and had it killed. She knew she'd never be free of him. He was her life.

What she hadn't counted on, in fact, what was inconceivable to her, was that his hard living would catch up to him. By his 40s, he had serious heart problems.

She hadn't seen Manny for several months when he returned the last time. He didn't look well at dinner. Afterward, they were sitting on the couch watching TV, and he yelled out in pain. As she tried to soothe him, he dropped dead of a heart attack, falling to the floor. Even when the paramedics couldn't revive him and proclaimed him dead on the spot, she couldn't believe it. This was a man who was invincible in her eyes. He'd thwarted every effort she'd made to get back at him or free herself from him. Nothing could harm him. He literally couldn't be dead.

Gloria struggled with depression and panic attacks, poverty, and nightmares over the next 2 years, but I was the first one she told that her husband was still alive and talked to her almost all the time. Manny was jealous of any man she talked to and called her a whore and threatened them, just as he had before the heart attack. He belittled and berated her until she was sobbing, promising to do better, just as he had before the heart attack. He threatened to beat and rape her, too, just as he had before the heart attack. He reminded her that he'd always told her she'd never be free of him.

I added an antipsychotic to her medication, which did quiet down her hallucinations of Manny's voice, and we worked to rebuild her self-confidence. She made some friends at the Village, and she helped us make fliers to send out. We helped her get a small dog, "Baby," that became her child. She dressed Baby in clothes that matched hers and carried him around in a baby stroller she got from Goodwill. Baby, at least, responded to her love and affection.

Nonetheless, Gloria only really cheered up when she found a new boyfriend, Stanley, who she assured us was "different from any man I've ever been with." Even though he *lived in a car and bummed money off her, she felt well treated by him. Manny wasn't convinced and got louder, trying to run Stanley off. When Stanley relapsed on crack, he became angry when she didn't want to have sex in his car. Manny was the one who told her to fight back and then get out of the car and run away. She was bloodied and bruised. Her dress was torn, and she only had one shoe left, but she did have Baby under one arm. It was 1 am.*

She didn't know where else to go; so, she walked the mile to her mother's house. Her mother, upset at being woken up, screamed and cursed at Gloria, "You can't stay here. You make your own bed. You sleep in it. I always knew you were worthless. Get your sorry ass out of here." She threw her out, slammed the door, and locked it behind her. "Don't you come 'round here like this again. You heard me."

Gloria walked awhile but had nowhere to go. Totally beaten, she sat in the middle of the street on the yellow line waiting for a car to come and hit her and kill her. It was only the thought of what would happen to her dog, Baby, still in her arms, that made her get up. She walked back to the Village and sat outside the rest of the night, waiting for us to open.

It's taken quite a long time for her to rebuild, this time without her mother or Stanley or any other man, but she doesn't have to do it alone either. We do let her bring Baby to work when she's our receptionist. Manny only comes back at times of weakness, and she doesn't give in to him anymore.

There are some people, normal people, who keep in contact with a departed loved one forever. For example, George Burns, the actor, was inseparable from his wife and longtime comedy partner, Gracie Allen. They performed vaudeville, radio, and TV together from when they met in 1922 until 1958 when she retired after a heart attack. When she died in 1964, George became very depressed and couldn't function without her. Like many long-term couples, it was as though part of him was missing without her. His recovery began by sleeping in her bed, instead of his, to feel her presence again. For the rest of his life, and he lived another 30 years until he was 100 years old, every day he planned how he was going to tell Gracie about his experiences in their monthly visits at the cemetery. He continued to share his life and his mind with his departed wife. He wasn't in denial. He knew she was dead, but in order to feel whole himself, he needed to keep talking to her. He also returned to his other friends, his work, and his life. He wasn't stuck in time, and he wasn't lost in his own reality. We each have to find our own adaptations to unbearable losses.

> Most people probably wouldn't notice Frances's developmental disability. She can read and write and do simple arithmetic. She might seem a little immature or overly dramatic or even vulnerable, but not "retarded." Nevertheless, she struggles to keep track of everything she needs to and sometimes doesn't really understand the reasons behind things, and subtle social interactions can sometimes get by her. She was educated in a combination of special education classes and "mainstream classes." She knows she has a disability but wants to lead a normal life and fit in with everyone else. Before she left high school, they gave her some vocational training; so, she was able to work at a grocery store for most of her life.
>
> Her parents had serious drug problems; so, Frances was raised by her grandmother when she was growing up. When her husband started beating her and she left him, her grandmother took in her and her three kids. They rarely had enough money and ended up moving between various hotel rooms and cheap apartments, but they always found a way to make it, even when Frances's daughter turned out to have autism and her son had severe diabetes and needed a lot of medical care.
>
> The kids were in their teens and Frances was 30 when her grandmother died.
>
> Frances was too depressed and overwhelmed to go to work; so, she lost her job. A couple months later, they became homeless. Her ex-husband, who Frances didn't trust at all, came to get the kids, and she reluctantly gave them

to him. She couldn't take care of their needs without a place to stay, and they'd have been sent to foster care if she hadn't given them to him.

We met her in the Cold Weather Shelter, trying to rock herself to sleep, holding a stuffed animal, crying uncontrollably. She was denied disability benefits, since she'd been able to work for the last 10 years. When they sent them all out of the shelter during the day, she'd get lost and confused, and she had no idea where she was. She repeatedly ended up in the ER with panic attacks.

We used our money to pay for a small hotel room for her, while appealing her Social Security denial. She isolated there, barely venturing out to get some food. We helped her get some cheap makeup, so she could feel like herself again. I gave her some medication to try to help her calm down, but it barely worked, and she got the pills confused. She kept talking about how much she missed her grandmother and how she would've taken care of all of this for her.

She was starting to make a little progress. She helped decorate our team area for the holidays. But one morning while walking along the beach, she stopped in the bathroom there and a man followed her in, pinned her against the stall and started to rape her. Fortunately, her screams drew a man passing by who pushed her assailant off her, and she ran away. She had no idea how she ended up 2 miles away at the hospital ER, where they called us to come pick her up. She couldn't stop shaking.

This time, I thought we might lose her entirely; so, I intentionally brought her grandmother back into her life.

"Imagine your grandmother is here with us sitting in that chair."

Her tears slowed a little, and she smiled as she looked at the empty chair.

"Can you see her there?"

"Yes, I can."

"What's she saying to you?"

"She's singing the song "Sunshine on My Shoulders" that she used to sing to me when I was scared as a child."

"Did you sing along with her?"

"Yeah."

"Go ahead, sing with her now."

She started singing along hesitantly at first. The shaking slowed down and stopped. She looked stronger.

"Could you ask your grandmother if she'd come sing with you when you're frightened in the future?"

"She said she would."

Over the next few months, everywhere Frances went, her grandmother came, too. They watched TV and ate popcorn together, like they used to. They went shopping together. Frances started to be able to function more and more. She started visiting her kids regularly and arguing with her ex about how he was raising them.

I didn't try to talk her out of spending time with her grandmother or try to medicate the "hallucination" away. It was more important that she could hold herself together enough to function and have relationships again. Sometimes, people have to alter reality a little to make it in this world. "Bargaining" was as far as she could go in her grief process for now, at least.

It seems like most of these stories you're sharing have all kinds of terrible things going on besides the grief and loss. You've included wife beating and rapes, poverty and homelessness, abusive boyfriends, and a really mean mother. You said this was a journey to ease me into this. Why did you pile on so much tragedy?

Here's where you're going to face a choice: Biological psychiatry wants you to believe that psychosis is a brain illness, "just like diabetes," and that all of the tragedy that I see every day is just "psychosocial factors" best left to social workers, so that it doesn't distract us from diagnosing and treating illnesses—and, perhaps more importantly, so that we don't have to feel so much of their pain and suffering. I believe that all that tragedy, rather than their genes, is a good deal of why those people became psychotic, instead of being able to grieve successfully. They would say that I've made Frances more psychotic, not less, by feeding into her delusions. I'd say that I've made her less psychotic, not more, by understanding so deeply what her loss of her grandmother really meant within our often-cruel society and helped her deal with the overwhelming tragedy that is her life, using every tool I have. If you want to keep traveling with me, you'll have to take off the "biological blinders" and share their tragedies.

Be prepared, our next chapter will go even further into how life's tragedies can lead to psychosis.

Here's a positive closing story for you before we move on:

> *Cherokee had been outreaching Alan on a bus bench where he'd been sitting for 2 years before Alan agreed to see me.*
>
> *"Two years sitting on a bus bench. Really? How does he live?"*
>
> *"People in the neighborhood know him and bring him by food and money. He goes into the McDonald's to get coffee or a hamburger or go to the bathroom, but then he's back out on the bench again. I brought him a blanket and some clothes for Christmas. He doesn't have any benefits, and this is the first time he's agreed to come in or see a psychiatrist."*
>
> *"Why? What's different today?"*
>
> *"He says the Demons have gotten too bad for him to handle."*
>
> *"OK. I'll give it a try."*
>
> *Alan was a short, somewhat disheveled, unshaven man, whose eyes kept darting around the room.*

"Hi, I'm Dr. Mark. Are you alright? You look like you're looking for something."

"Not looking, listening. I'm trying to tell if the Demons followed me in here. They were talking in the palm trees outside while I was waiting."

"Really? Are they still out there?"

"Probably."

"Let's go out and listen to them together."

"Would you do that?"

"Sure. How am I going to be able to help you if I don't know what's going on?"

We walked outside and stood together listening to the palm trees.

"I don't hear them now. Either they're gone or they're hiding."

"That doesn't really surprise me. I'm not really an expert in Demons, but one thing I've noticed is that they tend to be chicken-shit bullies. Do they only harass you when you're alone or feeling down and weak and leave you alone when someone else is around?"

He looked away from the trees and back at me and hesitated. "You might be right. They do always come when I'm on my own."

"Well, we've figured out one thing already that might help keep away the Demons. I could stand next to you all the time."

He laughed. "I don't think that's going to work."

"I don't either. My wife sure wouldn't like that plan. We better think of another plan. Maybe we can figure out how to strengthen you, so that they won't bully you. Let's go inside and talk about it."

By the time we finished talking, he'd agreed to take medications to strengthen his mind against the Demons. Unfortunately, the first four medications I tried created far more side effects than mental strength. In the meantime, however, we found out he used to be a housepainter; so, we gave him a paintbrush and a can of paint to fix the peeling trim on our building. The Demons didn't bother him while he was working, but he still wanted to return to his bench.

"Why that bench? We could help you get a room instead."

"I'm waiting for my mother."

"Your mother?"

"She went to see the doctor. She wasn't feeling well, and she hasn't come back yet."

"How long ago was that?"

"I don't really know."

It took a fair bit of detective work to find out that his mother had gone to St. Mary's hospital 2 years earlier, taking the bus from that bench, and that it was there that she had died of cancer she'd hidden from Alan. He'd been waiting for her to return ever since. His life had stopped. Time had stopped. Most of his memory seemed to have stopped as well.

Alan broke down into tears when I told him the news. I gave him a long hug. When he finally let go, he said, through the tears, "I was afraid something like that had happened to her."

That was the first step to letting go of her and rebuilding his life with us. He did a variety of handiwork for us and some of the members, and eventually got a job managing a local apartment building in return for free rent. He hung around with us a lot and started helping other members rebuild their lives. He kept taking his medications and the Demons stayed away. He even got a used car and started dating.

Even I didn't see the next twist coming.

A young woman came up to the front desk one day and said, "I'm looking for Alan Barber. I found out from the post office that he gets his mail here."

"Who are you?"

"I'm his sister. I haven't' seen him for over 2 years since he disappeared."

"Someone better find Alan. I think he's upstairs."

He didn't remember having a sister, but she looked vaguely familiar to him. She came back with a picture album.

Alan was stunned. Those wedding pictures sure looked like him. Who were those two kids he was playing with?

His sister told him, "When you didn't come back, Cheri took the kids back to Mexico and moved in with her family. She was heartbroken, but she didn't have any choice. She was broke and getting evicted."

This time, Alan's tears were tears of joy, breaking through his shock.

Cheri and the kids returned from Mexico and rejoined him. The last time I saw Alan, he was a proud father trick-or-treating with his kids.

CHAPTER 7

JOURNEY 2: PSYCHOTIC REACTIONS

Leonard had just turned 20 when he was hit by a car. No one came to visit him in the hospital, but that was mostly his fault. After dropping out of high school, he'd spent the next several years using and selling drugs, stealing, and running with gangs. His mother was at the end of her rope when she kicked him out for good. He'd blown every chance she'd given him, and she couldn't expose his younger brother and sister to any more of his problems. Also, she couldn't pay the rent when he kept stealing from her purse.

The doctors tried to save his leg, but it was hopeless. He ended up with a below-the-knee amputation. Since he didn't have any insurance, he couldn't have rehabilitation services. Since there was no one to call and he couldn't give any address, they drove him to a shelter in Skid Row and dropped him off in a wheelchair with a set of crutches, even though he'd never been to Skid Row before. That's just where human refuse is dumped in Los Angeles.

He was disoriented and confused and overwhelmed. He couldn't process what had happened to him. He was in shock.

The shelter was run by a religious group that insisted on the men going to morning prayers in return for food and shelter. They said they had good news: Christ died for our sins and he was bringing his Kingdom to Earth. Everything was going to be OK.

It was just the salvation that Leonard needed. He forgot about his past, about the drugs and gangs, about his estranged family, about the accident and his lost leg. Everything was OK. He became very cheerful—actually the most cheerful person I've ever met—and began trusting everyone. They were here to help him. And, remarkably enough, they did.

Somehow, he ended up on his crutches, but with nothing else at the end of the blue line subway in Long Beach. Instead of arresting these types of people, the "Quality of Life" police team, who assist people who are harassing the downtown businesses, helped him get a sober living and go to the General Relief office for benefits. They even took him to Social Security and arranged a doctor's appointment, so he could get a disability evaluation to receive SSI. They contacted Racy, our homeless outreach Mental Health Nurse Practitioner, who often did consultations on the street with them. He flirted with her and told her she used to be his girlfriend. When he was introduced to me, I was playing basketball in the parking lot in our little Village league alongside our members; so, he decided that I was his old middle school basketball coach. He's friendly with everyone he meets at the Village. We're all part of his life in one way or another.

I doubted that I could get him to take medications to help bring him back into reality, but I thought it would be easy to get him a prosthetic leg, so that he didn't need the crutches anymore. No such luck. I never got him to take a single step in that direction. After about 6 months, I figured out why: Going to a doctor and getting a prosthetic leg would've meant opening up to some of the reality of what had happened to him, how his life had been destroyed, and how he only had one leg and no future. He couldn't tolerate any of that reality. He'd created an entirely new reality, where the accident and the crutches were irrelevant, and he was happy in it. He never responded to any questions about his leg.

He still comes to the Village almost every day, flirts with the women, ignoring their rebukes, enthusiastically greets the staff with "hollering out to you," brushing aside our reminders that we're Village staff, not his family and friends. He doesn't even seem to mind being poor.

I was originally going to entitle this journey "Nervous Breakdowns" since it has its origins in quite old conceptions about mental illnesses, but a friend and colleague, Wayne Munchel, said, "What does 'nervous breakdown' really mean? Different people will have different ideas, depending on their experiences and their prejudices. You're going to trigger all the old stereotypes about mental illnesses and men in white coats taking people away when they have a nervous breakdown if you start there." He's probably right. Think for a minute about what baggage you're carrying with you about "nervous breakdowns."

One of my favorite questions when I meet someone new is, "When you first started having these experiences, before you went to any therapists or doctors and we started talking about mental illness diagnoses and chemical imbalances, what did you think was going on with you?" The answers I get are all over the map, but one of the most common is, "I thought I was going crazy. I'd been going through so much, I was under so much stress, that I couldn't handle it. I was afraid I was losing my mind." That's a description of the "psychotic reactions" journey.

On this journey, we'll start there and see if we can make sense of what's happening, so that we don't need the men in white coats or their asylums and we can join people in what's likely to be the most frightening time in their lives to help them recover.

When I studied at the Menninger's Institute in Topeka, I got to meet the then 89-year-old Karl Menninger. He was clearly experiencing some dementia, but the respect and love the staff seemed to have for him was pervasive, nonetheless. They gave me one of his books to read. What I remember most was his guiding paradigm, that mental illnesses are a result of our inability to adapt to some serious stressor. I remember him describing three levels:

- If we can successfully adapt to the stressor, then we won't have any symptoms.
- If we become overly defended, more distorted, or rigid in response to the stressor, then we will have neurotic symptoms.
- If we can't maintain our defenses or face the reality of the stressor, then we will have psychotic symptoms.

In other words, psychosis is the result of our normal defenses being overwhelmed entirely and unable to respond to the stress we're under.

Karl's brother, and cofounder of the institute, William, was a highly respected psychiatrist within the military who was given the job of creating diagnostic standards to help assess and respond to psychiatric disabilities in the military. The first *DSM*, released in 1952 based on his work, was a very short listing of conditions, including, under the category of "Disorders of Psychogenic Origin or Without Clearly Defined Physical Cause or Structural Change in the Brain," manic depressive reactions, schizophrenic reactions, paranoid reactions, and other psychotic reactions. Notice that all of these major psychiatric conditions were considered to be "reactions" to something, rather than today's conception that they are biochemical illnesses of our brains.

Both of these brothers, leaders of American psychiatry in the first half of the 20th century, would've begun their work with people with psychosis by trying to figure out what severe stressors these psychotic symptoms were formed in reaction to. How did their hallucinations, delusions, and withdrawal from other people and reality make sense in terms of what they'd been through?

> *Steven was only 8 years old when disaster struck.*
>
> *He was playing with his father's gun and pointing it at his 5-year-old sister when it went off and killed her, splattering her blood everywhere.*
>
> *Steven was shocked and started screaming.*
>
> *Their mother came running in, saw the carnage, cried out in horror, and dropped dead of a heart attack.*

> Ever since that awful day, Steven has heard voices calling him a "baby killer" and a "mother killer" and urging him to kill himself.
>
> He spends most of his days as an adult drinking heavily—trying, but failing, to silence the voices and forget that day.

Wait a minute. Isn't that called PTSD today, not psychosis?

That's an important differentiation to make on this journey. Consider this story by contrast:

> I was at USC listening to a panel of students who were veterans talking about their experiences going to college after combat. The most compelling speaker was a young man who was a Marine through and through. He had the crew cut, reflective sunglasses, fit muscular body, and stood at attention. He said, "Yes, sir" and "No, ma'am." He also had a small white dog, curled up by his feet.
>
> He had experienced severe difficulties returning to society. He was always on high alert expecting an attack from everywhere. As a result, he was often impatient and would lose his temper, cursing at staff and other students—and then, he'd get very apologetic and ashamed because he hadn't behaved as a Marine should, letting down his service's values. When he heard a helicopter overhead—not an uncommon occurrence in the high crime neighborhood where USC is located—he'd be instantly transported back to Iraq, taking cover, yelling instructions to everyone around him, thinking they were under attack.
>
> He tried every medication the psychiatrists could think of, all without much impact, and they made it harder to study on top of everything else. It didn't help that he had nightmares of being back in combat most nights. Finally, they suggested he get a dog.
>
> He recalled saying, "Yeah. A dog might be just what I need. A fighting dog. Do you have a Doberman Pinscher?"

"Well, we're out of Dobermans, but we have a white dog that would be close."

The audience laughed. That dog clearly was nothing like a Doberman and not a fighter. She'd been friendly with all the other panelists.

The dog proved to be an enormous help because it only got upset when there was something to get upset about. It wasn't hyperalert, and it didn't think it was in a war. It even stayed calm when he was upset. The student learned to emotionally check in with the dog before reacting. If the dog wasn't on alert, he could stand down, too.

Walking across the campus together, he was the perfect proud, but wounded warrior. He'd served us and was always prepared to protect us again, but with the dog's help soothing and reassuring him, he could return to civilian life and a college classroom.

So, what's the difference? He's out of touch with reality because of a trauma, too.

The student reacted to the terrible stress of combat by blocking the most overwhelming, life-threatening experiences out of his long-term memory. The terrifying emotions were still inside him, causing him to be hyperalert and overreactive whenever anything triggered them. They also kept sneaking back into his mind, as flashbacks and nightmares, despite his best efforts to keep them away. Notice how everything that he experiences that is "unreal" is actually a repressed reality from the past that he's experiencing in the present.

Steven is experiencing an altered reality that his own unconscious has created trying to cope with his overwhelming grief and guilt. He's not reexperiencing the shooting. He can't adapt to what happened. Similarly, Leonard isn't reexperiencing the accident or being dumped in Skid Row. He created a new reality.

PTSD is fundamentally a condition of unsuccessful repression, whereas psychotic reactions are fundamentally a creative attempt by our unconscious, using a dream-like process instead of rational thought, trying to adapt to an overwhelming reality.

In practice, it can be hard to tell the difference, especially if someone has both reactions to their trauma.

> *Christie had a very difficult childhood. She never knew her father, and her mother struggled to raise her and her older brother and sister. The kids always fought and wouldn't listen to her. Helpless, she'd end up sitting on the floor sobbing, begging them to behave.*
>
> *When Christie was 7, her 13-year-old brother started sexually tormenting her, instead of just beating on her. She got more and more agitated, screaming out at night, and misbehaving at school. Her mother wouldn't believe her, and still doesn't, "They just didn't get along. You know how brothers and sisters are." Christie started hitting herself in the head and rocking. She said she wanted to die. They took her to a psychiatric hospital, which was frightening, too. Every time they wanted to send her home again, she'd get extremely agitated. She wasn't very good at describing why she was so frightened of her brother; so, they sent her home anyway. She tried to keep away from him, but he'd catch her when no one was around and he'd beat and rape her. Over the next 5 years, she went back and forth between various mental programs and home. Her torture finally ended when he left home at 18, but she was severely damaged by then.*
>
> *She hadn't been able to focus enough to learn much in school, and she didn't have any friends. She was always depressed, frequently suicidal, and never felt safe. She gradually learned to find strong boys to protect her. She offered them her desperation, utter dependence on them, gratitude, and willingness to please them in any way to keep them—a powerful combination for the insecure boys, and later on, men she clung to. Many of her boyfriends resented our staff's presence in their lives and tried to keep*

her away from us. We helped her get a very small studio apartment of her own in a monitored building near her mother, trying to help keep her safe.

Her mother called us frantically late one afternoon, saying that Christie looked bad, and she was afraid she'd try again to kill herself. Laurel, her social worker, and I went to her apartment to see how she was. Her mother unlocked the door. Christie was huddled on her bed, with her blanket clutched around her. She looked at us in absolute terror, with what Laurel later described as her "Jack Nicholson eyes."

It was hard to make out what she was saying. She screamed for us to get away from her. We tried to calm her down. She picked up the clock radio from her bedside table and heaved it at me. It missed me by inches, shattering against the door. We made a hasty retreat out of the room with our hearts pounding.

Laurel turned to me, "Mark, what were you thinking when Christie threw the radio at you?"

I hesitated, regrouping, before explaining, "I was trying to figure out if that was a flashback response, and she felt like a kid again, thinking I was her brother coming to rape her or if she was paranoid and psychotic, and that's why she was frightened of us."

Laurel shook her head with a look of disbelief.

"Mark, I was thinking 'duck!'"

I think I see what you mean, but why is it important to be able to tell the difference?

Because PTSD and psychosis have different treatments. They even respond to different medications.

With PTSD, we try to help the person slowly let the repressed experiences back into their normal memories, to move them from the emotional parts of their brains where they got stuck into the normal long-term memory, so that they can deal with them, while maintaining safety and security. We try to help them convert those past experiences from "reliving as though I'm back there again" to "remembering a tragic event in the past." With the dog by his feet, the veteran can talk about his war experiences, instead of reliving them. We tend to prescribe antidepressants, antianxiety medications, and adrenaline blockers to decrease their reactivity to the relived experiences, so that they can feel less overwhelmed in the present and gradually stop repressing them.

With psychosis, we have to understand what overwhelming stressor or feeling they're trying to deal with that has transformed their reality, so we can strengthen their conscious rational responses that they'll need to distort reality less. We try to be a part of their world, hopefully a comforting part, so they'll move closer to a shared reality. We try to alter their beliefs about their experiences and their responses, so that they'll be able to better reintegrate them into reality. We can talk to Steven about disagreeing with his voices, forgiving himself for a tragic accident when he was just a child, and asking them to forgive him, too, and perhaps even get involved in anti-gun advocacy efforts, instead of trying to drown the voice in alcohol. We tend to prescribe antipsychotic medications to try to increase their conscious control of their mind and decrease their hallucinations and delusions. Leonard wouldn't let his reality evolve or take any pills.

So, which one worked with Christie?

Neither one, with us anyway. She found another protector, a mildly retarded young man, who took her back to his family home in Alaska to take care of her. I don't know what happened after that.

Living a nightmare

We get a glimpse of how our unconscious mind works in our dreams, and it isn't always pleasant. Sometimes, in our dreams, we overcome the worries of the day and our pleasurable fantasies come true, and sometimes, our worries grow and transform monstrously, overcoming and terrorizing us, chasing us in recurrent nightmares. Similarly, "psychotic reactions" can create lives of pleasurable fantasies (like with Leonard imagining caring friends all around him) or terrorizing nightmares. Both are unconscious, creative "reactions" to a reality we can't face rationally. Psychosis can go on for decades, intertwining with events and relationships as time goes on, making it almost impossible to untangle after years have passed. The "psychotic reaction" becomes every bit as real and important as everything else in our lives.

> When I first met Peter at Coastal, he was in his 50s. He was a large white man, about 6'2" and 325 pounds. He was wearing a large wooden crucifix around his neck and sandals on his feet. They didn't quite fit with the ironed slacks and button-down shirt and his neatly cut and lightly reddish dyed hair. He was also carrying a worn Bible with him.
>
> The psych tech and the nurse who had been with Peter for years told me that it was a bad sign that he had the crucifix and sandals on because those were warning signs that he was getting overly religious and psychotic again. This could lead to him fasting for days or even weeks, which is what got him sent to the hospital every year or so. They thought maybe I should raise his medication dosage in his shot.
>
> His sister was the real force in the family. When she heard Peter had a new doctor, she called me to make sure I knew that Peter had serious schizophrenia, not to believe Peter when he said things were OK, and to never, ever let him talk me into letting him stop his medications.
>
> The only clear image I have of Peter when he was young came years later when I went with Peter and his sister to his mother's funeral. Listening to the eulogy, I could tell that the elderly priest knew this family well. He had a mischievous smile for Peter and his sister that hinted at shared secrets. He included Peter in his remarks, "I used to be Peter's football coach in high school. You should have seen him then. He was a big offensive lineman. He was both very good at football and very popular with the girls." He turned to Peter who was standing beside me holding my hand and blushing a little. I'd never seen him blush before. "Do you remember senior prom? There was this girl. I can't remember her name. She had the biggest crush on you, but she wasn't very good looking, and she was far too shy to let you

know she wanted you to take her to the dance. I took you aside after practice one day and asked you if you'd do me a favor and ask her to go with you. I'm pretty sure she wouldn't have been your first choice, but you did it just to be sweet. Boy, did you make her day." Peter nodded and smiled, his only smile that sad day.

After high school, Peter put his charms to work, getting involved with a variety of business schemes and young women. By his early 20s, he fell deeply in love and got married. He needed more money if they were going to move on from their little apartment; so, he decided to invest in some Mexican gold mines. He thought it would be safe because their family doctor gave him the lead. Things didn't go well though, and he went down to Mexico to check it out. What he found there was far from reassuring. Organized crime was involved with the mines, and his life was in danger if he said anything to the authorities. When he told his mother what he'd discovered, she bought him a gun for their protection, a decision she never forgave herself for.

Late one night about a month later, Peter answered a phone call, but no one said anything. After he hung up, Peter and his wife heard some noises outside the apartment. Peter decided that the phone call was from criminals checking to make sure they were home before they attacked him. He locked the door, closed the blinds, turned off all the lights, and huddled frightened with his wife waiting to see who would come for them. After some more noises, Peter pulled his gun out of the drawer, loaded it, and pointed it at the door. His wife became frantic at this and whispered to him to put it down. When that didn't work, she tried to grab the gun from him. They tussled, and the gun went off in her face. Blood and pieces of her head splattered all over Peter. He screamed out in horror and jumped out of the second story window breaking the glass, and ran down the street covered with blood and glass. They never found out if anyone was at the door that night getting ready to attack them.

The next morning in the jail cell was the first and only time God came to Peter and talked to him directly. He told Peter that no matter what anyone said, his wife wasn't dead. She had run off and escaped, but he could never see her again. Everything that had happened was punishment for Peter's sins. God had selected Peter as the most sinful person on Earth, and as a result, he was destined for a very long, painful death as the Advocate of God after the second coming, which would be soon. That moment of personal contact with God was the most powerful moment of Peter's life. He knew his life would never be the same. Tearfully, Peter accepted his fate and has devoted the rest of his life to preparing for this horrific death.

The court took a different view. They found him incapable of standing trial, since he couldn't be convinced he'd killed his wife, and he was determined to be not guilty by reason of insanity because he was clearly delusional. They wondered if he'd been getting paranoid for a long time and if the entire story about the gold mine and organized crime, and the feared attack were all delusions. Maybe his psychosis hadn't been the result of his wife's death, but the cause of it. I never figured that out.

He spent the next 12 years of his life at a state hospital for the criminally insane. His mother took a bus 2 1/2 hours each way every week to visit him there for all of those years. That's why he stayed with her, at her beck and call, through years of dementia when I knew them. She never could bring him back to reality or convince him his wife was dead. I don't know why the hospital eventually released him, since they're usually very cautious about releasing psychotic murderers, but my guess is that Peter had been very gentle and considerate throughout the years, that he was never a threat to anyone, and that they felt sorry for his mother and let her bring him home.

Over the years, Peter's and his mother's biggest conflicts were over religion and prayer. He wanted to fill their house with religious icons and spend all day praying. She agreed to a few paintings and a figurine of the Virgin Mary on the TV. Sometimes, he'd be on bent knee for such a long time that he could barely stand. She'd beg him to get up. He'd want her to say endless rosaries with him to save her soul. Every day was some Saint's Day. His mother and his sister, now married and living nearby, felt that the more he prayed, the worse he got and they kept trying to limit his prayer. The fasts came when he would decide that he could live on just the blood and body of Christ, and if only they'd let him go to communion, he'd get all the nourishment he needed. He'd also cry all day at those times, contemplating the painful death God had destined him for. The medications did seem to dull those beliefs and some of his religious fervor, or at least, make him pliable enough to agree to eat food again. The medication also took all sexual drive away and made him impotent, which he considered a great relief and a gift in his new spiritual life, and, when I look back, was probably the main reason he took it.

Only once over the 20 years did I hospitalize Peter. He had been fasting for about a week and became more and more obsessed with the idea of prostrating himself, crawling on his hands and knees to the Sanctuary of Our Lady of Guadalupe Hidalgo in Mexico City to turn to the Virgin Mary for a miracle. As it happens, I've been to that church in Mexico City. It's one of three Catholic churches certified as miraculous in the Western Hemisphere, and even to this day, people do crawl for miles and miles to get there, but not an overweight man in his 60s, in poor health, coming thousands of miles from Los Angeles. I showed him how far away it was on the map and how much desert is between here and there. He promised not to go, but still insisted he didn't have to eat anymore. After a couple weeks, I told him he'd have to be in the hospital since he wasn't eating. As pleasant and understanding as ever, he said he understood, and went along with me in my car to the hospital. I told the nurses not to force him to do anything and treat him nicely. After a few days of me making him feel guilty for not being *home for his mother and for making me have to work late seeing him daily in the hospital, he started eating again, and I took him home. A couple years later, I happened to visit another of the miraculous churches, the Sanctuary in Chimayo, New Mexico, on Easter, and there were hundreds of people prostrating themselves, coming from miles away in every direction across the hills. I got a bag of blessed, holy dirt for him that day and brought it to him. He was forever grateful.*

His sister and I got to know each other. She'd call worrying about every sign of increased religiosity he showed (Peter was distressed that her soul was going to hell because she wasn't observant enough). She'd want to know how much dosage I was giving him in his shot and wonder if maybe it shouldn't be a little higher for a few weeks. I joked with the staff that I adjusted his meds depending on his sister's nerves, not his, but we got along. I think Peter kept it hidden from her that I let him talk about the Bible and religious right-wing politics with me. I also told him about my life and the outside world. Occasionally, I'd try to bring up the subject of his wife's death, but he'd always insist that she hadn't really died. Apparently, his mind could deal better with the daily nightmare of being an Advocate of God doomed to an eternity of torture.

After his mother died, it seemed there might be an opportunity for him to rebuild his life some. Maybe reality could compete with his nightmare. He was now free to drive himself to mass a couple times a week, and I guess he could still charm the ladies, because before I knew it, he was giving several old ladies rides to Church. He started talking about how now he'd be free to practice his faith more. That idea frightened his sister. She didn't want to lose him in a dangerous religious zeal again. She forbade him from going back to church, and he obeyed and sat back down on the couch, all alone with his Bible and a carton of ice cream.

Breakdowns in jail and prison

A lot has been written about how people with psychosis end up in jail and prison, instead of in hospitals. What's rarely talked about is how many people become psychotic in jail and prison. Incarceration is an amazingly traumatizing experience, especially the first time, and especially for people not used to coping with cruelty and violence. I've been inside Los Angeles's jails as a visitor and couldn't wait to get out as fast as I could. The clang of locking doors signaled we were entering a hidden and helpless world. The crowding was incredible, eight men in a room designed for two, in long rows of bizarrely lit cages. I could feel pain and suffering coming off the walls.

When astronauts go into outer space, we worry a great deal about how they'll do for prolonged periods in tight quarters with only a few crew members for company. They're carefully screened and trained to avoid psychological meltdowns. They're tested to ensure they're compatible and are given lots of psychological support. When convicts go into jail or prison, they're usually not very psychologically healthy in the first place. They have no training to make it in confinement. The guards tend to be punitive and abusive. They are disrespected and demeaned at every turn, and their cell mates are likely to be scary. America's founding fathers thought that confining anyone for more than 3 months was cruel and inhumane punishment. Now, prolonged confinement is our most common punishment, seemingly without regard to its destructive psychological impact. Solitary confinement, depriving people of all sensory stimulation, is a far too common punishment in our prisons and can go on for months or even years.

> Danny was never very smart, but he was good looking enough to make up for it. He was raised by his elderly grandmother. His teachers liked him and passed him even when he didn't really earn it. The girls liked him, too, with his wavy hair and bright blue eyes. Some of the guys took advantage of him, but mostly they treated him well.
>
> As he went through high school, he didn't have any serious plans of what he was going to do next and had no one to guide him. He didn't worry about it too much. He had a girlfriend, alcohol, and pot, and pricey Air Jordan shoes. What more did he need?

Danny didn't realize he'd made a serious mistake until it was too late.

He had gotten into debt with his pot dealer and made an agreement that he'd use his grandmother's car to take them to make a delivery in exchange for more time to pay up. He took the car keys without telling her and took off. When she found the car missing, she called the police and reported it stolen. When they found him driving her stolen car high with three other kids and a car full of drugs, they arrested all of them and took them to jail. When his grandmother tried to get the charges dropped, the police refused.

A couple of weeks later, I found out where Danny was from his grandmother. He was in an isolation ward in the mental health unit at Twin Towers Jail. He had regressed and was smearing his feces on the cell wall. They didn't know if he'd been beaten or just terrorized. He was cowering in the corner of the cell, mumbling to himself. The jail psychiatrist gave him heavy dosages of antipsychotics to try to help him. His public defender got him determined not able to stand trial, and he was sent to a mental health Board and Care in lieu of further prosecution.

Danny never really got back to his old self. His grandmother never really forgave herself.

When I hear family members say they're grateful that their adult child is incarcerated because at least they know they're safe there and getting the medications they refused in the community, I wonder if they've actually seen the inside of a jail cell. I've rarely seen anyone regain their sanity and rebuild their lives, while being broken down in an unbearably frightening, crowded small cage.

Adapting to the stressor and healing the breakdown

Not all breakdowns have to be permanent. Sometimes, Humpty Dumpty can be put together again. Remember my scuba instructor who became psychotic and was hospitalized and medicated for a month after his girlfriend left him? He recovered, put his life back together, and got off medications. Remember Dan Fisher, the psychiatrist who got so isolated and stressed out by his neuropsychiatry training and research that he became catatonic, thinking he was a lifeless chemical robot and was hospitalized with schizophrenia? He recovered and became a successful psychiatrist, husband, and father, and got off medications. They both needed to adapt to the stressor that broke them down in the first place to recover from their psychosis.

> Andy was beginning his last semester as a CSULB student. He'd done well overall even though he was a first-generation college student. He'd lived in the dorms as a freshman with financial aid and was now living in a crowded apartment with five other students who got along well. He was a psychology major because he thought psychology was interesting. The main problem he seemed to be facing was that a Bachelor's degree in psychology doesn't really qualify you for any job and his college days were ending soon. But he was going to enjoy his last semester and worry about that later.
>
> The group from the apartment got together for a party one weekend with some LSD dots on the beach. Everyone was having a great time. As sunset came, Andy could see the colors move like rays of love through all his friends. He couldn't believe how much he loved them. He hugged a few closest to him, and they hugged him back. He looked up into the clouds and saw shimmering, glowing white beings of love and light. He wasn't sure they were Angels. It was hard for him to describe them in normal words, but it felt like he was experiencing heaven on Earth.
>
> As it got darker and quieter, Andy felt a chill flow through him. Then, he descended into the worst darkness he'd even felt. It was as though he was all alone cut off from all of life. Was he dead? Or maybe in hell on Earth? He started screaming in fear, and several of his roommates tried to calm him down. They gave him some alcohol to relax and it did take the edge off, but he was still frantically looking

around him into the growing shadows. His roommates decided he was having a bad trip and took him home and put him in bed.

About a week later, he kept getting flashbacks, or were they panic attacks, or going crazy, or dying and going to hell? He'd be back in the darkness, cut off from everyone else, paralyzed with fear. He couldn't sleep because of terrible nightmares of hell. And it wasn't going away. Everyone else was fine. What was happening to him?

He was frightened enough to call his mother and tell her what had happened. She took him to the Mental Health Urgent Care Center where they gave him some Zyprexa, which did help him sleep, but the episodes kept coming.

They came together to see me at the Counseling Center. Andy did all of the talking while his mother sat quietly.

I began by asking him about his childhood and background and his studies, to get a fuller picture of him as a person, trying to make them both more comfortable, and looking for strengths, before going into his "bad LSD trip." He had grown up in the Church with his mother, but had drifted away in his teens as he'd realized he was gay and felt rejected by passages in the Bible. He hadn't dated much, basically staying in the closet. He had a 3.5 GPA but hadn't applied to graduate school, afraid of incurring more debt.

When he got to the part of the story when blackness descended on him, he started reliving it in front of us. His eyes grew wide, he began shaking and sweating. "Am I going to hell?"

"You're still in this room. Look around slowly at my posters." He nodded. "See the waterfall and the picture of the desert and the calendar and the dream catcher...." We systematically went around the room regrounding him, and he calmed down again.

Once he was back in the room, I could think about what caused that reaction. A drug flashback wasn't likely since it wouldn't have coincidentally come when we were talking about it. I was back at the two choices I had when Christie threw the radio at me: Was he traumatized by the drug experience or experiencing psychotic episodes losing touch with reality even though the LSD was likely out of his system by now and he had some Zyprexa that should be helping glue him back together?

"If I heard you right, you were having a deep spiritual experience with the LSD, that was heavenly, maybe even angelic, but clearly out of your control and experience, and then it went badly. I was wondering if feeling rejected by your Church for being gay might be connected to you now experiencing hell?"

He paused and sat quietly for a moment. "I hadn't thought of that. Maybe."

"This is the first time I've told my mom I'm gay." *We both looked over at her.*

"Honey. I'll always love you, regardless."

She did more than that. Over the next couple weeks, she talked to their Church minister who invited them both over to dinner at his home and told Andy that he doesn't reject people for being gay, and he doesn't interpret those passages in the Bible literally to mean that God does either. He welcomed Andy back to their Church, and he returned with his mother to Sunday services.

Over the next month, Andy stayed on Zyprexa, and we even added some Prozac to help with the overthinking, traumatic aspects of his experiences, and he gradually improved. There were no more experiences of hell during the day. His dreams were still vivid but no long nightmares. Now, they were about him having special powers and having a mission to accomplish in life, even though he didn't know yet what it was. He said that although he was no longer deeply immersed in his spiritual thoughts and experiences, he didn't want to entirely put this behind him. He thought it was important to find some ongoing spiritual purpose in his life.

Also, he said he'd decided that since God was love, if he felt love for someone, regardless of what gender they are, it was good, not evil. He felt peace with who he is for the first time.

He graduated that semester and got off all his medications, too. He still doesn't have any good job prospects with his Bachelor's degree in psychology.

Looking deeper

There's a problem with this journey: I have seldomly met a person who was doing perfectly well when something terrible happened to them, and as a result, they suddenly became psychotic, and that's all there is to the story. I was taught that when they did studies on people with schizophrenia, there weren't more stressors than usual in the period before they experienced their psychosis. People often look back grasping for straws, looking for reasons, and they come up with something that happened in their lives, but much of the time there was already something going on before that event happened. Their journey had already begun well before they "reacted." I don't know if that's true or not, but even in the stories I just told you, almost all of them had some challenges already with their self-identity and their relationships before their "first break."

Fair or not, starting with *DSM-III*, all the "reactions" were taken out of the diagnoses, and we haven't looked back since. Not only don't we look for stressors that people reacted to, we almost never look for meaning in people's psychotic symptoms or for the stressors they may be responding to throughout their lives. I think that's a big mistake.

Over the years, I've learned that I have to look beyond "psychotic reactions" and go on much longer, more complicated journeys with most people to figure out what's really going on with them.

CHAPTER 8

JOURNEY 3: DIFFICULTIES IN MAKING SENSE OF THE WORLD

Reggie was a strange, shy Black man in his 30s. About a year before Robbyn was killed, she was doing outreach looking for homeless people and met Reggie sleeping in Alondra Park. Alondra Park might have been a big beautiful park at one time, with a large lake, playgrounds, and a swimming pool, but not at that point. There were quite a number of homeless people sleeping under the trees, and drug dealers patrolled the parking lot as a stream of middle-class customers drove by. I guess the police figured it was best to keep all the undesirable elements in one place even if that meant I couldn't take my wife and baby for a walk there.

The park was next door to El Camino Community College separated by a large parking lot with a generous supply of lights, call boxes, and campus patrol cars trying to keep the students safe, especially after evening classes. When Reggie talked about being attracted to pretty female students and following them to school, it creeped me out.

Even though Reggie got a Social Security check, he couldn't figure out how to use it to get a place to stay or even enough food for the month. The money always seemed to disappear after about a week, and then, he'd panhandle outside the 7-Eleven. He admitted to drinking sometimes, but denied drugs, although he agreed there were plenty around. Mostly, he bought snacks. Maybe that's why they didn't run him off. Also, he was too shy to really scare off any customers.

Reggie's life wasn't always like this. He'd grown up in Tennessee in a small town. He'd never been very interested in school and dropped out in the tenth grade. I couldn't tell if he had a learning disability or was just disinterested. In either case, his reading level was probably about the third-grade level. He wasn't really able to hold a job or attract a girlfriend. He became progressively more isolated, and people noticed he talked to himself most of the time. When he was 19, he stole a car and went joyriding. He was sentenced to the state penitentiary for 18 months for grand theft auto. That's where the voices got really strong.

The way Reggie explained it, the voices had saved his life in prison. They warned him about which prisoners and which guards he should watch out for. They even kept an eye out for him while he slept, waking him when there was danger. He'd never lived away from his family before. The voices were the only friends he had in there. They even gave him a plan for after he got out—go to Hollywood and become a movie star. He spent a lot of hours in that prison talking about that plan with the voices until it became the most real thing in his life.

The day they released him, he got on a Greyhound bus for the 3-day trip to Los Angeles. He didn't even tell his parents.

He couldn't really account for the next 10 years of his life. All of his memories seemed vague and fragmented. I don't think he ever did anything real about becoming a movie star, but the voices kept telling him his big break was just around the corner. They didn't seem to notice that he was the most unlikely movie star ever. We couldn't figure out how he got Social Security or how long he'd been living in the park.

Robbyn was probably the only young woman who had talked to Reggie in years. She made a point of chatting with him when she made her rounds of the park and shared her cigarettes and her corn chips with him. She was kind and patient. She even helped him call his parents for the first time since he left Tennessee, but even though they offered, he didn't want to go back home. It took Robbyn about 6 months to talk him into deciding to use his check to move into a Board and Care.

On the first of the next month, Robbyn helped him cash his check and drove him to the Board and Care with a black garbage bag with his meager belongings, including the clothes they'd gotten at the Salvation Army the week before. She also helped him buy a carton of cigarettes, so that he'd be popular. That left him 50 bucks for the rest of the month. He thanked her effusively and said he'd be fine. I don't think he'd slept in a bed for years. He shared one of his cigarettes with her before she left him there.

Neither Robbyn nor I ever understood why he walked down the street setting fire to every mailbox on one side of the block. He probably didn't even know anyone on that street. He wasn't trying to hide. It was broad daylight, and he just slowly walked down the street deliberately lighting a match, throwing it into each mailbox on the curb, and then, he'd shut the mailbox, again leaving it burning. My guess is that the voices were directing him. The police caught up to him on the second block.

We got a call from the local jail. Reggie had told them to call us since we were the only people he knew. It turned out that helping get him out of jail was out of the question. Destroying US mail is a federal offense, and he'd probably be sent to Leavenworth Prison. I have to admit that the part of me that was worried about the female college students was somewhat relieved he was being sent away and that they were safe, but I was sure the voices would be his only friends again and have more time to take over his mind.

The sheriff was calling us for another reason, "This guy is being a smart ass. Whenever we take him out of his cell, he says he can only walk on the left side of the hallway. That *can't be part of his mental illness, can it? He's just making that up to give us a hard time, isn't he? I've never met anyone who couldn't walk on one side of a hall before."*

"I've never met anyone who said that before either and I've never heard him say it before, but that doesn't mean he's pretending. He's not a smart ass. He's just a confused kid listening to voices telling him to do things. Lighting fires in mailboxes doesn't make any sense to me either, but that's what they made him do and now he's going to be locked up for a long time as a result."

The sheriff wasn't having any of it. "I still think he's faking, and I'm not going to let him get away with it."

If we're going to travel further from shore than on our first two journeys, I think we should spend some time to look more deeply at how people actually become psychotic. We shouldn't just wave our hands and say people create an altered reality for emotional reasons and let it go at that. This journey focuses on analyzing the neurobiological processes that enable us to perceive reality and how those processes can malfunction and mislead us. This is my wife's favorite journey. She was a mental health Occupational Therapist who spent time helping people, with a variety of mental illnesses, adapt to their disabilities, so that they could function and interact socially better. She believes that the majority of people with schizophrenia have a sensory-integration problem—in other words, they have trouble putting together their sensory inputs into a coherent, accurate, functional reality.

This journey focuses heavily on the "experiencing reality" point of the triangle. In today's world, where we think of our brains as complicated computers and usually only consider that dimension of the psychosis triangle, it will likely seem more familiar and like a modern, scientific journey to most of you. It's filled with talk about brain processes. You'll notice, however, that even on this journey, I'll insist on seeing the humanity of the person and not just the malfunctioning of their brain.

Let's get started

While most of us would likely be more compassionate than Reggie's sheriff, his frustration with psychotic behaviors is quite common. It seems like we should be able to get people to understand that what they're experiencing isn't real.

> "Why can't he tell that no one is there? When he thinks someone outside is talking about him, we go together and open the door and see that no one is there, but he still doesn't realize it's not real. He'll make up some reason they're gone. We do it over and over again, and he just won't believe me."

Our most common conclusion is that "it's all in their heads," but that's not how it feels to people who actually hear voices. From their point of view, "voices" come in a wide assortment ranging from "mental tapes," usually from their childhood, that keep up a running commentary on what they're doing, to voices inside their head that they know are a projection of their own thoughts or conscience, to voices in their head that seem like they're being caused by something electronic implanted into their head, ears, or even teeth, to people talking outside their heads ranging from whispers to screams. Sometimes, they know who the voice is, but usually not. Sometimes, the voices talk to them, or echo their own thoughts, or make them say what the voices want to say out of their own mouths, or repeat everything when they try to read, so that they can't keep track of what they're reading. Sometimes, medications make voices quieter or further away or even help them realize that the voices aren't real. How can there be so many variations? And is it important to separate them out?

Let's start by talking about how the process of hearing someone speak to us works normally.

I know this may come as a surprise to you, but in reality, there isn't a voice coming out of anyone's mouth when they speak. There's air that is forced out of their lungs and shaped by their vocal cords and their tongue and lips to send sound waves across the room. These sound waves hit our eardrums and vibrate them slightly. That vibration is amplified by three small bones in our inner ears. One of the bones hits the end of our semicircular canals, which makes waves slosh around in the fluid in the canals. Those waves wiggle nerve endings that are dipped into the fluid in the canal that sends nerve signals into our brain where we start to process the signal: We figure out the sound is English and send it to our language center. We screen out extraneous sounds. We add in nonverbal inputs from our other senses. We rationally process what's being said to understand it. We add in unconscious experiences, emotions, symbols, meanings, etc. to give it impact. We focus our attention to amplify or discount certain portions. All of this processing happens incredibly rapidly and puts together a meaningful speech. Then, the most amazing thing happens—and this is perfectly normal—we project that speech outside of our head, so that we experience it as though it's coming out of the other person's mouth. It all happens so fast, the only part we're aware of is the end speech that we synthesized from external sensory input and internal experiences and projected out into the world.

Think about that for a minute before we go on because it's important to figure out why they can't tell it's not real—everything we hear (and see, touch, smell, and taste) is "in our heads" before we project it outward into the world. We are literally creating our perceptions of the world as we go along.

Here's the really tricky part: Our brain is perfectly capable of creating speeches without any sensory input. We do it whenever we dream. We can also create sights, smells, touch, physical sensations, feelings—entire worlds—and then, we experience them as real because both kinds of experiences are created in the same parts of our brain. We can't tell the difference between "real" and "imagined" sensations because both of them are creations of our own brains. We have no direct awareness of what's going on in our ears or eyes. We only know what our brain creates.

We can't even tell if our sensations are the same as someone else's in the same situation. Think about how people who are color-blind don't know they're color-blind until someone tests them. Why is that? Because our brains are very good at creating sensations that appear to be real and complete to us, regardless of what sensory input we're given.

So, how do we know what we're dreaming isn't real?

Because it's a dream. I can tell the difference between dreams and reality.

You can't tell dreams aren't real by the quality of the sensations of the dreams—the sights, sounds, smells, tastes, and touches feel exactly the same as "normal" waking sensations.

I can tell because I wake up.

Exactly, but what if we started "dreaming" while we were awake ... and these dreams started combining seamlessly with our experiences of our senses? Then, how would we be able to tell what's real and what's not?

Not as easy as you thought, is it?

> *Jackson had a serious manic-depressive illness, and when he was manic, he lost touch with reality. He started believing he had lots of money and property and got angry and even violent with people who disagreed with him. The police would be called, and they'd take him to a psychiatric hospital. The last time, I'd had to go to the mental health court with him three times to get the judge to order him to stay in the hospital and take medications against his will. It had taken over a month seeing him daily in the hospital to get him back to normal. As soon as he got out, he'd stopped the medications again and gone all the way back to the beginning within a week. We were going to have to hospitalize him again and start the whole process all over again.*
>
> *I thought I'd be proactive this time. While waiting for the ambulance, I pulled out a video camera and, with his permission, recorded him, so that I could show him how psychotic he gets off the medications, so that he'd stay on them next time. While I was taping him, he showed me how angels were coming out of the electric sockets in the wall and how he was able to defy gravity and float in midair.*
>
> *A month later, he was again medicated and ready to leave the hospital. Feeling clever and confident, I brought out the recording.*
>
> *"I want you to see how you are when you are off medications, so you can see why you need to stay on them this time."*
>
> *"OK. Let's see it."*

I played the recording for him. As we watched it together, I started feeling a little concerned that he might be crushed by seeing how crazy he really was. I wondered if he could handle it.

I needn't have worried. He said, "You recorded that from a strange angle and it's hard to see how I was floating."

What? I felt like screaming.

"It's not a strange angle. You're not floating. And what about the angels?"

"Oh. Angels don't seem to come out on tape. I didn't know that about them, but they're there."

"So, you don't think you were psychotic in that recording."

"No, but it has helped me in one way. I feel less angry at you for hospitalizing me that day. The recording helped me see it from your point of view. You were wrong, but I understand why you did it."

So much for my cleverness. I put away the tape recorder.

If we work really hard, and many people who are psychotic do work really hard at distinguishing reality, we can come up with a small set of techniques, each one, unfortunately, with serious pitfalls:

- Typical Context: Just like we know dreams tend to come when we're sleeping, some people learn that their hallucinations tend to come in certain contexts—for example, when they're under a lot of stress, drunk or high on drugs, jealous, half asleep, or in the middle of a panic attack—so, they should be more suspicious of reality in these "typical" situations. But, all of us distort things in those situations and think about how hard it is to sort out reality afterward. Do you tend to believe that feeling you got or what you thought you heard when you were stressed, drunk, and jealous, or not? We don't have an accurate recording to compare with what we remember. All we have is the distorted way we recorded it at the time. This is also why undoing past paranoia or even jealous suspicions is very hard to do.

- Typical Content: Just like dreams sometimes have repetitive content, hallucinations do, too (presumably because they're being generated from the same cells in the brain each time). If we know that we have recurrent dreams of forgetting to take a test or walking naked in public, when we wake up, we can be pretty sure that was a dream and not a strange memory. So, If someone learns that they have critical or paranoid voices, they can be suspicious of any critical or paranoid content they hear. Someone else might be suspicious of homophobic content or grandiose content. They don't have to be suspicious of everything they hear, just their "typical content." This tends to be easier if the content is far from their usual feelings and experiences and harder if it's similar to their "normal." For example, someone who feels inadequate is going to have a hard time discounting thinking that they heard someone laughing behind their back.
- Unrealistic Content: It's not that likely that Madonna came to my home last night or that I learned how to fly, making it pretty easy to discount those experiences as unreal dreams. This is the technique we expect people to use most of the time: "Why would the Mafia want to kill you?" or "If you really owned all of Long Beach, you wouldn't be homeless, would you?" Unfortunately, it rarely works because, like Jackson, most people are incredibly clever at coming up with any explanation except that they're psychotic. The more desperate the need for explanations, the more elaborate the delusional worlds people will create to confirm their sanity and the meaning of their experiences.
- Irrational Flow: Does it seem "dreamlike"? Psychotic processes are more symbolic, nonlinear, and emotionally driven than rational thought, more poetic and imaginative, instead of logical and linear. Unfortunately, if psychotic and rational thoughts are tightly entwined, it's going to be hard to separate them. Also, many people are drawn to this type of experience, suspecting they might have some special significance or spiritual wisdom, and are likely to pursue them rather than discount them.
- Trusted Other People: When I wake up, I can ask my wife if she heard the tree in the backyard fall down last night or if I just dreamed it. It's a lot less easy, though, to trust her answer if I'm

asking something like, "I thought I heard you talking to your friend on the phone about me last night. What did you say to her?" or "Did you really remind me to go to the store and I forgot or are you just saying that?" Not only do all of us have selective memories and distort reality somewhat to serve ourselves, we sometimes lie a little when we think it's for the best. Truly "trustable" other people are hard to come by. If someone is trusting you enough to be their reality test, try very hard to be painstakingly honest because, over time, it's more likely that you'll lose trust and become incorporated in their delusions than that you'll succeed in being a longstanding reality test for them. (Alternatively, you can try using a trusted dog to be your reality test, like the Marine veteran student with the dog in the previous Chapter, but the dog better not be hypervigilant if it's going to work.)

Altogether, these really aren't very good techniques, but they're the best we have. Too often, they can lead people into a vicious cycle of misinterpreting reality, building delusional explanations, pursuing alternative realities, losing trust in others, and isolating further. Not a good journey.

Given how difficult this is, many psychiatrists and others have given up trying to figure out what's going on, and label all psychotic people as having biologically determined "anosognosia"—a lack of insight into their own condition—and, therefore, decide that they are unable to participate in their own treatment realistically, and need to take more medications to restore their "reality testing," involuntarily if needed. Many people resist. Not a good journey either.

Instead, let's try to understand where the process is breaking down for each person and look for opportunities to intervene throughout the process, including, but not limited to, medications.

If we can pinpoint where along the steps someone is having trouble processing what they're sensing, we may be able to intervene preempting the creation of alternative realities. For example, if someone is likely to think other people on a crowded bus are talking about them behind their back, they can sit in the back row, put on head phones, and play a game on their phone to distract themselves.

There are people who have problems with sensory integration at each of the steps along the way. If we spend the time to differentiate their difficulties, we can take more focused action. When we're sensitive to each person's experiences, we can find a significant number of specific changes we can make in our usual medical model services that could decrease their distress and traumatization and facilitate self-reliance and recovery.

Here's a list of steps:

	Step	Description	"Treatments" and Other Helpful Responses
Experiencing Reality	a. Sensory perceptive	Our sense organs take in stimuli from our environment and send them to our brain.	Glasses, hearing aids, earphones Clear, unambiguous stimuli
	b. Intuitive and spiritual senses	In addition to our usual five senses, we have intuitive and spiritual senses that give us interpersonal and extra-personal stimuli.	Training—yoga, meditation, prayer Connecting with others with shared experiences, beliefs
	c. Sensory processing	Our brain finds the patterns in the information it is being given and makes a perceived reality out of it.	Using attention and inattention Pleasant, easy-to-read surroundings

Understanding Reality	d. Rational synthesis	We use our conscious, rational mind to analyze our perceptions logically and systematically.	Social skills training Cognitive Remediation Cognitive Behavioral Therapy
	e. Unconscious, "primary process" synthesis	Meantime, our unconscious mind is analyzing our perceptions and making sense of them irrationally, using emotions, symbols, etc.	Emotional processing Asserting our conscious will and decision-making
Creating Reality	f. Projection of internal reality into external reality	We experience the reality we synthesize outside ourselves often including our internal expectations and emotions.	Decreasing our emotional transferences and projections Improving our emotional reality
	g. Protection of self-perceptions	We sustain our sense of self, both good and bad, even as we grow and change.	"Alternative" self-identities Positive, "normal" roles
	h. Time perception	We experience our life's story as the flow of time as we move through it.	Emphasizing events to mark time Enhance personal narrative

Experiencing Reality

The first three steps in our tour are about how we take in information and experience reality.

a. Sensory perceptive

There are a large number of "hallucinations" associated with sensory damage that are usually not considered psychiatric conditions. One of Oliver Sacks's last books before he died was *Hallucinations*. It was filled with people, including himself, who had experienced a wide variety of hallucinations that weren't psychiatric. People with auditory nerve damage often hear a buzzing in their ears. Blind people sometimes "see" lights or colors. Horrible imaginary smells can torture people. Annoying music refrains can get stuck in our heads.

But why don't we usually diagnose these people as "psychotic," lock them up, and forcibly medicate them?

Two reasons, I think: 1) We understand what's causing their hallucinations, and 2) we're not afraid of them going crazy, and they aren't afraid of it either.

What difference does that make?

We tell them what they are hearing is "real" ... even though we can't hear it. We have clear neurological tests, biological explanations, medical staff, and patient roles for them that are reasonable for them to accept without admitting they're crazy and losing their basic self-identity. If the other steps in the sensory integration process are intact, they'll use that information to rationally synthesize a "shared world view" (like my nerve damage makes me hear buzzing no one else can, which is annoying, but if I focus carefully enough, I can still follow the same conversation everyone else is having), instead of an idiosyncratic one (like there's an implant in my head they turn on, so I can't hear them plotting against me) preserving their self-identity and relationships, so that they don't become psychotic.

We can sometimes teach people skills how to "correct" their sensory perceptions. If someone has a tendency to hear voices while in the shower, where the sound of the water is an indistinct, easily misinterpreted sound, they can turn on a radio and listen to music or talk radio, which are less likely to be transformed into voices. If we can give their brains enough easy-to-interpret sensory information, it can outcompete the distorted or even the self-created sensations. People can also learn to use one sense to fortify a questionable one. For example, if someone isn't sure whether someone is talking to them, it may help to look at them while they're talking and watch their lips move.

> *Patricia Deegan, who I mentioned earlier as a successful psychologist who has heard voices since childhood, spent a long time interviewing and taping people talk about how they cope with voices, and incorporated much of what she learned from them into the information and recovery-based training tools she developed at the National Empowerment Center. I've used one of these publications, "Coping with Voices: Self-Help Strategies for People Who Hear Voices that Are Distressing," with many people to encourage them to actively look for strategies that will diminish their voices and their impact. Some of the strategies she includes that likely work on the sensory level include humming or singing quietly to yourself, counting under your breath, listening to taped positive affirmations, putting an earplug in one ear at a time, actively listening to music that makes you happy, and turning up the volume of the TV. She also includes other strategies that likely work at other levels.*

Even with something seemingly as straightforward as sensory blindness or deafness, having a different perception of reality than other people do begins to transform our sense of ourselves and our reality—our self-identity. For example, it's interesting that even people with clear sensory loss often have a desire to say that they are not disabled. They prefer to describe themselves as differently-abled. Remember how Marlee Matlin's character in the movie "Children of a Lesser God" didn't want William Hurt to feel sorry for her as someone who was missing out on life because she was unable to hear? She wanted to share with him the beauty of the different world that she and other deaf people live in. There are various groups of people with sensory differences that are designed to cultivate a subculture that celebrates their altered experiences of the world.

The "Hearing Voices" movement and network emerged over the last decade from the Netherlands and the United Kingdom spreading to 26 countries at this point. It supports people who hear voices to avoid a pathological schizophrenic identity, instead normalizing hearing voices and helping each person through self-help groups, conferences, and websites to find meaning in their voices and strength in their ability to cope with and learn from their voices. Eleanor Longden's 2013 TED talk, "The Voices in My Head," dramatically describes this approach in her own recovery. We'll return to Eleanor in Chapter 15 when we incorporate finding meaning into recovery.

b. Intuitive and spiritual senses

We're all familiar with the "five senses"—sight, hearing, smell, taste, and touch—but there is another set of "senses" that are much subtler and are used primarily for complex interpersonal interactions. These can be called "intuitive senses." To illustrate this, here are a few examples: There are some hairs on the back of our necks that "stand up" when we "sense" that we're being looked at or are in danger. Sometimes, we get a "feeling" in our gut that someone is not to be trusted and we need to protect ourselves. Some people even "know" when someone they're closely related to is calling them on the phone or is in trouble and need them. We can get good "vibes" from someone. These intuitive senses are more likely to be processed unconsciously than rationally, and so, we may not even be aware of them. Nonetheless, they powerfully influence us and may cause considerable difficulty.

Some people, and families, seem to be born with stronger intuitive senses than other people, just like some people have stronger hearing or sight than other people. Normally, we don't train ourselves in how to use our intuitive senses effectively, relying on our five senses instead, and they tend to diminish through neglect. However, if someone has had to cope with substantial relationship-based danger and trauma along the way, they may, whether they realize it or not, strongly develop some intuitive senses and come to rely on them. This may lead to including them heavily in their synthesized reality.

Carl was constantly teased and beaten by his older siblings and cousins. He developed a "second sense" knowing when someone dangerous was around the corner or on their way, so that he could run away and protect himself. As an adult, he is anxious around other people, avoids crowds, feels abused by the world, collects injustices, and even became paranoid—believing that his cousins organized a conspiracy to monitor him and ruin things whenever he tries to get ahead in life.

He has spent more and more time isolated, allowing his inner thoughts to gain strength, and he feels inadequate to cope with other people and make decisions on his own. He interprets any obstacle, for example, a paperwork problem at the welfare office, as further evidence that his cousins are stopping him from getting anything positive in his life. His mistrust has gradually evolved into hearing voices that take over more and more of his life, both warning him and protecting him, and also urging him to not put up with this anymore, to confront the people who are persecuting him.

Underneath all of this paranoia is a young Black man who didn't fit in with any stereotyped role available to him. He wasn't really a tough gangbanger or a strung-out homeless man. If he'd had the opportunity, he'd likely have become an intellectual poet, skateboarding and listening to his favorite musician, Bob Marley (who outdid his overbearing family that didn't believe in him). The more I was able to relate to those parts of him, the more comfortable and the less paranoid he was with me.

Unlike the situation with normal five senses, most people don't really believe intuitive senses exist; so, children who have intense intuitive experiences may be told they're imagining things from the beginning or learn not to mention them to other people since others might think they're crazy. This can make it less likely for them to emerge with a shared reality. Indeed, the disbelief in these phenomena and the difficulty in funding careful studies to learn more about them, bemoaned by Rupert Sheldrake and others, make it difficult to separate reality from charlatanism to have a socially acceptable shared reality at all in this area.

Some people, seemingly without mental illnesses, would go well beyond what I'm describing as intuitive senses and say that they also have extra-personal, energetic, or spiritual senses. For example, they believe they can see or sense spirits and ghosts or God. They may have felt "the Holy Spirit enter their body" or "sensed evil in that man's soul." While Western science doesn't have any way at present to describe these phenomena, Eastern tradition might say that we get this information through our "third eye" or an "open Crown Chakra"—presumably "spiritual sense organs."

Many children have unusual experiences that would be labeled psychotic in adults, but I believe they have particularly strong intuitive senses or spiritual senses. For most children, these experiences fade away, unless they are reinforced by their family or culture, but for some they persist in hiding. They may start having two lives—one that becomes a personal world they rarely share with others and one within the public world. If we can understand that their psychosis began with these childhood intuitive experiences, we may be able to help them to integrate the two parts of their life, instead of using medications to try to suppress their experiences.

> *Melissa told me that she can remember as early as 3 years old being aware of the spirits of dead people around her. Her grandmother would help her identify who she was seeing. She also taught her how to protect herself from evil spirits that wanted to take her soul using crystals and potions.*
>
> *After her grandmother died, she stopped paying as much attention to what she calls the world of angels and spirits. Her adolescence was rather turbulent marked by having promiscuous sex, using drugs, and dropping out of high school. By the time I met her, she'd been homeless for a number of years and was living with an abusive older man in his camper along with their two big dogs.*
>
> *She always felt that she was doing poorly because she was neglecting her spiritual purpose in life—to find her first love from high school who was her soul mate to get together to restore the balance in the world of angels. She tried to make up for it by helping as many other homeless people as she could. She would give food, cigarettes, and money to many people and always had a kind word for everyone.*

> She resisted my attempts to get her to describe herself as having a mental illness, believing in a delusional world, and to take medications. They only gave her Social Security on appeal when I wrote that one of her signs of having schizophrenia was that she didn't think she did and that's why her applications didn't describe a diagnosis or a disability. She understood my tactics but didn't really agree with me. She used the money to leave the boyfriend but not the dogs and get a two-bedroom house that she kept subleasing to a stream of other homeless people, always on the verge of eviction.
>
> At times, she would disappear for a while and say she'd been spending time fighting evil spirits, but she never got to Arizona to look for her first love to bring balance back to the world.
>
> She said she hated talking about problems with psychiatrists since we always assumed she was psychotic and never believed her. But she never stopped believing that she could see spirits.

c. Sensory processing

Even if we have fully functioning eyes or ears or intuitive senses, our brain may still process the information coming in incorrectly—or exquisitely. Someone can have "perfect pitch" that helps them be a successful musician while someone else may be profoundly disturbed by the slightest of noises that keep distracting them and make them wonder if someone is intentionally persecuting them. We have incredible individual variation.

This is also where we start to put together a coherent picture of reality from the input we're receiving. For the most part, we have to ignore the vast majority of what's coming in and recognize useful patterns in order to put together a coherent picture. Unless someone shows us one of those strange visual illusions where I might see a cup while you see two faces, we don't even realize we're doing this ... even if we're getting it very wrong.

> *My mother-in-law had a stroke that wiped out the left side of her visual field—not her left eye, the left side of her visual field. She literally couldn't see the left side of things. She would do only the right side of her crossword puzzles. She could only read the right side of the menu. She got into several car accidents hitting things on her left that were invisible to her. She'd eat only the food on the right side of her plate. I could turn her plate around and then she'd see the remaining food and eat it, but she had no explanation for where the food had come from or why she couldn't see it if I spun it back around again. Rather than being fascinated by this neurological deficit and try to figure it out, she felt criticized, humiliated, got defensive and irritable, and withdrew. She couldn't face the idea that she was seriously distorting reality and didn't realize it. She never learned any simple coping skills to make the left side of the world reappear like spinning her own plate.*

Presumably, we can all learn to process information from our senses differently than we're doing it now. For example, at present, I can't detect the differences in the tonality of words in Asian languages. Even if I hear a word pronounced correctly, I can't replicate it because my brain can't process the difference between the way he's saying the word and I'm saying it. I assume that if I took enough Chinese language classes, my brain would learn to hear the differences. Similarly, I can't taste the difference between good and bad wines. I doubt the problem is in my tongue. It's more likely in my brain and I could be trained. Notice that I have to be trained both to detect the subtle differences in sensation and, then, to assign meanings to the differences. If I don't do both, I won't be able to speak Chinese or "appreciate" fine wines.

So, what's happening, if someone starts to hear voices and, then, they choose to strain to hear what the voices are saying? Do they train themselves to detect small variations in sounds that they then assign meaning to? And is it true that the more they train themselves to listen carefully for the voices, the easier it is to hear the voices? Often times, people who hear voices say to me, "Didn't you hear that?" and if I listen very closely, I can hear very subtle sounds that I didn't notice before and that don't have any language meaning to me even when I do detect them. "That's just the hum of the air conditioning. I don't hear anyone talking to us."

And what would happen if they trained themselves to be less sensitive to these subtle sensations, so that they couldn't detect them anymore? Or to be more likely to interpret the sounds as humming, instead of language? There are people who can identify the type of airplane flying overhead by the sound of its engine. Presumably, they'd be less likely to hear voices in humming engines than I would. Unfortunately, like my mother-in-law, most people usually recoil from the idea that they're processing the world incorrectly and could train their brain to process it more realistically. Even when I make it easy for them and give them a medication that quiets down the voices and makes the voices hard to hear (and neither they nor I know how that works), they may be glad they can sleep now without the voices keeping them awake, but more often than not, they're afraid they're going to miss something important going on with the voices. Many people will periodically stop their medications just to check in on what the voices are talking about. Even when virtually everything the voices tell them doesn't turn out to be true, they still may want to know what they're talking about.

> *Douglas has a great deal of difficulty living in Los Angeles because there are electric wires of a variety of types all over the place that he believes are damaging his body and his brain. He usually wears tinfoil lining the inside of his hat and clothes to protect himself from the invisible electric waves. He is able to block out some of them in his apartment by covering the windows and walls with tinfoil and putting rubber mats all over the floor to stop them from coming in through his shoes from the floor. He also believes that live green plants absorb some negative electric waves from the air. His landlord doesn't like the way he's fortified his apartment to protect himself. Douglas doesn't want me to give him any medication to make him less aware of the electric waves because then, he wouldn't know when they're at critical levels and he'd have no way of protecting himself from them. He tells me that if he was going to dull himself to be oblivious while he's being poisoned, he'd rather drink alcohol than take my pills. Unfortunately, I don't*

> know of any treatments that would make us either able to accurately assess the possible damage of electric waves or to become resistant to it.

Many years ago, psychiatric hospitals were designed to be a place of rest and recuperation and provide a healing environment to facilitate "moral" treatment. Attention was paid to the grounds and the foliage, to the color of the paint on the walls, and to the decorations. They included physical relaxation, art, and music, all designed to soothe and heal overstressed senses. As our lengths of stay have radically decreased and the primary mission of hospitals has become reducing dangerousness and ensuring safety, and as psychiatric hospital units were opened within busy medical hospitals becoming more medicalized and "efficient," and as treatment units were opened in crowded jails and prisons, there has been a severe assault to the senses, especially for people likely to be extraordinarily sensitive. When I think back to how I could barely handle walking into LA County Jail mental health units as a visitor because I'm bothered by the "suffering that seems to ooze out of the walls," I have to wonder how someone who can intuitively sense hateful feelings or someone who can "smell fear" is supposed to handle it. Crowded group homes and Board and Care facilities are often not much better.

> *In my opinion, the most visceral portrayal of psychosis from the inside ever made is David Lynch's classic film "Eraserhead." It seems likely to me that David himself was having psychotic experiences in order to make a film like this. He made "Eraserhead" as his first full length film, while a student at the American Film Institute, apparently wandering around, disheveled, missing classes, in his own world, living in the stables where the movie was filmed. He took years to make the film while trying to change his life, using transcendental meditation, giving up smoking and drinking, and becoming a vegetarian.*
>
> *On one level, the film's story is rather simple about a man meeting a girl, having dinner with her parents, getting married, and having a child together, but the entire movie has a profoundly disturbing quality, built on strange sounds and shadows. The hum of a radiator becomes a singing girl*

within it. The baby's cries turn it monstrous. It's all enough to explode the mind.

Later works by David Lynch also have extraordinary aspects that can be interpreted as emerging from his psychosis. Sexual feelings are distorted and frightening in "Blue Velvet," an unsolvable murder mystery that leads to more and more confusing characters, each with peculiar exaggerations in "Twin Peaks," and "Mulholland Drive" ends where it began, despite not including a flashback.

Regardless of the inspiration for these disturbing films, they can give us as viewers a vicarious experience of having sensory distortions, especially of sound, leading to a growing disorientation and psychosis.

Understanding Reality

The next two steps are about how we analyze the information we're taking in to understand reality.

Understanding reality is where I think most people who are diagnosed with schizophrenia begin to have their most significant difficulties: Their senses as well as their basic sensory processing are intact, but things start to diverge when they try to combine their own thoughts and imagination, conscious and unconscious, rational and irrational, with the information from their senses. I also think that this is the part of the process where medications have their most significant effects.

d. Rational synthesis

I was taught in medical school that if someone is psychotic, they usually hear voices, and if they're delirious (suffering from some kind of neurological brain damage or toxicity), they usually have other kinds of hallucinations—like seeing visions, smelling things, or feeling like they're being physically touched. This is such a strong differentiation that the presence of any other kind of hallucination besides hearing voices is a good reason to do a full neurological and medical workup. I've long wondered why hearing voices is different than other hallucinations. I now think that the reason is that auditory language requires far more massive processing, beyond basic sensory processing, to be understood than anything else. Our brain's systems for understanding sounds include all of our language centers and their supports that the other senses simply don't have. If our brain was a machine, we could say, "The more complicated something is the more ways it can break," but since we're talking about an ever-evolving biological system, it would be more accurate to say, "The more complicated the process is, the more likely it will diverge from the normal, expected responses." Indeed, most people's psychotic auditory hallucinations are language-based voices, not just sounds.

What about reading? Isn't that a visual process that requires complicated linguistic processing, too?

It turns out that most people with psychosis have impressive difficulty reading, too—which is very important if they're trying to study textbooks in school or learn psychiatric rehabilitation material by reading. It's not just that the voices and their anxiety are distracting, so it's hard to focus and concentrate enough to read. The voices have a tendency to act up when they're trying to read. The voices repeat the words or get stuck on certain phrases or try to convince people to look for hidden personal meanings. It seems to me that reading is actually wired through the verbal language processing centers. Think about it: When we first learn to read, we read out loud. If we find an unfamiliar word, we're urged to sound it out. Even as an adult, it seems to me that the words are being said somewhere in my brain when I read. That's why it's hard to read faster than that internal voice can talk and be heard and understood. One person I worked with who was blind and used sign language told me that she "heard voices," but she couldn't really describe what hearing them sounded like to her. It seemed as though her "voices" were actually sending and interpreting sign language inside her head, instead of talking out loud.

When we remember what we hear, or read, unless you're a rare person with a "photographic memory," it's not an actual transcript of what the person said. It's a synopsis of sorts that's been heavily edited by both rational and irrational influences.

Another area where understanding reality becomes very complex is understanding social cues. Beyond someone's words, we have to interpret their intonation, underlying emotions, nonverbal expressions, social context, and culture to create socially useful understandings. Many people with schizophrenia struggle so much with this that their lives are filled with so many frustrations and embarrassments, anxieties and awkwardness that they fear and withdraw from social interactions. This is a frequent path for challenges in experiencing and processing reality to negatively impact relationships, leading to a second dimension of the triangle collapsing.

Those problems with language and social cues sound more to me like autism than schizophrenia.

Presumably, people with autism have problems in these areas for the same reason people with schizophrenia do—because they're the most complex and difficult functions, even though the underlying malfunction is probably different.

It's interesting to contrast our approaches to autism and schizophrenia. We painstakingly spend hours and hours with children with autism teaching them language skill, social cues, and self-care for years and years, so that they'll be able to get along with others and not require as much lifelong care. Since they're children, we're hopeful and believe in their developing brains' plasticity and their capacity to learn. Often, our hopes and efforts are rewarded with true progress. Very little of that kind of painstaking effort is spent training people with schizophrenia. Instead, we rely on medications to make them less problematic, although medications do very little for language, social cues, and self-care. Often, our hopelessness is "rewarded" with stagnation and the need for ongoing custodial care. To be fair, the issue isn't really stigma and neglect of people with schizophrenia. We don't devote that kind of sustained effort training adults with any condition—not veterans with traumatic brain injuries, recovered drug addicts with brain damage, accident or beating or shooting victims, or even neurology patients with strokes or brain tumors or dementia. Perhaps it's because of funding systems or lack of family and adult school involvement. Perhaps it's because it's harder to force adults than kids to spend hours learning anything (after all, most kids think that being forced to learn is their normal life and most adults don't). Or perhaps it's because we just don't believe adult brains continue to be plastic, to learn, and to grow; so, we're more hopeful about kids than adults.

Dr. Robert Liberman has specialized in schizophrenia and psychiatric rehabilitation throughout his illustrious career at UCLA. For almost 30 years. he directed the Clinical Research Unit at Camarillo State Hospital, the same hospital Kenny was in as a child. After it closed, he continued his work at the Westwood Veteran's Administration Hospital. Much of his early work at Camarillo focused on creating Social Skills Training modules. These training materials helped people with significant deficits slowly build enough social skills to interact more successfully with others and relieve their isolation. They were translated into 15 different languages, and when I traveled around the world visiting mental health programs, Dr. Liberman was a great help, introducing me to people who were using his materials worldwide.

When the Village first began, we bought a copy of the training materials and started using them to train our members. They included tapes, activities, worksheets, and trainer's guides. We only got through training one cohort and then abandoned them on the shelf. Why? I'm almost ashamed to admit the answer—because they were boring. The lessons focused on small details and were repetitious, which is likely to be precisely what some members, those with processing difficulties, needed, but for everyone else, it felt far too remedial.

Today's incarnation of this kind of training is called Cognitive Remediation, and it's done mostly with computers, so that staff don't have to be bored, and the best versions look like video games, so that the clients don't have to be bored. Even still, they're not used much, primarily because, like all sorts of training, to be effective, they have to be used persistently—for at least an hour a day, for months. Helping our brain develop new circuitry to overcome deficits takes a lot of work. I did see Cognitive Remediation programs being used in hardworking Singapore, where patients worked on their computers several hours a day. When I asked the

> *staff if it worked, they said that it did, but only if the patients had the opportunity to practice the skills in real situations, too, not just on the computer. I think that's because they need to restore both their experience of social interactions and actually have real relationships—in effect, fighting the psychosis from two fronts, instead of just one.*

It seems to me that any kind of painstaking skill-building treatment needs to be specifically focused on what deficits and goals a particular person has if they're going to be sustainable and effective. Dr. Liberman's later work has focused on the issues of individual motivation, collaboration, patient-driven goals, and social context, while still retaining a skill-building emphasis. This is likely an area where a combination of technology-assisted approaches and highly individualized recovery-based approaches would be the most successful.

Another approach that belongs in this step is Cognitive Behavioral Therapy that I talked about in Chapter 4. CBT therapists are not trying to talk their clients out of their hallucinations and delusions by explaining to them how they're unreal and irrational. They realize and accept that these things are every bit as real to their clients as anything else is. Instead, they're allying with their clients, carefully understanding how they are perceiving reality, and then working to alter how they're making sense of it. They're working to make their client's synthesis more rational.

> *I recently worked with a young man who was experiencing intrusive thoughts that almost seemed like someone else's voice in his head, urging him to pick up a knife and kill his sister, who he'd always been close to, but who was now going on to college and had a new boyfriend. He was so frightened by his violent thoughts that he obsessed about them constantly and began to think that maybe he should kill himself to avoid hurting his sister. Instead, he decided to tell his sister, who said she wasn't afraid of him because she knew he loved her, but the family agreed to remove all the knives, so that he'd feel less at risk anyway. I worked with him, not to convince him that he wasn't having these thoughts or that they weren't real, but that they didn't represent his true self or any irresistible force. He could*

> observe these thoughts coming and going without getting upset, without acting on them, and without actively fighting to stop them. Once all the pressure and drama around them were relieved, he started experiencing them far less often. When he did experience them, he let go of them as strange thoughts that don't mean anything. The family was able to bring back the knives, and his sister promised to spend time with him and share her new life with him, even while she was busy with other new people.

e. Unconscious "primary process" synthesis

We tend to assume that our mind is rational and intentional, but that actually only describes a small portion of our mind's activity, mostly when we're connecting to our frontal lobes where most of our rational analysis and decision-making are generated. A good deal of the brain is concerned with rather mechanistic functions like breathing, digesting, metabolism, balance, temperature regulation, and certainly, we use those connections to understand some parts of our experience and take action (like pulling our hand away from a hot stove), but, as far as I can tell, those aren't the kinds of functions that lead to psychosis. It's the unconscious emotional connections that we care about here, the kind of functions that Freud was trying to uncover when he said that "dreams are the royal road to the unconscious." He described dreams, the unconscious, and psychosis as all using the same irrational tools to connect various thoughts, feelings, and perceptions, including wish fulfillment, symbolism, a part meaning the whole, metaphor, and emotional associations. He called this "primary process" thinking in distinction to conscious, rational "secondary process" thinking.

The vast majority of the daily synthesis we do is unconscious, rather than conscious ... and we can't even track our unconscious synthesis by going back and trying to understand how we came to those conclusions. The best we can hope for is to make some interpretations of what our unconscious might be doing based on our past experiences and self-awareness.

> Dolores worked for the Human Resources Department of a large company. For years, she did her job more rigidly by-the-book than most of the staff would've liked, but she stuck to her procedures since she knew she was right—and she

was. She always made sure she looked professional. She didn't have any friends and never dated. She lived alone. She didn't have any pets. She always looked after herself.

One day, her next-door neighbors were up all night drinking, partying loudly with some friends, laughing, yelling, and cussing. Dolores couldn't get to sleep and needed to work the next morning; so, she called the on-site landlord to ask him for help. He called the neighbors and asked them to quiet down, but that led to the neighbor woman coming down the hall and pounding on Dolores's door, "How dare you call the landlord on me?" A scuffle ensued that included the neighbor pushing Dolores to the floor. More frightened than outraged, Dolores called the police.

After talking to both Dolores and her neighbors, the police told Dolores that in situations like this, when two neighbors scuffle with different stories about what happened, that they'd have to take both parties down to the station to do anything and he'd rather not do that, saying, "How about if I get your neighbor to apologize instead?" Dolores felt betrayed and abandoned, but reluctantly agreed; so, the policeman left. When her neighbor came up, her "apology" was accompanied with a threat, "You'd better keep your eyes open from now on."

Her neighbor made good on her threat, or at least, it seemed that way to Dolores, making snide comments, knocking into her, taking things left at her door. After a few months, Dolores's lease expired and she left, although she'd lived there for 7 years. When she found a new place, it seemed to her that everyone knew about the problems she'd had, and they were harassing her there, too. One day, she saw her old landlord talking to the landlord of her new apartment, and she realized that he had been the one behind all of the harassment the whole time and had followed her there to get her. She went to the police repeatedly, but they "didn't do their job." She kept changing apartments, but the harassment followed.

All of this upset her so badly, she ended up losing her job. She ended up living in her car, and still no one would intervene to stop the elusive and indescribable "them" who kept harassing her unmercifully. The years went on.

By the time our outreach worker, Joanne, contacted her, she'd only agree to meet in various mall parking lots, so the people following and watching her wouldn't know where Joanne worked to get her, too, since Dolores liked Joanne. They had to communicate only in person because Dolores was sure her phone was tapped. Joanne had me meet her at a Starbucks to see if I could help. I was struck by how clean and well-dressed Dolores was. "I'm not a slob. Just because they won't let me live anywhere doesn't mean I don't try to take care of myself. The hardest part is when they poison my food and make me sick. Sometimes, I'll catch them at it and yell at the people in the restaurant to make them stop poisoning me. They pretend they don't know what I'm talking about, but at least that way, they know they can't take advantage of me. I know what's going on. I'll fight back. I may even have to get a gun to fight back with someday if they don't stop."

"I noticed that you don't seem to be looking around while we're here to see them. Are they following us now?"

"Oh. I'm looking alright. I just know how to not make it obvious. Didn't you see that girl passing behind me pick up her phone to tell them I'm here? I'm going to have to leave soon. When they find my car, they go through it and steal things they don't think I'll notice."

"I'm sorry. I didn't really notice her. I was focusing on listening to you. Why do you think they're doing all this to you?"

"Don't act dumb, like you don't know what I'm talking about. You know how the White people use the Blacks to get at the Hispanics. It's in the news every day. I'm a Hispanic woman who was getting ahead, and they didn't like it. They want to keep me down, but I won't stand for it."

All of her story made sense in a certain way, but only because she'd put it together that way. I wasn't going to be able to talk her out of any of it. Everything she said had happened probably did, but, at least to me, it didn't fit rationally, and I doubted that anything that was happening now really connected to the original argument with her neighbor.

I paused to decide what to do next and changed tactics, "How is all of this affecting you?"

She stared hard at me, and I worried she was going to include me in her plots. "I just told you they poison me. I end up throwing up for days while they laugh."

"Does it affect you mentally?" Sometimes, that gives me an in to try to talk about medications.

"No. I'm still strong, but it has given me high blood pressure." No luck there, either.

Both Joanne and I kept meeting with Dolores for about 6 months, but we didn't find any way to break into her world view. We got her to a doctor to get blood pressure pills. Even though she suspected him, too, she took the pills. We got her State Disability and then Social Security to have some money in her pocket to live on, but every time the paperwork got messed up, she'd take it as proof they were still trying to keep her down. Even when she had a check, she wouldn't try to rent anywhere because that would just make her an easier target. She kept waiting for the police to bring her justice and protect her, but I doubt they ever will. I also doubt her frustration will ever lead her to breaking the law or getting a gun or hurting anyone. No matter how persecuted and frustrated she gets, she still will try to do things the "proper" way.

At least, Joanne was one person Dolores could still talk to and blow off steam. No one else had been in her life for years.

> About a year later, we got a call from a public defender. Dolores had been arrested after repeatedly punching a woman who crashed into her car. She'd already been in jail for months (and refused all medications there, too). He thought he could get her out with 5 years of probation if she'd agree to see us. After all, we were the only ones she knew. Joanne helped her public defender get her released.

A good deal of the emotional tone of our lives, both pleasant and unpleasant, comes from our unconscious associations, rather than from our rational analysis. For example, the irrational, "dreamlike" quality of the early stages of being in love is probably related to being us more influenced by our unconscious primary process than usual.

Some artists attempt to work directly in primary process and give it a concrete form we can experience directly (for example, Salvador Dali and the surrealists, or James Joyce in his flow of consciousness passages in *Ulysses* or less intelligibly when his words themselves become distorted in *Finnegans Wake*), but Freud was probably right—the best way to directly experience primary process is our dreams.

He was probably also right that our conscious mind is in a constant battle to control and structure our unconscious mind, while the unconscious influences us far more than we realize.

While we sleep and dream, the unconscious generally has the upper hand, creating whatever it wants, although our conscious does intentionally intrude at times to wake us up to get out of the dream when it's too overwhelming. When we're half awake and half asleep, the balance is less predictable, and it's normal to see shadows moving around or hear our name being called in this twilight state. (I sometimes describe these "hypnogogic hallucinations" as being caused because our brain is "in-between gears" going from wake to sleep and, like a manual transmission car, it sometimes grinds instead of changing gears smoothly. We can also experience twitching legs or breathlessness or "sleep paralysis" or disorientation in that state, too.) When we're awake, the conscious mind has more control … unless we're psychotic. One way to look at this is that it's not so much that psychosis is a misperception of reality as much as that psychosis is more of a primary process perception of reality than we're used to when we're fully awake.

When some people take antipsychotic medications, it seems to influence the balance of control between conscious and unconscious. A typical pattern as medication "works" is from hearing voices so loud they're overwhelming or in their heads, to still hearing them while awake, but vaguer and only if they listen closely, to maybe just a whisper, to only hearing them when they're half asleep, to having nightmares but not voices, to sleeping restfully. One way of interpreting this pattern is that the conscious mind is gradually getting more and more control.

If any one of us goes without sleeping, for whatever reason, we start functioning worse. First, our bodies start feeling tired. Then, our rational minds seem fuzzy. We become irritable and less emotionally stable. After several days without sleep, even normal people can start hallucinating and become psychotic. When someone who has been sleep deprived does sleep again, the first thing the brain does is to catch up on rapid eye movement (REM) sleep and dream. Their first priority is to give the unconscious brain a chance to download what's overwhelming it and process what's been going on emotionally. Then, their brain rests their bodies. Many people who have psychosis will find themselves dramatically worse when their sleep is poor and dramatically better when their sleep is better. Unfortunately, using drugs or alcohol, or even medications, to artificially put themselves to sleep doesn't reliably create normal sleep, including crucially regular dream times for their unconscious to take care of emotional processing, especially over the long run. Sometimes, the most important thing I do with medications is help people get some sleep, so that their brains can recover their internal balance and not be as psychotic. Since many "sleeping pills" are addictive, they may work at first only to wear out over time as they become tolerant to their effects. Many times, I'm not able to help with sleep over the long run, and we're both frustrated.

Another way to influence the balance of control between conscious rational thinking and unconscious emotional, primary process thinking is through our will.

Do you mean that someone can choose not to be psychotic?

No, we can't will ourselves not to hallucinate or not to be paranoid, any more than we can will ourselves not to have unconscious feelings and dreams, or not to fall in love, but we can try to give them more or less attention and power over us.

There's a scene in the excellent movie "A Beautiful Mind" when John Nash, a brilliant mathematician who became increasingly psychotic as the pressures in his life overwhelmed him, forcibly rejects the two hallucinations, his "roommate" and a little girl (presented visually rather than auditorily so the film would work) that had been his main comfort and company while he was losing touch with reality. It's only then that he can return to real relationships, real teaching, and receive his Nobel Prize. When a representative of the Nobel committee comes to evaluate him, Russell Crowe, playing Nash says, "What you really want to know is if I'm still crazy." He looks back and the hallucinations are still lurking in the background, neglected but ready to return if he'd only welcome them. By force of will, he chose to keep them at bay, but they were still there waiting.

> *I was Lucia's psychiatrist in our Transitional Age Youth Program for 18- to 25-year-olds when she was 19. Both of her parents had been heavily into drugs when she was young, and she was raised by her elderly grandmother, who couldn't keep Lucia out of trouble. She ended up dropping out of school, was unable to get any reasonable job or apartment, and had two kids without any ongoing contact with their fathers. She was still far too much of a kid herself to take care of her kids. She'd leave them to go out dancing and drinking with her friends. She'd get frustrated when they'd cry or demand her attention or throw tantrums. She never really had enough of anything to take care of them. When the neighbors called DCFS to report her, they threatened to remove the kids unless her grandmother would once again step in. The pattern of child neglect was repeating for yet another generation. Reluctantly, Lucia and her two kids moved in with grandma.*
>
> *As I got to know her and we tried to help her grow up to take more responsibility for her life—getting her Graduate Educational Diploma (GED) and returning to school to become a nurse's aide, learning to understand that her kids were still just kids and how to care for them as their*

mother, and no more dating or staying out all night—she began trusting me more and talked about how she sometimes heard voices, especially when she was confused. Sometimes, she seemed to be observing her life, disconnected or "spaced out," instead of living it. Sometimes, she had mood swings that overwhelmed her. Sometimes, she just couldn't focus on her schoolwork. Most nights, she had nightmares. The most common one was of being chased through an empty house looking desperately for her mother and never finding her, until she woke up in a cold sweat. In my opinion, her unconscious was still actively working on her childhood traumas even though they were in the past.

We worked together to find some medications that she could use to help with these things, so that she could control them enough to do the things she needed to do to grow up.

Over the next few years, she aged out of our program and moved on. One day, I got a call from one of the adult Wellness Center therapists asking if I'd help out Lucia in an emergency, "She says you're the only one she trusts."

When she came into my office, she looked a little older, but hadn't changed that much. She'd been crying some, and she had the old combination of being scared and defensive. "It wasn't my fault. The voices made me do it." She sat with her arms crossed over her stomach, looking out the window, instead of at me.

"All right. Calm down and tell me what happened ... You want some candy?" I opened my desk drawer, and she chose a couple pieces.

It turned out that Lucia had earned enough of her grandmother's trust that she'd gone for a few days to Las Vegas with a friend for a vacation, leaving Lucia home alone with the kids. While grandma was gone, Lucia had slapped her 4-year-old son, and the kids had been taken away again.

Grandmother was mostly feeling guilty and blaming herself for leaving, but also angry at Lucia for not being able to handle even a few days on her own with them.

"I was taking my medicine and doing everything I was supposed to, but he was acting so bad, running around the house, and he knocked over a vase and broke it. The voices just kept telling me, 'Hit him. Hit him.' I kind of spaced out and the next thing I knew, I'd slapped him, and he was crying and my daughter was crying."

"Go back a minute. After he broke the vase and the voices started, but before you spaced out, what did you think you should do?"

She looked over at me and the tears started again, "I didn't know what to do. I just didn't know what to do."

"So, in that moment, did you back off and let the voices take over because you didn't know what to do?"

She paused and got very quiet, "I did."

"See how the voices took over? You gave them control."

"I didn't know that could happen like that ... I learned something today."

There's an ongoing balance in everything we perceive and do, between our rational processes and our unconsciously driven "primary processes." When our conscious mind loses control over that balance, we can end up living in a "altered" psychotic reality. This is also likely the mechanism by which hallucinogenic drugs, including marijuana, create psychosis.

Creating Reality

The next three stages are about how we turn our perception and synthesis of reality into the reality we live in.

Let's go back to my description of how normal speech works. We're ready to move on to this line, "Then, the most amazing thing happens—and this is perfectly normal—we project that speech outside of our heads, so that we experience it as though it's coming out of the other person's mouth."

To be honest, I don't know how we do that, why a speech that's put together inside our heads, in our brains, seems to be outside ourselves, but I do know, even though it's an incredibly bizarre idea, that we create the world we live in. I'm not saying that there isn't a "real world" out there, or even "I think, therefore, I am." All I'm saying is that the world that I perceive that I live in is the one I'm creating … and it's a little, or sometimes a lot, different from the world you're perceiving and living in. Ask any married couple and they'll tell you that their partner regularly misremembers and distorts things. It can be hard to live in two separate realities while sharing our lives; so, many couples fight a lot to prove they're right: "I wish I had a tape recorder, so you could hear what you actually said." "Don't' give me that, I'm not crazy. I know what you meant. Don't try to take it back now." "I know what I said." Remember way back in Chapter 2, Steve's "back of the hand" advice? It's very hard to really see the world the way someone else does. It's very hard to put down our way of seeing things enough to make room for anyone else's reality.

That's because we work so hard to create our own reality and put so much of ourselves into it.

Here's a whole other set of processes that can work "abnormally" and lead to psychotic and other extraordinary realities. All of them can make it much harder to engage with people and work with them, especially if we don't realize what's going on.

f. Projection of internal reality into external reality

Normally, we gradually create a series of emotional templates from our emotional experiences that guide our expectations and ongoing experiences of our world. Many of our strongest emotional experiences are from our early childhoods, and they can powerfully form our external worlds. For example, if we were raised by alcoholic parents who were always pretending everything was fine, while unpredictably blowing up into scary violence, we'll likely mistrust all reassurances and become hyperaware of small indications that something tragic is around the corner. Our friends will tell us to stop worrying and "loosen up," so that we can enjoy our lives, but we'll continue to project that "emotional template" and our self-protective response into every new situation we face. Like it or not, our internal emotional experiences form the foundation of our ongoing reality.

Freud called that phenomena "transference"—we're transferring an emotional reality from the past into the present. A good deal of psychoanalysis is built on the premise that if we can become aware of how powerful, and frequently, how distorted, our transference expectations are, we can refrain from projecting them into our current world. More often, however, we're "healed" by opening ourselves to having a very powerful "corrective emotional experience" that contradicts the old template and begins to change it into a new one. We then begin to create a new emotional world for ourselves. That corrective emotional experience can happen in very emotionally engaging therapies, including groups, or more commonly, with other people we become deeply emotionally involved with, like mentors or lovers.

This phenomenon goes beyond neurotically making ourselves miserable by expecting bad things from our childhood to recur. Because those past experiences are incorporated into our current reality, we push the people around us to conform to our reality, and they may well end up replaying our experiences, becoming characters in our emotional dramas, both wittingly and unwittingly. Then, we become "retraumatized," reconfirming and strengthening our initial templates, and setting ourselves up to recreate them even more in the future. Eventually, almost everything seems to be caught up in this underlying emotional conflict or wound. Repeatedly battered women who had abusive fathers are a reasonably common example of this pattern.

I've described the process using a traumatic early childhood template, but the same process occurs for positive templates, too. If we grew up believing that we're loved and valued, regardless of what we do, believing that we can be forgiven for our misdeeds and accepted as we are, we're likely to create our world within that positive framework. We'd be more likely to love and accept and forgive others and have more positive relationships overall. That underlying template is likely to make us happier and more resilient than a negative one. Unfortunately, it's also possible to meet someone later in life, like a battering husband, that severely damages our positive template and our future emotional world and our resilience.

"Psychotic transferences" aren't actually different processes than "normal" or "neurotic" transferences, but they are transferences that lead to such a big clash between world views that the consequences go beyond conflict with bosses or attracting a series of abusive alcoholic boyfriends to total disconnection. Let's go back for a minute to Dolores, the paranoid woman living in her car. We don't know what happened in her childhood that made her require rules to be followed rigidly to feel safe, or if it was originally connected to racist experiences, but we know that when that framework failed her, she turned to more and more unrealistic "templates." When she complains in a restaurant that they're poisoning her food as part of a plot by White people to keep Black people like her down, it won't just distort her relationship with the staff there and lead to them wittingly or unwittingly persecuting her. It will lead to them disconnecting entirely from her, saying she's paranoid and crazy. Since she doesn't have a template that includes the possibility that she's paranoid or crazy, she'll be unable to incorporate that into her reality and likely decide that they're saying that to discredit her and protect the plot they're part of and move to disconnect from them. "Psychotic transferences" are severe enough that neither side can accept the other one's reality enough to stay connected. The same disconnection can result from extreme positive distortions, too, like someone thinking they're God or have millions of dollars or own the city of Long Beach. It can be very hard to keep a relationship going with someone who thinks he's your boss and owns the company and doesn't need to use money while you think he's delusional.

> Joseph seemed to have inherited his schizophrenia from his mother and his stubbornness from his father. He also seemed to get his intelligence and Mormonism from both of them. He was in college learning to be a nutritionist when people began thinking he was crazy. He walked into class announcing that he had proof God is real and that he had personally received from God a diet that would ensure no one ever got old or died. His diet consisted of only eating naturally round foods and only prime numbers of each food—so, for example, he could eat seven grapes or three oranges (this diet turned out to be heavily fruit based, and it did reduce his cholesterol to the lowest levels any of us had ever seen before statins were invented). He was sent to a psychiatric hospital and permanently removed from his college. He told them he didn't have schizophrenia like his

mother because she heard voices and he didn't, but they medicated him anyway, which made his thinking fuzzy, too fuzzy to continue to work on his diet, which heavily distressed him, but they took it as a good sign that he wasn't as obsessed by his "delusions." Thus began a lifelong battle over diagnosis and medication.

Whenever he stopped his medications, he worked feverishly on a number of projects that seemed to invariably be a projection of some need or desire of his own. When he was interested in dating women, he decided he was going to open a school for young women to learn how to safely date and started posting advertisements all over. When he was scared by the possibility of pregnancy, he went to the Obstetrics ward at the local hospital to pass out fliers warning the expectant mothers about safe sex. Hospital security threw him out and pressed charges.

Once we were fooled. He asked us to give him a ride to the Mormon Temple, so that he could get his underwear blessed so he wouldn't think about sex and have "impure thoughts." We assumed this was another one of his projections, but took him anyway, only to find out that the Mormon religion does have special blessed undergarments for precisely that purpose. They didn't seem to work that well for Joseph.

When his mother died, even though he'd never seen the movie "Psycho," he tried to fight his grief and keep her alive by putting on her old dressing gown and slippers and pushed her walker down the street. He ended up finding an open school bus in the lot and fell asleep in the back. When the kids started loading the bus the next morning, he woke up. The kids were freaked out, and again, the police were called.

In all of these instances, he couldn't see what he'd done wrong, or why he was arrested or hospitalized, or why I was trying to get him back on medications. The reality he was creating matched his internal emotional reality perfectly since that's where it came from. We were the ones with the *problem, the ones who weren't understanding what he was doing. He didn't have a problem within his reality.*

His father responded to his mother's death by declaring he was going to lay down in a bed and wait to die to join his wife in heaven. He was moved to a nursing home, where it took two full years of stubborn refusal to go on with life before he actually died, leaving Joseph alone in the family house. Joseph's growing isolation and loneliness led to one of my favorites of his projections: One day, I found in my office mailbox a piece of paper with the words "niche license" on it. I suspected this was Joseph's work, since he regularly put papers of various kinds in our boxes; so, the next time I saw him, I showed him the paper and asked, "Joseph, what's a 'niche license'?"

"Everyone should have a niche in life, and this is your license to find yours, so you can be happy."

Even though we could never succeed at getting him to date (and being unmarried has serious implications for the afterlife in Mormonism), nor could we bring his mother back to life, we could help create a niche for Joseph. The wife of the local Mormon Bishop set up a prayer meeting at Joseph's home since he was too disruptive at the Temple. A friend of the family, whose brother had killed himself, converted his garage into a small apartment for Joseph to live in and his wife helped prepare vegetarian foods. (We didn't have a chance of finding a vegetarian, nonsmoking Board and Care.) We let him give the "Health Tip of the Week" at our weekly Wednesday morning community meetings. He became very active in our community garden project.

Over time, he felt more connected and even though he never agreed to more than tiny dosages of medications, he rarely disrupted the community or needed hospitalization. Even when he had cancer and recovered, he didn't have to create a separate reality. His emotional needs could be met within a more shared reality.

g. Protection of self-perceptions

Probably the most important goal in creating our reality is to create an ongoing sense of ourselves that is coherent and persistent over time. It especially takes quite an effort to convert our ever-growing childhood identity into a stable adult identity, usually during adolescence, and yet most of us succeed. But that is also precisely the same time that a great deal of psychosis first emerges. Here is where the dimension of experiencing reality directly impacts the self-identity dimension.

Even though every cell in our body turns over every 7 years, even though we change in size and looks, abilities and memories, relationships and homes, we usually manage to keep seeing ourselves as the same person throughout our lives. Even if that identity is no longer realistic, or is sorrowful, or highly dysfunctional, we usually keep it going throughout our lives. Occasionally, I'll meet someone whose self-identity seems to be lost in their confusion.

> *Juan was a young man who did very poorly without medications. He'd become very confused, unable to keep track of anything. He'd stop showering or changing clothes and started smelling bad enough to drive everyone away and to be teased by kids on the street. When we would try to talk to him about anything, all he'd say was, "I'm alright. I'm OK." over and over again. It was unclear if he was trying to reassure us or himself.*
>
> *He'd wander off, looking for family he hadn't seen in over a decade even though he had no idea where to look for them. Eventually, the police would find him and take him either to jail or to a hospital, where he'd be put back on medications again. He'd gradually clear up and be able to speak and take care of himself and he'd be sent back to us, but then, he'd stop his medications again. He never had any perception that he was different on or off medications.*
>
> *We could get him to live in a sober living group home where the woman who ran it liked him and could get him to take medications for a while, but sooner or later, he'd stop them again and seem to lose himself. Even at his best, he never really had any goals beyond finding his family. He seemed to be a lost soul.*

We're generally quite willing and able to make whatever distortions are required to keep our self-identity intact. I'm very protective of what I believe to be my enduring traits, both good and bad. I will object if someone describes me as cruel or mean and start a long self-justifying argument either with them or, more often, in my own head. I'll also object if someone says I'm good looking or kind. I just don't think I am (and I should know, right?). I suspect my unconscious is busy clearing away any experiences that don't fit my self-image, including even parts of my self-image that I'm not aware of, before my conscious has to intervene to make up elaborate rationalizations.

It may seem like people with psychosis have an inability to maintain a sense of self, but I think that if we're able to see it from their point of view, they've almost always adapted to protect an ongoing sense of self, often in the face of seemingly insurmountable challenges. It can be hard to understand what's going on at the time. For example, I remember a sweet, depressed woman, Vicki, who over the course of a few days became totally mute and catatonic, not moving an inch, telling me after she recovered that she thought that she had to stay still because she was such a bad person that every move she made or every word she said would spread evil and hurt the people around her, and she didn't want to hurt anyone.

> *I first met Taylor in the hospital. He was a tall, middle-aged, Black man who mumbled and growled more than talked. He had been picked up by the police and brought to the hospital for disturbing people panhandling too aggressively. He was wearing multiple layers of mismatched, very dirty clothes, and a faded Rasta hat.*
>
> *"I want to get out of here. I'm not dangerous to anyone. I have a place to stay. I'm not going to take any medications. There's nothing wrong with me. That lady just didn't like me asking her for money. I apologized. That's all I need to do. I know my rights. Fill out the papers, so I can get out of here."*
>
> *That was the most coherent speech I would hear from him over the next 15 years. He must have been very motivated to get out and back to his world.*

Both of us knew the drill. I couldn't keep him and medicate him against his will unless I could convince a judge he's gravely disabled—meaning that he couldn't provide for his food, clothing, and shelter because of his mental illness. He paid rent for an apartment, didn't seem malnourished, and had clothes on, dirty or not; so, unless there was something I was missing, I should let him go. On the one hand, I didn't want our relationship to start out on the wrong foot by testifying against him in court. On the other hand, he sure seemed impaired. I decided to take the extra step of going to his apartment to see if he was providing for himself.

I took Jim Wilwerth along for the ride. Jim had been a writer for Time magazine and wrote an important article about Clozaril, and a few years later had been sent to the Village to write about us. He was so impressed with our approach to people that he fell in love with the place and stayed on as a volunteer. He's been coming back every couple weeks, driving long distances, to lead a writing group for our members. At the time, he and I were exploring the idea of writing a book about the Village together. Unfortunately, his agent never found an interested publisher—"mental health isn't our kind of thing." At that point, however, we were just getting to know each other, and I thought visiting Taylor's home would be a valuable experience for him. Besides, I don't like going to places I don't know by myself for safety reasons.

The address we had was an aging housing court, with a series of small bungalows in a circle around a large tree. The landlady came out to greet us. "Yes, I know Taylor. He's lived here for a few years. Everyone sort of looks out for him. When he's hungry, he can come to me and I'll cook him some food. He doesn't take care of his place very well, but he doesn't bother anyone. I've gotten used to his mumbling; so, I can usually make out what he's trying to say. If he really wants something, he can talk more clearly. Sure, you can take a look at his place. He's in number 6. You don't need a key to get in, just push open the door. He took out the lock and he just pretends he has a key and turns it in the hole before he goes in."

She wasn't kidding. The entire knob was removed. Pushing the door open, however, wasn't that easy. Something seemed to be blocking it. I gave it a big enough shove to look in.

I'd never seen anything like it. It seemed that every square inch of the place was filled with stuff about 2 feet deep. We'd have to climb on it to go inside. "Take a look at this, Jim."

I moved out of the way, so he could see inside. After he looked, he just shook his head in disbelief.

"We came this far. We might as well go inside." I shoved the door open and climbed onto the pile of stuff and walked inside. Jim followed.

I had to walk stooped over to avoid hitting my head on the ceiling. "This isn't random junk. It's all things that belong in the room, but everything is broken into pieces and there are multiples of everything. See, there are pieces of three or four broken down couches and TVs over there and a pile of bicycle parts over here." I stopped to wipe a spider's web off my head.

"There also doesn't seem to be any rotting food. It doesn't smell and there are no cockroaches or rats as far as I can tell."

"Let's check out the bedroom." There appeared to be just enough room in his bed for him to lay down in. Several bowls of cigarette butts and a pile of beer cans, along with a radio, seemed to be the currently used portion of the room built on previous layers.

"I can't believe this place."

In the back of the apartment, the shower had some green water in the bottom of it. It wasn't clear if anything worked except the toilet. In the kitchen, the refrigerator had the door torn off and was filled with empty pizza boxes. The most concerning thing was the oven, half open, also filled with containers. "We better get the landlady to unplug the gas to this oven before he starts a fire here."

We climbed out the way we'd come in and squeezed out the door, returning to the bright sun and reality, somewhat dazed.

I started trying to pull my thoughts together, "I thought it was going to be obvious whether he's gravely disabled or not after we looked around, but now I'm not so sure. Is that really providing for his basic needs?"

"I don't know. The only time I've ever seen anything like that was when I was a war correspondent in Bosnia and people lived in caves."

"In a strange way, I think that apartment is a reflection of his mind. It's got pieces of what belongs there, but it's overcrowded and barely usable."

"That's a fascinating idea. I can really see what you mean. It's like being inside of him."

I debated with myself the whole next day until I finally decided to let Taylor go home, instead of taking him to court. We'd never have a chance to help him if we started out by keeping him locked up. I figured I could make a deal with him, maybe pay him $20 for each Hefty bag of stuff he took out of there.

I called the landlady to ask her to cut off the gas. She agreed and she was glad Taylor was coming home. "He's happier here than in the hospital, and he never comes out any different anyway."

I offered him a ride home in my new convertible. When we got there, he paraded around the lawn, waving his discharge papers over his head, with a giant smile on his face, reminding me of a victorious boxer. I drove away feeling pretty good about my decision.

Unfortunately, it turned out that Taylor was one of the most stubborn people I've ever met. I never talked him into the $20 Hefty bags or anything else he didn't want to do.

We got him a bus pass, so that he could come to the Village more often, instead of hanging out bothering people panhandling, but he lost it a week later and came asking me for another one. "We can't buy you more than one bus pass in a month, but if you want to do a little work around here, like washing the vans, to earn the money, you could buy another one."

He growled, "I ain't washing your car. Who do you think I am?" and stormed off. He wouldn't talk to me for 3 months after that.

He used to come to our Wednesday morning community meetings and dominate the microphone, grumbling incoherently for what seemed forever. We didn't want to exclude him because he clearly enjoyed being part of it, but he was ruining it for everyone else. Joe, the meeting leader, came up with the idea of having Taylor be the one who brought the microphone to everyone around the room, so that he could be included and have a role without needing to speak. He kept that role for years.

One of the team leaders got the idea that he could have a job carrying our interoffice mail each day between the Village and our administrative headquarters about half a mile away. He wanted a desk and a chair and a badge to go with the job, which we gave him, but administration didn't like how much he smelled when he came over there, and he refused to bathe or wash his clothes (I never did figure out where he'd get replacement clothes from); so, after a few weeks, he wasn't allowed over there anymore. He kept sitting at the desk and chair, wearing his badge, but we didn't pay him anymore.

At one point, someone recognized him and said he'd known Taylor when he was young, and he'd been treated at the VA. When he was on medications, he was even in college, but he'd stopped the medications years ago and refused to go back on them. He even had a brother who worked down the street, but he refused to talk to him.

Were we really helping him by helping him have connections and a role in his psychosis, instead of getting him back on medications and having a real role and family?

Years later, he landed in a different hospital, with a more coercive doctor, who did take the case to court, but the judge let him go anyway. That relieved my conscience somewhat, but I still don't know what would've been best for him.

A number of years later, a new team leader didn't like him hanging out pretending he worked there and took away his desk and chair. I didn't see him much after that, but the case managers kept making home visits regularly anyway. By then, his building had been torn down to build a more expensive one. Our case workers had to work several times a week with him to keep the new apartment reasonably clean, so that he wouldn't be evicted.

One day, several years later, he came in saying he was feeling sick. He said his chest hurt. The nurse took his blood pressure. That was the first time he'd agreed to have it taken. He'd refused to see any medical doctors over the years. His blood pressure was very high. We talked him into going with us to the ER to be checked out.

He asked to go to the bathroom first, where a few minutes later he slumped down and died, presumably of a heart attack. We pulled his pants back up and did CPR while we

> *waited for the paramedics. They pronounced him dead at the hospital. I suppose he had acted like a wounded animal returning home to die.*
>
> *We had a memorial service for him several days later. Many people came, including his brother and a 20-year-old daughter we didn't know existed. She appreciated the descriptions of her father and said she finally understood why he'd never been in her life.*

Even if someone is psychotic and living in a self-created reality the rest of us can't relate to, they generally protect their self-image anyway. This can be a powerful force, promoting ongoing delusions.

When I was in London doing a terrific clerkship as a medical student at the Maudsley, they told me a story about when long-acting antipsychotic injections were first used there. The first medication they developed was Modecate, a medication I'd never heard of. They used their network of public health nurses to do home visits to make sure their patients with schizophrenia received their injections every 2 weeks. Unfortunately, a significant number killed themselves, and the medication was stopped fearing it might be causing an increase in suicidality as a side effect. It took them quite a while to figure out that the real problem was that the medication had rapidly pulled people out of their delusional worlds and self-identities, forcing them to face a new, usually harsh, and shameful reality that they weren't ready for. The nurses had thought that their job was to make sure the patients received their medications and got rid of their symptoms. They didn't consider how their patients would adapt their self-identities and their lives to their altered experiences of reality.

The identity we usually offer people with psychosis to rebuild around is that of "mental patient." We tend to reinforce that new identity in every way we can—with family and individual psychoeducation, with treatment teams, and segregated "mentally ill only" living environments. We connect almost everything they might want or need to their diagnosis: We look for a place for their illness to be treated, instead of a home. We look for therapeutic activities, instead of work and play, and social support networks, instead of friends. Money to live on, prevocational rehabilitation, disabled student's services, driver's licenses, voting rights, jury duty excuses, parental rights, discounted handicapped bus passes, gun ownership, and even jail diversion are all based on the person's diagnoses and their identity as a mentally ill person. Mental health professionals bemoan society's stigma while we treat them as a walking illness in every way possible.

> Amy became psychotic in her teens while still in high school. She didn't respond to a series of acute hospitalizations; so, she was transferred to a continuation school, mostly learning at home, instead of returning to her classmates. She wasn't motivated to do her schoolwork on her own or to graduate. She drifted further and further into her own world. Her mother became increasingly frustrated and concerned and eventually succeeded in getting her hospitalized long term and transferred to a locked Institute for Mental Disorders (IMD) for 2 years to "get the treatment she needed." Unfortunately, none of that seemed to make much difference either, and Amy drifted further and further away.
>
> Her mother was very unhappy when the system transferred her from the IMD to an unlocked Board and Care, saying she hadn't tried to run away, was stable, and could be treated at a lower level of care. "This isn't my daughter any more. This is her illness talking to me, not her." She kept trying to figure out ways to get Amy rehospitalized.
>
> Amy responded by declaring, "That woman isn't my real mother. I don't know who she is, but she's stalking me. Keep her away from me." Amy refused to leave her Board and Care for over a year, fearful "that woman" would be after her and she'd be locked up again. She began to think more and more people were out to get her. She wouldn't come into the Village to see me; so, I went to see her at the Board and Care. I tried changing medications around, but nothing I did seemed to make any difference. She kept taking the medications without complaint anyway.
>
> Although her room was very small and barren—just two small beds and dressers and a closet without any decorations—it was never boring to talk with Amy. She had a very elaborate life in her own mind: She was a brain surgeon

who did surgery without anesthesia. She time traveled and visited different planets. She dated rock stars. She was in a government program getting paid for smoking (to be fair, in a strange way, I could see that one). I shared my life with her, too—my wife, kids, pets, job, and vacation trips. She remembered what I told her and asked me follow-up questions the next time I saw her.

One day, I bought a used fish tank at a swap meet for the office. I remembered that she had fish as a child; so, I asked her if she wanted to come with me to the fish store to pick out some fish for my office.

"No. No. I need to stay here."

"Come on. Come on. It'll be fun."

"No. I'm tired."

"But I could use your help."

After this went on for a long time, she finally gave me an opening, "How about if my roommate comes, too?"

I didn't really know her roommate. She wasn't my patient. Mostly, she'd either lay on her bed half asleep while I talked with Amy or went out looking for a cigarette.

What the hell. What's the worst thing that can happen? The fish store is only a few blocks away, and Amy hadn't left this Board and Care in over a year. I decided that it was worth the risk.

"Sure, she can come, too."

"OK, then." She got up, stopped to brush her hair, and found her roommate. They sat together in the back seat of my old Honda Civic, looking rather shy and overwhelmed.

They began to open up at the fish store, pointing to the different fish and discussing the various choices. I kept the price under control and included a practical catfish and algae eater to keep the tank clean.

> *When we were done, and I was paying for a box filled with bags of colorful little fish swimming around in them, Amy came up to me, "Hey, Dr. Mark, I want to thank you for getting me out of my room and bringing me here today. We had fun."*
>
> *"You're very welcome. It was my pleasure. What part of it did you like best?"*
>
> *"Well, there was a moment back there, when Kathy and I were picking out the fish, that I almost forgot that I had a mental illness and felt like a normal person again."*
>
> *I could feel my heart go out to her. My gamble had worked—if only for a moment—but now, I had something to build on and hope for.*

Many people with mental illnesses feel rejected and misunderstood, isolated and hopeless, unwelcome and useless. Their reality often reinforces those negative self-perceptions. Sometimes, their psychosis offers better alternatives. Sometimes, though, like in Chapter 7 with Peter the Advocate of God who was facing an eternity of torture, their psychosis builds on their negativity in truly cruel ways.

When we try to create efficient, medical model systems of care, built on data analysis and evidence-based practices, we run a serious risk of dehumanizing people and eroding their identities or driving them away. Recovery-oriented, person-centered, and client-driven approaches have a much higher chance of creating a collaboration that supports the creation of more positive self-identities that connect more easily to other people.

h. Time perception

I was taught in physics that Einstein discovered that time changes, depending on how fast we're traveling, and that it bends around the gravitational fields of very heavy objects like black holes. I was also taught that all of time may exist all the time, without beginning or end, and that there may be a number of dimensions and universes that exist simultaneously in different time dimensions. None of that makes any sense to me or matches my perception of time. (I don't even know if I've summarized them correctly.) Even the neurobiologists who claim that we only see time in discrete bits and fill in between to make it seem fluid, while subliminal messages can be snuck in too fast to be consciously perceived yet they get in our brains, don't really make sense to me either.

Like the vast majority of people, I perceive time as moving along in one direction—the future turns into the present and then into the past. It seems to me that I have no real control over time, although the speed of time's passage does seem to vary. I have noticed, for example, that the older I get, the faster time passes. I've also noticed, usually after my wife points it out, that if I'm not paying attention, I can "lose track of time." I've also noticed that if I really push myself, for example, by counting my breaths very mindfully, I can be more aware of the present moment, and time's passage seems to slow down.

It seems likely to me that we are actually creating our experience of the passage of time, like we're creating the reality around us and our enduring sense of self.

There are occasional glitches in the process. I've experienced "déjà vu" a few times, where it seems like I'm reliving a moment (but I can never remember exactly when that was). Or, for a few weeks after Robbyn was killed, it seemed to me that somehow I'd become detached from the flow of time that everyone else was in. They kept talking about basketball and movies at lunch as though the world hadn't stopped with her death.

I have met a few people whose psychosis seems to involve more elaborate versions of glitches like these. One young man worked very hard for 2 full years at a fast food restaurant to save money to buy a car, only to find that he'd woken up 2 years back in time. He was the only one who remembered the lost time. He had no record of having worked, and the bank didn't have his savings. He had to start all over again. He was so frustrated. He was sure that he'd lived and worked the 2 years, but all proof was gone.

Another young man told me that he lived in several different time dimensions at once. When he woke up in the morning, he had to figure out which dimension he was in. He had different jobs in different time dimensions. In some time dimensions, he owned whole blocks of property, and in others, he was extremely poor. Once he got confused and went to a large property in Long Beach that he knew he owned, but they told him it was a military base and called the police. He later told me that was the first time he'd been in that time dimension. He didn't know how many time dimensions there are. The police took him to a mental hospital, where they didn't understand what he was explaining to them about time dimensions and thought he had a mental illness. He didn't agree.

> *The incredibly creative, motion-capture animated, Amazon prime series, "Undone," gives viewers a vicarious experience of an altered sense of time and our ability to manipulate it. The central character, Alma, who has a family history of schizophrenia, childhood trauma, and a triggering severe head trauma due to a car accident, feels as though she's able to manipulate time trying to undo her traumas, while those around her are frightened and think she's increasingly mentally ill and needs medication and even hospitalization.*

To be honest, it's sometimes difficult for me to tell if those people have malfunctioning, or traumatized, minds, or if they're actually experiencing time more realistically than the rest of us normally do.

> *William grew up on a series of naval bases. His father was a violent alcoholic who used to beat him and his mother and lock him outside in the cold to punish him when he was small. As a result, he experienced the world very negatively, always on the lookout for someone abusing him. He saw himself as a victim of almost everyone he met, so he avoided most people. Every time I saw him, he had numerous complaints about someone or another mistreating him. He tended to spend his time alone, living in his car, with a small dog by his side. He was also very intelligent and played amazing classical guitar.*
>
> *What really made William unique, though, was his unusual sense of time. He said that he could perceive the flow of time as it went past him. He shared with me YouTube videos that showed our solar system moving through space over time, instead of my usual view of us revolving around a stationary sun. One day, I told him he might be interested*

> in Stephen Hawking's book, "A Brief History of Time," although I found it incomprehensible. He said, "I've read it, but I found it too elementary." Really, a homeless man living in a car who thinks Stephen Hawking is too elementary?
>
> He actively experienced a very long-term view of time. He'd consider the potential impacts of his decisions over hundreds of years. He thought we should live hundreds of years like they did in the Bible, if only we could avoid toxins. Unfortunately, the combination of this long view and his numerous fears made him virtually unable to make any decision. He would obsess about how the smallest risk—like additives in dog food or aluminum cans—could have potentially devastatingly bad impacts over long enough periods of time. Nothing was safe if he tracked its negative potential long enough.
>
> Even when I helped him get Social Security, although it wasn't clear to me he really had schizophrenia, he couldn't make decisions about how to spend the money. He couldn't decide where to live or even how to repair his car, and he couldn't trust anyone else; so, he ended up just as miserable as ever.

A far more common problem with people with psychosis than these unusual experiences of time is difficulty sustaining a sense of time passing throughout their lives, and this can badly impair their self-identity. It's fairly typical to be interviewing someone and get a coherent narrative, including time frames for their childhood and adolescence right up until their first hallucinations and delusions, but after that point, they relate a very vague history with lost time everywhere. Decades can pass without being able to piece together a reasonable chronology. I was even taught a name for this phenomenon in medical school, "failure of historicity," and was told that it was typical of people with schizophrenia.

This trait can be a very poor match for some of our treatment approaches. For example, we expect people to set goals every 6 months or once a year and track how they're doing in achieving their goals. That's not a good approach for someone who doesn't track time very well. Many clinics give psychiatrist appointments every 3 months and expect them to give us a clear update regarding their symptoms over the previous 3 months, while also expecting them to go on their own to the pharmacy to get monthly refills in-between appointments. We expect them to track their hospitalizations and list of medications and their responses over years to tell a new psychiatrist their "history." We're also surprised when they try failed approaches again and again, repeating their failures. Overall, standard "learning" approaches don't work nearly as well with people without clear chronologies to track cause and effect.

Certainly, time can be one of the hardest things for any of us to track. We have to be able to sustain attention, or time just floats by. When people become demented, one of the big things they struggle with is their sense of time. Long-term psychosis can be just as distracting as dementia. People may not have sharp attention or remembrances of external events and become lost in their internal thought processes. They may be waiting for something the voices have promised them or preparing for their grandiose destiny to arrive. That may make it harder to keep track of time in their lives.

There also may not be concrete events in their lives—like changes in jobs, marriages and divorces, children growing, vacations, new cars, moving apartments, etc.—to mark the passage of time. Their daily lives may pass unremarkably between meals, coffee breaks, and cigarettes, day and night. Even weekends are the same as weekdays. Maybe Amy "time traveled" between imaginary events because there were no events in her life, at least until we went to pick out fish together.

For people with long-standing psychosis, our standard mental status questions—what's the day of the week, date, and year, and who is the president—may be more useful in determining when the last time something notable happened to the person or when they were last connected to the external world, than in determining if they are "disoriented" due to cognitive deterioration.

Are we all a little bit crazy?

This concludes our most neurobiological journey.

In my opinion, the most important thing that emerges from this journey is that there isn't a "psychosis-producing" area or even circuitry of the brain. Even though it seems like people experiencing psychosis have incredibly abnormal brain functioning—as though the Devil got into them, or they have a split personality, or a chemical imbalance—they don't. Psychosis results from extreme usages of normal circuitry and processes, rather than from inherently pathological circuitry and processes. It's unlikely we'll ever find the underlying neuropathology of psychosis because it's based on circuitry we all use, and misuse, every day.

Using myself as example, I have challenges in almost every level of making sense of our world that we've discussed: I have serious sensory issues with my eyes (nearsightedness, corrected with glasses), ears (likely due to scarring from a neglected ear infection), and nose (I don't know why I have an impaired sense of smell). Although I can recognize and differentiate musical tones, and I can reproduce them whistling, I can't sing in tune. I struggle to mimic or remember words in a foreign language or learn any foreign language. I have a very good memory for events, but my father says I also remember events that never occurred (and I have good documentation that this has definitely occurred on a couple of incidences). My wife believes I don't pay attention well and that I distort and misremember most of what she says, but her biggest complaint is that I misinterpret her emotions and intentions, whereas I believe that I have particularly strong ability to sense and understand people's emotions and energies. I intentionally tried to stretch my sense of reality by going on a weeklong, almost silent Buddhist retreat and the sensory, structural, and relationship deprivation profoundly altered how I experienced the world (including, strangely enough, restoring my sense of smell), some of which lasted only days and some of which have become a part of me and my view of myself. All of these challenges could probably lead to psychosis if conditions were right. Like everyone else, I am probably on the "schizophrenic spectrum."

I believe that all of us have limitations on our ability to process time frames that are very short or very long, sizes that are very small or very large, emotions that are very different from our own, people beyond our own relationships, and especially, meanings beyond our own self-preserving ideas about ourselves, that make it difficult for us to accurately perceive and process reality. But we only become "psychotic" when the other two sides of the triangle—our relationships and our self-identity—fall apart.

If we look carefully at how people whose brains process reality differently, instead of just labeling them as psychotic and schizophrenic and trying to medicate them into normality, maybe we could better understand how the system is put together in the first place.

One day, I did a workshop for an audience with both people with mental illnesses and staff with Fred Frese, who I described in Chapter 1 as a man who recovered with schizophrenia to be a successful psychologist. He said that he didn't think that the "associations" that people with schizophrenia make are disabilities. He thinks they're altered abilities. He made his point with two demonstrations.

In the first demonstration, he showed us a green and white slide that was highly pixelated, so that we couldn't make out what the picture. It just looked like green and white blocks. As the slides went on, the pixels got smaller and smaller, and the picture started to come into focus. He told us to raise our hand when we knew what the picture was. On the fifth slide, the people with schizophrenia raised their hands. On the seventh slide, I raised my hand, and on the eighth slide, the "normal" people raised their hands. It was a picture of a dollar bill. He returned to the fifth slide and I still couldn't see the dollar and don't know how the people with schizophrenia could see it.

For his second demonstration, he asked us to say the first word that came into our mind when he said a word (a common psychiatric test of abstraction ability). He said "cat." We said "dog." He said "black." We said "white." He said "lion." We said "tiger." Well, that's what the "normal" responses are anyway. The people with schizophrenia in the audience had lots of different responses. "Cat" led to "lion" and "bark" and "meow." "Black" led to "Martin Luther King" and "night." "Lion" led to "Africa" and "mauling." Fred claimed those aren't pathological responses. They just show that the people with schizophrenia don't have connections that are as socially determined. They're more individualized. While this may be a reason for the speculated connection between mental illness and creativity, it can also get you into a lot of trouble if a waitress asks what she can get for you, and you jump to the conclusion that she wants to have sex with you or wants to help you run for president.

By focusing on breaking down into eight steps the process of "making sense of our world," I've outlined a neurobiological map to help understand psychosis, so that you can be more comfortable venturing even further afield. At this point, hopefully, we can understand "what" challenges someone may be and even some of the "how" things are going wrong, and we can better individualize our responses, but we haven't gotten into "why" they're having these challenges, which many people want to understand, but *DSM* rarely addresses these concerns. Like it or not, breaking down the experiencing reality dimension of psychosis into individual processes, like I've guided you through in this journey, simply can't answer "why." You'll need to go on other journeys to find meaning.

Chapter 9

Journey 4: Childhood trauma

Calvin didn't like talking about his childhood. He grew up as an only child in the back woods of Tennessee. His father was harsh when he was sober and unbelievably cruel when he was drunk. Calvin remembered times where his father would take him out in the snow, strip off his clothes, tie him to a tree, whip him with his belt until his skin broke open, and then, leave him freezing in the cold. Crying and praying, his mother would sneak out after his father had passed out to untie him, cover him in a blanket, and bring him back inside. Calvin spent a lot of time alone in the woods with stick figures he'd made, pretending they were his friends and family. He made up hours and hours of stories as they grew up together. He was always far more comfortable in the woods than at school or with other kids. Things were a little better at the Baptist Church. At least, that was one place he was sure his father would never show up. At age 15 when his mother died, he packed a few meager belongings and left.

He kept walking until he hit the ocean in Long Beach. Apparently, it took him 2 to 3 years to make it. Somewhere along the way, he decided that he was on a journey of Biblical proportions and that he was the hero of the story. When we first met him at the Village a few years later, he had a notebook filled with a convoluted book story about his journey called "A Black Man's Walk." HIs description of crossing the desert in Arizona, losing 30 pounds along the way, with nothing to eat or drink, and relying on God to bring him whatever he needed was particularly impressive, even in its fragmented state. I couldn't really imagine how that was possible. I don't know if he was delirious, psychotic, blessed, or perhaps all three.

There was no doubt he had a powerful personality. He was smart, sure of himself and his mission, and single-minded. He'd put together a "street-family" to live with in the park, noticeably missing a father, but seemingly filled with lots of true caring for each other. Dressed in a colorful collection of secondhand, donated clothes, he was ready to change the world.

He initially came to the Village when we first opened, excited by the chance to be a part of something new and important. Also, we had a clothing donation closet he used freely to take care of himself and his seemingly endlessly growing connections.

The first of numerous conflicts with our staff came when he said being mentally ill shouldn't be a criterion for getting help and services at the Village. It wasn't so much that he was trying to avoid the label of mental illness; sometimes, he'd talk with us about his depression and how he sometimes felt like giving up and committing suicide, and sometimes, he'd even agree to take pills for a few days. The issue was more that we had criterion at all, or even opinions or agendas of our own. If he needed something and we had it, we should give it to him. He'd never learned to be considerate of others. The stick figures always carried out their roles as he had directed them. When we didn't follow his directives, he'd get upset and confused and increase his demands and tell us that God was on his side.

Many of the rules at the Village—who could play pool, what visitors could come to the Deli, where you could smoke, and limits on the clothes closet—were created trying to deal with Calvin. Our director, Martha, was repeatedly besieged by either staff complaining about

Calvin or Calvin complaining about staff. When she made him the subject of our monthly "case conference," the room was packed.

In the face of Calvin's constant chaos and demands, most staff were more than willing to sacrifice our fledgling principles of "meeting the client where they're at," "client-driven services," "collaboration," "relationship building," "no fail services", etc. to restore order and our power, but Martha wasn't. She insisted that confronting and threatening him when he'd already been through far more than we'd ever know wasn't going to work. He wouldn't accept the reality of a desert in front of him. How was he going to accept a set of rules? Instead, she set us up, including herself, on an almost daily basis, to be his advocate, trying to partner with him to meet his goals.

She set an example for all of us when she helped him host a talent show for his homeless friends in our Deli on a Saturday. Wayne and Paul showed up as staff to support him, and also, of course, to make sure they didn't destroy the building. Neither one was comfortable as the building filled with a strikingly Black, enthusiastic, boisterous crowd. It wasn't like a criminal gang was taking over. These were the same homeless people we'd been trying to engage for months. Many of them had small children with them. It was a festive atmosphere. We'd never drawn a crowd this large before to our activities.

Wayne and Paul said it was incredible to watch him emcee the event. He knew everyone and made them all feel welcome. He encouraged the shy ones and moved the long-winded ones along. He led the crowd clapping and cheering along with the music and calling for "amens" for those telling their stories and praising God. Everyone had a great time. They felt free to be themselves.

Maybe we were missing something. Maybe that young Black man didn't need White mental health workers and our diagnoses to build his life and his community.

It wasn't so much that Calvin had stopped being demanding and ambitious, self-absorbed and unrealistic. It just didn't feel like an imposition anymore, a couple months later when I found myself with a broom sweeping the streets around our building as part of a crew he had organized as part of a city cleanup event. Our program could take his dreams seriously and help make plans to do them with him.

When I started working at our Transitional Youth Academy, with 18- to 25-year-olds who were already repeatedly homeless, jailed, or psychiatrically hospitalized, many of whom were "graduates" of foster care, the stories of trauma that I brought home started overwhelming my wife. I think that the first time she said, "They're just telling you those stories, so you'll feel sorry for them. That didn't really happen. You're letting them manipulate you." was when I told her about the young girl who had repeatedly been sold as a sex toy beginning at age 5 by her aunt and uncle in Guatemala and had never been taken to school or allowed to be with other children, until she was unmanageable at 10 when she was brought to Los Angeles and dumped here in a violent, feral, heavily damaged state. Or maybe it was the girl who at 14 conspired with her roommate at the state hospital to escape by setting fire to her mattress, so that the doors would open automatically and then had to spend the next 4 years in juvenile detention, without a conviction, because no one else would take her and she couldn't be released until her 18th birthday when she was taken in by an alcoholic older man who dressed her up as his doll. Or maybe it was the boy who said he was one of only two kids from his Russian orphanage who survived into his teens, when he was adopted by a wealthy family in Los Angeles who couldn't handle him. Or the woman whose mother beat her regularly, who wouldn't let her go out trick-or-treating on Halloween with her friends when she was 13, beat her especially severely when she complained, and then when she was broken down sobbing, comforted her by letting her suckle at her breasts while stroking her hair and telling her she loved her baby. I can't remember. Every week, there was a new tragic story. My wife isn't uncaring, but as a mother, she just couldn't believe that anyone would treat children the way these kids had been treated. It was just too terrible for her to imagine.

I don't always get it right either.

> Brenda told me that she didn't want to talk in my office. The white walls reminded her of juvenile hall where she'd been beaten by the other girls kept there. I agreed to see her outside in the alley. She was on high alert there, jumping at every sound, and looking around like a scared cat. Nevertheless, she started telling me her story. Her father was in prison for a gang-related murder. Her mother was in and out of jail for using and selling drugs. Her brother was shot in a robbery gone wrong. Her boyfriend had been lying in bed with her when a drive-by shooter got him, shattering the window and splattering his blood all over her.
>
> I tried to lighten the mood, "Does your family send Christmas cards to the prison guard union? It seems like you're supporting them single-handedly."
>
> She did not think that was funny.
>
> She glared at me and clammed up. Her next answers were barely more than grunts.
>
> I took a deep breath and waded in again, "I need to go back a minute. You were telling me about all kinds of tragic things that happened to you, and I made a joke about it. I'm sorry. That was a shitty thing to do. I've never experienced anything like you were talking about in my life. I'm a middle-class White boy from the San Fernando Valley. No one in my family has ever been to jail or shot. If I'm going to be able to help you, I'm going to have to relate to you and your life. To do that, I'm going to have to stop making jokes and really listen to what you've been through. Let's go back and try again."

She looked up at me right in the eyes and slowly nodded, "OK."

Say, doc, do we really have to do this? Haven't we talked enough about trauma? You've told me plenty of tragic stories already. I still can't get out of my head that kid who shot his little sister. Frankly, I don't know how you handle all that pain. Maybe I should skip this journey.

Well, you certainly wouldn't be alone in making that decision. My teachers in medical school skipped it. They taught me that you can't really drive someone crazy. They said that trauma can make someone neurotic or even give them a personality disorder or PTSD, but it can't make them psychotic. To be psychotic, you have to have an underlying biological illness, not a trauma. Families who were tired of being blamed for causing their child's schizophrenia and mothers who had fought the guilt of being labeled "schizophrenogenic mothers" skipped it. NAMI has heavily backed biologic models of mental illness and avoided addressing the impact of childhood trauma. Even Freud skipped it. When he was faced with a number of "hysterical" female patients who trusted him enough to tell him about their sexual experiences with their fathers, he decided that those were all fantasies and proof that they had Oedipal issues, rather than face the probability that they had been molested by their respectable fathers which likely caused their conditions. *DSM* has chosen to skip essentially the entire area of childhood trauma. PTSD was included to describe adult war veterans, not children. Each time they update and revise *DSM*, they vote to exclude "Developmental Trauma Disorder."

We all have our limits. Some trauma and suffering are more than we will let ourselves experience or share. We don't all have to travel everywhere. For example, I found that working with traumatized youth who were then getting each other pregnant and neglecting and abusing their kids was hard to face. I turned away from the couple who was so high on crack cocaine that they crushed their new infant to death rolling over him in their bed, not realizing it had happened until the next morning. However, there's a price to be paid for just handing people a map and telling them to find their own way, instead of traveling with them. About a month later, I was urging another young woman to get an abortion, so that she wouldn't continue the cycle of abuse and neglect she'd been exposed to. She looked at me sadly and said, "So, if you had been my mother's psychiatrist, you would've tried to convince her that I shouldn't even be alive." She needs someone besides me to be working with her on parenting.

It's important for us to keep reevaluating our own willingness and ability to travel. It's likely we all have blind spots about what we're avoiding. A group of students once did a study of outcomes at the Village and found out that White and Asian members were more likely to recover in our program than Hispanic members, while Black members were likely to deteriorate. We never looked closely at ourselves, or the community around us, to figure out why that was. Maybe, without realizing it, we're not the best guides for our Black members.

Certainly, not all mental illness is caused, or even contributed to, by childhood trauma, and every parent isn't responsible for their child's condition, but some parents, as well as other adults, and even other children, have done terrible things to kids, and it likely did contribute to their mental condition, even psychosis, and they should be blamed. If we all skip this journey, where are those people supposed to go for help? Who is going to join them on their journeys? Isn't it retraumatizing and abusive to tell people that we don't believe them, that they're making up those stories of abuse, so we'll feel sorry for them, so stop pretending and take your medication? Isn't it damaging to tell people they have a biological illness, instead of helping them work through the trauma they know impacted them and helping them update their childhood defenses to meet their adult needs? Shouldn't impoverished foster kids be given therapy, instead of ever-increasing amounts of medications, including antipsychotics?

OK. OK. Slow down, doc. I get your point. Maybe it would help if you'd tell me more about how you deal with trauma and abuse before we go on. You know, to prepare a little first.

Fair enough. Before we head out, here's my list of 10 lessons for dealing with trauma I've learned over the years.

Preparing to face trauma

1) In order to be effective, we need to respond to trauma stories emotionally as a fellow human being, rather than by creating some other artificial roles and relationships for ourselves. We can't hold them at a "professional distance" or maintain "strong boundaries" and expect them to really connect with us. Don't try to act like a therapist. Start by actually feeling whatever you're feeling: sympathetic, compassionate, desiring to help, comforting, protective, reassuring, sharing their experiences, desiring to heal, angry, wanting to bring perpetrators to justice, advocating for change, making sure it doesn't happen again, feeling guilty, feeling hurt ourselves, overwhelmed, damaged, self-protective, becoming part of their cycle of pain, frustrated, stuck in repetition, manipulated, traumatized by them, avoidant, or blaming. Don't block out any of it.

2) To protect ourselves from emotional burnout, we need to replace compassion with empathy. Remember the "back of the hand" story in Chapter 2? Compassion is feeling our feelings in response to their story. Compassion is when I tell you a story about a boy beaten in the snow, and you feel angry and sorry for him and want to help. It feeds our own suffering and our burden to help. Compassion is useful but draining. Empathy is a vicarious experience of their feelings, sharing their suffering, and leads to feeling quiet, connected, and stronger. Empathy is feeling what it would be like to be them, imagining hiding in those woods playing with sticks, and planning escape. Compassion burnout is common. I doubt empathy burnout exists. Carl Rogers even created an entire therapy around three things he believed make our relationships nurture healing—empathy, authenticity, and genuine affection. We should begin with these approaches.

3) Suffering itself is not a sufficient motivator for change. Having your suffering shared by others, feeling understood, empathized with, and sitting quietly with is a stronger motivator for change. Having someone take away your pain, fix your problem, or medicate it isn't generally effective without sharing the suffering that accompanies the experience of the pain, first and ongoing. Otherwise, they feel

objectified, misunderstood, minimized, and ultimately somewhat cheated by us. We need to connect to suffering, not just reduce the pain and other "symptoms."

4) We may feel suffering ourselves from sharing our clients' stories. They may trigger our own underlying traumas. Hiding our own suffering and trying not to feel deaden us and destroy the source of our own compassion and energy for our work. We need to value our own suffering, accepting and valuing ourselves as "wounded healers," understand and use gifts from our suffering, and accept and care for our vulnerabilities.

5) We can intentionally focus on creating a healing relationship between us to help heal their wounds, a "corrective emotional experience." This relationship has to be emotionally sustainable for us and winnable, so they don't drive us into hopelessness and suffering more than we drive them into hope and healing. It needs to be a partnership, not a battle.

6) We need to accept that there isn't a way to separate victim and perpetrator, good guys and bad guys. Virtually everyone is both. We need to replace pursuing vengeance and justice with pursuing acceptance and forgiveness. Forgiveness doesn't mean it was alright, we only forgive things that are wrong. Forgiveness is not for the perpetrator, they've likely already moved on or don't think they did anything wrong, it's for the victim. The weak don't forgive, only the strong forgive, and it makes them stronger.

7) We need to be able to see, appreciate, understand, and accept the traumatizing impact of all relationships. There's no such thing as "do no harm." We harm those most with whom we have the closest relationships. We need to cultivate an awareness of how we look to them, even if it's not how we perceive ourselves. We need to accept and take responsibility for our roles in inflicting more suffering, while working to minimize retraumatization, power struggles, and the use of seclusion and restraints. Rationalizing that we're acting in good faith, that we're good people, and that we're doing it for their own good is not helpful for them.

8) Promoting more social responsibility doesn't have to diminish self-responsibility—it can be social responsibility "and" self-responsibility, not "or." We do want to work together to improve

our world, but waiting for others to advocate for them, to change their oppressive social or personal circumstances is disempowering and reinforcing of victimhood. Diminishing self-responsibility is crippling, no matter how well intended it may be. People need to move from victim to survivor to recover. When we take responsibility for their lives, it burdens us and feeds both our and their resentments. It's also ultimately futile.

9) Excusing people from the burdens and expectations of self-responsibility is a very appealing and common way of coping and maintaining difficult relationships—it wasn't their fault because they're "sick." It may seem easier for me to keep working compassionately with someone who is acting badly toward me, especially dangerously so, if I decide that they're acting that way because they're ill, rather than out of choice. If I proceed even further to decide that they aren't responsible for understanding their illness and taking care of themselves and, therefore, I need to take care of their life and their treatment, I will have bound them to my care forever. We should desperately search for alternatives to this seductive path, highly individualized alternatives that build on and support whatever—even limited—free will and self-responsibility they have because without free will and self-responsibility, there is no recovery, only custodial care.

10) We cannot rid the world of damaging forces, no matter how much we might want to. We cannot ensure "this will never happen again." We cannot truly be safe. But that unfortunate reality shouldn't lead us to withdrawal, isolation, depression, or deadening of feelings, or we've given up on all of life. We can't block out or avoid just bad feelings and relationships—they all come together. Having fun together and enjoying life together can be a powerful motivator to keep all of us involved with life, despite the inevitable suffering, and fun brings us together. We can also create "protective factors"—a secure foundation from which to take risks, a self-identity, relationships and connectedness, and spirituality—to build resilience, so that we can make it through the inevitable next trauma together. Trust is the building material of protective factors—trust in ourselves, including our flaws and wounds, trust in our relationships even though we will hurt each

other, trust/faith in the world/God even though trauma and suffering exist.

I do have to warn you, before you decide if you're going to travel on this journey, that doing all of those things requires experience. You can't just be told those lessons. Most of them are counterintuitive and don't come naturally to most people. You're likely to be taught or read that you should do the opposite of what I recommended, but look back on your life experiences for the times that life has taught you similar lessons. Many of you will try to avoid these lessons if you can, looking for another path, just like most of us do, but I'm pretty sure you'll end up learning them at the school of hard knocks sooner or later. And you will likely be bruised along the way.

Let's go back to Calvin's story to practice:

> *How did you feel when I told you he was whipped and beaten naked in the snow? What feelings did you have? Instead of hiding those feelings behind some professional distance, share them, so you'll be a real part of their story: "It makes me tense up with rage, just hearing you talk about being treated like that."*

> *Try to connect your feelings to how he felt and how he feels now: "Did you feel angry, too, or were you too frightened and small, and felt more helpless than angry?" and "Did you ever stand up to him or take your anger out on others?" In this case, Calvin disconnected from his fear and anger and every other feeling. "It would be like I was watching him do it to me from a distance." "When I think about those times, it's like it happened to someone else, but I don't like thinking about them much anyway."*

> *How did you feel about his mother? (Often, it's the parent who "should" have been protective, who children feel angrier and more betrayed by, than the abusive parent.) Make sure you're on the same page he is, if you're going to ally with him. "Mom was just as much a victim as I was, but she escaped him, too. I know she's with God now. It's just too bad she didn't have a chance to have a good life, too. He took that away from her."*

Can you relate to running away as a way of coping with something unbearable? "I haven't been through anything nearly like you have, but I can understand that sometimes you have to run away to find yourself. In some ways, I bet you're still finding parts of yourself that your dad beat out of you or told you were worthless, but it is hard to get rid of the anger and resentment that way. I know that sometimes when I haven't been able to confront someone who hurt me, I keep replaying in my head what I'd say to them if I ever saw them again. Do you ever do that?"

Try to think of what he needs as a healing emotional relationship. Not someone to teach him to follow rules or be considerate of others or make better plans. Discipline is likely to be experienced as being violent to him. He needs someone to believe in him, to support him, to value him. His dad crushed the good parts of him; so, they need to be restored. "Tell me what your dreams are and let's try our best to work together to make them real."

Try to find a way to transform his wound into a productive gift. "I noticed something about you. Since you were beaten down as a kid, you try to notice the positive in everyone around you and help build it up. Even though that's something that comes from your pain, it's one of my favorite parts of you." *Telling him he needs to be considerate or fair might feel like a fancy way of devaluing him and will likely retraumatize him and bring out his anger and resentment.*

Anger and resentment aren't healing. Justice and fairness aren't healing. Acceptance and forgiveness are. "We'll work together on this, but that doesn't mean we'll always win, but we'll do the best we can and together enjoy what we can achieve." "I know the world hasn't usually treated you kindly, but it sure was great seeing you out there making our community a better place for all of us, whether we're always kind to you or not."

> *To be healing, these positive times have to be internalized, "It matters more what you think of all this, than what I think. Were you proud of yourself today when you look back at what you accomplished? I hope you can remember this good feeling when you have days that make you feel like giving up."*
>
> *"It feels like you've come a long way, but there's so much more to do. You have to find a way to get enough money and friends to fit into the Long Beach community and stay away from the police. And maybe even more importantly, you have to help make sure other kids aren't being hurt like you were. We have to do better."*

Notice how being attentive to his trauma—how it plays out in his relationships today and how healing can be incorporated into our daily activities with him—leads to very specific, individualized approaches with him ... and keeps us open and growing emotionally as well. That's the foundation of "trauma informed care."

How trauma can lead to psychosis

Now that you have that "luggage," let's look at how childhood trauma can lead to psychosis.

Remember our "psychosis triangle"?

The Psychosis Triangle

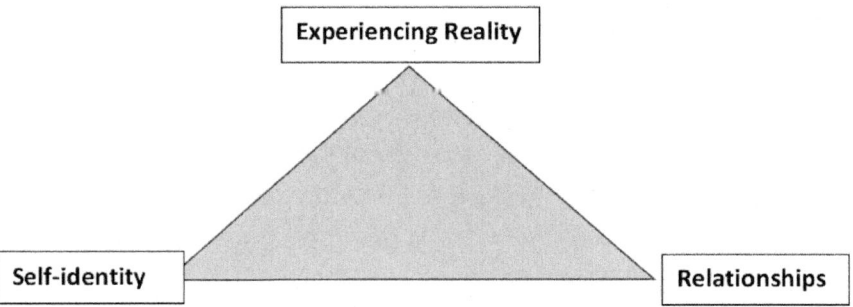

In the last journey, we were focused a lot on how problems beginning in the "experiencing reality" dimension can destabilize self-identity and relationships and lead to a collapse into psychosis. In this journey, most people's problems begin with relationships, spread to self-identity, and then, if severe enough, they can impact experiencing reality, too, and consequently result in psychosis.

Looking back at Calvin again, his childhood relationships were so destructive that he "reacted" by isolating and by cutting himself off from his feelings. He also tried to "adapt" by creating relationships and a self-identity with the sticks in the woods. He couldn't get any reasonable "mirroring" of his personal traits by either his father or mother; so, he projected them onto his imaginary scenarios as his only way of getting to know himself. That's better than nothing, but it dramatically altered his relationship with reality. When he walked across the country, he had only his conception of God and his self-image as a Black man left to guide his journey. By the time he walked across the desert, all three dimensions were in serious trouble, and he was psychotic. His recovery began by finding new relationships, both on the street and at the Village, and using them to rediscover and recreate himself. As time went on, his new reality, although still needy on the streets, was something he could experience in reasonably realistic ways. Notice that having healing relationships and positive roles was what he needed more than antipsychotic medications to recover. Although he'll likely always be somewhat fragile and vulnerable, he's no longer psychotic.

Prolonged childhood trauma has direct impacts on both lifelong relationships and self-identity as people grow and develop.

> *The Adverse Childhood Events (ACEs) Study was a large survey done by Kaiser Permanente along with the Centers for Disease Control and Prevention (CDC) between 1995 and 1997. They asked thousands of people, many now in their 60s or older, about their experiences of childhood trauma, including physical abuse, sexual abuse, emotional abuse, physical neglect, emotional neglect, violent treatment of mother, household substance abuse, household mental illness, parental separation or divorce, and incarcerated household member. They found the following: 1) lots of people experience childhood trauma (even these mostly White not impoverished Kaiser members), 2) childhood trauma tends to cluster, so that there is a subset of people who had multiple kinds of trauma, 3) there is a "dose response" to childhood trauma—the more kinds of trauma,*

the bigger the impact, and 4) the impact is pervasive and lifelong and quite dramatic, including health, suicide, productivity, smoking, substance abuse, and even early death from heart disease, for instance. A number of follow-up studies have found more and more impacts from childhood trauma.

Why would there be such a substantial global lifelong impact of childhood trauma?

The CDC developed the ACE pyramid that theorizes that adverse childhood experiences can lead to social, emotional, and cognitive impairment, which can lead to the adoption of health risk behaviors, which can lead to disease, disability, and social problems, which can lead to early death.

But what about psychosis?

It seems to me that for some small subgroup of people experiencing multiple adverse childhood events, the "social, emotional, and cognitive impairment" can be severe enough to lead to psychotic experiences. I also believe that it isn't just an issue of the childhood trauma "triggering" an underlying biologic predisposition to psychosis (any more than its triggering underlying predispositions for depression, smoking, diabetes, or stroke); sometimes, the trauma is so severe and so damaging that it can cause psychosis by impacting relationships and self-identity.

As I brought up in our last journey when I discussed "creating reality," our early childhood emotional experiences create internal emotional templates that guide how we interpret and experience new emotional relationships, which is called "transference." If we've experienced a lot of devaluation and rejection, for example, we're likely to interpret new people we meet as devaluating and rejecting, even when they don't intend to be and we're likely to attract people who do devalue and reject us. But that process, regardless of the positivity or negativity of the emotional projections, requires a coherent emotional template. Emotional experiences have to be reasonably consistent to be used to predict and attract the future.

There are three major ways this normal "emotional template" can break down:

1) There is no consistency of the early emotional experiences—like for the 13-year-old girl whose mother beat her and forbid her from going trick-or-treating and then comforted her by suckling her on her breast.
2) The emotions are too overwhelming to face—like Calvin being beaten in the snow.
3) There are no emotions to draw upon—like a woman whose mother had obsessive compulsive disorder and wouldn't let her daughter touch the ground as a toddler or play with anything she hadn't scrubbed repeatedly, and wouldn't let her leave the house or have any friends.

When relationships become chaotic and incomprehensible, or when people disconnect from all feelings and people because they're overwhelmed, or they're isolated and feel like they can't connect to anyone, their "relationship" dimension has become badly broken. These people aren't just miserably repeating their emotional templates. They're at risk of psychosis.

If we take the time to really ask people about their childhood experiences and their ongoing relationships, we can find people with psychosis with all three of these seriously broken relationship dimensions. (It might interest you to know that while most of these people would be diagnosed with schizophrenia or "schizoaffective disorder" today, there was a time when they might have been diagnosed with "borderline personality disorder with brief reactive psychosis" or even "pseudoneurotic schizophrenia," acknowledging that their path to psychosis was through relationships and childhood trauma.)

In the meantime, this same chronically traumatized child is trying to build a coherent sense of themselves. Faced with relationships that are severely inconsistent, overwhelming emotionally, or isolating and deprived, they're likely to have to spend a lot of effort just trying to find emotional comfort. If, as we'd expect in these scenarios, not enough comforting is available from outside, they're going to need to do a lot of self-soothing to even have a chance of creating any self-identity.

We can sometimes identify the age and developmental stage when a person was most traumatized, by observing what self-soothing skills they've utilized. For example, people traumatized as toddlers tend to self-sooth by rocking and head banging, while those traumatized in childhood resort to dissociating, or not paying attention to disconnect, or hyperactivity or precocious sexual behaviors to release tension. Preteens may act out their aggression by being cruel to animals or playing with fire, while teens cut themselves to either distract themselves from suffering or to feel again if they've become too deadened, try to overcontrol their eating and their weight, use drugs and alcohol to alter their feelings, become promiscuous, or even try to kill themselves trying to escape their emotional turmoil altogether. These are all signs that they're having serious problems achieving a reasonably stable emotional self-identity and usually, although not always, point to trauma as the cause.

When we're with someone on a childhood trauma journey to psychosis, we're most likely to see severe, ongoing impairments in relationships and self-identity, that intermittently lead to problems experiencing reality, rather than pervasive impairments in experiencing reality that intermittently lead to problems with relationships and self-identity, like we saw in the "difficulties making sense of the world" journey.

> *Bridget seemed to get into problems wherever she went. When we helped her get her own apartment, she'd keep breaking everything and getting into conflicts with the building supervisor. If she had a roommate, they'd be in the office blaming each other for everything from not cleaning up, to stealing each other's clothes, to letting strange men come into the apartment. If she was in a Board and Care with staff to take care of everything, she'd be constantly reporting them for mistreating her, and they'd want to know if I could raise her medications, so that she'd be easier to manage. Week after week, our staff spent hours and hours with her, dealing with her messes.*
>
> *Our staff, including me, weren't spared from her accusations, but she was at her most frightened and venomous with her parents. She was an only child. She said that her father had always been cold and critical to both her and her*

mother and that her mother had always been self-centered, making everything about herself, instead of thinking about Bridget's needs. No matter what Bridget complained about, her mother became the more wounded and neglected one. Whenever Bridget tried to get her father's attention, her mother would become physically ill and bedbound to make sure her suffering was the center of attention.

I don't think I ever knew the whole story, but when Bridget was 15, she got pregnant. Her father couldn't bear to look at her. Her mother worried about what people would think about her as a mother who raised a girl who got pregnant as a teenager. They took her out of high school, kept her away from all her friends, and hid the pregnancy. When the baby was born, they signed papers for it to be adopted immediately. Bridget didn't get a say in the matter. She didn't even get to see her newborn baby. She returned to school the next semester and was forbidden to ever bring it up again. Apparently, she went to the hospital repeatedly trying to find her baby, enough so that they filed a restraining order to keep her away. She felt that everyone was against her. She tried to kill herself and ended up in a psychiatric hospital, was diagnosed as paranoid schizophrenia, was put on a conservatorship, and was forced to take medications. She never finished high school.

The first time I met her parents was when the Board and Care hospitalized her, and I set up a family meeting hoping to figure out what to do next. I'd only known Bridget for a few months at that point. Her parents didn't pause for a kind word of greeting, let alone a hug, for Bridget before launching into their criticisms. The current issues of her losing her wallet and blaming the Board and Care staff were their entrée into a lifelong litany of Bridget's failures and the burden she'd been on them. Every possible solution I offered was met with some version of, "You don't know her like we do. We've already tried that, and it doesn't work with her." After an hour, I couldn't take anymore and told *them all that it was time for me to leave. Bridget begged me to stay, "Please don't go. They've been treating me nicely because you're here. When you leave, they'll stop being on their best behavior and go back to being mean again." I was flabbergasted and didn't know what to say. If that was their best behavior, what was being mean?*

Over time, I saw her father get so frustrated with her that he slapped her in the face in front of everyone to make her get in the car with him. I also saw her become so frightened of him, that she began to think he was really Darth Vader in disguise. She wasn't joking, she was terrified.

Over time, we learned to share Bridget, so we wouldn't get too frustrated—although it wasn't my best moment when I pushed her out of the office, slammed the door shut, and locked it behind her because she wouldn't leave to let me talk to anyone else—and we learned to keep her somewhat separated from her parents. We tried to be reasonably emotionally consistent and moderate, without being too distant and deadening. Gradually, new relationships and new emotional realities emerged. She even took some pride at being able to soothe herself.

People on this journey tend to engender the most conflict between themselves and their families. They're the ones who are the most likely to forbid staff to talk with their families and push for more confidentiality restrictions, creating rules that are applied to everyone else. They are often the most adamant, saying, "I have PTSD. I don't have schizophrenia. I don't need any antipsychotics. My mother is the one who needs them. I just need some real help." This agitates NAMI, a grass roots organization that excels in educating and supporting families of people with mental illnesses and advocating for their inclusion. They'd like to pretend that people like this and families like this don't exist. They're so afraid of losing the legitimacy of "mental illnesses are real illnesses that need treatment" and returning to a time of blaming families, that they end up keeping people on this journey from the "trauma informed care" that is the treatment that they need, pushing more and more medications and hospitalizations instead.

Remember, though, that there usually isn't a clear division between perpetrator and victim. Many children who are abused have things that are unusual about them that make them particularly frustrating or more likely targets. Many parents who are inconsistent, overwhelming, or isolating have serious issues of their own and may be doing the best they can. No matter what approach we take with these people and their families, we need to be prepared emotionally for difficult times.

Multiple personalities

It's time, at long last, to talk about multiple personality disorder, or as it's currently called "dissociative identity disorder."

Wait a minute. I thought multiple personality disorder wasn't real. Isn't it just something in the movies?

Some of my supervisors thought it wasn't real, too, but I've met about a dozen people who have it. That's not very many over all these years, but it's not none either. These people have such severe trauma at very early ages that it breaks down their identity into fragments. It's a very difficult condition to live with. Most of them don't even know they have it.

> *Margie was 4 years old when she was playing with her mother's makeup and jewelry, pretending she was grown up like her mother. Her mother had left her alone in their apartment, as she often did, while she was working as a prostitute. She came into the room, surprised and annoyed that Margie wasn't in bed. She was also drunk enough that the John she was with had to hold her up.*
>
> *He said as he was groping her, "Oh, look at the cutie. She's adorable. She's going to grow up to be beautiful just like you."*
>
> *Margie's mother didn't think it was adorable that her daughter was going to grow up to be a prostitute just like her. Through her drunken haze came the pain and the rage.*
>
> *She screamed at Margie to take the jewelry off and grabbed her. The beads of the necklace flew everywhere.*

> She grabbed a piece of steel wool and started rubbing the makeup off her face so hard that Margie's cheeks started bleeding. Now, Margie was crying and screaming, too.
>
> That's when Margie's father unexpectedly walked into the room. "What the hell is going on here?"
>
> He pulled out a gun and shot at the John and Margie's mother. Her shoulder shattered, spraying blood all over Margie.
>
> That's the last thing Margie remembers before she woke up in the hospital and a voice in her head said, "I'm Jenny. I took over for you and protected you. I won't let them hurt you."

What separates "voices" from "personalities" is that the personalities can take over the consciousness and voluntary actions of the person, whereas the voices can usually just talk or distract and confuse. The personalities tend to have "functions" somewhat like other traumatic voices—protecting, being violent, being sexual, and acting like a responsible adult. The person's "core personality" tends to be the frightened child, stuck in the emotional development of early childhood it was when it disconnected from the emotions that were overwhelming. Put those features together, and you have "dissociative identity disorder."

> I remember meeting Gloria, who was in her early 30s but looked and acted more like a teenager, with a cute smile, braids, and a gold tooth. She was struggling in our homeless Drop-in Center, couldn't get a job or enough money to get out of the shelter, and she was having a tough time keeping predatory men away from her. I gave her a little antidepressant that she didn't take regularly and practical support, including sending her to the hospital ER when her menstrual period had gone on for weeks and she looked pale. She turned out to be severely anemic and needed a blood transfusion. "You saved my life, Dr. Mark."
>
> A couple months later, I was told that Lynette had an appointment with me. I was puzzled since I didn't remember

anyone named Lynette, but sometimes I don't remember everyone. I asked for her chart, but we couldn't find it.

In strode a confident woman, wearing a business suit and heels. "You don't have a chart for me because I'm here for Gloria. She needs help. She's too much of kid to take care of herself and she's too shy to push you; so, I'm here to get you to help her."

"OK. How do you know Gloria?"

"I take care of her." She flashed a big smile.

When I saw the gold tooth and realized that Lynette was Gloria, I did a double take. I would never have recognized her. Her hair, makeup, clothes, everything was different, but most strikingly, her whole demeanor was different. Even when I knew who she was, she felt like someone else entirely.

"What do you want me to help Gloria with?"

"She needs you to help get her on disability. I've been looking for a job to support us, but no one is hiring. She's got to get money to get out of that shelter, and I can't earn any money the way things are now."

"OK. Tell her to go to the Social Security office to apply. You can't do it for her, but Nancy, her case worker here, can take her."

The next week Gloria came in to see me. "Hi, Dr. Mark."

"Did you get to the Social Security office?"

"How'd you know about that?"

"I was the one who told you to go there last week. Don't you remember"

"I wasn't here last week."

"Actually, I talked with Lynette."

> "Oh, that makes sense to me. When I realized I was at the Social Security office with Nancy, I wondered how I got there. I thought maybe Lynette went there and then left me to figure out what to do next. It was good she went with Nancy instead of leaving me there alone. What did you think of Lynette?"
>
> "She seemed like a very confident woman. She was looking for a job."
>
> "Yeah. She's always worked for us."
>
> "Maybe she could teach you how to do more things on your own, so that you could handle more things."
>
> "Oh, I don't think I can do things like she can, Dr. Mark."
>
> "Maybe you could learn."

There are very few therapists who specialize in working with people with multiple personalities/dissociative identity disorder—and they tend to work with people who have insurance, not homeless people. Their usual therapeutic approach doesn't rely on medications. Instead, an effort is made to reintegrate the personalities by having them become increasingly aware of each other and work together to help the core, frightened child's personality grow and become more and more independent, so that it doesn't need the interventions of the other personalities as much. This takes years of hard work.

Unlike people with multiple personalities who fragment their inner worlds, people with psychosis from childhood trauma externalize their fears and fragmentation. Calvin created an imaginary family in the forest to grow up with. Bridget suspected that everyone would ignore her needs and hurt her and that her father was Darth Vader. We can end up feeling like characters in their drama.

I think that our work with people with psychosis from childhood trauma could benefit from using integrative approaches like they use with people with multiple personalities, too. There is often a stunted, frightened, small child at their core. Instead of trying to medicate away their symptoms, which are actually compensations, we can look at how we could help that "inner child" grow and develop. Often, creating safety and security in the outer world, like helping Calvin and Bridget get a place to live and supporting their efforts to have a "family of choice" around them, can calm down the fear and the resulting psychosis more effectively than medications can.

Returning to our psychosis triangle, this approach relies on improving relationships and increasing security in order to improve self-identity with the expectation that improving those two dimensions will improve how they experience reality—in effect, reversing the causal process they experienced.

Social trauma

Childhood trauma can take a great many forms. and each person's journey evolves differently. As the three dimensions strengthen and weaken, their psychosis changes and evolves, coming and going. Once we join them on their journeys, we can have a multitude of impacts on their travels and their destinations.

> Sann was only 4 years old when the Khmer Rouge took over Cambodia, and yet, he was convinced we needed to understand what had happened then to understand him. We rented the movie "The Killing Fields" and watched it with him. During the screening, for the first time, he told us that his mother had starved to death because she gave him her ration of a cup of rice a day during the forced marches, so that he would survive. He made it to a refugee camp in Thailand as a 6-year-old orphan where he was reunited with his older sister. A couple years later, they immigrated to Long Beach, joining the largest community of Cambodians outside of Cambodia.
>
> As Sann grew up here, according to his sister, he was always different. He was quiet and withdrawn and seemed to be in a world of his own. He didn't make friends in school, and as he got older, he stopped going to school entirely. He wanted to work in the family donut shop, but they were worried about what he might do and if he could be trusted around other people. They kept him hidden. They knew he had a mental illness and knew he would be their lifelong burden. When he started talking to himself, they

reluctantly took him to a local Asian Pacific Community Mental Health Clinic where he was diagnosed with schizophrenia and started on antipsychotic medication.

They were afraid someone they knew would find out that Sann was crazy and bring shame to the whole family; so, they had him placed in a Board and Care, and they moved to Los Angeles. Cut off, he tried to kill himself, and then, they transferred him to the Village. We connected him with a Cambodian case manager on our staff. They arranged the movie event together. We tried to find a mental health expert to consult with from the local Cambodian community but couldn't find anyone to help guide us.

I knew that Sann was different from my usual person with schizophrenia, and I suspected his real problem was connected to his child trauma, but he didn't feel like the usual patient with PTSD either. I couldn't really imagine going through what he'd been through and how it would affect me, and I was pretty sure the psychiatrists who wrote the DSM hadn't thought about someone like him when they wrote it.

Sann would drift away into silence for long periods of time in the middle of conversations. The case manager said that Sann did the same thing with him, even if he tried talking in Khmer. His personal hygiene would drift away, too, not changing clothes or taking showers for days at a time. He'd hang out in the team area for hours at a time, not doing much. The staff started taking him with them when they went out on errands or social activities. After a while, he was a regular attender at almost any activity we had. He brightened up and made some friends.

Several of his friends lived in a subsidized apartment building a few blocks from the Village that MHALA developed and owned. He wanted to get his own apartment, too. With the help of his case manager, he moved. The more responsibility he had, the less he drifted away. The more friends he had, the less he drifted away.

His next big goal was to make a trip back to Cambodia to visit his family. We were somewhat hesitant, not knowing how it might affect him, but agreed to help him anyway. His family, usually rather avoidant of him, was quite supportive and made all the arrangements. I gave him enough pills to last 2 months.

When Sann returned, his case manager thought he looked stressed; he wouldn't respond to any of his questioning; and he asked me to assess him. Apparently, there had been an incident at customs when he returned. I was showing pictures from my vacation to Alaska to a group of members and staff sitting around my desk, and I urged Sann to go home and bring his pictures from Cambodia to share with us, too. He did, and we talked about visiting the ruins at Angkor Wat that I wanted to see, the native healers his family took him to, and his reactions at seeing his parents' graves. By the time we finished, he'd perked up again, and I had completed a good "clinical assessment" as well as learning a number of fascinating things and having a good time. He left, saying maybe we'd go together if he returned to Cambodia in 6 years.

I later found out that when the customs officer found Buddhist objects in his suitcase, he made Sann unwrap them to make sure they weren't smuggled antiques. Sann felt threatened, returning to a time when he was a refugee, unsure if he'd be allowed to come to America. At the urging of his grandparents, he'd also stopped his medications.

Over the next couple weeks, back in his apartment, with his Village friends, and on his medications, he returned to his usual self.

Over the next few years, his case worker left the Village, his closest friend and neighbor, a woman who looked after him and sometimes cooked for him, had a stroke and had to move out of her apartment, and the Village got larger; so, he wasn't as comfortable anymore. He couldn't rely on knowing everyone at outings anymore. When he drifted away and didn't pick up his groceries, or shower, or take his pills, his new case manager thought he was being lazy. He wasn't going to start doing things for Sann that he knew Sann could do for himself. Sann would have to experience the "natural consequences" of his laziness to get back on track. Instead, Sann isolated more.

I was no longer Sann's psychiatrist when I was called by his sister urgently, but I was the only staff she knew. Sann's apartment was a mess. He hadn't eaten except for a few bags of chips or bathed for weeks. He was walking around with feces in his pants. For the first time in a long time, he was mumbling to himself, too. I went over to see him, but I couldn't get him to even look at me, let alone talk. He didn't eat the burger I brought with me. We had to hospitalize him.

He did poorly in the hospital. The staff tried to force him to bathe and eat and change his clothes and go to group therapy, but he drifted away more and more. He just seemed frightened by their efforts. The psychiatrist there raised his medications more and more trying to break through, but nothing helped. He started shuffling his feet and drooling. They made his sister his conservator and put him in a long-term mental health facility.

About 9 months later, his sister called me again to tell me that she was removing Sann from the IMD against medical advice and sending him back to Cambodia. It was clear to her that Sann wasn't going to get any better locked up. She had to try something. I had no idea if that was a good idea or not. I wished them good luck.

The last time I saw Sann was 3 years later. He was fine again and wasn't taking any medication, Western or Cambodian. I asked him what had happened to him since I'd last *seen him. His family had arranged a marriage for him in Cambodia with a poor woman who had been taking care of her elderly, blind father. When her father died, she had no way of supporting herself. Sann still had his SSI checks directly deposited into his sister's account being sent to him. $830 a month might not have been much in Long Beach, but it was quite a lot of money in rural Cambodia. Even knowing that Sann had a mental illness and that she'd have to take care of him, the woman was willing to marry him, so that she'd have an income. Sann showed me her picture and said that they'd fallen in love over time. The next picture was of their two small children. He said he was happy. It seemed he had found someone who could understand his suffering and accept him as he is.*

Chapter 10

Journey 5: Losing balance

Nathan's therapist at Cal State Long Beach asked me to see him because she was somewhat confused. Nathan had been very psychotic a couple of months ago, but seemed to have recovered and was back to work and school, even though he hadn't taken any medications. She wondered if he really had schizophrenia, and if he did, how he recovered without treatment. Besides that, she knew she didn't like patients with schizophrenia, and she did like Nathan. Maybe the diagnosis was wrong.

Nathan was more than happy to meet with me. He, too, was confused about what was going on with him, and he appreciated the opportunity to meet with someone who could help him make sense of what had happened.

He told me that his parents were both very young when they had him and didn't know what they were doing. They'd both been sexually molested as children; so, they didn't have any good role models or families to rely on. He told me, "They learned to be parents with me while I was growing up." Unfortunately, that learning seemed to involve a lot of beatings when they were frustrated.

Nathan was also different from his parents: He had very light skin, so much so that many people didn't think he was Black. He was very intelligent, to the point of being nerdy, even though both of his parents had dropped out of high school. And he was gay. He said that he always knew he was gay, even as far back as 4 or 5 years old. None of that fit in with his family or his neighbors. It's not surprising they didn't know what to do with him. It's also not surprising that he didn't really know who he was growing up.

He tried to make friends by giving more to others than they gave to him and making himself desirable and useful to them. That approach was draining and unsatisfying for him. Also, other people tended to take advantage of him and tease him behind his back anyway. Not surprisingly, he didn't really fit in or feel like he belonged anywhere.

Nathan started writing poetry to express himself, which did feel satisfying, but made him stick out even more. He liked the sounds that the words made when they were next to each other.

College was his big opportunity to find himself. He was given a substantial scholarship since he was near the top of his class at his inner-city high school. He also worked at the local yogurt shop.

Nathan took full advantage of the opportunity. He was very involved in a Black student's group and joined in "Black Lives Matter" civil disobedience protests. He triple-majored in Poetry, Communications, and African Studies.

He made one close friend, Tony, who was the opposite of him, raised in a wealthy family, conservative, and studying business. They spent a semester abroad in London together. After the semester finished, they traveled together in the English countryside. It seemed like they were becoming more than friends. One night, after a few too many pints in a local pub, Nathan made his move, professing his love for Tony. Even when I met him, a year later, Nathan didn't know how to read Tony's response. Tony didn't rebuff his advances, saying he wasn't gay or not interested, but he didn't reciprocate either. He just got uncomfortable, quiet, and withdrawn. Nathan wasn't ever able to really reconnect with Tony.

When Nathan returned to school, he struggled with his loss and confusion. He had trouble focusing on anything else, including his schoolwork. He didn't know what it all meant. He started using marijuana daily to cope and that made him drift even further away. After a year, the marijuana started making him anxious and paranoid, instead of feeling relaxed and happy. He missed enough classes that he had to take incompletes and postpone his graduation.

He did continue to be involved in the Black protests even though they got more aggressive. For the first time in his life, he came into conflict with the police. "I wasn't just reading about police attitudes toward Blacks, I was living it, and it was frightening. I felt totally helpless." Even though they let him go without booking him, he carried his fear with him.

He became increasingly concerned about how he was doing and took steps to help himself. He began seeing a therapist. He cut way down on the marijuana. And he started to seriously meditate and pursue spiritual growth. The more he focused on emptying his mind, the more he began to have an awareness that he's part of a universal consciousness and that there are symbolic meanings in everything around him. The more he sought out these meanings, the more he found them, and the message was clear—there are powerful forces in the universe seeking to harm him that everyone was aware of except him and that are inescapable. His old fears had found a focus.

He became increasingly agitated and hard to understand. His therapist thought he was psychotic and having his first schizophrenic break and urged seeing a psychiatrist to get antipsychotic medications. He didn't.

His mother, unaware of his therapist or her recommendations, got more and more frightened. "She freaked out and took me to the county hospital ER to see a neurologist. She thought I had brain damage, maybe a brain tumor or a stroke." They did a brain scan that was normal, and they urged her to take him to the psychiatric ER. They went there together, but they were overwhelmed by the chaos in the crowded area, with police bringing in people in handcuffs, with people yelling out of locked rooms, with people laying on stretchers in the hallway, and they left without being seen.

Nathan's mother kept reassuring him that he was going to make it through this. She kept saying, "I'll stay by your side until you're better." Even though she was frightened, she was able to give him what one of my coworkers calls "unrelenting hope."

A this point, he made a very unusual choice and said, "I decided not to fight the paranoia, not to worry about who was after me or how they were going to kill me. I decided to open myself up and accept whatever happens." Like the old "Chinese finger traps," he found that the way to escape his persecution was to relax, instead of pulling harder and harder.

Instead of fighting, he spent a lot of time, with his mother by his side, sitting in nature, under a tree or in thick grass, trying to reground himself and reconnect to the wholesomeness and health of nature. Gradually, the fear receded and the symbolic meanings disappeared. A soothing reality reasserted itself. His speech became more and more intelligible. His thoughts cleared. He began to return to his normal routine and tasks.

When he returned to the therapist a couple months later, he seemed almost normal to her, and he was doing well in his classes again.

Nathan looked at me to make sense of all this. "Before I give you my feedback, I want to ask you if you received any gifts from this experience."

He looked at me strangely, "As a matter of fact, I have. Now, when I want to write poetry, I open my mind and all sorts of words and ideas and images and sounds come in, and I just write them all down without censoring them. After they're done coming to me, I go through what I've got and put it into a poem. I never had access to that other plane of inspiration before."

"Good. You deserve some reward for all the suffering you and your mother have been through."

"I know that we live in a time when we describe every mental condition in terms of illnesses and chemical imbalances and medications to fix those imbalances, but it hasn't always been that way. It has been for about 50 years, my entire career, but before that, we used a psychoanalytic model that talked about sexual and aggressive drives and childhood development. Before that, in the 1800s, we had a moral treatment model and talked about how people lost their ways with God and were lost souls. Before that, we talked about various humors like blood and bile being out of balance. That model is entirely out of fashion in the West now and has been for hundreds of years, but it's very popular in the East with things like acupuncture meridians, Tai Chi, and feng shui. All of these models have some truth to them and some strengths and weaknesses. For you, however, I think you'd be best understood with a developmental model. This model isn't nature vs. nurture. It's both. It says that you, like everyone else, are born with a variety of traits and a blueprint for development of your traits over time ... and then, life happens. Sometimes, it holds you back and you get stuck, and sometimes, it supports and encourages you. If we go through your story, I think we can trace your development and how several events along with your response to those events conspired to make you lose your balance recently and fall apart, and now, you're pulling yourself back together."

"As I understand it, you've always had trouble knowing who you are because you're so unique. As you've tried to connect to other people, you've had trouble with that, too, always feeling somewhat lost and alone and not fitting in. When Tony didn't work out, you really got lost. You turned to marijuana and meditation, which pulled you out into deeper spiritual waters that you couldn't handle at all, and you began drowning. Medication probably would've helped you at that point, but it was too scary and inaccessible for you. That might have been just as well, because a combination of pulling yourself out of the paranoia and seductive symbols, while regrounding yourself with your mother and nature helped you find solid ground again. You're not all the way back to yourself, but you're getting close. I don't think you need medications at this point, unless you start drowning again, but you need to keep regrounding yourself, instead of deepening the waters you're in. There's an old saying from Joseph Campbell, a mythology professor, that I like. He said, 'Psychotics drown in the same deep waters that mystics swim gracefully in.' You can dip your toes in the water with your poetry, but don't go swimming in the deep end again until you're much stronger. You need to have a strong sense of yourself and who you are, strong relationships, especially intimate relationships, to support you, and some spiritual wisdom to guide you, before you go into that deep water again. For now, my advice is: Focus on your degree, getting a better job, and finding a lover, instead of the deep symbolic reality of the universe."

He'd been following everything I said, nodding in agreement along the way. "That explanation really makes sense to me."

"Good." I relaxed and leaned back in my chair. "Hopefully, it will help you keep growing and developing into the person you're meant to be."

> "Thanks for taking the time to help me understand what I've been going through. You've been a great deal of help."
>
> "You're welcome. It's been my pleasure getting to know you. I think you're someone very special, but that means it will take extra work for you to really know yourself and what you're meant to do."
>
> Afterward, I told his therapist that I did think that Nathan had schizophrenia by our current diagnostic definitions, but that he had a good chance of making it anyway. "And, by the way, I liked him, too."

This journey focuses on the self-identity dimension of the psychosis triangle. It is the most "developmental" of our journeys. It's built on the premise that as we grow and develop as people, our mind continues to grow in its complexity and connectedness, but that a variety of challenges—both internal and external—can disrupt that growth and development. If that development is severely disrupted, we can lose our balance. Depending on how far our development has progressed when we lose our balance, it will have different impacts on our experience of reality and our relationships, and different "symptoms" of psychosis will result. Also, depending on how far our development has progressed, we can use different "healing relationships" to help recover our balance and return to growth and development.

Let's start by talking about how our ability to maintain our psychic balance develops normally.

When we are very small, we are dependent on the people around us, usually our parents, to provide what we need to survive and grow. Humans have a very long period of time of profound dependency for our basic survival needs. At this stage, we're not aware of how our needs are being met or even really what our needs are. We scream when they're not met and are content ("balanced") when they are being met.

As time goes on, we are more aware of ourselves—our bodies, sensations, and needs. This process is facilitated by adults reflecting our needs back to us and identifying them with us. We begin with, "That baby is always wearing a jacket because his mother is always cold" and move toward, "Are you cold, honey? Do you want a jacket?" An up-and-back process of "mirroring" helps build the baby's self-awareness. Two favorite toddler words, "mine" and "no," are reflections of growing self-identities and self-determination. This is the stage of "parallel play" where kids are playing next to each other, rather than "social play" or "cooperative play" where they're playing together.

Balance at this stage is between having our identity determined by someone else and forming our own self-identity. If enough needs aren't anticipated by others and identified for the young person, they can feel neglected, unimportant, overly reliant on others, angry, resentful, or depressed. On the other extreme, if they don't have enough self-determination and their needs are incorrectly identified and met by others, they can feel intruded on, even attacked or victimized, overly monitored, needing to fight for themselves, angry, resentful, or depressed. If this stage continues too long, people can feel very lonely or misunderstood, even if others are very actively involved—"no one understands me. There's no one I can talk to." Maintaining balance can feel as precarious as balancing on a unicycle, and if you fall down, it can be very hard to get back up by yourself.

Moving onward, when the toddler grabs a toy from another toddler yelling, "Mine," leaving them crying and going on with their own play, an attentive adult may try to help them grow by pointing out that the other child is crying, "Look they're upset," and try to help them build empathy as in, "How would you feel if someone grabbed your toy?" and compassion, "Give the toy back and apologize for taking it. Give them a hug, so they'll feel better again," working toward the Golden Rule—"Do unto others as you would have them do unto you." Gradually, the child realizes that they are part of a web of ever-changing, complex, personal relationships. They identify which kids they like and which ones they don't, who are their friends and who are not. They learn whose group or team they want to be a part of, how desirable or undesirable they are to others, and hopefully, what they can do to enhance their value to others and the quality of their relationships.

At this level, we spend a lot of time on our relationships—are we too clingy or distancing, giving too much or taking too much, hurting them or being hurt, loving or being loved enough, etc. We may have "assigned" family or relationship roles that we're trying to grow out of. Add love (often the entry to this level), sex, and even marriage to the mix, and we can become obsessed with this level, and it can be very difficult to maintain our balance. Maintaining balance can feel like standing with a group of people all in a bouncy house where everyone keeps moving and knocking each other over.

The third level is where our mind expands beyond connecting to just the people we're close to until it connects with the entire universe. We feel we are part of something much larger and more wonderful than just ourselves. This can be an expansive feeling while looking at a natural wonder—like a beautiful sunset, or an enormous whale, or a herd of bison—communing with, and becoming one with, the scene around us. This can be a spiritual feeling, for example, a sense of God being directly connected to our lives or letting Christ into our hearts. This can be a sense that the things that are happening aren't happening by chance, that there is some larger, inscrutable plan for us, and that everything is happening for a reason. In our current American culture, it is more common for people to have glimpses of this level, than to sustain living in it.

Balance on this level is between our self-will and our fate as determined by our place in the universe and, when achieved, can feel like profound peace and acceptance. We're balanced between feeling like we're exerting our own ego too much (instead of "letting the game come to us" or "letting God's will be done"), on the one hand, and feeling overwhelmed and small and lost in the awesome grandeur of God or the universe, on the other hand.

Our development doesn't necessarily progress to certain stages at certain ages. Some people never get out of the first levels. We also don't lose the lower levels, or their conflicts, when we progress to higher levels. For example, events or choices can isolate us from personal relationships or even deprive us of our basic needs. We may have only a tenuous grasp on a higher level that easily eludes us unless we're heavily supported and inspired.

We may react to the same situation from various levels, depending on what we're most comfortable or competent with. For example, most people in concentration camps ended up back at the very first level, being ignored and starved by people who had all the power over them, no matter whether they screamed or passively died. Others looked out for themselves, while struggling to maintain any sense of self after they were given numbers, instead of names, and were deprived of all of their clothing and belongings. Others spent their time looking out for others, sustaining relationships and a sense of camaraderie trying to survive for each other. At the highest level, we find Viktor Frankl's classic book about his experiences at Auschwitz, *Man's Search for Meaning*. He's inspiring because he emphasizes using meaning making in order to cope with deprivation, destruction of self, and pervasive sadistic relationships. He had worked a good deal of his life as a psychologist to develop that level in himself and his clients. Think about how you might have reacted if you were sent to Auschwitz. Which level do you think would've predominated? Would you have been able to maintain your balance at that level (which is a different question than if you would've been able to survive)?

Losing balance at any of these developmental stages does not necessarily lead to psychosis—although if things get severe enough that other adaptations don't work, psychosis is a likely outcome. Before we go through each of the levels, let me give you a "map" you can refer back to in order to help keep you oriented along the way.

	Major Symptoms	**Healing Relationships**	**Example Programs**
Failing to meet basic needs	"Failure to thrive" Passivity/"negative symptoms" Anhedonia	Attentively and respectfully meeting basic needs Empowering, hope, and personal goals	Charity and poverty services Personal service coordination Pursuing client-driven pleasurable goals
Personal imbalance	Paranoia Fear of sexual/homosexual assault Fear of explosion/destruction	Allying, instead of confrontation Assist in enhancing personal control and cohesiveness Break into isolation	Sustained engagement Personal advocacy Supported services Socialization

Relationship imbalance	Interpersonal symptoms—ESP, thought insertion and withdrawal, etc. Distorted "imagination" of relationships	Improve relationship skills Impact relationship imaginations Engage in "real" relationships and meaningful roles	Social skills groups and activities Person-centered therapy Psychosocial rehabilitation Clubhouse, school, work, "real roles"
Extra-personal/spiritual imbalance	"Spiritual drowning" "Hyper-religiosity" Expansiveness	Encourage returning to relationship level Contextualize spirituality Share spirituality	Growth-oriented crisis interventions Spiritual groups Spiritual skill groups—e.g., Bible study, meditation, yoga Spiritual healing

a. Basic needs—"failure to thrive"

When an infant's basic needs aren't met, they don't become psychotic. They can become passive and quiet, they have floppy muscles and slowly responsive nerves, and they don't gain weight, grow or develop. This syndrome is called "failure to thrive." If it isn't addressed, death often is the result.

Some infants, whose basic needs are being met, don't seem to ever be at peace anyway. This can occur for a variety of reasons—colic, exposure to intrauterine drugs, overly sensitive, etc. This can be very frustrating for the parents and caregivers, which can sometimes lead to a vicious cycle of deteriorating care and increasing distress that can lead to poor relationships, but, on its own, not likely to psychosis.

Some children are profoundly deprived. For instance, in the previous chapter, I described Sann, the man from Cambodia whose mother gave him her rice when he was 4 years old, starving herself, so that he would live. Sann might well have lost his balance at this stage, and that's why he'd sink into not eating or caring for himself and defecating on himself when he "lost his balance."

In adulthood, unfortunately, quite a number of people, especially homeless, incarcerated, and institutionalized people, do have trouble meeting their basic needs, or have them met in such inadequate or unresponsive ways that they are unable to ever feel content. As they regress into a passive state, needing others to meet their basic needs, they can lose all sense of self-identity, become isolated, and then struggle to know what's real or not, becoming psychotic.

I've met quite a few people who started hearing voices in jail or prison, especially in solitary confinement. Remember Danny in Chapter 7 and Reggie in Chapter 8 who both began hearing voices when they couldn't handle jail. I fear that far more people are regressing and losing their balance on the streets, or locked in jails and hospitals, than adapting in inspiring ways like Viktor Frankl would have done.

Most often, though, prolonged deprivation seems to wear people out or break them down, instead of making them psychotic, but sometimes, it's hard to tell whether someone who is beaten down and broken is psychotic or not.

> *It took some detective work on my part to put together Hank's story.*
>
> *He had scraggly, dirty hair and beard, with both bits of food and dandruff in it. His clothes were wrinkled and somewhat dirty, and he smelled like he hadn't showered enough to make the air around him heavy, but not really reek. He sat very passively, didn't say much, and lacked any emotional responsiveness. He didn't laugh, or even smile, at my lame jokes. He answered my questions with short, rather vague answers. It took a while to get even the basics of the story from him.*

He and his brother grew up together in a modest home in a quiet suburb of Los Angeles. Neither one had many friends or were remarkable in any particular way growing up. Neither one ever dated. Starting in high school and continuing after graduation, they both got quiet jobs, doing landscaping for the local Department of Parks and Recreation. Their retired mother made them lunches and drove them to work.

About 10 years later, Hank's father and then his mother died, leaving the two boys, by then 30-year-olds, alone. Hank tried to pay the bills as best he could. They went shopping together and cooked only a little. The house got messier. When the car broke down, they couldn't figure out how to fix it and couldn't get to work any longer.

About 6 months later, the sheriffs came to say that their house was no longer theirs. The bank had taken it from them because they hadn't made their mortgage payments, and they had to leave. Hank argued vigorously, claiming that he'd made all the payments. When the sheriffs were immovable, he started physically fighting with them, and he was arrested and taken to county jail. He didn't know what happened to his brother.

In jail, he drew the attention of the mental health workers even though he never had any hallucinations or delusions. He said that they said that he had schizophrenia because he didn't think there was anything wrong with him. They made him take antipsychotic medication.

His charges were dropped, but he was determined to be gravely disabled and placed on conservatorship under the Public Guardian's office. They placed him in an IMD for a year. They helped him apply for Social Security, and that was when they found out he had assets worth $125,000 for his half of the house that had to be exhausted before he could be on SSI. The Public Guardian spent it all on the IMD bill, leaving him with nothing. Then, he got SSI. He had no documented hallucinations or delusions at the IMD either, but his *conservatorship was renewed for a second year since he still didn't know he had a mental illness and wouldn't consent to treatment. Because he wasn't causing any problems, he was sent to an unlocked Board and Care with extra support from the Village. This combination is a "less restrictive setting" than the IMD and far less expensive.*

He said that he thought the banker who was working with him had lied and taken his house from him. I looked it up on Zillow and found out that his house had been bought for $250,000 a little before he was arrested and then resold for $450,000 6 months later. Of course, it didn't say if a banker bought and sold it.

I was also curious about what had happened to his brother whom he hadn't seen for almost 2 years by that point. I looked him up in the Mental Health computer and found that he was living across the county in a Board and Care in Downey. His worker, Gary, drove Hank there to see his brother. They were both happy to see each other after all this time. We suggested that they could live together, and they happily agreed.

I called the Public Guardian to tell her about finding Hank's brother—she said she didn't know he had a brother—and asked her for permission for Hank to move and live with him. Surprisingly to me, she replied that Hank had just moved, and she wanted to make sure he was stable here before he moved again. She said she'd consider it in 6 months. I objected. She was immovable.

Hank took the news passively. We told him we could take it to court and get the judge to order the move. He said he'd just wait and see what happened. Over the months, we kept driving him up there to see his brother, but he was never as enthusiastic as the first time. We never got him interested in doing anything else, or in improving his self-care, even though his case worker would pick him up and take him to any social activity we were doing. I gradually

> tapered off his medication that he hadn't ever needed, but that didn't help much either.
>
> He never did move in with his brother ... but he's very stable.

We can look at that story as someone struggling to get their basic needs met, an adult version of "failure to thrive." Maybe more of what is labeled as schizophrenia is from a failure to meet their basic needs than we realize.

Wait a minute. That guy doesn't seem to ever have heard voices. In my simple way of looking at things, he's not crazy, he's just way too passive.

I see what you mean. Let me go back a minute. Remember how I said that our standard description of schizophrenia includes both "positive symptoms"—things like hallucinations and delusions—and "negative symptoms"—things like emotional blunting, lack of energy and motivation, poor self-care, isolation, and "anhedonia" (the inability to enjoy anything)? Some people have more positive symptoms and some have more negative symptoms, but they're all lumped together into schizophrenia. We'll talk more about this in Chapter 12. It turns out that our medications are only really effective against positive symptoms, not the negative ones. They may even make negative symptoms worse. From the point of view of social safety and order, that's not a big problem since passive people are far less frightening and disruptive than delusional people. From a rehabilitation point of view, however, it's an enormous problem, because it turns out that the ability to live independently and work depends a great deal on how severe someone's negative symptoms are, and very little on how severe their positive symptoms are. In other words, people who hear voices have a much better chance of holding a job than people who are disheveled, emotionally blunted, and isolated. This reality is one of the main reasons that our current medication-based treatment system achieves so little rehabilitation and recovery.

If instead of looking at negative symptoms as part of the "schizophrenia syndrome," we look at it from a developmental perspective, they look stunningly like "failure to thrive" infants. Most people don't have a lot of negative symptoms early in their illnesses. Negative symptoms tend to come later, often after the positive symptoms "burn out." But by that point, the person has probably been beaten down a lot. They're likely to have lost most of their connections to other people and their self-identities, and they may be reduced to getting their basic needs met in inadequate and poorly responsive ways. Remember also how Dr. Robins was such a good interviewer because he engaged people enough for them to come alive and their negative symptoms disappeared. The first time Hank visited his brother, he came alive and his negative symptoms went away, but after his needs were ignored again, he became passive again.

"Anhedonia," another fancy clinical word that means unable to experience normal enjoyment from things, is often included as a key "negative symptom," even though many people without schizophrenia, especially depressed or detached people, have it, too. Maybe it's really a symptom of getting beaten down because your basic needs aren't being met, like "learned helplessness," except that the lack of pleasure and rewards has gotten so pervasive that nothing registers as pleasurable anymore. Anhedonia may be the mental equivalent of trying to get a severely deprived infant to eat again after they have given up.

If you walk around an average Board and Care home or homeless encampment, you'll see lots of people sitting passively. From the perspective of this journey, they don't have biologically determined "negative symptoms." They may stir enough to ask if you have a cigarette. They've regressed into a passive state and can't get their needs met well enough to thrive and grow anymore. They're slowly dying like the neglected, dried out plants around them.

Like the successful moral treatment programs that preceded us, successful recovery programs like the Village tend to emphasize helping people meet their basic needs in respectful, humanizing ways. We also emphasize getting people to have and express goals and hopes and wishes and then helping them achieve, enjoy, and celebrate them. We do that both for people who have given up and become hopeless and for people who are irritable, grumpy, and easily frustrated. By doing that, I believe that we're helping people move from chronic deprivation, to meeting their basic needs, some modicum of contentment, and even some pleasure. Many visitors to the Village remarked about how full of life and laughter and even joy it was.

Our members have a chance to regain their balance and function on a higher level.

b. Personal balance

At this level, our basic needs are being met, but we're doing everything on our own. Maybe we never learned how to reach out to others, or our efforts failed and we retreated into solitude and mistrust. If we're going to succeed on our own, we have to have a reasonably coherent sense of who we are, believe in and use our abilities to influence our own situation to be able to get what we need and keep dangers at bay. It can be hard to maintain psychic balance on our own. If we become too fragmented, helpless, frightened, aggressive, or endangered, we can lose our balance.

For many people with schizophrenia at this level, their world can be a very lonely, isolated place. The most common psychotic reaction to losing personal balance is paranoia.

I get paranoid sometimes. Does that mean that I'm doing things too much on my own and don't have relationships to help me stay in balance?

It might, but before I can be sure, I have to really know what you mean by paranoid.

Many people come to me saying that they're "paranoid," but I go further to separate out paranoia from other kinds of fear:

- Paranoia is a very personal fear—fearful that I'm definitely the one who's going to be destroyed, not just the world coming to an end, for instance—but it's often very vague who is doing the attacking beyond an unclear "they" or why they're being targeted. It's also often an incredibly intense feeling, demanding some sort of response.
- There's a difference between paranoia and normal fear. I remember a man who repeatedly came to the Homeless Drop-In Center, reporting that he was scared that the police had him under surveillance and were going to arrest him. I assumed he was paranoid and offered him antipsychotic medications, which he refused, saying they would just slow him down and make him less

aware of what the police were doing. A few months later, I got word that he'd been arrested. It turned out that he'd neglected to mention to me that he'd been selling heroin out of his apartment. The police really did have him under surveillance, and they caught him. I hadn't noticed that his fears were probably too specific to be paranoia—also, he hid essential information from me. (By the way, "just because you're paranoid doesn't mean someone's not out to get you.")

- There's a difference between paranoia and social anxiety. A common presentation of social anxiety is feeling like other people are talking about you. You may imagine that people are laughing at you behind your back, or saying embarrassing things about you, and then stopping when you get within ear shot or denying it when you ask. They may seem to be commenting on your appearance or making fun of you. These feelings are likely built on your insecurities, especially interpersonal insecurities. Those feelings are all different than feeling like people are plotting against you and wanting to hurt, torture, or kill you (usually with paranoia, it's vague as to what the destructive intent is, but it's very personal). Social anxiety can progress to delusional proportions, but it's an interpersonal phenomenon, not a personal destruction.
- There's a difference between paranoia and hypervigilance. Many people have lived in dangerous environments, ranging from having a beating and alcoholic father to spending 20 years in prison, and, in order to survive, developing a highly sensitive danger warning system. For these people, it's the world that's a dangerous place (and those of us who don't know that are naïve), rather than that they've been personally targeted for destruction.
- There's a difference between paranoia and blaming. Many people try to deflect responsibility and blame onto others when something goes wrong. (This can look paranoid, for example, when an elderly person is sure that their misplaced glasses have been stolen.) Also, if someone tries to put the responsibility back on them, they may get defensive and angry and feel like they're being unfairly picked on. The feeling of being at risk of undeserved punishment is not the same as being fearful of being destroyed either.

If you're going to be that specific, I guess I'm not really paranoid after all. I've never analyzed it like that.

But Dolores in Chapter 8 who lived in her car and thought her old apartment manager or her neighbors were having her followed and poisoned is paranoid.

By this selective definition, paranoia is clearly a symptom of losing personal balance and feeling like you're on the verge of personal destruction. The world is closing in, with destructive intent, and you need to do everything you can to fight for yourself to survive. This isn't an issue of not getting basic needs met or problematic relationships or losing connection to God. This is a personal destruction.

Paranoia often occurs in a vicious cycle with anger. The more paranoid someone gets, the more resentful and the angrier they get, and the more likely they are to resort to violence to protect themselves. This raw aggression may, in itself, be frightening and needs to be blamed on someone else, and gets projected outward, feeding the paranoia even more. The more the person gets angry and tries to fight, the more they're persecuted. (Notice how Nathan, at the beginning of this chapter managed to escape this vicious cycle by accepting the possibility of destruction, instead of fighting it, but that's a rare reaction.) Voices often escalate both sides of this vicious cycle, urging aggression and violence, on the one hand, while warning of pervasive dangers, on the other hand.

Paranoia of this type can be sexualized as well. This is the selfish, aggressive, possessive kind of sex that leads into rape, not a loving or even relationship-based sex. I've met several elderly women, who lived alone and became more and more insecure, and then, they started having delusions that someone was coming in at night and "sexually violating" or "sexually assaulting" them. For men, this can be expressed as the delusion that they're being homosexually sodomized. Freud noticed a connection between paranoia and homosexual delusions and that fed into one of his convoluted theories about the casualty of homosexuality. In my view, these delusions aren't expressions of repressed homosexuality. They are expressions of fears of personal violation and destruction—more aggressive than sexual. Occasionally, I've seen positive, caring actions or words become misinterpreted by a very paranoid person as the first steps of a sexual attack, causing them to react very defensively.

So, how do you help someone like that?

Creating and sustaining a relationship with someone who is paranoid is one of the most difficult challenges in mental health. Most of the time we fail, and the person drops out of all contact with us. Nonetheless, it's essential to have a relationship if we're going to be helpful. Many people who are paranoid, in my focused sense of the word, also have some of the other kinds of "paranoia." They can be socially anxious, or fearful, or blaming, too. All of that makes it harder to connect with them (but also gives us some other things we can try to improve). Medications, which may or may not be effective with these people, are hard to begin or maintain without a strong relationship. Even more importantly, creating relationships have a chance of helping the person move up to a more interpersonal level where it may be easier for them to maintain their balance, instead of them continuing to "go it alone."

The two biggest relationship pitfalls in dealing with paranoia are as follows: 1) feeding into the vicious cycle of anger and paranoia by confronting them and increasing their defensiveness and 2) getting incorporated into their paranoid delusions by trying to take over things for them, which can feel like we're challenging their independence and self-determination.

Remember Reggie, the man at the beginning of Chapter 9, who was incarcerated for lighting fires in mailboxes? He'd just lost the only relationship he'd had in many years with Robbyn, the homeless outreach worker, and was likely to return to his long-term isolation. The sheriff's plan, "I think he's faking and I'm not going to let him get away with this," is likely to unintentionally land him in both pitfalls and dramatically worsen Reggie's condition. He'll frighten and anger Reggie while he's also breaking him apart. The sheriff will probably never be aware of the harm he's doing.

Here are some practical strategies I've learned to try to proactively avoid those "pitfalls":

- When I talk with someone who's paranoid, I don't face my chair toward them; so, I'm not immediately in direct confrontation with

them. I sit almost side-by-side with them; so, we're allied facing the world together.
- I also sit fairly far away from them to avoid being invasive. (I have extra chairs in the office, so they can choose to sit further away, instead of in the usual chair next to my desk.) I avoid leaning forward or being too piercing with my questions.
- Sometimes, I'll even make a playful offer to trade chairs to decrease the sense of my power over them, giving them my chair at the desk. Some people take me up on the offer, and I go with it.
- I'll sometimes leave the office and walk outside with them, so they don't feel like I have them on my home court where I have all the power (also, it's somewhat safer to be out of a small office as long as other people are around to call out to).
- I'll make it a point to talk about things that they're comfortable with and subjects in which they can feel like experts, instead of what's wrong with them.
- I'll openly explore their fears, rather than disparaging them by calling them paranoid or delusional.
- I'm especially interested in hearing about how they've dealt with this terrible persecution so far. What have they figured out to increase their safety and security, if anything? Do they react with anger, and does that make it better or feed into a vicious cycle?
- I'm also interested in the role of voices, if they have any, in this. Are the voices helpful, essential, misleading, or even part of the persecution (for instance, like implanted devices that won't let them sleep)?

Tyrone was one of the Village's first members. He started out by telling us that the Long Beach Police Department was following him wherever he went. He couldn't leave his apartment to do his laundry or go to the doctor's office or get a hamburger or anything without a police car appearing within a few minutes. They'd been doing that for years. (Strangely enough, that seemed to be more or less true when we did anything with him in the neighborhood. Maybe it's just because he's a tall, somewhat disheveled Black man walking around in a high crime neighborhood with a large police presence. Who knows?) Also, whenever he went anywhere, they raised the prices just to "punk him." He knew a hamburger really costs 50 cents and a load of laundry is really 25 cents. They just raise the prices when he comes in, so he'll always be broke.

It took me a while to figure out he lived in a world without inflation and that every price was fixed at the levels they were at 20 years ago when he first came to Long Beach. Even his Section 8 subsidized rent was too high by his evaluation.

"Where did you come to Long Beach from?"

"I came from Alabama when my aunt died. I was born in Mississippi, but when my mother died when I was 3, I was sent to Alabama to live with my aunt. I stayed there until she died, too, when I was 19, and I decided to see what California was like. I took a Greyhound bus."

"So, you were totally alone and on your own when you first came here."

"I still am. I learned you can't trust anyone."

"I assume you learned that the hard way, at the school of hard knocks."

"You want to see the scars?" he pointed to his arm. "Here's where I was stabbed when I first got here." He pulled up his pant leg, "And here's where I was shot." He lifted his shirt, "This was another stabbing. That's all from being jumped. And now, I've got the police after me, too."

He also had complaints about his health. "I have sarcoidosis that I'm getting treatment for from a specialist." *Although I could I barely remember what sarcoidosis is, except that it was often thrown into test questions in medical school along with lupus, since it could cause a lot of different symptoms, a long-lost medical school fact resurfaced.* "Do you have the lines on your fingernails?"

He looked at me with a smidgen of appreciation, nodded, and held out his hands, "Yes, I do." *I acted like I knew what I was looking at, to keep the few credibility points I'd gotten.*

Journeys Beyond the Frontier | 267

"But that's not what's wrong with me. Because of the sarcoid, my lungs can't handle cigarette smoke, and there are people smoking everywhere I go."

"Smoke bothers me, too. How do you avoid it?"

"I can't. People follow me wherever I go just to blow smoke on me. I'm getting fed up with it. Also, they poison my food."

"Who poisons your food?"

"I can't ever catch them at it to stop them, and since the police are in on it, too, I couldn't get them arrested even if I did catch them." I made a mental note not to offer him any food.

"I notice you're taking some Navane. What do you take that for?"

"All of this gets to my nerves, and it's hard to relax. I'm always on edge, and it's hard to sleep. Taking Navane helps me with that, but it has to be the pink ones."

"I think I can arrange that."

I warned the team nurse, Joyce, that Tyrone was very paranoid and could be dangerous, so she shouldn't do things with him by herself until we really get to know him.

I noticed he played a lot of pool at the Village; so, I decided to meet with him and play pool, instead of talk in my office, even though I'm a bad pool player, saying, "I could use some pointers." To be frank, he did improve my game over the next 6 months. He became comfortable with me in the process and began to think of me as a friend.

"You look like you've lost some weight. Are you getting enough to eat?"

"Not really. I just had to throw out a hamburger I bought because it was poisoned."

"So, how do you get food that isn't poisoned?"

"You want to know the best way to avoid being poisoned?"

"Sure. How do you do it?"

> "First, you get on a bus and go to a store they're not expecting you to go to. Then, you go in the frozen food section and go through the frozen peas and grab one of the bags near the bottom, not the top one."
>
> "Why peas?"
>
> "Because peas are very hard to poison. You'd have to inject the poison with a small needle into each one individually. So, there's a good chance they're safe."
>
> "Good to know in case someone tries to poison me."
>
> Joyce came up to me one day, "I don't get why you thought Tyrone was dangerous. You don't usually give that warning; so, I took it seriously, but he's a total gentleman. I think he'd sooner sacrifice himself to protect me than hurt me."
>
> "You know, I think you're right. I was worried at first about him just because of the paranoia, but we're both on his good side, and even though he's paranoid, he's not aggressive. Not everyone who's paranoid is, but it was worth being a little cautious to start with."
>
> The three of us were close for a long time. Tyrone never stopped thinking he was being cheated and poisoned and followed, but he did a lot of fun things with us. Joyce even took him to a local jazz festival. He always treated us well, even when he was clearly suffering.

I got an elusive compliment that made my often futile efforts seem worthwhile one day, when one of our members who struggled with paranoia every day told another staff, "I can't quite get myself to be paranoid of Dr. Mark, even though the voices keep telling me to, because I like him so much."

Say, doc, if you, with all your experience and fancy techniques, often fail to connect with people who are paranoid, how are the rest of us, especially family members, supposed to be able to do it?

Honestly, it's one of the hardest things to do in the whole guide, and one of the most important. This might be depressing, but let me spend some more time on it, so that you get a fuller picture. At least, if you understand what's going on and what the pitfalls are, you'll have a chance.

Many people first experience psychosis during their late teens, when they are still developing their ability to connect to other people and have meaningful relationships. For some of them, their failure to move on to the next level—balancing within relationships—precedes their overt psychosis and, for some, their tenuous foothold in interpersonal relationships falls apart because of their psychosis.

A common scenario has a vulnerable person who is experiencing their first psychotic symptoms being traumatized by their first hospital treatment and then being returned to their families—who are quite understandably frightened, overwhelmed, and confused. While the family focuses their efforts on understanding the diagnosis and treatment options, making sure their adolescent child takes their medications and follows their doctor's orders, and trying to track symptoms and side effects, too often the affected child drifts into their own world and regresses developmentally. Meanwhile, friends, lovers, fellow students, and coworkers may hang in for a while, but they tend to disappear. Families are likely to become more watchful and protective. The adolescent's autonomy decreases. They may cling to what's left of their autonomy with further withdrawal, refusing their medications, altering their wake–sleep cycles to be up all night and asleep all day, building a wall of irritability, using drugs, or moving further into an altered reality, but in their impaired condition, they're probably not in any shape to make it on their own. They deteriorate further, lose their balance, and get more paranoid and aggressive, especially targeting their family, likely the only people left in their world. This can become an extremely burdensome and frustrating downward cycle. Most violent acts by people with schizophrenia are targeted at their families, especially mothers, within this sort of scenario.

As this cycle progresses, families often get frustrated that the hospitals won't take their child back until something dangerous has happened. They get frustrated that their child is released before they're well (or rebalanced) again; so, the process starts up again. They also often get increasingly frightened, convinced that "someone is going to die next time." The recommendation to "call the police if you're in danger" leads to incarceration and further anger, resentment, and deterioration. By now, everyone says they're powerless and blames the incurable illness or the person's noncompliance. (By the way, one of the reasons that the Finnish Open Dialogue model I mentioned in Chapter 3 is appealing is because it attempts to directly target and strengthen the web of relationships around the person with psychosis to avoid this common scenario. Rarely in our common practice is the focus placed on sustaining the person's web of relationships and their autonomy.)

I'm going to attempt to tell this next story as much as possible from Randy's point of view, from "the back of the hand," to try to give you a sense of what paranoia is like for the people who are dealing with it.

> *Randy described his childhood in Pennsylvania as "fine" and denied any history of abuse or violence. Randy did, however, describe his father as "disaffected and antisocial," and his mother as "OCD and psychologically affected." He also said that his mother has become increasingly withdrawn and less comfortable in public settings as she gets older.*
>
> *He said that he was socially popular throughout elementary school, with his social problems beginning in junior high when other kids started bullying him. He said he coped "by enduring it" and socially isolating himself. He "skipped out of high school for the vocational track" and moved to California, but he missed academics; so, a few years later, he went to community college majoring in Philosophy, where he says he was a victim of harassment and persecution by his peers and professors throughout his academic career. He dates the beginning of his systematic persecution to his writing a thesis on media and ethics, which he felt drew the anger of his professor who felt exposed and the larger philosophy field. He says he was not allowed to graduate and was put on a secret list to be targeted for Internet harassment. He became obsessed with the phenomenon of Internet stalking and believes himself to be one of a number of people whose lives have been mercilessly ruined by this phenomenon. His whole life fell apart, and he tried returning home to his parents.*

Randy says his relationship with his family is strained. "My family is actively "trying to break me—make me think I'm crazy." He believes that after he returned home, his mother "put something in my food." An argument ensued that resulted in Brett's arrest for domestic violence, even though "only words had been exchanged. It was a set up." He said he was in county lockup for 48 hours. He was forced into 3-month anger management by the court Randy felt had been illegally influenced: "The court situation didn't seem legal. My dad had someone who worked in the Mental Health Board there. My mom had her NAMI buddies there. She's obsessing over it. She's not a doctor. She doesn't know what she's talking about." At some point, he said that his mother "started writing to the anger management staff that I was suicidal. All I'd said was, 'If you don't stop harassing me, I'm going to kill myself.'"

He describes having several arguments with his family that consisted of his parents being "manipulative and abusive" over the phone. "They were accusing me of threatening them—and I was, because they weren't being supportive." "My parents didn't believe I had social problems. They think I have a mental problem and I don't have one; so, I've tried to stay away from them."

Randy also describes another incident in which he was left home alone for a short period of time, during which he took his parents' car and drove to the emergency room with a "whole bag of meds." "I was prescribed so many meds: Seroquel, Xanax, Lunesta, Klonopin, Geodon—That was the last straw. I had gray vision, balance problems, it scared the shit out of me. I stopped taking everything; so, I went on a Klonopin withdrawal and went to the emergency room. Then, my parents came in, saying I was suicidal; so, I got stuck in the hospital again."

That time, his parents got him on court-ordered every 2-week antipsychotic injections. That didn't seem to help either, and it was always a fight to get him to the clinic to receive the shots. When the year-long court order expired, he left again for Los Angeles. I don't think that his family knew that the outcome of getting him forcibly medicated was going to lead to a permanent separation a year later. But what were their alternatives?

Randy was referred to the Village by a friend of the family and barely agreed to see us. He was homeless and had no money and was miserable. He said he was unable to work because any time he tried to apply for a job, the Internet stalking group would find out and spread rumors and ruin it for him. The same thing would happen if he tried to date a girl. They were able to track him with an intricate system of devices implanted into street signs, billboards, and traffic lights. They could alert each other by sending coded messages that after a while, he started learning to decode, but he still couldn't make them stop. Also, they would put chemicals into the air, his food, medication, clothes, etc. that progressively poisoned him and gave him a chemical sensitivity syndrome, which plagues him.

Randy wouldn't agree to any mental health treatment or apply for Social Security because then no one would ever believe him in his efforts to catch and bring to justice his persecutors. We put him in a Safe Haven program that uses HUD funds to provide temporary shelter for a year in an apartment with a case manager, hoping that over the course of a year, he would trust us enough to accept mental health treatment and Social Security. Instead, it took 4 years for him to agree to apply for Social Security for his "chemical sensitivity." He only agreed to occasional Ativan to calm down and Ambien to sleep but never any antipsychotics.

He kept the apartment (because we kept paying for it), but he profoundly altered it. He taped all the doors and windows shut to keep outside chemicals out. He refused any air conditioning or heat to keep gas from being pumped in. He washed his own clothes by hand in his room because he didn't trust laundromats and then hung them to dry, creating a damp, mildew-infested apartment with mold growing around it. He had a cat whose behavior he used as a criterion to judge the quality of the air, and if the cat seems upset or poisoned, he bleaches everything, including the cat. It wasn't a happy cat.

"My parents don't call me, I call them. They only give me financial support if I see counselors and get help. I get angry about it." Randy does not agree with those conditions because he does not believe he needs mental health services, but he accepted them anyway, fearful of losing a relationship with his mother. Randy also reported having had a long-term friend that he lost because "they got to her and turned her against" him. Randy admits that the only people he interacts with now are "the people who are paid to talk to me." He often says that his social life consists only of meeting with Village staff. Other than that, he has no one to interact with.

Randy reports being a victim of various forms of harassment, including verbal, sexual, and social. "People on the street yell things to upset me. Like yesterday, someone yelled, 'Your mother is a sexual terrorist.' Someone would only say something like that to hurt me, knowing that she is the only person I have a relationship with." Because of this constant verbal harassment, Randy has learned that he either has to watch TV or, when outside of his apartment, listen to music on his headphones to get from place to place to "drown out all the harassment."

He has particular problems relating to women. He thinks that a number of women he comes into contact with are coming on to him and being seductive and saying things to him, and then, as he starts to get aroused, they make fun of him and humiliate him. He is often in an aroused, aggravated state as a result.

Because of Internet and social harassment, Randy also says he suffers from a physical health condition. "Since I first arrived in California, I started developing a health problem that's never been adequately diagnosed: chemical sensitivity." He experiences symptoms such as "muscle and joint soreness, disorientation, fluctuating blood pressure, and stress and makes me want to get away. People use this information against me. I don't tell them my problem, but they seem to know. They wear the chemicals on their person and say, 'I'll put some stuff on me and then fight you.' Total strangers tell me this on public transit! When I go to the gym just to do yoga, I get muscle and joint pain for days after that happens." Randy can unexpectedly feel these symptoms at any given point and time, and once he does, he has to "immediately leave the environment."

Randy tried to work through the Village's job development program at our onsite Deli but had "an allergic reaction to the chemicals in the atmosphere" and walked off the job back to his apartment. These same allergies had interfered with his ability to maintain housing in the past. He would constantly rewash his roommate's clothing, against his roommate's consent, in order to get rid of the chemicals that would cause him to have an allergic reaction. He says that the last time he was hospitalized, 6 years ago was because of a severe allergic reaction, "People were using something in the apartment that they knew was intentionally causing a problem for me."

His parents called me once, concerned about how Randy was doing since he sounded even more aggressive than usual. I wondered if Randy wouldn't be better returning to his hometown. His father said, "He's allowed to come visit us, like for Christmas or something like that, but he can't stay in the house. He's just so unpleasant and aggressive. It always ends up with a fight. It's like having a dog pee around the house to mark his territory." After they hung up, I thought that he's clearly had enough of Randy. It's hard to blame him, though, after all that Randy put them through.

> *We finally got Randy to agree to apply for SSI for "chemical sensitivity." I turned in an additional confidential report saying he really had schizophrenia with a special alert warning them not to share it with Randy because he would feel betrayed by us and it could psychologically harm him. They gave him a copy anyway and he got so angry, he dropped out of our program permanently and abandoned the apartment. The last I heard he was homeless in Van Nuys.*

There's no doubt that helping people at this level tends to be quite difficult. Notice, however, how many of Randy's psychotic symptoms are actually extreme versions of understandable problems getting along with others at this low developmental level. He's trying to be self-reliant and doesn't see himself from other people's perspectives; so, he isolates and he's always sure he's right and everyone else is wrong. He has trouble trusting other people, refuses well-intentioned help, and is traumatized and further distanced by coercive help.

Paranoia isn't the only symptom people have who have lost their balance on a personal level. They can also feel like they are profoundly dangerous, capable of destroying the entire world or breaking it into pieces. These sorts of feelings develop from feeling like their minds are going to explode, rather than feeling like they're under attack—two sides of the same coin.

> *Elyn Saks is a highly accomplished woman by anyone's standards. She graduated top of her class at Vanderbilt, received a Master's degree from Oxford, and a Law Degree from Yale. She's a fully trained psychoanalyst and a Macarthur "genius award" winner. She's currently Associate Dean and Orrin B. Evans Professor of Law, Psychology, and Psychiatry and Behavioral Sciences at the University of Southern California Gould Law School. The fact that she's done all of this while living with schizophrenia makes it all the more remarkable.*
>
> *I won't repeat her story here, since you should read her autobiographical book, "The Center Cannot Hold: My Journey Through Madness," except to tell you that she's had really severe symptoms, including paranoia, delusions that she*

was destroying the world, and multiple hallucinations—all severe enough to require repeated, lengthy hospitalizations during her education. She describes her erratic behavior, her incoherent speech, her demons, and especially her violent delusions graphically. You can also get a taste of her remarkable journey by watching her TED talk.

It's only because she's bravely shared her psychosis with us that we can try to learn from her example at all. It seems to me that what she's describing when she says that she believed that she'd killed thousands of people, that she was God, and that she had been tortured and cut up into little pieces is a severe, long-standing psychosis from losing her personal balance. That's why I've put her journey in this part of my guidebook.

She is doing ongoing research on people with schizophrenia who, like her, are very successful and responsible. We need to understand how they're doing it and what we've done to help them succeed. Each of them has a different story to tell.

She believes that she's succeeded for three reasons:

1) *Excellent treatment*—both ongoing psychoanalysis for years and medications. The passages where she describes how her psychoanalyst shared her nightmarish world, so she wouldn't be alone and could recover, are truly inspiring. The passages where she tries again and again to get off medications but becomes psychotic again are heartbreaking. The passages where she describes being forcibly restrained even though she never did anything violent are brutal and agonizing—and ultimately seem so unnecessary.

2) *Her family and friends* who bring meaning, depth, and helped her navigate her symptoms. I think they also stopped her, along with the meds, from drifting back into a place where she'd have to balance herself. Along with her psychoanalysts, they've been a web of relationships she can be psychologically balanced within. The first time I ever heard her tell her story, at a psychiatry conference, I went up afterward and said, "I wanted to let you know that I thought your speech was quite good, but what's really amazing are the multimedia slides that your husband created to accompany

your story. Not only must he really understand what you've been through to create them, he has the skill and artistry to put it together visually, so we can all experience some of what you went through, too." She said, "I'll let him know. He'll think that's funny, that you liked his slides better than my lecture." I'm still convinced he's been a special companion for her on her journey.

3) An enormously supportive workplace at USC. I've been to several excellent conferences she's put together there and had lunch there with her one afternoon. As Joseph in the previous chapter would put it, she's found her niche. The work she does, and several academic books she's written, focus around the topic of decision-making and severe mental illness. This is precisely the key issue for people losing their balance at this stage. How do we guide them and even protect them at times, without violating their self-determination and dehumanizing them? We're far too sloppy, thoughtless, and insensitive when we act coercively. Elyn is helping to show us how we can do better.

No matter how difficult it is to connect with people on this level, having someone in their lives can make an enormous difference. Elyn Saks probably never finishes her education without her friends reaching out to her even though she's a genius. Nathan, who I began this chapter with, probably doesn't recover without his mother. Dolores back in Chapter 8 doesn't get out of jail without her connection with her case worker, Joanne. Even when it's frustrating, they need us. If they can regain their balance and climb up to the next level, they can recover like Elyn and Nathan did.

c. Interpersonal balance

Most of the time, the majority of us function at the level of Interpersonal balance. We maintain our psychic stability by balancing an array of relationships. We know we need other people and we actively work on our relationships. We regularly reassess the quality of these relationships: Are our relationships draining or supportive? Are we giving more than we're getting? Are we more in love with them than they are with us? Do we really know them, or are they "playing us" to take advantage of us? Are we feeling guilty? Helpless? Abused? Unappreciated? Avoidant? We shuffle our relationships and our commitments hoping to improve things for ourselves.

In our earlier journeys, we focused on how negative events and relationships can lead to psychosis. This journey is more about how we manage our relationships, especially the difficult ones, can contribute toward our loss of balance and can precipitate becoming psychotic.

Broadly speaking, we tend to manage our relationships in three distinct, but interacting, ways:

- Thinking: We think about ourselves, our relationships, and our lives, sometimes more rationally and sometimes less, sometimes more orderly and sometimes less. Cognitive Behavioral Therapies and Problem-Solving Therapies, which are very popular at present, focus on improving our overt thinking processes.
- Imagining: We create and imaginatively experience ourselves in situations, both past and present, including sensations and emotions. These internal experiences can be distressing—for example, with flashbacks of traumatic memories, or out-of-control ruminations, or anticipatory anxiety—or very positive and useful—for example, relaxation visualization techniques, pleasant daydreams, or even purposeful imaginative practice, as utilized by some musicians and public speakers. Psychoanalysis used to focus on creating an imaginary relationship with the analyst by depriving the client of a "real relationship" with the analyst in order for people to understand the power and the content of their imaginary relationships and even healing them "within the transference regression." Guided Imagery tends to work on this level.
- Behaving: We actively talk, move around, and interact with other people and our environment in the present (the past and the future can impact our actions, for example, replaying old traumatic patterns, but we can only actually act in the present). Behavioral Therapies and Communication Skills Trainings, like Non-Violent Communication, impact this level. Role Playing in therapy tries to move thinking and imagining into behaving. Most "advice" we receive is recommending changes in our actions.

I believe that most people who lose the ability to maintain their relationship balance and become psychotic are struggling to control their imagining function.

Before I came to the Village, I vaguely remember working with a woman who was somewhat shy, somewhat overweight, not very attractive, and who lacked self-confidence. She was in her 30s and lived with her elderly parents. What I do remember well is that she had an imaginary boyfriend (although I don't remember how I knew that he was imaginary, since she thought he was real). She would come to my medication visits, repeatedly complaining about how badly he'd treated her: He didn't like the dress she was wearing and made her change clothes over and over. He would promise to be someplace and then not show up. He would belittle her and threaten to break up with her. She was in terrible distress because of him almost all the time.

Frustrated, I remember telling a co-worker about her, "If she's going to have an imaginary boyfriend, at least she should be able to have a good one. She's stuck with this terrible one. I don't even know how she could break up with an imaginary boyfriend."

Now, I would say that she had to have a mean boyfriend because her self-identity and her relationships didn't allow the possibility of her being loved and her being lovable, and I would work with her on broadening her self-identity to expand her imagination of her possible relationships.

Imagining is probably the most important, and problematic, function in our relationship balance even if we're not psychotic. In most relationships, we spend more time interacting with people in our imaginations than we do in our actions. In any relationship, there are four people involved: Me and my imagination of who you are, and you and your imagination of who I am. Most people aren't aware of this and assume that they are interacting with the actual other person and not their imagination of the other person, thereby resulting in many misunderstandings and hurtful feelings.

Being in love is probably the ultimate of this phenomenon. Our imaginations of our loved one become all-consuming and incredibly real. I had a supervisor who would say, "Love is psychosis." Have you ever tried to get someone to see the flaws in their beloved that everyone else can see, except them? It's basically impossible. They're pretty much "delusional." If we're fortunate when we're in love, the experience is reciprocated and the other person is also entranced by their imagination of us. Most of us are familiar with the sensation of "falling out of love," realizing we've never seen the other person as they really are. Commonly, we then feel betrayed, shamed, or humiliated. Sometimes, the other two levels remain: We still think fondly of the person and behave considerately toward them, although the imagined eternal loving bond has melted away. "I still love him, but I'm not in love with him anymore." The relationship has lost its pervasive existence on the imagination level.

What we rarely appreciate is how often we have negative imaginations of other people, including our loved ones. The person who once was imagined to be so wonderful, after that's been punctured by some hurt or betrayal, or even just the reality of who they are, may take on a new negative identity in our imagination. This can fuel considerable hatred in breakups and divorces. But it's not just disappointment-driven negativity. Some of us carry around negative expectations and imaginings about relationships for various reasons, including our beliefs and imaginings about ourselves. For example, our own insecurities may lead us to imagine that our partner is always thinking negatively about us, criticizing us to their friends, and looking for someone to replace us. These beliefs can continue to fester until we're filled with jealous imaginings. Then, we feel angry and betrayed, and we treat our partners badly even though it's our imaginations of them that we're angry with, not their actual selves.

My point in this relationship discussion, besides giving you free marital advice, is that all of us are on a continuum with delusional relationships all the time. There's no clear demarcation between "ideas of reference" (other people's actions and events are meant for us), like, "She's sending out signals to me" or "The restaurant had a last-minute reservation cancellation because this relationship was meant to be" and "delusions" like "Alicia Keyes put lyrics in her album just for me to tell me that she wants to be with me. When I didn't figure them out correctly, she figured out how to talk to me in my head. Sometimes, she even comes in secret to see me." or on the negative side, between "I'm getting the same kind of bad feeling I got in my last relationship. I'm pretty sure she's losing interest." and "I can tell by the number of letters in the street signs that he's sending messages to let them know I'm coming, so they'll poison my food."

People may have struggles in how they think about relationships and how they behave, too, not just in their imagining of relationships and their psychosis. They may need to work on skills in all three areas, not just reducing their psychosis. Programs should include services in all three areas tailoring them to what each person needs. For example, the woman with the mean imaginary boyfriend might benefit from a Women's Group that focuses on positive thinking in relationships and a social group that goes out dancing in addition to working directly on her imaginations of herself and her relationships.

Psychosis emerges at this stage when our relationships aren't working well enough for us to sustain our balance. Different stages of life can bring different challenges to deal with.

Common risky times in life include the following:

- Some children develop imaginary friends and narratives either when they're isolated or when they don't really understand what they're dealing with around them.
- The interpersonal challenges of adolescence are particularly likely to create crisis.
- Massive stressful life changes, like immigration, having children taken away, homelessness, or becoming physically disabled, can be destabilizing.
- Other life developmental stages—like having children, mid-life crisis, empty nest, retirement, or aging and multiple losses with isolation and loneliness—can be too difficult to negotiate and adapt to.

Notice how Becky "loses her balance" in different ways at several points of her life, as she increasingly tries to cope overusing her imagination:

> I had been warned to be careful with Becky before I met with her, "She doesn't like men; so, I don't know if she'll trust you enough to talk with you. She can get very irritable or she can just clam up and not say anything."
>
> When Becky came into the office, she wouldn't sit in the chair by my desk. (Later, she said that's because she's

obsessively organized, and my desk is a mess; so, she couldn't handle being near it or looking at it.) She was, however, attracted by a set of magnetic words on a cabinet that are designed to play with and be put together to make poems or small messages. (In my defense, if the office is going to have enough strange things like that laying around to connect to people, it's going to be a mess ... Becky didn't buy that explanation either.) She spent most of the session playing with the words, moving them around, with her back turned toward me, but also answering my questions. It seemed that if she could keep herself distracted and didn't have to look at me, she could keep from getting too anxious and still interact with me.

Since she was facing away from me, I couldn't see her emotional reactions to these remembrances.

Becky told me that when she was born, both of her parents were in their teens. They moved around a lot since her father was in the military, including to Texas, Germany, and Alaska. Becky had substantial racial issues growing up being the only Black girl in several settings. She has an early childhood memory of sitting by herself, looking through a fence at the White kids playing, wiping off her tears with her sleeve, so they wouldn't see them. She says she was a willful child and was on restriction a lot as a child for misbehavior. She was somewhat aggressive in school and didn't do well even though she was smart. Because of the moves, she had to make new friends often. Beginning at age 5, she started talking with imaginary friends and hearing voices that continue to be with her when she's lonely. She also escaped into reading a lot and tended to have a lot of magical thinking, believing things could happen, both good and bad, just because of what she was thinking. In school, she had trouble focusing. Nonetheless, she completed high school, and even took some courses at a community college. She says she was close to her father until he died while she was in her teens, but had an up-and-

down relationship with her mother, who helped her out at times and avoided her at other times.

Becky had her first child at 20 but says she didn't feel like she could be a mother; so, her mother cared for her son and took him to Germany with her. She's regretted that decision ever since. In her early 20s, her second son was born and Becky did keep him and has been very close to him over the years (that father is in prison). Becky worked at Wendy's for about 10 years while raising that son.

She got married at 25 to a man who was 35, and they had two more kids together, but gradually, their relationship fell apart. She felt mistreated by him and pressured to have sex when she didn't want to. He didn't like her going out with her friends. He made promises to her and didn't follow through. Overall, she feels that her husband traumatized her and took her innocence. Since then, she's more easily fed up with people, gets impatient, feels like the world is unjust and she's gotten a bad deal, and lashes out as a result. When she's most upset, her voices feed into her negativity about others. They urge her to be aggressive or to leave people. She realizes that makes her less desirable to be around and hard to hold a job. She also realizes that just walking away and escaping and isolating isn't getting her anywhere either, and she's fed up with not having anything. She fantasizes about going back to how she was when she was young, before she met him.

They got divorced, and he kept their two kids. She was ordered to give him $150 per month in child support payments from her Wendy's paycheck. She couldn't survive as a single parent of her remaining son, pay her rent, or hold on to her job.

When I met her, Becky had been homeless about 5 years and unable to work. Over the last couple years, she'd gotten more and more depressed and withdrawn, hiding behind dark glasses, and avoiding people. She stopped reading to escape and lost touch with her voices of imaginary friends, and she misses them. She feels irritable and defensive, especially around men, almost all the time. She gets into serious arguments with strangers she passes on the street. Nonetheless, out of desperation, she got married to a homeless man, hoping he would take care of her and they could get subsidized housing together, but it didn't work. They lived in his car together which was very hard for her since she is obsessively organized and he hoards things. She didn't really want to sleep deeply in the car and keeps lookout all night for police lights. She's gotten more hypervigilant over time. She can't tell if she's imagining people watching them or if it's real. Her husband handles their money. She doesn't really know what he does to get money since he lost his welfare benefits and food stamps.

As Becky's kids have grown up, bouncing around between various homes, they resent her for being a bad mother. Her youngest daughter, who had spent some time with Becky's first husband, some with her grandmother, and most recently in foster care is now 16 years old and is aggressive and disrespectful to Becky. She had a baby a few months ago, and when Becky came to see her first grandchild and tried to give her daughter advice and support, her daughter became enraged. The two of them escalated into a physical fight in the hospital obstetrics ward. Becky was arrested and jailed for 34 days and sentenced to 5 years of probation, including being referred to the Village program. There's a restraining order keeping Becky away from her daughter and granddaughter (her daughter went to a DCFS placement for teenage foster mothers with their infants).

As I started to get to know her, the most striking thing was how little who she was matched this story. She's an impressively smart, sensitive person. She understands a lot about relationships and her role in her problems. She can often see other people's perspectives. She's creative and fun, *generous and helpful. Sometimes, she wonders what her life would've been like if she'd had a stable family and gone to college. So do I.*

Our staff started interacting with that potential person, instead of with the aggressive, overwhelmed failure. At first, she tended to feel safer with the staff than the other members. We gave her a clerical job in our team area, copying and printing things for us. We gave her and another member money to go to the 99 Cents Only Store to get holiday decorations for our team area. She sat in on interviews for new staff and was very insightful and helpful. She was part of a photography project where a professional photographer took pictures of people in our community, including our members and staff, that really captured each person's essence. Most of the members had never had a real photograph of themselves. She started mentoring the newer members and reconnecting in more positive ways to her scattered family. She was even able to interact with her daughter on Facebook and take pride in the grandbaby's pictures.

We also helped with the practicalities. We helped her get on Social Security disability and get a Section 8 subsidized apartment for her and her husband, so they didn't have to live in the car anymore.

I've tried to get her to take low-dose risperidone to decrease her irritability and be able to sleep. When she took it, she got into far less arguments with her husband and everyone else around. The aggressive voices went away. As her life improved, she'd stop the medicine, and then restart it when she'd start to isolate and get irritable again and the voices returned. As her depression lifted and she had new friends and roles, she didn't miss her imaginary friends and the voices as much. Nonetheless, she still tends to do better with medicine than without it.

We'd expect that the symptoms of losing our relationship balance would be relationship-based symptoms. Classically (in the 1950s), these were described as follows: thought insertion (where it feels like other people are putting thoughts in our heads), thought withdrawal (where it feels like people are taking thoughts out of our heads), and thought broadcasting (where other people can hear our thoughts), along with having other people read our minds or being able to read their minds, and knowing what someone else is going to do or being able to psychically control them, etc. But if we rely on checklists of symptoms like these, we're likely to miss the mark. Each person's "interpersonal psychosis" symptoms are every bit as individual as their interpersonal relationships. Those checklists are the equivalent of evaluating your relationship using the quizzes in the magazines at the grocery store checkout line.

Losing control of imagining looks different, depending on what's in the person's imagination, good and bad. The symptoms any given person has will depend both on the culture of relationships around them For example, when I visited Communist China in the 1980s, many patients had delusions that the government was spying on them, hiring their families to monitor them and even torture them—all of which seemed to be common activities of their government. Back at home, I met a woman from New Orleans who was suffering because a woman who wanted to steal her husband from her had put a voodoo curse on her that had been affecting her ever since. Believing that implants are put into your body or brain to track you or send messages is common in American society with so much digital tracking around us. Nonetheless, the most common negative imagining in Downtown Long Beach, in Becky's world, continues to be the tried-and-true, "He was looking at me funny like he was going to mess with me. I'm not going to let him punk me. My voices warn me who to watch out for and tell me when to attack." It's a place with far more relationship-based violence than any other kind of violence.

> *A classic description of the process of progressively more bizarre imaginative ruminations leading to increasing detachment from reality and psychosis can be found in Franz Kafka's novel, "The Trial." It's revealing to be inside the head of the protagonist, Joseph K., as he experiences all of his problems coming from outside forces and relationship*

misunderstandings, leading relentlessly to a progressive loss of his external moorings. We can join him and see the novel as a reasonable, allegorical reaction to the culture and events in Prague at the time, or we can see the novel as a description of psychosis from the inside focusing on the role his imagination has in progressively distorting the challenging reality around him. Like many people, the narrator never entertains the notion that he has created his own nightmare. He is too overwhelmed and engrossed in the details of his strange experiences to get any perspective. Indeed, all of Kafka's novels have this claustrophobic feeling of being trapped within these worlds, without any external place to stand to gain perspective or external person to relate to. My guess is that Kafka himself had to have been psychotic to have portrayed in so much detail these "imagination-induced relationship–imbalance" journeys of psychosis.

I would further guess that the oft-discussed link between creativity and madness has some of its roots in this particular type of psychosis journey. It seems likely to me that people who have impressive abilities to imagine—whether they imagine never built electromagnetic machines in "mind experiments" like Nikola Tesla or turning into a giant cockroach like Kafka—are at risk of overly imagining their relationships and clashing with the actual other people they're trying to relate to, eventually losing their balance entirely. If they, as many people do, respond to their own distress by blaming those around them, and increasingly feel misunderstood, and even persecuted, they're likely to regress and try to make it on their own and lose their personal balance, too, ending up paranoid and isolated.

When people start experiencing extraordinary things—like being able to make a couple at a bus stop start arguing with each other or making an attractive girl look at you just by using your thoughts, as one young man I knew did, or like feeling everyone's emotions as they walked by them down the street, as a young woman I knew did—they're likely to spend more and more time thinking about these experiences, trying to figure out what's going on, changing their behavior to see if it's "real" or take advantage of it or protect themselves from it, and especially imagining what might be happening and what it all means.

> I saw Robert Altman's film, "Images," about 40 years ago. It's a haunting portrayal of psychosis, but the part I remember the most clearly is that there was a point in which the main character knows she hallucinates and starts acting out fantasies, like having sex with an ex-lover and killing her husband, to intentionally enjoy the "unreal" reality. But ultimately, she can't tell which reality she's been in. Has she really killed her husband? Which of her selves is real?

People often report the strange sensation that there are now two parallel realities—the normal one they can share with everyone else and the new, often more real and more special, reality only they are experiencing. They may seek to hide this new reality from others (if there are voices, the voices themselves often urge keeping them hidden from other people). People may become more defensive or isolated if their new reality is confronted. They may also feel pushed into resolving the dual realities by diving deeper into their personal world. Sometimes, with treatment, as their personal reality drifts away, they may feel guilty for having driven themselves deeper and deeper into their psychosis in the first place, while also feeling they've lost something very special and ethereal. They may have a yearning for the old times, wondering if maybe there's some way to go back and make it work out. Unfortunately, mental health professionals, families, and friends rarely have conversations about these feelings to share them or help them work through them. All of this just seems too strange and too crazy to get involved with. Also, there's the lurking fear that we'll somehow make it worse or feed into it if we have these conversations. As a result, these feelings are almost always left to internal, often unsatisfying, ruminations.

> Nev Jones is someone who is not afraid to have those intimate, detailed conversations about hearing voices and other extraordinary experiences. Probably that's because she has so much personal experience of her own. Her mother had chronic severe psychosis and Nev, always fearful of following her mother's path, was diagnosed with schizophrenia 7 or 8 years ago. She told the Chicago Reader, "I did hear voices, but other aspects of my

experience *were more distressing. For example, physical objects seemed to develop their own agency. It was as if chairs were alive, beds were alive, bricks in a building had their own intentionality."* She didn't hide from her experiences or try to deny them; instead, she worked hard to overcome them and function. Medications didn't help her much, but that hasn't stopped her from developing a lot of personal ways of dealing with her experiences. She's now a respected published researcher on the qualitative experiences of psychosis, finishing her PhD, a strong advocate working to improve treatments for people with in the early stages of psychosis, and the founder of Chicago Hearing Voices. I believe that it is precisely her willingness to get involved, in highly perceptive ways, with people's unique experiences and their personal reactions to those experiences that makes her a powerful force in mental health today.

Let's return to my parallel with the most common out-of-control, "imaginary relationship" experience—falling in love. When we fall in love, we do all of the same things I just described above for psychosis—we have two parallel realities, one normal and shared, and one special and personal. We often keep love hidden, for fear others won't understand it or belittle it, and love often thrives when pushed into isolation, "We'll go somewhere away from all of them. As long as we're in love, all we need is each other." Later on, as our love drifts away, we may feel ashamed for having been so gullible, while also feeling like we've lost something very special and ethereal. Maybe there's some way to go back and make it work out. My point: None of this is too strange or too crazy to get involved with. Most of us even have a lot of practice with these conversations. And these are some of the most important conversations we can have with people if we're going to travel alongside them.

Whether we're talking to someone about a seductive "too good to be true" relationship or a relationship–imbalance-based psychosis, our strategy is similar—to impact how their imagination has put it together, so that it can include normal reality without separating the two. "Be reasonable. How are the two of you going to support yourselves on a tropical island? Neither of you has any money." and "Maybe you should date for a while longer and really get to know her, or try living together first before you get married" are similar to, "Be reasonable. If you're developing psychic powers to influence people with your thoughts, you'd better show some restraint and use them for more mature purposes than making people argue, so you can laugh at them or get a date you didn't earn." and "Maybe you need to avoid really toxic people if you're picking up on everyone's emotions, or you could take a little Abilify to block out some of those emotions if they're getting too overwhelming. That may be more emotional sensitivity than you can handle without burning out."

For the woman I described with the mean imaginary boyfriend, we'd probably want to try to get her to date someone else, preferably someone real, to show her that she isn't stuck with the imaginary guy. To do that, we'd have to help her imagine a better relationship—and how she'd be in that relationship—or she won't even try. But if she ever got into a real relationship, it's likely she'd imagine him and interact with him as though he's negative toward her because that's what she brings to the relationship—unless we've really changed her imagination. Usually, we need reality to help. He'd have to treat her well, and she'd have to be open to being treated well, for her to have some chance to break out of her stagnant imagination—"He's different than all the other men I've known"—and be open to creating new imaginings. Note that, almost counterintuitively, she'd usually have to be open to more "reality input" in order to expand her imagination. This point becomes very important with people with relationship imbalance psychosis because they also usually need more relationship reality input to impact their imaginations to regain their balance. When we deprive people of "real relationships"—whether it's pretending to like ballet for our girlfriend, mental health professionals maintaining "professional distance" and hiding our authentic reactions, or families tiptoeing around their psychotic family member out of fear of "doing the wrong thing" or "setting them off"—we're not giving them the reality they'll likely need to adapt their imagination to normal reality.

With Becky, we not only imagined a different life with her, we created different real relationships that helped counter the childhood loneliness, the abusive boyfriend experiences, the inability to take care of her children, and the feeling that the world is a dangerous, destructive place requiring constant vigilance. How did we do that? For a minute, stop and think about just one of the interventions I mentioned in her story. We included her in our interviews of new staff members for the team. Can you guess how she dressed for those interviews? How professionally she acted? How important and valued she felt? How it changed her view of herself and her capabilities? How many times she retold that story to other people, including a visiting dignitary from the federal government. Think about the little girl—crying at the fence alone while the other kids played—being brought into the room as a valued part of our interview team. Every one of those role interventions I described impacted her as she gradually changed her life and her imagination of her life until she no longer needed either the imaginary friends or the aggressive, protective voices.

> The clubhouse approach, pioneered by Fountain House in New York, is a crucial approach for working with people, like Becky, for whom we're trying to get their relationships and roles back in balance by imagining and experiencing real relationships in which they can thrive.
>
> Normally, clubhouses are a supplement to traditional mental health services and are excluded from the usual private and public medical insurance funding sources. As a result, they tend to be run by passionate, creative, nonprofit organizations and need to attract private donations to continue: Fountain House was first established by a small group of patients released from Rockland State Hospital in the 1940s who wanted to keep supporting each other, as they had in the hospital. It's been growing ever since. Step Up on Second Street was established in Santa Monica by Susan Dempsey, the mother of a man with schizophrenia who wanted him to have a reason to leave his Board and Care home and a productive place to spend his time. My first in-depth exposure to a clubhouse was at LAMP in Skid Row when I was doing my psychiatric residency. It was founded by Mollie Lowery to give the homeless, mentally ill men who were being dumped in Skid Row a place to belong. You may have seen LAMP in the book or movie, "The Soloist."
>
> Instead of being a clinic where mental health professionals treat needy patients, clubhouses only function if everyone

helps out. Their "members" aren't useless. They're essential. The place literally can't function without them. Everyone contributes their strengths. Some people answer the phones, sort the mail, keep the place clean, make lunches, decorate the walls with paintings, run fundraising campaigns, show visitors around, and welcome newcomers. Everyone there has a mental illness. Clubhouses often keep away professionals, especially psychiatrists, out of fear that they will unintentionally turn all the people helping each other and running the place back into useless, needy clients. The clubhouse approach has been replicated all over the world. I even saw one in India. It works because it forces the voices and delusions to exist around the edges of their positive roles and relationships, instead of thriving in a vacuum created by negative roles and relationships.

The Village's first director, Martha Long, was recruited from her position across the country as the assistant director of a clubhouse program in Fairfax, Virginia. Under her guidance, we decided that we needed to have a clubhouse culture for our entire program, for all of our members (that's why they're called "members," instead of "clients" or "patients," because they have "membership" to belong in the clubhouse), regardless of diagnosis or what services they needed. Every staff, including me as the psychiatrist, had to adapt to working within a clubhouse atmosphere. That decision, as far as I know, had never been made before in community mental health.

This turned out to be a crucial decision because it opened up the possibility for every person to have a variety of authentic relationships and roles, including people with schizophrenia. Our imaginations of what was possible for them changed radically and, in the process, they more often recovered their relationship balance and regained control of their psychosis. For people like Becky and many, many others, clubhouse services aren't just a pleasant adjunct, it is their most essential service—having a place that *cheerfully welcomes them into new relationships and roles and then provides the personal, emotional support they need to reimagine and remake their lives while adapting to their psychosis. It is the main tool in their recovery and the main tool we have to help them avoid detaching and living entirely in their own realities or drifting into isolation and paranoia.*

As increasing efforts around the world emerge to try to work with young people at high risk of developing psychosis or who are experiencing early symptoms, it's been interesting to watch as the emphasis in many places has moved from promoting early medications to creating environments that are supportive and help young people get back on track developing relationships and roles, while working through their psychotic experiences. Australia, inspired by Dr. Patrick McGorry's leadership, has created a number of pioneering efforts, including the headspace programs, designed by youth, often in shopping malls or in virtual e-headspace. Programs like these, similarly to the Village, provide a place to integrate a number of clinical, case management and rehabilitation services within a culture that helps their members keep in relationship balance despite the outside world's hostility and rejection.

d. Extra-personal/spiritual balance

The next level of development is a level where we've let go of our personal egos and agendas and even our interpersonal relationships enough to appreciate that we are a small part of something much larger. Our balance on this level is maintained by "connecting with the oneness of the universe" or "turning our will over to God to be his servant." At this level, it is our faith and acceptance that keep us balanced. Although this level has been visualized and described in relatively similar terms by both secular and spiritual seekers of almost every type, it remains elusive. It is a level very few people are sustaining, at least in our culture. Most of us have merely glimpses of this level, which can, nonetheless, be profoundly moving and inspiring. Some people keep seeking transcendence for a lifetime after catching a glimpse of it.

A relatively common, nonreligious experience of this level is the feeling you may have had when you looked out on an awesome natural scene and felt like you were both very small and somehow also very large, becoming one with nature around you. Looking at stars on a clear night can sometimes evoke this reaction. Another extra-personal experience is when it seems like things are happening in your life that can't just be a coincidence, as though there must be some purpose behind it, the world is guiding you and providing for you to achieve your destiny or fate. An accessible description of this level is also in John Lennon's song, "Imagine."

Our culture is currently in a strange and unique situation with regard to achieving and sustaining this level of development: We don't have dominating, trusted religious institutions that are reliably guiding and supporting people on this level, but we have a sizable number of people trying to find their own individual paths, using a patchwork of connections to a whole range of spiritual mentors, beliefs, and practices. This combination leads to a considerable number of stumbling seekers.

Many of our communities, having to choose between "church and state," at least officially, use mental health workers, instead of religious workers, to evaluate and "support" people who describe themselves as in profound spiritual states. The primary question mental health workers concern ourselves with is whether the person is psychotic or religious, not how they got to this state and what support they need and from whom, in their current condition. This is a very flawed methodology, in my opinion. It seems likely to me, for example, that if St. Francis of Assisi lived today in America and tore off his clothes in public in protesting his father, a successful silk merchant, after being traumatized in war and seeing visions while held captive, he would've been diagnosed with schizophrenia and forcibly hospitalized and medicated. Maybe he could've been safely returned to an interpersonal level of balance and not gone on to wander homeless, living in rags, never speaking to his father again, preaching to birds and animals, and ultimately dying of an eye infection at age 44. Or maybe he would've continued to be very stubborn and rebellious, repeatedly refusing treatment, getting courts to release him, while continuing to frustrate his family. It's unlikely, though, that he, and his handful of homeless followers, would be sanctioned and supported by the Pope and the Catholic Church in today's world as they were then.

> *It was the first time I had to go to the Mental Health Court to testify that a patient should be kept in the hospital involuntarily and continued to be forcibly medicated, but I wasn't nervous. I was familiar with this court and how the law worked. After all, my father used to be the commissioner in that court room. Also, I'd already won the small "probable cause" hearing in the hospital.*
>
> *It seemed an open-and-shut case to me. Jerry's wife had called the police to have him brought to the hospital because he had been praying incessantly for weeks on end. She had tried calling their minister, but he couldn't help. This wasn't normal prayer. He wouldn't listen to anyone and said God was talking to him. He was clearly psychotic. On the hospital ward, he knelt in the corner for hours on end praying, so much so that he had trouble straightening out his legs when the nurses got him to reluctantly stand up to get something to eat or shower. They said at night when they did bed checks, he was usually lying awake praying, too. He didn't really want to talk with me except to ask me to let him go back home. His wife wanted him to be fixed first. I started him on Haldol to see what I could do to help.*
>
> *I had to admit, though, he looked pretty good in court. He'd cleaned himself up well and was dressed neatly. He talked to his public defender, and we all went into the courtroom. I testified first.*
>
> *"In your expert opinion after examining Mr. Miller, did you determine that he has a mental illness?" I'd only been a psychiatrist for a month, but both attorneys had stipulated that I was an expert.*
>
> *"Yes, I have."*
>
> *"And what is his diagnosis?"*
>
> *"Schizophrenia."*

"On what basis do you make that diagnosis?"

"He has hallucinations of God's voices and religious delusions that aren't shared by his congregation or family that are impairing his daily life." I knew that for a religious belief to count as a delusion, it had to be unshared. (By the way, that criterion now seems to me to make less and less sense in our culture, but I wasn't worried about that then.)

"Is he gravely disabled due to his mental illness?"

"Yes. He isn't focusing on activities of daily life. His wife can't take care of him like this. It's getting worse and worse. He's even hurting his legs by kneeling too long."

"No more questions."

Now, it was the public defenders turn. "Does he have any other hallucinations besides hearing God's voice?"

"Well, no. Not that I know of."

"So, you're concluding that he hallucinates because he's talking with God. Is that right?"

"Yes."

"Moses talked to God. Would you say that he hallucinated, too?"

Quick as a whip came my sarcastic response, "I don't know. I wasn't Moses's psychiatrist." The whole courtroom laughed. I told you I was comfortable in that court room. I was feeling pretty clever.

"No further questions."

Now, it was Jerry's turn.

"When did you first start talking to God?" I never thought to ask that question. I wondered what he'd say.

"Well, ever since I was a small boy and my mother taught me to say my bedtime prayers."

"And does he answer you?"

"When I've been good, he does." A couple people laughed at that.

"And what kinds of things does he tell you now?" I never thought to ask that question either.

"Oh, just little things to help me, like don't spend your money all in one place or don't forget to take out the garbage."

"Do you have a home?"

"Yes, I do."

"And do you get enough to eat?"

"Yes, I do."

"And do you have enough clothes?"

"Well, I do when I'm not in the hospital."

I was shocked that I lost the case. The judge found that even if he was psychotic, he wasn't gravely disabled as a result. His wife would have to tolerate his prayers. She probably wasn't happy about it, but I never actually met her, so I don't really know.

Looking back, I'm pretty appalled by how I handled that case. I never made any real attempt to understand him from his point of view (or to understand his wife either). I never built a relationship with him (or his wife). I never even got any details about his relationship with God or what had changed recently that caused this crisis. All I'd done was make a diagnosis based on family displeasure and forcibly medicated him because I could ... until the judge stopped me. It wasn't that I'd done a poor job because I was new and inexperienced. That's all that anyone was doing. My supervisor commiserated with me and criticized the judge.

So, what are you saying, doc, that all those crazy people, like that guy, Jerry, are really saints in disguise? Next *thing you're going to tell me is that man yelling on the corner really is Jesus Christ. Give me a break.*

No. What I'm saying is that there is a real spiritual level, but it seems to me that more people are losing their balance on this spiritual level than have sustained their balance.

Some saints seem to sustain themselves on that level, but others, even some venerated saints like Mother Theresa, only had brief periods in their lives when they felt the ecstasy of being in touch with God and their fate. For most of Mother Theresa's life, she was depressed, feeling desperate for contact with God, and in prolonged "crisis of faith." But she had enough personal and relationship strengths supporting her vision that she didn't lose her balance and fall into psychosis.

I want to base this section of our travels on the premise that our brains have wiring intended for spiritual usages and that our minds can and do connect to realities greater than ourselves, but these states are precarious and difficult to sustain. Remember Joseph Campbell's quote that I shared with Tony at the beginning of this chapter, "Psychotics drown in the same deep waters that mystics swim gracefully in." In my view, the waters are real, but they're deep and difficult to navigate. There's a big difference between telling someone that their deep spiritual experience is "all in their head," "imaginary," or "psychotic" and telling them that they've been blessed to have a glimpse of the deep waters that surround us all, but that they don't really know how to swim in those waters.

I also want to include the premise that in order to experience extra-personal/spiritual realities, there must be a loss of self-consciousness and personal control. This can occur before the self fully develops, in brief moments of inspiration and letting go, in times of breakdown and crisis, as a result of drug use breaking down self-consciousness, or as the result of intentional transcendence practice. Let's consider these various pathways to end up in those "deep waters" in more detail with some examples:

➢ Some people seem to have access to extra-personal/spiritual levels very early in childhood and retain it as a part of themselves. If this is supported by the people around them, like for the two women I described in Chapter 4—Maria from a small village in Mexico who had the blessing of knowing what was ailing people and who was sought out as a healer at a young age, and Christina, the intuitive doctor carrying on her family's tradition in England—they can have a high likelihood of integrating extra-personal/spiritual experiences as a stable part of themselves. In many cultures, like for these two women, this calling includes a healing ability, but other callings, for example, to be the reincarnation of the Dalai Lama or to be a honey gatherer dangling on a rope ladder in the cliffs in remote Nepal, are possible. These people are probably the subset of "psychotic" people who become shamans or holy people in other cultures. I sometimes remind people in our culture who are looking for their spiritual calling and niche, that even in cultures that do support shamans, as often as not, the shamans live a lonely, impoverished life at the edge of the community and are more involved with sacred realities than with family, friends, and material joys. I ask them if that's really the life they're seeking.

➢ Some of these children aren't supported, "Ghosts aren't real. You're just imagining that Auntie was in your room last night" or meet overt hostility, "Don't talk like that. People will think you're crazy." Sometimes, they grow up in challenging, conflictual environments, and these conflicts take on spiritual aspects, "My mother told me I was a Demon child because my father left her, and I reminded her of him. Sometimes, she couldn't stand to be around me." Or "Don't play like that, the Devil is trying to enter you." Especially as they enter adolescence, and try to solidify a conflicted identity, these people can experience themselves as being personally involved in spiritual warfare. It may become disconnected from the original conflicts and seem as though the entire fate of humanity or the world itself depends on them winning this fight. Remember Melissa in Chapter 8 who I described as having unusual spiritual senses that persisted her entire life? She never succeeded in reconnecting with her first true love, an act she believed necessary to resolve the spiritual warfare she believed was going on all around us.

Anthony took a different path:

Despite coming from a broken family in the ghetto, Anthony showed a great deal of promise as a child. He excelled at both the guitar and the judo classes that his mother took him to. He even got good grades in school up until high school. It looked as though he might beat the odds.

Unfortunately, he didn't. The draw of drugs was just too much for him. He did manage to graduate from high school, but by that time, he was using speed regularly, staying out on the streets a lot, arguing with his mom, and acting more and more strangely. He ended up spending the next few years in and out of jail and psychiatric hospitals. He didn't cooperate with either the drug rehab or the medications they gave him.

"I don't need any of that shit," Anthony told me when we first met. "I'm a warrior angel in the third level of heaven. I bet you don't even know what that is."

"No. I don't."

"They're relying on me to defeat the Demons who have invaded."

"You? How did you get to be a warrior angel?"

"You don't get to be a warrior angel. I've always been one. Here, look at this video of me as a kid in a judo match. You'll see how I levitated in the middle of the match. I couldn't do that if I wasn't an angel."

He handed me his smart phone to look at what appeared to be his mother taking a video of about a 9-year-old. It was filled with static. "I'm sorry, I don't see the levitation."

"Well, you have to know what you're looking for. It's not a very clear video, but it's there."

"Did you know you were an angel back then?"

"No. I've needed the speed to open my eyes to know what's really going on."

"But the speed makes you not able to sleep and all irritable and you end up in jail."

"The war I'm in in heaven is more important than all of that. Maybe we'll drive off the Demons soon and I can focus on my life here again."

"I hope so."

Anthony kept sinking. He stole his nephews' Christmas gifts from under the tree to get money for his dealer; so, his mom kicked him out. He pawned his last possession, his guitar, that he had said he would never part with. The next time he was jailed, they offered him the choice of going to Beacon House, a strict drug program for 6 months, instead of prison.

Six months of Zyprexa and off speed cleared his head (and made him gain 30 pounds). He said the spiritual battle was still going on in heaven, but he needed to take care of himself first if he was going to be of use there. He started working out. We helped him get his guitar out of the pawn shop. He did his moral inventory and made amends reconnecting with his family. He even started a relationship with a woman he met in a 12-step meeting, although his sponsor thought it was too early in his recovery for a relationship. Nonetheless, after he graduated, he moved in with her.

By the time their baby was born about a year later, she had relapsed on drugs, but he hadn't. DCFS called me, wanting to know if he could take care of his infant daughter; so, I asked him, "Are you going to stay clean and on meds to be there for her, or are you going back to your spiritual war?"

"My dad wasn't there for me. I'm going to be there for Lisa, whatever it takes."

I advised them to give him a chance but keep the case open. He took over custody of his daughter and moved in with his sister to get help raising her. He got a good paying job as a garbage truck driver that he held for years. When his *daughter was older, he became her soccer coach and taught her to play the guitar, too.*

Years later, I asked him if he ever second guessed his decision not to be a warrior angel.

"My daughter is my angel now."

➤ Some people's first spiritual experiences are in response to adolescent struggles to develop on the relationship level. Cracks in their self-consciousness open the door to spiritual experiences.

Jerome still believes that he's meant for something more than the life he has.

"Why are you so sure?" I try to be hopeful, but I'm not seeing it, and if I don't see where we're going, I'm going to have trouble helping him get there. Jerome was raised by a welfare mom. He did poorly in school, reads at about a 4th grade level, and dropped out of high school to hang out smoking pot. He's a nice kid, but he's never really had a job or a serious girlfriend. At about 18, he was hospitalized for psychosis, and since then, he's been on antipsychotic medications, SSI, and still lives with his mom. He helps out some with the rent, but mostly he spends his money on stuff like new headphones and shoes that seem to disappear later in the month anyway.

"I'm going to be a rap star."

"You and every other young man you hang with. What's going to make you special?"

"God told me."

"Really. When did this happen?"

"You know, when I was first hospitalized?"

"Yeah."

"Well, that wasn't just a mental illness. God really did talk to me then."

I nodded, "Go on."

"I was just sitting there, like usual, you know, smoking pot, not knowing what I wanted to do, when out of nowhere, the clouds opened up, and I saw this ray of light coming down onto me. I had this feeling, kind of like this voice, from God, that told me that the light was from the spirit inside me and that I should take off my clothes and let the light shine out, so everyone could see it. The more clothes I took off, the brighter it got. I became more and more excited. Like really excited, you know, and tore off all of my clothes, and then, I ran down the street to show my grandmother, to share the good news with her. As I was running, I sort of lost track of time, and it seems like all the people around me were cheering me on, but before I could get to my grandmother's house, the police stopped me and put me in their car, and the spiritual light went out. The whole experience exhausted me. I'm not really sure how I got to the hospital or what they gave me then, but after that, the light never came back, and they were sure I had a mental illness. They wouldn't believe it was real."

"But you know it was."

"I absolutely do. They can say whatever they want, but now, I know that the spirit of God is in me and he wants me for something special."

I could visualize what he was talking about. *"So, what you need to do is find something, whether it's rap music or something else, that brings out that light of your spirt again, even if it's only in a small way, so you know you're meant to do it."*

Jerome looked up at me. *"You get it."*

Our standard response to these spiritual experiences within adolescent identity crises is to label them as "first break" psychosis, the first step of a life-changing chronic, disabling psychotic illness guiding them to adapt to their new seriously mentally ill adult identity. Instead, we could help them, and their families, value those experiences and help integrate them into the positive adult identities that they were struggling to find in the first place. Many of these people are probably the people who would not go on to chronic illnesses and medications if we helped them grow up instead. These people are also probably one of the main groups that explain why people do better with spiritual explanations than medical ones.

- Sometimes, people are in an extreme crisis, having lost everything, and can't hold themselves together, or have been driven to the point of suicide and, in desperation, reach out to God for help.

"I was really going to kill myself. I'd been planning it for months and collected up the pills to do it. I hadn't talked to my mother for 2 years at that point. I'd dropped out of school. There didn't seem to be any point in going on. Everything I did failed. I went into the small room I was renting and turned on the light, but it didn't go on. I said out loud, 'All right, God, I'll give you one last chance to keep me alive.' At that moment, the light went on, but it seemed much brighter than before, like a flash of light and I heard God ... well, not so much heard as felt ... it's hard to describe ... and he told me two things, 'You've been fighting me all the way. All you have to do is give your will over to me and I will take care of everything.' And I felt this sense of love wash over me, but much more powerful than any love I've ever felt. It's like a thousand times more powerful than a mother's love for a child. If you would've asked me anything, I would've known it in that moment. I was connected to everything. Then, God told me the second thing, 'Your grandfather is going to die for your benefit.' The next day, my father called to tell me that my mother's father had died. I knew he'd been sick, but not sick like that. I still don't know how that was supposed to benefit me. After that happened, I meditated for up to 10 hours a day, trying to achieve that state again, but I never have."

Or sometimes, transcendence comes unbidden as people break down.

> *"I was taken to jail and I broke down into tears. My best friend had just betrayed me, and I was taking the rap for the stolen car that he did. He left with all of our money There was no business without him. I didn't have anything. Nowhere to go. No one to call. I'd been drinking some, but I wasn't that drunk and I didn't have delirium tremens. I knew what was going on. They had me go over to talk to the mental health worker, and I could tell something was going on because he typed so fast. No one can type that fast. I don't know if he was an alien or what. Anyway, they gave me this pill. It was a special pill that made me totally calm and totally aware. It was a blue pill. Doc, I need your help to find out what that pill was. It's what I need to be whole again. It's like I've been broken and searching my whole life, and then, I wasn't. The psychiatrist put me in a holding area, but it wasn't to watch me. She knew that in that state, I could calm everyone and heal their suffering. I talked to all of them and fixed them. I'm sure she did that on purpose. She was watching me do it through the little window in the door. They ended up taking me to a normal cell, and I never saw anyone from mental health after that. About 5 days later, I was released. I've had spiritual experiences ever since I was a kid. I've heard God and I've even seen the Devil, but this put it all together. Everything made sense. I really need you to find out for me what that pill is. I've got a bad feeling about what's going on with me now. I don't like that apartment they showed me. I had a vision of the whole building collapsing in an earthquake. I think they're just putting all the homeless people there on purpose to get rid of them. If I had that pill, I'd know what's going on. I'd know what to do."*

Either way, it's usually such a powerful, positive experience that the crisis seems unimportant in comparison. They tend to focus on how to recapture that feeling instead of doing something about the crisis, or even seeing how the transcendent experience connects to the crisis (for example, I think the purpose of the first man's grandfather dying was to bring him and his mother back together, but he didn't see that. He also didn't see how he was still letting his ego run his life, looking for the love and attention he felt deprived of, instead of realizing that love is all around us if we're open to it).

> Some people have serious imbalance problems and resultant crises throughout their lives and try to incorporate spiritual solutions throughout their development, trying to strengthen their balance. While this can sometimes be reasonably effective, the result can be also become an ill-fitting mismatch of pieces, none of which are functioning well, together creating a precarious, poorly adaptive structure. It's worth trying to determine what their struggles are at each level to help them strengthen those levels, rather than focusing on their alluring, but more than likely "fool's gold" spiritual elements.

> *When I first met Charlie, he was wearing a tie dye shirt and a Celtic design necklace. He told me that his name was really Sunny Day, and that he was there to help me in my spiritual development. He sat in my chair in a lotus position and said he was a human mirror; any problems that I think he has are actually my own problems being reflected back to me. He couldn't guarantee that I would do anything about my problems, but he would spread sun onto my day. If I didn't want his sunshine, he would just leave.*
>
> *Admittedly an unusual opening gambit, but I'm always up for a challenge. "So, how much would I have to pay you for your mirroring and sunshine services."*
>
> *"I don't believe in money. It restricts my freedom. If I'm tired, I just find somewhere to sleep. If I'm hungry, I just take food from the store."*
>
> *"Doesn't the store get mad at you for stealing?"*
>
> *"I'm not stealing because I only take from institutions that have more than enough, never from people. I often*

give food away to homeless people who need it. I'm not hurting anyone. I'm actually helping to free everyone by breaking down the social laws and structures."

"So, you're an anarchist?"

"I don't accept labels. I believe in love and freedom. Do you like being labeled as a psychiatrist?"

"It's part of who I am and one of my roles, but not a full description of who I am."

"Well, I don't need a psychiatrist. I don't have a mental illness."

"How about if we try to get to know each other as people instead of as labels?"

"OK. You tell me about yourself first."

"I grew up in Los Angeles. I'm the oldest of five children. Both of my parents were lawyers. We went on a lot of camping trips to National Parks when I was a kid. How about you, where did you grow up?"

A long process of give and take over several sessions led me to his story. Perhaps the strangest thing was that his emotional tone didn't change, no matter what he was telling me about. It wasn't that he didn't have any emotions. He'd get easily angered and even walk off if he felt he was misunderstood or challenged in any way, but when he talked about his past, he used the same above-it-all attitude that he'd used to describe his stealing food.

He was born as Charlie in Chicago, but he spent most of his childhood in the deep south traveling around, rather poor with his mother. He was often hungry and had to sleep outside. He describes his mother as being very obese and an alcoholic and not very functional. Most of the time, she lived with a very violent boyfriend who often beat both of them. When things got out of control, he was sometimes sent to live with his aunt and uncle in Atlanta.

His behavior as a child was very poor. He almost burned down his house, frequently playing with fire. He was cruel to cats at times, even throwing one by the tail through a window, breaking the window. He did very poorly in school. He did have mental health contact as a child, but without any consistency.

When he was 16 years old, he discovered his mother unconscious from a suicide attempt. After significant hesitation, he called paramedics to save her. Then, he was so distraught he went to the bathroom and took a pile of her pills, trying to kill himself. When his mother regained consciousness, she ended up leaving for Oklahoma again with her boyfriend, abandoning Charlie in a run-down hotel room to fend for himself since he couldn't cross the state line to join them because he was on probation in Texas due to his frequent legal troubles, primarily stealing.

He dropped out of school in the 11th grade and accumulated increasing legal problems and was sent to juvenile camp, juvenile detention, and then, when he was 19, 3 years of state prison, he says, for buying marijuana from an undercover policeman he thought was a homeless man. In prison, he was out of his league, beaten, terrified, depressed, and traumatized. After he got out, he came to California.

His first memory of sexual arousal and erection was at 8 years old, wearing his mother's clothes. As a teen, he repeatedly exposed himself in front of older women he was attracted to but who didn't respond to him. His behavior apparently became more aggressive, masturbating in front of unwilling women, and he was convicted as a sex offender and, now, must register for the rest of his life. At this point in his life, he says he still doesn't understand sexuality or how to express himself appropriately; so, he is trying to avoid all sexual feelings and contact to avoid getting into more trouble.

He used lots of drugs, especially hallucinogens, but also cocaine, trying to expand his mind in his 20s. He also had a variety of spiritual experiences, both good and bad. His favorite was an Amazonian Ayahuasca experience. He read a lot of spiritual texts on his own without really sticking with any group. He was homeless almost entirely, wandering wherever his spirit took him.

For a while, he felt an internal split between the good and bad inside him, cut and colored his hair and beard differently on the two sides, and made split clothes.

In his 30s, he seems to have initially settled down a little, working at a Guitar Center for a number of years. It's hard for me to tell if this was a real job, since he said he came and left work whenever he wanted to and was paid mostly commissions. He claims he was their best salesman, but also said he was fired the same day he quit the job a few years ago. He insists that he shouldn't have to do what any boss tells him to do, keep any schedule, or have his freedom restrained in any way. He doesn't expect to find a job like that again.

In 2007, he met the "love of my life" at Burning Man in Nevada, but like everyone else, she left him, too. He became severely depressed, crying every day, and was still homeless.

He has come out of this with a new philosophy, name and identity. He now believes in not being connected to anything material. He is "Sunny Day" now. He stays wherever he gets "good vibrations." Usually, he sleeps wherever he sees an open door or window or porch, especially if he finds a couch. When I met him, he was sleeping in a storage room behind a local church. He's not very well tolerated by other homeless people. He bristles at the notion that there's anything wrong or criminal about any of this. He believes he's not hurting anyone and actually holding up a mirror to society, so it will become a better place.

His ambition at this point is to become a professional astrologer, reading people's fortunes and bartering for what he needs. He dominates any conversation, brooking no dissent, rapidly becoming agitated if anyone disagrees with him or questions his self-defined role in life.

Even though he describes himself spiritually, he has no foundation on any of the other levels. He never even had his basic needs met, and wasn't really meeting them now. We spent considerable time working with him to agree to be on Social Security and in an apartment, instead of stealing and being homeless. A jailing for shoplifting helped convince him. He had no idea who he was inside and bristled at every attempt to get to know him, still a frightened, violent child. We began to find roles for him, combining spirituality and practicality. He made a mandala drawing for each of us that we put on the walls. We started to build connectedness and relationships. He has a long way to go to swim safely in deep spiritual waters.

➤ When I meet someone who seems genuinely spiritual, they seem to glow with higher levels of love and compassion even while they're struggling practically. They aren't filled with fear or anger. They don't create conflict with others. But, opening yourself up to spiritual levels can be risky even if someone has been reasonably well adjusted at other levels. Even monks and nuns are usually relieved of worldly concerns to fully immerse themselves in spiritual pursuits. I've forgotten where I saw this advice, but it fits these people, "A state of deep spiritual contemplation may not be the safest way to cross a crowded street." At times, I've found myself unsure if I should be protecting someone while they journey spiritually or trying to draw them back into the shallower water of interpersonal relationships. When I offer them Abilify to "make the water shallower, so you're not drowning," am I really helping them or keeping them from the journey they're really meant to be on but can't handle?

I know that psychiatrists aren't supposed to have favorite patients, but even though I haven't seen her for years, Abbie is still my favorite. I worked with her for about a decade. When we met, she was in her late 30s and she lived with her elderly mother, a self-proclaimed "Victorian" from England. They looked out for each other, but things could get difficult when Abbie was lost in her own world, especially as her mother aged.

Abbie had a serious mental illness, that, on the face of it, acted like the books say mental illnesses are supposed to act. When she was on medications, she did so well you couldn't tell that she had an illness. She took care of a dog, was an artist, and even worked as a secretary at the Village. Everybody liked Abbie because of how compassionate and sensitive she was. One Christmas, she gave each of us an individualized handmade card giving thanks for us. Mine said, "Thank you for trying to help us grow, even though it's sometimes in ways we're not sure we're ready to grow." She reconnected with her teenage daughter who lived with her ex-husband in Portland, even visiting and going to one of her dance recitals. I never figured out if Abbie ran away with a musician lover when her daughter was a small child, destroying her marriage because she was mentally ill when she met him, or if she became mentally ill when the affair ended, leaving her lost and alone.

When Abbie was off medications, she believed that Jesus was calling to her to join him in heaven as his wife. She would be lost in bliss during those times, sometimes naked, not eating or talking for days, often climbing higher and higher to get closer to heaven. When she was like that, I'd worry that she'd get in trouble climbing naked on the roof of her house, which was across the street from a high school, but she never did.

Sometimes, I'd force her to go to the hospital and take medications to get her "well" again. Unfortunately, it took about 6 weeks of being on meds to recover; so, it was a substantial investment in time, money, and coercion each time we hospitalized her and forced her to take medications to bring her back. I remember one day we called the ambulance and the police to drag her out of the backyard, wrapped in a sheet, and tied down to a stretcher. I called the charge nurse, Mary, to arrange the admission. She knew Abbie well and liked her, too. She told me not to worry about Abbie. They'd take good care of her. Two of my favorite nurses, Joseph and Moses, were on the evening shift. I thought it was ironic that we were stopping Abbie from joining Jesus by sending her to a hospital to be with Mary, Joseph, and Moses, and started laughing. Her mother, who was usually very fond of me, glared disapprovingly at me. I told her why I was laughing, and she said, "I get the joke, but remember, Abbie is suffering and humiliated to be taken off like this, and it's insensitive for you to be laughing at her while she's in pain. Even though she's not talking, she knows what's going on and she'll remember it." I apologized to both of them.

I spent a lot of time in the hospital with Abbie over the years. I remember one time when a careless workman left a ladder he was using to replace the light fixtures unattended, and she used it to climb naked into the crawl space in the ceiling, and we had to call the urban SWAT team to get her out. Another time, the recreation therapist was trying to get her to participate, and Abbie was sitting silently on her bed with the sheet over her head. Suddenly, Abbie pulled off the sheet and said, "Val, the way you care about me and the other patients and respect us, you should be working at the Village, instead of here in the hospital," and then covered her head again and wouldn't say anything else. Val did follow her advice and came to work for us and became one of our leaders. I also remember a time when she told me that one of the staff at the hospital had raped her, but she didn't want to report it since she didn't think anything would happen anyway, and she was embarrassed talking about it. I assured her that I believed her and would support her, but maybe I should have pushed her harder to report whoever it was.

It also took 3 months of being off medications for them to totally wear off; so, we didn't usually know when she'd stopped taking them. She didn't really have any serious side effects. She just didn't like taking pills and didn't think that she needed them. For a while, we gave her long-acting injections of medications every 2 weeks because she couldn't be trusted to take the pills, but she eventually refused those, too.

Sometimes, instead of hospitalizing her, I'd leave her at home in her own world. Her mother actually preferred that to being alone for weeks while Abbie was in the hospital, especially as she got older. I would come to see Abbie at home about every week or two since she wouldn't come into the Village when she was like that. Her mother could convince her to put on clothes for my visits. Sometimes, I would try my hardest to convince her to rejoin our world, but it's hard to compete with Jesus. Once she was in His thrall, she wouldn't come back without being forced to. I don't know if the times she spent like that helped make her special or just wasted a lot of time. I do know that she wasn't worried about it. But we were. Sometimes, we'd just sit together or go for a walk. For a while, I would end my week by watching the sunset Friday evenings with her and her mother in their backyard.

Sometimes, Abbie got into very serious problems when she was off medications. One day, again looking for Jesus, she drove a car out into the desert, ran out of gas, and then started climbing a nearby mountain without any food or water. It took the police several days after our missing person's report to find the car and then, using a helicopter, to find her up in the cactus covered, rocky slopes. I met her the next morning back in the hospital, badly sunburned and dehydrated, but otherwise fine. Hard to believe. She didn't *talk much and didn't argue when I put her back on her medications.*

Sometimes, people who are living at this spiritual level, even if they're drowning, can bring out the spiritual in us, too, as we try to connect with them. Could it be that Christ was looking after her and keeping her safe? I sure don't know, but I don't think I betrayed her spirituality by giving her medications and bringing her back to shore. Whether medicated or not, she had an innocent spirit that reminded me of the stories of the young Bernadette seeing visions of Mary at Lourdes. There was a purity and sweetness about her that would always touch everyone around her.

When she first began at the Village, Abbie liked spending time with the staff more than the other people we were serving. She was middle class, smart, college educated, well dressed, from a good family, and, except for her illness, she had more in common with us than with them. One day, after a number of years, she told me that she no longer thought of herself as different from the other patients. I asked her if that was because, after she'd gotten to know the other people, she respected them more, and felt they were up to her level, or because she'd been through so many hard times and tragedies that she'd been beaten down to their level. She looked at me quizzically and replied, "Neither one, Mark. I realized that there weren't two levels in the first place."

When her mother died, her sister came to sell the house and have Abbie move to Colorado with her. At the time, Abbie was on her medications and doing well. Abbie, her sister, her two adorable kids, and I went out to lunch at a fancy garden restaurant nearby. We had a very pleasant time getting to know each other. Afterward, I remarked to Abbie, "I've gotten used to you for all these years with your illness, but when I saw you here with your sister, I realized how much of your life you've missed by being ill. You could've had a life like hers." She thought for a moment and then said, "Mark, I didn't think that I missed out on anything until you said that. I thought I've been living my life." I didn't know what to say to that.

After she left California, I heard that she'd climbed a mountain in Colorado in the snow without a coat but survived, and that her niece and nephew like having her around. Her daughter visited her sometimes. As far as I know, she's still living her life. She's been on a strange journey, and I feel blessed to have shared some of it with her.

➢ The deep waters of spirituality are, I believe, extra-personal levels, beyond our normal sense of time and space, cause and effect. That's why they're so "deep." It's possible for people to encounter suffering and healing that are more profound than we're used to on this level. Sometimes, when I've had the courage to swim out and join them, rather than urging them back to shore, I've been able to make a bigger difference than I would've thought possible, to restore peace and balance.

Penina means "pearl" in Samoan. I didn't realize when I first met her how well the name fit her.

Penina grew up in Samoa, an only sister with six brothers. She always felt less valuable than her brothers. She looked up to them and tried to get them to accept her, but they always responded by looking down on her. Nonetheless, she was a beautiful, joyful child, full of life.

When Penina was 18, though unmarried, she got pregnant, bringing shame and scorn raining down on her and her family. She had her first "mental breakdown" and was sent pregnant to a mental hospital for about 6 months. After her son was born, she was sent to Los Angeles to live with a brother who was already here. He agreed to look after her, which he did, although in a quite bossy way, until she found a man to marry. Her husband helped her pay the rent, but he had a bad temper and beat her at times. She adored him anyway. She took care of her son and worked as a child day care worker—a job that she loved but didn't pay very much. Her brother told her that if she hadn't gotten pregnant, she could have done better, and found a better man.

About 10 years later, Penina's husband got cancer, and after a year died, leaving her again unable to pay the bills. She took a second job at nights at a shelter, where the homeless people loved her because she would sit with them and listen to their stories, while helping to clean them and cut their nails. She found a new boyfriend whom she didn't really love, and who didn't have a steady job, but he treated her well. Her family's scorn and shame again rained down on her. She signed up for classes to become a teacher's aide in the evenings, trying to better herself, so that she could be independent. Between two jobs, school, parenting, and her guilt, she didn't have any time to sleep and fell apart. She began talking non-stop, laughing at nothing, which frightened the people where she worked; so, they took her to the psychiatric emergency room where she was diagnosed as manic, hospitalized, and medicated.

She was released after a few days, but still couldn't handle things and was again hospitalized. This time, she lost her job, and her son went to live with her brother. She was sent to our program.

Penina was very reluctant to see me or take any medications. She thought she could handle things on her own if we just gave her a chance. She was angry at her old coworkers, and felt betrayed by them since they'd hospitalized her, when she didn't think anything was wrong with her. We were able to give her enough emotional support and some State Disability income to pay her rent, and I was able to get her to take just enough medication to pull her out of the episode over a few months. She kept trying to go to school to prove she was worthwhile. Every day, she met her son at school and walked with him to her brother's house and made sure he did his homework.

We were impressed by how hard working and devoted she was. We also just plain enjoyed being with her. She returned to work, got her son back, and got off medications. We all hoped that, in the same way she recovered in a matter of months as a teenager, and she then stayed well for over a decade, maybe it would happen again.

Instead, she became very depressed. She only got out of bed to take her son to school and walk him home and make him dinner. She lost her job again and quit school. Her boyfriend became frustrated with her not talking with anyone or wanting to be with him. He began seeing someone else. She began thinking about suicide. Voices of spirits started urging her to do it. We made home visits, trying to reconnect. I tried to get her on antidepressants. Nothing worked for almost a year. Then, she became manic again.

I tried to explain to her that she had manic depression. She'd been going through episodes—first manic, then depressed, then manic again. She needed to be back on lithium (even though it made her beautiful skin break out and gain weight) to stabilize her moods, or she'd go through the whole thing again. She told me it was a Samoan evil spirit that was tormenting her that she couldn't get rid of.

"Where did the spirit come from?"

"He came with me from Samoa. He has been bothering my family for many generations. In the early 1900s, he was in a tidal wave that destroyed all the homes in my village and killed several people in my family. Years later, he came with the German colonists, and he impregnated and shamed my grandmother. He always paid for her house, but he never married her."

"But what does any of that have to do with you? You weren't even born yet."

"The same evil spirits are always with us. He got into me because I was weak and did wrong things."

"Is there a way to get him out of you?"

"Oh, yes. There's a ceremony." She found a video for me on the Internet.

"Well, I don't know how to do that. I've never been to Samoa and don't know your culture, but is there a way I can help you get rid of the evil spirit anyway?"

Her face filled with joy, *"Yes, we can do it together. First, I have to bless you, so you can bless me."*

"OK."

She began singing in Samoan and put her hand on my head.

"Now, can I help you?"

She looked around my desk and found a flower and a picture of a little girl that said, *"You're beautiful."* These will work. *"Say you're a beautiful girl."*

I put my hands on her head, *"You're a beautiful girl."*

"You are a good girl."

"You are a good girl."

"Leave her alone."

"Leave her alone."

"Set her free."

"Set her free."

We went around and around like this for about 20 minutes, each time she was louder and stronger, until she said the spirit had left her and wouldn't bother her again.

"You can keep the flower and the picture to keep you safe."

Journeys Beyond the Frontier | 319

Her voices never returned, either depressed or manic, but her mood swings continued. It took several more months and losing everything again to pull it back together. She still doesn't really take medications, but she's broken up with her boyfriend completely and freed herself of guilt. She's gotten some money and a new apartment and a clean start. She is closer than ever to her son, her pride no longer tainted with shame. She's working at the Village. The spirit is gone.

When I last saw her, glowing and beautiful again, wearing a flower in her hair, driving to the Village to work, it seems to me that the grain of sand that was such an irritant to her family has truly developed into the pearl she was meant to be.

Closing thoughts

We've come to the end of the longest, and my favorite, of the journeys. Perhaps I've lingered along the way more than I should have.

I like this journey the best because it is the most "developmental" of the journeys. It fits most closely with my model of our brain being the physical record of the journey we've been on. In this journey, each of us develops in our own ways, interacts with different people and circumstances, achieves and loses our balance in different ways. If we look closely enough at people's psychosis, we can understand where they've been and what they need. There's a lot of hope in this journey.

This journey also highlights the nuances and challenges of having helpful relationships with people on strange journeys. It's not enough for me to see a young woman in my father's court in need of companionship. To really be a valuable fellow traveler, I need to work on my relationship skills. For each level along the way, there has been relationship challenges:

> ➤ How to help people meet their basic needs in respectful, humanizing ways while empowering and reengaging them hopefully and enjoyably in the world

- ➢ How to connect with someone who is paranoid without further frightening and fragmenting them, helping them regain control, rather than controlling them
- ➢ How to use "real" relationships to build their imaginations of what their relationships can be
- ➢ How to wade into deep, highly individualized spiritual waters knowing when to help bring someone back to shore and when to help them "swim gracefully"

Other psychiatrists can pursue brain scans and genetic testing, trying to diagnose and treat people with psychosis. I'd rather spend my time learning to be a useful guide, traveling supportively alongside people as they change and develop, helping them regain their balance when they've lost it.

This journey could lead us to seriously consider a "public health" approach to help people avoid losing their balance at each level, to prevent psychosis, and, not so incidentally, to improve everyone's mental health in the following manner:

- We can fight childhood poverty, reducing childhood hunger and homelessness.
- We can increase paid family leave and supports, so there is more and better parental contact to improve "mirroring" and building a personal identity.
- We can aggressively support families, especially those dealing with substance abuse, poverty, mental illness, death, divorce, homelessness, incarceration, and domestic violence to improve children's basic safety and security.
- We can work to eliminate child abuse and traumatization and decrease exposure to guns and violence in other ways than removing kids from their families.
- We can improve children's socialization in schools, including combating teasing, bullying, sexual mistreatment, and racism.
- We can improve mentoring, helping young people find and develop their core gifts, and enhance initiation rituals to welcome and include them as valued members of our community.

- We can improve social connectedness and "social capital" in our communities, focusing on enhancing welcoming, acceptance, and inclusiveness.
- We can improve rituals and connectedness with natural rhythms and cycles of our days, seasons of the year, years of our lives, and lives of our heritage and ancestry.
- We can improve our connection to nature, art, and religion, gaining comfort with feeling small, because we're also connected to things larger than ourselves.
- We can improve our spiritual skills, practice, and experiences, including focusing on gratitude, acceptance, forgiveness, calmness, compassion, humility, prayer, and enlightenment.

I wonder if we did work on all those tasks and by doing so helped people avoid losing their balance, how many severe, disabling "cases" of chronic schizophrenia would there still be?

We're not helpless. We don't have to just wait for better psychiatric medications. We can all help each other be in balance.

Chapter 11

Journey 6: Drugs and alcohol

Maggie was a feisty, middle-aged White woman who knew what she wanted and didn't want to be told otherwise. To her credit, she was willing to live with the consequences of the choices she made. Her highest priorities seem to be smoking cigars and drinking brandy. As long as she had those, she seemed oblivious to her surroundings—generally living in squalor in a run-down single room occupancy hotel. From time to time, she'd get into an argument with a neighbor or the hotel staff and get thrown out. Her case manager worried that Maggie was running out of choices. Maggie wasn't worried or, at least, she didn't act like she was.

What interested me most about Maggie was that she believed she was God.

"Really, you're God?"

"Yes, I am."

"How long have you believed that you're God?"

"For all of eternity, of course. I existed before the Heavens and the Earth."

"I heard that you pray. How do you pray if you're God?"

"I pray to myself, 'Oh, Holy me, please bless me,' and I answer, 'May my will be done. Go in peace.'"

I just shook my head. I had to hand it to her, her approach had consistency.

I couldn't figure out a way around it when she wouldn't kill the cockroaches that were overrunning her room because "they're all my creatures. I can't kill my own children." She got evicted again.

She refused to take any antipsychotic medications because she wasn't crazy. It was either Ascendin (an unusual old-fashioned antidepressant that sometimes did help with psychotic depression, but that she wanted to use for sleep) and Xanax (a very short-acting antianxiety medication she used when she ran out of money for brandy) or nothing.

She had long moved on to another treatment team and psychiatrist, when I was called about a decade later and asked if I would make a home visit to see her. I remembered her fondly even though she was stubborn and a pain in the ass; so, I agreed.

She couldn't come to the Village because her physical state had progressively deteriorated. She had chronic painful arthritis and could only walk with a walker. She lived on the second floor and couldn't get down. Her case manager was looking for a new place for her, but prices had gone up and Maggie had a bad reputation and she couldn't really come down and help with the apartment search. She hadn't been out of her room for a couple months.

I sat on her couch and we began to chat, catching up. She was an older, more disabled, in more pain, version of her old self. She still paid a neighbor to bring her cigars and brandy, but not nearly as much. She was facing her life of chronic pain as well as could be expected but wanted me to give her Ascendin and Xanax again to help her sleep and ease her anxiety. I agreed.

As I was parting, I couldn't resist asking her, "Maggie, I remember that when I used to be your doctor, you believed you were God. You haven't said anything about that today. Do you still believe that?"

She just laughed, "Oh, no, Dr. Mark. I was really crazy in the head back then. I was using lots of LSD, almost every day."

LSD? Really? I hadn't suspected a thing.

"I haven't used any of that for years now and I stay in reality."

"OK, why did you stop?"

"I just got too old for it; I expect. I couldn't be an acid-head forever."

"Your life was really messed up back then. You never even had an apartment like this and you kept getting kicked out of every hotel you were in. Do you wish you'd done things differently?"

"Not really. I've lived a good life and I've lived it my way. How many people get to be God in their lives? Now, my body's wearing out and this pain is killing me, but if I can get into a one-story apartment and get to the doctor's office more often, maybe things will be better. In the meantime, I can still enjoy a cigar and a glass of brandy. Thanks for coming by, Dr. Mark. It's been nice seeing you again after all these years."

"It's been my pleasure. You take care."

I'm not alone in not suspecting or including drugs and alcohol often enough. I saw a study once done in my local county psychiatric emergency room that found that about 70% of all the people who came to that ER, who had no mention of drugs or alcohol in their chart, tested positive for some substance. Sometimes, like with Maggie, I miss it because they don't fit my preconception of what someone using drugs is like. Sometimes, it's because they lie and tell me they're not using them even when they are because they don't want to be seen as an alcoholic or addict—or maybe because they don't see themselves as one. They may be hiding it from themselves, not just from me.

But, so many of the stories you've told in this book include drugs and alcohol. You must be pretty good by now at opening people up to have these conversations.

I have gotten a lot better over the years, but this is a journey it took me a very long time to prepare for. I certainly didn't have the luggage I needed when I started.

Like most people, I didn't become a doctor or a psychiatrist to help people with drug addiction. I don't use drugs or alcohol. I don't like them. I don't like the destructive effect they have on people. I don't usually like how people behave while they're using them.

Nonetheless, I was the only student who chose to spend a couple weeks at a 12-step treatment program as an elective at my medical school. Besides that, however, I had very little education on substance abuse in medical school or psychiatry residency. It's not that we didn't see people who had problems from drugs and alcohol (probably over a third of every patient at USC–LA County Hospital where I did my residency had some problem from drugs or alcohol or two thirds if you added cigarettes). We just never addressed their substance abuse directly, except by telling them to stop their use or go to a 12-step program.

When I began my career, community mental health clinics routinely told people they had to be clean for 3–6 months before we could begin psychiatric treatment. (The substance abuse programs usually told them that they had to be free of serious mental symptoms for 3–6 months to benefit from drug rehabilitation.) In residency, we were instructed not to give anyone psychiatric medications who was actively drinking or using drugs because the combination could be dangerous. We'd be putting ourselves at risk if something bad happened, and nothing was going to work until they got clean anyway. (The substance abuse programs, except for River Community, a small "dual-diagnoses" program in an old Civilian Conservation Corps camp in the mountains, refused to accept anyone who was taking psychiatric medications.) Meanwhile, our ER was full of people high and psychotic who didn't fit anywhere in our system—so, we sedated and released them, while cursing the police for bringing them to us in the first place.

It's not just our treatment system that people with both mental illnesses and substance abuse have trouble fitting into. We all have a set of pervasive beliefs about people with mental illnesses and substance abuse that require artificially separating them:

- Mentally ill people are victims. They're not responsible for what they do and deserve treatment, not jailing. Addicts and alcoholics have no one to blame besides themselves. They can stop whenever they choose, "Just say no" and begin a program with step 1: We admitted that we were powerless over alcohol or drugs and that our lives had become unmanageable.
- People with mental illnesses may not know they need treatment and should be forced into treatment, including in locked hospitals for their own good. People who use drugs and alcohol are responsible for not making that choice and recovering. They should be confronted, punished even with jailing, and allowed to suffer enough that they "bottom out" until they choose recovery.
- Psychiatrists and mental health professionals treat people with mental illnesses in hospitals and clinics paid for by health insurance and the public. Recovered addicts counsel people who are using drugs and alcohol in programs that take away your freedom and autonomy and try to break down your way of doing things yourself, so that you can turn your life over to a higher power and work your recovery program.
- People with mental illnesses need to be taken care of and are entitled to disability payments and housing supports, but will rarely recover. People using drugs and alcohol are explicitly excluded from social security disability and most public housing programs, but can recover if they stop drug and alcohol use.
- People with mental illnesses need day treatments to keep occupied. People using drugs and alcohol need to get a job and stay clean and take care of their responsibilities.
- People with mental illnesses deserve accommodations for their disability. People who use drugs should be tested to make sure they're clean to return to school or work.

But what happens if you're both mentally ill and substance abusing? You're likely to get the worst of both worlds: blamed and hopeless, rejected by both sets of staff, neglected on the streets, excluded from disability and subsidized housing along with jobs, while being drug tested and jailed anyway. Almost no one wants to spend time or resources on the people on this journey.

Maybe that's OK. Most of those beliefs make sense to me. Why should we waste resources on this journey, with people who are using drugs and alcohol when they can't be helped anyway?

You're going to need some more luggage before we really set out on this journey. Notice how you have a vicious circle going there—since they can't be helped, we're right in excluding them from anything that might help them. That's the same place most people, including me, start. You didn't say that about the other journeys, even though some people think that everyone who is psychotic is hopeless and we shouldn't waste resources on them.

You have a point there.

We have some work to do before we head out. Let's start with the "they can't be helped" part of the circle.

When the Village first began, some of our most problematic members were people who both had serious mental illnesses, including psychosis, and used drugs and alcohol. They were missing their appointments, not taking medications, getting dragged into psychiatric hospitals and jails, having medical problems, being violent, having their kids taken away, trying to kill themselves, even dying, at far higher rates than anyone else in the program. We weren't allowed to disenroll them until they got clean—the only mental health approach I'd been taught. We had to figure out something, and fast.

> *Patrick had been homeless his entire adult life. He didn't talk much; so, I never got all the details of his history, but he was taken away from his parents when he was young and raised by an elderly grandmother when the Department of Children's Services placed him with her. He didn't have any friends in school. Apparently, he'd never been in a sit-down restaurant or a movie theater in his life. He*

didn't know how to ride a bicycle or drive a car. He missed a lot of school along the way, dropping out in the 10th grade. It was never clear to me why he left his grandmother's home, where she was, or even if she was still alive. I don't think Patrick knew.

Our homeless outreach worker found him on the streets a year before the Village opened, got him some SSI money to live on, became his payee, and moved him into a small apartment on the block where our Homeless Drop-in Center used to be. The staff there guided Patrick through the process to apply to be a Village member, hoping he'd get more resources and a chance at a better life. He couldn't do much by himself.

We did have more resources. We set him up with an account at our Village bank that used his SSI to pay his rent and utilities and gave him weekly money draws for food, cigarettes, and whatever else he wanted. We helped him sign up to make sandwiches at our Deli to have a job a few hours a day. It was his first job.

We took him out for his birthday, but he got overwhelmed by the attention and snuck out and walked home.

After his first payday, he didn't show up for work; so, his case worker went to his apartment.

He was badly hung over. "I'm sorry I missed work. I'm not feeling well. I'll come tomorrow."

The beer cans littering the room made it clear this wasn't a one-time problem.

The burn marks on the carpet next to his bed worried us. It didn't take much imagination to see how, drunk and smoking, he could someday start a fire and burn down the apartment.

"What should we do about Patrick?"

The team was motivated and energetic. The ideas flowed. "We can control his money more closely, so he can't buy beer." "We can hold his next paycheck." "We can take him to an AA meeting to get him sober." "We can get him a smoke alarm."

Patrick didn't have much to say about any of our proposals, but he did thank us for giving him another chance at work. We tightened our financial control and visited more often. He started hiding his beer cans.

A few weeks later, he got in trouble for stuffing a sandwich in his pocket at the end of the shift. When he was confronted, he didn't have much to say. He was suspended for a few days and watched more closely. "Maybe he needs a job coach." "Or to come to social activities." "Or a sober companion."

When the landlord saw us visiting him, he pulled us aside and told us he didn't like how Patrick was looking at a 13-year-old girl down the hall when he was drunk. When Patrick was confronted again, he didn't have much to say. We became really alarmed and tried to make sure he didn't have any extra spending money for beer. We doled out his money daily with supervision on how he spent it.

He disappeared.

We checked out his old homeless sites, but he wasn't at any of them. No one had seen him.

Why would he run away when we were just trying to help him have a better life? He had his own apartment and a job for the first time.

We kept searching for him. Social Security hadn't heard from him either; so, after a few months, we started returning his checks.

Four months later, they informed us he'd died in Miami. It took a fair bit of effort to find out that he'd drowned in a *drainage culvert when there was a scheduled water release.*

It was hard not to feel that we'd driven him away—with all our control and monitoring and "good will"—driven him to his death as it turned out.

Maybe the few "dual-diagnosis" programs that existed knew what to do ("dual diagnosis" meant having both a mental health diagnosis and a substance abuse diagnosis). We started looking around: I went to visit River Community. We got in a van to visit Jerry Vaccaro at UCLA and the Westwood VA to learn about their approach. I went to an all-day training by Ken Minkoff, then working at Harvard, who told us all something like, "Stop looking for someone else to be the dual-diagnosis program. We are all the dual-diagnosis program. People with both mental health and substance abuse challenges are the norm, not the exception. Build your services around them, and you'll be able to help everyone." We sent our substance abuse specialist to look at NIMH's dual-diagnosis programs, and he came back with Fred Osher's four stages:

- Engagement: This is for people who don't tell you they have a substance abuse problem, but they do. Build a longstanding relationship with them, try to help them work on their goals to earn their trust, help them get enough support and services to stay alive and as healthy as possible, while being nonjudgmental and accepting of substance abuse, so that they'll feel safe enough to open up.
- Persuasion: This is for people who admit that they use substances, but they maintain it's not a problem for them, and for people who say substance use does make problems but they don't want to or can't stop using now. Instead of our "normal" approach that tries to convince them to stop using by confronting, avoiding "enabling," and waiting for people to "bottom out," we learned to try to partner with them to try to improve their lives and help them learn from each inevitable loss, while promoting the option that their lives could be much better without substances. We try to "raise their bottoms," helping them visualize a better, sober life and how they could get there.

- Active treatment: This is for people who want to stop using, but can't do it alone or in their usual lives. These people are finally ready for step 1. The 12-step treatment programs are the most common active treatment programs, but there are other choices. People may need to be temporarily removed from their lives, usually voluntarily, to avoid triggers for using, "people, places and things," as their pleasure centers get used to being without their substance of choice and they develop other ways of maintaining their moods. They may need to do serious work with the shame and guilt that have been built up over time. They may need to face their mental conditions, including trauma, and address them in different ways, too.
- Relapse prevention: This is for people who have stopped using and want to sustain sobriety. Relapse can often be a part of recovery, but it doesn't always mean you need to go back to active treatment. Each relapse is an opportunity to learn what further changes need to be made. Building protective factors, both inner and outer, are crucial aspects.

That sounds like a more productive and humane approach than come back when you're clean.

It is. Over the years, we have added harm reduction and motivational interviewing to our arsenal.

Harm reduction is an approach used during the engagement and persuasion stages to try to help people avoid permanent or lethal damage while we're trying to convince them to stop using. This may include things like giving them clean needles or condoms, arranging "wet housing" where they can live while using, jail diversion to avoid permanent legal records, and helping with supportive medical care. People who have been raised on the concepts of enabling and bottoming out often have serious problems with the harm reduction approach, especially if it goes on for years and years, because it can seem like we're just helping them use without consequences, so they'll never stop. While there will always be some people who will never stop using, the harm reduction approach is not intended to be giving up on eventual recovery. People with more left to lose have a better chance of stopping than people who have lost everything long ago and are chronically hopeless.

Motivational interviewing is a technique for the persuasion stage. It maintains that stopping using is a difficult, life-changing decision, and like any difficult, life-changing decision requires quite a bit of time and ambivalence to make and implement. Motivational interviewing describes a series of normal stages in decision-making: precontemplation (not even thinking about changing), contemplation (thinking about changing but no concrete plans), planning (making plans for change but not taking any action yet), action (actually making the change), and sustaining (not going back into old ways). Instead of confronting people, trying to force them to change, which usually increases their resistance and resentment as they dig in their heels, we can meet them where they're at, whichever stage that is, and gently push them forward.

Armed with these strategies, we began having significant success. Perhaps just as importantly, we stopped being as frustrated and angry at people who were using drugs, since we had a productive, hopeful approach for everyone, regardless of what stage they were in. When we were less frustrated and angry, we made better decisions and treated them better.

> *A number of years ago, when I presented this approach to the State Mental Health Advisory Board, a very impassioned, sincere lady rose and told me about how when she was deteriorating from alcoholism. her doctor had given her an ultimatum that she had to stop drinking or he'd stop seeing her, and she did stop. As a result, her entire life has turned around. She asked why I didn't do this with the people I was working with, instead of using those four stages.*
>
> *Three weeks later, she was long gone, but I figured out the answer: While it may be acceptable for her to attribute her recovery to her doctor and for him to become her "Higher Power," it isn't acceptable for her doctor to believe that.*
>
> *I, too, on occasion, have had the skill, timing, and good fortune to do something that drastically facilitated someone's recovery. More often, however, the addiction progresses, and the person deteriorates, despite my efforts. If I begin*

> to believe I have power over substance abuse, I will ultimately have to blame the people I work with for their lack of recovery. I will either conclude that they don't really want to recover and tell them to return when they're really ready to get better, or conclude that they're manipulating me to get something besides assistance with recovery from me and I'd better closely guard and limit what I give them to avoid "enabling" them and strengthening their illness, instead of their recoveries.
>
> These two reactions, both of which stem ultimately from a failure to accept our own powerlessness, are the defenses that underlie much of our substance abuse treatment policies today and keep us from creating an effective treatment system.

Now that we have some real tools to help people and some successes, it's time to look at the exclusion side of the circle.

> Paul was a young, good looking Italian man. I saw him go through the same cycle several times in the first year I worked with him. He'd find some woman who would fall in love with him and he'd move in with her. Things would go well for a while, until his drinking started making bigger and bigger problems. She'd try to help him stop, but when it didn't work, she'd leave him. He'd go back to his mother's house again, feeling depressed and abandoned. After licking his wounds, he'd find another girl and the cycle would start all over again.
>
> Samantha was his latest victim, I mean, girlfriend. "Doctor, can you please help Paul? He's a wonderful man. He has so much potential, but he has this drinking problem. He knows he has a problem and he wants help. Can't you please help him stop drinking?" Her big, beautiful eyes pleaded for him.
>
> I pulled back in my chair. My first reaction was that I'd seen this scene before. He's trapped you like all the rest. Get out while you can. After another look at her eyes, my second reaction was she's not ready to hear that and you're not

being very helpful anyway, Mark. Think of something more productive to say.

As I often do when I'm stuck, I tried to imagine myself in her situation. Remember the back of the hand story? What would it be like to be her and be "in love" with someone who is a self-destructive alcoholic, lost in his addiction? After a moment, I was surprised to realize that I couldn't do it. I wouldn't stay with any active substance abuser no matter how much I loved her. (Try it for a moment and see what you imagine for yourself.) That's when I tried to imagine being with an actively disruptive mentally ill person with psychosis, who wouldn't take their medications, and I realized that I could do that. (Try that for a moment, too, and see what happens.) It struck me that on some deep emotional level, I'm able to open my heart to people with mental illnesses but not to those with substance abuse, and that inability is probably getting in the way of helping them. (I told this story once as part of a presentation to a room of mental health and substance abuse workers trying to integrate services. Almost all the mental health workers were like me, they could imagine being with the mentally ill person but not the person using drugs, and almost all of the substance abuse workers were the opposite, they could imagine being with the person using drugs but not the psychotic person. Very few people, even in that room, could imagine being with both. How did you come out?)

I see myself as helping people by accepting them and connecting with them wherever they are and then trying to guide them into recovery. How could I do that effectively if I was unable to accept them and connect with them until after they stopped using drugs? That would be like a tour guide who has never been where you are, won't meet you there to begin your trip, and then if your trip goes poorly, he says you must not have wanted to travel in the first place. A caricature perhaps, but that sounds like the problem with a lot of our dual-diagnosis treatments.

> This isn't just my personal problem. I'm "normal" for American culture today. In the movies, "A Beautiful Mind" and "Shine," we admired the tenacious, accepting wives of poorly compliant disruptive mentally ill men. They seem almost heroic, and ultimately, their love is portrayed as very healing. In contrast, in the movie "Leaving Las Vegas," we do not admire Nicolas Cage's girlfriend, played by Elisabeth Shue, as she sticks with him while his alcoholism destroys them. We wonder what's so terribly wrong with her that she would stay with him. We don't find her love healing. It might even be enabling. Maybe he would've done better without her, we speculate. A number of years ago, I was a visiting lecturer in Amsterdam. One of the psychiatrists there, who was telling my fascinated teenage sons about their liberal marijuana policies, also told us that in Amsterdam, Shue's character is admired. She is acting exactly as they believe a loving, connected partner is supposed to act. In that moment, I realized that, on a very deep level, their cultural view of drugs was different than ours, not just their policies.

If we really want to help these people, we are going to have to, at least within our treatment centers, create a "counter-culture" that accepts them and connects with them. If we look to learn from 12-step groups, probably the most effective help available, we can see that they are profoundly accepting and connecting, while maintaining a strong rule of anonymity to keep out the larger rejecting society. The nods of recognition and the shared laughter as they tell their devastating stories are the beginnings of healing.

> Gabor Mate is a physician who has worked for a number of years in Vancouver's impoverished Downtown Eastside with people with serious childhood trauma, mental illnesses, substance abuse, HIV, or commonly all of the above. His book about his experiences, "In the Realm of Hungry Ghosts," describes how his personal compassion evolved into a harm reduction-based, counterculture of acceptance. He describes his understanding of the biological impacts of trauma and addiction, alongside his description of his own unusual emotional development beginning as a

> displaced infant in the holocaust in Hungary. His profoundly personal approach has brought him both significant acclaim and conflict with the prevalent Canadian and American policies or rejection and punishment.

At the Village, we tried very hard to create a counterculture of acceptance. Nearly all of my teammates were "abnormal" in their reaction to substance abuse, mental illness, homelessness, and even jailing. Some have experiences of being an addict or mentally ill or both. Some have been raised by family members with addiction or mental illness. Some have been homeless or in jail. They've formed "abnormal" attitudes because of deep personal experiences. I'm not saying that all people with these experiences become accepting. In fact, many become even more rejecting or judgmental than the rest of us. But some do. And it's very hard for us "normals" to break away from our societal culture of rejection.

We spend considerable time during our job interviews trying to find out if potential hires are able to be accepting and can connect with people actively abusing substances. "Will you get frustrated or angry?" "How will you handle it?" "Will you become punitive? Cut people off from services or medications?" We can't have a psychiatrist work with us who threatens to get people's Social Security cut off, if they don't stop using drugs.

When new staff at most places do try to help people who are using drugs, they are criticized and made to feel there's something wrong with them. "You're naïve, you'll learn." "They always look for new staff to take advantage of." "You're not helping, you're enabling them." Most places, in effect, actively train their staff to reject and exclude substance abusers. They can't really help people on this journey.

I see what you mean by the two sides of the circle—feeling confident you're able to help people who are using drugs and alcohol, on the one side, and accepting them even when they're using, on the other, without pushing them away. Wow, that's a lot of hard work to do.

Yes, it is.

Different substances have different impacts on psychosis

Once we get equipped with enough competence to accept our powerlessness and enough acceptance to avoid moral judgments, this journey can appear to be a very biological journey. Each of the drugs and alcohol have unique biological impacts on psychosis, much of which we can attach to our understanding of how we perceive, understand, and create reality that we went through in Chapter 8. Keep in mind, though, that even biologically, there are enormous differences in the settings drugs are being used in, the goals of using them, and the individual responses to any given substance. Even on this journey, we will still have to consider the impact of the experience of altered reality on the person's self-identity and their relationships to really understand the psychosis any given person is going through.

Here's a map of the different classes of substances and their impact on psychosis to help keep track of where we're traveling:

Substance	Desired Effect (besides pleasurable "high")	Impact on Psychosis
Hallucinogens: PCP, LSD, mushrooms, ayahuasca, peyote	Expanded consciousness, spiritual enlightenment	• Direct effect on experiencing reality—can be short- or long-term • Hard to dose • Situational impact—can be positive or negative, depending on the stimuli, internal state, and intent
Ecstasy	Heightened sensations and emotional connection, including sexual	• Usually experienced as pleasurable alterations without loss of ability to distinguish reality or loss of self-identity

Marijuana is a hallucinogen, too (also synthetic cannabinoids—K2, spice, etc.)	Loosen conscious control Decrease social anxiety Calming Sleep Spiritual uses	• Direct effect on experiencing reality—mild, short-term, often pleasant • Calming/sleeping impact can make it easier to deal with voices/psychosis • Can have negative short-term effects feeling out of control and/or panic and paranoid • Long-term usage can lead to more of the negative effects like panic and paranoia "turn on you" • Long-term regular usage increases risk of long-term psychosis; often, the person is unaware their psychosis is worsening because they still have pleasant, positive effects, too
Stimulants—="meth"/"street speed" and prescription stimulants (Adderall, Ritalin, Vyvanse, etc.)	Energy Focus Power	• Commonly causes psychosis that can be very severe, both short term and long term • Paranoia common • Usually higher than prescription dosages

Journeys Beyond the Frontier | 339

Cocaine—crack	Euphoric mood	• Mostly indirectly leads to psychosis through severe mood changes, either euphoric while intoxicated or depressed while wearing off • Can disrupt self-identity
Heroin—opiates	Decreased pain Direct pleasure center stimulator Rush	• Indirect through delirium/confusion • Often improves voices • Withdrawal can worsen psychosis by increasing distress
Alcohol	Calming Reduces social anxiety Stop thinking about problems Sleep Disinhibition	• Often improves voices acutely • Calming/sleep can make psychosis and voices easier to handle • Wearing off can worsen anxiety, sleep, and psychosis • Withdrawal hallucinosis—if the psychosis and hallucinations go on too long, they can become permanent • Indirectly impacts experiencing of reality through delirium/confusion
Nicotine—cigarettes	Calming/soothing when smoked slowly Energizing/activating when smoked rapidly Improves focus	• Usually improves voices • Withdrawal anxiety and agitation can increase psychosis

Hallucinogens: PCP, LSD, mushrooms, ayahuasca, peyote

I'm beginning with hallucinogens because alterations in perceiving reality are the intended impact of these substances. From a strictly biological point of view, these are psychosis-creating substances.

When I was in college at Caltech, I saw the tail end of the LSD era. It was like coming to a party the next day after everyone had left and only the trash remained. There were a handful of students who were rumored to have been brilliant before they fried their brains on daily acid and a collection of dorm walls painted with enormous glow-in-the-dark planetary scenes. I watched one group who took some LSD together, but they seemed to have no idea what they were doing and wandered off with minimal impact. Maybe the dose was too low. Maybe this stuff is impossible to dose safely. It didn't seem worth risking my brain for. But maybe I was missing something really special. What about Carlos Castaneda and his peyote-induced shamanic journeys? Or Timothy Leary and his LSD trips? Or "deadheads" following the Grateful Dead around the country? Or Ken Kesey's Electric Kool-Aid Acid Tests? I was left to imagine what might have been if only I'd been born a decade earlier.

I had a chance to meet R. D. Laing in his later years, when I saw him on a mental health panel in Los Angeles. His remarks were so abstract and ethereal, including curing schizophrenia with love and an alignment of the planets, that I couldn't tell whether he was psychotic or enlightened or both. Afterward, I went up to him to ask about using LSD. He said he thought its only value was for psychiatrists to experience what psychosis is really like. I've never tried it, even when I read that Steve Jobs thought that it had helped him immensely.

My first clinical experiences with hallucinogens was with a very different hallucinogenic drug, PCP (Phencyclidine), better known as "angel dust."

When I was a resident at LA County–USC General hospital in the mid-1980s, Los Angeles was in the midst of a terrible "angel dust" epidemic. It struck me as bizarre that a drug that was so devastating could be so popular. PCP was originally developed as an anesthetic but had to be abandoned when people got psychotic and even violent in postoperative rooms. It is extremely powerful in very small amounts, which made it cheap. Dipping a few drops on a cigarette, making a "Super Kool" or a "Sherman," created a hallucinogenic high for about $20. It also makes it impossible to dose. We were taught that 10% of people who used it got temporarily psychotic for up to a few days and 1% got permanently psychotic. The police used tales of PCP-induced violence, imperviousness to pain, and superhuman strength to justify increasingly ruthless tactics in the streets; but when someone was really high, they brought them to us, instead of to jail, to be dealt with. When they brought in someone who was "dusted," often a repeat admission, we tied them down to a bed and gave them a series of shots of a heavy cocktail of Thorazine, Ativan, and Inderal to "get them horizontal" for a few days before waking them to see if they were going to recover. About a quarter of all our admissions were PCP psychosis.

I remember one young man who was one of the unfortunate one in a hundred who'd gotten permanently psychotic. He couldn't focus on anything. He kept getting scary visual hallucinations like seeing demons flying around the room. He couldn't sleep. He was anxious all the time. In a rare moment of clarity, he started tearing up and told me, "I can't believe I did this to myself. I was the smart one in my family. I got A's in school. I was going to be the first one in my family to go to college. My mother had such big dreams for me. We all did. And look at me now. I've lost it all. I can't think straight. I can't do anything. I've let them all down. And I'm going to have to live locked up forever, like a bird in a cage who never got to fly." He was 25 years old.

Eventually, the epidemic calmed down. The poor people in the ghetto were supplied with cheap crack and meth instead. They moved on. My guess is that very few of them were really trying to expand their consciousness or get psychotic anyway. They just wanted a cheap high as a diversion. Maybe its anesthetic properties or the superhuman mythology around it gave it some appeal, but fortunately not enough to keep it going.

I've met a number of people who have used LSD or "magic mushrooms," but I usually found that out while taking a history. The hallucinogenic effects were rarely the reason the person was seeing me. They described a variety of both pleasant and unpleasant, euphoric and terrifying experiences, dramatic visual and other hallucinations, profound alterations in the flow of time, and even glimpses into "the nature of the universe." These experiences sometimes had lasting impacts on their metaphysical beliefs, but almost never made them "psychotic" without repeated, prolonged usage.

Why not?

To understand that, I think we have to go back to our triangle. These drugs clearly impact how we understand and create reality, especially at the higher levels (remember unconscious, "primary process" synthesis, projection of internal reality into external reality, and time perception from Chapter 8?), but they usually do not have a long-term impact on the other two dimensions of the triangle—our self-identity or our relationships. After we recover our "normal" perceptions, we attribute all the altered perceptions to the drugs, rather than deciding that there is something fundamentally wrong with us … or reality or God. It was a "trip," good or bad, not a change in our self-identity or relationships, even if there are flashbacks. Remember Andy back in Chapter 7, who had a psychotic reaction to LSD where he experienced heaven and hell? His mother, minister, and I helped him get past his crisis by solidifying a positive gay identity and accepting relationships in his church. I did meet one person who, while using LSD, saw the thin veil of reality part revealing a dark underlying reality, where there is no God, or hope, or love. As a result of that insight, he was persistently depressed and had trouble finding meaning in everyday life, but I still wouldn't describe him as psychotic.

If the hallucinatory experience is more internalized, there is the same risk of drowning "in the same deep waters that mystics swim gracefully in" that we saw in people who lost their balance in level three and ended up with "spiritual psychosis" in Chapter 10. Once again, the pathway to psychosis includes not just altered reality but also a breakdown in self-identity and relationships.

> *Samantha viewed herself as a modern mystical healer. She wore flowing white clothes, including a veil, and was adorned with mishmash of new age symbols and crystals. She didn't think she should have to deal with any everyday demands of life, like getting her own groceries, paying the rent, or doing the laundry. Someone of her stature should be above all of that. Our case manager seemed like the perfect person to serve her. When their conflicts got to the*

point of her swooning on the floor, overwhelmed by all "the pressure he's putting on me," she was brought to see me, "Maybe you can get her to take some medications."

She was born male in Missouri and named Sam by his parents. He never fit in, even before he started wearing makeup and wearing feminine clothes and was gang raped. A suicide attempt by pill overdose didn't work to escape her reality; so, she turned to LSD for spiritual enlightenment on an almost daily basis for several years.

She left Missouri, lived in a commune for a while, and discovered peyote, which she liked even better than LSD. Over the years, her masculine physical body seemed to dissolve away and was replaced with a feminine energetic body.

The boundaries between her and other people increasingly dissolved away as she felt spirits touch when bodies touched. Emotions of other people passed right into her, leaving her wracked with tears in a corner, or overwhelmed by panic. Instead of trying to protect herself, she embraced the role of empath. She used more and more hallucinogens and engaged in every mind-altering group ritual she could find. She went on long meditation retreats and became a healer.

Unfortunately, she had no community and no customers. She told me that her most recent healing was with a man who she did a 5-hour healing to help him have a bigger penis. The neighbors and the landlord wanted her out. She had stopped eating, and she had to keep moving her fingers up and down her body touching herself to keep the energy in her body flowing and to maintain connection with the physical reality of her wispy body.

I tried to offer Samantha antipsychotic medications to help her be more grounded and better "glued together," but that was the opposite of what she wanted. She wanted to transcend reality, expanding her consciousness further, exploring her healing gifts and her spiritual purpose in life.

> "Can you give me a medical marijuana card? Marijuana helps me relax and sleep without dulling me." We barely agreed on a compromise of sleeping pills. Her case manager wasn't pleased. That wasn't really going to help her get along. Why hadn't I gotten her to take antipsychotic medications?
>
> I pointed out to Samantha that shamanic healers in their own cultures and communities tend to live lives of isolation on the edge of their village, and she didn't even have a community or village to be a spiritual healer in. She was going to experience more and more rejection and isolation on the path she was on. She wasn't pleased. That wasn't really going to help her get along either. Why hadn't I gotten everyone to accept her as a mystic healer?

If we look at how indigenous cultures use hallucinogens from this perspective, we can see how the risk of psychosis is minimized by 1) only using them occasionally for certain prescribed purposes, 2) using them with careful supervision of the personal self-identity aspects (e.g., in initiation rituals), and 3) using them within a web of supportive relationships.

When I was in Peru, I saw advertisements for tourists to legally take ayahuasca administered by an indigenous healer. Ayahuasca is a complex hallucinogen found in the Amazon rain forest. I read that traditionally, small hunter–gatherer extended family groups lived in relative isolation from each other. Over time, if the chief felt that the amount of internal tension and conflict was getting out of hand and more than he could manage, he'd consult with the medicine man and arrange an event where the entire clan would use ayahuasca and alcohol from fermented fruits along with drumming and dancing to create a lowering of boundaries between the individuals and a shared consciousness. Apparently, after some verbal and physical fights and sexual liaisons while under the influence, everyone woke up somewhat dazed the next day, not remembering exactly what had happened, with all of the tension resolved.

In contrast, the tourists do not know each other, and the medicine man doesn't know them either. There is no expectation of a shared experience—of shared consciousness, aggression, sexuality, or anything else.

Instead, each person is on their own journey. Afterward, each person integrates their experience however they are able to.

Although the drug itself is the same, the impact of the experiences is likely to be very different.

Perhaps we can learn something about how to reduce the risks of ongoing psychosis after acute changes in reality, whether drug-induced or not, from these traditional precautions. What if our emphasis, instead of just sedating and shortening the experience as much as possible, was on helping people integrate the experience as much as possible, improving their underlying conflicts and dynamics to enhance their developing self-identity and improving their relationships, overcoming conflicts and tension? What if instead of universally repressing these episodes and labeling them as pathological illnesses, we viewed them like the traditional Peruvian leader as opportunities for personal growth and relationship consolidation?

Apparently, Carl Jung spent several years exploring his unconscious, without drugs, basically on his own, while others feared he was psychotic (documenting it in *The Red Book*) with the goal of personal individuation and development and found beneath his personal unconscious the collective unconscious, universal archetypes, and synchronicity, which have widely influenced Western psychospiritual thought ever since.

> Based on experiences guiding people on LSD trips, the personal growth path was tried at a short-term crisis residential program for people with psychosis called Soteria in northern California between 1971 and 1983. It was used as an alternative to hospitalizations and medications. Six or seven people lived there at a time or an average of 4 to 5 months. While only medicating 3% of residents, the outcomes both in terms of 6-week symptom reduction and 2-year recovery rates were as good or better than the outcomes for people hospitalized and medicated. The staff were non-mental health professionals chosen for their ability to relate warmly and intensively to residents "meeting them where they were at" without fearing or pathologizing them. They focused on helping them make sense of what they were going through. There were also a number of volunteers and ex-residents

> who were welcome to assist as well. Soteria has been a lightning rod for controversy ever since its success apparently drove its founder Loren Mosher from his positions of prominence in the psychiatric establishment. Its results have been replicated elsewhere, especially in Europe, but its basic approach has never become a well-funded part of the mainstream system, while insistence on more and more medications has continued to grow.

Before we leave the interesting intersection of indigenous practices, hallucinogens, and psychosis, I want to touch briefly on the common speculation that people who are diagnosed with schizophrenia in our society would have become shamans in animistic societies. In my opinion, we're only talking about the relatively small group of people who we discussed in Chapter 10, who have level 3 spiritual experiences in childhood, or occasionally later in life, people who "show signs of being touched by spirit," not people who use a lot of hallucinogenic substances. I suspect that some of these childhood level 3 people (like Maria, the Mexican healer, or Christina, the intuitive physician I described at the beginning of Chapter 4) could be carefully mentored to have personal roles and relationships that encompass ever increasing amounts of altered reality and shared consciousness experiences, including using hallucinogens, meditation and prayer, retreats featuring isolation and deprivation of sleep and food, rituals incorporating drumming, dancing, and trances, etc., so that they can function effectively within an altered reality, if we knew what we're doing. While they may appear to be psychotic at any given point, it seems clear to me that this is a very different journey from the ones we've been discussing in this guide—a journey that is generally unavailable within our society and that we usually only have glimpses of. Powerful community roles can protect from losses of self-identity and relationships. Maybe Samantha really could've been a spiritual healer in another time and place, but not in our current communities. Nonetheless, there are stories of a few "psychotic" people who have been helped, even in our society, by shamans working with them. There are likely many things we could learn from their mentoring techniques for emerging shamans that we could use to help fortify some people who are currently diagnosed with schizophrenia.

My bottom-line warning about hallucinogens: They're very hard to dose or use in any reasonably safe way. You didn't work for any of those experiences or insights; so, if you have more than an interesting trip, or use them regularly enough to become part of your life, you're likely to drown in deep waters.

Ecstasy

I don't have enough experiences working with people who use ecstasy to include more than a basically speculative paragraph about it. Although I've met a number of people—all young people—who have used ecstasy, none of them came to me because of the ecstasy or reported that it had sent them on a psychotic journey. They rarely even describe the altered mental state in terms of psychosis. I don't know how much of the difference between ecstasy and hallucinogens is due to neurochemical differences between the compounds (it seems like ecstasy alters how reality is perceived more than how it's understood and created), how much is due to the social context in which it is used (generally in large highly stimulated groups at clubs and raves), and how much is due to the young developmental stage the users are at and their goals (usually enhanced emotional closeness and sexual experiences, rather than consciousness expansion), but the outcome is usually described as a body-altering experience or a sensation-altering experience, rather than a mind-altering experience. Similarly, the dangers they faced seem to be related to their bodies and fears about their bodies, more than their minds and fears about their minds. The old fogy in me wants to conclude that ecstasy fits our current youth culture that cares more about amplifying superficial social and physical contacts than it cares about personal growth, consciousness expansion, and spiritual exploration.

Marijuana and synthetic cannabinoids

Many people in our society have used marijuana, and almost all have had positive, pleasant responses—feeling relaxed, less uptight, more sociable, and happier. Most people don't stop to wonder how marijuana creates those effects or why it's classified as a hallucinogen.

Hallucinogen? Come on, doc, that's just old scare tactics. This is pot we're talking about. Lots of states are legalizing it.

I'm not talking about whether marijuana is a "good drug" or a "bad drug," whatever that means. I'm talking about how it works. Its effects are primarily to decrease our sense of being separated from others and lower the internal self-absorbed worries: Let your thoughts flow more freely, wandering beyond your personal hang-ups. Loosen up. Chill out. It's not that important. It's kind of funny when you don't think about it as hard.

OK, I'll buy that. But why call that hallucinogenic?

Because decreasing our sense of separateness, while often pleasant, is also decreasing our self-identity, one of the three functions in our psychosis triangle, which can, in turn, weaken our experience of reality.

Consider these observations about marijuana from a psychosis perspective:

- Some people's first reaction to marijuana is to feel more anxious or panicky or even paranoid. These are commonly people who hold themselves together with large amounts of monitoring and controlling themselves and everything around them. Weakening their primary coping strategy exposes them to their underlying fears.
- After sustained use, marijuana sometimes turns against people. Instead of making them feel calmer and happier, it starts making them panic or paranoid. (I don't mean being afraid of being caught using. I mean feeling you're in danger of being attacked or falling apart.) I've seen this in people who are having other issues in their lives—they're under more stress, or in depression, or have lost some stability and security in their lives—so, instead of feeling calm, they feel out of control. I've seen other people who it seems like years of marijuana usage itself has eroded enough of themselves and their lives that they're frightened, instead of cool. (By the way, full panic attacks are often a compelling reason to stop marijuana use entirely.)
- People often start using marijuana socially, and it can help them feel more relaxed with other people and more sociable. Besides,

everything is funnier. If they start using it on a regular basis to decrease the anxiety they feel when they're by themselves, usually from their own ruminations and insecurities, or use it to help sleep (both of which it usually does rather well), over time they can start feeling less and less solid about themselves, and have weakened their self-identity function. Motivation may slide away, and apathy may take over. Ambition decreases. Aggression decreases, which is usually a good thing. (You rarely see two stoned guys say, "Let's take this outside.") Isolation increases, which is usually a bad thing. The relationship function in the psychosis triangle weakens, too.

- Some people experience marijuana as a "spiritual drug." It helps them feel more connected to the infinite. Unfortunately, if they also have sloppy spiritual practices and support, they're at risk of losing their balance as they're less and less grounded.
- People who have an experience of psychosis are much less likely to recover and more likely to have repeated episodes if they're using marijuana (and it's not just because they're not taking their medications, though that happens, too). With weak self-identity and relationships, when something else goes wrong with experiencing reality, it's harder to recover. The psychosis can increase personal and relationship anxiety, which feels better on marijuana, even while experiencing reality is getting worse; so, the person uses more and more and slips into a vicious cycle, using more and more marijuana to decrease the anxiety from the psychosis that it's causing. (This negative impact on people with psychosis is a big effect and, in my opinion, will likely be one of the worst unintended effects of legalizing marijuana.)

My overall point here is that marijuana has built into its "good" effects the potential for its "bad" effects and that the "bad" effects are predominantly ones that can impact psychotic journeys: loss of motivation and self-identity, isolation, panic, and paranoia. That's my explanation for the clear statistic that prolonged marijuana usage, especially if begun at young ages, significantly increases the odds of having a long-term psychosis.

Aren't there different strains and synthetics that can get around that problem?

Yes, there are, and no, they can't (at least not yet).

I've heard a number of people say that marijuana is "natural," unlike the pills; so, it's better for them. What "natural" means, in practice, is that you're getting many different cannabinoids in different combinations and different dosages. Hallucinogens are already hard to dose because of the individuality of response, but this makes it even harder. (By the way, if you're a novice, don't start with edibles thinking they're safer because they're cute. Edibles are much harder to dose than smoking or vaping because they don't really take effect for about an hour; so, you don't know how stoned you are when you eat more and you can't get rid of it after you've eaten too much.) There are generalizations, like Sativa contains more tetrahydrocannabinol (THC) than cannabidiol (CBD), which makes it more stimulating and more likely to provoke paranoia, whereas Indica contains more CBD than THC, which makes it more calming and more likely to decrease energy and relationships, but every plant is somewhat different and there are many active ingredients besides THC and CBD in marijuana. It's possible we will eventually find that some cannabinoid, perhaps even CBD, is a useful compound that doesn't increase psychosis, but since marijuana has been illegal, and still is illegal federally and in many states, it hasn't been researched and developed as carefully as it could be by legitimate pharmaceutical companies. Instead, there are synthetic cannabinoids that are primarily designed to get around legal restrictions against recreational use. Good "highs" are the goal more often than safety. It's also possible that to really understand marijuana, we'll have to research it holistically, rather than reductionistically. It may well be that for marijuana (and perhaps other complex herbal compounds), their total impact is more than the sum of its parts.

> *Evan came to a major university on a basketball scholarship with dreams of the NBA filling his head. His classes were less important than his performance on the court. As the best player on the team, he had minor star status. He lived in an apartment building with some of the other players. Free tennis shoes and coeds were scattered around.*
>
> *This didn't quite feel like the heaven it could've been. He was far from home, and truth be told, he was more a shy momma's boy than a player. He followed his NBA idols; so,*

he knew what his life was going to be like, but he couldn't always silence the gnawing doubts. Was he really a star in the making?

The team had a regular drug testing policy that had caught several of his roommates, including the one who always seemed to have plenty of pot around to give to anyone, so Evan rarely used. But this was a special occasion. A childhood friend was visiting from back home. Part of Evan wanted to be his old self and part of him wanted to show off. They ended up smoking a lot of his roommate's stash, with a couple girls, while watching horror movies.

Maybe there was something wrong with the pot, or maybe it was just exceptionally strong. Evan's friend, who was a regular user back home, started getting anxious and paranoid. That movie wasn't helping. He got up and went to bed, saying he felt strange about 1 am. Evan kept smoking. When did the girls leave?

When he woke on the couch the next day, he didn't feel right. He was groggy and edgy at the same time. He had a vague sense something bad was going to happen to him. Maybe he'd be caught on the next drug test. No, it was more pervasive than that. Nothing felt quite right. Maybe it'll go away by tomorrow.

But it didn't. He felt strange going to class the next day and couldn't focus on the lecturer. Every time his phone buzzed, it startled him. Something was wrong, but he was scared to tell anyone.

His thoughts were going faster and faster. He didn't get much sleep that week. The longer it went on, the harder it was to focus.

He couldn't shake the thought that he was being watched and going to get in trouble and lose everything he'd worked for. He put a piece of tape over his computer's camera just in case they were using it to watch him. He knew it sounded crazy, but it couldn't hurt.

When the game came on Thursday night, his timing was off. Actually, it was more like everything seemed slightly out of sync. Some things went a little fast and some a little slow. He couldn't find the flow of the game. Nothing was coming naturally. He ended up sitting out most of the first half with fouls.

He began to wonder if he'd blown his future.

After the game, his phone kept sending him the message that he didn't belong in college anymore. It was time for him to go pro. Who was sending these messages? Was it just his imagination?

"Everything will be fine if you go pro."

That's a reassuring message.

"The pressure will be gone without this college and its rules and its classes that you don't need anyway."

That makes sense.

"Get on a plane now and get out of here. Take your shoes and your ball. That's all you need."

His friends stopped him at the airport and called the coach who called the police, and he was taken in handcuffs to a psychiatric hospital. He'd always promised himself he'd never be that Black man in handcuffs, but there he was.

"My life has fallen apart. I don't know what's next."

The nurse in the hospital forced him to take a shot. What's in it? She just said, "It'll help you calm down."

He fell asleep.

When he woke up, his first thought was that he had to call his family to get him out of this nightmare. *I need to go home before I really do go crazy. I'm going to lose it here.*

> *Evan's mom did show up and she pretended to be calm, telling him everything would be all right while she was screaming inside, "What did they do to my son?"*
>
> *She did take him home, and it took several weeks for him to get back to himself.*
>
> *They didn't know what to do next.*
>
> *The coach, perhaps unreasonably, doubted his star would ever be safe to play again.*

My two bottom-line warnings about marijuana:

1) If you're not going to do anything with your life anyway or you just get into trouble, go ahead and get stoned every day. Sit on the couch, calmer, not worried about your life, eating chips. But forget about any ambitions you may have had. Remember: Pot is not a performance-enhancing drug.
2) If you're dealing with psychosis, or even if you have family members who deal with psychosis, find another way to deal with your anxiety, stress, depression, loneliness, irritability, paranoia, or whatever you "need" the pot for. You could get further and further out of balance and more and more lost the more you rely on pot.

Stimulants—"meth"/"street speed" and prescription stimulants

Methamphetamine, with its appealing combination of power and pleasure, has insinuated itself into our society through a variety of cracks, ranging from disruptive foster kids to college students trying to focus on their studies to gay men enhancing sex to loners isolated in the desert or in forgotten rural communities to professionals pushing their limits, with an impressively destructive impact, including causing quite a bit of psychosis.

At the Village, in common with many other places, our speed users were predominantly survivors of serious child abuse, many of whom had been prescribed stimulants as children for hyperactivity, some are stuck at level 1 personal development, fighting for their survival as outcasts in the hostile, impoverished fringes of our society. Power, aggression, focus, energy, drive, and a pleasurable, sexual high can pose as precisely the solutions that they need.

Even when she was strung out on speed, Candice was an attractive young woman featuring long, curly, but somewhat unkempt, blond hair, sensuous movements even though she was quite underweight, and a sense of desperation and longing that cried out to be rescued, or at least taken advantage of.

When she was 9 years old, she'd been too frightened and ashamed to tell anyone that her 15-year-old cousin started forcing her to have sex with him. She barely knew what he was doing to her. She knew it hurt. She knew it felt wrong and that it wouldn't have been happening if she wasn't a bad girl. She knew it was her fault. She was ashamed and knew she'd be blamed if she told anyone. That's what he told her and that's what she believed.

The teachers noticed her behavior deteriorating in school. She wasn't paying attention in class. She got in fights with the other kids. She was biting her nails and pulling her hair out. They asked her what was wrong, but she didn't tell them.

Her parents took her to their pediatrician, who said it sounded like she had ADHD, "which is common at her age," and prescribed her Adderall. It mostly made her feel dead inside, which frightened her—what if she was dying inside? But she didn't tell anyone that either. She was quieter in school; so, her problem was apparently solved.

As she went on to middle school, she hung out with the other outcast kids and barely passed her classes. No one ever wondered what she was really capable of. She could get the attention of older boys and even if she couldn't feel the sex, she could feel noticed by someone. The boys were happy to give her alcohol and then marijuana, and she could feel drunk and high—until it wore off. If her emptiness got too bad and she couldn't feel anything, she'd cut herself on her thighs to feel something. She needed to draw blood for it to work.

Things deteriorated at home. She got into screaming fights with her parents punctuated by slamming her door shut to her room, so they couldn't see her tears. They thought she was a self-centered, sullen teenager who didn't appreciate what they'd given her. They were frustrated and angry with her most of the time. She withdrew further. They grounded her. She cried to herself and cut some more. Then, she got piercings and a tattoo to show them they couldn't tell her what to do.

By 16, she dropped out of school and moved out with her boyfriend in a garage behind his mother's home. His mom would let them use the bathroom, but he'd stolen from her too many times to let them live in the house. They used a lot of speed together. He wouldn't tell her where he got money from, but they never had enough. A couple years later, she agreed to start prostituting, so they could get more money. By then, she was only living for the next hit of speed anyway.

She started staying up all night, thinking she heard people outside. She'd awaken her boyfriend to go check, but he'd just get mad and tell her she was imagining things. Maybe she was. But it seemed more and more clear that people were outside waiting for their chance to attack her. If she stood behind the window, then she could catch a glimpse of them. Sometimes, they parked cars across the street to watch her. Meantime, her life narrowed down to having sex with whoever he brought by and begging him to get her more speed. She missed a lot of meals. She'd go days without showering.

When the police busted him for buying speed, they brought her to the Village to get help.

She couldn't focus on anything we said. She was picking at her skin on her arms as her eyes darted around the room. We brought her a hamburger, which she ate voraciously. It was a little hard for her to eat since her hand muscles jerked suddenly without warning. She also yelled out angrily at no one we could see. It wasn't clear if she could understand us, but she seemed to agree to us paying for her to be in a hotel room and bring her dinner, get a shower, and think about changing her life.

The next morning when we stopped by to pick her up, the manager told us she'd already checked out.

We went back to the garage, but her boyfriend's mother told us we'd just missed her. She taken off with one of their friends.

A couple days later, we caught up to Candice. We offered to get her into a rehab to get off drugs and get her life back on track.

"This is my life."

"It doesn't have to be."

"Yes, it does."

"Can't you imagine anything else in life? You can get away from these people and selling your body for drugs. You don't deserve this."

She looked down and shook her head and quietly said, "Can you get me something to eat? I haven't had anything to eat today."

I looked down and shook my head feeling defeated, "Sure."

A couple weeks later, her boyfriend was released. He beat her up.

Gradually, Candice made a connection with us. She'd come by for a sandwich or to talk. She told us about the sexual abuse as a kid. We took her to the ER when she got an abscess on her arm where she was skin popping the speed. We kept offering rehab, but she'd say it wasn't for her.

Her weight went down. She looked more and more strung out. She started mumbling to herself. Now, we couldn't even really ask her if she wanted to get clean or not.

At our weekly team meeting, Candice was often brought up as a "member of concern." "Can't we do anything to save Candice? She's going to die like this."

We'd been round and round about her, but we couldn't stop ourselves from going through it again. It's hard to accept being helpless and watching someone die.

"Why can't we put her on a 5150 and send her to the hospital?"

"You can't force someone into inpatient drug treatment, like you can for psychiatric treatment."

"Why not?"

"As it happens, there's a law they passed at the same time as the 5150 mental health law for involuntary treatment of drug addiction, but no county has ever opened a facility to take them in. Medi-Cal won't pay for it, and the county doesn't have the money to put every addict who's killing themselves in the hospital over and over again. Besides, drug rehab takes a lot longer than 72 hours, or even 14 days."

"But, by then, she might be clear enough to agree to rehab. We can't even ask her the way she is now."

"We can't lock someone up, just to detox them and ask them if they want rehab. I don't think there's really a chance she'd say yes anyway. She's always turned it down."

"Can't we get her arrested for using drugs and then sentenced to receive treatment?"

"They might arrest her boyfriend again, but they don't usually arrest attractive White women. They're seen as the victims, not the criminals."

"I bet if she was your daughter, you'd find a way."

I paused before quietly answering, "I bet if she was my daughter, I'd destroy myself trying. Since I'm not, I'll just keep hanging in there, even though I don't have much hope."

As it happened, 6 months later, they did arrest her. She spent 6 months in jail and then was sent to a residential drug rehab in Santa Monica for 6 more months. When the judge released her from the program, she returned to Long Beach. I saw her a couple weeks later. Although she looked and sounded good—she'd gained weight, her skin healed up, and she wasn't paranoid or twitching anymore—it was clear she was drifting back to her old habits.

"Don't you remember how bad your life was, how messed up you were, how you had to prostitute and got beaten up? Please, don't go back to that. You can live in a sober living group home with other people trying to stay sober, make some new friends, maybe go back to school."

"They have rules, don't they?"

"Yeah, but not as many as at the rehab. No drugs or overnight guests. One meeting a week. Share the chores. Let them know if you're going to be out for the night. You know, stuff like that. Nothing too strict."

"I'm not following any rules or doing what someone else tells me to do. I'm going to live my own way."

"But you'll end up with some guy telling you what to do and hitting you when you don't."

"That won't happen again. But I'm not putting myself in a program any longer. It's been a whole year. The judge said I don't have to."

I looked down and shook my head. I didn't really have anything else to offer her. "No, you don't have to."

A couple of years later, I heard that Candice had been institutionalized in an IMD. She was chronically paranoid and

> *had difficulty talking coherently even off speed. Her brain had probably been permanently damaged by the speed.*

At its most dramatic, psychosis from speed can be every bit as severe as schizophrenia, and often more difficult to treat with medications. It often takes staying off the speed to recover and eventually even that might not be possible. Use the speed again and back come the delusions, voices, and paranoia.

Stimulants are prescribed as a treatment for AHDH for both children and adults, but in much lower dosages than street speed. When I began training, the main stimulant being used was Ritalin, which was used entirely for hyperactive children. I was taught that the "paradoxical" effect of a stimulant calming a child down stopped working at puberty, and after that, it made them more hyper and jittery, just like everyone else. Ritalin was especially useful for young boys who wouldn't sit still in class until they "outgrew" their hyperactivity and could sit still without the medication anymore. Medicating children like this potentially could avoid lots of relationship problems in school, disrupting classes and getting disciplined or even suspended. They could avoid an identity as a bad kid, that could influence their entire life trajectory. (I wonder if Tom Sawyer would be diagnosed as ADHD today and how his life would've been different if he had taken stimulants.) Unfortunately, Ritalin also had lots of side effects, including decreased appetite and repressed growth in height. Some kids complained of feeling like zombies, while others developed tolerance. Standard practice developed to only medicate the kids when they needed to be well behaved in class and not on weekends or in summer. Needless to say, parents, day care programs, and summer camps all wanted well-behaved medicated kids during their time together. Also of concern was that some of the pills seemed to be being "diverted" to the kids' parents or sold on the street. Cylert was developed as a longer-acting stimulant to try to decrease abuse potential.

From those beginnings, prescription stimulants have mushroomed. The original Ritalin and Cylert are no longer on patent and, therefore, not very profitable, but they have been replaced by an entirely new crop of stimulants, including Adderall and Vyvanse, and more are in the pipeline. ADHD was added to many kids' list of diagnoses, including the majority of kids in foster care. Some of those kids went on to become the traumatized, dropout, homeless, addicted adults I saw at the Village. The pharmaceutical industry countered that frightening observation with studies showing that treating with stimulants as kids actually reduced the incidence of stimulant abuse when they grew up. That would be reassuring, but is it true?

The pharmaceutical companies moved to further increase their market and profits. No longer is hyperactivity the main target. Poor attention span has largely replaced it. (I suspect that smart phones are largely responsible for turning hyperactive, disruptive, bored kids into sedentary kids who can't pay attention to anything besides their phones and video games.) Since our attention span is steadily getting shorter, more and more people are having problems and therefore "diagnosable." If we look back across the last 100 years, we can see a progression from a generation who listened to the radio and tracked the leisurely pace of baseball as the national sport, moving on to my generation who grew up training our brains to watch TV and Sesame Street's short attention span segments, and we respond to the pace of football, and now we're being replaced by a generation raised on video games, surfing the Internet, and iPhones for whom even basketball isn't stimulating enough.

Also, people don't tend to outgrow inattention, so adult ADHD was promoted as an under-recognized diagnosis. More and more adults are now on stimulants, without weekend or summer breaks, presumably for the rest of their lives, with no end in sight.

Stimulants have also been marketed as brain enhancers, or "nootropics," for people with no diagnosis at all, competing successfully with herbal stimulants and highly caffeinated energy drinks. Many college students use stimulants with or without prescriptions to stay up all night studying or have more energy and focus while taking tests. After all, why should ADHD-diagnosed students have an advantage over them? My college students estimate that over half of their peers are using stimulants to improve their academics.

It seems likely to me that our next drug epidemic will be stimulants, fueled by both prescription and street supplies.

I don't know if that epidemic will include a lot of psychosis or not. It seems likely that the lower dosages of stimulants used in prescription strengths compared to street speed—where the effect is often intentionally enhanced by snorting, skin popping, and injecting—are less likely to cause psychosis, but we don't have unbiased, long-term information to know. What I'd really like to know is this: If a college freshman is prescribed stimulants to improve their attention and studies in school, what are the odds that they'll lose control and become psychotic before they're seniors? I know it's not zero. What percentage would be an acceptable risk?

> Kathy begged me to see the Johnson family because his parents were so desperate for help and didn't know where to turn, even though Timothy wasn't eligible to become a Village member; so, I agreed.
>
> Timothy's father told me the story, while Timothy fidgeted, his eyes darting around the room, and his mother quietly cried. He wanted me to know, that even though they were from Compton, they weren't the stereotypical ghetto Black family. They both worked. They were responsible and had raised Timothy to be able to move up in the world. He'd done extremely well in troubled Compton High School where most students drop out, graduating near the top of his class. The state of California has a program to encourage students like Timothy by giving them a guaranteed admission to the University of California if they were in the top few percent of their high school. Timothy was proud to go to UCLA to study engineering.
>
> Unfortunately, the competition and the academic standards at UCLA were well above what he was used to. Even with a support program for first-generation college students, he began falling behind. The pressure grew. He'd never had trouble with school. That had always been his refuge. He could count on A's, but no longer. He wasn't even passing. He couldn't pay attention when he tried to study longer and longer hours. The lectures confused him as he fell further behind.
>
> He went to the Student Health Service and told them he was having problems concentrating and needed help. They diagnosed him with ADHD and gave him Adderall. It helped

a lot. He had more energy. He could focus better both in class and at home. Maybe he wasn't sleeping much and was somewhat more irritable, but he was making it again. He didn't get his customary A's, but he did get some B's.

The next year, his courses got harder. The intense mathematics classes in his engineering major were overwhelming. They raised his Adderall dosage. He got C's.

By his fourth year, he'd lost control. He'd failed several classes and ended up on academic probation. The Adderall was the only thing that helped him, but they wouldn't raise the dosage any further. He started buying more from other students.

When he became paranoid and pulled a knife on another student, he was given a medical withdrawal and sent home in shame. Without the Student Health Service, he had no insurance or access to Adderall. He panicked. He couldn't live without it. He started buying it off the street.

His parents had taken him twice to the hospital because he was high, aggressive, and paranoid. The hospital staff advised him to go to a drug program to get off the stimulants. He begged them to prescribe more Adderall to him, so he'd be well again. He promised to use it responsibly. He said he needed it to go back to college and get his life back. The hospital staff told his parents they couldn't do anything and sent him home after sedating him. His parents began locking him out of the house during the day while they were at work since he was breaking and stealing things and barricading the house.

I didn't do any better with Timothy. He wouldn't consider anything except getting more Adderall from me, and I wouldn't consider that. I didn't think I had any chance of helping him taper off as an outpatient, especially since that wasn't what he wanted to do. All I'd be doing if I gave him more Adderall would be to add more fuel to the fire.

> As they left, I felt really sorry for both Timothy and his parents. His biggest break, being admitted to UCLA, turned out to be a curse when he turned out to be out of his league. But did he deserve to have his whole life ruined as a result? Wasn't that mostly the Adderall's fault?

It isn't just college students who are at risk with stimulants. There are lots of people, including successful people, who are seduced by having more energy, more focus, more brain power, than they've ever felt before. And since the doctor gave it to them, it must be safe. Even as people around them start questioning if these pills are good for them and if they're really in control, they're sure they have everything under control.

Notice how, even for stimulants, it's not as simple as "bad drugs poison your brain and cause psychosis" (or for those of you old enough to remember the commercial where they cracked an egg into a hot frying pan and said, "Here's your brain on drugs. Any questions?").

My bottom-line warning about speed: It's the "solution" to all your problems that can literally drive you crazy or even kill you.

Cocaine—crack

While there are certainly people who experience psychosis directly from cocaine, usually transiently while high, I couldn't come up with any stories like that to share with you. From what I've seen, cocaine's impact is more likely to be an indirect one, destroying a life rather than destroying a brain.

Cocaine is quite possibly our most psychologically addictive drug. A combination of a rapid onset very pleasurable, stimulating high that is short lived followed by a deeply unpleasant, depressing crash drives people into ever more desperate searches for more.

I've been told repeatedly that Cocaine Anonymous meetings tend to be harmful because just hearing other people talk about their experiences with cocaine triggers overwhelming urges, leading to people leaving the meeting and using again. I've never heard that excuse for not going to other 12-step meetings. Escaping all triggers, "people, places, and things," seems to be crucial to abstaining from cocaine. Otherwise, the temptation is just too great.

Even experienced drug addicts can't seem to control cocaine. The continuous quest for more becomes the only thing that matters. I've even met people who said they went back to speed because they couldn't handle crack. (Crack is a cheaper, less pure "ghetto" cocaine.)

This is another variation on the theme: Crack isn't the solution, but once you're on crack, you only have one problem—how to get more crack.

> Andrea came to see me because her Section 8 worker told her to, not because she believed any good would come of it, or from anything else for that matter. With her Section 8, she only had to pay $220 out of her $830 SSI check for rent, but she had again spent it all on crack and not paid her rent. She knew that was stupid, but she couldn't stop herself. The only thing in her mind was how to stay high for another day.
>
> She was ashamed and kept her head down and her eyes on the ground to avoid seeing how she looked in my eyes. She knew I'd tell her to stop just like everyone else, but I didn't. I tried to meet her where she was at without judgment. Her silences made the conversation one sided, "How are you going to make it on the street after they evict you? ... Have you been homeless before? ... Do you know where to go? ... Do you have someone to protect you, so you won't be raped?"
>
> She furtively looked up at me and then back down. "No, Owen is in jail."
>
> "How long is he in for? ... Was he living with you? ... Will he be mad when he finds out you've lost the apartment?"
>
> She broke down into sobbing. I stopped questioning her and offered her a Kleenex and then sat quietly for a long time.
>
> She barely got out the words, "We killed our baby."
>
> "What?"
>
> She looked up at me, pleadingly, "I tried so hard not to use when I was pregnant, but I just couldn't stay stopped. The

baby was so small and kept crying all the time. We didn't know what to do .... We didn't have anything to take care of a baby with, and we were both still getting high all the time. One morning, I woke up and the baby was lying in bed between us, all blue and not moving. I freaked out, but there was nothing anyone could do. Manny was dead. He was only 2 months old. They told us that X-rays showed that Manny had several broken bones, but I don't know how that could've happened. They pressed charges on us. Owen got a year in jail. He took the blame, because he knew I couldn't make it in jail. I got probation, but I'm not calling in like I'm supposed to. I just keep getting high."

She stopped talking again. I took a deep breath. How am I supposed to accept someone who killed an infant after breaking his bones because she and her boyfriend were too busy getting high? I have to try, "Shit, that's a heavy burden you've got for the rest of your life."

She looked up at me questioningly.

I softened a little bit, "I'm not sure I could get clean knowing that's what I'd have to face, but if you decide to try and sign into a program, I'll try to be there with you."

She looked up at me gratefully, "Thanks for understanding, but I just can't do it."

"Then, we'll be with you on the street, too."

A couple months later, she was evicted. I saw her once or twice after that, but then, she disappeared. I don't know what happened to her. When Owen got out of jail, he came looking for her, but I didn't have anything to tell him.

While cocaine may make someone psychotic, that's not likely to be their biggest problem.

My bottom-line warning: A cocaine user's only real problem is how to get more, and their only real solution is to get away from it, probably far away.

Heroin—opiates

Heroin and the other opiates, both legal and illegal, biologically skip the middleman. Unlike the other drugs on this journey that indirectly stimulate our pleasure centers, opiates go straight to our pleasure center, binding directly with our opiate receptors. And pleasure only partially describes their impact. It's a profound sense of peace, safety, and wellness. This is one of the most primitive parts of our brain. It tells us whether we're alright or not, safe or not. When it's activated, it sends signals throughout our brain and body telling us everything is fine, relax, be happy. Nothing bothers us. Even the physical pain and psychological panic of a heart attack can be relieved with an injection of morphine in the ER while the doctors work to save our life. Opiate addicts commonly say that they need "their medicine."

Disturbances in any of the three functions in our psychosis triangle don't bother us either: Voices aren't so bad, paranoia is blunted, loneliness and isolation, confusion and self-doubts, none of it is as disturbing. No other substances, even the indirect pleasure stimulators like the benzos and all the rest of the illegal drugs and alcohol, can sooth us and take away the distress like opiates can.

> *Diane was desperate. She already had two felony convictions for narcotics, and California is a three-strike state. If they caught her using heroin again, she'd be incarcerated for life, and she was only 24. She couldn't stay off it, even though they were going to drug test her, and she couldn't go to a program because no matter what medications they gave her, and they'd tried everything in jail, there was no other way to calm down the voices that were torturing her or even to be able to sleep.*
>
> *"Isn't there anything you can give me, so I can stay off the heroin and not be a psychotic mess?"*
>
> *"Have you tried methadone?"*
>
> *"They won't give it to me anymore. I used while I was on it. I mean, isn't there some psychiatric medication you can give me?"*

"I can try, though I doubt everyone else whose tried before me are idiots. Let's start by you telling me your story."

"When I was about 13 or 14, my parents were both working. After school, they had me stay with my uncle who was about 20. He started forcing me to have sex with him every afternoon. He told me that if I told my parents, he'd just say I was lying, and they'd believe him and not me, and then, they'd beat me even more than they usually did. After about 6 months, I couldn't take it anymore. I hurt all the time. I couldn't stop crying. I couldn't sleep because of the nightmares. So, I told my parents, but he was right. They believed him and not me, and they did beat me more. And he kept abusing me. So, I got a gun and I shot and killed him. They put me in juvenile hall until I was 21."

I held up my hand. "Wait a minute. I have to ask you something."

"What?" she asked softly.

"I've met so many other women who wished they had the guts to do what you did, to kill him, and they keep wondering what would've happened if they had; so, I have to ask you, 'Did it work?'"

She hesitated, "Well, it made him stop."

"That's important, but that's not really what I'm asking. Did it make the terror or the shame or the dirtiness or the emotional pain any better?"

"No. It sure didn't. That's why I'm here today. I still can't get rid of any of it."

"I can take all the Seroquel and Trazodone or whatever else they give me, but he still haunts me. I still hear his voice taunting me. I still feel vulnerable. I still feel ashamed and like it was somehow my fault. I still can't sleep."

I put together a new combination of meds for her, but what she really needed was emotional healing, probably all the *way to acceptance and forgiveness to finally be freed. There was no magic in my pills. She was caught using heroin again and sent to prison.*

I feel sorry for her and I don't know what she should've done. I don't think she should have to accept being abused or forgive her uncle, but that's not an excuse to use heroin. You have to face life, not become a junky, no matter what happens.

Well, I think most people would agree with you, but let's look at ourselves a moment before we throw the first stone. I think almost no one is "living life on life's terms" without artificially manipulating our pleasure centers to sooth ourselves and feel calm.

Everyone is not a heroin addict.

That's true, but heroin isn't the only way to manipulate pleasure centers, it's just the most direct—along with the other opiates. I'll often ask new people I meet what they do to manage their moods, so they'll be less edgy and restless, to feel calm and relaxed. They'll often look confused and ask me what I mean. "People have discovered and invented quite a few ways to manage our stress. Here are some common choices: all street drugs, alcohol, nicotine, caffeine, sugar, carbohydrates, dark chocolate, sex, love, risk taking, very strenuous exercise, prayer, meditation, gambling, basically anything you can be addicted to. My go-tos now are dark chocolate and meditation. How about you?" Then, they get what I mean and come up with their choices. I claim that almost everyone is using one or more of these things in a very intentional, carefully dosed, frequent way to artificially feel good. And that you're likely addicted to whatever your choice is, meaning you're sure you can't feel good without it and will start craving it as soon as you don't feel good, and in most cases, give in to your craving, reinforcing it.

Well, that's probably true.

We attach different morals to different things on this list, but they're not biologically or psychologically that different. We make up rationalizations to defend our choices, but it's really not that different listening to a smoker explain why it's worth a 35% chance of dying to keep smoking, an alcoholic explain how drinking beer isn't the same as hard liquor, or Bill Clinton explain how getting a blow job behind his desk wasn't really sex.

What I think is fair to say is that the choices we make, purposely or not, of what we use to artificially manipulate our pleasure centers, and then likely get addicted to, is one of the most important predictors of our physical and mental health. None of them is free of side effects. And none of them is as deadly as heroin and the other opiates.

With the push for doctors to prescribe opiates more liberally for pain relief, including chronic pain, many more people have ended up using opiates regularly, and addictively. And many more are dying as a result.

Why are opiates deadlier than the other choices?

Some of that is due to their other effects on the body, like slowing breathing or decreasing appetite or slowing our gut, but I think the problem is related to how effective they are at altering our basic safety system. I think our brains and our bodies have trouble making all the ongoing adjustments needed to respond effectively to a world of stressors when we're messing with the alarm system. People who use a lot of opiates just seem to get more and more unhealthy. I've had a number of patients who chronically took benzos and opiates, who died without any clear cause in their 50s and 60s. They always had a lot of health issues, but more than that, they always seemed unhealthy. I remember reading that half of all heroin addicts die by the time they're 40 if they don't stop using. I don't know if that's true, but I sure haven't met many elderly heroin addicts.

> *Samuel had three highly intertwined traits that made him difficult to work with.*
>
> *First, he had a nasty personality. He was very impatient and demanding. When he didn't get his way, he rapidly turned to swearing, threats, and even spitting to try to intimidate and bully people into giving him what he wanted, usually money ... now. As a result, he had no friends, and even most of the staff tended to avoid him.*
>
> *Second, he was chronically paranoid, complaining about people stealing from him and beating him up. Because he*

was so unlikable, and so often in debt, it's likely much of the time, he really was being assaulted. Occasionally, he even had the bruises or black eyes to prove it, but it would've been unlikely that everyone he claimed was persecuting him really was.

Third, he was a heroin addict, and he never seemed to have enough money to support his habit. We generally only had the pleasure of his company when he wasn't high and didn't have money to get high again ... now. He was also chronically physically unwell. He'd lost a lot of weight. His pants barely stayed up with his belt cinched up. He had a chronic cough, too.

One day, Samuel suddenly got severe chest pain and panicked. He called 911 to get an ambulance to take him to St. Mary's hospital ... now. The ER doctors agreed that he might be seriously ill. They suspected a pulmonary embolism, a potentially fatal blood clot in his lung, and began a workup and treatment. Samuel was overwhelmed, frightened, confused, and probably withdrawing on top of it all. He reacted in his usual way, with swearing and threats. The ER reacted in their usual way, by sedating him with a shot of Ativan. When he tried to fight them off while they were giving him the shot, they tied him down and called a psychiatrist to put him on a hold, so he could be kept there to get the care he needed to save his life. That's when the spitting started, and they put a mask over his face. They were scared to sedate him more with his breathing problems.

Once he got to the medical ward, still tied to the bed, the battles continued. When they tried to untie him to go to the bathroom or eat, he tried to pull the tubes out and hit them. When they tried to change him when he soiled himself, he kicked them and accused them of sexually molesting him. When they tried to feed him, he spit the food at them.

Needless to say, getting the workup done and him treated was a prolonged process. A couple weeks later, his lungs were much better, but he'd lost an alarming amount of weight—and he didn't have any to spare—and the hospital staff began to worry he was going to die there. They decided they needed to put a feeding tube in him, since he was refusing to eat, but they didn't know how to go about getting the legal approval to do that over his objection; so, they called me.

I reviewed the situation with our team nurse who had been going to see him relatively regularly, or at least regularly enough to be totally frustrated and burned out by this whole situation. Fortunately, I hadn't been involved; so, I could stand back and be somewhat calmer. I pointed out that forcing him to have a feeding tube was just going to escalate the conflicts and leave them without any way of sending him home eventually—and it seemed his lungs were no longer in acute danger. He was just very weak now. Instead, I recommended offering him a trade: Start him on Methadone in the hospital to restabilize his pleasure centers, so he'd calm down and be relaxed, while watching his breathing, in return for him agreeing to be fed twice a day by the case manager on our staff he liked best. The hospital staff was taken aback. They didn't know he was a heroin addict and they usually didn't start Methadone on the inpatient ward, although they'd maintain patients who came from the Methadone clinic. They also didn't like using outside staff to do their nursing functions. Both Samuel and the hospital team were desperate enough to agree.

He began to improve. He was really hungry and ate a lot. He'd never been "refusing to eat." He'd been tied down and lashing out at them at every opportunity.

He was impressed how well the Methadone worked to help reduce his agitation and his cravings for heroin and agreed to try it on an ongoing basis after he was discharged from the hospital a couple weeks later. He also had enough clarity and calmness to feel gratitude toward the staff that was feeding him. They gradually untied him.

> That crisis became a major turning point in his life. He got off heroin altogether. Perhaps not surprisingly, once he did, his mood stabilized, and he was less impatient. He was broke and beaten up less and less often. He began eating regularly and gained weight. The paranoia gradually went away. He became less nasty. The staff and other members stopped avoiding him. He even made a couple friends.

(Both of the last two stories predate Suboxone, which is a better prescription opiate substitute than Methadone, both of which are widely used to keep your opiate receptors stimulated without having to keep getting high, which can break the behavioral cycle around using, compensating for but not healing the underlying pleasure center problem.)

One of the big problems in getting off anything you've been using to maintain your pleasure center is that you won't feel good without it, even if your life is OK. You've built up a "highway" of circuits catering to your simulator of choice that's empty, and craving, when it's gone. Try talking with a "dry drunk" or an injured athlete who can't exercise or someone who's trying to give up cigarettes or dieting. They're all irritable and feeling unwell. They're all desperately looking for something else to use, so they don't relapse. The 12-step group meetings include "buffets" of replacement pleasure center stimulators—coffee, sugar, cigarettes, doughnuts, empathy, prayer, and sometimes even sex—trying to help people hold it together until their "normal" circuitry that's withered from disuse comes back to life. Then, they can feel pleasure and wellness from everyday stimulation. Even still, the empty highway for their substance of choice is likely always going to be there waiting for them to relapse. (Incidentally, the most dangerous time for opiate addicts is often after they've had a prolonged period of abstinence, long enough to reduce their tolerance, and then they relapse and use their "normal" dosage, only to find it much stronger than it was, unfortunately, sometimes even lethally.)

Opiates are particularly difficult to substitute for, except with other opiates like Methadone and Suboxone, because they've imbalanced the pleasure center itself, not just altered the pathways that stimulate it. So, if someone who has a psychotic condition finds themselves without a supply of an opiate they've become accustomed to using—whether it's because they used up their prescription too fast, they ran out of money to buy more off the street, or they're confined in a medical or psychiatric hospital or jail—they're at risk of feeling irritable and unwell, exacerbating their psychosis, and raising their antipsychotic medication may not be that helpful.

My bottom-line warning: Over time, opiates disrupt our pleasure centers and our ability to feel well without them. That makes it very hard to recover from anything else, including psychosis. It also kills people.

Alcohol

Alcohol is perhaps the most popular substance people use to calm down and relax, deal with stress or social anxiety, dull our feelings, enjoy ourselves, make it easier to fall asleep, fill us with "liquid courage," or even stabilize and stimulate our pleasure centers.

On the positive side, for the vast majority of people, alcohol is easy to dose and affects us in predictable, reliable ways once we learn how to use it. It appears that only about 10% of people get addicted to it, becoming dependent, and potentially become "alcoholics." We don't know what's different about those people, although we know it strongly runs in families. We don't even know where the difference is, whether they metabolize it differently in their livers, or if it impacts their pleasure centers differently, or they have a reduced ability to judge how intoxicated they are, for instance.

In the absence of a clear diagnostic test or biologic explanation for alcohol dependence, we tend to drift back to personal and moral weakness to explain the differences. Rather than explaining alcoholism as the progressive dependence and poisoning of a person, we describe it with step 1 of the AA 12 steps: "We admitted we were powerless over alcohol—that our lives had become unmanageable." *DSM* includes a list of signs of the progression of being unable to control drinking—drinking in the morning, when alone, to feel normal, to deal with hangovers or delirium tremens—and its consequences—social, legal, functional, relationship, and health. *DSM-V* even eliminated the distinction between use and dependence, relying entirely on negative consequences to categorize the severity of the "disorder."

On the negative side, alcohol damages almost every part of our brains and bodies. Because alcohol is a "normal" and apparently controllable part of so many people's lives, we often don't realize how pervasive its destructive forces are.

I was working as a resident in the outpatient psychiatric clinic at LA County Hospital when an unusual patient came in to see me. Lawrence had been sent over by Goodwill Industries. Lawrence was 21 years old and developmentally disabled. He was working at Goodwill in a sheltered workshop with other developmentally disabled young people. His job was to sort the shoes that were donated and put a size and price on each one and display them in the thrift store. Unfortunately, he'd gotten into the habit of drinking beer at the liquor store next door at lunch time. Just a couple beers made him aggressive, and he was getting into fights in the afternoon almost every day. They told him not to drink over and over, but he kept sneaking over and doing it anyway. After 3 years working there successfully, he was going to get fired and lose all his friends. Also, he was a big man, and they were afraid someone was going to get hurt. In desperation, they sent him to me to get him to stop drinking.

I read the note and confirmed the story with Lawrence and, then, sat back puzzled. I didn't know what to do. I hadn't been taught how to get people to stop drinking.

A crazy idea came to my rescue, "Let's go for a walk up to the hospital wards, so you can see how alcohol affects people."

We walked into one of the wards with six beds to a room. I told the nurse what I was doing and asked her if it was OK to introduce Lawrence to the patients there. She said beds 1, 2, and 5 had alcohol-related problems.

Bed 1 held an older man in the end stages of kidney and liver failure. His skin was yellowish, and he had a swollen belly because fluid was backed up behind his cirrhotic liver. He also had a stent in his arm, so they could hook him up to the dialysis machine since his kidneys weren't working either. He was laying there, groaning with his tongue sticking out of his mouth, not able to talk to us.

"Alcohol did that to him?"

"Yes, it did. Years of drinking destroyed both his liver and his kidney, and now, toxins are building up everywhere in his body, poisoning his brain, and he'll die in a matter of months. It's too late for him to stop drinking and reverse the damage now."

Lawrence was starting to look a little yellow himself.

Bed 2 held a man in his 20s who had been riding a motorcycle drunk and crashed into a wall, breaking lots of bones. He had casts all over his body and was in traction. The skin we could see was heavily bruised. Lawrence just stood there with his mouth open. I don't think he'd ever seen someone this badly hurt before.

Bed 5 held a woman in her 40s. She had a tube going through her nose into a big glass jar hooked up to a suction machine. We could see little pieces of her stomach lining floating in the jar. She drank so much she had ulcers, and her digestive acid was destroying her stomach lining. She was also in terrible pain.

Lawrence started to gag and ran to the bathroom and threw up.

When he returned, they started talking. She told him how alcohol had destroyed her life, and how she was going to try to stop again. He told her that he'd just started drinking and was getting in trouble. I stood back as they bonded and even prayed for each other.

Two days later, I got a call from Goodwill, "Lawrence just keeps talking about the people he met and how bad alcohol is for you and how he's never going to drink again. Can we send some more people over to you?"

I hesitated before answering, "No, that was a one-time only deal. I'm glad it worked out, but I think I was lucky."

That's a good story, but what does that have to do with psychosis?

Hopefully, it gives you the background to understand how alcohol and alcoholism impact psychosis. Here are the main points:

- "Normal" alcohol intoxication is likely to make psychosis better since it reduces anxiety and stress.
- If someone is addicted to alcohol for years, they can have withdrawal symptoms, delirium tremens (DTs), that can include paranoia and hallucinations.
- Out-of-control alcohol use can cause damage to a person's self-identity and relationships, which can reduce people's resiliency and make it harder to deal with reality, so they drift into psychosis.
- In large amounts, alcohol's damaging effects on both the body and the brain can lead to psychotic symptoms.
- Both of the last two consequences are far more likely to occur in people who become dependent on alcohol, that is, alcoholics, than to everyone else.

OK. That makes sense.

Let's talk a little more about some of the damaging effects on the brain that can lead to psychosis. Almost everyone is familiar with the pleasant effects of alcohol going into their brains and the unpleasant effects of it leaving, also known as a hangover. Within reasonable dosages, neither one leads to psychosis. If you drink far too much (usually an alcoholic who can't evaluate or regulate their intake or whose tolerance has gone down, likely due to liver damage, on the one hand, or an inexperienced young person drinking way too much and way too irresponsibly, usually influenced by peer pressure, on the other hand), you can "black out." This is different from "passing out," which is falling asleep uncontrollably because of too much sedation. In a blackout, you look like you're drunk and you're walking around functioning, but afterward you can't remember anything that you did. While that's a quite toxic and potentially dangerous state, and you can be quite confused, it's not really psychotic. You'll be yourself again after the alcohol wears off.

If you've become dependent on alcohol, you don't just get hangovers when it comes out of your system, you get withdrawal symptoms, otherwise known as DTs. DTs can include quite serious symptoms, e.g., shaking, severe anxiety and insomnia, seizures, and "delirium," including hallucinations, usually visual, and delusions, usually paranoid. These are seeing "pink elephants" you've heard of (although I've never met anyone who saw pink elephants). DTs can be quite dangerous, even deadly, and should be treated in a medical ER or hospital. The treatment is primarily sedatives, often Librium since it slowly leaves your system over a couple of days, to counteract the alcohol withdrawal, but may also include anticonvulsants or antipsychotics. DTs peak about 2 days after stopping drinking and then gradually resolve. The key question here is: "Did the hallucinations and the paranoia occur when you were really drunk or 2 days after you stopped drinking?" Most people will be surprised when they really think about the answer because they assumed they were psychotic because they were drunk, not because they were withdrawing.

Once someone gets to true DTs, they've generally been dependent on alcohol for a number of years, they're clearly alcoholics, and significant brain damage has occurred … but they can still recover if they can stop drinking. If they continue drinking, the DTs will happen more and more regularly with increasing severity until maybe 10 years later, they are shaking, anxious, sleepless, having seizures, hallucinating, and paranoid all the time. This used to be called "alcoholic hallucinosis." Once you've arrived at this point, the odds are the damage is permanent and medications are relatively useless.

> Marsha was creating a giant fuss on the medical ward; so, they called me in as a psychiatry consult. I was still in residency training; so, I had no idea what was going on. They said she was an alcoholic in DTs. They had been sedating her with Librium. And they had an IV going with fluids and vitamins. She started screaming that there was a Harley Davidson motorcycle gang outside her room waiting to kidnap her. She was flailing around trying to get out of the bed, pulling on the IV lines and the curtains around her bed, trying to see her pursuers and run away from them. The nurses called the code team, who were a bunch of big men, and they were busy tying her down to the bed in "four-point" leather restraints by the time I got there. Strangely to me, she seemed more terrified of the imaginary men outside the room than the real ones inside the room.

After they finished tying her down, they left me alone with her.

As I sat down next to her bed trying to figure out what to say, I realized that she was old, well maybe middle-aged, about my mother's age.

"You've got to help me. They're still out there and now I'm helpless. They're going to get me. You need to untie me. I need to get out of here." She was tugging at the restraints on her arms and thrashing her legs around.

"Who's going to get you?"

"The gang. Didn't you see them when you came in? They're right outside with their Harleys."

"How could they have motorcycles in a hospital hallway?"

"What?" She looked around confused and terrified. That's when I realized that she probably didn't even know she was in a hospital or who any of us were.

"Let's slow things down a little. You're in a bed in county hospital. I'm a doctor, and Sally here is your nurse. These are your medicines in these bags." Her gaze followed my finger pointing to the IVs, and she seemed to calm down a little.

"I think you were brought in by an ambulance when someone called because you had a seizure. Is that right?"

"Yeah. I get seizures when I forget to take my Dilantin and Phenobarbital."

"Have you been drinking, too?"

"I'm not really sure since I get blackouts, but I don't think I've had anything since Saturday night. What day is it now?"

"It's Monday afternoon."

There was a crash in the hall outside, and suddenly Marsha was screaming again, "They're out there. They're out there. Please. Please help me."

I got up and looked out the door. "It looks like a patient in the hall on a gurney banged into a door. It's fine."

"I tell you what. I can't untie you, but I can get someone to sit in your room to watch over you and make sure you're safe." She looked doubtful. "I can also get you some more medication to help you relax."

Some Valium in her IV and more Librium kept her quiet for a couple days. We were able to untie her.

I was surprised a couple days later when the nurse told me that when she tried to get Marsha to take a shower, Marsha thought the showers were a gas chamber and we were going to kill her, but she went in anyway. I guess she thought it was hopeless to resist anymore, and she didn't want to get tied down again.

The social worker found her adult son in Texas. He was pretty burned out on her. He said she'd been an alcoholic for years and she'd been getting worse and worse, and the paranoia was getting worse and worse. Nonetheless, he agreed to take her to live with him in Texas.

As the days went by, even though Marsha's acute DTs ended, she continued to be paranoid. I added some Haldol, but it didn't seem to do any good. Until then, I hadn't known you could get permanently paranoid from drinking.

I never really understood how her son got the airplane to let her on when she was telling them that he was kidnapping her and planning on killing her, but they did.

My bottom-line warnings: Alcohol is a very popular, relaxing, pleasurable substance that is addictive only for some people, alcoholics. It can separate us from reality temporarily in blackouts, DTs, and chronically in alcoholic hallucinosis. Also, it poisons almost every cell in our brains and bodies, even if we're not alcoholics.

Nicotine—cigarettes

I hesitated before including nicotine and cigarettes in this chapter, but there are a few things about them that I think are worth commenting on.

First, nicotine is likely the most common drug used by people with psychosis. It turns out that the vast majority of people with severe mental illnesses smoke, far higher than the percentage of people without mental illnesses. This is likely because it's such an effective mind-altering drug. If they smoke it slowly, it's relaxing and makes it easier to withstand the anxiety and insomnia they're often facing. If they smoke it fast, it can be stimulating, counteracting the sedating effects of their medications and of their negative symptoms. I once heard that they did a study at UCLA that showed that nicotine was the only substance that reliably improved the cognition and memory of people with schizophrenia. Psychologically, it's an incredibly helpful drug. But that's not the end of the story.

Second, it helps stabilize pleasure centers and counteracts the dopamine blockade that the antipsychotics, especially the older ones, cause that can blunt the ability to feel pleasure. Cigarettes are ubiquitous and almost affordable (although increasing taxes on cigarettes have driven many people to roll their own or use small cigars). Cigarettes form an essential part of the economy and social interaction in almost all places where people with serious mental illnesses live and congregate.

Third, nicotine is impressively addictive. Despite increasing efforts to address smoking, I can't think of anyone I've actually helped get off cigarettes (even though I have helped lots of people get off other drugs and alcohol). When money runs out at the end of the month, and no one has any more cigarettes to beg for, and they've already borrowed from the Board and Care operators, everyone gets irritable and goes into withdrawal. One woman I knew kicked a nurse in the head opening up a big gash because she wouldn't take her out on a cigarette break fast enough. Increasingly, we're eliminating cigarettes from psychiatric and medical hospitals, sending lots of patients into withdrawal. People are hospitalized at the worst times in their lives, when they are the most aggressive and out of control. While I sympathize with the goal of getting them off nicotine, is that really the best time? I knew a man who refused a surgery on his neck, which would've saved him from progressive paralysis and death because he wouldn't go without smoking for the surgery and the lengthy bed-bound recovery. In the "old days," we often took advantage of their addiction and "bribed" people with cigarettes to take their medications. Other people can use cigarettes to control them, too. I found out that two young women had repeatedly allowed the janitor at their Board and Care to have sex with them in return for cigarettes; when they tested positive for syphilis, they were too scared to let anyone but me give them the shot.

Finally, the gut-punch line is: Cigarettes account for the majority of the 20–25 years of early death we see in people with schizophrenia. Cigarettes are aging them, making them physically ill and disabled, and literally killing them in their 50s and 60s. They are ruining their hearts and lungs and blood pressure and causing cancer. From a physical point of view, cigarettes are the most dangerous thing in their lives by far.

My bottom-line warning is: We can't just ignore cigarettes while they're killing so many people.

Closing story

> The last time I gave a lecture about working with people who use drugs and alcohol, after I finished, one of the other lecturers came up to me and said, "You know how you said you don't like people who are using drugs and alcohol."
>
> "Yeah."
>
> "How do you like people who have recovered and have long-term sobriety?"
>
> "Oh, they're some of my favorite people. They often have a calmness and stability and a spirituality about them. They tend to clean up shame and guilt, instead of letting it fester. Many of them seem to be able to be in the present, able to really connect and be vulnerable, without too much fear of what the future will bring. I guess it's an acceptance of their own vulnerability and powerlessness."
>
> He paused before he responded, "You do realize that those are the same people you said you don't like … at a different time in their lives, don't you?"

I believe that the most important things I've learned traveling with people on journeys of substance abuse are the humanizing aspects, not the biological specifics, of how certain pleasurable chemicals can impact their perceptions of reality and their lives. Sticking with people on these often frustrating and tragic, but sometimes truly inspiring, journeys can help make us all better people.

CHAPTER 12

JOURNEY 7: PSYCHIATRIC ILLNESSES

Rachelle was a very sweet young woman. Her parents were very sweet, too. There was no serious trauma or substance abuse in her past, just a psychotic illness that seemed to come out of nowhere when she was in her late teens. Her parents did the best they could to adapt to this new reality, and so did she. They were all used to the idea of coping with a brain illness they couldn't see because she'd been diagnosed with dyslexia when she was a child and had learned to cope with that. They listened carefully as they were told that she had a disabling illness, but could have a good, if sheltered, life, with medications, Social Security disability payments, and good care.

I met her as one of the very first members in the Village because her parents were always on the lookout for opportunities for Rachelle, and they signed her up as soon as they heard the Village was going to open. I met her at her Board and Care, which was widely regarded by NAMI parents to be the best one in Long Beach. Physically, it wasn't much different than the others, maybe a little cleaner, and it did have a nice courtyard with a basketball hoop. The residents seemed a little younger than the other Board and Cares, maybe a little cleaner, too, and certainly less disruptive. There wasn't any yelling or swearing at each other. The usual vaguely threatening atmosphere wasn't in the air. Also, they were strict about throwing out people who used drugs, so that kept things quieter. They even ran a few activities for the residents. There was a psychiatrist who stopped by to see them for a few minutes every month or every 2 or 3 months to renew their medications.

Rachelle had been living there a few years.

I found her laying drowsily in her boyfriend's arms on a lounge chair in the sun in the courtyard. Not bad.

I introduced myself and her boyfriend excused himself, and Rachelle and I sat and talked. She said she usually hung out at the Board and Care, and sometimes went down to the MHA Social Center. She was looking forward to the changes the new Village program would bring. She worked a stipend job at the Social Center 3 hours a week, answering phones and making lunches for homeless outreach. The job was only 3 hours a week, so she wouldn't earn more than the $65 per month threshold she'd have to report to SSI. They'd deduct money from her check if she made more than that, and there was always the fear that Social Security would decide she wasn't disabled anymore and take away her SSI entirely. She liked the job, and most of the time she felt up to it. Sometimes, the voices, which were always there in the background, would get worse and be mean to her, and she'd get demoralized and depressed and stay in bed, instead of coming in. She was usually glad if she made the effort to come in to work, the voices even tended to be quieter, but she wasn't always "up to it."

She told me she'd been taking Navane for about a year to keep the voices down. She also told me she was allergic to lithium.

"Lithium? Why were you on lithium?" Lithium isn't an antipsychotic. It's a mood stabilizer.

"Back then, they thought I had manic depression and gave me lithium, but it made me really sick. I got tremors and diarrhea and got confused, and my kidneys shut down. They had to put me in the hospital. They told me if I took it again, I could die."

"Did all that happen on your normal dosage of lithium, or were you toxic on too high a dosage? Do you know what your lithium level was?"

"Sorry, I don't remember any of that. I think it was Dr. Carl. Maybe you could get the records from him."

Good luck with that.

"What's your diagnosis now?"

"Some doctors say I have schizophrenia, and some say schizoaffective. I think it's schizoaffective on my chart now. I don't really know what the difference is."

"What happened to the mania?"

"I don't know. I haven't had any episodes like that in several years. I guess the Navane works."

"But you still hear voices."

"Yeah, but I've learned to deal with them most of the time, except when they get too bad."

"Do they ever take a break and leave you alone for a whole day?"

"No, not that long."

"How about an hour?"

"Yeah, sometimes an hour or even 2 hours, if I'm lucky. It helps to be distracted. They're usually better when my parents visit on weekends and take me out."

I called her parents to get more history. They remembered the same story. She'd originally been diagnosed with mania, not schizophrenia or schizoaffective disorder. She used to go days without sleeping with high energy, talking a lot, but not anymore. She'd gotten very sick on lithium; so, she'd never taken it again.

I explained to both Rachelle and her family that there was some chance that her real diagnosis was still manic *depression, or bipolar disorder as it was now called, and that she might do better if I added a mood stabilizer to her medications. We were using a couple of seizure medications for mood swings, Depakote and Tegretol, and they were much safer than lithium. She'd still have to have her blood tested to determine safe medication levels, but they didn't cause kidney damage like lithium.*

They agreed to try. When we got the Depakote level up to a therapeutic level, the voices went away entirely. She was also less depressed and slept more regularly.

In the meantime, Paul Barry took over the Village's employment program. He said, "No more 3-hour-a-week stipend jobs. That's not enough to develop good work habits or a working identity."

"But they're too ill to work more than that. Rachelle doesn't always make it for her 1-hour shift."

"She can do it. It takes practice and work hardening."

It turned out he was right. With some time and support, she was working 15 hours a week. She felt like a worker. Her identity began to change. We included her in our staff functions, like our Christmas party, our staff meetings, and retreats. He helped her fill out the Social Security forms, so she still had most of her check. Overall, she had more money than before and was prouder of herself.

When an opportunity came up a couple years later to get an HUD-subsidized apartment she could afford, in a building we had developed, she moved out and had her own apartment for the first time. She even had us over for lunch once. She became friends with the other residents. She still usually had a boyfriend around to keep her company and feel safe. Not bad.

She's still sweet and so are her parents.

Finally, you tell a good story, the way it's supposed to go. Someone without a lot of strange background gets an illness. You do a careful history, fix her incorrect diagnosis, and get her on the right medications, so her symptoms go away, and then she's able to do more work and even get an apartment of her own. That's what a psychiatrist is supposed to do.

I can see why you like that story. It does go the way things are supposed to go according to the medical model. This is the kind of story they tell in all the educational materials, in the pharmaceutical advertisements, on TV, and in our anti-stigma and fundraising campaigns. Effectively treating a correctly diagnosed illness is the foundation of a better life.

But, to be honest, I'm hesitant to take you on this journey. This is the "illness-centered" journey that is dominating our current culture and the one I'm rebelling against. Unlike the other journeys that we've been on, that I believe usually expand our humanity and increase our connectedness, this journey tends to decrease our humanity and connectedness. This journey urges us to see people as "cases" of some illness. I waited so long to take you on this journey, so you'd see there are other journeys before we headed out on this one. Sometimes, it can be very hard to see any other perspectives when the medical model is so pervasive.

Here's the "brochure" for this journey, available everywhere mental illness education is provided:

- If you're experiencing hallucinations or delusions, it must be caused by a mental illness, not a psychological, emotional, or spiritual process.
- All mental illnesses, especially psychotic illnesses, are brain illnesses, caused by malfunctioning brain chemistry.
- If psychosis persists, it's likely to be schizophrenia (or schizoaffective disorder), which over time may lead to physical brain damage, often including shrinkage of brain volume and cognitive deterioration.
- Schizophrenia causes a great deal of disability, social costs, and increases your risk of homelessness, jailing, violence, and suicide.

- Like people with many other deteriorating neurological illnesses, for example, dementia, many people with schizophrenia lack insight into their own condition; so, they will often need others to make treatment decisions for them, many times including involuntary hospitalization and medication.
- Medications, if used early and aggressively enough, can not only prevent relapses but also, in some cases, chronic deterioration and disability.
- Families are very important in coordinating and providing treatment and ongoing support; so, they often need psychoeducation and support.
- Rehabilitation can help achieve some success in school, work, and other life area, if the illness can be medicated into sustained remission.

Even though I don't agree with almost anything in this brochure, that doesn't mean you can't have a good experience anyway. Many people have rewarding trips they bought after reading misleading travel brochures, but it still would've helped them to know what the trips are really like.

Wait a minute. You don't agree with almost anything in that list? I've heard almost all of that everywhere. I thought that's all true.

This is the approach I criticized in "Chapter 3: What am I rebelling against?" but I'm not returning to it now just to criticize some more, although I will discuss a few more of those assertions in this chapter and a few more in Chapter 16. For now, notice how even though every one of them is tenuous at best, all those assertions fit together to justify our current system like a Jenga tower that would collapse if any of them were removed. That's why they're all defended so vociferously. Also, that's why many people who reject any of those propositions, reject all treatment entirely, including medications. As Patricia Deegan put it in the June 2020 issue of *Psychiatric Times*, "A prescription for noncompliance arises when a message of hopeless chronicity is paired with a psychiatric medication. You have schizophrenia. You will be sick for the rest of your life. You must use medication for the rest of your life. This common message is a prognosis of doom. Many people will reject this hopeless forecast by rejecting the medicine. In rejecting the medication, they reject the prognosis of doom as well."

Nonetheless, an illness-centered approach is a legitimate approach. There are many people who have benefited profoundly from this approach, especially those people who agree with its underlying assumptions and have learned how to make it work for them. I'm returning to it now to help those of you who are on this journey get as much as possible out of your journey while avoiding some serious pitfalls. For everyone else, at the very least, you will need to accept having a psychiatric diagnosis if you want to have any services or benefits paid for, and you should know what those diagnoses mean, and don't mean.

Even though this journey may seem very familiar since it's so pervasively promoted, there are three things I'd like you to bring along as luggage to try to decrease some of the conflicts before we start:

1) Understanding the connection between the medical model and involuntary hospitalization,
2) A sense of how illness diagnoses and medication choices are related, and
3) A caution about the common dehumanizing impacts of this approach.

1) Understanding the connection between the medical model and involuntary hospitalization

There has been a linkage made between the medical model treatment and involuntary hospitalization by both proponents and antagonists that doesn't necessarily have to be there, but often is. Many people who are against forced treatment and locked hospitalizations are also antagonistic to psychiatrists, medications, and the medical model overall. Many people who promote illness-centered, medication-based treatments also promote involuntary medications and hospitalizations.

There are a few reasons for this linkage:

Hospital and institutional treatment don't have to be medical model, but at present it always is. The medically directed funding demands it. There are no more locked moral treatment hospitals or custodial institutions without at least the trappings of psychiatric care. Institutional psychoanalytic treatment programs, like Chestnut Lodge used to be, are long gone. Even personal growth-oriented crisis residential treatments, like the Soteria model, are quite rare. Most psychiatric hospitals are resistant to implementing trauma-informed approaches, relying instead entirely on diagnosis, medications, and restraints and seclusion, if needed. At the same time, jails are hiring large numbers of mental health workers and prescribing large amounts of psychiatric medications complying with court orders to give humane medical model psychiatric treatment even to those people being punished. Since all involuntary treatment facilities are medical model, anyone who is trying to decrease or eliminate forced treatment is going to find themselves battling psychiatrists and other medical model staff.

Deinstitutionalization occurred at about the same time that *DSM-III* was adopted and the biological psychiatrists took over from the psychoanalysts; so, they often found themselves fighting the closure of state facilities and defending them despite widespread abuses, even though the biologic psychiatrists largely inherited, rather than created, these problems. When biologic psychiatrists insisted that the medical model be the model used in Community Mental Health Centers under their psychiatric direction—day hospitals, day treatment, treatment teams, clinics, involuntary treatment commitments, etc.—more battles ensued. Today, psychiatrists are in relatively short supply in CMHCs and even at many state hospitals, especially in any leadership positions, but the medical model reigns supreme, nonetheless.

Some older psychiatrists, now frustrated by the limited services available in the community, including a lack of psychiatric hospital beds, and the high levels of noncompliance with medical model illness-centered treatments, look back nostalgically upon the days of asylums, when they were in charge and could easily force someone to take their medications and take care of them, protecting them from their illnesses and the stressors of community life. They've become some of the leading advocates for expansion of involuntary treatment and hospitalization, including E. Fuller-Torrey and Richard Lamb.

Meanwhile, "consumer survivor" groups that once focused on the trauma and abuses in the institutional system have evolved into "consumer staff" and "peer advocates" within the Recovery Movement are now more focused on the abuses of cursory diagnoses and medications (including careless prescribing, overmedication, and forced medication), but involuntary hospitalization remains the most abhorrent practice to them.

Less than half of people with psychotic experiences agree they have a mental illness and almost all illness-centered psychiatrists don't have any alternatives to offer you if you don't agree you have a mental illness, leaving most people experiencing psychosis either untreated or coercively treated against their will in our current illness-centered psychiatric system.

Why do so many people with psychosis not believe they have a mental illness?

- Some people don't agree with their diagnoses for biological reasons. "Anosognosia," the inability to see you have a disability because of your disability, is diagnosed in over half of all people with schizophrenia by biological psychiatrists. They rarely look beyond that, assuming they'll need to force treatment on all of those people if they're going to be treated at all. (I read an analysis of the large CATIE study of antipsychotic medications that "explained" the outcome that over half of all the patients stopped their medications within 6 months by saying that proved there's a biological factor in schizophrenia that causes noncompliance. This conclusion was arrived at despite that fact that all the people in this study agreed to be in the study and had been treated with antipsychotic medications before the study. Most of them just didn't like their medications.) In my experience, anosognosia does exist, but far more rarely than 50%, whereas not liking your medications is far more common than even 50%.
- Some people disagree with their treatment plan for psychological or emotional reasons. They may think someone else has the problem, not them. They may think of themselves in different, usually more positive, ways than others see them. They may be too frightened or ashamed to face certain truths about themselves. These emotional defenses, described as "lack of insight," "denial," and "resistance," were commonly blamed by psychoanalysts when they struggled to collaborate with their patients. Motivational interviewing, an approach developed for people with substance abuse, tries to look at things from the person's own point of view,

emphasizing how what appears to negative, like using drugs, might actually be serving a positive purpose for the person, making it hard for them to give it up. (For example, having a spiritual mission as an advocate of God might help Peter in Chapter 9 with guilt feelings for accidentally killing his wife and, therefore, be hard to part with.) Today's biological psychiatrists are trained to equate lack of insight with either being too ill and needing more treatment to relieve their anosognosia or psychiatric ignorance, needing more psychoeducation. (For example, someone who comes from a family who believes in spirits, but not in mental illnesses, needs to be educated out of their superstitions and ignorance.)

- Some people disagree with their diagnosis because they're actually on a different journey, and an illness-centered explanation doesn't fit their experiences or their needs. Since psychiatrists have been trained to think that an illness-centered approach is the only possible journey, they rarely try to collaborate on any other basis. (When Los Angeles County was in the process of creating a network of crisis residential programs, I recommended designating one of them as a place for people to go with spiritual crises, staffed with mental health workers, including psychiatrists using medications, who would be willing to work with people on that basis. After all, these people were frustrating all of our standard approaches, and countywide there are a lot of them. My recommendation wasn't adopted.)
- Some people disagree with their medications because they think their medications are causing more harm than good. Having the patients create the goals for medications, instead of the psychiatrists (client-driven treatment), can reduce this problem by helping the professionals see the impact of treatment through their patient's eyes. Patients often value decreasing psychosis less than psychiatrists do and resent side effects more than psychiatrists do. The side effects may be hindering their quality of life more than the symptom reductions are improving their lives. (At its most extreme, this conflict has led to a bitter battle raging between people who think that the primary cause of cognitive deficits in people with schizophrenia is due to ongoing psychotic symptoms damaging healthy parts of the brain over time and

people who think that the medications themselves are causing brain damage. I once met a Canadian psychiatrist in her 90s who had helped bring Thorazine to Canada and who told me that cognitive deficits, like we see today, didn't exist before antipsychotic medications. Researching this is difficult because it's likely that people, who have more serious underlying illnesses and might therefore have more cognitive damage, are also likely to be prescribed more medications, which might also cause damage, whereas people who are able to successfully get off their medications might have less serious illnesses in the first place. Careful statistical analysis, for example performed by Dr. Nancy Andreasen, seems to indicate that the medications are, for the large part, to blame, but the individual variation in her data is considerable.)

My bottom line: If more psychiatrists looked beyond the biological reasons for treatment refusal and developed more approaches to building collaboration, we wouldn't be so frustrated, so resentful that we don't have more coercive powers to lock up more people and forcibly medicate them, and we wouldn't be in so much conflict with the consumer/survivor movement and other civil rights advocates. After all, most people don't become psychiatrists because they want to lock up people.

2) A sense of how illness diagnoses and medication choices are related

Medications have been promoted almost entirely within a narrow-minded illness-centered perspective. People have an underlying chemical abnormality that the medications treat. End of story. But that wasn't always the end of the story.

When antidepressant medications first became widely available, there was an effort to divide depression into "exogenous depression" (which meant that some events outside them caused their depression. Their depression made sense. Almost anyone would've become depressed in the same situation.) and "endogenous depression" (which meant that the cause of their depression was likely within their own brains; there wasn't any external reason for their depression. It must be caused by an internal chemical imbalance.). The hypothesis was that we should give therapy and support to improve lives to the people with exogenous depression and medications to the people with endogenous depression. It turned out that the medications didn't care why you were depressed. They helped relieve depression and other problems that often cluster with depression (like poor sleep, appetite, concentration, energy, and low sex drive), no matter what the cause.

This was a key moment, when narrow-mindedness overwhelmed plausibility. The oft-repeated conclusion was that all of these people have an underlying chemical imbalance that the medications are correcting, some people just need more stressors to trigger their illnesses than others, and they all should be medicated. The more plausible conclusion, that didn't have to be neglected, is that the medications don't correct underlying conditions at all. Medications provide valuable relief from distress, regardless of the underlying cause. They can be just as useful helping people who don't have an illness as those who do, so long as they have the distress the medications relieve.

You lost me, doc. Are you saying that medications don't treat illnesses, but that we all should take them if we're distressed enough? Isn't the way you know that you need to take medications because you have an illness that they treat?

I told you that you'd have to reevaluate what you know before we go on this journey.

Let me try to explain with a medical example:

If you go to the doctor with swollen legs and you can't sleep laying down because fluid fills your lungs, the doctor is likely to prescribe a diuretic medication, a "water pill." This medication pushes your kidneys into creating more urine and draining the fluid. He doesn't prescribe this medication because there's something wrong with your kidneys. He's actually making your kidneys produce more urine than they should normally, making them function abnormally because it will help with your edema (or your "dropsy," if you like old-fashioned diagnoses). If he's not absurdly old-fashioned, he'll try to figure out why you have edema. Maybe you have congestive heart failure because your heart is too weak to push the blood around or because it has a leaky valve. Maybe you have cirrhosis and liver failure and your liver can't filter your blood efficiently enough and it's backing up. Maybe you have venous insufficiency because there's something wrong with your blood vessels and they can't carry your blood around. Or maybe you do have a kidney problem and it's holding on to too much fluid. Regardless of the cause, you may "need" the diuretic pill to relieve the swelling, so that you don't overwhelm your heart and drown your lungs. But if you're going to recover, you're probably going to need some other treatment for the underlying pathology, too.

Now, let's return to the depression. You may be depressed because of grief or being repressed or because you have chronic pain or because your husband is beating you ... or because you have a major depression illness. You may "need" an antidepressant medication to avoid committing suicide and have enough energy to go on with your life, regardless of the cause of your depression. But if you're going to recover, you're probably going to need some other treatment for the underlying issues, too.

So, the medications relieve your mental symptoms but not the underlying cause, just like the water pill relieves the swelling symptoms but not the underlying cause?

Exactly, but since *DSM* doesn't include causes in its descriptions of major mental illnesses, it leads you to assume that relieving the symptoms is exactly the same as relieving the entire condition.

When antidepressants were first invented, therapists worried that if their clients were given antidepressants that relieved their suffering, they wouldn't work in their therapy. It turns out, that happens a lot. It also happens that if antidepressants relieve your symptoms, your insurance won't pay for therapy to deal with your "life issues." This kind of thinking makes more sense if you believe that the antidepressant is correcting an underlying chemical imbalance and that it's actually treating your illness, than if you believe that you're suffering less, but that you still have underlying issues that haven't been addressed. The shame here is that studies repeatedly show that people who get both therapy and medications do better than either one alone. You have more energy and hopefulness with an antidepressant to actually be introspective and make changes in your life—whether it's going through the phases of grief or standing up for yourself or doing rehabilitation exercises to decrease your pain or leave your beating husband. And if you don't make some changes, it's more likely you'll never get off your medications. You might even start complaining that your medication has "pooped out" and doesn't work as well as it used to.

Our current outcome, lots of people with somewhat relieved depressions taking antidepressants indefinitely and not changing anything in their lives, has the "narrow-minded" explanation that we've discovered that depression is a much more chronic illness than we had previously thought and that people should be very cautious about stopping their antidepressants because their illness is likely to relapse, ignoring the more plausible explanation that you never had an illness in the first place. You didn't dig deep enough to figure out why you're depressed, and you didn't do anything about it; so, you never really recovered. Currently, almost all psychiatrists, and all pharmaceutical companies and their educational materials and advertisements promote the narrow-minded explanation, instead of the more plausible one. We've all seen advertisements that say if your antidepressant isn't working well, you should add another medication, usually an antipsychotic medication. We've never seen an advertisement that says if your antidepressant isn't working well, you should figure out what's wrong with your emotions or your life and make some changes.

I'm confused again, doc. Should we take medications or not?

I think medications are very helpful, even lifesaving, for lots of people and they should take them, but that doesn't mean that all those people have mental illnesses or that their medications are treating an underlying chemical imbalance. Almost always, there's something else in addition to medications you should be doing to address what's really wrong underneath, and when you do, you 're more likely to get off your medications.

When lithium was first gaining popularity as a treatment for manic depression, I was taught to tell people that their manic depression was being caused by a lithium deficiency; so, they needed to take lithium pills to correct it. I refused to tell anyone that because it just isn't true. No one has a lithium deficiency because no one has any lithium in their system naturally. Nonetheless, lithium pills do very effectively treat manic depression. We just don't know how or why. Similarly, the fact that the early antipsychotic medications block dopamine doesn't necessarily mean that psychosis is caused by a dopamine imbalance either. It just means that blocking dopamine often helps decrease psychotic symptoms. We just don't know how or why. In general, it seems to me that the process by which our medications of all kinds work tends to be much simpler than the process by which we became ill in the first place. Knowing how Tylenol works doesn't really help understand why I have a headache. Take the Tylenol to relieve the headache and then figure out what's really causing the headache because I can assure you it's not a Tylenol deficiency or imbalance. Yes, take the antipsychotic medication to relieve your psychosis and then figure out what else you can do because it's unlikely your problem is just a genetically based dopamine imbalance.

Ironically, our current psychiatric diagnoses, like many medical diagnoses, are far more useful for defining what your cluster of suffering consists of and what medication is likely to relieve your suffering, than they are for defining your underlying pathology or guiding your non-medication treatment. If you live in many places where there are no treatments or support besides medications, the current *DSM-V* is all you really need to choose your medications. Or, if you're like Rachelle, the woman I introduced in the beginning of this chapter, with nothing clearly wrong besides the symptoms, a careful *DSM* diagnosis and well-targeted medications may be all you need to get your life back on track.

The heart of this journey, therefore, is about how to distinguish between the few *DSM* diagnoses that include psychosis as part of their defining symptom cluster, so that medications can be used more effectively.

The silver lining is that people don't have to agree they have a mental illness to "need" medications. They can "use" medications effectively if they have the right kinds of distress, regardless of the cause. Taking off the "narrow-minded" blinders of the current illness-centered medical model doesn't mean that we lose all the benefits of modern medications; it means that more people can use them and that their medications can be part of their deeper recovery.

3) A caution about the common dehumanizing impacts of this approach

Despite the fact that medicalizing mental illness has been widely touted as lowering stigma and reducing shame and guilt because an illness isn't a moral or personal weakness and it isn't anyone's fault, the illness-centered, medical model is often experienced as profoundly dehumanizing. It doesn't have to be.

The main problem is that the more we "humanize" the illness, the more we "dehumanize" the person. In Patricia Deegan's words, "If we reduce a person to being an illness, then there is no one left to do the work of recovery. Once I became my diagnosis, there was no one left to recover." When we attribute to the illness the ability to pursue its own course, regardless of who has it, we devalue the person's contribution to their own life and we demean them. In today's society, there are a whole stack of determinations that psychiatrists are expected to make, depending on their diagnosis: Can someone with that illness drive a car safely, be trusted with a gun, make financial decisions, serve on jury duty, hold a job, go to college successfully, raise a child ....? The list goes on and on. The widespread underlying assumption is that we can determine all those abilities just by knowing their diagnosis ... and, of course, if the diagnosis is schizophrenia, they can't do any of those things.

> *I'd known Bruno for a few months when he popped the question, "They took away my driver's license when I was put on conservatorship in the hospital 8 years ago. My old psychiatrist wouldn't fill out the form to say I could get my license back. Will you?"*
>
> *I'd never even seen the form he shoved at me before. "Why didn't he fill it out?"*
>
> *Bruno rolled his eyes, "He didn't want the liability."*
>
> *I looked through the form trying to find something about mental illness on it. It seemed this form was mostly for blindness and seizures. But there was one part that wanted to know if the applicant had a neurological or psychiatric condition that impaired their decision-making decision (like intermittent loss of consciousness), and if they did, if it was stabilized on medications for over 6 months.*

I looked up at Bruno. Well, he certainly had issues with decision-making, but I wasn't sure that had anything to do with his psychiatric condition. Actually, I wasn't too sure what his psychiatric condition was. He was just too complicated. He'd had a lot of childhood trauma and he was very overweight, was floridly gay and clung to guys he clearly shouldn't. He was "all over the place" emotionally. He used to use a lot of speed. He denied it now, but he sure sweated a lot, but maybe that was because he was carrying around a lot of extra weight. And stable wasn't a word I'd ever use to describe him.

"I need the car to get to the hairdresser's shop. I borrowed some tools, and they'll hire me on commission. You want me to work, don't you?"

Hmmm. Was this a real job? I couldn't keep track between being a spray can artist and a deacon in some church I never heard of. I wondered if he'd wear his church collar while he cut hair.

"Doc?"

I'd better focus. He does take his meds, well mostly, and he's always begging for addictive benzos I don't give him. He shakes, but he hasn't heard any voices. He's kind of hyper. He doesn't sleep well. He breaks down into tears sometimes, like when he's dumped. What does all this have to do with driving anyway?

"Can you drive?"

"Sure. I drove for years before they took the license away. To tell you the truth, I even drive now, but I want to do it legally, so I don't get in trouble."

I got a brainstorm. "I tell you what. If you bring a car here, I'll drive around with you and see if you can drive." I know I'm not a driving instructor, but I don't know how to figure out if he can drive from his diagnoses. After all, it isn't his illnesses that are driving. Let's see what he can do.

> The next Friday, he drove up in a massive, beat-up old car, the kind I'd usually call a boat. The passenger's side door was stuck closed; so, he had to get out, and I slid across from the driver's side. He got in.
>
> I did my best imitation of a driving exam. We drove a few miles around the neighborhood, and he did fine, despite the challenging vehicle.
>
> "OK. Good enough. I'll fill out the form."
>
> "Can I borrow $75 from the Village to take the test? I'll pay you back out of my haircut earnings."
>
> I groaned, but we loaned him the money. He passed the test and got the job. He was paying us back very slowly with lots of nagging, when he quit his job. Stable is not a word I'd use to describe Bruno.
>
> In the end, I made a person-centered decision, instead of an illness-centered decision, and avoided dehumanizing him in the process, even though it made it messier.

When we focus on treating the illness instead of the person, it can seem like we're valiantly battling a powerful illness: We can get totally engaged in the fight and lose track of the person entirely. They're just the battlefield. Sure, they might get bloody or damaged in the process, but that's not important. After I beat this illness for them, they'll be fine. Hell, they'll be grateful. Besides, it's the nurse's job to look after the patient while the doctor fights their illness. Those are tolerable side effects. Don't complain, I'm winning this battle. I'm going to add another pill and really get control. It's time for the big guns. Even if they agree that they have a powerful illness that needs to be subdued, they might feel beaten up by this process.

There are some person-centered practices we can use that can reduce the dehumanization:

- I can let you choose the symptom and suffering that we're going to target and what side effects you most want to avoid.
- We can identify together growth and recovery goals that will be facilitated by reducing symptoms and how you'll get there.

- I can give you choices of medications you can try and advice on how aggressive or how cautious to be with them.
- I can read my medication visit notes out loud to you to start the next session, so we can be learning and collaborating and problem solving together. You can keep track, too, and even help write the notes, if you want to.
- I can let you be the judge of what's working and what's not for you, and I can ask you how you're making those decisions, so I learn what's important to you.
- We can talk about what you can do to make the medications more effective and how you'll fight the illness, too.

The medical model has often been touted as radically reducing stigma about mental illnesses, helping us emerge from dark times of exorcising demons, or blaming moral failings, or "schizophrenogenic" parents. By describing people as having a biological illness, hopefully they receive more compassionate care and less moralizing, shaming, and blaming. Unfortunately, when we objectify mental illnesses, we dehumanize the people who have them, reducing them to "cases." We also create two artificial categories—normal and mentally ill, which have to be differentiated and separated. This segregation creates additional fear, stigma, and loss. Segregation, even with compassion, leads to more stigma, not less, because of decreased relationships and connections. Segregating people with mental illnesses into separate group homes, institutions, hospitals, and even separate jail and prison wards, even if done to enhance treatment accessibility, increases stigma.

The inherently dehumanizing aspects of the medical model also have tended to undermine hope and empathy.

> In a 2014 post, "We are Whole People, Not Broken Brains" in the Mad in America website, Dan Fisher (the psychiatrist who has recovered from schizophrenia I introduced you to in Chapter 1) included a picture of a t-shirt with this caption:
>
> "This is a t-shirt sold at a recent NAMI Texas conference. Under a figure with an Indian-like design emanating from the person's head is the caption: 'Mental illness is a broken brain.' You can tell from the words under the heading ['It is

not bad character. It is not bad choices. I can't just buck up. Don't judge ... learn'] that the design was intended to reduce stigma and discrimination. Unfortunately, describing emotional distress as due to a broken brain has the opposite effect. This description has been shown by research to actually increase stigma and, even more devastating, it robs people of hope."

He goes on to say, "When a psychiatrist tells a young adult that they have a life-long mental illness, hope crumbles. They are often told that their mental illness is like diabetes. This is not a fair comparison. Diabetes is due to a defect in a body part, the pancreas. It is understood, however, in diabetes, that the person can continue to play an active role in their life with diabetes. They can work on their diet, exercise, stress, connectedness, as well as medication. On the other hand, mental illness literally means that your mind is sick. It is as if your very personhood is declared sick. Your mind, unlike your pancreas, is not just a body part. Your mind is the whole of who you are. Your mind is an expression of your whole self, which enables you to run your life. Your mind enables you to relate, set goals, dream, and have hope. If you and the people around you believe that your mind will be defective and sick for the rest of your life, you are left without hope of ever having the agency to build a life. This dire prediction can become a self-fulfilling prophesy."

Until the medical model can overcome the four premises I rebelled against in Chapter 3—so we value their humanity and input, we work to understand the process behind their distress instead of just giving it an illness name, we relate to them and connect on an emotional level, and we're hopeful about their ability to recover and lead meaningful lives—it will inadvertently be adding more stigma, instead of reducing it. Adherents to the medical model need to relentlessly ask ourselves if we're partnering, understanding, connecting, and being hopeful. Just being compassionate isn't enough.

That's enough preparation and packing. It's time for us to move on. If you bring along a reticence to lock up people, a broader view of illnesses and medication usage beyond correcting underlying chemical imbalances, and a pervasive need to focus on humanizing the people we work with, instead of their illnesses, this journey can have a lot to offer.

Here's what we're going to look at along the way:

1) Neurobiology of schizophrenia—from dopamine imbalance to disturbed circuitry, positive and negative symptoms
2) Natural history of schizophrenia—stages of a chronic illness
3) Impact of age of onset—Does schizophrenia express itself differently depending on how old and how developed someone is when they first get it?
4) Diagnosis and prognosis—separating out "good prognosis" and "bad prognosis" schizophrenia and the creation of schizoaffective disorder
5) Secondary psychosis from other psychiatric disorders—depression, mania, anxiety, and eating disorders

1) Neurobiology of schizophrenia—from dopamine imbalance to disturbed circuitry, positive and negative symptoms

In our current form, the illness model proposes that a set of symptoms, including hallucinations and delusions. define a brain illness called psychosis. If it persists for more than 6 months, it's schizophrenia. Efforts in the past carefully catalogued a variety of hallucinations (including hearing sounds and voices, seeing colors and shapes, being oversensitive to touch or strange sensations emerging from their bodies, or problems being overwhelmed by or processing sensations) and delusions (including ideas that everything refers to you, that there are hidden patterns or meanings to events, that thoughts are being put into or taken out of your head, that your thoughts are being broadcasted or that you can read other people's thoughts, and that you have pervasive grandiose and paranoid thoughts). Since we're no longer looking for hidden meanings of these symptoms, since no particular symptom is either definitive to rule in or rule out schizophrenia, and since all of these symptoms seem to respond to the same medications, it seems there's no longer any need to carefully describe them. All of the subtypes of schizophrenia, once based on which symptoms were most predominant, have been discarded as useless.

This simplistic approach leads to a direct treatment approach: Assess the prevalence and the severity of hallucinations and delusions and alter the antipsychotic medication to try to minimize them as much as possible. If the psychosis is minimized, their illness is stabilized or even in remission. Stay on your meds and try to rebuild your life. If you still have a lot of symptoms, raise the dosage, change to another antipsychotic medication, or even take more than one in hopes that will minimize the psychosis.

Since all antipsychotic medications block dopamine and their potency is closely related to how much they block dopamine, the widespread conclusion is that the psychosis is caused by an overabundance of dopamine—the "dopamine hypothesis." This formulation makes a nice pairing with Parkinson's disease—a severe, progressive movement disorder characterized by stiffness and shaking that is thought to be caused by a deficiency of dopamine. Medications for Parkinson's that increase dopamine, like L-Dopa, reduce the movement symptoms. Making the picture more compelling is the observation that L-Dopa sometimes leads to psychosis in people who never had it before, presumably by increasing their dopamine, and that antipsychotic medications sometimes lead to "pseudoparkinsonian" movement symptoms in people who never had it before, presumably by blocking their dopamine. In the early years, antipsychotic medications, like Haldol, were even invented by finding medications that made rats stiff, since they'd likely to be dopamine blockers.

That makes a lot of sense to me. Why did you tell me while we were packing not to believe that?

Because our brains aren't that simple. First of all, these two disorders seem to be in very different areas of our brains—one that controls emotions and thinking and the other one that controls coordination of movements. It turns out that our brains use dopamine for lots of things—including, for example, telling women when to release prolactin hormone to cause breast engorgement and milk production to nurse infants, which explains why antipsychotic medications can cause breast enlargement and milk production in both men and women, block menstrual periods, and lead to impotence. Visualize for a moment that dopamine is the equivalent of electricity in your house. Not everything runs on electricity, but a number of things in different places do. Say your toast was getting burnt in the toaster and you went outside and lowered the electrical current in your whole house and then you wondered why the TV and the microwave weren't working so well. Medication side effects are like that: You don't like that you're hearing voices; so, you take a pill that blocks dopamine everywhere, and then, you wonder why your movements are stiff and your breasts are enlarged.

Second, keep in mind that electricity doesn't just work within certain appliances. It also transfers energy between parts of your house. Dopamine is like that, too. It doesn't just work within certain brain areas. It also transfers energy around the brain in circuits. The next efforts in conceptualizing schizophrenia try to put together a disturbed circuit that includes several areas of the brain:

- The connections between the temporal lobe, which is involved in perception, and the limbic system, which is involved in emotions and memory, may be where hallucinations and delusions—"positive symptoms"—are caused.
- The prefrontal connections to the frontal lobe, which is involved in judgment, abstract thinking, and self-concept, may be where disordered thinking, poor emotional integration and relatedness, and self-care—"negative symptoms"—are caused.
- The connections to the lower levels of the midbrain, which are involved in biological regulation, may be where disordered sleeping, eating, energy levels, catatonia, and even the rare person who craves water, drinking extreme amounts—"disorganized symptoms"—are caused.

This might explain why medications that affect almost entirely dopamine tend to have a dramatic impact on reducing positive symptoms, but no impact or perhaps a negative impact on negative symptoms, leaving us with a lot of patients whose psychotic symptoms are stabilized but they're not very interactive, emotional, or functional. The second-generation antipsychotic medications, which affect multiple neurotransmitters in addition to dopamine, have sometimes been reported to do better with negative symptoms, perhaps because they're impacting all this intertwined circuitry in more complex ways.

There is also the theory that there are people who have only a partial expression of schizophrenia: People with only strange ideas and experiences have what is sometimes called schizotypal personality disorders, while people with only passivity and isolation have what is sometimes called schizoid personality disorders. Neither of these diagnoses are given much attention today, but it is interesting to note that the early genetic studies of schizophrenia tended to find relatives of both types in the family trees of people with schizophrenia.

OK. I can follow that, sort of. I don't know where all those areas of the brain are, but I get the idea. But what advantage did we get by making it more complicated?

We didn't make it more complicated. It is more complicated. The circuit model explains more of the illness than the dopamine imbalance model and can help direct treatment better. Even biological psychiatrists can see that there's more going on than just hallucinations and delusions from too much dopamine.

2) Natural history of schizophrenia—phases of a chronic illness

Standard teaching describes the unfolding of schizophrenia in a series of stages:

- Prodromal stage: Before any positive symptoms emerge, many, but not all, people who go on to have schizophrenia have a significant period of social anxiety, awkwardness, and isolation. "They were always somewhat different than other kids." They may seem to be drifting away, into their own worlds. Marijuana usage is often a part of this period.
- First break: This is when the first positive symptoms emerge, but often they're not recognized or hidden, and to be fair, it may be more of a subtle slide than a dramatic break. "They're just going through a stage." Some early interventions target reducing the "duration of untreated psychosis," which currently averages about 2 years in our country because they believe if they can medicate people earlier, their brains will have less damage and they'll go through less trauma and destruction.
- Treated psychosis: This is where positive symptoms are being actively targeted to control them. This may be easy and

straightforward, but more often, there is a great deal of conflict and frustration during this period, getting on and off medications, refusing and rejecting treatment, and going in and out of acute hospitals without stabilizing. Medication treatment advocates a push for the use of long-acting injections, involuntary medications, and even conservatorship and longer hospitalizations in order to stop this roller coaster, while trying to build insight with psychoeducation.

From here, several long-term paths emerge:

- Remission: The positive symptoms are successfully treated with medications, and with caution and ongoing medications, the person can return to life.
- Partial remission: There are some positive symptoms that don't seem to respond to even good medication treatment, leaving the person in a reasonably stable, but disabled condition.
- Relapses: Sometimes, people who have attained either partial or even full remissions have a return of their positive symptoms, which if not rapidly restabilized can lead back to conflict and frustration.
- Burning out: Many people as they get older seem to have fewer and fewer positive symptoms, or at least, respond less dramatically to them. The energy behind their hallucinations and delusions wears out, and they're left with lots of negative symptoms, limited relationships, and low functioning.

In recent years, increasing attention has been paid to:

- Early death: It appears that people with schizophrenia, on average, die 20–30 years younger than people without it. A good deal of the blame seems to go to cigarettes, poor diet, inactivity, hypertension, high cholesterol, and diabetes (often contributed to by second-generation antipsychotic medications), and social isolation. More and more emphasis is being placed on smoking cessation and accessing ongoing medical care to try to prevent this.

If we look at the entire progression of schizophrenia, we can see that conceptualizing it as a circuit, involving several interacting areas of the brain, instead of just a dopamine imbalance leading to psychosis, can lead to a more nuanced and effective approach to treatment. Here are a couple of examples:

1) There are two competing approaches to prevention and early intervention in the prodromal stage. One is to try to identify people at genetic risk of developing schizophrenia and giving them antipsychotic medications even before they develop positive symptoms, preventing them from ever emerging. The other approach tries to improve the social interaction and the personal development of people in the prodromal period, without antipsychotic medications but perhaps with more antidepressant and antianxiety medications, focusing on keeping them stronger, so that they don't "break." If we conceptualize an entire circuit, instead of focusing on just dopamine and the positive symptoms, the prodromal period is legitimately a part of the illness. Circuits connecting the emotional parts of the brain and the emerging frontal lobe's self-identity and "higher" interpersonal functioning are struggling to be formed, and we'd expect the second approach to be more effective.

2) Similarly, much of the disability that emerges after treatment and the "burnout stage" are more clearly conceptualized as persistence of negative symptoms. It turns out that negative symptoms predict employment disability more than positive symptoms do. In general, people who hear voices or have delusions have an easier time getting and holding a job than people with no motivation, emotional tone, poor self-care, and apathy. Therefore, vocational rehabilitation doesn't have to wait until all the positive symptoms are gone, and adding more medication to the already passive person isn't going to make it easier for them to work. They need more interpersonal stimulation and motivation to become more activated, not more suppression of positive symptoms and sedation.

OK. I guess I see how the circuit model works better than the dopamine imbalance model, even though it's more complicated. Do the three sides of your psychosis triangle fit into the different areas of the brain, too?

Yes and no. Remember back in Chapter 4 when I talked about the difference between the brain and the mind? My triangle is a description of our mind. The circuit model is a description of our brain. But it is likely that brain changes in these circuits correlate with the mind changes in the triangle.

Remember back in Chapter 8, Amy, the young woman who I took with me to the fish store trying to give her a momentary relief from her mentally ill self-identity, so that she could "feel like a normal person"? When seen from an illness-centered perspective, that kind of "psychosocial rehabilitation" intervention is directed at relieving negative symptoms by stimulating circuitry connecting to self-identity and interpersonal functions in the frontal lobes that our antipsychotic medications are so usually ineffective at impacting.

I want to spend some more time describing the stages of schizophrenia in an actual person; so, using these stages, let's look at Amy's history:

> Amy went through a **prodromal stage** in high school where she isolated from other students. She tended to be somewhat disheveled and ate by herself at the cafeteria. Her mother was concerned about her, but she kept insisting everything was fine. She started staying up at night, and it was hard to get her to go to school in the mornings. She talked less and less to her family and locked herself in her room. When she started talking to herself in her room, her mother became alarmed, but she didn't know who to turn to. She called the family pediatrician who recommended taking her to a psychiatrist. Amy was outraged by that suggestion, "I'm not crazy. I don't need to see a psychiatrist. Just leave me alone!!" She slammed her room door behind her. It was getting harder and harder to even get into her room.
>
> The next suggestion was to call the psychiatric emergency team, but they explained that they could only get involved if Amy did something that was dangerous to herself or others. Otherwise, Amy would have to make an appointment and come in on her own. Now, we're in the **period of untreated psychosis**. Her family was unsure when a "psychotic break" had occurred, but it was clear Amy

wasn't their sweet little girl anymore. She'd sneak out at night to eat out of the fridge. She wasn't going to school at all anymore. When she did talk to her family, she was angry and swearing, using language she never had before. Her mother was reduced to tears.

She hadn't heard anything from Amy for about a day or so—she wasn't really sure—and she wasn't getting any response from Amy, when she decided to break through her door and found Amy laying on the floor with a bottle of pills and a note by her side that said, "I can't handle them coming every night and raping me anymore. I have to leave this world." She was still breathing, but shallowly.

After the ambulance came to take her to the hospital, her mother was left wondering, as she drove to the hospital as well, what that meant: Who was raping her? What had happened to her daughter? She would never find out, even when it became a recurrent overwhelming fear for Amy. For years, Amy would spread salt on the floor around her bed to keep the rapists away. Later that day in the hospital ER, Amy and her mother met her first psychiatrist. He explained that he was putting Amy on a 72-hour-hold, and when she was "medically cleared," she would be transferred to a psychiatric hospital for further observation and treatment. He didn't explain that they'd send her to any available psychiatric bed, in this case 10 miles away, or that no one would call her to tell her when and where her daughter was transferred. Thus, began her **period of treated psychosis**.

The psychiatric hospital had very limited visiting hours: 2:00–3:00 pm and 7:00–8:00 pm daily. It was scary for her mother to see the other patients, yelling or shuffling around the ward. A few, blankly staring at the TV, were sitting in the day room where her mother could visit with Amy. Amy didn't seem to react much to anything.

"What is that you're wearing? Where did the clothes I brought for you go?"

Amy just shrugged, "Things disappear around here."

"And where's your hairbrush? Your hair is a mess." Sometimes, when we're afraid of losing it, we focus on small things, trying to get a grasp on something.

"They took it away from me because I'm on suicide precautions. That's where my shoelaces went, too. They said they'll give them all back when I'm discharged."

The night staff couldn't tell her mother what her treatment plan was. She never met the hospital psychiatrist because he didn't make rounds during visiting hours.

Amy would only spend 6 days in that first hospital. She returned home quieter and even somewhat apologetic, "I don't want to talk about it. Can I just go to bed? These medications make me tired."

"Sure, honey, you just rest. Is there anything I can get you?"

The psychiatrist, who had seen her in the hospital, wasn't going to be her psychiatrist in the community. She'd have to make an appointment with someone else. The social worker at the hospital gave her a list of possibilities, along with a prescription for a month's worth of pills. No one had an available appointment within a month, and Amy didn't want to go anyway. She didn't like the pills and stopped taking them within days, "I'll be fine without them." No one at the hospital could tell her mother what to do next. They advised her to take care of herself and recommended she go to a NAMI meeting to get support. "I'm not trying to get support for me. I'm trying to get treatment for my daughter."

Amy slipped away again.

When her mother called them, the emergency team told her that she'd have to wait for Amy to do something else that was dangerous in order to hospitalize her again.

She did start going to NAMI meetings and heard that her story wasn't unusual. She learned how to exaggerate to get Amy into the hospital.

"When there's an angry fight, tell the police she threatened you. Even tell them she hit you or threw something at you, if you have to."

"When she wanders away, tell them she was walking in traffic and almost got hit."

"Tell them you're frightened of her."

"But I'm frightened for her, not of her."

"If you can get her hospitalized enough times, they might put her on a conservatorship and transfer her to an IMD for long-term care, where they'll keep her long enough for the medications to work."

"You have to keep track of the medicines each hospital gives her and make a record to take to the next one when she's admitted each time."

Amy's mother learned fast. She got Amy hospitalized repeatedly over the next 6 months.

Amy also learned fast. She learned to tell the hospital staff that they didn't have her permission to talk to her mother or tell her where she was.

Her mother learned to call the patient pay phones at all five of the local psychiatric wards and ask the patients if Amy was there.

Amy would refuse to let her in when she came to visit.

By that point, no one knew what medications helped Amy and which ones didn't. She started claiming she was allergic to every antipsychotic medication she'd been on to make it harder for them to give them to her.

Finally, her mother succeeded in getting one of the hospitals to file for a conservatorship and take her to court, so the staff would have to talk with her regardless of what Amy said, so she could make psychiatric decisions for Amy, and especially so Amy could be kept longer than a couple weeks in the hospital.

Amy was driven to the courtroom where my father used to work. Her mother was anxiously waiting.

"I can't believe you would do this to me. Locking up your own daughter, when I haven't committed any crimes. What are you here for, to lie about me again? Just stay away from me, you bitch." The court bailiff came over to tell her to quiet down.

Amy didn't say a word during the hearing, even when her lawyer tried to get her to. The conservatorship was granted.

A month later, Amy was transferred to the IMD. There wasn't too much to do there, except a few groups they made them go to. Most of the patients dozed off during the groups, but if you went to them, you gradually moved up levels and that's how you got to leave eventually. The psychiatrist came by about once a month to see her and ask how her medications were working. Amy stopped caring enough to fight and just took what they gave her. The nurses reported she wasn't talking to herself anymore, she wasn't agitated, and she wasn't suicidal. When the county DMH administrators came around trying to find out who could be discharged to make room for all the people sitting in hospitals waiting months to get into the IMD, Amy was a natural choice. She was stable. She was in **partial remission**.

Her mother was extremely angry when she heard the plan to send her to a Board and Care because she could be treated at a "lower level of care" in a "less restrictive setting." "She isn't back to herself yet. She hasn't recovered. You must have more medications you can try. You can't give up on her like this." But they did.

About a couple weeks after Amy was discharged, I met her. She was freed, but she wouldn't leave the Board and Care. She said she was frightened her mother or the police would come and lock her up again. She refused to talk to her mother, and as far as I could tell, her mother gave up and didn't try to contact her again. I never met her mother.

It took me about 6 months to get her to go to the fish store with me, but that was the start of her coming out of her room and connecting with other people. She'd come to a few activities if a staff member picked her up and stayed with her the whole time. She balked at taking one of the jobs at the Village, but she did agree to help set up for our Thanksgiving dinner. She was gradually coming out of her shell and spending less time with her delusional life and more time with the rest of us.

About a year later, I got a call from a public health nurse. Amy and her roommate Gloria both had tested positive for syphilis. Amy was refusing the penicillin shot to treat it, but said she'd let me give it to her.

"Will you come out here and meet us to get her treated?"

"Sure, if you bring the medication, but how did she get syphilis? She almost never leaves her room alone."

"We're still investigating, but it looks like the janitor at the Board and Care was giving them cigarettes in return for sex."

When I came by to give her the shot, they told me the janitor had been fired. The owner of the Board and Care "sold" it to family members and changed the name, so they couldn't be prosecuted. There was nothing we could do to prosecute anyone.

We tried to talk Amy and Gloria into moving to a different Board and Care, but neither of them wanted to. This Board and Care had become their home.

About a year later, a new Section 8 subsidized building opened, and we helped the two of them move together into their own apartment, for the first time in either of their lives. They required a lot of help from their case workers— help getting the bills paid, shopping, cooking, cleaning, doing laundry, and taking their own medications—but gradually they learned more and more. They got to know their neighbors and made some friends.

About 6 months later, I got a call from the local county psychiatric emergency room on a Saturday afternoon, telling me that both Amy and Gloria were there, "We've got these new rules that say if someone is a Village member, we're supposed to contact you before we hospitalize them. What do you want me to do? Both of them are on 5150 holds from the police who went out to their apartment, and both of them are very psychotic."

*My wife wasn't very happy, but I drove over to the hospital to see if they had **relapsed**. Gloria apparently had been drinking since the night before and was much more agitated than her usual self. Amy was frightened by the change in Gloria, but otherwise she was her usual self— rambling, delusional, and passive. She said she was scared of being locked up, even though it had been a few years, and she desperately wanted to go home.*

"I think Gloria should be hospitalized for a few days until she recovers, and here's a list of her meds. They probably don't need to be changed. She just needs to sober up, but I can take Amy home."

*I arranged for a case worker and a life coach to check in on Amy and bring her a pizza and make sure she took her medications over the weekend. Amy and Gloria were back together by the next week, although neither one wanted to talk about what had happened. That was the last time either one was brought to the psychiatric hospital. Amy had been **stabilized and "burned out."***

> *I worry that she will face **early death** because she still smokes a lot, doesn't eat well, doesn't exercise, and is somewhat overweight, but we can work on that, too.*

Amy is a classic example of the stages of chronic schizophrenia. But is that really the "natural history" of an illness or the results of our current, highly flawed treatment system? We've grown so accustomed to patients like Amy that we believe their course is inevitable: That's just what schizophrenia is like.

Let's unpack and use one of our pieces of luggage: The medical model doesn't have to be a coercive model of care.

Let's go back for a moment and wonder:

- What if Amy had gotten comprehensive school-based support when she was struggling in high school and first isolating?
- What if instead of telling her mother there was nothing we could do, we sent out mental health workers, peer outreach workers, and a family support worker for her mother to help them adapt to Amy's changing mental state, trying to keep their relationship, her friendships, and her school career from deteriorating (like Finland's Open Dialogue does)?
- What if her first hospital saw its main responsibility as engaging both Amy and her mother in the mental health system successfully? What if they practiced "welcoming first" instead of adhering to universal "safety first" protocols, helping Amy figure out what's going on and what her goals are, and introducing her and her mother to community providers?
- What if her first hospitalization triggered her being referred to somewhere like the Village to give continuity of relationships and care in the community to help them avoid multiple destructive hospitalizations, instead of making her "fail first"?
- What if the IMD was a rehabilitative facility, instead of a custodial one, that engaged them meaningfully around collaboration and recovery, like the clubhouse I started this book with, instead of focusing on compliance and unattainable cure?
- What if the Board and Care was more like the old "halfway houses" teaching her the skills to manage her own apartment and get to

know her community, instead of warehousing her with minimal staff who took advantage of her?
- What if the Village had hired a family advocate to support her mother and perhaps even help them reconnect in a positive way?
- What if she hadn't had me to avoid that last hospitalization and had gone through the whole cycle again because of a "relapse"?
- What if we'd focused on healthy living throughout, so she had a chance of stopping smoking?

How much of Amy's course of illness, and numerous others like her, is actually the result of our inadequate treatment system, that we continue to excuse by saying that schizophrenia is a chronic, incurable illness? Even an illness-centered journey might turn out a lot differently if it offered more engaging services and relied less on coercion without ongoing relationships.

3) Impact of age of onset—Does schizophrenia express itself differently depending on how old and how developed someone is when they first get it?

> *In the desert of Death Valley, plants have developed a variety of strategies to survive with very little water. The creosote bush is very vulnerable when it's young. It needs a few years of abnormally high rainfall to begin life at all. It sends out roots that are very good at absorbing whatever little rain does fall and also releases a chemical that kills the roots of other plants around it, so that it will have very little competition. It can grow quite large and live for decades, usually with a barren buffer zone around it, where it's eliminated all the other plants and spread its own roots.*
>
> *Sometimes, schizophrenia reminds me of the creosote bush. Hallucinations and delusions need to have an opportunity to even begin. Normal circuits aren't growing well. Maybe there is too much isolation or interpersonal anxiety. Maybe there is too much stress or grief. Or maybe there is too much marijuana stimulating psychosis and inhibiting normal emotional growth. After it emerges, many people can overcome it and repair the damage developing normal circuitry. But for*

some people, it keeps growing and then starts poisoning the area around it. Emotions don't grow normally, and nerve connections don't get made. Brain size shrinks. Even if medications successfully suppress it, and especially if they don't, it's hard to overcome the damage and rebuild normal circuitry. Too often, the other struggling plants are further stunted in the arid and repressive environments people find themselves in, including devastated overwhelmed families, the streets, Board and Cares, and jails.

It's time to bring out another piece of our luggage. Let's consider the person who has the illness and not just their illness. Specifically, let's consider how the illness might impact someone differently at different ages and stages of development. There was a theory when I was in training that has disappeared over the years, that autism, childhood schizophrenia, schizophrenia, paranoid schizophrenia, and paranoid disorders of the elderly are all the same illness with onsets at different ages. Whether you believe that all of these conditions are caused by the same illness or not, looking at the person's underlying development at their age of onset can be a useful way of understanding their particular symptomology, how to interact with them, and how to target rehabilitation efforts (all these age ranges are approximate and overlap).

- Birth to age 5—"Autism spectrum": At this point, there is very little personal development in place. This is when a sense of self and an awareness of the existence of others emerge. If our "creosote bush" schizophrenia illness emerges at this point, the child may struggle to develop language, or lose what they have developed. They may have limited social interactions, problems with pronouns, and an inability to see other people as distinct individuals. They may only be able to handle things that are highly routinized and be unable to adapt to changes. True hallucinations and delusions don't develop since they never get that far in abstract, creative experiencing of their worlds. There are considerable challenges and rewards in focusing on their underdeveloped sensory integration, self-identity, and interpersonal relationship circuitry trying to challenge their illness and help them aggressively "outgrow" it.

- Ages 6–14—"Childhood schizophrenia": At this point of development, there is a sense of self and increasingly of others, but it's very concrete. The schizophrenia illness inhibits normal fantasizing and imaginative learning, taking over those circuits, leaving the person rather rigid and concrete. Their "delusions" may seem like "confabulations" or childlike stories or even willful lies. Their interactions with others are stilted, so they may seem socially awkward or isolated, with a limited personality, and hard to influence. I suspect that Clozaril and some atypical antipsychotic medications may be more effective than more purely dopamine blockers because there's more impairment in interpersonal circuitry than reality perception. Similarly, focusing on "stop making up stories and lying" may be less effective than attempting to stimulate more externally directed and interpersonal creativity.
- Ages 15–25—"Chronic schizophrenia": At this point, the brain is specializing, pursuing certain activities and self-images, and emotional relationship styles, while "pruning" other unused pathways. The frontal lobe functions—decision-making, problem solving, meaning making, self-direction, morals, etc.—are developing as they're connected. If these developing circuits are taken over by their schizophrenia illness, we'd expect them to have elaborate distortions of meaning, perception, and decision-making, creating a personalized world, cut off from emotional connections and normal development. This results in the classic schizophrenia symptoms—hallucinations, delusions, emotional blunting, and social isolation. Since their brains are developing so actively, aggressive early treatment, including heavy interpersonal involvement, trying to recapture as much of their circuitry as rapidly as possible from the illness, is warranted.
- Ages 25–50—"Paranoid schizophrenia": Given the late age of onset, lots of development has already been completed and is more likely to remain intact. The schizophrenia illness is limited to the edges. These people are often described as seeming to be "perfectly normal unless you ask them about their paranoid system." Their paranoid delusions tend to emerge with stress and center around issues of dangers specifically targeted at them. Their interpersonal connections become impaired not because of social

awkwardness or inability but because more people become involved in the plots against them. Support that targets increasing their sense of personal safety and security, rather than confronting their paranoia or pushing medications, is more likely to have an impact and keep the relationship going.

- Ages 55 and older—"Paranoid disorders of the elderly": These conditions tend to emerge as dementia begins. The schizophrenia illness takes advantage of a shrinking brain and the growing feelings of personal vulnerability. "Sundowning," when cognitive functions deteriorate at night, are particularly susceptible times. Delusions are usually personal attacks—being poisoned, stolen from, or raped at night. As dementia worsens, this can sometimes "improve" as the connections needed to create and sustain these paranoid ideas wither away, too. Supporting their personal sense of safety and security, often by maintaining familiarity and routine, along with trying to maintain their health and cognition as much as possible, is better than confronting them. Antipsychotic medications have "black box" warnings that their usage in the elderly is associated with premature death, presumably because of their underlying physical and neurologic fragility.

If we keep in mind Hippocrates's teaching, "It's far more important to know what person the disease has than what disease the person has," we have a better chance of effectively treating their illnesses and helping them rehabilitate and adapt.

4) Diagnosis and prognosis—separating out "good prognosis" and "bad prognosis" schizophrenia and the creation of schizoaffective disorder

> *I was giving a presentation to a group of psychiatrists who work part time at a crisis stabilization unit in Orange County. To attract the doctors, the presentation was held at a very fancy restaurant, paid for by a drug company that did a little commercial before I began, and they were busy enjoying quite good filet mignon while I talked. As I described the recovery model and how I thought it could be promoted in the crisis unit, one of the psychiatrists looked up from his food to make his only comment, "I've been working for 30 years and*

> *there are some people I've been treating for years and years who have 'real schizophrenia' who are never going to get any better or recover, no matter what we do."* The other doctors mostly nodded in agreement.
>
> *I wonder how they know who those people are when they see someone with psychosis come into the crisis unit, meeting them for the first time.*

Since before the word "schizophrenia" was invented, there has been a conflict between the highly variable prognosis that outcome research and population studies describe and the clinical judgment that "real" schizophrenia has a terrible prognosis.

I was taught a rule of thirds: "one third get better, one third stay the same, and one third get worse." In *Surviving Schizophrenia*, Fuller Torrey says the prognosis more nearly approximates a rule of quarters than a rule of thirds and quotes a 30-year prognosis of "25% completely recovered, 35% much improved, relatively independent, 15% improved, but requiring extensive support network, 10% hospitalized unimproved, and 15% dead." Other long-term prognosis studies like the Vermont longitudinal study I quoted in Chapter 3 are even more positive, describing recovery rates of two thirds. (Keep in mind that all of those numbers reflect the outcomes with poorly funded, fragmented, coercive mental health services. No one knows what recovery rates could be realistically possible with better services and supports.)

Almost all mental health professionals resolve this conflict emotionally, relying on their clinical experience, siding with hopelessness. Fuller Torrey's first line in his guide to schizophrenia is, "When tragedy strikes, one of the things that makes life bearable for people is the sympathy of friends and relatives." Why is he pleading with us to be sympathetic, instead of pleading with us to expect and fight for recovery?

> *After hearing a very caring psychiatrist working on Skid Row tell an audience that he doesn't think that anything he does really touches the people he's working with or makes any difference, but he does his best anyway, a mother in the audience stood up to say, "I like you, but I'd really rather my son had a doctor who had hope for him."*

Do you think that hopelessness, like coercion, is an unnecessary handicap of our current medical model that doesn't need to be a part of this journey?

Probably.

The biologic psychiatrists who created *DSM-III* wondered about how to tell who was a "good prognosis" and a "bad prognosis" schizophrenic, too, and they applied their epidemiologic and genetic tools to the question. Their observation was that people who had a rapid onset, without a lot of prodromal symptoms, and relatives with mood disorders, instead of psychotic disorders, were most likely to have a good prognosis. Their conclusion (unlike mine, which would be that people who still have two points of the triangle, self-identity and relationships, relatively intact have a better chance of regaining the experiencing reality dimension and recovering) was that these people were misdiagnosed as having schizophrenia and that they really had mood disorders with psychosis, and that's why they did better. Their conclusion had history behind it. There was a long-standing argument between more biologic European psychiatrists who more often diagnosed mood disorders with psychosis and American psychoanalysts who diagnosed almost everyone with psychosis with schizophrenia. Their findings seemed to indicate that the European biologists had been right all along. Also, this conclusion matched Kraepelin's original division between the better prognosis manic depression and the dismal prognosis dementia praecox (which became schizophrenia). All that was needed to complete the analysis was a way to reliably separate out mood disorders with psychosis and schizophrenia. Then, we'd be able to correctly identify and label the people with hopeless schizophrenia. Unfortunately for them, even with their "research validated tools," they couldn't do it. They were back to the same dilemma that has plagued the illness model from the beginning—it isn't possible to definitively diagnose schizophrenia. Hopelessness is easier to diagnose in retrospect.

Ever the pragmatists, they created a diagnostic category, schizoaffective disorder (combining the words for "schizophrenia" and "affective," which means mood, disorders), to use when they couldn't tell which diagnosis the person actually had. It was the only diagnosis in *DSM-III* that didn't have any criteria attached to it because it was a gray area between the two secure diagnostic categories—schizophrenia and mood disorders with psychosis (manic depression and depression with psychosis). By *DSM-IV*, they created a set of diagnostic criteria for schizoaffective disorder that basically lists the various ways you can be confused—for example, when someone with "bipolar disorder, with psychosis" doesn't seem to get better even when they're not manic, or when their psychotic symptoms don't match their moods. (My personal opinion is that many of these people with schizoaffective disorder who are "confusing" when viewed from an illness-centered perspective like we're using on this journey are actually on other journeys, often including trauma, overwhelming grief or stress, and/or drug abuse and if we changed our perspectives, their presentations would then make sense.)

Clinicians, looking for a way to avoid giving people the hopeless diagnosis of schizophrenia, started using schizoaffective disorder more often, especially for people they like. The drug companies, always on the lookout for larger potential markets, got their newer, more expensive antipsychotic medications approved by the FDA for mood disorders as well as schizophrenia. People with schizoaffective disorder can be, and often are, now prescribed antipsychotics, mood stabilizers, and antidepressants all at once.

In my view, the major stumbling block here is that we're unwilling to recognize that there are a lot of people with schizophrenia who have good prognoses, even better than some people with mood disorders. Just because schizophrenia is our most frightening, stigmatized illness doesn't mean it's a hopeless illness.

So, how do we know if someone is going to recover from schizophrenia or not? Isn't there such a thing as chronic schizophrenia?

My honest answer is, I don't know. And that's mostly because I don't know how much of the chronicity of schizophrenia is due to our mediocre treatment system, social rejection, and treatment avoidance and how much is an inherent feature of the illness.

> About 15 years ago, I made the mistake of going to Syracuse, New York in November to give a series of lectures. As a native Californian, my body wasn't prepared for the cold

and the snow and within a day, I had a severe cold. Instead of getting better when I returned, the infection settled into my sinuses and blocked my ears. Over the next few weeks, I kept going to work even with a runny nose and a fever. My hearing deteriorated. I "knew" I'd be fine, so I didn't go to a doctor or take any antibiotics. And I was right. After about a month, I successfully fought off the infection and recovered. Unfortunately, ever since, I've had a 30% reduction of my hearing, worse in the right ear than the left. I assume that was caused by scarring in my eustachian tubes as I healed, but I've still never gone to see a specialist and probably never will.

Did I have a chronic illness, or did poor choices and a lack of resistance and treatment lead me to be permanently disabled by what should've been an acute illness?

How many people with "chronic schizophrenia" are permanently disabled by poor choices, and a lack of resistance and poor treatment for what should've been an acute illness? Since virtually no one is getting good treatment for all three dimensions in psychosis (or the entire circuitry of schizophrenia, if you prefer to look at it that way) from the beginning, the answer could plausibly be everyone.

I'm not sure if that idea makes me sad, or hopeful, or both. How about you?

5) "Secondary psychosis" from other psychiatric disorders—depression, mania, anxiety, and eating disorders

Bipolar disorder (or manic depression) with psychosis

Let's move on to the mood disorders with psychosis.

These disorders are on the hopeful side of Kraepelin's divide. The assumption is that their depression or mania gets so severe that it causes people to become psychotic, so if we can successfully treat their underlying mood disorder, either depression or mania, their psychosis will go away and not return unless their mood disorder returns.

Let's start with mania.

I learned that mania was characterized by a very stereotypical presentation, including severe hyperactivity, high energy despite a reduced need to sleep, pressured, rapid, loud speech, impulsiveness, grandiosity, irritability, impatience, and hypersexuality. "Manics" were also often entertaining and funny. The women changed clothes a lot and wore makeup in the hospital, and we had to watch out for them having sex on the ward. When I went on a trip to China visiting their psychiatric hospitals, I could easily identify their manic patients without knowing a word of Chinese. They showed the same traits as manic patients in America—hyperactive, loud, singing, laughing, flirting. (That similarity convinced me that mania is a biological condition that could appear and look the same anywhere, but nowadays bipolar disorder is so broadly used that it incorporates many nonbiological causes and the old stereotypical presentation is hard to find.)

The psychosis comes in at the most extreme phases of their illness for several possible reasons:

- For some people, their thinking goes faster and faster until they can no longer control it rationally. They begin to put words together that just sound the same ("clanging" or "rhyming"), or that build on what someone else just said to them ("echolalia"). The association between words becomes "loose" or "disorganized." They can also get lost examining the details of things, like the grain in a wood tabletop, and have terrible trouble paying attention and tracking what others are saying.
- For some people, becoming disinhibited and grandiose brings out their most egotistical and unreasonable sides. Freed from needing to worry about what other people will think or consequences, their fantasies can become real to them. They really believe they are a beauty queen or have a million dollars or are married to the president or can fly. They become delusional.
- Many people use drugs and alcohol mostly, or even only, when they're manic and disinhibited. Usually, they're using substances that make them more disinhibited, overstimulated, or sped up, including most problematically, amphetamines. Their goal in using drugs might not be to get psychotic, but neither is it to calm down, relax, or sleep off their mania. After all, mania is usually a very pleasant state for them, even if it isn't for the people around them.

- Some people have modest trouble staying in reality—maybe they're on a mild version of one of our other journeys—and when they become manic, disinhibited, and less coherent, that's enough to tip them over the edge. Now, they're sure that their sister or the police are persecuting them or that there really is an inheritance being hidden from them, instead of just suspecting it. These people are more likely to be diagnosed as schizoaffective than manic with psychosis because their delusions may not be based in their mania itself, "mood congruent," but in other buried parts of their minds. Similarly, just treating their mania with medications may not resolve these delusions as easily since the delusions can cling to other parts of their minds.

Doris was one of the very first Village members. (She would loudly insist she was the first member if she read this.) The first time her social worker, Brenda, met her, she was calling angrily, complaining that her family had locked the door on the refrigerator and were keeping her locked in her room, hungry. Appalled, Brenda drove over and rescued Doris, put her in a hotel room at our expense and bought her some food. Satisfying Doris once she found a source of help was like trying to put a genie back in a bottle. She had new demands every minute. She ate up every bit of food within moments, no matter how much it was, and wanted more. She called everyone nonstop, demanding something.

She loved talking, even all night. She called our emergency line nonstop, keeping the on-call person up all night. When they started calling her once to check in and tell her that was her only call that night and then wouldn't respond to her numerous calls, she got the numbers for the 24-hour complaint departments of all the chain department stores. She called them so often they knew her by her voice.

She collected phone bills she couldn't pay; so, we took away her phone. By the time we got back to the office, she'd gotten two more phone contracts from the mall. When we asked her how she was going to pay the bill, she just laughed.

She took everything that wasn't tied down, even if it wasn't hers, including her neighbor's bicycle and everyone's cigarettes. "People should learn how to take care of their stuff if they want to keep it."

Once she signed up for a Medi-Cal managed care plan. She found out that if she threatened to kill herself, they'd do almost anything. After a while, she was injecting herself with her insulin, saying it was a suicide attempt, in order to get a "smoking permitted" cab to take her to the hospital in time to watch her favorite TV show. I had to get her un-enrolled, afraid she'd end up accidently killing herself. We didn't respond to her suicidal threats; so, she didn't make any. Instead, she learned that we'd respond to requests for hourly work to make money. She was still a pest, but at least she was pestering us about doing something positive. We gave her a mop.

I was never sure if all of those behaviors were mania or just selfish survival skills she'd picked up as a kid, when her father always had other women and families he supported ahead of her mother and sisters. Where she grew up, everyone grabbed what they could to survive.

I do know now that none of that was her "full blown manic episodes." Those would come by about every 5 years and last about 6 months of living hell. When the first one came, she was convinced she was in love with her preacher, and she kept interrupting his sermons and following him around. At the same time, she said she was Doris Jorgenson, married to her young male case worker, Eric Jorgenson. At first, he was amused, but his naïveté wore off as she became more and more impulsive, grabbing him and jumping out of his moving car when he drove her places. I remembered that, in a quiet moment, she'd told me that just because she's fat now doesn't mean she still doesn't get lonely and wish she had a man in her life. With the disinhibition of mania, that wish became her reality.

I pulled together a meeting of everyone in Doris's life to try to figure out what to do—her sisters and kids, preacher, and our staff. Her sisters said that in the past, she'd always been hospitalized and heavily medicated when she was like this for the 6 months it took her to recover. I explained that I wanted to avoid caging her up like that and that maybe if we worked together, she could be cared for in the community. I did raise her medications substantially, and we supervised her medications carefully, handing them to her in individual packets and watching her take them in front of us. (When she was manic like that, she could burn off huge dosages of medications, much more than she could handle normally, but she also tended to get diarrhea, which added to the confusion and the mess. Her second social worker, Laurel, first met her helping her try on adult diapers.)

None of it worked. We simply couldn't contain her. Even when I broke down and did hospitalize her, she drove them crazy. One day, she saw me coming up to the ward to see her and ran naked, slamming into the large, locked, shatter-proof doors ... and shattered them (keep in mind she weighed about 250 pounds).

I got her somewhat stabilized with even more meds and tried releasing her again.

This time, she was caught stealing in the grocery store and started screaming at the security guards when they accosted her, until the police were called, and she was arrested. Her sisters were mortified, and blamed me. "If you would've kept her in the hospital like we told you to, she would never have been arrested. Now, she has a criminal record and has shamed our whole family."

"I'm sorry, but we don't have long-term hospitals any more to keep people for 6 months."

When she got out of jail, they didn't want her either; she was mad at all of us and said she was going back home to Detroit to her mother, and she got a Greyhound bus ticket.

She was taken off the bus and hospitalized in Colorado and again in Kansas and never got to Detroit. Kansas shipped her back to us.

After 6 months, she went back to being her annoying, but lovable self, a handful but not psychotic, and back on normal dosages of medications.

New staff—who were frustrated by her antics, forever working with her to find new places to live, when she burned out wherever she was by being too demanding—didn't believe me when I told them they were lucky they didn't have to deal with Doris's mania, just her personality.

Her kids were the same ages as mine, and she often asked about my kids and told me about hers. I reflected on what a huge difference in upbringing and opportunities my kids had and hers did. Mine had a stable place to live with two parents, lots of money and activities, good schooling, and both grew up very successful. Her kids bounced around various relatives, and even occasionally foster care. None of them had ever met their fathers, and Doris hadn't had any boyfriends since they were small children. They had to learn to fend for themselves and deal with their always self-centered mom. The two boys dropped out of school and got in trouble. One ended up in juvenile hall, the other moved in with an older woman, and they had a kid he couldn't support. Eventually, she kicked him out, and he came back to try to live off his mom's Social Security check, but she was always a step ahead of him, taking advantage of him more than he could take advantage of her. Her daughter did better and was trying to become a nurse, while trying to take care of her mother, too, until she became pregnant and had to drop out of college. As the years went on, Doris saw less and less of her kids.

It's not that she didn't love her kids. She just couldn't tone herself down to be there for them. Whenever we talked, Doris would always close with, "Kiss your kids for me" and *a big lovable smile. Then, she'd grab a handful of candy out of my desk drawer and run away giggling.*

One last detail about Doris I'd like to share with you. Not surprisingly, given her appetite and weight and meds, she developed diabetes. Our mental health nurses checked her sugar levels and gave her insulin daily keeping it under control ... as much as anything in her life could be said to be under control. Her sisters, who were also overweight, but not mentally ill, didn't have our support and they all died from their diabetes, while Doris lived on.

Major depression with psychosis

When someone is manic enough to be psychotic, they're usually very difficult to manage and keep out of trouble, but they're also usually fun to be with. We smile and laugh with them in spite of ourselves. Manic "war stories" are often our favorites. When someone is depressed enough to be psychotic, they're often withdrawn and difficult to connect with. When we do catch a glimpse of what they're going through, it's often so discouraging and painful that we back off. Depression with psychosis is usually not just a very painful state but also a very isolated state. That combination makes suicide a definite risk.

Like mania, depression can lead to psychosis in several, often overlapping ways:

- Depression can get so severe that thinking can be slowed down dramatically, like they're in mud. It may be hard to concentrate and focus or sustain attention long enough to work things out. Rational thought may become too difficult to sustain and be replaced with automatic or reflexive responses, intuitive guesses, or even unconscious thoughts and feelings taking over. It can just be easier to believe they're going to fail everything or that everyone hates them and thinks they're no good, than to work through the subtleties of what's really going on. Someone may seem to have a thought disorder, just because they're so depressed they can't keep their thinking moving fast enough to keep up with a conversation or

even to remember what they were trying to say by the time they get there.
- Depression can lead to obsessive thoughts—for example, everyone is making fun of them or they can't do anything right, which can increasingly take on a life of their own. It can become impossible to go out with friends because everyone is staring at them—even if their friends reassure them that no one is really looking at them. They can become more insistent. People can start calling them crazy. They can start believing everyone is talking about them, too—and they might be by then. Somewhere in here, they've become psychotic, or in clinical language, their "ideas of reference" (thinking everyone is talking about them) have become "delusions of reference" (believing everyone is talking about them). It's a slippery slope.
- The depression can start impacting their body directly. We have emotions in both our brains and our bodies. Bodies experience our minds in far less rational ways than our brains do, in general, and that can lead to psychosis, too. For example, when someone breaks up with someone, they become depressed, but they also become "heartbroken," often literally feeling an emptiness and a tightness in their chest. Their heart rate can go up as the sobbing breaks out. Once someone starts focusing on their bodies, they can start to get confused—thinking that they're having a heart attack—rather than understanding those physical feelings as emotions. Depressed people often come to doctors with various physical complaints, only to be told, "It's all in your head." They can start examining their sensations even more closely, looking for evidence the doctor is wrong. Soon, they're sliding down another slippery slope. I remember one very depressed man who believed that his body was actively rotting and emitting a terrible smell. He thought everyone was denying they could smell it just to be kind to him, but they really could. He couldn't see how he was experiencing his body as actively expressing his emotional state. His depression was rotting his life away.
- Depression can severely narrow some people's conscious focus. They can't remember the good times anymore. It seems to them like they've always been depressed … and always will be. Hopelessness

sets in. Only things that confirm their depression seem to be able to get through. Flaws get magnified, slights get magnified, setbacks get magnified. There's no longer any place for rational hope or happiness. The world the rest of people seem to be living in has been exposed as a fraud—at least for them—replaced by a very dark, discouraging reality. As rational thought becomes more and more limited, some of the most depressing thoughts can seem to have come into their minds by themselves, or have been put there by someone else ("delusions of thought insertion"), or they're someone else's thoughts that they're overhearing, either inside or outside their heads ("hallucinations"). Occasionally, it can even seem like their own thoughts are being removed by someone else ("delusions of thought withdrawal"). The more distorted reality becomes, the more elaborate explanations become to explain what's happening.

Evan couldn't really remember a time when he wasn't depressed. Nothing that traumatic happened to him growing up, but he doesn't think he was happy as a child anyway. He didn't really have a good reason not to be happy. He just wasn't.

Part of the issue might have been that he didn't grow up with much happiness around him. His father worked as an engineer and tended to sit by himself, slowly drinking, most evenings. He wasn't much of a presence. His mother had periodic depressions, when she'd end up in bed for months at a time, and he'd have to get himself to school and most of the time feed himself, too. She said medications helped her, but he thought she was addicted to her Prozac and Xanax and blunted by them. She felt guilty she didn't have more energy to do more with him and his younger sister. His sister had some eating issues in her teens and even started cutting herself. After a while, she'd moved in with her boyfriend and seemed a little happier. She wasn't making much money walking dogs, but they were living with his parents, so they didn't need much money.

Evan had always been very smart in school, at least when he cared enough about the subject and the teacher to pay attention. Mostly, he read a lot of books on his own and played complex computer video games. He hesitated to tell anyone, but he had long ago decided that he didn't like people. He could see how self-centered and inconsiderate and even cruel most people are, and he didn't see why he should either forgive them for that or spend any time with them.

Alice was the only person he liked. They'd met years ago at a Starbucks. He wasn't sure what was really different about her than everyone else, but it had something to do with the way she could be really present without needing to say much. He never felt judged by her.

When he started feeling suicidal more regularly, it was hard for her. She never told him he was wrong for feeling that way, but it pained her to see him like that. As the years went on, he tried a variety of antidepressant medications, even though he was sure they wouldn't work, because it was worth trying anything, so that she wouldn't have to share his depression. When he saw how broken up she was when he took all his pills trying to kill himself, he promised her he'd never do that again, and he didn't.

He'd sit by himself playing blues on the harmonica for hours at a time. We got him involved in our Village band for a while and he sure played well, but even that didn't seem to break through the depression.

I tried more combinations of medications, but got nowhere. I learned to accept him the way he was, too, just being there for him. I was the one person he could share his suicidal thoughts with, knowing I wouldn't hospitalize him or tell Alice.

"I'm not sure it's really what you'd call hallucinations, but sometimes it sure seems like someone is on my shoulder telling me to kill myself. You know, like the cartoons with a demon on one shoulder and an angel on the other, except I don't have an angel, just the demon."

Sometimes, he'd let himself be seduced by suicidal thinking, imagining how he'd do it and what it would be like to have his pain stop. He never imagined there'd be anything after death; except for Alice, he didn't have anything he liked about living or any reason to stay alive; so, he took comfort in thinking about the end of everything. Both he and Alice knew that when she died, he'd kill himself.

"Be careful daydreaming about death. The thoughts will get stronger that way and be harder to resist."

"That's true, doc."

Over the years, it got harder and harder for him to concentrate to read. He'd have to read the same page over and over again. He lost interest in video games, too. He could go days without remembering to eat and nights without sleeping, his mind going around and round, but mostly nowhere. He was tired all the time. He'd have to make a special effort to have sex with Alice.

From time to time, he'd think he was dying, but the doctor never found much wrong with him.

I learned to schedule his appointments with me at the end of the day, so I wouldn't have to pull myself together to see anyone else after being dragged down by him.

Sometimes, it's not clear with depression and psychosis which one is the cause and which is the effect. The most common approach is to diagnose them as schizoaffective, depressed type and prescribe them both antipsychotic and antidepressant medications and assume it will work, regardless of which condition is "primary" and which is "secondary." If our only treatment is going to be medications, that's probably good enough, but if we're going to try to help guide them to recovery, we should try to go deeper. Evan clearly has severe depression leading to psychosis, but there are two other possibilities to keep in mind:

1) Their psychosis is causing them to be depressed. Certainly, experiencing psychosis can make someone's life more difficult in a number of ways, and they can sink into depression as a result. For

example, hearing voices may make it impossible to concentrate to read or to fall asleep at night. As a result, school performance may go down. Falling grades, shamefully telling parents, even failing classes and dropping out can follow, leading to giving up and sinking into depression. This pattern is often described as "secondary depression." Just treating the depression with medications, for example, is unlikely to make the voices go away, too, on a strictly biochemical basis. This leads to a not uncommon stalemate, where the person is only willing to take antidepressant medications because they're "not crazy," but they're not improving, while others want them to take antipsychotic medications, often focusing in on only the psychosis and assuming everything else will be fine once the voices are gone, while irremediable harm is being done to their lives. It is possible that if someone's depression is improved enough that they can rebuild their self-identity and relationships, they may improve their experience of reality, too, so don't give up if they won't address their issues with reality directly. If their life improves, starting with their depression, they might not need to distort and escape from reality as much, even if losing touch with reality was what led to their depression in the first place.

2) Both the depression and the psychosis may be caused by something else. They may really be on one of the other journeys—say experiencing severe grief or life events they can't adapt to or have lost their balance. Lowering either the depressive and psychotic symptoms may well help them to recover, and likely should be done, but they're not really going to climb out of their hole without doing more work on whatever is underlying both conditions.

I believe that if we're far more careful in understanding exactly what the person is experiencing, going far beyond the basic "objective" criteria, exploring their subjective experiences, we can usually understand how their depression interacts with their psychosis. Taking the time to uncover these processes not only helps us direct treatment efforts, it can also help distressed people understand what's going on within themselves and how they can work with us to recover.

Anxiety disorders (obsessive-compulsive disorder, panic disorder, dissociative disorders, and PTSD) and eating disorders (anorexia and bulimia)

Today's *DSM-V* psychiatric taxonomy doesn't include any of these disorders as potentially including psychosis, even though they can lead people to seriously lose touch with reality:

- People with obsessive-compulsive disorder can have fixed beliefs that can dramatically impact their lives—like they have to check the door exactly eight times or someone will break in, or they'll catch AIDS if they don't wash their hands using a ritual that takes 20 minutes and wear gloves when shaking hands.
- In the midst of a panic attack, someone can start to feel like their body isn't really theirs ("depersonalization") or like the walls are shimmering or moving all around them ("derealization") or be so convinced they're having a heart attack that they go to the ER over and over, despite reassurances and normal tests.
- Someone who is incredibly anxious can disconnect from either their thoughts or their feelings and often lose memory of the episode ("dissociation")—for example, I worked with a man who had a severe anxiety condition his whole life that was poorly controlled with benzodiazepines. His life fell apart when an ex-lover killed himself, and he ended up in a shoe store wearing a shoe box as a hat and the shoes were hanging from his ears. He regained awareness as the security guard gave up on questioning him and calmed him down instead, but he had no idea how he'd gotten there or what he was doing.
- Someone who has a post-traumatic reaction to a life-threatening situation may feel like they're back in the situation—for example, when having sex with a husband, their body may feel like they're being raped again or when they're walking around a college, they may feel like they're back in Iraq with explosive devices and snipers hiding all around them ("flashbacks").
- Someone with a severe eating disorder may insist that they are overweight even when they aren't—for example, when asked to draw their image on a mirror, many people with anorexia will draw one much bigger than they are and then be confused why they

don't fit into it when they look in the mirror—and literally starve themselves to death based on that distorted belief.

Why aren't all of those experiences diagnosed as psychosis? What's the difference between them and the psychosis from schizophrenia, schizoaffective disorder, and mood disorders?

Here's where we have to look beyond the idea of delusions as "fixed, false, unshared beliefs" and return to the old "definitions" of psychosis and schizophrenia I told you about in Chapter 3: Psychosis means we don't understand either biologically or psychologically what is wrong with the person and schizophrenia means we can't emotionally connect to the other person and what they're going through. For all the conditions in this section, we believe we have some understanding of what's wrong with the person—obsessions, dissociations, panic, PTSD, and anorexia all more or less make sense to us. Even more importantly, most of us have had experiences that seem to relate to what these people are going through—at times, we've felt like a superstitious ritual really had an impact, we've felt driven to check something "just one more time to make sure," we've been in shock or grief enough to feel disconnected from the normal flow of time and reality, we've felt if only for a moment that we were reliving a frightening or tragic moment in our lives, and we've looked in the mirror disgusted with our appearance and refused to believe anyone's reassurances.

As a fortunate result, when we meet someone with any of these conditions, we don't usually feel lost and confused about what the problem is and, even more importantly, we feel we can relate to them. We don't need to invoke psychosis to describe them. These people aren't "beyond the frontier." We're not afraid they're going crazy ... because they don't have "real" psychosis or schizophrenia. Their diagnoses are relatable enough to treat them within our normal medical model parameters. For people with "real psychosis," we are often lost, confused, and struggling to relate to them. Then, their diagnoses aren't relatable enough to treat them within the normal medical parameters. People with "real psychosis" aren't hopeless because their illnesses are actually more extreme and untreatable, but because the people are more frightening and harder to connect to.

The same thing is sometimes true from the person's point of view and sometimes not: Sometimes, people with these conditions (and also those with mood disorders) feel like they understand what's going on and aren't totally isolated in their experiences, and sometimes, they don't. When they don't, we should probably be working hard to relate to them, break through their isolation, and help them see themselves within their diagnoses. If we can bring them back on the map, with conditions they can accept and feel accepted with, they can engage with treatments, especially directed toward their conditions.

Wait a minute. Isn't that what we try to do with all diagnoses, give people enough information about their illnesses and stories of other people they can relate to, so they'll cooperate with their treatment? Isn't that what psychoeducation is all about? Why are you making it sound like it's different for schizophrenia than it is for anxiety disorders and eating disorders?

You're absolutely right, except that it's not me that's making it sound different; the difference is built into the way the model is applied. I'm not the one who said people with anxiety and eating disorders aren't delusional or psychotic and people with schizophrenia and severe mood disorders are delusional and psychotic. I'm not the one who said that people with anxiety and eating disorders can be understood and treated with a combination of biological, emotional, interpersonal, and social interventions, whereas people with schizophrenia have a degenerative brain condition and should be treated with medications and custodial care. I'm not the one who said people with anxiety and eating disorders can understand what's wrong and participate meaningfully in their treatment and recovery, while people with schizophrenia can't. I'm not even the one who said that public funds shouldn't be used to treat people with anxiety and eating disorders because they don't have "serious, persistent mental illnesses (SPMI)" like people with schizophrenia, schizoaffective, and mood disorders do—even though panic disorder with agoraphobia, obsessive-compulsive disorder, chronic PTSD, and anorexia can be incredibly disabling, treatment-resistant, and even life-threatening conditions.

Journeys Beyond the Frontier

In fact, one of my main purposes in writing this book is to expand our ability to understand and relate to people with psychosis and other extraordinary experiences, so that this artificial barrier ceases to exist. I believe that we can help everyone with a combination of biological, emotional, interpersonal, and social interventions. Everyone can come to some understanding of what's wrong and participate meaningfully in their treatment and recovery. Everyone with serious suffering and impairment deserves publicly funded services if they can't afford them.

I'm not going to get into the variety of approaches we currently take with people with anxiety and eating disorders because that would require another book, but I do want to highlight a point about medications usage with these people: Even though we have a wide range of new, second-generation antipsychotic medications that have been tested on schizophrenia and mood disorders (even getting FDA approval for mood disorders without psychosis), there is relatively little testing or usage of these medications for extreme experiences connected to anxiety and eating disorders.

Rigid, extreme obsessions and compulsions, dissociations, derealization, depersonalization, and dangerously distorted body images are rarely treated with antipsychotic medications. Usually, these conditions are medicated with either addictive benzodiazepines and other anti-anxiety medications, or with selective serotonin reuptake inhibitor (SSSRI) antidepressants that tend to be anti-rumination (anti-overthinking) medications, none of which was specifically developed for these extraordinary experiences. There is the exception of Seroquel, which is a very sedating antipsychotic medication, with complex molecular properties, that is widely used in relatively low dosages to sedate and calm and put to sleep lots of people. Seroquel's "off label" usage is widespread enough that it creates budget problems for public mental health systems and questions of mistreatment of traumatized veterans, but it hasn't been systematically studied either.

It seems to me that each of these extraordinary experiences likely has different underlying biological mechanisms that might be responsive to different antipsychotic medications, if only we knew what we were doing better. We continue to be handicapped by a diagnostic system that lumps together various biological pathways with similar symptoms and pharmaceutical research that is dedicated to increasing market share and profit, rather than increasing effective, targeted usage.

Or maybe, we'd find out that none of our pills impact any of these experiences. At the rate we're going, we'll never know.

I want to be sure to leave you at the end of this journey with an appreciation that the narrowness of our current "illness-centered" medical model, not medical psychiatry in its entirety, is what needs to be rebelled against. The "medical model" can potentially be reformed and refocused to the point where it could inform all of our journeys.

At its best, the "medical model" uses scientific methods to discover and describe the pathological processes that lead to psychological distress to find ways to intervene and improve things. While psychiatry purports to work within a holistic "biopsychosocial" framework, it's understood that because we emphasize breaking things down to understand them, using a "reductionistic approach," we'll likely focus on biological or even chemical processes and interventions.

At its worst, the "medical model" creates "illnesses" out of clusters of symptoms, without regard to why they cluster or underlying pathology, and then acts as though those "illnesses" are independent entities that can destructively infiltrate people's minds with their own life forces and purposes. This model includes the clearly incorrect assumption that if an illness has been named and put in *DSM*, there must be an, as yet undiscovered, underlying genetic and biochemical pathological process that causes that particular illness. Somehow, clustering expressions of distress (like low mood, poor sleep, concentration, appetite, and sex drive) is presumed to magically make them symptoms of an illness, instead of just the common expressions of distress that they are.

I'm not saying that scientific, medical evaluation of suffering to find a variety of interrelated causes and pathways is a bad thing. I'm saying that's not what our current "medical model" psychiatric establishment is doing.

In my view, there are a few people who have psychiatric illnesses that are relatively autonomous conditions, not directly caused by one of the other processes I've already discussed, but not the vast majority of people who are diagnosed today. The promoters of the autonomous illness model did large-scale, multi-center, house-to-house surveys of common expressions of distress like anxiety and depression, and instead of coming to the plausible conclusion that many people experience serious mental distress, they came to the oft-repeated "narrow-minded" conclusion that 40% of everyone will get a mental illness sometime in their lives. For people who experience psychosis, their analysis is even more narrow-minded—all of them are believed to have a mental illness (except maybe a few who use drugs, and even many of those are often characterized as having triggered an underlying, latent psychotic illness).

The biggest shames in all of this are as follows: 1) It is almost impossible to research anything except these illness constructions; so, we can't discover what's really going on and improve our treatments, and 2) we can't get either government or private insurance to pay for any treatment services unless you first agree that you have one of these mental illnesses lurking within you. Don't bother to come for help for overwhelming grief, or events you can't handle, or a life that's falling apart, or from carrying the scars of childhood trauma. We're only paid to treat mental illnesses.

Chapter 13

Journey 8: Brain Damage and Other Neurological and Medical Conditions

When I was doing my psychiatry residency training at LA County–USC, one of my clinical rotations was consultation–liaison psychiatry. This rotation consisted of going around the hospital responding to various medical and surgical residents' requests for psychiatric consultation. Usually, a psychiatric consultation meant, "Get this patient off my ward. Take them away. They're crazy. There's nothing really wrong with them. I'm too busy for this shit." Some of them were demented, or high, or John Does "found down" somewhere and brought in by the paramedics. Frequently, a language barrier was also involved. Only about a third of new admissions to the hospital could tell us a coherent, "chief complaint" in English. It was my job to take the time to figure out what was really going on. Ward 6300 was where many of these patients were put while we figured out what to do with them. About a third of the patients on this ward were tied down with leather restraints. I used to enjoy going around with my "restraints key," untying them like a great liberator.

One morning my patient for consultation was Juan. He had just come illegally from Mexico about 6 months ago and was staying with his cousin, Carlos, who was the one who had brought him to the hospital and was sitting in the room with him. Carlos spoke both English and Spanish; so, he got to be the interpreter between Juan, who only spoke Spanish, and me, with my rudimentary high school Spanish.

Juan had come to Los Angeles, looking for work, but it had been hard going. He'd found some day labor but seemed to be getting discouraged. He didn't know anyone besides Carlos and was lonely. He didn't have much money. He'd sit in bed a lot. As the months went on, Carlos had more and more trouble getting him to do anything. He wouldn't eat. He wouldn't go out looking for work. He didn't talk much. He just didn't seem like himself; so, he brought him into the hospital to find out what was wrong.

I got this story mostly from Carlos, rather than from Juan, and it seemed like Juan was depressed to me. Nonetheless, I started to do a brief mental status exam to see how his brain was working, using Carlos as my translator. I asked him what date it was, who was the president of the United States, where we were, what 3 + 5 and 5 + 8 were. He stumbled through those questions as most people do.

Then, I pointed to my watch, "Que es esto?" (What is this?)

"Un reloj." (A watch.)

"Bueno, and que es esta parte?" (Good, and what is this part?) I pointed to the watch face.

He looked confused.

I traced the watch hands, "Que es el nombre de estos?" (What is the name of these?)

Again confused. Carlos tried to explain what I was asking in Spanish that I couldn't follow, but he couldn't get an answer that made sense either.

I pulled my keys out of my pocket, "Que son estos?" (What are these?)

He answered something I didn't understand, and Carlos laughed.

"What did he say that was so funny?"

"He said those were chicken feet."

Chicken feet, really? This may just be a language issue, but being depressed doesn't make you not know what watch hands are or think that keys are chicken feet. Maybe something was wrong with his brain.

"I'm going to order a CT scan of his brain to see if anything is wrong."

The CT scan showed a tumor growing in the side of his brain that had blocked one of the main veins, and his brain was getting squished against his skull. Unfortunately, the news from the neurology consult was bleak. "We can drill a hole to relieve the pressure, but that tumor is inoperable and will kill him."

I heard that he died 6 months later.

In some ways, this journey is the most frustrating of all of them for me. It seems like we should know more than we do. I can tell you stories about people becoming psychotic connected to sundowning or delirium from hypertension or seizures or brain inflammation, but I can't really tell you how any of that works. Why do all these things happen?

I think that we're struggling to make more progress because each of these people has conditions that cross the mind–body divide, and we're not very good at feeling connected to our bodies enough to integrate mind and body to understand how they interrelate. We've made some progress in the direction of understanding how minds can impact bodies, but the people on this journey are likely predominantly in the other direction—we need to understand how their bodies (including the neurons in their brains) affect their minds ... and we're just not very good at that. Our training doesn't connect body and mind.

Because of this persistent disconnect, the main piece of luggage you need for this journey is a "dual passport," so that you can travel within two different systems. In California, and many other places, we divide the patients into different departments and silos. For most of my career, including the entire time at the Village, I've been a part of our county-run mental health system. As I mentioned in Chapter 12, that system is supposed to focus on people with serious persistent mental illnesses (SPMI). We specifically exclude people with primary diagnosis of developmental disorders (they go to Regional Centers), alcoholism and substance abuse, dementia, and medical and neurological disorders. The reason I've met so few people with primary medical and neurological conditions may be that they're supposed to be excluded from the public mental health system. As a result, of all of our eight journeys, this is the one I have the least personal experience with. In fact, most of my stories in this chapter, like that first one, come from my training in the medical hospital, part of the Department of Health Services, not the Department of Mental Health, when I had a "different passport."

But how do you know that people aren't coming to mental health thinking they have a mental condition when they actually have a physical condition?

I don't really. To be fair, given the stigma around mental health, far more people are going to present the other way around, thinking they have a medical condition when it's really a mental health condition. Nonetheless, when I was in England years ago, the British Health Service gave every new mental patient a medical and neurological evaluation, including lab tests and a CT scan of their head, to make sure they weren't missing a medical or neurological condition before the patients were treated in the mental health system. I've never seen a system in the United States that does anything like that. Personally, I can't remember ever successfully ordering a neurological evaluation or a head CT scan for a psychotic patient. Not only are they in a separate system than I am, there are hardly any neurologists in the public sector, and outpatient CT scans are distinctly hard to get. I'd estimate the wait at my local county medical center for a neurologist to be about 6 months, and then, they'd have to order the head CT scan. They won't take an order from me as a psychiatrist. (Don't get me wrong, if someone shows up to the medical ER in acute distress, including people with new severe headaches, they'll get a head CT scan to make sure they're not having an intracranial hemorrhage or a stroke). Also, I've rarely met a brand-new patient in public mental health, like Juan. Almost everyone had already been in treatment for long periods of time. Presumably, if they had a dangerous neurological condition, they would've deteriorated or died by the time I met them.

The main tool we use in practice to separate out neurological and psychiatric conditions is a Mental Status Exam, like you saw me doing with Juan. If you have a purely psychiatric condition, the nonemotional functions of your brain should be intact: You should be "oriented"—know who you are, where you are, what day it is, and why you're here. You should be able to do simple arithmetic, spelling, remember the president, and remember words for a few minutes, and sometimes draw a few pictures. If there is a doubt, we can get fancier.

What we're doing is differentiating between psychosis (and other psychiatric conditions) and delirium (basically a confusion caused because your brain is medically or neurologically compromised, or toxic, including drugs and alcohol). Besides testing basic functions, we assess level of consciousness. If you're drifting in and out of consciousness or hard to arouse, that probably isn't just a psychiatric condition either. Blood tests can also help find medical conditions.

As a psychiatrist, I also had a fair bit of purely medical training, and I learned how to tell who's "sick" and who isn't. If you're delirious for a medical reason, you're likely to be "sick." (I remember one woman I saw at Coastal who was referred to a panic disorder group I was running. She seemed confused and disoriented during the interview and was having trouble finding words. Besides that, she seemed "sick" to me. I called in her therapist and asked her if the patient was always like this. She talked to her a few minutes and said that this was unusual. I sent her to the local ER, not knowing what was wrong but knowing something was wrong. It turned out her potassium level was severely out of balance and she was on the verge of a heart attack.)

I honestly don't know if that's enough to be sure I'm not missing people whose journey is really medical or neurological but who happen to be in the mental health system anyway. And psychiatrists have the most medical and neurological training of anyone in the mental health system.

Developmental disorders

There are a variety of ways in which our brains can develop abnormally both before and after birth.

On the most extreme edge, I did a special rotation in Pediatric Neurology in medical school at Washington University because it had a specialty clinic that drew in patients, primarily newborns and infants, from hundreds of miles away around St. Louis. I saw an amazing array of tragic malformations of young brains, mostly vastly more severely impaired than any psychiatric patient I ever saw, and many of whom died later in infancy.

But there are many more people with subtler malformed or malfunctioning brains of far lesser severity who do survive and grow up in our communities, often with extra support from Special Education and Regional Centers as they grow up. Some of these people go on to have mental disorders, some with psychotic experiences. Our standard approach is to say that, of course, having a developmental disorder doesn't protect someone from also having a mental disorder, and there are unfortunate people who just happen to have both. They are "dually diagnosed" people. We may try to coordinate their treatment, but we conceptualize them as having two independent conditions, both in need of specialized support and treatments. There may need to be some adaptation of their treatments—they probably can't use sophisticated psychoeducational, or cognitive behavioral approaches. They may need lower dosages of medications because their "damaged" brain is more sensitive. They may need more support to take medications regularly and to adapt to their conditions.

I don't think that should be the end of the story.

It seems to me that people with developmental disorders are more likely to struggle with life than other people. Grief may be harder for them. (Remember Frances back in Chapter 6 whom I urged to stay in touch with her dead grandmother because she couldn't cope without her?) They may have trouble adapting to serious stressors and have psychotic breaks. They may have more trouble maintaining their emotional balance. And I would certainly expect them to have more trouble processing reality as a direct result of their underlying neurological condition. For many of these people, I think we'd be better off describing them as having a developmental disorder with psychotic experiences, rather than describing them as having two separate disorders—a developmental disorder and a psychotic disorder. Consider these two examples:

> Brad had an IQ of a little less than 70. He could read and write and socially interact with other people. He was overly concrete and repetitive, which could get annoying, but he

did well enough to manage his own apartment and even had a few girlfriends along the way. The main problem with trying to get along with Brad was that he'd take everything personally and negatively. If I didn't call him back right away, he'd be convinced that I think he's worthless and hated him. He wouldn't (or couldn't) listen to any other possible explanations. If I didn't sit at his table in the Village Deli, he'd take it as a personal affront. Over the years, a few of us, including most notably the director, Paul Barry, learned how to combine overly dramatic apologies, feigned guilt, humor, and pretend to take affront back at him; so, we were able to keep caring, but prickly relationships going over many years.

When he was a teenager, his father was somewhat frustrated and disappointed in his development. He wasn't doing very well in high school and getting into problems with other kids. Brad took his father's natural and caring responses very badly. He would spend hours and hours ruminating on his father's negative comments and slights real and imagined. His father realized what was happening and tried to reconnect and make it up to Brad, but nothing seemed to work. Brad got worse and worse and decided his father was literally trying to poison and kill him. He didn't talk with his father for the last 2 years they lived in the same house or for the 20 years since he moved out into his own apartment. Brad wouldn't talk with any of us about his father, fixed in his paranoia.

I think that Brad's intellectual and emotional abilities were too weak to handle the normal adolescent issues with his father, while at the same time, he couldn't establish a positive identity within the community. With those two aspects of the psychosis triangle weakened, his experience of reality was impacted, too. With the ongoing network of caring, accepting, inclusive relationships at the Village, he was able to feel like he belonged even though every day was a test, and while he was there, he never became paranoid of any of us.

Many phenomena that we call psychotic in adults are more or less normal at certain childhood developmental stages—for example, thinking that things that are out of sight no longer exist, "stranger anxiety," talking to stuffed animals and imaginary friends, making up elaborate stories and claiming they really happened, having premonitions, or confusing dreams and reality.

> Patrick wasn't diagnosed as either mentally retarded or autistic, even though he was obviously strange his whole life. In California, the Regional Centers have responsibility for administering service funds for people with developmental disabilities. Their responsibility has been diagnostically delineated—mental retardation (IQ less than 70), autism (not "spectrum"), cerebral palsy, and childhood-onset seizures. By those criteria, Patrick was ineligible for their services. The school districts generally give up on our impressively inadequate childhood psychiatric diagnostic system (Featuring diagnoses like oppositional defiant disorder and conduct disorder and attention deficit disorder, with or without hyperactivity, it's even worse than the adult system I've been ranting about.) and serve these students under the broad heading of Severely Emotional Disturbance (SED). Patrick had an Individualized Educational Plan (IEP) throughout his schooling and even for a few years of "transitional services" after graduation, when they got him a volunteer job at the local VA hospital.
>
> The main challenge managing Patrick had always been his "lying." When he was little and he would lie and say he didn't do something when he was caught, it didn't seem that abnormal, but the lies gradually expanded to anything he was uncomfortable about. For instance, he described in detail conflicts he had at home with a brother who didn't exist and lamented his parents' losing their jobs in the financial recession, even though it didn't happen. Some teachers confronted him with his lies and pressed him to tell the truth, and, especially when he was younger and well connected to the teacher, that seemed to work to bring him back into

truthfulness. As he got older, however, he would get more adamant in his insistence in his accounts, and most people started backing off and confronting him less and less.

By the time I met him, he was 20 years old, and it was very difficult to know what was true and what wasn't. He related everything in the same way. He described details of his experiences as a volunteer at the VA hospital, even though I later found out from his mother he hadn't been going for months. He showed us a whole pack of pictures of his two dogs he had at home and described their antics— except that they didn't have a dog. I don't know where he got those pictures from. If I tried confronting him, he typically wouldn't either get upset at being challenged or back down. He'd just continue as though I hadn't said anything.

Sometimes, I tried to figure out the reasons for the lies (or should I call them "confabulations" or even "delusions"). He didn't want to be nagged by us about taking care of himself, or doing his chores, or budgeting. He probably wished he had a dog. He was probably just trying to fit in when he told stories about using drugs and getting beaten up when he couldn't pay for them, when nothing like that happened. When he told me he was thinking about killing himself, should I take that seriously or assume it's made up, too, perhaps as another way of getting attention or respect?

It was very difficult to have a meaningful conversation or relate to him or work on teaching him anything when we had to check everything he said to see if it was true or not. I wasn't sure whether to prescribe him medications or not, and when I did, I never knew when he was taking them or not to see if they made any difference. I began to dread seeing him and became more and more passive to avoid being so frustrated.

He found new people to show his dog pictures to.

I'm not sure whether to call Patrick psychotic or not, but it sure makes more sense to me that his "delusions" emerged from his developmental disability, as he held on to normal childish behaviors long past normal, rather than that he happened to have two separate "dual diagnoses"—a developmental disorder and a co-occurring psychotic disorder.

Seizures and other neurological conditions

It may seem like there should be a considerable overlap between the training and practice of psychiatrists and neurologists since we're both working on the same brains, but that isn't the case. Psychiatric residents are required to spend 2 months of our 4 years of training in Neurology and neurologists have no required psychiatric training. At least in the public sector, we rarely work together. Like for developmental disorders, we're more likely to describe the patients we share as having dual diagnosis—one neurological condition and one psychiatric condition, each needing separate, specialty care, rather than trying to combine their symptoms into a single condition we can collaborate in treating. Perhaps not coincidentally, the only neuropsychiatry textbook I read was a British book.

Seizures are probably the most common neurologic symptom I've seen in my psychiatric patients, and I've been carefully taught that occasionally, someone may have seemingly psychiatric symptoms (like visual hallucinations or mood swings or irritability) that are a result of their seizures, but seizures are never the result of any psychiatric disorder. (I assume that Kraepelin would've been surprised by this since apparently about 30% of the patients in his psychiatric hospital in Germany in the 1890s had seizures—Remember him? The German psychiatrist who called schizophrenia "dementia praecox" and decided it was a deteriorating condition of the brain.)

> An elderly Chinese man, who spoke only Cantonese Chinese, had been admitted to LA County–USC half a dozen times over about 3 months, usually for seizures. They always stopped after a few days back on medications, and he was sent home only to return again. The interns suspected alcohol withdrawal seizures, just because that was the most common cause of seizures there. If you can't communicate with the patient, play the odds. Only once did

they catch an English-speaking family member who said that he never drank, but that he had a lot of bizarre behaviors. He sometimes had hallucinations and would be paranoid and confused.

That's why the next time he was admitted, they called me in as a psychiatric consult. I knew that sometimes, psychosis can be a prodrome of seizures (especially seizures that begin in the temporal lobes of the brain (temporal lobe epilepsy), which are usually very hard to detect with an electroencephalographic (EEG) brain wave test. I also knew that sometimes, seizures can relieve psychosis (that may be why electroshock therapy works sometimes with psychosis). Needless to say, my Chinese was far too limited to get a clear history from him. Cantonese Chinese is far less common than Mandarin Chinese; so, no one was available as a translator. No one knew when his family might stop by and there was no phone contact.

When I came back to the ward the next evening at the end of the day, just hoping there would be a family member there, I was amazed to see down the hall a young woman sitting, intently reading an Essential Cantonese textbook. She was there because her mother was ill. I asked her if she'd be willing to try to help me talk with my patient.

With her help, I figured out that he didn't have any of his psychiatric symptoms, except during the day after he had a seizure. The hallucinations and paranoia were a direct result of his brain recompensating after his seizures. He didn't need any antipsychotic medications—they often can make seizures more frequent. Instead, we had to raise his seizure medications and he had to take them more regularly. We spent enough time with him that he understood how his symptoms fit together and how he could fix both by treating his seizures more aggressively.

That case, however, is unusual. Since most people's seizures have no known cause, and often no other neurological symptoms, and since most psychiatric disorders have no known causes, it's very difficult in practice to know if there's any relationship between the two. We just don't understand enough about the brain's functioning to figure out what's really going on most of the time.

> Rosa was taken by ambulance again to Harbor General's ER because of a seizure. She'd fallen and hit her head again. When she was there, she created a scene because she refused to take any medications again, saying that she was talking with God and he told her not to take any medications. The seizures were how he was purifying her brain. The doctors, on the other hand, told her that they thought the seizures might be because she'd had gotten a fungal infection, Coccidioidomycosis, in Guatemala, which had been effectively treated, but she had residual cysts that they could see on her CT scan of her head. She didn't agree. They put her on a psychiatric hold and transferred her to the psychiatric ward where they forced her to take antipsychotic medications, so she wouldn't endanger herself, but legally they couldn't force her to take seizure medications.
>
> When she was released a few days later, she found that she'd lost her job. The apartment manager who had been hiring her under the table to do housekeeping wasn't willing to risk her having another seizure on the job and getting hurt. She said God would provide, and she stopped all her medications again. When she didn't pay her rent, she was referred to us as at risk of becoming homeless.
>
> I worked with her for about 6 months. I tried everything to convince her to take either her antipsychotic medications or her seizure medications without much success and referred her back to the Neurology clinic. When they saw her a month later, they found again that her medication blood levels were almost zero and told her to take them more regularly and scheduled a 3-month follow-up visit. They didn't respond to my letter asking if they thought there was any

connection between her seizures and hearing God's voice. I doubt they knew. I didn't.

Her boyfriend and her family were very upset with her but couldn't get anywhere. They wanted me to put her back in the hospital to make her take both medications. I didn't see how locking her up for a few days again would help, and then, she probably wouldn't come back to see me. I decided to focus on getting her to take her seizure medications and gave up on the antipsychotic medications. I tried to understand what she believed was happening to her spiritually but didn't get very far. I'm not sure whether there was a language barrier, or whether she didn't trust me enough to share her experiences with me, or maybe it didn't really make sense to her either. Her case worker, Mauricio, speaking in Spanish, instead focused on getting her and her boyfriend a subsidized apartment through the Department of Health Services—something they provide to repeat medical ER patients to try to help stabilize them. It took 4 months to do the paperwork, but finally, they had an apartment and moved in together. She was very happy. I urged her to take her medications.

Two weeks later, she was found dead in her bed, at age 28, by her boyfriend. I suspect a seizure killed her. If God had anything to do with it, he never let me know.

It's not just our medical system that separates neurological and psychiatric treatments; our legal system does, too. Psychiatric holds are only for treating psychiatric illnesses. Medical illnesses can only be treated involuntarily over the very short term in life-or-limb threatening emergencies on the spot or by court order with a Probate conservatorship, an entirely different court and process from the psychiatric conservatorships (at least in California). Generally, you're allowed to endanger yourself medically or neurologically unless you're dying.

Head trauma

It's reasonably common for people or their families to date the onset of their psychiatric condition to a head trauma. We usually discount that explanation. We assume they're just reaching for straws, trying to come up with something besides a psychotic illness to explain what's happened to them or their loved one. We explain to them that head trauma doesn't cause psychosis. Their head injury is likely irrelevant. Besides, even if a head CT scan showed something, we don't have any significant public neurology treatment or rehabilitation system in the community; so, it doesn't matter anyway.

Over the decades, driven by soldiers coming back from Iraq and Afghanistan exposed to homemade improvised explosive devices, known as "IEDs," like roadside bombs, and by brain-damaged and suicidal retired pro football players, we've learned more and more about the range of problems that can occur with severe head trauma and concussions. Mood changes, irritability, poor sleep, anxiety, and even suicidality can result. Why are we sure psychosis is impossible?

> When Daniel was about 25, his off-road ATV flipped over. He wasn't wearing a helmet, and he was knocked out. He was taken to a hospital, where he was medically stable, but only responsive to deep pain. He remained in a semicomatose state for about 6 months. He eventually woke up but was still quite impaired. He stayed in a rehabilitation nursing facility, gradually improving for another year. When he finally returned home, there were changes in him: He was a little bit slowed and blunted, he didn't have his old sense of humor and didn't even smile much, and his memory was never as good as it used to be.
>
> He lived with his father for a few years but wasn't doing much during the day anymore. His motivation seemed to be gone. His father helped him apply for Social Security disability and helped him move to a mental health Board and Care.
>
> As the years went on, he complained more and more of poor sleep and wanted more medications to help him sleep. The workers at the Board and Care insisted that he did sleep, but he told me that was because they weren't there

at night. How would they know? No matter what dose of medications I put him on, it was never enough. He'd call our after-hours on-call system, waking up our staff, complaining he couldn't sleep. Frantic, he'd walk into the Village to see me because he said he hadn't slept for 3 days.

Part of the problem it seemed to me was that the lone nighttime, live-in staff at the Board and Care gave out the bedtime medications at 8:00, so they'd be finished for the night, and that was too early to go to sleep. I helped Daniel get permission to hold onto the pills and take them later, but he said that didn't work either. I even got desperate enough to try some much older, very sedating psychiatric medications—Thorazine, Mellaril, Elavil, and Sinequan. When he dangerously overdosed on Sinequan pills and had to go to the ER with a dangerous heart arrhythmia, I found out that sometimes he'd stack up several nights worth of pills and then take them all at once, trying to knock himself out. The staff found stashes of pills in his dresser.

We kept trying to help him rebuild his life, despite his sleep problems. He got a part-time job on the Clean Team, a project we arranged with the city of Long Beach, where some of our members helped them keep the downtown streets clean for modest pay. He even met a girl on that job, and they started dating. She lived in a different Board and Care.

Eventually, they decided to try to move into an apartment together and got engaged. But she couldn't handle his sleep complaints either. She also said that he slept most of the night, but he never thought he slept. Even though we had the pharmacy put his medications into special bubble packs, where pills were packaged separately and labeled by date and time, his pills were always mixed up because he'd take extras late at night when he was desperate to sleep.

Food was a problem, too. Now that they weren't being fed by the Board and Care, he insisted on eating only nonfat milk, peanut butter and jelly sandwiches, oranges, chips, *and Oreos. She tried cooking other things, but he wouldn't eat them. His health deteriorated. He got more obsessive at home. He quit his job.*

The arguments grew, and he started blaming her for everything. He rarely bathed or changed his clothes. She hung on anyway.

When he started getting overtly paranoid of her, complaining she was lying about him, trying to poison him, and cheating on him, none of which was true, she couldn't handle it anymore. Her family and her mental health team increasingly urged her to leave him. And eventually, she did.

He moved back into the old Board and Care, beaten down, depressed, and heartbroken.

He still complained he couldn't sleep.

He never got any neurological evaluation or treatment after he was initially discharged from the facility, but neither did anyone I worked with at the Village, including a man who was beaten in the head with a pipe because a group of drunken men thought he was gay. He, too, gradually became more and more rigid in his thinking, withdrawn and obsessive, eventually drifting into paranoia. How do we really know that head trauma doesn't lead to psychosis?

Medical conditions

Medical conditions can affect our brains either directly (The classic example is tertiary or neurosyphilis, which occurs when the bacterium spreads from the genitals to the blood stream into the brain. Before antibiotics, neurosyphilis was a widespread, devastating condition. It's estimated that a third of Kraepelin's patients had neurosyphilis. I've only seen one case, a woman in her 80s, when I was in medical school in St. Louis.) or indirectly (The classic example is pellagra, a disease that was widespread especially in the South where poor people ate mostly processed corn, and that is caused by niacin deficiency. It first drew serious notice in Mount Vernon Hospital for the "coloured insane" in 1906 where the patients were only fed corn, which explained why the staff didn't get it. I've never seen a case of Pellagra psychosis, although we still routinely give B vitamins to undernourished alcoholics to prevent it.).

In practice, however, it can be very difficult to separate out direct and indirect effects. For example, if someone has lupus cerebritis, they have inflammation of the blood vessels in their brain presumably causing mental symptoms; they likely have inflammation of blood vessels impacting other organs as well, which could, in turn, impact their brains; or if someone has HIV in their brains and mental symptoms, they're likely to have a weakened enough immune system to have other widespread infections, too. And how about people with cirrhosis, usually from longstanding brain-damaging alcoholism, who have impaired liver function and, as a result, toxins are building up in their blood, so high they impact their brains, too? Usually, these people are so sick that all we do is add a little antipsychotic medication to their aggressive medical treatments. But could there be subtler forms of these illnesses that still impact their brains, or could there be some people who happen to have more mental susceptibility? I've never gotten a helpful response to a letter I've sent to a medical specialist, asking if their medical condition might be impacting their mental state.

> *I met Tammy on the medical wards at LA County–USC doing a psychiatric consultation. She was clearly psychotic. She was hearing voices and seeing things. She was talking about people who weren't there and seemed to think she was in Jerusalem. We couldn't get a clear history out of her. I checked her laboratory test results, and everything seemed to be in order. Also, she didn't seem "sick"; so, this wasn't likely to be a delirium.*
>
> *The only issue in the way of transferring her to the psychiatric unit was her blood pressure, which was elevated at 160/110, not dangerous, but not normal either. I told the medical resident that I'd put her on a hold and transfer her when he got her blood pressure down.*
>
> *"Oh, come on! Give me a break. You can see we're really overcrowded here. You can treat her blood pressure over in*

psych just as well as I can, and she won't get in trouble there. Please, just do me a favor and take her off my hands."

I tried to convince my supervisor, the attending psychiatrist, but she was firm.

"I'm sorry, I tried. Let me know when her blood pressure is stabilized, and I'll take her."

When I returned 2 days later, her blood pressure was down to a slightly high, but respectable 135/90, but there was no longer any reason to send her to psychiatry. All of her symptoms had disappeared. She was perfectly oriented, and the hallucinations were all gone.

"I get a little loopy when my blood pressure gets out of control."

Even though I was somewhat puzzled as to what had just happened, we sent her home.

About a month later, I got a call from a medical resident on another ward to come see Tammy. She was psychotic and needed to be transferred to psychiatry. Her old chart hadn't made it up to the ward yet.

"What's her blood pressure?" I asked smugly.

"What difference does that make? Let me see ... It's kind of high 160/115. No big deal."

"You're not going to believe me, but I know this patient. If you get her blood pressure down, all her psychiatric symptoms will go away. I'll check in on her in the meantime."

Once again, when her blood pressure was normal, so was her mind.

"Tammy, you need to do a better job of taking your blood pressure medications."

"I know."

One of my hopes is that as we move toward more integrated care, where medicine, neurology, and psychiatry are all in the same clinic, we'll all get more experience thinking about how these conditions can impact people in more holistic ways and improve our understanding and treatments for them.

Hormonal conditions

Hormonal changes can clearly affect our moods and mental states. We see this in a wide range of conditions, including premenstrual mood changes, aggression in men with genetic conditions that alter testosterone levels, depression and lethargy with low thyroid levels, or hyperactivity and irritability with high thyroid levels, and anxiety and panic attacks in patients with adrenal tumors secreting bursts of adrenaline. But we usually don't see psychosis unless the person is very sick and delirious.

A common exception is postpartum psychosis, which I've seen estimated at 1–2 per 1,000 births, although it's hard to know since this is another condition that has been removed from the *DSM*, lumping it in the rest of psychosis. Sometimes, it seems to be a disorder of its own, with extraordinary experiences occurring for only weeks after birth, and sometimes, it can be an exacerbation of an already existing mental disorder or the first precipitation of a mental disorder that's just beginning. In any case, postpartum psychosis is often handled as a psychiatric emergency to protect the infant and mother. For example, I knew a woman who had occasional manic and depressive episodes. When she gave birth to her son, amid lots of stressors, she lost touch with reality and walked with her infant into the ocean trying to drown both of them. Fortunately, she was seen and stopped, and after considerable hard work, her mental illness stabilized, and she safely returned to being her son's mother. It's not always that dramatic, or even shared with anyone by the mother.

> *Rosalia was a 20-year-old, single woman living in poverty on her own, working as a waitress in Florida when her hard-drinking, conservative, musician fiancé got her pregnant. She had been using birth control pills, hiding them from him because his Christian religion was antagonistic to birth control, but he'd found them and taken them away from her. He expected to be the man of the household, and to make all the decisions, and to be always supported by Rosalia. She reluctantly went along. This was the man she loved and*

intended to marry. She had dreams of their life together and having a family, but not this soon. Abortion was out of the question; so, too soon or not, she was having a baby.

She stopped using alcohol and marijuana, but couldn't stop her cigarettes entirely (which says something about the addictiveness of cigarettes or its effectiveness in reducing stress or both). She bought every book and magazine she could find about childbirth and child-rearing. She'd been the youngest in her family and didn't have much exposure to infants growing up. Her boyfriend said he didn't need to read any books. They didn't have any health insurance, and her fiancé wasn't going to "get on welfare or charity help"; so, she arranged for a midwife at home she paid for herself.

The baby's kicks within her told her the infant was growing, and she began to get excited by the possibilities.

The birth was somewhat difficult because the umbilical cord was wrapped around the baby's arm, but the midwife handled it well at home. Her fiancé paced around, coming in and out, but couldn't focus on supporting her during the 14-hour labor. She later said, "It wasn't too bad. I just wished he was there more for me." Her baby girl was just fine.

Nonetheless, those first days were overwhelming. "This small being was entirely dependent on me for life." The first meconium stool, green goo squirting everywhere, freaked her out. Her fiancé left to get drunk. "I can't believe you don't know how to be a mother. What's wrong with you?"

She did enjoy nursing her baby, feeling proud that she could provide for her, and spent hours lying in bed with her daughter, Simone, by her side, stroking her.

Sometime, in those first weeks, Rosalia started hearing music when nothing was there. The first time it happened, she went outside thinking a band was playing. Maybe the neighbors were having a party. But no, nothing was happening. "I got scared and wondered what was going on."

The next day, I thought the car radio was on, but it wasn't. "I checked my phone, but the music wasn't coming from it either."

Rosalia also started hearing whispers and mumbles like someone was talking behind her. It wasn't exactly scary, but it was weird. It was like they were commenting on what she was doing with her baby or giving her directions, but it was always too muffled to understand. When she told her fiancé, he was convinced there were evil spirits trying to harm their baby. "But it wasn't like the voices were critical or anything. I couldn't even make out what they were saying."

A couple weeks later, during a phone argument with her fiancé, begging him to come home, suddenly it sounded to her like there was music in the background.

"What's that music? I can't believe you just turned on your car radio, while we're talking."

"There's no music here …. Are you starting to hear things, too?"

That's when she first learned she better not tell anyone about what she was hearing. She was having enough problems as it was.

When she started seeing vague shadows in the corner of the room, while lying awake with her daughter all night, she started leaving the light on.

All of that went away after about a few weeks or a month or so. It was hard for her to remember exactly. She ended up leaving her fiancé about 6 months later, as his drinking worsened. She couldn't trust him with the baby; so, she moved to California with her older sister's family. She'd gotten herself together and was going to college, mostly so she and her daughter, Simone, could have a better life together.

She'd come to the college counseling center to talk about her struggles and had told the psychologist about her postpartum hallucinations. She also told her that very rarely in the 5 years since then, maybe three times a year, she'd hear music or mumbling like that again, but it would always go away and wasn't causing any problems. There didn't seem to be any pattern. The psychologist didn't know what to make of all of that. Was she psychotic? Was this mild schizophrenia? Should she be taking medications? She referred Rosalia to me to help her understand what was going on. Rosalia was relieved to finally have someone to talk to about these strange experiences and who might be able to explain it to her.

I told her about how our brain creates voices and music, "real" and "imagined," and then project them outward into the world the same way I described it to you in Chapter 9 with the sound waves, the eardrums, inner ear bones, canals with fluid, and lots of nerve cells.

"You had a lot of reasons for your brain not to be working quite right back then. Your hormones were badly out of balance. That commonly leads to strange experiences just by itself, but you also had some sleep deprivation and weren't eating well; so, you were further physically out of balance. You were isolated, which can lead to your brain imagining more things. You were also under a great deal of emotional stress, which was probably stirring up your unconscious. I'm not sure what was going on in your brain, but your fiancé's music was one of the things you fell in love with, and you sure could've used some commentary and calm, uncritical advice. I think you were yearning so hard, your mind tried to create what you needed."

"That makes a lot of sense to me."

"You'll have to do a checklist when it comes back again to see if any of these fits then: How's your body's health? Are you sleeping and eating? Are you sensory deprived? Are you under great stress and yearning?"

"Two more things before you go: One, if you're afraid of this happening more and more and going crazy, the most *important thing you can do is stop using marijuana, especially the Sativa. Marijuana is a hallucinogenic drug. That's how it makes us high. It's weakening a part of your brain that's not so strong in the first place. Marijuana might not be as dangerous as it's sometimes made out to be, but one of the bad things we do know about it is that it's associated with ongoing psychosis, especially when you use it when you're young. Second, we do have medications that can help you stay in reality if this ever does start happening more often or impairing you. The medications have much fewer side effects than they used to; so, you don't have to be that afraid of them. It's not like drugging you up. I don't think you need them now and I hope you never will, but they're there, if you do. If you have another child, right after the birth will be the time of greatest risk because your hormones will be all out of balance again."*

Aging and dementia

If we live long enough, all of us will find that our brains are deteriorating and that dementia is creeping up on us, and more and more of us are living longer and longer. Aging and dementia create challenges in all three dimensions of psychosis—experiencing reality, self-identity, and relationships—in interacting ways as we deteriorate. When we're trying to work with someone elderly who becomes paranoid or hallucinates, we need to consider all three dimensions:

> **Experiencing reality**
>
> o Is the neurological damage impairing their ability to experience reality?
>
> o When they misplace their glasses or their wallet, do they start suspecting that someone is hiding them from them or stealing them?
>
> o As their hearing deteriorates and they have trouble distinguishing voices from background sounds, do they start filling in the gaps and imagining what's being said to them and then get angry and insist they're right when they're contradicted?

- Do they forget that their beloved brother has been dead for a decade and imagine they're talking to him, keeping him alive in their minds?

Dr. Murphy was well dressed and well-mannered when she came into LAC–USC Hospital, but her heart was progressively failing. She was having trouble walking more than a block or sleeping without being propped up with several pillows because she couldn't breathe well. Decades of smoking had caught up to her by her late 70s.

We all enjoyed talking to her, since she had been a college professor and had a lifetime's worth of interesting stories that she told with grace and intelligence. She was kind of a grandmotherly figure for us. Over the first few days of her hospitalization, we readjusted her heart medications and she began to feel better.

One night while I was on call, I got a call from the night nurse on her ward that she was agitated and confused and had wandered down the hall.

"Are you sure you mean Dr. Murphy? She always seems so mentally sharp to us. What's going on?"

"Well, she's not sharp with us. She's always somewhat confused on night shift, but never quite this bad before. Can you give us something to knock her out, so we can get her back in bed and keep her from hurting herself or someone else?"

"I'll come on up."

I'm not fond of "knocking out" patients, just to make the nurses' life easier and I suspected they were exaggerating, but when I got to the ward and heard Dr. Murphy screaming at them, I stopped in my tracks. She was accusing them of imprisoning her. She didn't know who any of us were or where she was. She'd pulled her IV tubing out, getting out of bed.

I did order a sleeping pill and she did sleep.

The next morning, she was back to her charming self. She didn't remember anything from the night before.

The attending doctor told us, "That's called sundowning. Lots of old people do it. They become much more confused and agitated at night. Don't forget this experience when you meet a family complaining that grandma is a terror and you see a harmless lamb in your office."

- **Self-identity**
  - As their function deteriorates and their roles diminish, do they struggle to maintain their self-identity?
  - Do they imagine they're still in their old house or need to get dressed to go to work, when it's been years since they moved into a nursing home?
  - Do they get angry and imagine they're being attacked when someone helps them change their diapers or bathe them?

Toward the end of the second year of medical school, they let us go into the hospital and examine patients on our own and try to figure out what illnesses they had. My roommate, Tom, and I were assigned to a very old woman in the neurology ward of City Hospital in St. Louis, a run-down impoverished hospital, for run-down impoverished patients. She looked like she weighed about 80 pounds, curled up in bed, moaning quietly, seeming to be oblivious of everything around her.

"Good afternoon, Mrs. Wright. Tom and I are medical students. How are you today?"

No answer.

"Are you feeling any pain?"

No answer. I wasn't sure she'd even noticed we were there.

"Would it be alright with you if we examined you?"

Still no answer.

We tried to examine her as best we could without moving her. Sometimes, when we touched her, she'd moan a little more. We warmed up our stethoscopes before putting them on her chest through her hospital gown. I don't know if it mattered to her.

The entire exam was a letdown. Where was the excitement of helping people, of doing real clinical work with real patients?

Finally, I had a stroke of genius. I took my stethoscope and put the earpieces in her ears. Then, I talked into the bell, "Good afternoon, Mrs. Wright."

She looked around startled, her eyes darting from side to side, "Whaaat?" she croaked.

I grinned at Tom, "How are you today?

"Whaaat?"

My grin faded, "Is there anything we can do for you today?"

"There's something in my ears bothering me. Take this thing out of my ears."

I was crestfallen. I'd managed to be the first person to communicate with her in who knows how long, and she wasn't thrilled. All she wanted was to be left alone.

The next day on rounds I pressured the resident, "There must be something we can do, some medication we should try. How about a stimulant to get her going again?"

"She has end-stage dementia. There's nothing we can do. No pills will bring her back. We can help her be fed and hydrated and reasonably comfortable, but we can't reverse her illness."

So much for being a powerful, healing doctor.

- ➢ **Relationships**
  - o Have they detached from relationships with people in their lives in the present and turned inward relating to their memories and their recreations?
  - o Have all their friends died and the loss and loneliness become unbearable?
  - o Have familiar people become frightening and potentially threatening because they no longer recognize them?
  - o Are they being cared for by an endless parade of strangers who they can't identify in an unfamiliar place?

Something was going to have to be done about Annabelle.

Annabelle had been a Village member for 20 years. She was a very anxious, somewhat shy Japanese woman, who had been brought to the United States when she was about 18 when her parents immigrated to Los Angeles. Apparently, she was already having problems in Japan, isolating and had dropped out of school. Her parents were very protective of her. They had kept her away from all mental health services, but when they died, she was moved to a Board and Care and referred to the Village. She was overwhelmed by these events and wary about her new housemates and our members. She gradually made friends at the Village and came to outings and holiday celebrations.

"I haven't seen Annabelle for a long time. What's going on with her?"

"As she's getting older, she's having trouble keeping track of things. She doesn't check her sugar levels or give herself her insulin the way she's supposed to. When we tried to get a visiting nurse to give it to her, she wouldn't let her in. She said she didn't know who it was, and she wasn't going to let a stranger in. Our team nurse can't go give her injections twice a day, 7 days a week."

"I wonder if I talked to her doctor, if she could be lowered to one shot a day. Maybe we could increase her pills instead."

"That's not really the biggest problem, though." Wonderful.

"She's getting more and more paranoid. Sometimes, she doesn't let us or the building manager in. She's started calling the police several times a week, complaining about intruders, when it's just a neighbor or a staff. The police want us to make her stop calling. The building gets in trouble if there are too many police calls, and it scares the other residents. They're threatening to throw her out."

"We've tried giving her some antipsychotic medications, but it doesn't seem like they're really helping. We even tried the long-acting shots since it's pretty clear she's not taking her pills regularly."

"Last night at 2 am, she started screaming that a man was in her apartment trying to rape her. Everyone's had enough of her."

There was nothing I could do. We ended up moving her to a nursing home for people with dementia where they kept her pretty sedated.

It is usually very hard to separate out the different dimensions as we try to help people sustain or regain their equilibrium. Too much keeps deteriorating.

It takes special staff, and families, to persist with aging and demented people in the face of all these challenges and find sustenance in treasured moments as they pass by. A medical specialty of gerontology has evolved to help engage and support these staff. Within the mental health system, specialized Older Adult programs and Older Adult Full-Service Partnerships have been developed in Los Angeles. Medicare funding available for people over 65 provides some needed resources.

Closing thoughts

These last two journeys have taken us closer to shore, to seemingly more familiar waters, in sight of the reassuring medical model fleet. And yet, it still feels like we're too far away to connect. I think, like for all of our journeys, our lack of understanding is due to our emotional limitations, more than our scientific limitations.

I have met and read the books of two exemplary doctors who are inspirational in their integrative practices: Rachel Remen and Oliver Sacks. They have strong medical foundations, but have moved far beyond it, relating deeply to their patients, and becoming healers in the process.

> *Rachel Remen was raised in a family of multiple doctors (and incidentally, a mystical Kabbalistic grandfather); so, she knew she was going to be a doctor early on. Unfortunately, she also has had Crohn's disease, a chronic severe intestinal condition, that has required numerous serious operations beginning in her youth. When she began medical school, she'd already spent a great deal of time as a patient. Many of the customary dehumanizing practices in hospitals and medical education were very disturbing to her. She wrote about these experiences in her bestseller, "Kitchen Table Wisdom." It wasn't that she wasn't able to separate out her personal experiences to become an emotionally detached, professionally distant doctor. She didn't want to. She didn't think that was a route to healing.*
>
> *She went on to establish the Commonweal Institute and led 2-week retreats for patients newly diagnosed with cancer to help them emotionally react to their new diagnosis and build a relationship with it, before they began their medical treatments, and retreats for burned out doctors who no longer felt they were helping people and had lost touch with their passion. One of her core premises is that what suffering patients need to heal is not a detached professional with no serious problems of their own who gives them orders to passively follow to be cured, but rather someone who cares about them and whose compassion they can feel, likely*

because of their own personal experience and suffering, a "wounded healer" to walk alongside them.

Oliver Sacks was a neurologist who you may be familiar with from Robin Williams's portrayal of him in the movie, "Awakenings," or his numerous books filled with his unique brand of case studies. He brought his unusual mind to the process, including significant autistic traits, a passion for observing and mastering scientific details that rivaled Darwin's, a substantial amount of substance use, and an unending curiosity about the functioning of the brain. In each of his case studies, he describes what's understood about the underlying neurology of the condition, the history of how the condition was discovered and described, and most crucially, painstaking detail of how the person he's treating experiences their condition and how it impacts their lives. He includes someone with a song going round and round in their head, torturing them on permanent replay, someone who can't remember anything more than a few moments, so they forget everyone they meet, an artist who became color-blind and moved on to create powerful black and white paintings, and an autistic woman who used her exquisite sensitivity to help design more humane cattle slaughterhouses. Many of the people he describes, he stays in touch with for years, and he appears to develop true friendships with. I'm not alone in feeling profoundly moved by his painstaking descriptions.

I hope that if you're on this journey, you manage to find doctors who, like Rachel Remen or Oliver Sacks (or Gabor Mate who I included in Chapter 11), have developed the ability to integrate a deep understanding of medicine, along with profoundly compassionate healing relationships.

As we arrive at the end of the journeys that I'm going to take you on, one of the things that I've come to appreciate more than I did before is how each and every one of these journeys requires emotional and relationship preparation and luggage. It's unlikely anyone—whether traveler, companion, or guide—will be totally prepared for any journey. Hopefully, we'll all learn and grow along the way.

CHAPTER 14

PUTTING TOGETHER YOUR JOURNEY

I was consulting with a Full Service Partnership (FSP) program in Los Angeles. They were presenting one of their most challenging cases to me: Robert had schizophrenia and he used heavy drugs. He would get into fights with and even beat up his girlfriend, and then, when the police were called, he'd tell them he had a mental illness, so that he'd be sent to the hospital, instead of to jail. When the first of the month would come around, he'd tell the hospital staff that he wasn't hearing voices anymore and he wasn't a danger to himself and others anymore, so he's fine to leave, and they'd discharge him. He'd pick up his Social Security check (he refused to let anyone be his payee, and Social Security wasn't about to get into a fight with him to force the issue) and get high. Then, he'd go back to his girlfriend's apartment and start the whole cycle all over again.

Since he was so difficult and all the staff had enough of him, they gave him to the newest, least experienced case manager, who was way out of his depth.

I broke into his case description to see if I could help, "Do you know anything about how he got like this? What he was like growing up?"

The case manager looked a little sheepish, but answered honestly, "You know, I don't. Even though I've worked with him for over a year, I've never really had a chance to just sit with him to really get to know him. I'm always too busy trying to deal with whatever crisis is going on. You know, talking to the police, or the hospital, or trying to find him another place to stay."

"That's too bad. Let me ask you something else. Do you know how he looks at himself?"

Now, the case manager looked more confused than ever, "What do you mean 'looks at himself'?"

I told him Steve's back of the hand story: You'll be able to start helping me when you see nails and knuckles and hair because then you'll be seeing the world from my side instead of from yours.

"How would he describe himself?"

He squirmed some more and hesitantly said, "I guess he's manipulative ... and noncompliant ... and dually diagnosed ...."

"Stop. That's not what I mean. No one has ever described themselves as manipulative, noncompliant, and dually diagnosed. That's how you see him. That's your side of the hand, not his."

The young case manager fell silent. Finally, a hard-boiled psychologist in the back, who'd been silently pretending he knew nothing about this, said, "I think Robert would describe himself as a misunderstood prophet of God."

The young staff, suddenly revived, said, "Yeah, he's always getting in trouble preaching on street corners with his bullhorn. The police are called. People get angry at him. Do you know how to make him stop doing that?"

"I don't know if I know how to make him do anything, but I do know that a treatment plan for a misunderstood prophet of God will look a lot different than a treatment plan for a manipulative, noncompliant, dually diagnosed patient ... and he'd be a lot more likely to cooperate with that plan."

It's time for you to start describing the journey you're on and where you intend to go from here. If you're the person experiencing psychosis or some other extraordinary experiences, you need to be able to describe your journey from your point of view, what you see on the "back of your hand," using your words, so that it fits what you feel you've been going through. Enough of my stories. It's time to create your own story. If you're a companion or a guide, you need to describe their journey, using their point of view and their words, so that it fits what they feel they've been going through. We need to meet them where they're at, rather than try to convince them that we know how to create their journeys for them.

This chapter is very different from all the others. It's a worksheet and a set of instructions designed to help people observe their own lives, using the perspectives of the psychosis triangle and the eight journeys to create a map of the path they've been on and become the author of their own journeys. It is OK for other people to collaborate in creating your map and journey, but the job of the other collaborators is to reflect accurately on what the person on the journey is going through, not to define their journey for them. Think about the difference between a mother who notices her child is cold and responds by putting a sweater on them and a mother who puts a sweater on her child because she's cold. When someone accurately sees and hears us, we can see ourselves through their eyes, perhaps even seeing things about ourselves we hadn't noticed or thought about, but if they try to impose their view of us on us, it feels repressive and can lead us to withdraw.

Let's start by returning to our psychosis triangle, shown below:

The Psychosis Triangle

Journeys Beyond the Frontier | 475

Step 1: Assess yourself in all three dimensions.

Experiencing Reality: Are you having a lot of conflict or suffering dealing with reality around you? (Note: For this step, it doesn't matter whether other people are experiencing reality differently than you are. For example, it doesn't matter if you are being spied on and followed everywhere you go or if you're paranoid and imagining being spied on and followed; either way, it's a serious problem.) Are you having disturbing experiences? For example, are you hearing voices, feeling like you're going to die because of signs you're interpreting everywhere around you, or obsessing about the end of the world?

Self-identity: How is your self-identity? (Note: For this dimension, it's your view of yourself that matters, not someone else's. There may be serious differences in both directions—you may feel more confident about yourself than others feel about you, or others may see strengths in you that you don't see. These differences will likely impact your relationships, but this dimension is about self-identity.) Do you have a clear idea of who you are? How about more serious self-evaluation: How's your self-confidence? What roles do you have and how do they fit you? What are your gifts and wounds? What meaning does your life have? Do you have a sense of how you're growing and changing over the course of your life?

Relationships: How are your relationships? (Note: Include both good and bad relationships, close and less close relationships. If you're being bullied and excluded at work by your coworkers, stalked by your ex, loved and supported by your spouse and your sister, and belittled and humiliated by your parents and kids—or any combination life has happened to throw at you—include them all. Even include people you feel connected to, like an ex you're stalking or a celebrity you're obsessed with, even if other people tell you it's not a "real" relationship.) Do you feel pressured or supported? Are you giving or receiving? Are you moving toward people or away from them?

Which dimension(s) are weaknesses/deficits for you? Which dimension(s) are strengths? Check the boxes.

Fill out Step 1 shown in the table below:

	Experiencing Reality	Self-identity	Relationships
Step 1: Assessment			
Current situation (provide brief descriptions in each dimension)			
Weaknesses/deficits			
Strengths			
Step 2: Current Situation			
Risks/crisis			
Needs for help/support			
Step 3: Origins			
How it started (provide brief descriptions in each dimension)			
Initial weaknesses/deficits			
Initial strengths			
Step 4: Journeys			
Journeys that have impacted you (check and provide brief description)			
1. Grief			

2. Psychotic reactions			
3. Difficulties making sense of the world			
4. Childhood trauma			
5. Losing balance			
6. Drugs and alcohol			
7. Psychiatric illnesses			
8. Developmental, neurologic, and medical conditions			

Step 5: Core Journey

(Circle Core journey, most problematic cell, and other impactful cells above)

Step 6: Formulation

Write a short personal formulation.

"Title" of your formulation:

Step 2: Are you currently in crisis or at high risk?

Think about each of the three dimensions again. Currently, is something happening, either inside you or around you that's changing in a bad way? Are you going through something challenging? Are you scared of something? Are you at risk of something bad happening or falling apart? Are you in crisis? What's the cause of the crisis? Do you need help and support now that is different from what you've been getting?

Fill out Step 2 shown in the table.

Step 3: Origins. How far back does this go? When and how did all of this start?

Are the problems you're having familiar to you, or is this the first time anything like this has happened to you? When have you experienced this before? Looking back, are there situations or problems that have led to your current difficulties? Go back to the origins.

Which dimension did things go wrong first? Even if it's a long time ago, try to remember what happened. How did it spread to other dimensions? Or perhaps, how did strengths in other dimensions stop it from spreading, containing it, or even reducing the original problems?

How does that compare to your assessment of your current situation? What's changed? What's the same? Do you have the same or different strengths and weaknesses?

Fill out Step 3 shown in the table.

Step 4: Which journey best describes what you're going through? How have other journeys impacted you, too?

Let's go through all the journeys one by one. Think about how each journey has impacted you in each of the three dimensions—experiencing reality, self-identity, and relationships. Think about the past and the present. You may have to look back at the chapter about each journey to remind you what it was about. If any given journey doesn't apply to you, or you just don't connect with it, just skip it and leave it blank.

1. **Grief:** Have you experienced major losses and grief?

2. **Psychotic reactions:** Have there been major stressors in your life that were hard to adapt to?

3. **Difficulties making sense of the world:** Do you make sense of the world in unique ways? Does that create problems for you?

4. **Childhood trauma:** If you experienced childhood trauma, neglect, or abuse, how has that impacted you as you've grown and developed?

5. **Losing balance:** Which developmental level are you usually on—meeting basic needs, personal, relationship, extra-personal/spiritual? Have you gone backward in levels? Have you struggled to maintain your balance or lost your balance and fallen?

6. **Drugs and alcohol:** If you've used drugs and/or alcohol, what impact have they had on you?

7. **Psychiatric illnesses:** If you have a psychiatric illness, what impact has it had on you?

8. **Developmental, neurologic, and medical conditions:** If you have a developmental, neurological, and/or medical condition, what impact has it had on you?

Put a check mark and provide a brief description in any relevant box in Step 4 shown in the table. (For example, childhood trauma may have affected your relationships by making you mistrustful of others; drugs and alcohol may have affected both your relationships because you put drugs before your family, and your self-identity because you've become consumed with shame and guilt; and a manic illness may affect your experience of reality because you become grandiose when you're in a manic episode, but all the other boxes may be empty.)

Step 5: Finding your journey

Look at the boxes you filled out in Step 4.

Are lots of boxes filled out or just a few? Have you been on the same path throughout your life or have you traveled on more than one path? Have you moved from one path to another as your life has gone on or have you added journeys on top of each other, so that by now, you're experiencing problems from more than one journey at once? (For example, by this point in your life, are you experiencing problems from the impact of childhood trauma, ongoing drug usage, having a psychiatric illness, and losing your spiritual balance?)

Even if you have a complex picture, does one of the journeys feel like it fits you the most and is the core of what you've been experiencing? Do other journeys need to be included because they've had so much impact? Can you put together your core journey and the other important journeys by describing how the other journeys fed into your core journey? (For example, your core journey could have been about your difficulty finding a spiritual balance ever since you were a child, but you've been weakened by childhood trauma that made it hard to grow and develop, drugs that gave you glimpses of a higher reality that you couldn't sustain, and manic illness that exploited your spiritual desires to convince you that you're God, when you're not.)

Which of the three dimensions is the most problematic and active in your journey? (For example, your spirituality might impact your self-identity because you're not sure who you are, and it impacted your relationships since people couldn't relate to your spiritual journey; but, for the most part, it's been hard to carry on in everyday life and reality since you're consumed with spiritual thoughts and experiences. You're so busy exploring and building your spiritual powers that you forget to eat or bathe, let alone holding a job and paying the rent.)

Return to Step 4 shown in the table.

> ➢ Circle the name of the journey that fits you best, your core journey.
>
> ➢ Circle the one cell on the grid that is the most problematic for you.

> Circle other cells that have impacted you the most seriously and have fed into your core journey.

Step 6: Creating a personal formulation

Think about the descriptions you've written in the table. Look back at where you started. Look at your core journey, which dimension is the most problematic, and how other dimensions feed into your core journey. Look at where you're at now.

Think about how things have changed for you over time throughout your life. Can you track the changes within a journey? within a dimension? between journeys? between dimensions?

Are things starting to fit together for you? Can you see a path that describes the journey you've been on?

Look back at the story I began Chapter 4 with, Patty's story. I created a brief formulation of her journey for her, and she asked me to write it down. Can you create a brief formulation of your journey and write it down at the bottom of the table?

Using her own words, I titled Patty's formulation "Pain in the Ass." What's the title of your formulation, in your own words?

Fill out Step 6 shown in the table.

Once we've taken the step of describing the journey we've been on, we have begun the process of moving from being merely a character in our own stories, and likely the passive victim of genes, events, and other characters around us, to being the author of our own stories, capable of shaping for ourselves where we go next.

How does it feel to have a personal formulation?

Moving on to recovery

Spending the time and effort to put together a truly biopsychosocial formulation with people is a key step in overcoming disconnection and hopelessness, so that we can move on to recover.

On January 13, 2020, the Washington Post Magazine published a lengthy article, "What Schizophrenia Does to Families: A mother, a son, an unraveling mind—and a mental health system that can't keep up" that Abigail Jones apparently worked on for 2 years. She describes a typical tragic case of schizophrenia in a typical way: Aaron was a well-liked, athletic, young man who became psychotic in college and drifted through a life of drugs, impoverished treatment facilities, violence, and finally, institutionalization, accompanied by his long-suffering mother. They all believe he's been on a tragic, hopeless illness-driven journey. None of them even know there are alternative explanations or approaches.

But since it's a very long article and Abigail is a very good writer who really tried to make the story come alive, she included a lot of personal details that enable us to put together a very different narrative: Aaron's parents were very young and struggling when he and his sister were young. They had to travel around a lot with his father's military job. Aaron never settled down anywhere. Even though he was popular, he didn't feel it was deserved. It felt as though they were relating to some other kid, not the real him. He was athletic, but never had any reasonable training, equipment, discipline, or guidance to have more than a few moments of success out of which he and his family built a life goal of being a star quarterback. As a senior in college, his dream was shattered. He wasn't given the starting position or even a scholarship. He had no backup plan. He retreated to using a lot of marijuana, and a psychiatrist diagnosed him as having schizophrenia, "It's a full-blown case. ... My practice is full, but you have to get him help. Things are gonna get worse." His family didn't believe the diagnosis or follow up, and neither did Aaron. The college expelled him after an aggressive incident, leaving him with nothing. Aaron thought that the movie "Varsity Blues" (about an insensitive football coach destroying his players' lives) stole his life. In a variety of run-down facilities, he tried to rebuild, using the only two things he knew—getting a girlfriend and using drugs, but even as the professionals found him "high functioning" and urged more independence, his failures and frustrations grew. His mother was terribly afraid she'd be blamed for his occasional violence, and the entire family felt burdened by him. Eventually, his mother talked his girlfriend into pressing charges after a fight, so she could get him into jail and then to an institution to be safe. She brought his album of high school athletics with her when she visited, crying, and Aaron was unable to handle his familiar feelings that he'd lost everything, disappointed everyone, and was just being passed from ward to ward. His mother reassured him that she'd keep driving long distances to see him and not abandon him like the other patients' families had.

Let's put together a formulation for Aaron using what we know:

His self-identity was always the weakest dimension. When the mostly imaginary identity of football star fell apart, he had nothing to fall back on, and he still doesn't. His psychotic reaction was deepened as his grasp on reality was weakened with a lot of drugs, especially marijuana. After he was kicked out of college and his family was overwhelmed, he had no normalizing relationships. All his relationships, including with his mother, became illness-centered, with no chance of rebuilding a normal self-identity. All three dimensions were destroyed for years. Now, stuck in the hospital for years, he can hardly remember who he is, and the sports clippings recall only an imagined identity. He's isolated from the world. The reality of his life, especially his current reality, is unbelievable to him, even when medications and staying off drugs keep him from drifting away.

A reasonable name for this formulation would be "The boy who tried to be a football star, but failed; so, he's nothing without his dreams."

When I put together the formulation like that, we can not only see how and why he broke down, we can see lots of things that could've been done, and maybe still could be done, to help him recover—things that are invisible and ignored from their illness-driven perspective. Instead, they've been told, "Scientists don't know exactly what causes schizophrenia because the brain is so complex."

It's still a sad and challenging story, but we can connect to him, and there's hope; so, he can still recover.

Part III

Creating Your Own Journey of Recovery

Chapter 15

What we do matters—
Three intertwined dimensions of recovery

When I was in medical school, I looked through the file cabinet of psychiatry electives other students had done. One student's description of his time studying at the Maudsley Institute in London ending with "and the side trips to London weren't bad either" leaped out at me. After considerable planning, there I was at the historic Bethlem Royal Hospital, the oldest psychiatric hospital in Europe and the one that led to the creation of the word "bedlam" because in Victorian times, families would come for picnics outside the hospital while being entertained by the bedlam within the walls. I met students there from all over the world. Even though we all spoke English, our different accents still made it somewhat hard to understand each other.

One day, in a steep auditorium that looked like it could've been used a century ago to present the Elephant Man, one of the attending staff presented a set of three identical triplets at Grand Rounds, two of whom had schizophrenia and one who had manic depression. The staff were fascinated by how it could be that three genetically identical people could have developed two different major psychiatric illnesses.

The first two brothers did, to all appearances, have schizophrenia. They had been in college when they had their first "psychotic breaks" consisting of hallucinations, delusions, and paranoia. They were successfully medicated and accepted the doctors' prognostication that they would be disabled their entire life, slowly deteriorating, and that they needed to stay on their medications to keep their illness under control and avoid too much stress. They had dropped out of college, gone on disability benefits, and moved together into a group home for people with mental illnesses. They obediently attended their activity groups and went on the outings. Over the years, they did deteriorate slowly. The days ran into each other. Smoking and coffee became the highlights. They gained weight and became more and more dulled and lifeless. Clearly, classic schizophrenia.

The third brother was quite different. He, too, had his first psychosis in college, but for some reason, he was much more rebellious. After his first hospitalization, he threw away his medications, saying he didn't need them and returned to college. At first, his decision seemed to pay off. He graduated and began a job, but unfortunately, his psychosis returned in a few years. He was again hospitalized and medicated and again rebelled after discharge. This time he got married and worked a few years before his life fell apart again. Over the years, the pattern continued—several years of normal life interrupted by brief, highly destructive psychotic episodes when he was agitated, grandiose, unreasonable, and lost everything. Clearly, classic manic depression.

I don't believe for a moment that these brothers had different illnesses, genetically based or otherwise. I believe that the decisions they made—and I don't really recommend either path, although those are, in fact, the two paths we offer to most people with psychosis—so profoundly altered their life's journey that they ended up in different diagnostic categories.

A diagnosis isn't a destiny. The decisions that all of us make—people with psychosis, families, mental health professionals, and the communities we all live in—and the actions we take, matter.

You could easily get the impression looking at our current mental health system that the two choices these brothers made are the only choices available—either you comply and take your medications or you don't, and you try to figure it out on your own. Hopefully, as we've gone through our eight journeys, you've picked up some more ideas of how you can improve your journey. This chapter will focus on using our psychosis triangle to develop your plans to recover, regardless of which journey you're on.

The Psychosis Triangle

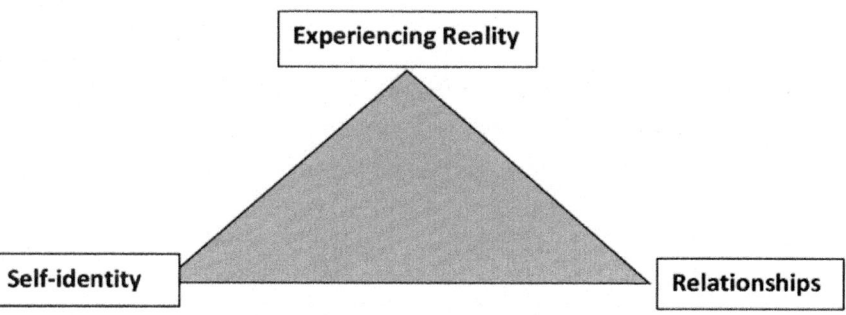

We're going to build three paths to recovery, one for each dimension.

How do I decide which dimension to use for my path?

The short answer is that a solid recovery uses all three dimensions.

But which one should I start with?

It may seem that you have to begin with the experiencing reality path: "First, you take your medications, and then, you can work on other aspects of recovery" is a common refrain today. But it wasn't always that way. Before there were medications, moral treatment approaches in 19th century America focused on rebuilding the self (and the soul) and for centuries in Geel, Belgium, they used an adult foster care system to give people with serious mental illnesses family relationships and roles within their community. Today's clubhouses, psychosocial rehabilitation, open dialogue, and recovery-based programs all focus on the self-identity and relationship dimensions. Building meaningful roles often combines self-identity (how we view ourselves within a role and what roles we're meant to be playing) and relationships (how others relate to us within our roles).

Most of us would naturally think that we should begin with the dimension that is most problematic, where the person is suffering and struggling the most—a "deficit-based" approach—but that means going straight to their most painful, impaired area. Almost counterintuitively, there can be advantages to beginning instead where the person is most confident and has the most skills to build on—a "strengths-based" approach. For example, someone may be ashamed to admit they hear voices, but more than happy to work on decreasing distractibility, so that they can hold their job, whereas someone else may not be willing to discuss their history of child abuse and how it impacts their interpersonal relationships but would like to take medications to be less paranoid.

Courtney Harding, who I introduced you to before as the lead researcher of the Vermont Longitudinal Study that demonstrated a high rate of recovery among discharged state hospital patients with schizophrenia, focuses her clinical work on building recovery by exploiting strengths, rather than by reducing deficits. She advocates creating a historic lifeline for patients that highlights their skills and accomplishments, and then centers service plans around building lives based on people's strengths.

Here's a quote from her article, "A Celebration of Strengths," published on the Foundation for Excellence in Mental Health Care website, an excellent place to find inspiration and practical advice:

"Think about it. Wouldn't you rather have people appreciate your strengths and help you grow with those attributes rather than focusing on all the deficits that we, as fallible humans, have? The irony is, if you mostly ignore the problem areas and focus on the strengths, goals, and aspirations that a person has, problems are gradually found to be tolerable to the person and lessen over time while dreams begin to come true. Ignoring problems is exactly the opposite of what clinicians have been repeatedly taught and at first it doesn't make sense to our ears because we learned to "fix broken things." But living broken things can indeed fix themselves when clinicians, family members, and friends hold up mirrors which reflect the healthy and competent parts of ourselves. And that is the secret of rehabilitation."

My overall recommendation is to begin wherever the person is most engageable. Where will they agree to begin?

Wait a minute. Isn't that feeding into their illnesses and wasting time while they deteriorate? What happened to "first, take your medications, and then, we'll work on recovery"? I liked that idea.

That idea is built on the assumption that they have an illness that exists only in the experiencing reality dimension. What if I said, "First, help them rebuild their sense of self, their hope, and self-responsibility before we try to get them to collaborate on medications and coping with voices" or "First, help them get out of their isolation and feel they can trust other people before we try to convince them that other people don't believe they're a prophet of God"? All of these approaches are likely to work for some people and not for others. Don't forget that over half of all people with psychosis don't engage in our current approach. Having more choices would likely improve our odds of engaging people.

> The first person I met when I walked into LA Men's Place (LAMP) in Skid Row was Jack, one of my old residency clinic patients. Jack had always done poorly at the clinic. He would wander in months after missing his appointment, usually dirty and hard to understand, asking for refills on his antipsychotic medication, Stelazine. He couldn't say when he took the pills or how come a 1-month supply had lasted so long. He couldn't say what the pills did for him. He just said he needed them; so, I'd write him another refill without really knowing what was going on with him. I figured it had to be doing more good than harm even if he took it irregularly. He was on my list of patients to be transferred to the next resident, but I wasn't at all sure that another resident would keep helping him like that.
>
> Jack was in the kitchen, stirring a huge pot of soup for lunch for the program. He looked clean, and he was talking coherently to the other people preparing the meal with him. I was shocked. He'd never looked this good at the clinic.
>
> "Hi, Jack. How are you doing? I was worried about you. Did you end up seeing one of the other doctors at the clinic after I left?"

"I'm doing fine. I'm making soup."

"I can see that, but I was asking about your treatment. Where are you getting your meds from now?"

"I'm not in treatment. I'm making soup."

I was starting to get a little frustrated. "You're doing so well, you must be getting meds from somewhere. Maybe Dr. Drucker at Skid Row Mental Health is seeing you?"

"Nope. I'm just making soup."

I may be a little slow, but I finally got around to, "OK. Tell me about making soup."

"Well, you see all these guys here."

"Yeah." An impoverished, disheveled, mostly psychotic group of men meandered around. Some were working like Jack was, a couple were playing chess, one was reading a book, and several were talking to themselves. More were outside smoking. If you saw the movie, "The Soloist," you saw scenes filmed at LAMP that included the actual people who are part of the program there.

"Well, most of them don't have any money. If they get a check, it's all gone by this time of the month. It's likely they won't have anything else to eat today besides this soup. They need me; so, I've pulled myself together to make their soup every day. They're depending on me. I haven't needed any medications since I've been making soup."

At the time, that story made no sense to me. You can't recover from psychosis making soup and stopping your medications. I'd learned that first, your illness has to be treated, and then, you can do something meaningful. Now, I know that as often as not, recovery goes the other way around. You find something that gives your life meaning. That helps you pull yourself together. Then, you have a better chance of facing reality.

Wherever we start, after engaging someone in one dimension, we should strive to spread out to the other two dimensions to solidify recovery. Here's where our investment in any given approach can get us into trouble because we can be self-righteous and dismissive of other approaches. It's not just our medication-based approach to recovery that often sacrifices self-identity and relationships along the way, leaving considerable additional damage to address to integrate recovery (for example, by forcing them to accept damaged personal identities as schizophrenic patients and isolating them from other non-mentally ill people, except professional staff). Many personal recovery programs are antagonistic to medications, believing them to be antithetical to empowerment and personal growth, rather than a potential tool for promoting empowerment and personal growth. Many social justice and relationship-based approaches conceptualize medications as dehumanizing and repressive and dismiss professional therapist relationships as "unreal" and "dependency creating." We have to be more broad-minded and accepting of each other to integrate recovery approaches that successfully impact all three dimensions.

When we're doing well, the experiencing reality dimension can provide an effective and adaptable basis for understanding ourselves and our relationships to other people and the world around us; the self-identity dimension can provide a secure foundation of who we are and what we value, guiding us as we relate to others and the world; and the relationship dimension can provide a positive, supportive network of mirroring, caring, and hope that nurtures us and promotes our growth and exploration.

One more thing before we start on our three dimensions of recovery: There are many more tools to achieve recovery than just medications. Too often, we define treatment as taking medications. Too often, we seem to use a 2-step approach to recovery: "Take your medications and shut up." Too often, we act as though there's nothing helpful we can do if they won't take their medications—and as long as they're taking their medications, we're doing our jobs. The truth is that almost no one recovers just by taking medications alone. They almost all have to do something else, too. Otherwise, they're just sitting there waiting for the medications to kick in, or for their medication appointment to get their medications adjusted, or even waiting to get off medications to go on with their lives.

I asked hundreds of people what they did to help themselves recover, and I put their answers together into this list that I used to have pinned to the wall in my office:

14 Things You Can Do to Rebuild Your Life

1. Talk to other people, instead of isolating.
2. Actively build security in your life—money to survive on, safe housing, connections with family, friends, and spirituality.
3. Actually feel feelings and emotions, instead of deadening them, medicating them, avoiding them, or getting high.
4. Learn some emotional coping skills.
5. Learn to "use" medications, instead of just "taking" medications.
6. Engage (or re-engage) in activities that make you more fun and interesting.
7. Take responsibility for your own life and make some changes in yourself.
8. Go to work even when you're not feeling well.
9. Do things outside of being a mental patient and outside the mental health system.
10. Improve your physical health and wellness.
11. Love other people—family, partners, and kids.
12. Work on acceptance and forgiveness, instead of blaming and vengeance.
13. Give back by helping others.
14. Find meaning and blessings in suffering and reconnect with God and spirituality.

I'd ask people to pick out any one or two things from the list they'd be willing to work on with us and offer to help with whatever they chose. Each one of these items can open up a rich path.

Self-identity—building a secure and effective self

Many people's sense of self is severely damaged by the time they've been dealing with psychosis for a while. For some people, their self-identity began fragmenting or drifting away well before their psychotic experiences, opening the door for the psychosis to occur. Even if someone had a strong self, going through psychosis is not just a medical condition. It's a profound human experience. It can shake them to their very core, causing them to doubt who they are and whether they have control of their own minds, fearing they're "losing it" or "going crazy," wondering if they can trust themselves. The boundaries of experience can become expanded far beyond anything they've known before, sometimes in ecstatic ways and sometimes, in agonizing ways. Trying to live among other people with an altered experience of reality, trying to fight to restore themselves, and trying to deal with the treatment system can all leave them even more lost and frustrated. In their battered state, they can be overwhelmed and defensive, hiding away, barely daring to hope. Much of what's left may be used just to protect themselves from exposure, shame, and further damage.

At the Village, as we started trying to figure out how to support people on their personal journeys of recovery, we often began with rebuilding their self-identities. We figured out that people needed to go through four stages to get their identity back and recover:

- **Hope:** They have to see the possibility of a better future for themselves to work hard to get there.
- **Empowerment:** They have to believe that they are strong enough to achieve a better future and that their efforts will be rewarded.
- **Self-responsibility:** They have to make their own decisions and take actions to grow and recover. They can't be caretaken into recovery.
- **Attaining meaningful roles:** They have to have meaning in their lives, apart from their disabilities and destructions. It's not enough to move from being a victim to a survivor. They have to develop other ways of relating to people, too. Otherwise, they're always defined only by their struggles and they haven't really moved on and recovered.

Debbie had struggled a lot through her childhood. She grew up in the ghetto. Her mother had a serious mental illness and her father was drug addict. They fought over her, threatening each other and threatening to commit suicide if she wasn't living with them. Her first sexual experiences were all rapes. She got so emotionally disturbed she had to spend 2 years in a group home as a teenager.

When we met Debbie in her mid-20s, she was filled with rage. One day, in the hospital, she even kicked a nurse in the head when she wouldn't get her a cigarette quickly enough. She opened up a huge gash that needed stiches, and that nurse never really recovered from the incident. Nonetheless, we kept working with her. We focused on her strengths, instead of trying to fix everything that was wrong with her.

A year later, we were taking her out to lunch celebrating her getting A's on her first set of midterms at Long Beach City College.

She said, "Dr. Mark. I want to thank you."

"Thank me? What for? You did all the work. You put yourself out there, going back to school. You're the one who was studying. You even made it through when you saw an old friend from childhood who said, 'Don't think you're fooling anyone by being here. I know who you really are. You're street and you're a whore.' You're proving to him and everyone else that you're more than that. All I did was sit on my ass back at the Village."

"Well, you were kinda helpful, too."

"Oh, yeah? What did I do?"

"Well, I used to come into your office and complain about stuff. You know, my dad is no good, the meds are no good, the apartment is no good, my boyfriend is no good, the Village is no good. And you'd sit there and say things like, 'I can see you at LBCC. You're pretty smart. You could fit in there. Those army fatigues you're wearing look weird here, but they'll fit in there. You're not that much older than the other students. I know someone at the disabled students' office who can help with the registration and red tape. I can see you at LBCC.'"

> She paused, and then said, "You just kept talking about how you could see it until I could see it, too. And when I could see it, then I could do it."

Notice how in just 6 months, Debbie had made serious progress in all four stages, and how all four were essential for her to do well at school.

We put together an entire recovery program around these "four stages of recovery." I even wrote a small book called *A Road to Recovery* that described the four stages and some practices and programs that promote them.

Along the way, we learned that contrary to common practice, people can't be caretaken into recovery, no matter how well-meaning their family and staff are and how compliant they are, because without hope, empowerment, self-responsibility, and meaningful roles, they can't build a positive identity. We can caretake people into safety or security or stability if we're lucky, but not into growth, maturity, and self-responsibility. Many times, psychosis begins before the person has fully matured and derails the process. Families, who ordinarily have a built-in ambivalence about their children growing up and facing the consequences of their own decisions, often become so frightened by psychosis and the destruction it can lead to, that they tilt heavily toward the protective, caretaking side. Professionals tend to push families even further into caretaking, recruiting them to take on case management and medical monitoring responsibilities. But going too far the other direction, neglecting people and kicking them out to figure it out by themselves aren't likely to work either. They need guidance to recover.

> Sometimes, after a successful treatment, someone will thank me, "Dr. Mark, you're the best doctor I ever had. You really listened to me and understand what I'm going through. You helped me find pills that really help me. You got me on SSI, so I don't have to work. You found me a Board and Care to live in where they take care of everything. I know I can always count on you to be there when I have a problem. I don't have to figure it out for myself, you'll tell me what to do. I don't have to make any

decisions. You'll take care of everything for me. Thank you so much!"

Wait a minute! What happened there? That started out so good. They were saying nice things about me. And then, it got vaguely creepy. Or vaguely crippled. What went wrong?

Sometimes, after a successful treatment, someone will thank me, "You know, I wouldn't wish this condition on my worst enemy. The suffering, the loss, the destruction—it's more than I ever imagined I could go through. But fighting this has helped me find strengths in me I never knew I had. Some of the things I'm most proud of about myself, I got in this struggle. I've learned what's really important. If not for this, I might have become a lawyer like my brother. There have been gifts for my wounds. I wouldn't wish it on anyone, but it's been a blessing in disguise. It has made me who I am today. I'm proud of myself in ways I never was before this."

That's what a real recovery sounds like.

And when do those two paths diverge? The first time I meet someone. If I tell them, as I was taught to do, "I'm so glad you came to see me. It's hard to face the stigma of mental illness and seek help. We're going to be able to help you here. I'm a good doctor. I have a lot of experience helping people like you." Then, we're headed down the first path, to vaguely creepy and vaguely crippled. If instead I say, and I say this to almost everyone I see the first time I see them, "I can already see the strengths you're going to be able to use to overcome this," we're headed down the second path. They leave that first visit, beginning to believe in themselves, instead of believing in me.

Here's what someone building a strong self-identity sounds like:

- Don't take care of me. Teach me how to take care of myself and get caring for myself.

- Don't make decisions for me. Guide me to make better decisions as I learn from my successes and failures.
- Don't protect me from risk. Walk alongside me and help me prepare for risks and learn from my risk-taking.
- Don't shield me from responsibilities. Help me meet and increase my responsibilities.
- Don't keep me away from the stresses of the world. Help prepare me for the world and help the world welcome me.

Think back to Jack who was cooking soup a few pages ago. LAMP helped him begin his recovery by believing in him enough to give him the job of cooking soup, even though he wasn't "prepared and likely to succeed," and he rose to the challenge. He believed he could do it, too. Making soup only works to build self-responsibility if how he cooks matters. Is there someone else looking over his shoulder, correcting all his mistakes, saying that's the best he can do because he's mentally ill, and making sure there are no consequences for his failures? If so, he'll never build self-responsibility. If instead, he starts to take responsibility for everyone's lunch, he starts to own the process and the results. The lunch starts to reflect on him—"You're a good cook." He starts seeing himself as "the soup man." Because he performs his tasks responsibly, he can take pride in it, and he can start to define himself by his role. Then, he's likely to start making changes in his life in order to preserve his role—making sure he gets up on time and shows up sober, cleaning up for the job, maybe even taking medications, so he can concentrate to work.

> *The Village used to do "immersion" trainings almost monthly where a whole variety of people would come from all over the world to experience for 3 days firsthand what we were doing. Part of the experience was "buddy time" where they'd spend part of a day following us around one-on-one. When there was a psychiatrist in the group, they'd be assigned to be with me.*
>
> *"Let's spend lunch going over to a restaurant down the block where one of my members is working. The biscuit sandwiches aren't low calorie, but they're really good."*
>
> *"Sure."*

"Sheila has serious schizophrenia. We got her out of the state hospital where she'd been for over a year. Even with Clozaril, she still hears a lot of voices."

"Wait a minute. I thought you said she was working there. She can't do that if she's still hearing voices."

"Why not? She's been there for 4 months so far, hearing voices all the time. We have members with all kinds of symptoms who are working. They have to do their jobs and, probably more importantly, they have to act like workers, but they don't have to be symptom free." He looked puzzled.

We sat down at a table by the window and looked over the menu. Sheila came by to take our orders.

"Hi, Sheila. This is Dr. Williams. He's visiting the Village today; so, I brought him here for lunch."

"Welcome. This is the best place to eat around the Village. Dr. Mark always orders the biscuit sandwiches, but I like the waffle sandwiches better. What can I get for you today?"

After she took our orders without writing down anything, he watched her working the busy room with the same puzzled look on his face. When she brought us our sandwiches, he said, "I have to ask you, how do you remember our orders with the voices talking to you? Don't they distract you?"

"If the voices start talking to me while I'm working, I tell them I'm busy now and I can't talk to you now. I get a break at 1:30. I'll talk to you then. They wait."

I laughed. "Sounds good to me."

While she's working, her identity as a worker is so strong it keeps the voices away.

Of course, the voices or the paranoia may return, no amount of medications can ensure it won't, but hopefully, they'll be strong enough to deal with it.

> Chris's father came to visit me. Chris had left a year ago to move to Georgia to be a peer advocate there, to help other people with psychosis.
>
> "How's Chris been doing?"
>
> "Just great. He hasn't had a single relapse since he left."
>
> "Really? He used to have relapses every few months, no matter what medications we tried. What's he on now?"
>
> "Oh, his meds are the same, and he still has times when the voices get worse and he gets paranoid, but now he uses his WRAP plan and he gets over it without going to the hospital or ruining his life. He knows when he starts hearing voices, not to isolate, to raise his meds for a few days, to stay away from pot, to get some extra sleep, and to remind himself that his work is valuable, to help him pull back together. Calling me is even on his plan."
>
> "So it isn't that he doesn't have relapses, he's just developed the resiliency to handle them when they come."
>
> "He believes in himself."

Roles are often the core of how we define ourselves. There are many possible roles in our society, but by far the most common, enduring, meaningful roles are romantic, work, family, and spiritual roles. Many of us have lifelong images and plans for these roles: "I'm going to get married and have three children." "I'm going to be a truck driver." "My parents raised me to be Catholic." I think that one of the reasons that psychotic experiences often emerge in adolescence and early adulthood is because that's when there can be serious problems achieving the roles we imagined. Even though many young people are taught that if they work hard and know what they really want and follow their passions, they can succeed at anything, that just isn't true for many people. Disappointments, both in ourselves and in the world around us, abound.

Conversely, regaining a stable self-image and recovering from psychosis can be grounded in attaining meaningful roles. Being a good husband, father, truck driver, or Catholic can provide a strong structure to build self-identity around in ways that being a "good patient" just can't. A recovery program must include the opportunities for attaining these meaningful roles if the self-identity dimension is going to be the focus. Most of these roles will have to be beyond the protective walls of the program. They need to be in the community. Therefore, programs have to include more than just a "social center" or "clubhouse" or "worksites." They have to support people working at Walmart, exercising at the YMCA, trying to get a date at a local happy hour, going to Long Beach City College, and praying in their temple.

Experiencing reality

Antipsychotic medications are breathtakingly successful in altering how people experience reality. They often dramatically reduce hallucinations and delusions within days or weeks, regardless of the underlying causes. For many people, they also help organize thinking, reduce anxiety and agitation, and improve sleep and self-care. It can seem almost miraculous to watch minds return to normal functioning and old personalities return: "The medications gave my son back to me. Thank you so much."

The amazing impact of medications is why working on this dimension is now the most popular, and unfortunately, usually the only dimension that is seriously addressed in recovery efforts. As a result, "treatment" today tends to become a battle to get people to take medications they don't want, think they don't need, and often even believe make them worse.

> "How many of you have been in the situation where you've sent someone to the hospital against their will and they get medicated there and their symptoms are massively reduced and they come out and they realize that they can function fairly normally and regain, to some extent, their former self? They say, 'Thank you so much for taking over my life and hospitalizing me when I was out of control. Now that I'm on medications, I can see how impaired and mistaken I was. I'm going to follow my doctor's orders and stay on my meds now and take care of my illness now. I'm so grateful to you.'"
>
> Over and over, rooms full of staff just snicker and groan. No one raises their hands.

"Come on. It can't be none. Haven't any of you ever had an experience where forced hospitalization and medications got someone to see how sick they were and how much they need medications?"

Reluctantly, one or two hands go up.

"OK. And how many of you have had the experience that you've sent someone to the hospital against their will and they get medicated there and their symptoms are reduced, but they don't see any difference anyway? They aren't grateful and they feel betrayed and they're mad at you and say they'll never trust you again and they refuse to see you anymore."

The room fills with the laughter of recognition. Every hand goes up enthusiastically.

Mental health systems have created a number of "illness-centered" strategies to improve "medication adherence" (formerly called "medication compliance," but that sounded too strong-armed):

- Medications have been invented with less bothersome side effects.
- Psychoeducation efforts are directed at patients and their families to try to promote understanding of their illnesses and the ongoing need for medications.
- Long-acting injections (ranging from lasting 2 weeks to 3 months) have been invented, so the medication doesn't have to be taken daily.
- "Assertive case management" (ACT) staff go into the community, reminding people of their appointments, bringing them to appointments, or even dispensing medications, sometimes including injections, in their homes.
- "Assisted outpatient treatment," also known as "outpatient commitment," allows a psychiatrist to get a court order requiring someone to take their medications, under threat of rehospitalization, to stay living in the community.
- Anti-stigma campaigns are directed at describing mental illnesses as equivalent to physical illnesses, emphasizing that there is

nothing to be ashamed of and that people with mental illnesses are deserving of effective treatments.
- Outreach campaigns, like Mental Health First Aid and QPR Suicide Prevention, encourage people in the community to recognize the signs and symptoms of mental illnesses and persuade their friends to come for treatment.
- Psychiatric medications have been integrated into other social service systems, most notably forensic, health care, substance abuse, and children's services, to increase their accessibility.

But all of these approaches are really attempting to make the person do what we want them to do—take their medications—regardless of what they want. Let's talk about a more collaborative, "client-driven" approach instead.

Let's start in the same place we began building self-identity—what are their goals?

> When my younger son was in elementary school, we complained to an expert in gifted student education that he wasn't motivated, "He won't do any of his homework. He says, 'I already know what my teacher is teaching. I get A's on the tests. Just because the other kids have to do all that repetition to learn something doesn't mean I should have to.' He doesn't show his work because he figures it out in his head, not on the paper."
>
> She smiled and nodded knowingly, "Hold on a minute. Before you decide he's not motivated, I have a question for you, 'Is he motivated to do what he wants to do?'"
>
> "Sure. He'll spend hours mastering a level on Donkey Kong and reads all the Harry Potter books as soon as they come out. If he wants to do something, there's no problem."
>
> "So, this really isn't an issue of motivation, it's an issue of priorities. Neither you nor the teacher have convinced him that what you want him to do is more important than what he wants to do."
>
> "Ain't that the truth?"

> "It's the truth for all of us."

The reason for being "client-driven," instead of "professionally driven," isn't just to be empowering, it's so people will actually work on their plan. Too often, we write down a plan we think is important and they don't do anything, and then, we call them unmotivated or treatment-resistant and then write down the same goal and plan for the next year. We need to start with their goals, so they'll be motivated to pursue them. By the way, the opposite is true, too. If the patient makes up the plan, instead of the staff (or the parent or friend), there's a good chance the staff (or parent or friend) won't be motivated to work on their goal, but we're not as likely to get labeled as unmotivated or treatment-resistant.

Making goals believable to them creates hope and making goals meaningful to them creates the resilience to keep pursuing the goal, even when inevitable challenges occur. Pursuing goals that are theirs, believable, and meaningful to them is what "client-driven" means, not that staff have to do whatever the client wants.

> *A man came in one day, saying, "I'm hearing voices, can you help me?"*
>
> *My first set of questions wasn't, "Can you tell me more about the voices? Are they inside your head or outside? Do they talk to you or to each other? Do they only come when you're depressed and they're depressing or when you're manic and they're grandiose? Do they come when you haven't slept or had a seizure or used drugs or a couple days after a drinking binge or after you've stopped your medications or on the anniversary of some trauma?"*
>
> *I know all those questions, designed to figure out his illness diagnosis, but that's not where I start. I start with their life and their goals, "What difference would it make if you weren't hearing voices? Why do you care about stopping them?"*
>
> *"I'd like to date women."*
>
> *"Well, so would I, but my wife objects. What do the voices have to do with dating?"*

"Every time I try to talk to a woman to ask her out, the voices start up. They tell me that I'm fat and ugly and no good, and they ask me, 'Who do you think you're fooling? She'll never go out with you.' I get so discouraged, I don't even try."

"That makes sense to me. By the way, I don't think that the voices are your only problem with dating women. It would be better if you were cleaner and dressed nicer. It would be good if you had some money to take her out with. And if you get lucky, it would be good to have either a car with a big back seat or an apartment to bring her back to. But we can work on all these things at the same time." Notice that I'm not telling him he has an illness we have to get under control before he can start living again. We're working together on his goal of dating women.

"I do have several different medications that might help with voices. They tend to have different side effects, and some work better for some people. Have you ever taken medications for voices before?"

"Yeah, I have, and they helped. That's why I'm asking you for pills."

"Great, what were those pills?"

"I don't know. I think it was a blue pill and a white pill."

Have you ever noticed that if you ask someone about street drugs, they can often tell you every detail about them, which strain of marijuana it was, whether it was the ecstasy with the smiley faces or the stars, etc., but if you ask them about their psychiatric medications, they often can't tell you anything except, "I think it was a blue pill and a white pill"? I've been trying to think about why that might be ... and I don't think the answer is because their dealer is running medication education groups every Thursday at 3 pm.

I think it's because we "use" drugs and "take" medications. On the one hand, when we use street drugs, we have some goal in mind—to get high, feel happy and have a good time, forget about our problems, get rid of anxiety, focus better, have better sex, date women—and afterward, we judge whether it was "good shit or bad shit," depending on how well we achieved our goals. On the other hand, when we take medications, it's usually because someone says we have an illness we need to treat, that we may or may not agree we have or believe needs treating. They also tell us that the medications have side effects we need to adjust to, that it will take a while to see the effects and even then, sometimes we won't notice the effects ourselves, and that someone else like our parents or our psychiatrist will have to tell us whether it's working for us. When we use street drugs, we talk with our friends and use the Internet and get a lot of misinformation and learn by trying stuff. When we take medications, they tell us to ask our doctor or maybe the pharmacist any questions we might have, and don't self-medicate. It's much harder to learn that way, and it certainly doesn't lead to self-involvement in the process.

"If you know the pharmacy and it's not too long ago, we can call and try to find out what the pills were. If not, we'll have to figure out together what pills will work best for you. They vary in how relaxing or sedating they are vs. how energizing they are, but more energizing pills might make you shaky or restless. Also, some may cause more weight gain and issues with cholesterol and diabetes than others do, while other ones have more sexual side effects. Which of these issues is most important to you?"

"Also, you can start with a low dosage and work your way up slowly, like getting in the pool starting at the shallow end, but it might take longer to build it up to a dosage that actually works for you. Or you can start with a full dosage, like jumping in the deep end of the pool, which might be harder to get used to, but might get those voices down faster and you dating faster."

"I don't want to get restless. Coffee does that to me, but I also don't want to be too sleepy. How about something in the middle, and I have diabetes in my family, so we should probably stay away from that."

"That sounds like Risperdal might be the place to start. We'll have to watch out for shaking and sexual side effects. How low or high do you want to start?"

"I can handle things. We can start out in the deep end."

"OK. Then, let's try 3 mg of Risperdal one at night, and I'll see you in a couple weeks and see how it goes."

When he returns (remember that is the most important part. If he doesn't come back, I have to go back and do better engagement), my first question isn't, "How are the voices?" My first question is, "Did you date any women?" Remember we're doing goal-driven medications, not symptom relief-driven medications.

He said, "No."

"Why not? What happened? You're looking sharper today and I saw you got a little day labor earlier in the week helping another member move; so, you had some money in your pocket. What went wrong?"

"It was your fault, doc."

"My fault? It's my fault I didn't get laid this weekend, but how is it my fault you didn't get laid?" (Yes, I talk like that.)

"It was those medications you made me take."

"Medications I made you take? Wait a minute, those were medications we agreed might help you get a date. How did they end up working backward?"

"Well, they did make the voices quieter, I gotta thank you for that. They're just whispers now, but now my hands are shaking so badly that I'm embarrassed to talk with anyone."

"OK. So, our first attempt didn't work perfectly, but we learned something. Let's keep working on it. We have some more choices today. We can move to a medicine that causes less shaking but more sedation and diabetes like Zyprexa. We can add some Cogentin or Inderal to see if it helps with the shaking, but they might cause other side effects. Or we can lower the dosage and see if you end up with a little more voices but no shaking, which might be the best balance for you." Notice that third choice doesn't appear in an illness-centered perspective. I'm offering to intentionally make him "more ill" to make him more functional and especially to help reach his goals.

He makes another choice, and we'll see how that goes.

Down the road when he's doing better, he might ask, "Hey, doc, when can I get off these meds?"

"Well, that depends on your goals. If you figure out how to not get intimidated by voices, so you can keep them quiet and date even with them, you can stop the meds. Or if you decide you don't want to date women after all, you don't need the medications. Or if you get married and you don't have to worry about dating anymore and the voices don't interfere with anything else important in your life. I'm not here to make money for drug companies. You should take medications as long as they help you have a better life and meet your own goals."

Notice how he didn't have to agree he has schizophrenia or psychosis to use medications. He just needed to have a goal, that I'd be motivated to work on with him that might be helped with medications.

Once we free ourselves from the constraints of the medical model, we can find lots of collaborative uses for medications. Here are some examples of medication usages within various formulations from our journeys:

- The pills strengthen you mentally, so you can handle the stress you're under without fragmenting as much. They help "glue" you

together. They also keep your sleep/wake cycle and basic functions under better control.
- The pills help your mind filter the amazing range of stimuli, including physical stimuli from your body, and internal thoughts that bombard it, so you can think more clearly and more linearly, and have an easier time maintaining your personal balance and homeostasis, but this might make you feel less creative.
- The pills slow down your ability to jump rapidly between various thoughts and mental associations, so your thinking will be more grounded and normal and less ethereal and idiosyncratic. This may help you feel less lost, confused, and alone, and help you be more productive.
- The pills help strengthen your rational, conscious mind, so that your unconscious mind is more under control in both your sleep and waking hours.
- The pills help you stay in reality, so you're better able to deal with it, instead of escaping into your imagination.
- The pills help strengthen your personal boundaries, so you won't pick up on other people's feelings as much as you walk by and they won't impact you as much. This may make you less intuitive and lonelier, but will make you more emotionally grounded and independent. This also makes it harder for other people to influence your mind outside of your personal control, regardless of the way they're trying to do it.
- The pills help make the "spiritual waters" you're swimming in shallower, so you won't drown, but you also won't have as much contact with the immensity of the spiritual world.
- The pills help strengthen you, so the devil can't fool you or bully you as easily.
- The pills decrease the ability of voices to impact your self-consciousness and take over more of your mind.
- The pills partially counteract the disorganizing influence of drugs, alcohol, seizures, and other medical and neurological conditions.

These aren't clever ways of manipulating people into taking medications who don't have insight into their psychiatric illness. They are authentic hypotheses for mechanisms of action for how these pills actually work.

Remember that the classes of medications we now use have been named to correspond to the illness-centered model that corresponds to their FDA approval and their marketing campaign. For example, "antipsychotics" were originally "major tranquilizers" when the goal was to sedate institutionalized patients (or sometimes housewives) and now they've been rebranded as "mood stabilizers," so they can be marketed to people with major depressions and bipolar disorder without psychosis. These class names aren't really any more legitimate than my psychological descriptions. These pills are all so complex neurochemically that there isn't a clear correlation between their biochemical actions and their psychological impacts. My descriptions haven't been studied, not because they're outlandish but because the medical model is impressively narrow-minded and it controls all the pharmaceutical research funding. (I once met a psychiatrist in Beijing who was busy studying various "antidepressants," categorizing them by their impact on the Yin–Yang balance in various energy meridians. He combined his findings with his ability to diagnose people using his traditional Chinese medicine model to give his patients more targeted medications than our neurotransmitter system is able to do.) It wouldn't surprise me if some of our "antipsychotic" medications are better than others at some of my mechanisms of action, but I'm never going to see them systematically studied in any way outside of our incredibly broad *DSM* syndromes.

Keep in mind that medications aren't the only tool available. For example, some people might improve their experience of reality with better sleep, coping skills, cognitive reframing, using fewer drugs, talking with friends, relaxation, less isolation, etc. A package can be put together, through shared trial-and-error for each person. There are several tools to assist with shared decision-making, even anticipating when a person loses self-control in a crisis:

> *Two mental health professionals with serious mental illnesses developed self-help tools that, although they're not specific for psychosis, have been used quite successfully to help self-manage psychosis on an ongoing basis.*
>
> *Patricia Deegan, who I cited earlier in the book, created a software tool, Common Ground, that can be used to help people prepare for short psychiatrist visits, so they can be*

more personalized and based more on shared decision-making. She also has a concept of "personal medicine" that helps people create an entire personalized toolbox, including medication and non-medication tools to promote their recovery.

Mary Ann Copeland created Wellness Recovery Action Plans (WRAP). Either individually or in groups, people discover what works for them. They create an evolving set of simple, safe wellness tools they choose from, depending on what level of distress they're in: 1) develop a list of things to do every day to stay as well as possible, 2) identify upsetting events, early warning signs, and signs that things have gotten much worse, and by using wellness tools, develop action plans for responding at these times, 3) create a crisis plan, and 4) create a post-crisis plan.

In addition, Psychiatric Advance Directives have been developed analogously to Health Advance Directives. People can proactively create a plan at a time when they're doing well, to have serious input into their care in the future if they face a serious crisis and become so impaired they aren't able to collaborate at the time. They can specify, for example, what hospitals and what medications they would prefer, who should be informed of their crisis, and even who they would designate to speak on their behalf. Many times, these plans are developed collaboratively with a mental health professional. Different states vary as to how legally binding Psychiatric Advance Directives are.

But what if you tried all those techniques and they still won't take their medications and are too out of touch with reality to function? I've heard that most people with psychosis won't take their medications regularly.

And I've heard that most psychiatrists aren't goal-driven, person-centered, client-driven, formulation-based, and collaborative … but I'll try to answer your question anyway.

Remember that the point of this dimension of recovery is not to take medication to treat an illness, it's to alter people's experience of reality. Just because medications can change our perceptions of reality while we're taking them doesn't mean that they change our experience of reality.

Unfortunately, all people are heartbreakingly unable to change our experiences of reality—even when our perceptions are changed. Our memories remain stuck in how we initially perceived events. We resist any changes in our understandings of reality, inclining to distort our perceptions, instead of changing our minds. We get stuck in denial and resistance, instead of learning and adapting. It's probably even harder to restrict our views of reality (to stop believing we perceived something) than it is to expand our view (to see new perspectives or have "enlightening" experiences), but even with so-called transformative experiences like using a hallucinogenic drug such as psilocybin mushrooms or with a spiritual awakening, consider how hard it is to actually sustain a meaningful change in our lives.

Integrating a new experience of reality is very difficult (especially if you're focused on how to get out of a locked hospital), making working on this dimension often incredibly frustrating for staff and families. Before medications, it was largely considered hopeless to help someone by confronting and altering their experience of reality directly. Since medications can forcibly alter perceptions of reality without the person participating, almost all of our focus in treatment has gone into "How can we get them to stay on their medications?" even when they don't see how their perceptions have changed.

I was taught the compelling metaphor that, "A patient with a broken arm can use their brain to see that their arm is broken and needs treatment, but someone with a broken brain can't use their broken brain to see that their brain is broken, and so, they don't see that they need treatment. It's our job to give them the treatment they need anyway."

The fancy biologic word for having a brain that's too broken to know it's broken is "anosognosia." Here's a quote from the Treatment Advocacy Center's website forcibly making this argument:

> "Anosognosia, also called "lack of insight," is a symptom of severe mental illness experienced by some that impairs a person's ability to understand and perceive his or her illness. It is the single largest

reason why people with schizophrenia or bipolar disorder refuse medications or do not seek treatment. Without awareness of the illness, refusing treatment appears rational, no matter how clear the need for treatment might be to others.

Approximately 50% of individuals with schizophrenia and 40% with bipolar disorder have symptoms of anosognosia. Long recognized in stroke, Alzheimer's disease and other neurological conditions, studies of anosognosia in psychiatric disorders is producing a growing body of evidence of anatomical damage in the part of the brain involved with self-reflection. When taking medications, insight improves in some patients.

Improving access to treatment for people too ill to seek help, including involuntary treatment when legal criteria are met, is one of the ways the Treatment Advocacy Center is working to fix the mental health system."

From that perspective, there are only two options: 1) keep raising the medications until their insight improves, or 2) force them to take the medications they need, regardless of their reasons for refusal and however rational those reasons might seem to them.

But what if this isn't a neurologically determined lack of awareness or even a psychologically determined lack of insight? What if the "part of the brain involved with self-reflection" isn't broken? What if "self-reflection" depends on our personal temperament, development, and situation? And what if "self-reflection" is most effectively done with someone who is listening carefully to you and mirroring back what you're experiencing? Then, maybe we could create a treatment plan that proactively and collaboratively targets the multitude of individual variations of self-reflection, while we're prescribing medications that alter how they experience reality.

Let's learn from a couple examples away from psychosis: battered women and alcoholics. Both groups of people suffer terribly. Neither one likely has neurologic damage causing anosognosia, but both are incredibly frustrating to treat primarily because they show the same breathtaking inability to change their perception of reality that we all have. Like many people with psychosis, their inability to change frustratingly perpetuates their suffering. Unlike people with psychosis, we have no medication that we can use to alter their reality. We have to do it entirely emotionally if we're going to help them break out of their reality.

Battered women are usually in love with their abuser. Like anyone in love, they were initially attracted primarily by their imagination of who their man was, and crucially, how he made her feel. Likely, they were also blinded by this love to seeing undesirable traits and "warning signs" that were there from the beginning. They were likely also "resistant" to hearing the concerns of their friends. In some cases, their man used the friends' negativity about him to justify isolating her from her friends. He may well have also claimed that his jealousy, his dominating and controlling behaviors, and his angry outbursts were all because he loves her so much he couldn't bear to lose her, an explanation that fit with her love-distorted reality. (It made sense to her because it's exactly the explanation her mind came up with, too.) By the time serious physical abuse occurs, fear has usually become a part of the picture. But somehow, even with threats, beatings, and rapes, which should all be intolerable, as often as not, she won't leave him. Even if they're separated, she's likely to return, usually because he says that he's sorry and didn't mean to hurt her and he'll change because he loves her so much. She's impressively blind to the reality of their relationship, as she continues to cling to her initial love-struck perception.

How do battered women's programs try to change her experience of reality?

They try to keep her away from the isolation he's imposed on her. They try to avoid confrontation and shaming. They try to help her accept that she's been distorting reality without blaming her. They use peers, who have been through the same experiences, to normalize what she's going through. They encourage lots of sharing self-reflection with other people, for example, through journaling and self-help groups. They try to create experiences that remind her of what she was like before this relationship and what she stands to recover if she leaves him for good. They emphasize how hard the process of leaving is, how returning to him is a setback, but also an expected part of recovery. They encourage her to be more positive about herself, to love herself, and not to need a man's attention for validation. They emphasize a hopeful vision of the future, she can attain. They believe in her until she can believe in herself. She may have to just take it a step at a time on her own until her self-image is stronger.

It's a long, hard process, but many battered women do change their experience of the reality of their relationship and recover.

Alcoholics often have a distorted perception of how alcohol affects them from the beginning, minimizing their experience of their own drunkenness and its consequences. They also often have initial extremely positive experiences with alcohol, their new best friend, a social lubricant, "liquid courage." Alcohol gave them a whole new sense of who they are and what they're capable of. Over time, ugly consequences emerge, but they minimize these, too. They can't give up what alcohol does for them. As addiction takes hold, they no longer have that good feeling and need to drink just to feel normal. Even that doesn't change their perceptions of their alcoholism. They insist it's not addiction, they can stop whenever they want. Even when their demonstrations of control fail, they rationalize and excuse. When loved ones confront them with their addiction, lack of control, and deterioration, they usually respond with anger and accusations. The alternative reality everyone else sees is simply too painful to consider as moments of "bottoming out" prove.

How does AA try to change their experience of reality?

They try to keep up high levels of contact, avoiding isolation, urging going to lots of meetings sharing self-reflections and getting a sponsor to share even deeper with, even at odd hours. They try to minimize shame and blame, while urging taking self-responsibility, including doing a moral inventory and making amends. They lean heavily on the shared experiences of alcoholism to normalize the experience without needing to admit an internal moral or personal flawed nature. They give hope for recovery through shared example. Relapse is a setback, but an accepted part of recovery. They urge faith, "fake it until you make it," "keep coming back and working the program and it will work for you." They urge loosening the need to control everything in your life, turning it over to a higher power to replace alcohol as something to rely on.

It's a long, hard process, but many alcoholics do change their experience of the reality of their addiction and recover.

The similarities between these two programs are striking despite their very different social contexts and histories.

My take-home lesson is that for many people with psychosis, we're going to have to develop a long hard process if we're going to change their reality, alongside the help of medications, like we've done for battered women and alcoholics.

Go back for a moment and reread the very first story in this book, the one about the clubhouse in Montana. Listen to the things they said they started doing to help themselves when they stopped believing that medications alone were going to do it. Don't they sound like the people in battered women's programs and Alcoholics Anonymous? They're normalizing, reducing shame and guilt, sharing hope and empowerment, and accepting setbacks. Clubhouses are often seen as good places for socialization or psychosocial rehabilitation or development of employment skills, but they're also often the most powerful "treatment" environments for "accepting illnesses." By being places where people with psychosis can drop in and be accepted as they are, self-reflecting, connecting with others going through similar journeys, all learning and growing together, while having fun and being productive, for many people they are the best environment for changing their experience of reality and sticking with their medications.

Too often, we relax after the person has found medications and other things to improve their perception of reality. Their side effects are reasonably low. They're "stable." We can spread out their medication visits and give them prescription refills lasting months. Too often, however, while we're not paying much attention, they stop their medications or something else important changes and they "relapse."

We see a similar problem with our analogous groups: Alcoholics often relapse after getting sober at a 30-day program, and battered women often return to their abusers after being separated and living at a shelter. Motivational interviewing calls this stage of change "sustaining," and it takes prolonged effort and a tolerance for failure—"relapse is part of recovery."

Probably the most important thing to focus on in the "sustaining change" phase is changing our self-identity and personal narrative, so that the change becomes part of ourselves. Often, someone can't just stop drinking; they need to develop a recovery identity and lifestyle. Often, someone can't just leave a battering partner; they need to develop a sense of self-sufficiency and personal value to get free. Consider also the difference between creating a beautiful wedding and exciting honeymoon and becoming a "married person" who can sustain a new identity and life.

We've already talked about how hard it is for people to build a strong self-image as a psychotic or schizophrenic person with all the real and imagined limitations and hopelessness that identity implies, but it can be done, and we can help people get there.

> *Kay Redfield Jamison wrote a compelling memoir about her struggles with bipolar disorder, "An Unquiet Mind: A Memoir of Moods and Madness." I was most struck by how this very bright woman—she's a MacArthur "genius" award winner—who was a psychologist at UCLA and had written a textbook on bipolar disorder found it so difficult to use medications to manage her own illness and life. She writes about how seductive her mania has been for her, and how, even after she learned the hard way that she needed to take lithium to be stable, she couldn't trust her own judgment while she was manic to convince herself to actually take her medications. She got to the point where she turned her own personal judgment over to her psychiatrist (even when he was long-distance), taking whatever medications that he told her to, regardless of what her opinion was, especially when she was manic, and it worked out for her.*
>
> *Before she released her autobiographical book, she stopped treating other people as a psychologist. She writes that she couldn't expect that her clients could trust her judgments for them, once they learned that she couldn't trust her judgments for herself. Although she had been doing it for years secretly, once she made public her inability to be rational about medications in the heights of mania or the depths of depression, she stopped treating people herself. She couldn't integrate her vulnerability while ill into her self-image as a professional psychologist.*
>
> *Even though Kay is living quite productively with her mental illness, on a recovery journey which features the ultimate in scholarly understanding and impressive trust in her*

> *psychiatrist and compliance with his medications, it seems she'd have to go beyond those pathways to find an adaptation that would allow her to go on as a practicing psychologist.*

The standard illness model assumes that if the illness is treated thoroughly enough, that will be enough for the person to be well again. That's because we rarely include this step—"Support adaptations to their changed perceptions of reality and develop a recovery narrative"—and, as a result, many people relapse again and again. If we've gotten to the point of stabilizing our experience of reality primarily through coercion and compliance, they're unlikely to have enough hope, empowerment, and self-responsibility to adapt to their new realities and roles. That's a crucial reason why integrating those same factors into this dimension and our medication practices is often needed to sustain recovery. If we chose instead to enforce long-acting injectable antipsychotics that force the person into a changed perception of reality without their participation and we do everything we can to avoid relapses, instead of learning from them, we risk building a recovery that is weak in both dimensions and likely to feel rather lifeless, as though something important has been lost along the way without having ever been processed or even grieved.

> *Mark Vonnegut, son of the famous writer Kurt Vonnegut, became severely psychotic as a young man and wrote a dramatic book in 1975 about his struggles called "The Eden Express: A Memoir of Insanity." It's a messy story with elements from many of our journeys, including childhood trauma, losing balance, drugs, and psychiatric illness (diagnosed both schizophrenia and bipolar). I especially remember how frightened he was when he had done everything the psychiatrists had told him to, stayed on medications and away from drugs, and ended up relapsing into another psychotic episode and hospitalization anyway. He'd given up on his autonomy, been compliant, and still he was back in the same mess.*
>
> *He didn't write another book until 2010, "Just Like Someone Without Mental Illness Only More So," which also features a lot of wry observations reminiscent of his father. By that*

point, he was a Harvard medical school graduate, a pediatrician with a wife and children. To my reading, the point of this book is that he never stopped having psychotic experiences, but he sustained a productive, satisfying life anyway: "None of us are entirely well, and none of us are irrecoverably sick. At my best I have islands of being sick. At my worst I had islands of being well. Except for a reluctance to give up on myself there isn't anything I can claim credit for that helped me recover from my breaks. Even that doesn't count. You either have or don't have a reluctance to give up on yourself. It helps a lot if others don't give up on you." He learned how to act normal, so people wouldn't be upset and try to help him poorly, and how to accept who he was and that his life, just like anyone else's, is built on small moments, not great accomplishments and events. Here's another quote: "Note to self: being Kurt's son, being an ex-mental patient, getting into Harvard, having written a book, and being a doctor are all things that in and of themselves do not make a life. If you lean on them too hard, you'll find that there's not much there. But if you add up a lot of things that aren't in and of themselves enough, it almost starts to add up to something …."

Both books are worth reading, the first for how lost someone can become in psychosis without giving up on themselves and the second for how an honest person struggles to make sense of an insane life that sounds a lot like the struggles of a sane one—thus, the book's title, "Just Like Someone Without Mental Illness Only More So."

Maybe needing to find meaning and adapting to reality isn't limited to people with psychosis and other extraordinary experiences. Maybe sustaining a meaningful life isn't that easy for anyone.

Return for a moment to the identical triplet brothers that I began this chapter with. It's not just the "compliant" schizophrenic brothers who would benefit from developing a new path and way of relating to their treaters. The other brother, the rebellious manic-depressive brother, would, too. He shouldn't have to leave all treatment support, including medications, to find his own path and identity. If we've been diverse in our understandings of how medications are helping people, they can be diverse in how they include medications in their lives and how they adapt to their extraordinary experiences of reality. We'll have to use all the options we've learned on our various journeys to help put together a larger array of meaningful adaptations with people.

> *If you want to hear an impressive version of overcoming psychosis and meaning making, spend 20 minutes listening to Eleanor Longden's 2013 TED talk, "The voices in my head." After several years of profoundly unsatisfying illness-centered, hopelessness-creating treatment, she puts together a childhood trauma journey that features befriending the voices as representatives of her most painful, innermost, blocked-out emotions so that she can reintegrate herself.*
>
> *Eleanor is both a beneficiary and a leader of the Hearing Voices Movement and the Hearing Voices Network. This is a worldwide, largely self-help movement designed to give people an alternative to a schizophrenic illness identity and a supportive space in which to understand their own identity as "voice-hearers." They do not begin with a presumption of pathology or illness, but unlike many in the anti-psychiatry movement, they do expect that hearing voices will lead to a great deal of confusion and suffering. Overcoming that distress is the primary goal, whether the voices disappear or not. Hearing voices are meaningful experiences, not meaningless pathology, and "voice-hearers" need to work together to develop an understanding of the voices along with a meaningful personal narrative and identity.*
>
> *In my opinion, they are not saying that they are modern day shamans living in a separate spiritual reality, but instead, they are insistent that hearing voices is a highly impactful, meaningful experience that requires serious, ongoing effort to integrate successfully into their lives and identities.*

> *I think the rest of us, especially psychiatrists, should strive not just to get out of their way by not imposing hopelessly ill identities on them, but to actually collaborate in their meaning-making efforts. We can learn from the example of Marius Romme, the Dutch psychiatrist, who accepted the voices of his patient, Patsy Hague, as real and helped her make sense of them, beginning the Hearing Voices Movement.*

If we come from the all too common point of view that suffering is something to be eliminated, this step doesn't exist at all. If you've figured out how to adapt to reality and gotten rid of your distress, you're done. It doesn't matter whether you've accepted that you have an illness that medications help you control or you've finally realized that you can't handle drugs without risking your sanity or you've come to terms with childhood trauma by recovering your deepest feelings that fueled the voices, like Eleanor did. If the pain is done, you've recovered.

If instead we come from the point of view that suffering happens for a reason, that it's something we should learn and grow from, that we have more to gain by welcoming our suffering than by trying to exclude it, then we must continue onward, pursuing the meaning of our suffering. What is this experience supposed to be teaching us? Why did I have to go through this?

Not everybody will feel this need for meaning, but many do.

Some alcoholics will be satisfied with the medical explanation that they have an illness, that is heavily genetic, and have to stay sober for the rest of their lives to avoid bringing it back to life. Others will wonder if the alcohol was hiding something deeper within them. Were they using it to self-medicate something else and then became addicted and lost control? Did their childhood trauma impact them more than they thought it did, and if they're going to sustain sobriety they're going to have to deal with it? Was alcohol and drugs a "spiritual shortcut" that revealed their underlying craving for spirituality that ultimately brought them back home to God?

Some battered women need to just get out of their abusive relationship, and then, they'll be fine. Others continue with a tragic pattern of recurrent abusive relationships, and they have to figure out what is making them so vulnerable. What keeps driving them into the same hell? What do they need to learn to not just make this episode of suffering stop, but to stop the cycle of suffering?

Instead of viewing everyone who has recurrent relapses as treatment non-compliant and lacking insight, we should take another look to see if there mightn't be something underlying going on that's driving them into psychosis over and over again. Maybe they need deeper insight to recover. Maybe their wounds are deeper than what we're seeing or maybe their biology is more dysfunctional than our medications can restore on their own.

> The first time I met Ryan, Gail, one of our homeless outreach workers, brought him in to see me in the basement in our Homeless Assistance Program. "Pay extra attention to this guy. I know he looks like any other drunk, but he's someone special." I spent a lot of time with him getting to know him. He was from a small town in Colorado. He had a religious upbringing, even becoming a junior pastor in his local church, but he couldn't control his alcohol. Over the years, he'd drank more and more and been in and out of hospitals and "drunk tanks" throughout the West, eventually ending up with hundreds of other people in the park in Long Beach where Gail bicycled around, giving out lunches and looking for people to help.

> Over the next week, several other homeless people had also told me they were glad I was seeing Ryan. He needed my help. I wondered what was so special about this guy.

> By then, he'd been picked up by an ambulance for the umpteenth time and taken to the ER at St. Mary's and sobered up there. He was given Librium to help avoid DTs and released to the streets. He came in to see me. "I saw you last week? I don't remember any of it. Probably I was in a blackout. I do strange things in blackouts. The last time I was in one, I hugged one of the trees, thinking it was my brother." Wonderful.

> Ryan said he couldn't stop drinking because without the alcohol, he couldn't stop hearing the voices which tortured him, convincing him he'd committed terrible crimes. They'd

even get him to go to the police to confess to things he hadn't done. He couldn't sleep with them. They kept his heart racing. "Only alcohol works to quiet them down, but then I get sick from the alcohol."

Over the next couple years, it seemed he might be right. We'd gotten him SSI to live on, and he was sharing an apartment with one of our other members. He'd hang out and try to help other people. I'd tried lots of different anti-psychotics and antidepressants, even large doses of my most sedating pill, Seroquel. He'd stay sober for a few weeks or even a month or two, but ultimately, the voices would get too bad for him and he'd go back to drinking, and then, it was only a matter of time before he was blacked out, and in the ER again.

Ryan showed up looking both miserable and ashamed. "I'm sorry to bother you, Dr. Mark, but the voices are really bad, and I don't know what else to do."

"It's fine. I wish you were doing better. What are the voices talking about anyway?"

"You know, the usual. They want me to confess to stabbing that homeless guy last week."

That isn't really "the usual." I rarely see someone with voices urging false confessions. "You didn't stab him, did you?"

"No. I've never committed any of the crimes they accuse me of."

"I wonder why they think you're guilty."

"I'm not the one who's guilty."

My breath stuck for a moment. "Wait a minute. You said you're not the one who's guilty. Who is guilty?"

He sat there stunned. Then, the tears started streaming down his face. "My mom is."

"Your mom?" I couldn't remember reading anything in his chart about his mother. What's going on?

"What did your mom do?"

"She used to sexually abuse me when I was little. It went on for years." The tears continued to flow.

I passed him a Kleenex. "So, why do the voices blame you for what she did?"

He stopped and looked up at me, "I don't know. Maybe because she would blame me and said I couldn't tell anyone."

"Does anybody know besides you?"

"No. This is the first time I've told anybody. I've known you for so long and I'm desperate. I'm sorry."

"What are you sorry for?"

"Because I feel like I've betrayed her by telling you."

"What do you think she'd want you to do now?"

"I don't know." The tears started up again.

"I tell you what. Let's try something unusual to see if it can help us figure this out. See that chair next to you?"

He hesitated. "Yeah."

"Let's pretend your mother is sitting in that chair. Can you imagine her there?"

"Yeah."

"OK. Now, ask her what she wants you to do."

He looked over at the empty chair, which no longer seemed as empty. I waited to see what he'd say next. He seemed to be taking this very seriously.

"She says she's sorry, and she wants me to forgive her."

I paused. "Do you think you can do that?" More tears. Another Kleenex.

"I can't. I just can't do it."

We'd come this far. I had to think of something else. "Hold on. Didn't you used to be really religious, even like a junior deacon or something like that?"

"Yeah. So what?"

"Well, I'm not here to preach Gospel to you or anything like that. I'm sure you know the Bible better than I do, but isn't part of the point of Christ that he's supposed to forgive people for us when we can't do it ourselves?"

"Yes. He gave his life for our sins. We can all be forgiven." He looked a little brighter.

"OK. Can you ask Christ to forgive your mother, even though you can't do it yourself?"

He nodded. "I can do that."

"Go ahead."

I waited for what seemed like forever. Finally, he smiled and looked back at me.

"What happened?"

"Christ forgave her."

"Good. And how did that affect your mother?"

He looked back at her empty chair. I waited some more. "She's very grateful. She praised Christ and thanked me."

"Is there anything else she wants?"

"She wants a hug."

"Can you do that?"

"I can." He got up and hugged the empty chair, and as he did, it seemed as though an enormous weight was being lifted from his shoulders. He let out a huge breath, and a calm settled over him.

He dried his eyes and thanked me before he left.

Ryan never heard voices again, and he never drank again. We tapered him off his medications. He began to make plans to get a job.

Four months later, Ryan was sitting, eating dinner with his roommate when he choked on a chicken bone ... and died.

We had one of our best Village funerals for him. About 50 people showed up. Even though none of them knew about what had happened between us, they all said that he seemed like he was changed these last months, like he was at peace. "Maybe it wasn't so bad that he died now. It almost seemed like he was here to do something, and he did it and was free to go now."

Maybe. Something did feel finished and right about him dying then.

Before we leave this section, here's a table contrasting the standard illness-centered approach to medication prescribing and my person-centered approach, so you can see the differences:

Illness-Centered Prescribing	**Person-Centered Prescribing**
1. Take a history and collect objective signs and symptoms. 2. Make a diagnosis. 3. Obtain Informed consent (may include family psychoeducation). 4. Prescribe medications. 5. Assess impact on target signs and symptoms of diagnosis and creation of undesirable side effects. 6. Adjust medications until effect maximized. 7. Continue effective medications to avoid relapse and deterioration.	1. Engage the person in the process, building a trusting relationship. 2. Find out their goals to motivate them and build hope for positive change. 3. Create a shared story of their lives, a "formulation" that stands up to self-reflection and makes them feel understood. 4. Work together, using shared experience and decision-making, to learn how they can use medications and other tools to achieve their goals, change, and recover.

8. If medications have been effective and the patient is motivated, may add rehabilitation to overcome disabilities and recovery services to enhance quality of life.	5. Support adaptations to their changed perceptions of reality and develop a recovery narrative. 6. Help them internalize the meaning of their changes, so they can be self-sustaining.

Relationships

Let's begin with two very different expressions of the power of relationships:

> The Harvard Study of Adult Development, begun in 1939 and including as one of their subjects sophomore John F. Kennedy, is still collecting data and reporting 80 years later on the most important determinants of health and wellness. They found out that even for things like heart attacks, relationships were more important factors than the traditional health risk factors like weight, blood pressure, and exercise. The Harvard Gazette reported in 2017: "The surprising finding is that our relationships and how happy we are in our relationships has a powerful influence on our health," said Robert Waldinger, director of the study, a psychiatrist at Massachusetts General Hospital and Professor of Psychiatry at Harvard Medical School. "Taking care of your body is important, but tending to your relationships is a form of self-care too. That, I think, is the revelation." And that's for all of us.

> Dan Fisher and I were in St. Louis doing a recovery training for the Veterans Administration. At lunch, he drew a picture that looked like this one, trying to express the profound difference between being alone, with your mind, words, and heart going round and round in hopeless circles and sharing your mind, words, and heart with another person. This difference was the key to his recovery from psychosis.

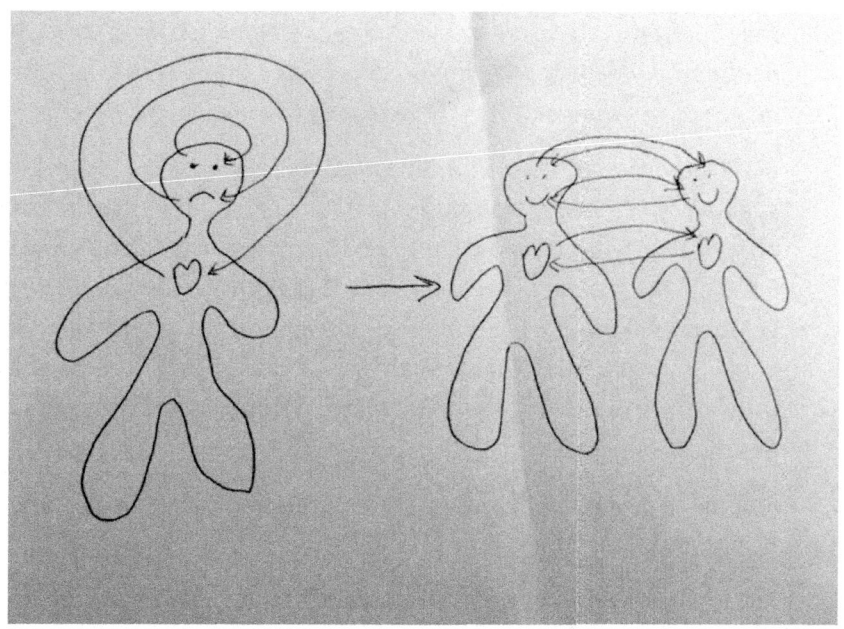

There's still something about this simple drawing that, for me, goes beyond words, bringing out something of the primal power of relationships. We are profoundly different when we're isolated than when we're connected to others.

Dan and others have promoted a relationship-based public health approach to improving mental health, emotional CPR. From their website, emotional-cpr.org:

"Emotional CPR (eCPR) is an educational program designed to teach people to assist others through an emotional crisis by three simple steps:

***C** = Connecting*

***P** = emPowering, and*

***R** = Revitalizing.*

The Connecting process of eCPR involves deepening listening skills, practicing presence, and creating a sense of safety for the person experiencing a crisis. The emPowering process helps people better understand how to feel empowered themselves as well as to assist others to feel more hopeful and engaged in life. In the Revitalizing process, people re-engage in relationships with their loved ones or

> *their support system, and they resume or begin routines that support health and wellness which reinforces the person's sense of mastery and accomplishment, further energizing the healing process.*
>
> *eCPR is based on the principles found to be shared by a number of support approaches: trauma-informed care, counseling after disasters, peer support to avoid continuing emotional despair, emotional intelligence, suicide prevention, and cultural attunement. It was developed with input from a diverse cadre of recognized leaders from across the U.S., who themselves have learned how to recover and grow from emotional crises. They have wisdom by the grace of first-hand experience."*

When we look at people with psychotic experiences, relationships are an important dimension in three interrelated ways:

1. Maintaining relationships and reducing isolation can be a powerful tool for "prevention."
2. Reestablishing relationships is an important part of recovery.
3. Lack of relationships and isolation are important factors leading to negative outcomes, including suicide, violence, drug use, homelessness, poverty, incarceration, and early death.

We'll focus on recovery in this chapter and on negative outcomes in the next chapter.

Our lives are all sustained by a network of relationships—friends, family, coworkers, neighbors, teachers, etc. I don't mean the "safety net" of relationships that catches us when we fall. I mean the web of relationships that gives our daily life context, company, and resilience. For some of us, this web is quite strong and extensive. For others, it may have a few strong strands, but beyond those is quite weak and fragile. Some people's webs have seen better days. Time, trauma, and neglect may have taken their toll. Most people dramatically restructure their web in adolescence and early adulthood, moving from the web created for them by family, schools, and hometown neighborhoods to webs of their own creation. Especially in our society, this can be a vulnerable time (and, in my view, explains much of why we see mental conditions of all kinds emerging then). Many people enter adulthood with weakened webs from childhood, as well as considerable social anxiety and limited relationship building skills; so, they are more likely to find themselves cut off and alone as they emerge from childhood.

There are many ways to be cut off from our web of relationships as adults. Isolation, regardless of cause, makes the emergence of psychosis more likely, and psychosis makes rejection and isolation more likely. Many young people with psychosis find themselves in a vicious cycle as a result. Maybe a distraught family or a loyal friend tries to hang on, often while others urge them to "set limits" and "stop enabling," but oftentimes, people with psychosis too often drift away alone.

Once people are cut off from their communities and their relationships, they tend to bounce along alone, going through the "rapids" of life, getting thrown around and bruised and battered, as though they are in a "river of suffering" flowing through lots of terrible destinations. It can lead to homelessness, drug use, poverty, incarceration, suicide, violence (both as victims and perpetrators), and even early death. It's very difficult to make it alone in our society, especially if you're experiencing psychosis.

Most connected people in our communities want to make sure this river goes nowhere near where they're living. Keep those people away from me. Not in my backyard. They may be compassionate and willing to build programs and supports for people floating in the river, as islands of respite in the river, so long as the river isn't diverted toward them; so, most programs built to help people are built within the river, isolated from any normal community relationships. State psychiatric hospitals, homeless shelters, jails and prisons, and public housing projects are all designed to support people while not providing any realistic bridge back to the community. That way we can all feel like we're doing something to help without having to actually have a relationship with any of the numerous suffering people in the river. When we see people floating by, we want to be able to call someone else to take care of them out of sight.

A problem with building programs out of sight is that eventually they run out of funds and they run out of compassion. When the economy struggles, the first thing to go is likely to be the programs for people out of sight, who are too isolated to have anyone to advocate for them. They just don't matter enough to the community because they're no longer really thought of as part of the community. It's even more tragic when compassion runs out, and it always does sooner or later. State psychiatric hospitals turned into "snake pits" with forced electroshock therapy and lobotomies, medical experimentation, and dumping bodies in unmarked graves in the back. Housing projects turned into corrupted, decayed, crime-ridden places that the police were too fearful to enter, creating generations of lost children. Jails and prisons mistreat mentally ill inmates, beating, isolating, and sometimes killing them. Creating programs, no matter how well intentioned, to help psychotic people be cared for and live isolated from their communities are, unfortunately, doomed efforts.

Instead, what we need is a bridge, so that people can return from the river of suffering back to the community. Fortunately, in many communities, that bridge exits. It may be terribly disorganized and falling down in places, but it is there. There are numerous people, like the homeless outreach staff at the Village or Long Beach's "Quality of Life Police," who are standing in the water grabbing on to people and pulling them out of the river and passing them on to many other people who help them climb back up the cliffs to rejoin our community. Although "normal" people avoid the river, there are also an amazing diversity of helpers and programs who are "abnormal in a certain special way," so their hearts go out to people we've all been taught to avoid and reject. These people include immigration workers, substance abuse sponsors, people who do prison outreach, people running transitional living programs, mental health workers, and especially an incredible number of family members refusing to give up on their loved ones. Most of these people aren't really aware of how many other people are also working on this bridge and struggle alone, too often burning out, but there are lots of us. Notice that as a person crosses this bridge, they move from drifting isolated to connecting with only a few others who reach out to them, to working on their relationships while connecting with more supportive people in largely sheltered settings, to connecting with people in the community in "natural" settings, thus rebuilding their web of support in the community.

Regardless of why the person is isolated and drifting away, the bridge from the "river of suffering" back to the community has three main stages, each with different kinds of helping relationships and relationship tasks:

- ➢ Engaging—standing in the river and pulling people out, breaking into their isolation and hopelessness;
- ➢ Rebuilding—assessing the damage, learning to connect again, healing, building skills, and practicing roles; and
- ➢ Arriving—welcoming back, developing and finding community niches, roles, and connections.

A colleague and friend of mine, Wayne Munchel, who ran our Transitional Aged Youth Academy, called these stages: Rocking In, Tuning Up, and Rolling Out—much cooler names than mine.

For people with psychosis and other extraordinary experiences, there will be some special considerations at each stage, but many of the strategies that help anyone who is isolated and lost will work for people with psychosis, too. A good deal of the "packing" we did for our journeys was about being able to have strong relationships with the people we're trying to support.

- ➢ **Engaging**

Many people who are in the river, isolated and flailing around, have tried to adapt to their isolated lives as best they can. They may be easily overwhelmed or frightened. They may be focused entirely on daily survival, or daily drugs and alcohol. They may be paranoid. They may have been in the river a long time, or even their whole lives. They may not think they have any chance of getting out of the river. They may not believe that anyone really wants them to get out of the river and return to their old life. And if they were born in the river and have always lived in it, they may not even believe there is a shore or be able to tell when they've gotten there.

If we respond by building a program in the river, we'll reinforce that we're not really interested in helping them get out. We don't want to have a "real relationship" with them. We're just with them because it's our job.

If we respond by yelling out to them from the shoreline, telling them that we'd be happy to support them if they can change and get themselves out of the river first, we'll reinforce that we don't understand what they're going through and aren't likely to be very helpful. If we tell them they have to be clean and sober or medication compliant, or remember to make their appointments, or "calm down," we're standing on the bank yelling out to them.

A helpful relationship is most likely to form if we swim out into the water with them (as many times as it takes) and offer to help them to get to shore. This means "meeting them where they're at"—whether it's offering practical charity, helping them do benefits paperwork, calling their public defender, listening to their paranoid psychosis and trying to understand what it's like to be them, just letting them sit silently next to us, or sharing lunch. Oftentimes, family and friends and peer outreach workers who have flailed in the river themselves can do this better than mental health professionals and feel more authentically helpful than professional staff who are focused on their own required paperwork and productivity. Far too often, staff are busy making a treatment plan for someone who is unengaged, instead of making an engagement plan. And if staff have never been in the river, they may not even believe there are places where you can't stand up in the river or be able to tell when someone needs help getting to shore, before they can start climbing up the banks.

> *I worked for several years on the Village's Welcoming team, with an amazing set of coworkers all dedicated to connecting to new members to the Village. Here are our guiding principles and practice that we created together at a team retreat in 2014:*
>
> *"Our team's signature gift is that we welcome people who have become outcasts and who feel misunderstood, devalued, rejected, and isolated.*
>
> *We believe that:*
>
> 1. *Each unique outcast person has overlooked, special gifts and value if the effort is made to welcome them to share their lives with us. We believe this because each of us have been outcasts and our value has been overlooked too.*
> 2. *The more challenging someone is to connect with the more rewarding that connection is likely to be when it is made for both of us—especially if it is the first time they've connected with someone.*
> 3. *Successful approaches to building relationships with people include:*

a. *Listening, above all*
   b. *Trusting our own feelings and instincts while exploring other people's worlds and sharing our worlds with them*
   c. *Approaching people with warmth, kindness, and caring—including hugs*
   d. *Being nonjudgmental, accepting, and tolerant*
   e. *Searching for truth and meaning in their unique perspectives rather than imposing our own*
4. *Healthy, healing relationships include:*
   a. *Relentless hope*
   b. *Mutual trust*
   c. *Reciprocity*
   d. *Multiple shared roles, activities, and interests*
   e. *Helping people reconnect to their families and their past to more solidly know who they are*
   f. *Becoming sources of safety and security, sometimes even becoming surrogate families*
5. *Small precious moments of connection, shared joy, mutual admiration and gratitude lead to treasuring the time spent together and each other.*
6. *These connections and relationships lead to increased self-awareness and valuation, achieving personal goals, and rebuilding lives."*

That was a special team.

➤ Rebuilding

Now, we're on the shore, but there's usually a long way to climb back up the hill to return to the community. There's usually lots of damage. There is usually a history of lots of failures and mistrust. There are usually lots of bad habits to get rid of and new ones to develop. They haven't experienced a lifetime of rejection for no reason, and they are likely to have been scared and scarred by it. We're going to fall a lot and sometimes slide all the way back into the river again, but we have to keep getting back up and working our way up the hill.

This stage tends to bring out the "Fixer" in all of us. After all, we have an abundance of tools to help people rebuild, whether we learned them in school or our own lives. The needs and goals are clearer than in engaging or arriving. Let's get to work, together.

But, if we're not paying attention to our relationships, they can undermine even the best laid plans.

It can be hard to watch someone fall while we're helping them. We may want to take responsibility for them and bring them everything they need, so they don't have to climb. We may want to protect them from falling again and again. We may lose faith in them, coming to believe they're too damaged or "ill" to make it. We may give up on them, sometimes without intending to or realizing it. They may feel guilty for being such a "burden" on us and others in their lives (a not uncommon suicide motivation).

They can become frustrated and blame us for their failings. They can resent needing help and get stuck in "angry dependency." They can remember overly fondly their time in the river, when they didn't have any responsibility or accountability, "When I didn't have to deal with any of this B.S., I was free to do whatever I wanted to do." They can feel judged and like they're being pushed to do things they don't really have to do.

We can become frustrated and blame them for their failings. We can resent that they need help, accusing them of laziness or not working as hard as we are. We can overly fondly remember their time before they drifted away in the first place and wonder when things are "going to be normal again." We can feel overburdened and like we're being pushed to do things they don't really need us to do.

If the relationship is built entirely on supporting the rebuilding process, all of this is likely to prove to be too much work. There needs to be some fun and joy, too. There needs to be some other roles besides helper and helped in the relationship. There needs to be some strengths included, some positive accomplishments to be shared and celebrated together.

> The Village had an annual Golden Duckies Award ceremony to celebrate our members' accomplishments over the past year. The duckie came from a Sesame Street video where Ernie wants to play the saxophone, but every time he tries,

the rubber duckie he's holding squeaks. An array of celebrities from the 1970s urge Ernie to "Put down the Duckie." Ernie doesn't have to give up his beloved rubber duckie forever, but if he's going to learn something new, he's going to have to give up an old way of doing things and leave his comfort zone. That video was played at our very first retreat in 1990 when we were planning the Village and became one of our enduring symbols.

For our members, the achievements honored at our red-carpet event—including getting their own apartment, managing their own money, completing a school degree, holding a job, taking care of family, living free from their drug of choice, and even graduating from the Village—almost always required a putting down of old habits to open up the possibility of these achievements.

Instead of hiding in the shadows, members invited their families to share in their accomplishments at the Golden Duckies, often with media coverage. Community partners have also been honored (including one year, the apartment managers who took a chance on renting to our members, and another year, the mayor's wife who had publicly disclosed her own struggles with mental illness to reduce stigma appeared in a show of solidarity).

Each Village team selected their "member of the year," and the award was presented to them by their primary service coordinator who told the story of their relationship and their struggles together that led to the member's inspiring accomplishments. Universally, both partners clearly cherish their relationship and agree that working together has benefited them both enormously.

Tears of joy flowed freely.

It's all hard work, too hard to do alone.

- **Arriving**

Now, we've climbed the hill. There have likely been an array of accomplishments. Maybe they've learned to use medications to improve how their mind is working for them. Maybe they've sustained sobriety. Maybe they've gotten their own apartment or completed a job training program. Maybe they've become their own payee. But their life is still largely within the supports of the system. Their relationships are mostly with other people with mental illnesses or staff or family. It may seem easier for them and us for them to stay with us, but the more they can rely on natural supports or be self-sufficient, the less they will be dependent on the vagaries of mental health funding and services. The less they are "out of sight" and disconnected from the larger community, the less vulnerable they are to us running out of compassion. People living successfully with psychosis are an incredibly powerful force against stigma. I'd rather fight stigma by having successful workers scattered around local business talking about their experiences than by giving a psychoeducational lecture about psychosis to the Kiwanis Club.

Mental health staff have to leave their offices, and families have to leave their homes and NAMI meetings, if we're going to help the people we're working with truly connect to the community. And the connections can't be out of pity or compassion if it's going to be a true part of the community's web of relationships. It must be out of valuing us and them as individuals.

If the people we serve are going to be welcomed, mental health centers can't have their entire relationship with their communities be based on protecting the community from dangerous mentally ill people, clearing out homeless people, and asking the community for money. The Village has participated in neighborhood cleanups and tree planting. We had a community garden plot. We've helped with the local arts council's open house studio tours. We've run a water stop at the Long Beach marathon and helped raise money for cancer. Even better, a Wellness Center in a poor Hispanic neighborhood of Los Angeles ran a fundraiser, so the high school students nearby could go to Washington, DC. I'm sure those students won't look at people with mental illnesses the same after that. We can help people practice contributing and being good neighbors, instead of being a burden, so they'll be able to do it on their own.

Mental health centers and families also have to do some community development to increase the likelihood of the people we support being included. One of our staff, Erin von Fempe, joined the Board of Directors of the local YMCA. We helped them when they needed a large meeting room or some of our homemade cookies, and they gave us discounted memberships that we could use to bring our members there. Our members could use the YMCA the first few times with a staff member and then on their own. Many places have people who are their natural "welcoming hearts" who can be recruited to help. A man at the local bowling alley welcomed us to play there after one of our community integration staff, Izzy, courted him. Unfortunately, It can be hard to get funding for this kind of community development work.

> Kathy, one of our best job developers, made it a point to find people who worked at the businesses she was finding jobs at who could be "natural supports" for our members. She'd look hard not just for someone who was kind but also who knew the business and its expectations and pressures and who was already a respected part of the workplace.
>
> "Hi, my name is Kathy. I am with a company called Preferred Staffing that helps individuals looking for work to match their interests with the right job ("Preferred Staffing" is the nondisclosure company name we use, so our members don't have to tell the employer and the rest of the job site they have a mental illness if they don't want to.). I've been observing your business here and figured out that you appear to be, what we call around my company, "the heart" of the operation. You seem to be concerned about others, add a positive tone to the atmosphere here, and are generally seen as an unofficial leader."
>
> "That's nice of you to say. I don't know if that's all true but I'd like to think it is."
>
> "It seems to be pretty true to me. The individual that I recommended for the job is Sally Perez. Sally starts next Tuesday. Sally badly wants to be good at her job. But she's also nervous that she'll make mistakes and worried that

she doesn't know anyone here. She's worried about feeling lonely here. Now, I know that you weren't always a veteran around here, and I'm figurin' you felt some of the same things when you started."

"Yeah, I guess the first week can be the hardest."

"I'm thinking the same thing. I was wondering if you'd reach out to Sally after she starts and kind of take her under your wing in the beginning—you know, introduce yourself, show her around and introduce her to others, check in to see how's she doing ... stuff like that."

"I can do that. When does she start?"

"Tuesday at 11 am. I'll be dropping by later in the week as part of our regular practice just to see how she's doing. I'll check in with you then just to say hi. And thanks. As I expected, it's very kind of you."

This approach aims to create "natural supports" that will evolve into mutual relationships. Notice how Kathy isn't recruiting someone who is compassionate toward people with mental illnesses trying to work. She's recruiting someone who is helpful to new employees, who may turn out later to tell her that they have a mental illness. An outside job coach providing support may be easier for the service agency to manage but stands out like a sore thumb causing the individual being supported to seem (and probably feel) very different from other workers. The support of someone already on-site who is known and respected by other employees can be a natural bridge to the new employee's social orientation and acceptance. Volunteering to stop by later in the week and check in with her is a very nice way of telling her that this is an important task she's agreed to do and that this will not be the last time the coworker will see the job developer for follow-up.

A "support group" in the clinic at this stage isn't where you come to get support. It's a place to come to figure out how to build connections and support in the community, so you don't need to come back to the group anymore. This is the stage when the staff who gets a call asking for reassurance or emotional support, instead of giving it themselves, helps the member problem solve as to who they can contact as a "natural support," so they won't need to rely on the staff anymore. We need to be prepared to say goodbye to them and help teach them to say goodbye to us. We may still be old friends for them, or we may run into them in other roles in the community, but they should have a reliable web of relationships of their own in the community by the time we say goodbye.

Before I leave community integration, I want to tell you the story of Geel, a small town in Belgium:

> *Legend tells us that back in the 6th or 7th century, a Celtic king's wife died, and he sunk into a deep depression. His advisors, unable to lift his spirits, came up with the idea that he should marry his teen-age daughter, Dymphna, because she was as beautiful as her mother, and it would be like his wife coming back to life. Strange as it may seem, the King liked this idea. More understandably to us, Dymphna didn't like this idea, and she ran away. The king's soldiers chased her and when they caught her, they had her beheaded. Over the centuries, many people prayed to Dymphna for help with their mental problems, and apparently, many miracles occurred, enough for her to be canonized as a patron saint of mental illnesses and the Church in Geel to be consecrated as a healing center in the 13th century. The Church has posted a series of rituals that need to be performed to be healed and testimonials from those who have been healed.*
>
> *Apparently, this center was popular enough to draw suffering pilgrims from far and wide (creating the same "magnet effect" that any good program does, drawing ever more people), but, unfortunately, it seems it didn't heal everyone. Soon, the "sick house" attached to the Church was filled and the town faced a problem of being inundated with homeless people with mental illnesses.*

By the 15th century, the town developed a truly unique solution to this now familiar problem—they welcomed the mentally ill pilgrims into their homes as "foster care" adults to live with them as long as they liked. These mentally ill foster adults were likely sometimes treated well and sometimes not so well, as they shared in the family's life and work, which was mostly subsistence farming. When the father in the family died, the foster adults were passed on to the next generation along with the home and land, livestock, and other belongings. This system continued throughout the centuries.

At its height, apparently almost half of all the people in Geel had mentally ill people living with them. Two things happened as a result.

One is that the people living in Geel learned to live with people with mental illnesses. Over time, their fear went away along with most stigma. They learned to relate to these people who weren't sorted by diagnoses, as people, including their peculiarities and disabilities. I sat in a restaurant in Geel where a woman was talking to herself at one table. At the next table, a family with two small children carried on, without fear or whispering, as though nothing abnormal was happening ... and in reality, nothing was.

Second, the people without mental illnesses in Geel were stigmatized by neighboring communities for living with and being tolerant of people with mental illnesses. I heard the saying, "Half the people in Geel are mentally ill, and the other half are half mentally ill." It's a common occurrence that people who live and work with people with mental illnesses are suspected of being mentally ill themselves.

This system thrived for hundreds of years, but when I visited Geel and went to an international Adult Foster Care conference there in 2000, the system was withering away. The rise in modern, biologic psychiatry and medications damaged the system in two ways:

First, the "referrals" dried up. People thought that this foster care system was old-fashioned and keeping people away from the professional, medically based care that they really needed. Mental health professionals, who in current times are far more often the point of first contact rather than a church, routinely refer people to live in professionally run group homes, institutions, nursing facilities, and hospitals, not adult foster homes. Preference is given to finding a place where their illness will get the treatment it requires, rather than a place where the person will get the home, roles, relationships, and self-identity that they need. They never have a chance to experience living in a tolerant, inclusive community anymore, since treatment takes precedence.

Second, with the advent of medications, people are less tolerant of aberrant behavior. "Why don't they just take their medications?" or "Why can't the doctor get their medications right?" become the pervasive questions. People no longer feel they should have to tolerate and accept behaviors that medications can alleviate.

Also, over time, the town of Geel has become more modernized and prosperous. It's no longer a close-knit, subsistence-farming community requiring lots of manual work. These social changes are undermining the community and family structures that for hundreds of years supported the adult foster care system in Geel.

At the arrival stage, in many ways, our community can become our client. How welcoming and inclusive is our community? Is there a strong web of relationships tying people together or a pervasive loneliness and isolation? Are there roles available for a wide diversity of people to contribute and take pride in our contributions? There's an ancient Greek saying that you can judge a civilization by how well it treats its weakest members. Perhaps it should say, you can judge how weak a civilization is by how many of its members can't find a way to be included and contribute.

I previously quoted Joseph Campbell, a deceased professor of collective mythology, as saying, "psychotics drown in the same deep waters that mystics swim gracefully in." In his most famous book, "The Hero with a Thousand Faces," he describes in depth a mythological hero's journey that almost every culture seems to have a version of: The hero finds himself in some serious trouble in his village and he's forced to leave the village, either in exile or to accomplish some seemingly impossible tasks. Either way, he finds himself wandering in the wilderness facing a variety of monsters, both internal and external. He is often helped by a wise character like an old woman or a wizard living beyond the pale. He may also be tempted by evil spirits or demons. He finds himself changing, transforming, and growing as his journey progressed. Eventually, he is able to complete the seemingly impossible task, and live through it.

Now comes a crucial point in the story: He returns home to his village, with his wisdom and accomplishments, and is welcomed back to share his transformation and what he has learned during his journey as a hero. If he isn't welcomed back, it doesn't really matter what he learns or accomplishes, he's still a wanderer or an exile. He isn't a hero. And if he isn't welcomed back, the village doesn't grow and benefit from his journey either. They are still missing one of their own.

Too often, in our current world, people are rejected in times of trouble, wander without finding wisdom or accomplishment, and are never welcomed back home as someone of value with important things to share with the rest of us who stayed home, especially if their journey has included psychotic experiences. Nonetheless, more and more often, people are sharing their journeys of recovery, and we're all growing and benefiting as a result.

A clinical tool to bring the three dimensions together

Our standard treatment forms emphasize an illness-centered approach: Chief complaint, history of present illness, and psychiatric history, mental status exam, medications, treatment goals and services are all aligned with illness-based financing, accountability, and treatment. Here is what an alternative person-centered recovery-based form that integrates all three dimensions might include:

Recovery-Based Treatment Plans Checklist

- **Relationship Engagement**

    Is the person engaged in a trusting relationship with staff?
    What are the challenges?
    What strategies are proposed to further engage them?

- **Hope**

    Are they hopeful about their future and the impact of services?
    Can they describe, in concrete, believable terms, a better future?
    How does their description compare and contrast with the staff's description?
    What strategies are proposed to build hope?

- **Goals**

    What goals do they want to pursue?
    How do those goals fit in with their growth and recovery?
    How can their goals move forward?

- **Recovery Path**

    What path(s)/actions are they willing to pursue?
    How can they be supported in those paths/actions?

- **Motivation**

    What stage of motivation are they in regarding those hopes, goals, and paths (precontemplation, contemplation, planning, action, sustaining)?

- **Level of Shared Decision-Making and Self-Responsibility**

    How do their perspectives compare and contrast with the staff's perspectives?
    What choices can they be given?

What strategies are proposed to empower them?
What stage of self-responsibility are they at?
What supports do they need at this level of self-responsibility?
What strategies are proposed to enhance their self-responsibility?

- ❏ **Community Integration**

    What community integration goals do they have?
    Do they have housing needs?
    What community services can be included?
    What community development is needed?

- ❏ **Strengths Building, Resilience, and Self-Efficacy**

    What internal and external strengths do they have?
    What protective factors can be built?
    What strategies are proposed that are strength-based?
    How can self-efficacy be enhanced?
    How can strengths-from-struggles be built?

- ❏ **Flow and Graduation**

    How are they dependent on staff/family directly providing support?
    What strategies are proposed to reduce that dependence, either with increased independence or community supports?
    What is the next lower level of service, or out of services, they can graduate to?
    What is the plan for flow and graduation?
    How will changes in staff/family relationships be supported?

One last time, let's return to Omar, from the beginning of Chapter 3. Notice how I was working within the illness-centered model. I made the assumption that he had a psychotic illness that had appeared without cause in his late teens and that he was doomed to suffer with it forever, at best repressing it with medications. I never learned anything about his self-identity or relationship factors to make sense of his experiences and understand what journey he was on. As a result, I didn't do anything to help him with his self-identity or relationships, even though both were badly damaged by the time I met him, and, as a result, he didn't really have a chance to recover. Look at the enormous difference between the "effective" treatment I gave him—basically take your meds, accept disability, and reduce stress—and the recovery-based treatment plan I just described.

Bottom line: I'm rebelling against the sheer laziness and neglect of our standard approach. We need treatment relationships, individualized formulations, and three-dimensional biopsychosocial recovery plans.

Closing story

My closing story for this chapter is one of my favorite people, Gail, who I introduced you to at the beginning of the book when we were talking to our state legislature together and they didn't believe she had schizophrenia. Her story is very complex, and not always positive, as she journeyed to recovery. Before I started writing this story, I called her—she's 70 years old now—to ask if she wanted me to use her real name or a pseudonym. It took her a while to remember who I am. We hadn't seen each other for years, and to be fair, I probably played a much smaller role in her recovery than she played in my growth as a psychiatrist. She doesn't share her story anymore to try to help others, but she still wanted me to use her real name.

> *Gail's parents met and fell in love at a military party. Her father was a successful soldier who looked good in his uniform. Gail was the youngest of four children. She was born 2 months premature and remembers always being sickly as a child. Since she needed more care than her siblings, sometimes she ended up living with her aunt, instead of her family, when they moved around a lot. When she was about 10 years old, she was put in a Catholic boarding school. She learned to be strong and self-reliant and private and to handle whatever came her way, including dyslexia and seizures.*
>
> *When she was 12 years old, she started hearing God talking to her. She's still not sure it really wasn't God. She was able to keep to herself the voice she was hearing for almost 2 years, until He told her to jump out of a two-story window, which she did. Surprisingly, she wasn't hurt, but she was sent to the first of a series of psychiatric hospitals, including Napa State Hospital, where she was usually the youngest one, but young patients weren't necessarily separated from older ones. This was the "snake pit" era with over 50,000 people crowded into California's state hospitals. Psychiatric medications hadn't even been invented yet.*

Her mother died when Gail was in her mid-20s, and Gail blamed God. She also gave up on her life. She ended up at Camarillo State Hospital. Gail responded somewhat to the new medications. Even though God wasn't talking to her anymore, she did hear a lot of other voices, mostly derogatory and belittling her. They made it hard for her to focus on what other people were saying to her. They also warned her that the staff and the patients were out to get her. She got more and more paranoid.

Unbelievably as it sounds today, one day the hospital staff, just for fun, voted on which patient was the least likely to ever be discharged from the hospital, and it was Gail. At that point, she'd lost about a year of her life, almost mute, not remembering hardly anything that happened. She figured she'd better fight for her life or she really wasn't ever going to get out. She says that her recovery began with one lowly staff "who just talked with me" and "a cooking group at the hospital."

It took a couple years, very high dosages of Prolixin, one of the original phenothiazine "major tranquilizers," and the new deinstitutionalization movement for her to be transferred to "community care" at a locked nursing facility in West Los Angeles. Gail learned to hide her symptoms, follow orders, and always pretend she was fine, to get more and more privileges until after a couple more years, they discharged her to a Board and Care.

She wasn't going to waste her second chance at life. She kept her appointments with her psychiatrist and her case manager and stayed on her medications. She learned how to function even with the voices. She'd sit in the back of buses, so she could see everyone come in. She gave herself enough time to get off the bus if she got scared and take the next bus without being late. She never rode at 3 pm when the high school students got off school and crowded the bus. She bought a Sony Walkman to drown out the voices.

She enrolled at Santa Monica Community college and worked hard to get an AA degree after 4 years, while maintaining her own apartment on Social Security disability. She faced each challenge as it came, never giving up.

In the mid-80s, she moved to Long Beach where rents were lower. Her new case manager recommended that she go to the Social Center to meet people and keep busy. The Social Center was one of MHALA's first projects. MHALA had noticed that many people with serious mental illnesses, especially those living in Board and Cares, had almost nothing to do during the day, nothing to look forward to, and nothing to do for fun. The treatment system focused on their symptoms, their medications, and disabilities, rather than their strengths and joys. Their lives focused on cigarettes and coffee. MHALA got volunteers, originally described as "blue-haired old ladies," to go for a couple hours a week to a Board and Care to run a "club"—usually sewing or art projects. This proved to be so popular that the number of clubs expanded throughout the county, and the members themselves, the people with mental illnesses who were thought of as disabled and incapable, began running their own clubs and organizing their own events and outings. The Social Center became the hub for the Long Beach clubs.

Gail walked in that first day with an attitude. She didn't need any help from anybody. She was tough and could manage her own life. She had her degree and apartment keys to prove it. She was wearing army fatigues and big boots, and she kicked the door open announcing her entry. Joanie, the director, was sitting on one of the sunken couches talking casually to the members who had dropped in. She looked up at this new, glaring person and totally disarmed her by smiling broadly, and welcoming her with a cup of coffee, without making any demands of her. When Gail decided it was time to leave, Joanie invited her back and offered her a hug. It was the first hug Gail had been offered in years. Joanie was the best hugger I've ever met. She hugged slowly and deeply, making you feel warm and cared about and safe and comforted. For many years, we said that Joanie's hugs were our most important tool in creating an environment where broken and untrusting people could feel safe enough to be vulnerable enough to heal and regrow.

Joanie became Gail's new inspiration and source of hope. Gail became one of her most solid volunteers. She began by getting snacks for groups and worked her way up to meal planning and cooking for the Project Return camping trips. When Gail told her that she got depressed every Christmas time, thinking about her dead mother, often ending up back in the hospital, Joannie put her in charge of the holiday meal for the homeless people MHALA had at their storefront Homeless Assistance Program. That was her best Christmas in years.

She also was part of creating an improv acting group, the Project Return Players, who helped fight stigma with their acting, bringing mental illness and its challenges to life for audiences. They even got to be bit players in a small movie Walt Disney's grandson made about how difficult it is to help homeless people in Skid Row, decades before homelessness became a popular subject. Gail's character expressed her trauma and frustrations by yelling at the food kitchen staff, instead of being grateful.

When MHALA was working on the proposal for the Village program, they took the very progressive approach of including people with mental illnesses in their planning process and their advisory board. The consumer movement had been urging "nothing about us without us," but most agencies didn't trust them enough to include them. MHALA did, and they brought unique and valuable perspectives and inputs. Consumers are far more likely to identify personal caring and even hugs as essential services than professionals are. Even with her diagnosis of schizophrenia and ongoing voices, Gail was put on the MHALA board. The first time I met her was at a 2-day retreat that brought together all the new staff and showed us the Duckie video to inspire us to put down old ways of doing things, including overprotecting people, in order to create the new mental health program they'd envisioned. I'd never sat in a meeting with a person with schizophrenia as my colleague, instead of my patient. I'd never sat in a meeting where her opinion was valued as much as mine. I'd never been asked to work alongside coworkers with mental illnesses before. This really was going to be a different program.

Gail was also one of the first members of the Village, and I was her psychiatrist. She was still taking very high-dose Prolixin and still hearing voices almost all the time, but she was functioning anyway.

"I read that there's a new medication, Clozaril, for schizophrenia that works better than the old ones. Can I try it?" It was really more of a demand than a request.

"To tell you the truth, I've never used it before. I have heard that it's a more powerful medication, but I've also heard it can be deadly, and you need to take weekly blood tests to be on it."

"I can do that."

"Would you like to learn about it together to see if it might help you?"

She gave me a surprised look and after a brief hesitation said, "Sure."

Together we read the material the FDA released about Clozaril. We learned about the drug monitoring system that makes sure you don't stop making white blood cells and get infected without any defenses. We watched the tapes the drug company created with vignettes about people who were taking Clozaril. (That was back when I still trusted drug companies to give out accurate information. It was before Eli Lily intentionally hid the diabetes side effect of Zyprexa while trying to get us to prescribe as much as possible and as fast as possible. They paid millions in fines when they were caught, but they'd already made billions.) We talked together to an old colleague of mine who does psychiatric research who said that he wouldn't give it to her because it might increase her seizures and that if we waited another year, Risperdal was going to be released and she could try that instead.

"So, we've both learned that about a third of people who don't respond to other meds respond to Clozaril. We've also learned it has a lot of side effects in addition to the potential of making you stop producing white blood cells, including seizures. If it were me, I'd likely take my friend's advice and wait, but I'm not leading your life. I don't know how terrible it is for you to be hearing voices. You seem to be functioning well to me. I also don't know how frightening it would be for you to have a seizure. It's reasonable to either take it or not. I'll help you either way. What do you want to do?"

When Gail used to tell this story, this was her favorite part because she knew she really had the power to choose her own treatment and her own priorities. That had never happened to her with a psychiatrist before.

She chose to try the Clozaril. We began slowly, and within a few days at our starting dosage of 50 mg, the voices went away for the first time since she was a teenager. Since the "therapeutic" dosage is usually about 300–450 mg, I kept increasing her dosage producing lots of side effects along the way. Eventually, I decreased the dosage back down to 50 mg, which worked fine and the side effects went away again. She only had one seizure, when she was in a car accident. By the way, she eventually did try Risperdal, but it didn't work. The voices came back. When Seroquel came out, it did work, and she got off the Clozaril.

The point isn't that it turned out she was right, and I was wrong. The point is that an empowering prescriber gives real information and real choices and shares decision-

making, so people learn to use medications, instead of just taking them. Gail wasn't the kind of person who could be forced to do anything, but she was absolutely the kind of person who would fight for her own recovery, if given the opportunity.

She was able to function better without the voices, and she began working regularly at the Homeless Assistance Program as an outreach worker, riding her bicycle to all the local parks finding homeless people and bringing them in to see me. (Remember Ryan earlier in this chapter who she found hugging a tree in a blackout and who used Christ to forgive his mother and relieve his voices?) She also signed up at Long Beach City College to take culinary classes to learn to be a real chef and baker.

She was working with Manny, a very large man who was developmentally disabled and had a short temper. His family couldn't handle him, so Gail was helping him mange his money. One day, an argument about money got out of control and he got mad and shoved her. She lost her balance and fell backward, putting out her arm to break her fall. Her arm broke in two places as she hit the wall. Her arm never really healed, and as a result, it was too weak to lift pots and pans, and she had to give up on her dream of professional cooking.

Soon after that happened, Gail got me my first speaking job. Dr. Steve Goldfinger, who was for many years active in mentoring young psychiatrists, put together a daylong training to encourage them to work with homeless people. Gail was part of a panel of people who had been homeless, sharing their perspectives and insights. She told them that she thought I would be a good role model for their panel of psychiatrists working with homeless people. We went up to the training in San Francisco along with my wife and two small children. We were also invited to go to Napa State Hospital to talk about the Village and the recovery model, so we all drove up there the day before our conference training. It was interesting to see the hospital through her eyes as an ex-patient, instead of through my eyes as a psychiatrist. I saw the therapeutic aspects and the treatment teams and their clinical challenges. She saw the barbed wire and the guard towers and saw the patients as prisoners.

If you've been tracking Gail's story as it's moved between the three dimensions—her self-identity, as she built hope and empowerment and self-responsibility and meaningful roles, her improved experience of reality, as her medications were improved taking away her voices, and her growing relationships from isolation and kicking in doors to helping so many people and having so much fun doing it—check out her multiple relationships with me at this point in our lives: I'm her psychiatrist prescribing medications. I'm her coworker at the Homeless Assistance Program. We're fellow speakers at the state hospital and psychiatric convention where she got me the job. She's riding in a car with my wife and family exposing my young children to what recovery with schizophrenia looks like. And I'm cutting her food at dinner since she still has a big cast on her right arm and can't do it herself.

Traditional programs and professional ethics forbid "multiple roles" or "lowering professional boundaries." They're concerned that the patient will get confused and might think we're really their friends and not just paid professionals. They're concerned that their psychodynamic treatment might be impaired if their "transference reaction" to us is contaminated—in normal language, their fantasies and imaginations about us based on their childhood experiences and illnesses might be interfered with by so much "real relationship," so they won't be able to actively experience their regressed fantasies as much—which isn't a useful technique for most people anyway and can be quite harmful for people with psychosis. Also, they're concerned that without strong "boundaries," I won't be able to stay safe and ethical.

By ignoring those prohibitions (but not my ethics or safety) and creating multiple relationships, I'm actively encouraging her to be more than a mentally ill patient. Her relationships are actively growing, so she'll be able to connect to more and more people in the community in more and more productive ways.

With her chef career gone, after Joanie retired, Gail got a promotion to be the director of the Social Center, which had become an entirely consumer-run program by then, Project Return: The Next Step. She no longer needed the intensive supportive services of the Village, and she became one of our first two graduates. As a full staff, she got Kaiser insurance. She told me she was training her new young psychiatrist to act like me and give her choices and help her direct her own treatment. That was also when the scene I described at the very beginning of the book occurred where we were lobbying together in Sacramento.

She met her wife working for Project Return. Gail says it was love at first sight. They invited me to their informal wedding. Some years later when homosexual weddings became legal, they were legally married. They bought a condo of their own. Gail became noticeably less aggressive. She got rid of her Samurai sword collection and her guns at her wife's request. She even changed from being a Republican to a "conservative Democrat." The two of them adopted two troubled kids, a 14-year-old boy and a 9-year-old girl.

All was not roses. Gail's physical health deteriorated badly. She's had several strokes, chronic bronchitis, progressive blindness in her eyes, and the last time I saw her, about 10 years ago, was at her retirement party where she was basically wheelchair bound. I never really figured out what was wrong with her physically or whether her smoking or her psychiatric medications had an impact on her physical health. She moved with her wife to be near her wife's family in Minneapolis.

I reached her on the phone in Minneapolis. Her physical condition is terrible: She's had both legs amputated, she has painful lower spinal fractures treated with an indwelling pain pump, she's legally blind, and she has a urinary catheter. She couldn't get along with her brother-in-law, so she's now in a nursing home. She's waiting to get a motorized wheelchair but manages to get around on her own anyway. I was surprised, though maybe I shouldn't have been, that none of this was really getting her down. She was adapting and getting along as best she could, like she always had.

What was getting her down was that her wife had died of liver disease 3 years earlier. Gail thinks about her every day and misses her terribly. She even started smoking cigarettes again. She was the one real love of her life. Gail told me that for about a year after her wife died, she wanted to die to join her, too, but wouldn't ever commit the sin of killing herself. She'll have to wait to join her wife. At the time, she was also very angry at God for taking her wife from her, but she was more accepting now and has even returned to church.

"How has your voices and mental illness been?"

"It really hasn't been a part of my life. I take very low milligrams of medications and it hasn't bothered me in years."

"What are you most proud of?"

"My kids. They're both doing really good and come to see me. I'm a grandmother now, and another grandchild is on the way."

"Do you have any advice you want me to share with people reading your story in my book?"

"Never give up. Keep going no matter what happens."

Chapter 16

Practical travel tips— Facing today's challenges

In 2000, my family embarked on the most ambitious trip of our lives. I found a friend to take my job for 4 1/2 months. My wife, Terry, and I took our 12- and 13-year-old sons out of school for a semester, and we went to over 20 countries in Europe, Asia, and Africa. My main goal was to help my kids broaden their view of the world and themselves. To create some personal contacts and a little funding for the trip, I arranged visits with psychiatrists and rehabilitation programs in 12 different countries. (Thanks to Dr. Liberman at UCLA for many of the contacts who had translated and were using his skill training modules around the world.) I generally gave my four stages presentation (after a while, the kids could do annoying parodies of my stories), and we often had interesting personal visits with our hosts. I don't think we'll ever forget eating shawarmas at the house of the first Jordanian psychiatrist, celebrating May Day with a picnic at an Italian villa converted into a psychiatric rehabilitation program, visiting windmills and talking about drug policies with a Dutch psychiatrist, or a banquet complete with dress kimonos, taiko drums, and folk dancing in Japan.

I am familiar with the historical progression of American psychiatry from the moral treatment era in the 1800s, to the Victorian, mental hygiene institutions of the early 1900s, to the medical treatment, protective asylums in the mid-1900s, to our present, highly conflictual, civil rights, deinstitutionalization era. Like most ethnocentric Americans, I tried to put other countries into a framework of "developing" along the same lines, but somewhere behind us. Particularly seductive was the analogy between present-day Japan, with its focus on social order and appearances, modernization, hiding underlying social ills and relying on massive institutionalization, and our Victorian era.

I had two problems with this approach: First, some countries are in places America has never been. For instance, Jordan has a combination of an extremely strong family culture and a government-funded modern medical model psychiatric treatment system. In America, our families were already deteriorating as psychiatric medications were being developed; so, we never had both at once. In Italy, there is a very strong psychoanalytic training and practice within their psychiatric system, including their rehabilitation programs, whereas in America, psychoanalysis was well into decline as rehabilitation emerged and there is virtually no overlap in training or practice between the two.

Second, many of the special things I saw were never part of American mainstream development. These included the Maori influence in New Zealand, family foster care in Geel, Belgium, a mosque-based community center and mental health treatment in Cairo, the Netherlands's decriminalization approach to substance abuse that we're now increasingly adopting in America, and a residential vocational training program in Japan. I began to try to organize my experiences by common issues, rather than by stages of American development.

My list of "common issues" from the trip included family support and burden, treatment and medication availability, especially in the community, institutionalization and abuses, basic life supports and homelessness, fear of violence, shame and stigma, substance abuse, legal responsibilities and criminalization, and rehabilitation.

What I found was that although there may be general principles and values that cut across various countries and settings, what is actually possible is highly variable. Many of the programs I saw not only were highly adapted to their particular circumstances but also dependent on the distinct qualities of their leaders. In India, I saw a sophisticated community-based empowerment, recovery program being run by a young psychiatrist in the basement of his parents' retirement apartment building with a combination of professional staff, trainees, consumer staff, and volunteers. In rural Egypt, I saw a small private psychiatric hospital attempting to integrate itself into the local village by including farming activities, teaching local children, community volunteers, and even giving small business loans to the villagers. This program was led by an Egyptian psychiatrist from a prominent family in his mosque. In Malaysia, where family stigma and shame, mental health laws, and a reliance on long-term hospital institutions make rehabilitation and return to the community almost impossible, they were making wicker furniture in a self-help ward in the hospital and in an embattled transitional apartment program outside the hospital walls. In New Zealand, there was a "new marae" community center that was built from scraps of discarded lumber by a group of troubled adolescent Maoris, so they would have a place to belong and be accepted since many had become detached from their home "marae" when they moved to the city.

The one universal I am sure about is the quality of my hosts. They were all doing incredible work in very difficult situations. I may not really understand what they go through, but I can feel their heart and souls, and I was truly inspired by them. I am very honored to be their colleague and only wish that they could've had the same opportunities I had to be inspired by each other.

This is the part of a guidebook where they usually put the practical tips: how to get a visa or a hotel room or change money or a train pass, or specialized advice for handicapped or gay and lesbian travelers, or a calendar of special events and holidays, or how to stay safe. Each book has very specific information that needs to be regularly updated.

I can't do that in this book. I hope I've shown you by now how journeys with psychosis depend more on the people and community and culture and laws and resources more than they depend on the symptoms or diagnosis. The same person can have a very different journey in different places or times or by making different choices. There is no specific set of information that applies to everyone.

Almost every story that I've told you occurred in Long Beach, either at the Village or one or MHALA's other programs or at CSULB, and they occurred in the 40 years between about 1980 and 2020. Even within that period of time, things have changed: We had a recession that made it impossible to find any jobs but kept apartment prices down. We had an economic recovery that made housing amazingly unaffordable. We have new programs in California from the Mental Health Services Act, a tax on millionaires that doesn't exist in any other state. AB109 moved thousands of people out of our prisons into our communities. We've had Obamacare expanding Medi-Cal and Trump's presidency increasing divisiveness. MHALA has moved on in new directions detaching from my era, but life goes on. There are new programs and new leadership always emerging somewhere.

You are living somewhere and sometime that is unique to you. The practical details of your journey are unique to you. The most I can do here is to share my practical perspectives on some of the common issues you're likely to face along the way. I can't tell you what to do where you are.

Here's a list of the common issues I've included in this chapter:

- ➢ Families
- ➢ Medications and psychiatrists
- ➢ Psychiatric hospitals
- ➢ Finances—poverty, Social Security, and homelessness
- ➢ Violence

- Suicide
- Physical health, medical illnesses, and early death
- Education and work

That ought to cover most of your hopes and fears.

Families

Every family is a unique web of relationships embedded in a particular family background and heritage. These relationships profoundly impact all of us in a myriad of ways.

Standard family therapy theory includes the idea of "triangulation"—parents take out their conflicts and problems on their children. Sometimes, they also include the idea of "reverse triangulation"—the child creates problems and the parents take it out on each other. (If you haven't had kids yourself, you're more likely to connect to the triangulation idea, and if you have had kids yourself, you're more likely to connect to the reverse triangulation idea.) Adding in siblings (or extended family members) creates even more complexity and possibilities. There is even the concept that an entire "family system" is "sick" but only one person is the "identified patient" carrying the secrets and pathology for the entire family.

Historically, psychiatry has spent a great deal of time working in both directions: "How are parents and other family members causing or exacerbating psychosis?" and "How are families responding to the burden of caretaking someone with psychosis?" Either or both may be relevant in any given family. Some families fight bitterly over assigning blame, guilt, and shame, creating enormous suffering. Medication usage and other services can also be drawn into these conflicts.

Here are a few prominent examples of approaches to reduce family conflict and damage:

- R. D. Laing, an extremely influential and controversial psychiatrist, spent a great deal of time analyzing communication patterns in families with people with schizophrenia, uncovering pervasive "double-bind communications" fed by underlying family secrets and hypocrisies that he believed led to their schizophrenia as they attempted to respond to these self-contradictory communications. While his claims that psychosis is a rational response to an irrational world and that "schizophrenogenic" mothers cause schizophrenia have been largely discounted, there remain some efforts to teach families clearer, more direct communications. Theoretically, better communications could lead to less conflict and distress, clearer relationships, and an easier time forming and sustaining a self-identity, without the need to emphasize blame. Nonviolent communication is a current example of a communication skill.

➤ High vs. low "expressed emotions" is another family-directed "psychoeducational" approach that enjoyed some popularity and research documentation of effectiveness, although it's less common today. This approach asserted that the higher the expressed emotions in a family—especially hostility, blame, and disapproval—the more the person with psychosis will feel stressed and overwhelmed, and defend themselves with more withdrawal and/or anger of their own. If, instead, the family has low expressed emotions—including more acceptance and approval—the person with psychosis will be less overstressed and less defensive.

➤ "Family burden" theory describes how having a family member with psychosis usually exerts a large "caretaking burden," of a variety of kinds, including financial and emotional loss of time and attention, fear of violence, guilt and shame on the entire family, often with lifelong implications. (I once was sitting in a lecture about family burden next to a person with serious mental illness who started crying and said to me, "I knew I'd been hard on my family. I didn't know you all actually researched all the ways I've been a burden and quantify how burdensome I am." Keep in mind that feeling like a burden to others is sometimes a powerful rationale for suicide to relieve the loved one's burden, even though suicide actually increases their burden and guilt.) Historically, families were not expected to bear this burden and could "put family members away," but that's rarely an alternative now—leaving jailing and homelessness the more common consequences of avoiding burden. The vast majority of the "burden" of deinstitutionalization has fallen on families. There may, or may not, be ways in which your local mental health system can relieve or share these burdens. The roots of NAMI, and still a crucial function, is to provide family support and understanding and a place to share thoughts and strategies about family burden. Burden affects everyone in the family, usually both directly and indirectly, including, for example, lost opportunities for siblings due to the oversized needs of the family member with psychosis. (I think we could learn something from AA's concept that alcoholism is a family illness impacting everyone in the family; so, they have specialized services in Alanon, Adult Children of Alcoholics, and Alateen groups.)

Families vary in how empowered they feel in general, which can have an impact on how they respond to a family member with psychosis.

Some families are so fragmented, beaten down, impoverished, and/or hopeless in their overall lives that someone with psychosis can become just another burden to silently bear, on the one hand, or someone whose needs can't be afforded or met and they need to leave, on the other hand. Sometimes, Social Security disability checks may be a substantial resource for the family, which may make the person more valuable and/or create more conflicts and unhealthy incentives.

Some families are used to being able to handle any challenges that come their way and aggressively seek out treatment knowledge and resources to help their family member. They're likely to try to push through the limitations of our psychiatric treatments, trying every possible medication and treatment program, and breathlessly following research and pharmaceutical advances looking for something better for their family member. They may minimize the risks involved, they're so desperate and certain positive results are essential and possible. They're also likely to try to push through the person's resistances to diagnoses and treatments, pushing for conservatorships and involuntary treatment programs, including institutions. They may find themselves very frustrated with both the limitations of our treatments and the lack of availability and funding of services that could potentially help their family member, if only they could find them.

These families are more likely to view acceptance as helplessness and failure than their more impoverished counterparts. Their drive can sometimes be incredibly helpful, and sometimes it can tear apart families.

Try to be aware of how much caretaking and treatment expectations and efforts may be adding to the communication difficulties, the expressed emotions, and the family burden, on top of what the condition itself is leading to. For example, becoming someone's payee may sound like a good idea, to protect them from financial irresponsibility or drug use, but it may create severe conflicts and resentments, while also making it harder for them to develop true responsibility.

I think many families focus almost exclusively on medications. This is understandable since all of the information they're likely to find, whether from their family member's psychiatrist or NAMI literature or public information or drug advertisements is likely to overemphasize medications and the "experiencing reality" dimension of their problems. I believe that many families are overlooking major opportunities in the other two dimensions—self-identity and relationships—which were likely more in focus before the diagnosis of a mental illness.

> Several years ago, I received an e-mail from a mother, telling me that her adult son with schizophrenia was returning from Japan. He'd gone there to get a medication only available there, but it hadn't worked; so, he was returning to California. He wasn't sure where he wanted to live. She had read something I wrote and wanted a recommendation of where he could find a psychiatrist here who would help him get cutting-edge medications. I told her that although medications are important, he should decide where to live, not based on psychiatrists but on where he could make a home for himself and where he could visualize a hopeful future. "Recovery is built upon hope and home." She wrote back thanking me for my advice, saying that I'd helped her realize she'd gotten too narrowly focused on medications and wasn't considering what else her son needed to rebuild his life.

Traditionally, people developed their identity and relationships entirely within the expectations and experiences of their families. They were likely to stay within the same community, learning their jobs and other roles by observing their parents and other family members. They practiced the same religion as their parents. They married people either chosen by their parents or at least approved of by them and sharing their culture. They raised children within their extended families in the ways they were raised, perpetuating their traditions.

In our current American society, it's more likely that people will try to form their own identities, especially as they move through adolescence. They try to find their own internal passions and gifts and purpose. They learn skills at school and work separate from their parents. They partner and marry for love. They try to develop their own personal spirituality and their own child-rearing methods.

An advantage of our current society is that it is far less repressive and far more empowering. It's more likely to lead to a diversity of personal expression and adaptability in the face of social change. A disadvantage is that the vast majority of parents have only a limited ability to accept their children diverting from their expectations and imaginations. The emerging adults often find themselves torn in two, growing in certain ways around their friends and staying with their childhood behaviors, feelings, and expectations around their parents. This tearing apart can be a very painful and difficult process for both parents and children and often weakens extended families and cultures.

This tearing apart of self-identity in late teens and early 20s is likely one of the reasons that psychosis emerges at that point in life, especially in our society. It can also complicate rebuilding and recovery efforts.

Families generally have serious problems adapting their expectations to the realities of the emerging psychotic experiences their family member is going through and the uncertainty that brings for their future roles. It may feel as though their dreams for their child are being shattered just as they were emerging. They feel compelled to help their child conquer this illness to get them back again, regardless of the cost. Psychosis wasn't part of the plan.

At the ages that many people would be using their peer group, friends, students, coworkers, and especially romantic partners to test out and develop their emerging identity, psychotic experiences can isolate them from their peers, leaving them with only their family and its broken dreams and mental health staff who tend to pathologize all their feelings. Instead of exploring their emerging feelings and talents, they are usually being socialized into their new identity as a chronic mentally ill patient.

It's not that their "normal" developmental feelings are gone. They're just likely to be ignored, replaced by concerns about mental health. For example, I recently read a *New Yorker* article, "The Challenge of Going Off Psychiatric Drugs," about a Harvard student who tried to kill herself in her freshman year, which launched her mental health career with multiple diagnoses and multiple medications. It was only when she got herself off medications 14 years later that she realized she'd had all of her sexual feelings blocked by medications all that time and lost all those years of normal sexual feelings and experiences, both good and bad. While she, and everyone around her, were focused on battling her mental illness, her development had been stunted.

In my view, families should place a higher priority on helping their impacted family member avoid becoming developmentally stunted. They should try to keep as many growth and exploration experiences available while trying to sustain some peer influence. It may seem bad to be around peers with mental illnesses, but the crucial consideration is to determine if these "peers" are older, disabled, chronically mentally ill people who have given up on other roles and identities besides "chronic mental patient," or if they are other young people who can still relate to each other in a range of roles, including friends, students, coworkers, and especially romantic partners. Like it or not, most psychotic experiences are powerful enough to impact identities forever, even if the "symptoms" resolve. Help them develop an emerging adult self-identity that includes their psychotic experiences.

In the same way that families everywhere struggle to accept emerging identities far from their expectations and imaginations, most families struggle to accept and actively promote emerging identities that include psychotic experiences. Families usually view them as having an "ill self" and their "real self," maintaining the hope that their illness can be cured and then their real self will reemerge, while most recovery integrates the psychotic experiences, rather than excising them.

Families naturally assume that the only identities that include the psychotic experiences are impaired, ill, burdensome, and unable to achieve adult roles. Virtually all traditional cultures have that expectation, and our current medical culture is usually no better. Nonetheless, recovery is a reality. Meeting people living successfully with psychosis will help expand your expectations and imaginations. Then, families won't be pressuring them to stop being ill and functioning normally as much. Instead, they'll be pressuring them to take more responsibility for growing with their experiences. Adaptation will still be hard for both families and the impacted person since this isn't the life journey any of you expected or imagined.

"Overprotection" and risk aversion are enemies of exploration, growth, and development.

"Normally" in our society, families, especially mothers, are the primary voice for protection and risk aversion. "Normal" mothers are supposed to remind their children to wear a jacket when it's cold. "Normal" fathers are supposed to be wary of their daughter's dates. Both spend a lot of effort making sure their kids are ready before they give them the car keys … or a credit card. However, psychosis magnifies every risk and makes every misstep potentially more tragic. Parents' natural tendencies to protect tend to be magnified. "We don't want them to get sick again or have to go to the hospital again."

"Normally" other adults, like teachers and coaches and job supervisors, mentor young people to take risks and grow, to develop their potential and move beyond their families. However, the adults a young person with mental illness is surrounded by and influenced by tend to be mental health staff who are likely to be caretaking and risk aversive, too. They're likely to promote stability, instead of growth, and safety, instead of opportunity.

"Normally" friends actively encourage risk taking, experimentation, and growth, often alarmingly so. Parents find themselves in the uncomfortable position of looking around their child's peer group, desperately trying to find someone with some "common sense" to watch out for their child. Too often, people with mental illnesses lose all their friends and have no peer group outside the mental health system.

As a result, counterintuitively, families of people with psychosis have to take on more promotion of growth-directed risks for their children than "normal" parents naturally do, while looking for growth promoting other adults and peers to positively influence their children.

Started in 1979 by two mothers of sons with schizophrenia, NAMI, the National Alliance on Mental Illness, is an impressive grassroots organization of over 1,000 self-help, psychoeducational groups, predominantly led by family members of people with serious mental illnesses. NAMI provides support to families as a supplement, or even an alternative, to mental health professionals who too often exclude, undervalue, ignore, or even blame family members for their family's mental illness. NAMI groups have largely embraced the "medical model" as a hopeful, evidence-based, non-blaming approach to help their family members and support each other. Largely funded by pharmaceutical companies, they run lots of local programs and are a powerful national advocacy organization. NAMI is actively evolving, including more people with mental illnesses and more recovery-based approaches and programming.

I've seen a number of NAMI groups, but my favorite has been the group in Davis, California. I was there giving a speech for their annual awards ceremony, celebrating the accomplishments of their impacted family members and their supporting family members. This group functioned like a PTA for its local mental health center. Instead of focusing on assisting the professionals in their tasks, they actively volunteered in roles they excelled at and the staff didn't have time for or consider it part of their jobs. They ran a bicycle club and an art group, led camping outings, and taught job interview skills. The parents in longstanding leadership roles, contrary to my usual experiences at NAMI, weren't the ones with the most impaired children, often on conservatorships or in institutions, who initiated new members into the depths of suffering and burden they're likely to face. Instead, the parents in longstanding leadership roles in this group, mostly UC Davis professors or staff, were the ones with children who were doing well, who had returned to school or work, who actively participated in the clubs and groups, and who were positive role models and peers for newcomers.

Medications and psychiatrists

I think medications can be an important, positive tool to promote recovery with psychosis for many people. They have an unparalleled ability to assist with:

- making experiences more in line with sensory input and shared reality,
- decreasing hallucinations, delusions, and paranoia,
- making thinking more organized, rational, and easier to consciously control,
- improving anxiety and sleep, and
- improving basic daily functions like grooming, dressing, and eating regularly.

Unlike for many medications, the responses to psychiatric medications are highly variable and individual. The target dosage has a sizeable range not easily determined by a person's height and weight. Because of variability in the porousness of our blood-brain barriers that keep most substances out of our brains, there is a high variation in correlation between blood levels of medications and brain levels, except for lithium that travels relatively easily through membranes. Once a substance is in our brains, it seems like different people respond differently anyway. There are even genetically based cultural differences in medication responses.

What all this means is that everyone is likely to need a significant amount of personal trial-and-error to find the best medication and the best dosage for them. Think, for example, about how difficult it is to know how much alcohol someone who has never drank should drink to get pleasantly buzzed but not out of control drunk, black out, or have a hangover the next morning. We all had to learn our own "dosage curve" by drinking and, for better or worse, experiencing the consequences. Carefully dosing psychiatric medications is just as important as carefully dosing alcohol.

I described in the previous chapter a person-centered approach to prescribing. Unfortunately, you are more likely to encounter profoundly limited psychiatric accessibility than shared decision-making. Given that more and more psychiatric medications are being prescribed with less and less stigma, most psychiatrists have been converted into prescription machines, doing 15- or 20-minute medication refill visits every couple months or so, seeing hundreds of patients, most of whom they don't remember or have any personal connection with. Many psychiatrists have rebelled against this job description, including me, and currently over half of psychiatrists don't accept any insurance, public or private, because of the billing requirements and limitations. In the public sector, you're likely to see different psychiatrists as they cycle through. If you're in one of the 50% of counties in America, mostly rural, that have no psychiatrists at all, you're likely to use telepsychiatry, talking to a psychiatrist through video equipment who is living somewhere else. A good provider seen virtually is likely better than a poor provider in person.

Many places have started using Mental Health Nurse Practitioners to prescribe since there is such a shortage of psychiatrists and since they're cheaper; so, let me spend a moment describing nurse practitioners (NPs) to you. When the shortage of psychiatrists started looking worse and worse, there emerged the thought that experienced mental health nurses, who were doing lots of the daily treatment work in hospitals and clinics and knew a lot about medications, could be given a couple years of specialized training, and then, they could prescribe under a psychiatrist's supervision, extending our capacity. This has proven very popular, but there aren't that many experienced mental health nurses; so, they started training less experienced nurses, and even creating accelerated RN–MHNP combined programs to graduate more and more providers. It became more and more difficult to get psychiatrists to provide oversight and supervision for all of them. (Many psychiatrists are antagonistic, feeling that NPs are undermining them, and that if someone wants to prescribe medications, they should go to medical school.) Gradually, the training and supervision requirements have been relaxed, so now there are more inexperienced, minimally trained, unsupervised NPs. This is unfortunate, since there are many quite good, experienced, well-trained NPs out there, some of whom I prefer to most of my psychiatrist colleagues. If you're seeing an NP, check on their experience, training, and supervision. By the way, even though there has been an increase in medical schools and the creation of more and more doctors overall, the number of psychiatrists has been almost flat despite the massive shortages.

Your public sector psychiatrist isn't likely to have time to connect to you, to really understand you, to create a clinical formulation explaining what's going on with you, to learn your goals and priorities, or to carefully try various medications at various dosages to maximize their impact. They're unlikely to be available between visits for problems or questions, or dosage alterations. They're unlikely to coordinate with other providers you've had, including hospital and urgent care psychiatrists.

If you have some money, you might consider investing in an expensive psychiatrist for the short term, learning as much as you can about how you respond to medications and what works best for you, so that you can use the normal prescription machine system after that.

All of this means that you are less likely to benefit and more likely to be harmed by medications than you need to be. You might develop a more negative attitude about medications than is warranted because they've been prescribed poorly to you.

If you try to take a more active role in your medications so they'll work better for you, you may be shut down. Many psychiatrists aren't open to having their prescriptions questioned by people with psychosis, or their families. This is a "seller's market." They can stop seeing you, but you may not have any other choices besides them. They can enforce conditions on prescribing to you—like coming to groups or not using drugs or alcohol or getting lab tests (some of which might really be helpful, even though you didn't choose to do them).

You can do things to "help" your psychiatrist be more "efficient" in the tasks he and the billing system are prioritizing without challenging them:

- You can find and fill out a symptom checklist.
- You can create a symptom history for them, describing when certain symptoms come and go.
- You can create a summary of your psychiatric history (you'll have to request the records yourself and keep track of them and summarize them yourself, since they usually won't take the time to read them).

- You can create a list of all the medications you've been on, and the dosages they were tried at, and what impact they had. (This is the most important thing to give them, especially if you can combine it with a symptom history.)
- You can bring to each session a current list of your symptoms and side effects and what, if anything, has changed since your last visit.

As you get to know your provider, you'll learn what questions they're going to ask and can prepare the answers in advance. They might start respecting you more and listening to your opinions more, and they might spend more time talking with you with all the routine questions out of the way ... or they might not.

Here are some poor prescribing practices you should watch out for:

1) If a pill isn't working even when you increase the dosage, they keep increasing higher and higher and continue it indefinitely, instead of stopping the pill and trying something else.
2) If a pill creates serious side effects, they add other pills to counteract them, instead of stopping the pill and trying something else. (Cogentin and Artane should rarely be used. They impair memory and create other side effects, and there are many other pills you can try to avoid the movement side effects and stiffness that they're counteracting.)
3) They didn't ask about sexual side effects, and you didn't tell them. They're almost always a serious enough reason to stop the pill and try something else.
4) They prescribed stimulants. They're destabilizing, dangerous, and addictive, especially with emotionally isolated, unstable people and often make psychosis worse.
5) They use benzodiazepines long term. Even though you may like them and they "help," their effect will wear off if you keep using them and they're addictive and impair intellect.
6) They start more than one pill at the same time or make multiple medication changes at once (even if you're in a hospital). That makes it impossible to know how each pill affects you either—good or bad.

7) They use more than one, or rarely, two pills in the same class at the same time. Three or four ineffective pills are likely to be more harmful than one ineffective pill.

Given all these difficulties, many people will start looking to the Internet for answers and will likely become even more confused. First, realize that most information out there, including virtually all of the research studies, have been created, either directly or indirectly, by the pharmaceutical companies, by people they subsidize, or people who have bought into their paradigms. Even materials on mental health advocacy sites will likely include pharmaceutically supported materials (check out the ads on the page you're looking at) and "facts" copied from pharmaceutically supported studies. Currently, there is almost no independent research being done on medications. This is a problem because various major pharmaceutical companies have shown themselves to be more than willing to withhold important information about effects and side effects, slant their outcomes, and create "advertising-driven" studies. They are willing to pay large fines for their behaviors, so long as their profits continue.

Second, on the other side, there are lots of personal narratives, sharing horror stories of various side effects. Just like with reviews for anything else, most people who bother to write a review either really like, or more often, really hate a product. When people feel mistreated, poorly medicated, harmed, frustrated, and powerless, they post their negative experiences. Also, remember that most people who are taking antipsychotic medications never had a psychotic experience. They've been caught up in the pharmaceutical companies' efforts to expand their markets and profits.

Bottom line: It can be very hard to get the benefit from medications that you could and should be getting.

I'm sorry if this section sounds overly negative and defensive. Aa a psychiatrist, I wish my profession was doing a better job, and was being supported to do a better job. None of us wants to think of ourselves as doing poorly, but I've heard too many stories of people being kicked out of practices or just leaving them hanging without meds when they missed an appointment or when their insurance was cut off, of people being prescribed several meds simultaneously after brief evaluations, and of people being diagnosed with schizophrenia and being given up on, when that wasn't what was wrong, or there was another hopeful path available. When people used to tell me that I was the first psychiatrist who actually took the time to listen to them, I didn't believe them. I thought they were just being nice to me. Now, unfortunately, I do believe them.

Psychiatric hospitals

Psychiatric hospitals have changed considerably over the years. The vision most people have, primarily from old movies, is of large old buildings with extensive grounds far out of town, where people are taken by "the men in white coats" to be taken care of for long periods of time. Those were the old state hospitals, the asylums. For many people, the asylum image is not a benign protective one, but instead, a "snake pit" where people were neglected, abused, shocked, given lobotomies, and experimented on medically, and ultimately, their bodies dropped into unmarked graves on the grounds.

Beginning in California in 1972, civil rights legislation had a large impact on the ability to hold people for long periods of time against their will for their own good, setting up time limits of a 72-hour hold, a 14-day hold both for either danger to self, danger to others, or gravely disabled, a 90-day hold for danger to others, and a 1-year conservatorship for gravely disabled (meaning unable to take care of your own food, clothing, or shelter). Note that widespread homelessness didn't exist then, and welfare benefits were enough to actually live on. Courts are supposed to determine if people have the mental capacity to provide for or to collaborate with someone to have basic needs met, not if they have the financial resources to provide for their basic needs. We're not supposed to be locking people up in mental hospitals just because they're too poor to live anywhere.

The states had to pay for the entire bill for state hospitals, but if they put people in psychiatric units in general medical hospitals for less than 30 days, they could bill medical insurance, including Medicare and Medicaid/Medi-Cal for the hospitalizations, offsetting a good deal of the costs, assuming the hospitalizations were "medically necessary." These financial incentives diverted almost all the non-incarcerated people from state hospitals to short-term psychiatric units in general hospitals. Many people thought it was better for people to be in these acute hospitals, integrated with medical care, that were usually local, and highly professionally staffed and overseen, and didn't institutionalize people for long periods. However, these hospital units tended to be much smaller, without grounds to walk around, and most of the ancillary services—like art occupational, recreational, and art therapy—were dramatically reduced. Instead of the "rest cure" ideal from the old spas, the unit atmosphere became a crowded, highly structured, medical setting featuring medications as the dominant treatment, involuntarily if necessary, using seclusion and restraints if necessary—just as a delirious, acutely medically ill patient would be treated. The idea of "milieu therapy," that the atmosphere of the unit itself was healing, was lost along the way.

I've seen the average length of stay in hospitals gradually decrease over the 35 years of my career from about 14 days to about 5 days. Many people blame this decrease on the legal restrictions, but the laws haven't changed. The decrease is actually the result of the progressive cost-cutting assault by all insurances, but most relevantly in the public sector Medicaid/Medi-Cal cost cutting that impacted all medical and psychiatric hospitals. When I was a resident, we had voluntary patients on the hospital unit and got paid for them. That was stopped because Medi-Cal decided that if you're mentally well enough to agree to be treated in a hospital, you can probably be treated in a crisis residential setting instead; so, hospitalization isn't medically necessary, and payment is denied. Never mind that there isn't a packaged payment rate for crisis residential services in Medi-Cal. As "denied days" got more and more common, most of the more humane hospitals went broke and the rest learned to only take involuntary, acutely dangerous people and sedate and release them rapidly, so they'd be sure to get paid for every day the patient was in the hospital. They also learned to have their staff do hours and hours of paperwork to document "medical necessity," even though that meant spending very little time with the patients.

The same short-term, "revolving door" that occurs in all our medical units occurs in our psychiatric units, too, but it's even worse because we're only hospitalizing involuntary people. Almost everyone is going to stop doing whatever the hospital is forcing them to do there as soon as they get out (usually taking meds, including sleeping pills and sedatives, and not using drugs and alcohol) and they're likely to be back to where they started very soon. Certainly, some heart patients and kidney patients stop their treatments and bounce back into the hospital, too, but not as many, since most of them were voluntarily in the hospital in the first place.

Add to this picture that everyone in the hospital must be dangerous to themselves or others every day they're in the hospital for the hospital to get paid. Imagine the war zone that results. Staff are frequently assaulted and need to be on the lookout. They get good at overpowering patients, restraining and secluding, and forcibly medicating them to sedate them to keep them from hurting themselves or the staff. "Safety first" became the mantra as anything remotely like a weapon, including shoelaces and belts, was removed. A bunker mentality emerged among the staff as they take care of each other against the common enemy of the patients, and they have little use for people outside of the hospital, including outpatient clinicians and families, who don't know what they're dealing with day after day.

That's the current hospital environment to which these people are brought—people with psychosis who may be overwhelmed and confused and suicidal, or feeling like their world is falling apart, or who are hyperalert and paranoid, or ignoring their self-care, or having trouble relating realistically to other people. Maybe they couldn't handle their life anymore. Maybe the people around them needed a break or were frightened or begging that they get back on meds, or maybe the police brought them in because they were acting strangely or strung out on drugs in public. Today's psychiatric units are very likely to be frightening and traumatizing for the patients, and even actively physically assaultive. They're a hard place to heal.

> *I once did a consultation at a VA hospital where, as a result of a couple of suicides on the unit, they had created an extreme "safety first" environment. Virtually anything homelike or comforting was removed from the unit, and there was heavy surveillance, including cameras in every room. The bleak result felt more like a prisoner interrogation unit than a place of healing for desperate people. Some suicidal veterans, many of whom were very resistant to revealing their suffering, were so distressed by this hospital environment that they quickly hid their suicidal thoughts again to be released from the unit, never to return to any VA mental health services. The staff I talked with agreed*

> that very few of the patients really needed that level of safety assurance and that every one of them would've benefited from a "welcoming first" environment, but the risk-aversive administration and culture, going all the way up to the Congress, wouldn't permit that.

We have a terrible mismatch between what the community expects of hospitals and what we need, and what the hospitals are capable of providing.

Almost all the time, I think that the chance of benefit with hospitalization is so much less than the chance of traumatization, building anger and resentment, disengagement, and even increased hopelessness, dehumanization, and suicidality that I don't hospitalize people unless they're in actual physical danger in the community.

> Trauma-informed services, that we talked about in Chapter 9, have been applied to acute hospitalizations with the goal of reducing seclusion and restraints. Instead of seeing the patients as dangerous people about to attack us if we lower our guard, staff are urged to see patients as frightened people, who may be lashing out trying to protect themselves, and who are likely being retraumatized by being in the hospital. From this perspective, most of patients' violence is likely heightened by staff confronting, frightening, and agitating them, and it can be lessened by allying with the patients, soothing and comforting them. Most hospital staff reject this approach, saying that we'll be assaulted even more if we fail to contain and control the patients, and in untrained settings that does seem to happen. However, if there is a unit-wide commitment to this approach and the entire unit's culture is changed, including every staff, the amount of seclusion and restraints drops to almost none, and so does the incidence of staff assault and injury. I've personally seen this work, in the most difficult setting imaginable, the high assault ward at the well-funded, staffed, and led Oregon State Hospital (for "the criminally insane") where a dedicated team of staff progressively helped very violent people build self-control, instead of controlling them. SAMHSA has produced trainings for trauma-

informed inpatient care. Nonetheless, I don't know of any of my local psychiatric hospitals that have attempted this transformation. Instead, the battlefield mentality persists. Ask your local psychiatric hospital if they use trauma-informed techniques, especially the SAMHSA toolkits.

Psychiatric hospitals look very different from the perspectives of patients, staff, and families:

- For the patients, the hospital mostly feels like a jail. Most of the time they've been brought there by police, often cuffed or restrained in a police car or an ambulance. They are being held there against their will on a legal hold. There are legal criteria they need to meet, or their hold will be extended. There are legal hearings in the unit or even in a courtroom, where they can fight their case with a lawyer defending them. The psychiatrists are the ones who have the legal power to release them whenever they choose to, so they're experienced as the ones who are holding them and prosecuting them. There are a lot of rules—patients can't walk around freely. Many of their belongings, including cell phones and cigarettes, are taken away. There are limited opportunities to go outside. They must follow orders. Visitors are limited. They can be punished with seclusion, restraints, and forced drugging, if they misbehave.
- For the staff, the hospital mostly feels like a treatment facility, albeit a dangerous one that is overloaded with paperwork and regulations. They make treatment plans for each patient, based on their diagnosis. They work hard to get patients to understand and comply with their treatments. They have individual and group therapy sessions and activities. They need to get patients better, to reduce the symptoms of their illnesses, so that they can discharge them safely to a lower level of care.
- For the families, the hospital mostly feels like an imposing, powerful, locked institution. They may have initiated the hospitalization, often out of desperation, with high hopes that their loved one will be treated effectively and returned to health. They often feel excluded with limited visiting hours and contact with their family, and with staff who refuse to talk with them because

of confidentiality. Staff are rarely collaborative, beginning their own medications and treatments, without regard to the family's knowledge and experience. Families are confronted with their family member's complaints of abuse and overmedication, while being blamed for putting them in there in the first place. Staff may describe the family as undermining or sabotaging, rather than empathizing with the difficulties they've faced. And then, usually, their family member is released, far too early, far from the health they'd hoped for, overmedicated, with confusing aftercare plans they may or may not have been included in or informed of.

These perspectives are so different, it's often very difficult to even have a conversation between these groups, let alone a collaborative strategy and plan.

Peer supporters and peer advocates have been used in a number of psychiatric hospitals to try to bridge these perspectives. These staff generally have often been patients in the same hospitals earlier in their lives and recoveries. As such, they understand in a deep way the patients' experiences and can both advocate for them and help engage them in what they need to do to recover, in ways the professional staff often can't reach them. They are also walking beacons of hope and perseverance. Peers have been powerful agents of change in many hospitals. More rarely, hospitals hire family peers and advocates to better engage families. Look for hospitals that have peers and utilize them.

I recommend re-envisioning psychiatric hospital units as "refugee centers." Today's hospitals are not where people are taken when their treatment team thinks a "higher level of care" is "medically necessary." They are where people are taken when they've become so unbearable, either to themselves or the people around them, that they are forced to leave their homes, families, and communities (if they have one ... at least, in Los Angeles, many, if not most psychiatrically hospitalized patients, are homeless). Hospitals are being used as refugee detention centers for people with mental conditions. Let's accept that reality and use it to bring the three perspectives into alignment. Here's how we can all fit together:

- Patients have been rejected and excluded from their lives. They need to focus on how they need to change, so that the conflicts and distress can be resolved and they can be welcomed back.

- Staff has a number of duties to run a refugee center, including charity, treatment, documentation assistance, facilitating community housing and connections, and advocating for community inclusion. Drug detox, psychiatric medications, and sedation are only a small fraction of their treatment responsibilities.
- Families are often the most active representatives of the community as a whole. They often know why the person was rejected and excluded, what the conditions for reintegration might be, and are the often the ones most likely to work hard to achieve that reintegration.

The funding should be based on "social necessity," rather than "medical necessity," and the legal processes should be mediative and restorative, not adversarial and punitive.

In addition, this refugee-center perspective can be used for longer hospitalizations and institutionalizations. Many of the problems we see in long-term hospitals and nursing homes resemble the problems of long-term refugee camps, for example, creating an internal black-market economy, high levels of coercion and abuse, hopelessness, agitation and radicalization, social isolation, loss of meaning, and pervasive passivity. It is far preferable to help the patient be reintegrated rapidly than to create a long-term refugee, while attempting to treat their symptoms more effectively.

If someone has repeated crises and hospitalizations, they may develop an understanding of the best ways to help them recover from the next crisis. They might write down their preferences in a Mental Health Advanced Directive, including which hospital to be taken to, what medications to be given, who should be informed about the hospitalization, and who they would like to be a surrogate decision maker if they're too impaired in the midst of the crisis to make decisions for themselves. While the legal status of these advanced directives varies from location to location, at least they give an underpinning for possible collaboration during a crisis.

Not everyone having a crisis needs to be locked up, nor do crisis interventions need to wait until the person can be involuntarily hospitalized, if your area has some alternative crisis programs, especially crisis residential programs. These can be much more like homes and sanctuaries, instead of like battle zones. In my view, it was a shame we weren't able to follow the advice of

Steve Fields, longtime leader of Progress Foundation, which runs a series of crisis programs in small apartments in San Francisco, who wanted to use a sizeable portion of the Mental Health Services Act money to fund crisis residential programs that Medicare and Medi-Cal won't pay for, so we could begin to wean ourselves from our reliance on hospitals for crisis care.

> *When I first began working at the Village, we had to pay for hospitalizations out of our overall budget. We wrote a contract with Community Hospital of Long Beach for $350 per day (now, it would be over $1,000) and the Village psychiatrists were given hospital privileges. We admitted patients to ourselves and paid for their stay using our own criteria, rather than "medical necessity." While this was hard work for us to go to the hospital after a long day at the Village and share on-call on weekends, it provided seamless, targeted care for our members. We always knew why we'd admitted them and what we needed to accomplish for them to be discharged back into the community. Sometimes hospitalizations were shorter and sometimes longer than they would've been, but the hospital administration knew the bill would be paid by us and left us alone. The hospital served the community treatment team's needs, rather than being its own fiefdom.*
>
> *There was an initial fear that we would go broke paying for hospitalizations, and I was under a great deal of pressure not to overspend. We became very creative in finding alternatives. We had a lot of team meetings where we said, "Is there anything we can do for them that would cost less than $350 and be more effective?" Most of the time, the answer was, "Yes." I could go over to their house with an injection. We could have a family meeting to problem solve. We could have a peer go over to their house with a pizza and keep them company, so they wouldn't get suicidal. We could put them up at a hotel for a few days to give everyone respite. We only used the hospital when it really was necessary. We reduced hospital costs from about 25% of the*

total budget to 7%, saving enough to buy payees, job developers, and community integration specialists.

When the Village integrated Medi-Cal funding, that system was eliminated, and the hospitals no longer worked with us. Eventually, it got so bad that I withdrew from Pacific Hospital in protest.

In those first years, I focused on handling crisis effectively while limiting hospitalizations. Then, I heard a presentation by Dr. Carl Bell, a recently deceased, wonderfully inspiring, Black, child psychiatrist who worked in the poorest communities in Chicago, fighting the pervasive violence and childhood trauma there. He said that instead of focusing on risk factors and traumatic events, we needed to focus on protective factors and resilience. Trauma didn't lead to nearly as much distress and disability if the child had protective factors because they'd be able to withstand the stressor, instead of being driven into crisis. He identified protective factors as:

- Having enough money to make it through the month and extra for emergencies,
- Having a reasonably safe, secure place to live,
- Having a family (it didn't have to be a perfect family),
- Having other adults who cared about them (like a coach, teacher, or minister as a "protective shield"), and
- Having some self-identity as something besides being a bad or messed-up kid.

I adapted his list to the adults I was working with and added one more:

- Having some spiritual practice or supportive beliefs.

After that lecture, instead of spending a lot of time doing crisis interventions, I spent a lot of time proactively building income with SSI applications, finding housing, reconnecting with families, finding other supportive adults, including us, helping people find productive roles, including within our

> Village community, and rebuilding spiritual practices. Once those were established, the crises and the hospitalizations almost stopped. I'd love to see a study of how many of those protective factors people who go to psychiatric ERs and hospitals have. I'd bet that the vast majority have none or one and that almost none have a handful.

Finances—poverty, Social Security, homelessness, and incarceration

There's an old argument over whether mental illness leads to poverty or poverty leads to mental illness. I remember in training being taught about a study from the early 1900s that showed that people with schizophrenia grew up spread across social classes, but they ended up highly overrepresented in lower classes, describing that process as "downward social drift." I also remember a more recent study that showed on a block-by-block analysis of schizophrenia that the incidence was highest in neighborhoods with the most wealth discrepancy, where people were more likely to be rejected and discriminated against because of their poverty. If everyone was poor, or rich, there wasn't as much negative pressure as when there were rich people to feel superior to the poor people and the poor people internalized their inferiority. It's beyond my abilities to really separate out chicken and egg between poverty and mental illness. My presumption, and the basis for this section, is that serious mental illnesses and poverty form a vicious cycle each one worsening the other, and that, without some kind of protection, usually from families, people with mental illnesses are likely to end up impoverished and that poverty will make their mental state worse. In my opinion, we are currently living in a society with some of the highest wealth inequalities and the weakest family structures ever, feeding this vicious cycle.

Many people with psychotic experiences struggle to work consistently and be self-supporting. After a while, their family may no longer be able to support them, or perhaps they never could, and they need government assistance to support them. The federal system we have to help them is Social Security Disability or SSI if they haven't paid much money into the Social Security system out of paychecks and SSDI if they have. The two systems have differences: Medicare comes with SSDI and Medicaid (Medi-Cal in California) comes with SSI; and while SSDI payments depend on how much you paid in while working and can be up to several thousand dollars a month, SSI payments depend on your poverty (so you can't have much savings and you get somewhat more money if you're living in a licensed Board and Care, somewhat less on the street or a hotel, even less in an apartment, and even less if you're married or being supported by your family. Also, you get different amounts in different states). The two programs also have different work incentive programs.

The criteria for either kind of Social Security Disability (and it's the same application) is permanent total disability due to a medical or psychiatric condition (excluding a substance abuse condition). While these criteria make sense for many disabling medical conditions, they're more problematic for back pain and mental conditions—currently, the two leading causes of disability. How do we know that someone with a mental condition is going to be disabled and unable to work forever? How do we know if they're psychiatrically disabled or just "unemployable"? The current system, established in the 1970s and only changeable by an act of Congress, has a medical determination process based on the medical records submitted to them or the evaluation of doctors they hire. Medical records only include things written by psychiatrists or psychologists, not social workers, case workers, families, or the person themselves. If you think back to the previous section on medications, how much time do you think a psychiatrist is going to spend on their records to document psychiatric disability, or write up disability evaluations? Not enough to be approved is usually the answer. You may have to do some of the leg work to collect your medical/psychiatric records. There are several government services and even law firms who will help with the process, sometimes even helping you hire your own psychiatrist to do the evaluation, for part of your "back check." (A "back check" is the money you're owed for all the months from when you first applied for Social Security, a "protected filing date," and when they granted the Social Security.)

It may seem like the best approach is to apply as early as possible when things go wrong, so you're not more of a financial burden than others can bear and so you don't end up homeless, but then, they'll say you don't have enough of a psychiatric record to be sure you're permanently totally disabled. Many clinics and doctors say you must be in treatment for 6 months or a year before they can say you're permanently totally disabled. The process, even assuming you don't need appeals to be approved, takes months to complete. How do you pay the bills and avoid homelessness in the meantime? How do you maintain enough stability to keep going to that doctor or clinic in the meantime?

Even if you get SSI, it's not enough to live on in any major housing market in America. It's so low you're usually eligible for food stamps. In California, it's currently about $950 per month and the cheapest rent in a crime-ridden, drug-infested, dangerous neighborhood is about $1,200. You'll be hard pressed to even share a one-bedroom apartment at market rents.

You might think about working to supplement the SSI, but they'll deduct $1 from your check for every $2 you make; so, you're working for half wages, and there's always the possibility that they'll decide you're not permanently totally disabled anymore and take away your check. It takes so long to get SSI that many people won't risk losing it to try working. (Although losing it is less common than you might expect, or fear, because the Social Security Administration is too busy to do too many reassessments.) Also, it usually takes so long for them to make the work deduction that you end up with an additional deduction to pay back "overpayments."

In summary, SSI is the only major program to financially support disabled people who haven't worked regularly. Its funding is inadequate to live anywhere and it's a trap, leaving you permanently dependent on it. If a family can support someone for long enough to have a chance to get back on their feet, either completing some education or getting a job, they should try to do that to avoid the trap of SSI. If someone has no choice besides SSI, I tell them not to give up and live on it forever, even though the government has just determined them to be totally, permanently disabled. The system has a built-in hypocrisy: It has work allowances and even work programs for people "permanently, totally disabled." By the way, most of the work programs, like the Plan to Achieve Self-Support (PASS) program, are so much work for the overburdened Social Security office staff that they're almost never used.

Social Security does have a system within it for people who don't spend their money on food, shelter, and clothing (by determination of a doctor) to have a payee appointed to be responsible for managing their money for them. This often creates a great deal of conflicts and extra work for the Social Security office, so they don't like doing it unless the person agrees, or it was part of the initial disability determination. Being a payee can also create a great deal of conflict and extra work for whoever agrees to do it. Social Security prefers family members, but beware that being someone's payee often ruins your relationship with them. My main piece of advice, if you are in that position, is to act like a banker, making sure payments and records are kept for the three basics, not like a therapist or caring family member trying to make sure they use their money wisely or therapeutically. There are some agencies who will be payees for people, usually for a small amount of money (but even $50 per month feels like a lot, if you're only getting $950). Think about what a monthly budget looks like for $950—be sure to include cigarettes and a cell phone.

To avoid homelessness, you'll have to live with family, do some kind of shared housing, or get a Section 8 housing voucher. Section 8 vouchers were created to replace the old public housing projects, which had become crime infested, drug ridden, terrible places to raise children. The housing project I saw in St. Louis across the street from the mental hospital was so dangerous the police wouldn't go in it. The new appliances that were bought for the apartments rotted in the basement while drug dealers stole the residents' Social Security checks. Section 8 vouchers were meant to allow people to rent apartments in scattered settings, instead of in a public housing slum. Unfortunately, when this transition was done under President Reagan, apparently 90% of the money was removed. (I'm personally convinced that the people we currently see on the streets and in jail weren't the people who were released from mental hospitals without adequate community support. I think they're people who used to live in the public housing projects before they were closed down. Once they were out of the projects, the "war on drugs" easily captured them, and they were doomed.) Almost every city's Section 8 waiting list is closed almost all the time and has enough people on it to last decades anyway. Even if you get a voucher, in Los Angeles most often from the homeless Coordinated Entry System, you'll have to find a landlord who will take it, which has become almost impossible, too.

Putting all these factors together, the majority of people being served by the LA County Department of Mental Health are currently homeless or at risk of homelessness. LA County has over 50,000 homeless people and even with millions of dollars and numerous programs to help them, the numbers keep growing because more and more people are impoverished every day, including nearly everyone with a mental illness or any other disability. Families need to realize how hard it is to avoid homelessness and how destructive homelessness is to prioritize avoiding it.

Once someone is homeless, they are at a much higher risk of jailing. Many activities like sleeping, urinating, defecating, fighting with a partner, passing out drunk, using drugs, talking to voices, or owning a gun—that are relatively easily tolerated for people who have somewhere of their own to live—lead to evictions in group settings and arrests when you're homeless. Most people in LA County Jail are homeless. Jail is where someone is held before their hearing if they can't make bail and after sentencing if they've committed a relatively minor crime with a sentence of less than a year of incarceration. Poor people, especially homeless ones, can't make bail, so they're stuck in jail. About 95% of cases are plea bargained, rather than tried. If you're in jail because you can't make bail, you're in a worse bargaining position. The district attorney can just continue the case and keep you in jail until you plead guilty. I've heard that the average sentence is twice as long for people who can't make bail as for those who can. (By the way, there are active efforts around the country, including in Los Angeles, for "bail reform" to address these problems.) Once you plead guilty, the odds are good you can get out early since the jail is overcrowded and they discharge people after serving a fraction of the sentence. But then, of course, you have a conviction on your record, making it harder to get a job, apartment, or Section 8 voucher. You may have missed a rent payment and gotten evicted. If you stay in jail for over a month, they cut off your SSI checks and you have to get them restarted.

Incarcerations make it much harder to get off the street. Being on the street makes it much easier to be incarcerated. Many people are caught in that vicious cycle. The court system has created special homeless courts to try to expunge people's records, trying to undo some of this damage.

Sometimes, family members think it might be good for their family member to be arrested to force them to get treatment. I think that's almost always a bad idea. The damage done by jailing to their lives, their mental state, and their relationship with you vastly outweighs the benefits. Hardly anyone comes out of jail more mentally healthy than they go in. Taking fragile people and locking them in small crowded cages with lots of other distressed people overseen by guards intent on coercing and frightening everyone to keep them under control is a recipe for destruction, not healing. Even if you meet a mental health worker, and many jails have substantial mental health staff, you still don't have to take medications unless you're put on a hold and transferred to a forensic hospital unit.

If you or someone you care about is arrested while taking medications, it will likely take a good deal of advocacy, and maybe a number of days to get them evaluated in jail and their medications restarted. Putting in the effort to directly contact the mental health staff in the jail is almost always worth it because there's a good chance that they'll slip between the cracks otherwise.

The best opportunity for jail diversion is often in the community before the arrest is made. Many police departments have specialized mental health teams, consisting of a social worker and a policeman, that have access to both systems and can often divert people from jail to hospitals, which are generally dramatically better than jails. Some cities have police teams just for homeless outreach or to help local businesses that are being harassed and they can assist with jail diversion as well. If you have someone you care about who is homeless or a public nuisance, it may be worth the effort to get to know those policemen personally and work out long-term strategies with them. Oftentimes, they have contacts with local mental health and substance abuse programs.

Many people with psychosis face bigger challenges around finances, homelessness, and jailing than from their mental condition. As a result, many mental health programs have diverted resources from treatment to "case management," "benefits assistance," and other "poverty services."

> *The most highly developed form of case management teams is ACT (Assertive Community Treatment) teams, which began in the 1970s in Madison, Wisconsin, with early deinstitutionalization efforts. Drs. Leonard Stein and Mary Ann Test realized that previously hospitalized patients couldn't be relied on to show up to clinic appointments, take their medications regularly, and manage their lives independently in the community after they were discharged. The hospital had a built-in structure to ensure that all of this was done. The community didn't. They created teams*

of case managers, who traveled around the community with their small case load of patients, about 10–20 patients per case manager, helping them to organize and handle all of those tasks, overseeing and supervising them. With that innovation, over two thirds of the previously institutionalized patients could be successfully discharged to the community and treated at far less cost. Although the ACT model was developed outside of the mainstream psychiatric establishment, it has spread throughout the world.

Over time, ACT teams have evolved somewhat. Led by the Village program, California has emphasized two of these evolutions (having an array of services integrated into the case management team, like substance abuse, housing, employment, and medical care, and using a more collaborative approach in working with patients) creating Full Service Partnership (FSP) teams. Throughout California, these teams, funded by the Mental Health Services Act tax on millionaires, has served thousands of people, the majority with psychosis and other extraordinary experiences, reducing homelessness, jailing, and psychiatric hospitalizations by about 70%.

Violence

There are two intertwined issues in coping with violence—safety and security—avoiding being hurt and handling the fear of being hurt.

It can be muddling to deal with both of these aspects of violence together. For one thing, the situations we're the most frightened of, for example, mass shootings or psychotic people acting on the command of violent voices, are rather rare, while the situations that more often lead to violence—for example, family confrontations, anger and frustration at dependency on other people, drug, alcohol, and cigarette cravings, or arguments over money—we think we can handle because they're "normal" problems. Even when someone is having psychotic experiences, their violence is more often driven by "normal" reasons than "psychotic" ones. And the victims are most often the people around them, primarily family members, just like for "normal" violence.

If we can resist the fearmongering hype that every mass murderer is mentally ill and every mentally ill person is a potential mass murderer, neither of which is true, there's something potentially reassuring in that last paragraph: Non-professionals, especially family members, who are the ones most likely to be hurt, do have some "normal" skills they can use to decrease the odds of violence. They don't have to be entirely dependent on police and mental professionals to keep them safe. So, let's start there with a few example scenarios that can become violent and how to break the cycle:

- *Blaming can fuel anger and violence.* Most of us have an unfortunate tendency to respond to things going poorly by blaming someone else for our personal failings, especially the people around us, turning our frustrations outwardly against them, instead of taking self-responsibility. Most of us respond to being blamed, by defending ourselves and retaliating against the other person, often adding more failures and frustrations, including our own, to the fire. Instead of either side actually working on the problem, looking for opportunities for hope and growth, all our energies go into the fight we start feeling we must win. Often, the same unresolved issues lead to the same fights over and over again. And that's for "normal" people, especially families. If we add to the picture some paranoia or some voices urging us to defend ourselves more aggressively than we're inclined to, the blaming fights become supercharged, and less likely to be resolved. Shared responsibility can break the cycle. When we acknowledge our own contributions to the problem and resist blaming, we're at the very least not adding fuel to the fire, and we may be creating a space for everyone to back down and take more self-responsibility.
- *Depending on others to help us can at first be positive and seductive, but as time goes on, our lack of ability to do anything for ourselves or get what we really want becomes frustrating.* If we believe that we can't do something, but that the other person can do it for us, then we can become focused on their withholding help from us and resent them. This can apply to something like giving us the pills or drugs we want or money to go out or even to something emotional

like needing help to calm ourselves down. Since no one can meet our needs perfectly, frustration and anger are inevitably going to emerge from longstanding dependence. Also, the person being helped may feel compelled to rebel and assert their competence and independence even when it's unrealistic. On the other side, the helper may feel like they're being taken advantage of and the person could do more for themselves and resent them. Both sides may test each other, each seeking to prove at least to themselves that their resentment is justified, and the conflict escalates. Mental conditions can decrease the ability of each side to accurately understand each other's capabilities and needs and make it harder to find a shared understanding. Empowerment can break the cycle. Helping people define their own goals and what help they would like to meet those goals, instead of the helper telling them what they need, can help make us allies, instead of foes.

- *When we get frustrated at our inability to get someone else to do what we want them to, we too often try to "make" them do what we want by threatening them with punishment and "consequences."* Threatening punishment is the lowest of the four levels of motivation: avoiding punishment, seeking rewards, rewarding ourselves, and pursuing a higher purpose or value. Mental health staff and law enforcement are especially vulnerable to using punishment and coercion because we often have overt physical power on our side. Coercion may work temporarily and even create a sense of control, but it's likely to build anger and rebellion over the long run. Motivational interviewing, attempting to ally with the person wherever they're at, while looking for opportunities to move up to one of the three higher levels of motivation can break the cycle. Unfortunately, mental conditions may alter priorities and especially "higher purposes" while also reducing our ability to understand each other. Addiction also often profoundly alters motivations and priorities. It takes perseverance and empathy to keep looking for higher levels of motivation.

- *The most powerful threat is often to kick someone out and exclude them.* "This is my house. You'll follow my rules if you're going to live here." ("Tough love" seems to me to overly rely on this approach.) This approach implies that the other person doesn't belong there and doesn't have any shared ownership or responsibility for the home or environment. It also weakens relationships. Without shared relationships, ownership, or responsibility, there is far less inhibition of violent and destructive impulses. Shared commitment can break the cycle. People are less likely to destroy "their" homes, programs, and families than someone else's homes, programs, and families they no longer feel a part of.

- *Some families, groups, neighborhoods, and cultures have higher customary and acceptable levels of violence than others.* Swearing at each other, threatening, throwing things, and even physical and sexual aggression may be the norm. These violent atmospheres are more likely to trigger violence and less likely to be restraining. Violence begets violence. Weaponizing the environment, especially with guns, increases the likelihood of severe damage. Many times, whether we're family, staff, police, or potentially anyone, we're only aware of the other person's violence being problematic and not our own because our violence feels justified and reasonable to us. Reducing our own violence and the overall violence and weaponization of the environment can help calm things down.

All of these scenarios are rather common and most of us are used to the scenarios we live within, whether it's due to an alcoholic angry father, chronic marital arguments, a resentful, rebellious teenager, a disruptive relative, or our feuding neighbors. Our lives may have a "nasty equilibrium" to them. However, if someone in the scenario starts experiencing psychosis, or is drunk or high, they may not be able to sustain themselves within the "nasty equilibrium" they live in any longer. They'll misplay their "role" and destroy the precarious balance. Many of the aggressive delusions and hallucinations I've seen seem to me to be exaggerations and distortions of what was already going on, rather than meaningless psychosis.

When a policeman, psychiatrist, payee, drug dealer, or a girlfriend, etc. is added to one of these "nasty equilibriums," they're also likely to misplay their "roles" or be pressured to play conflicting roles by various people, and tend to destroy the precarious balance, too. The outsider may be resented.

The outsider may feel a need to exert their control. The outsider may inadvertently provoke more violence.

I think that the puzzling statistic that people with serious mental illnesses are much more likely to be the victims of violence than the perpetrator may be more understandable if we consider the entire equilibrium that they are part of.

Now, let's return to our initial differentiation between safety and security, between violence and fear of violence, and try to add fear into the picture. When we're frightened, our decision-making changes:

- We're more likely to make rapid, "impulsive" decisions acting on our emotions, instead of thinking things out. Our immediate defensive reactions may include counterattacks that aggravate the situation.
- We may have a more limited range of vision and thought as our fear creates focus and leads to more rigid thinking, and we lose the patience needed for thinking about alternatives.
- We're likely to do things that have an impact in a short-term focus, overlooking long-term consequences and goals.
- We're likely to be risk aversive, considering "safety first," limiting engagement and inclusiveness, not giving them the chance to regain self-control.
- We're likely to see the other person as our enemy, losing our ability to be empathetic or "trauma informed" and then react defensively, escalating blaming.
- We may try to take control, either by being protective and caretaking, rather than collaborative and growth oriented, or by being demanding and pressured, rather than thoughtful and measured in our responses.

All of these common reactions potentially escalate the actual danger, even though they're designed to protect us. But our fear also decreases our self-awareness, so that we can't see what's happening within us as it happens. Some of these fear-based reactions end up included in our ongoing rules and practices to "reduce risk," persisting long after the fear has subsided, and better decisions could be made.

It's risky to continue in a situation where we're frightened, whether it's a family situation or a clinical relationship or even police on patrol, and we should try to avoid these situations over the long term, rather than figure out how to continue on even in fear. I've sometimes been critical of colleagues who use a lot of self-protective practices that distance them from the people they're trying to help, but I'd rather they do that, than work in fear and have their judgment chronically impaired.

When California moved to release "nonviolent" prisoners from our jails and prisons, we experienced a large increase in violence in our Homeless Assistance Program (and "nonviolent" means that their most recent conviction was for a nonviolent crime, not that they haven't been violent and aren't dangerous. Our legal system, despite being incredibly elaborate and expensive, is not effective at assessing or preventing dangerousness.). A number of staff and clients were threatened, physically assaulted, traumatized, and/or left. We had to make physical and practice changes to reestablish both safety and security to function effectively, even though we unfortunately reduced our accessibility and openness in the process.

> *A few years ago, for the first time in almost two decades, I was assaulted by one of our members. Annie had a history of severe childhood sexual trauma and was manic, irritable, and disinhibited without her medications. She tended to attack any male she thought was threatening her—which was basically any man. We didn't have access to her records, but it appeared that she'd spent years at Pullon State Hospital as an "incompetent to stand trial" inmate on several occasions, but she was released each time at the end of each sentence. (Someone can't be held in the state mental hospital longer than the maximum sentence for the crime they're accused of. Contrary to popular opinion that they're getting off lightly going to the hospital, on average people who are "not guilty by reason of insanity" spend twice as long locked up as they would have if they could've pled guilty.) Annie had been kicked out of a half-way house for female parolees for being too aggressive there and she was sent to us, homeless and refusing all medications. She was repeatedly hospitalized by the local police for*

assaulting people, and then released within a few days, since hospital staff didn't want to be assaulted either. I, and all of our male staff, were avoiding direct contact with her and we only worked with her outside the building, so she'd be less likely to hurt other members. Nonetheless, one day I walked by her on my way to lunch, and she suddenly slugged me in the chest.

We petitioned to remove Annie from our program, which county administration was reluctant to do, since no one else was willing to work with her. I filed a restraining order to keep her away from me and the Village. Going to court to get that restraining order was an eye-opening experience for me. The entire staff—ranging from the clerical workers, who literally sat doing their nails while people waited hours in line, to the female judge who showed no compassion for the difficulties the victims were having in finding and safely serving their attackers with notice of the hearing—were demeaning in the extreme. I could handle this treatment, but 90% of the people there with me were battered women, seeking protection from their partners, or ex-partners. Their common feeling that they are worthless and to blame and deserve being beaten was being confirmed by the court's treatment of them. Their safety clearly didn't matter to anyone. Many walked away without getting their restraining order to be beaten and blamed again.

I, however, persisted and my director, Paul, served Annie the restraining order papers in the hospital where she was again. The hospital staff were too scared to give her the papers themselves. They insisted on him giving her the papers in a room with six staff there, right before they released her back into the community closing the door behind her; so, if she got mad, she couldn't take it out on them.

A couple weeks later, she again attacked someone on the street. I called the mental health worker in the jail to explain the situation, my refusal to work with her, and the

> need for involuntary treatment in a high security environment. I was told that given her modest charges, they wouldn't be able to keep her very long. Then, I got the dreadful piece of advice that families are frequently and thoughtlessly given, "Hopefully, next time she'll do something more serious and we can hold her longer." Really, I'm supposed to hope she does something terrible to someone? I hope she doesn't do anything more serious, but I was powerless to protect myself any further than I had or to protect our community at all. I never saw Annie again.

Families often feel stuck with a family member who is violent and/or frightening who they can't forcibly send to be locked up and treated somewhere. They're told that police and emergency teams can't do anything unless there is an immediate threat or violent act. They're advised to kick the person out and get a "restraining order" to keep them away. Most families can't follow through on this cruel and rejecting advice. If they vacillate, sometimes letting their family member stay and sometimes not, they can be accused of sabotaging the plan, violating the restraining order themselves, and they may lose credibility with the police and mental health services who may stop trying to help them.

"Call the police" is only an effective safety and security strategy if we have a good, trusting relationship with our police, if they're funded well enough to respond rapidly, and if the community policing standards of acceptable violence aren't significantly higher than our own. Racially biased violence perpetrated by the police is a serious enough problem that many people, especially Black people, won't call the police out of fear.

Before I close this section on violence, I want to say a few words about mass murderers since they attract so much attention and are traumatizing our entire society, even though I've never met one and am unlikely to meet one. From the same media-driven accounts all of you are familiar with, it seems to me that these murderers have a variety of mental states and ways they experience reality, but they almost always have limited self-identity and relationships. Often, they've experienced lots of rejection and isolation and have reacted with bitterness and resentment. Usually, it's not hard to see why and it's hard to really blame the people around them for rejecting them. Sometimes, their anger is incorporated into their identity and relationships, especially if they find hateful virtual groups on the Internet to connect to. I think we should focus our interventions mostly on self-identity and relationships, battling isolation and resentment, rather than on diagnosing and medicating psychiatric illnesses. (If they can't handle people, or people can't handle them, I'd start with emotional support animals. I'm serious: I don't think I've heard of a single mass murderer who has a pet.)

> For the last 10 years, LA County DMH, along with local school districts and police have created the START program (School Threat Assessment Response Team) to try to prevent school violence. Their services include training and program consultation, early screening and identification, assessment, intervention, and case management and monitoring. We'll never know if this approach has actually prevented any mass murders, but, at least, it's offering targeted help to at-risk students that will benefit them, even if they were never going to hurt anyone.

Suicide

Suicide prevention as a public health issue has arrived. There are public service announcements, celebrities talking about their suicide attempts, "zero suicide" initiatives, and even fundraising walks to prevent suicide. School children are taught about warning signs of suicide and how to get help for themselves and their friends. All of this is all the more remarkable, since suicide is perhaps the most unthinkable act there is, even more so than mass violence: No current culture condones suicide for any purpose (and we look back with horror on human sacrifices to the Gods or Hindu women throwing themselves on their husband's funeral pyres). No child game pretend "plays" suicide. Even military "suicide missions" are extraordinary and largely avoided. Suicide doesn't appear to have any evolutionary purpose. No other animal commits suicide. Suicide is truly "beyond the pale." For the longest time, people thought asking someone about suicide might make them do it.

How did we get to where we talk and think about suicide so much now?

Mostly, I think, because death by suicide is deeply traumatic for those who knew and cared about the victim. The combination of unthinkable and unbearable leads people to devote the rest of their lives to preventing further suicides. (Active Minds and the JED Foundation are both high-profile, nationwide organizations originally founded by a family member of a college student suicide victim.) Once the curtain has been pulled back and the awful reality that suicide can and does happen stares us in the face ... and we courageously stare back at it, we start to realize how pervasive and terrible things really are. Here are some typical US national yearly suicide statistics (even though getting accurate numbers is incredibly difficult, most studies have about the same outcomes):

- Suicidal thoughts   9.8 million   4%
- Suicidal plan   2.7 million   1%
- Suicide attempt   1.4 million   0.5%
- Death by suicide   44,000   0.017% (about 1/6,000)

I was taught a medical model approach to suicide (created by the same Drs. Robbins and Guze at Washington University who so heavily impacted the creation of *DSM-III*). They said that people who actually killed themselves were fundamentally different from people who had suicidal thoughts, plans, or even attempts. The people who actually killed themselves were almost universally mentally ill or hopelessly physically ill. Virtually everyone had major depression, substance abuse, schizophrenia, chronic pain, or was receiving dialysis. Therefore, suicide prevention was almost entirely an issue of identifying people at risk and, then, giving them appropriate psychiatric and medical treatment for their underlying conditions, which would remove the cause of their suicidality. Virtually, no one who isn't "sick" kills themselves. Their postmortem analysis was widely accepted and embedded in our suicide risk assessments.

> Even today, QPR, our most common suicide prevention approach, relies on getting at-risk people professional treatment for their mental illness. CSULB uses it. QPR's website says, "QPR stands for Question, Persuade, and Refer—the 3 simple steps anyone can learn to help save a life from suicide. Just as people trained in CPR and the Heimlich Maneuver help save thousands of lives each year, people trained in QPR learn how to recognize the warning signs of

> a suicide crisis and how to question, persuade, and refer someone to help. Each year thousands of Americans, like you, are saying "Yes" to saving the life of a friend, colleague, sibling, or neighbor. QPR can be learned in our Gatekeeper course in as little as one hour."

The strangely common reaction of people who knew suicide victims and had recent contact with them, "I just saw them and didn't see anything wrong with them," has been conceptualized as our lack of ability to identify the common signs and symptoms of mental illnesses to see who needs professional treatment. (I, too, reacted that way when I heard a fellow psychiatric resident killed herself the day after I had lunch with her.) But is that true?

In 2018, the CDC released a suicide fact sheet designed to increase public focus on suicide because the suicide rates are going up dramatically (over 30% in half the states since 1999). Instead of medicalizing suicide, they normalized it. They said that 54% of people who died of suicide didn't have a known mental illness (which leaves us to speculate whether they had an "unknown" mental illness). Instead, they categorized suicides by "factors contributing to suicide with or without known mental illness":

- Relationship problem 42%
- Crisis in the past or upcoming 2 weeks 29%
- Problematic substance abuse 28%
- Physical health problem 22%
- Job/financial problem 16%
- Criminal/legal problem 9%
- Loss of housing 4%

That's a strikingly "normal" list of factors, so much so that we're given the impression that suicide could occur in almost anyone's lives, and that suicide victims might not seem any different from any of us. But is that true?

I'm inclined to try to integrate both approaches: It's likely that people whose mental distress is severe enough to give them a diagnosis of a mental illness have a much higher risk of suicide than people who are less persistently mentally distressed (although children and adolescents might be an exception to this, since they're more impulsive overall) and that "normal" life tragedies are what push them over the edge.

Before I worked at the Village, I knew about one person a year who killed themselves (perhaps surprisingly, they were split about evenly between fellow students and patients). But then, we had no suicides for the first 10 years of the Village.

I was so pleased I wrote an article for the California NAMI journal titled "Challenging the Suicide Status Quo," which hypothesized that our outstanding results could be attributed to our attention, not to the objective, illness-centered risk factors, but to the subjective, person-centered risk factors—hopelessness, feeling trapped without choices, facing loss or risk of loss, isolation, alienation, emotional or physical pain, lack of resources, powerlessness, giving up, and betrayal. Perhaps our program was providing "universal suicide prevention" by giving everyone an ongoing emotional, "no fail," relationship with a staff member who wouldn't let them disappear or drop out, and who was relentlessly empowering and hopeful, while pursuing resources and community connections with them.

Ironically enough, shortly after I published that article, the Village had its first suicide. Arthur was a sweet young man, who was always cooperative and friendly. He spent time hanging out with us, but never really got his life going. He never had a regular girlfriend, completed a school program, held a good job, or had his own apartment. One day, he took a risk and asked a waitress for a date; he saw her weekly at the local diner and had a crush on her. He nervously bumbled his request. She politely turned him down. The next day, he returned to apologize, but he bumbled that, too, and she was flustered and walked away. The third time led to her telling him he'd better leave her alone; she knew he had a mental illness and was going to call the police if he kept harassing her. He was devastated. He'd had enough of being the nice guy who finishes last. He stopped his medications, changed to a "bad boy" wearing a black leather jacket, and started hanging out with drug users. He got more depressed and had trouble thinking straight. I hospitalized him, trying to restabilize him, but we couldn't get him back on track. Over the next few months, he got kicked out of the place he was living in, kept using drugs, got dirtier and dirtier, stopped hanging out with us, and ended up homeless, sleeping in the park. He tried to withdraw from the Village. We kept reaching out to him over and over. He ended up hanging himself.

We had a funeral with his family that included a large crowd of people who knew him both from the Village and when he was younger. I wondered if he would've killed himself if he had realized that so many people liked and cared about him.

As staff, we were emotionally shaken, too. We hired a consultant to help us figure out if we'd made mistakes we could learn from. After he heard the story, the consultant wanted to know why we'd kept reaching out to him in the park, when he'd given us an "out" by withdrawing from the program. We knew he was at risk and we had a chance to disconnect to protect ourselves from blame and liability. Why hadn't we taken it? I was so naïve that it took me a few minutes to understand what he was asking us. We were trying to figure out how we could've saved Arthur, not how to avoid liability. I didn't realize that most suicide interventions are actually designed to reduce liability, not to help the person. We stopped listening to him and comforted each other instead.

So, what should we do about suicide?

First, look back at those suicide statistics and notice that 99.6% of people who think about suicide aren't going to kill themselves. The vast majority of people we talk to about suicide do not need their lives to be saved by risk prevention. They need support for whatever they're going through. We need to make sure we're serving those 99.6% well, not just preventing deaths. Similar to substance abuse, we need a full spectrum of responses targeted at each of the "motivational interviewing" stages of making the decision to kill yourself and acting on it. Each stage needs a different approach; so, there is no one-size-fits-all answer (including psychiatric hospitalization):

- *Precontemplative:* These people are the majority of us who are not even thinking about killing ourselves. A few simple screening questions answered honestly can identify these people who do not need personal suicide prevention efforts. We can do some public education preventatively, so that if they do start to think about suicide, they won't feel it's that strange and "beyond the frontier" and would be willing to share their feeling honestly with someone else.
- *Contemplative:* These people have thoughts of suicide, but not plans. These thoughts can either be "death wishes"—"I wish I wouldn't wake up tomorrow"—or "suicidal thoughts without intent"—"I have the thought that I could turn my car into traffic and kill myself, but I'd never do that." Thoughts like these can sometimes bring relief to people who feel trapped in their suffering. At least, there's a way out. They may indulge in these thoughts or be seduced by them. That's a bad idea, though, because suicidal thoughts, just like every kind of thoughts, grow the more we pay attention to them and indulge in them. Even if we never kill ourselves, having chronic death wishes or suicidal thoughts make for bad musings. We don't want to encourage them to stick around inside our heads. People who are at a contemplative stage are paying attention to the idea of suicide more than the actual action and its likely consequences in reality. A few nonjudgmental questions about the likely damage a real suicide would do can help emphasize that suicide isn't a realistic choice for them. Ask what they think would happen after they die? If it's going to hell or they don't know, maybe it's not worth taking the chance. You can't change your mind and come back. (Check out Kevin Hine's videos. He jumped off the Golden Gate bridge and then changed his mind and is one of the few who miraculously survived.) "Giving up" by killing yourself is most often an illusionary solution. Spend the time thinking about how to make life worth living, instead of how peaceful death away from your problems will be.

- *Planning:* These people are developing concrete plans for how they could kill themselves. They're probably scared of going ahead with killing themselves, and they should be. There's a lot of things that could go wrong. (As a psychiatric resident, I had a job of going around the medical hospital talking to the patients who had tried to kill themselves, but failed, to help them figure out what they should do next. I saw all kinds of methods fail: One man put a gun to his temple and shot, but he slipped and blew out his eye and part of his brain, but he lived. Another man jumped off a freeway bridge and landed on a car, fracturing his hips and spine, and he was crippled, in chronic pain, impotent and peeing into a bag after that. Someone swallowed razor blades and someone else drank bleach. Both ended up in terrible pain with a tube replacing their esophagus and trouble swallowing solid food after that. Someone else cut his wrists severing all his tendons; so, he couldn't use his fingers anymore. After I met enough people like that, I learned that nothing is foolproof. I also began to believe that we don't get to choose when we die any more than we choose when we're born.) If someone is not afraid of dying, maybe they've been trained as a soldier or a gang member, maybe they've been through something very traumatic that took away that fear, or maybe they've gotten so hopeless they've stopped caring. Help them care again. There's also the pain to be frightened of and the reality of how suicide will affect the people, and animals, they love. Contrary to popular opinion, suicide is almost never a selfish decision. Almost everyone is trying hard to stay alive and thinks everyone would be better off without them, but they're wrong. Suicide isn't an "easy way out" of your problems and the living do suffer. Help them make a "safety plan" of what they can do, instead of killing themselves—how can they distract and comfort themselves? Who can they reach out to? How can they get rid of their guns and other weapons?
- *Taking action:* These people actually make suicide attempts. Suicidal actions can be anything from writing a note, giving away possessions or pets, practicing putting a noose around their neck, or buying alcohol, pills, or most dangerously, a gun. However, it's important to distinguish suicide attempts (which are intended to end their life) from self-harm behaviors, usually cutting or burning

themselves (which are intended to focus sensations on their bodies, either to escape from unbearable feelings or to escape from emptiness or numbness. Some people even say that after they've cut or burned themselves, they no longer feel like they want to die. Taking suicidal action is the most dangerous stage and calls for rapid action to stop them. Now, the safety plan is put into place by the people who care about them, rather than by themselves, and/or they need to go to a crisis program or hospital. Everyone who mentions that they have thought about suicide doesn't need to go to the hospital. That self-protective, risk-management practice scares people away from talking about suicide and increases their isolation and risk. But people at the taking action stage may well need involuntary hospitalization. Do be aware, however, that the riskiest time for suicide seems to be shortly after hospital discharge and a traumatic, unhelpful hospitalization may increase the risk of suicide, rather than preventing it.

- *Maintenance:* These people have long-standing suicidal thoughts, plans, and/or actions that have become part of their lives on an ongoing basis, not just impulsively or in acute crisis, and often make their lives miserable. They are likely to resent others telling them why they should stay alive or giving them suggestions on how to handle their suicidality, "I've already tried that. It doesn't work for me." They more often need someone to be with them, to empathize and share the burden of their suffering, more than they need any concrete problem solving or "answers." There may be things that make their suicidality better and worse, or make them more or less likely to act on it, which can be addressed and improved—for example, staying away from alcohol when they're depressed or keeping their guns at someone else's house might be lifesaving, even though neither one decreases suffering. Involuntary hospitalizations, especially repetitively, aren't likely to help long-standing suicidality. Focusing on strengths and protective factors may be a more useful approach. (I remember one man who used to call the on-call line night after night, saying he was suicidal. One day, he took an overdose of pills and got frightened and called the paramedics to take him to the hospital to rescue him because he realized he didn't really want to die. He then took some risks coming out as gay to his parents, dating, and enrolling in school. Months later, I asked him why he was no longer calling the on-call line, and he said, "I'm too busy living now, to have time to think about killing myself.")

- *Resolution:* These people have gone through a time of suicidality and may have made a serious attempt but are no longer suicidal. They don't need suicide prevention, but they may need help making meaning out of the experience, finding meaning in everyday activities after their life-and-death struggle, and reconnecting to other people who haven't been through suicidality and might not understand. It can be tempting to hide both scars and stories, but secrets in the shadows have a tendency to come back to haunt us. ("Live Through This" is a website that since 2010 has been collecting "raw, honest stories of survival, and pairing them with portraits of those survivors in the moments just after telling their stories—putting faces and names to the statistics" that can help break through the shame, isolation, and stigma of being a suicide attempt survivor.)

Suicide rates continue to climb, especially among young people. Soon, we may be entering an era when almost all of us have had some serious exposure to suicide. I wonder how we'll react to that or how it will change us. I've had much more exposure to suicide both personally and professionally than most people and although I suspect, and hope, suicide will never become accepted and routine, it's not as far beyond the frontier anymore.

I recently went to a walk for suicide that felt like every other charity walk my wife drags me to. Most of the participants were high school students, most of whom knew someone who killed themselves. The American Foundation for Suicide Prevention has beads of different colors to identify each person's connection to suicide, so we can find people who share our experiences: White—lost a child, Red—lost a spouse or partner, Gold—lost a parent, Orange—lost a sibling, Purple—lost a relative or friend, Silver—lost first responder/military, Green—struggled personally, Blue—support the cause, and Teal—friends and family of someone who struggles. It was a moving moment when they had people wearing each color raise their beads in turn, while noting how many other people were wearing the same beads and could relate directly to your suffering.

There are so many ways for suicide to impact all of us.

Physical health, medical illnesses, and early death

The news that people with schizophrenia and other serious mental illnesses die on average 20–25 years younger than the general population hit all of us like a punch to the gut about 15 years ago. How could that be? How could we not have noticed that? I checked the Village records and, sure enough, our members were dying in their late 50s and early 60s, too. The strangest thing was that when I thought about the people who had died, although I'd been to many of their funerals, I didn't remember ever reacting that they had died young. To be more accurate, it hadn't really struck me that they were relatively young. They hadn't just died young, they'd aged young. So, what was going on?

The initial stigmatizing view, that they were dying from drug ODs and violence and suicides, just wasn't true. These people were mostly dying from "natural causes"—mostly cancer and heart disease, just like everyone else. But why were they dying younger? Maybe from "hard living" in poverty and on the streets, always under stress, beaten, using drugs and alcohol?

I started going to lectures to try to figure it out and found myself listening with a large group to Dr. Ken Duckworth, the medical director of NAMI, from Harvard. He said that over 90% of the early deaths could be accounted for by the normal cardiac risk factors that had been identified decades earlier in the Framingham Heart Study, a multigenerational study that began in 1948:

- Smoking cigarettes
- Obesity
- High cholesterol
- High blood pressure
- Diabetes
- Lack of exercise

Each of these factors statistically can take years off your life, and worse than that, they interact with each other, each one increasing the risks of the others, so the combined risk of several factors is much higher than just adding up the risks independently (which means, by the way, that even if you can't get rid of one of the factors, say smoking, you could still lower its negative impact if you took care of the others, for example, by lowering your weight, cholesterol, and blood pressure). People with schizophrenia and other serious mental illnesses routinely have lots and lots of those risk factors, which accurately predict they die decades early.

Then, he delivered the knockout blow: Both these risk factors and the resultant medical conditions go largely untreated. If someone without serious mental illness smokes and is overweight and gets diabetes and high blood pressure, they get a stack of pills from their primary care doctors to try to keep them going. Far too often, people with serious mental illnesses don't have primary care doctors or get routine ongoing medical care. And they're not referred to specialists. Dr. Duckworth asked us how many of us had a friend or relative who had an angiography procedure for heart disease. Almost everyone raised our hands. Then, he asked us if we knew anyone with schizophrenia who had an angiography. Even though we were all mental health professionals, only two people raised their hands, and they knew the same person. People with schizophrenia aren't getting treatment for their conditions.

Bottom line: They are dying and aging early because they have poor health habits and they don't get primary care or specialty care to save them from the consequences.

A large movement began then to try to address this problem by integrating health and mental health clinics, so people could get their psychiatric and primary care and specialty care at the same place. But should the psychiatrist move into the medical clinics, "co-location," or the medical doctors move into the mental health clinics, "reverse co-location"? It may not surprise you to learn that the federal payment rates are much higher in the medical clinics than in the mental health clinics—so, mostly psychiatrists moved into health clinics, creating "integrated services."

In my opinion, this hasn't really worked for people with schizophrenia and other psychosis. The main reasons they weren't getting medical care in the first place had to do with the stigma and discrimination of the medical practitioners against psychotic patients, the inflexibility of their clinic systems, and their inability to handle people with severely disorganized and/or disruptive behavior. Those clinics and their staff didn't change their attitudes or their culture to better engage and serve people with psychosis and other extraordinary experiences. Co-location worked to get psychiatric medications prescribed to many more depressed and anxious patients in the health clinics, but the psychotic people still weren't welcomed and largely still receive their mental health services in specialized mental health programs, including ACT programs.

Reverse co-location has worked, when we could find a primary care doctor willing to work within the atmosphere of a mental health clinic, and when we could figure out how to pay them as well as the health clinics can. What many programs like the Village have figured out is that we have to use our own staff to take people to medical appointments, help support them while they're there so they don't get kicked out, help teach them how to use their medications and often even dispense their medical medications for them, back at the mental health program or in their homes for them to get effective medical care. We developed rather expensive, time-consuming "supported medical care." Many mental health workers resent having to spend so much time on medical care; so, we needed to hire more nursing staff. The Village's medication management system that helps people take their psychiatric medications is handling 1/3 medical medications and 2/3 psychiatric medications—without any way to bill the medical system for any of those services. Most Community Mental Health Clinics can't divert scarce mental health treatment resources to either reverse co-located or supported medical care; so, people are still dying early.

Additionally, there have been efforts to try to address removing those risk factors directly. What if we ban smoking in our psychiatric facilities and try to run smoking cessation programs? What if we run exercise and healthy eating programs? Well, at least in my hands, not much happens. Before we blame the medications—and clearly the second-generation antipsychotics that we use now, especially Zyprexa, Seroquel, and Clozaril, that contribute to weight gain, high cholesterol, and diabetes in alarming numbers, while lots of our medications contribute to sedation and weight gain—or their symptoms, keep in mind that these "healthy living choices" programs don't work very well in the general population either.

I think we need to make a mind shift here from treating illness to enhancing health. Health is not the absence of illness. Taking blood pressure, diabetes, and cholesterol medications and an inhaler for lung disease don't make you healthy, they just protect you from some of the consequences of your unhealthy life.

Health Is Not the Absence of Illness

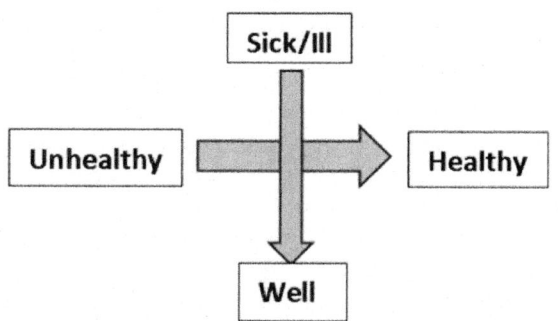

Some people have serious illnesses but are healthy.
Some people don't have illnesses but are unhealthy.
Some people have illnesses and are unhealthy.
Being unhealthy can lead to a lot of illnesses and kill you.

Look back at those Framingham cardiac risk factors. For the vast majority of people, mentally ill or not, they are the result of unhealthiness, not independent illnesses. So, how do we help people be healthier?

We can take a deficit-based approach and work on risk factors. For example, the Adverse Childhood Events Study (ACES) shows that childhood trauma has a substantial impact on lifelong health; so, we could try to help people overcome the impacts of their traumas. We also know that anxiety and depression contribute to cigarette smoking, emotional eating, and hypertension; so, we could try to impact their emotions (presumably while also reducing the usage of metabolically detrimental medications). Getting more "natural" pleasure in life while developing safer pleasure center stimulators to rely on than opiates, benzos, cigarettes, drugs, alcohol, sugar, and carbohydrates—like prayer, empathy, love, dark chocolate, and caffeine—might help. (This third one is particularly promising, in my opinion, since many of our members who died early were people on opiates and benzos, in addition to these other risk factors, but it's also very challenging.)

Or we can take a strengths-based approach. For example, the World Health Organization (WHO) Department of Ageing and Life Course says in their website:

> "*Healthy Ageing* is about creating the environments and opportunities that enable people to be and do what they value throughout their lives. Everybody can experience *Healthy Ageing*. Being free of disease or infirmity is not a requirement for *Healthy Ageing* as many older adults have one or more health conditions that, when well controlled, have little influence on their wellbeing.
>
> WHO defines *Healthy Ageing* "as the process of developing and maintaining the **functional ability** that enables **wellbeing** in older age". **Functional ability** is about having the capabilities that enable all people to be and do what they have reason to value. This includes a person's ability to:
>
> - meet their basic needs;
> - to learn, grow and make decisions;
> - to be mobile;
> - to build and maintain relationships; and
> - to contribute to society."

I quoted this for two reasons: First, because they've landed back on the very same factors I've been emphasizing throughout this book in the self-identity and relationships dimensions, and second, because they completed the circle—the reason these people are dying early is because they're aging early and that's because they're living and aging unhealthily and that's, to a large extent, because we're neglecting those five abilities for most people with psychosis. If we're predominantly illness- and deficit-focused, we're going to be very limited in our ability to impact people living long and healthy lives. Ultimately, if they are impoverished, repressed, passive, isolated, and excluded, they're not going to be healthy or long-living.

Education and work

A good mental health program will hopefully tell people to go to school or work, instead of telling them to just stay at home on disability to avoid pressure and relapses. Unemployment is really quite bad for people. It's depressing, hard to structure your life, and hard to find meaning in it. Families may agree, even if they're somewhat scared, thinking that it would be good for you to go to work or school. "It'll give you something to do. It might be therapeutic. But we don't want it to be too stressful or cause a relapse. Maybe we can find something to do at the mental health center like a 'sheltered workshop,' or maybe you can volunteer or take an easy class 'for fun.' Just make sure there's some mental health worker watching over things to make sure everything is alright."

That widespread, appealing, protective approach might indeed help people who are in the early stages of recovery, building hope and empowerment or working their way up the hill back to the community, but it isn't a good way to build self-responsibility or meaningful roles or reconnect with the community. For those recovery stages, you have to find "real jobs."

In "normal life," we don't work because it's good for us though it likely, indeed, is. We work for money and meaning, two things that almost all of us, including people with psychosis, badly need, and are both often hard to find anywhere else. (Most of us, meeting someone new at a party, identify ourselves first by what we do for a job. After that may follow our family and romantic relationships and, then, our other passions. Introducing yourself as on disability for a mental illness is a terrible conversation starter.) If people get stuck with "therapeutic" work, they may be left without enough money and meaning.

Unfortunately, many of the jobs in our current economy that don't require specialized skills, training, or experience don't provide enough money and meaning either. Minimum wage, while higher than Social Security disability, doesn't pay the rent either without two or three jobs or two or three roommates, but it's still likely to be a substantially higher standard of living. Also, many people are afraid of losing their SSI checks entirely, that may have taken years to get, if they try to work. After all, then they'd no longer be permanently, totally disabled. In reality, it's quite rare to lose SSI by trying to work unless you start making a significant amount of money and don't need the SSI anymore, but it's still a scary possibility. Even when SSI doesn't stop the checks, they do make deductions for working, which unless you're very careful, can lead to mandatory deductions for "overpayments" or even checks stopping for a while, either of which can lead to not begin able to pay the rent and wondering why you even tried to work. Even if you do it all correctly, when $1 is being deducted out of the SSI check for every $2 that are earned, so that the net pay is about half of minimum wage, it can be hard to keep people motivated to look for a minimum wage job or hold onto it. Oh, and by the way, if you lose the job, it may take months for your SSI to be restored to your full payments—another chance to be evicted.

Yet, minimum wage is precisely where most people, psychotic or not, have to start.

It seems to me, we often begin with people who don't have any special skills, training, or experience by doing elaborate assessments of their job interests and their passions, so that we can help them find a job match with enough meaning to sustain them. Then, we face the stark reality of what minimum wage jobs are available—for someone with holes in their resume and perhaps obvious mental health symptoms that may further restrict their opportunities. We might tell them that the job is just an entry job, a first step, but we likely won't tell them that if they hold that job for 6 months, the State Department of Vocational Rehabilitation will close their case as a success and not give them any further training or job placement assistance to move onward. (The situation is even more difficult with VA benefits.)

No wonder people, and their families, so often get discouraged and want to know if they can just stay at our clubhouse or day treatment, or maybe volunteer somewhere. But if they give up, their best chance at money and meaning is gone. We've learned to sit with our members, and sometimes their families, to do the math to explain why they should take a minimum wage job, even part-time, despite all these challenges. Here's an example of the math:

- Basic SSI check = $944/month.
- Working minimum wage at 20 hours at California's minimum wage of $13/hour = $260 per week or about $1,092 per month.

- SSI check deduction will be $1092 − $85 = $1007 divided by 2 = $503.
- New SSI check = $944 − $503 = $441.
- New combined income = $1,092 + $441 = $1,533, which is $589 more than you had without the job, and may be enough for a small apartment or a used car or a girlfriend (or all three, if you can get her to move in with you and share the rent!).

Why does it work out to be so much more than you probably expected? Because you're so poor on SSI that even part-time minimum wage work pays enough to substantially improve your quality of life.

Here are some tips to try and help you get a good job:

- If you're not responsible and don't have good work habits, start with a job that tends to be an entry job, hiring mostly young people, because they're used to helping people build work habits. If you start a work training program within mental health or a volunteer program, ask yourself if this program is going to help you develop good work habits or practice poor habits while excusing them. Expect to be fired repeatedly until you do develop responsible job behaviors. We used to tell people that the average American takes until their sixth job to hold one for 6 months. Don't blame your firings on your symptoms or stigma or your medications. You need to act like a worker to hold a job.
- If you can be responsible, you can probably get and hold a job, unless we're in a recession. It's likely not going to be the job you want, and it'll pay poorly. We had a recruiter from Target come to the Village, and he said, "If you can do three things—show up to work, do what you're told, and not steal anything—you'll be ahead of two thirds of the new employees we get who we end up firing for one of those three things."
- Once you're responsible and have proven you can hold a job, you can decide if you want to try to move up through job experience or go back to school for training. School isn't for people who think work is too hard. To succeed at school, you usually need to be more self-directed and self-disciplined than at work and you're not usually getting paid. School is for people who are responsible and

who want to make a temporary sacrifice so that they can get a higher paid and more meaningful job, not for irresponsible people.
- There's a difference between support and accommodations. You may be able to get support from the Department of Vocational Rehabilitation or a job coach or even from friends and family (after all, most of us got support getting and holding our first jobs from friends and family, why shouldn't you?). Accommodations are alterations at the job site provided by the employer and require disclosing your "disabling" condition to them, something you may or may not want to do.
- If you have noticeably strange or interfering symptoms or behaviors, you're entitled to accommodations, but then you're going to have to have something important to offer the employer to get them to go out of their way for you. Figure out what you really have to offer and sell it, or figure out what you have to do, so that you can fit in and be productive without disclosing your condition and using accommodations. As Fred Frese put it, "The best time to self-disclose is when you have tenure." Instead of starting with a job that requires you to always be on and "give 110%," choose a job you can keep even when you have some bad days, as one job developer with mental illness told me, that "requires 70%, so you'll have a cushion."
- Even if you were taught that you can be whatever you want to be if you know what you want and really work hard at it, that may not be true, especially at first. Instead of giving up entirely if you can't find enough meaning in work, try to find some meaning outside of work, so your work doesn't have to be as satisfying, and/or find an employer whose mission and purpose you find meaningful, so that you can feel good about your job even if you're only a small cog in a big process. It may matter to you if you're doing clerical or janitorial work for a company making spaceships vs. one making cigarettes. One of the reasons people are attracted to working within mental health is that we have a good mission.
- The longer you work, the more your life will be centered around your job and its requirements, instead of your illness and its symptoms. You'll learn to structure your spare time, your tasks, your meals, your vacations, even your symptoms, around your

work schedule. You'll become a worker who happens to have a mental illness, instead of a person with mental illness who happens to have a job. That's when working really pays off by propelling you into those later stages of recovery.

Frustration should lead to advocacy

Taken together, the practical sections in this chapter describe an impressively challenging, if not outright dismaying picture. Recovery depends both on each person's efforts and on our community's and the system's availability. Martha Long, the founding Village director, used to say that most of what we do to help people, far more than treating their illnesses, is to try to remove the obstacles to them getting the services and supports they need to get the lives that they want. Larry Davidson, a longtime champion of the Recovery movement and prolific writer at Yale, has similarly oftentimes suggested that social exclusion and discrimination are often more profound barriers to recovery than the illness itself. The point of overcoming disability isn't just to reduce suffering but to be able to pursue your own goals with as little interference as possible. Teaching a blind person to read Braille is hardly of use if there aren't any signs in Braille where you live and work.

There's so much more to feel damaged by and angry about beyond the psychotic experiences themselves. Many of the people I've known spend far more time trying to get their basic needs met, than trying to get well. All the staff I've worked with spend more time trying to help people get their basic needs met than trying to help them get well. There are frustrating obstacles everywhere we turn.

Many of the first organizations of people with mental illnesses called themselves "survivors," but unlike cancer survivors, they didn't mean that they'd survived their illnesses. They meant that they had survived their mental health treatments and their community's stigmatizing, rejecting reactions to them. They've organized themselves for several decades using a civil rights model to push for changes.

Advocacy is our strongest tool to improve things. Sometimes, we're advocating for an individual person—trying to help them get their SSI check straightened out, or to get a support animal to bring warmth to their lives, or to get a cardiologist to treat them, or any of a million other daily needs and tasks. Sometimes, we're advocating for changes in the system—like Jim Pries who worked tirelessly as a lawyer and executive director for Mental Health Advocacy Services in Los Angeles until his recent death, fighting many legal causes, including making the welfare office more accessible to people with serious mental illnesses. Sometimes, we're advocating for our communities to be more accepting, inclusive, understanding, and compassionate—fighting stigma and discrimination. I've had the privilege to collaborate with amazingly courageous advocates all around the world who keep fighting each day to make things better for all of us.

> *Certainly, not all people with mental illnesses can speak eloquently for themselves, most can't, but we have to be cautious that when we're advocating for them, we're really helping give them a voice and not just speaking for them.*
>
> *Josh is a man who often sat dominating one of the tables at the Village Deli with an array of books and papers. On seeing him, most people would not see what he sees—a serious lifelong philosophy student working on a book describing the intersection of early Christian theology and quantum physics. After all, this isn't a Starbucks, and he doesn't have a laptop computer he's writing on. He's a rather dirty, homeless middle-aged Black man, his clothes covered with food stains, and the table is a mess. I, however, like talking with people like Josh; so, if I wasn't too tired, because it's hard work keeping up with Josh's conversation, I'd sometimes pull up a chair, and he'd happily clear some space for me at his table. Listening to him could be rather like following one of my Caltech professor's lectures in his field's esoteric jargon.*
>
> *"I've been closely watching the Village for over 20 years, from when it was a Homeless Drop-in Center before it was the Village. While other programs have come and gone, the Village has consistently helped hundreds and hundreds of people."*
>
> *"Why do you think that is, Josh?"*

"I think that's because we're in a particularly strong spiritual space grounded in the wisdom of the early followers of Christ, but can you tell me the story of the history of the Village?"

I took a breath and began, *"The Village's parent organization is Mental Health America of Los Angeles, which was originally founded by Clifford Beers in 1909. MHA's primary mission has always been an advocacy mission."*

His eyes lit up, and he clapped his hands together joyfully. *"That's it! I was right. The reason you're so successful is because you're grounded in advocacy, giving voice to the weak and marginalized who have no voice. You've stayed true to that, instead of losing your way like so many other programs do."*

"I should tell you that Clifford Beers was a person with a severe manic-depressive condition, including paranoid and grandiose delusions and repeated suicidality. He spent years in psychiatric hospitals and even wrote a book about his experiences called 'A Mind that Found Itself,' which both highlighted how brutal and unhelpful treatment could be and also helped destigmatize serious mental illness because he was a Yale graduate who was willing to openly share his experiences when he was released from the hospital. With the aid of powerful friends like psychiatrist Adolf Meyers and philosopher and the 'father of American psychology' William James, they created the National Committee for Mental Hygiene, a forerunner of MHA, which spearheaded efforts to improve the understanding and the care of people with mental illnesses, to improve research and training, and to reform laws regarding people with mental illnesses."

"So, someone like me partnered with someone like you to make things better for everyone."

I hesitated and then nodded, *"They were more famous than you and me, but basically, yes, they did."*

> After all these years, I still think it's worth spending the effort to listen to someone who thinks differently than everyone else. They might see something I can't. By the way, even though Josh won't believe that he has a mental illness or accept any government disability money, that year we got him to accept an HUD Section 8 housing certificate, so that finally, he got off the street and into a place of his own, "so I can have a quiet place to study and write." I also included him in interviews for new staff and in strategic planning meetings for the Village. He adapts to the roles, although he's still dirty, and makes incredibly valuable contributions, for example, saying that one young woman we were considering hiring as a personal service coordinator might have trouble working with people on the streets or in their homes in the rough neighborhood we were located in because her older brothers had always protected her and he wasn't convinced she could protect herself. He also was hesitant about another older woman who seemed to think she knew what other people needed without asking them first. "She might create barriers for people, instead of going with the flow and working with people in whatever ways they can accept."
>
> One of the most special things about the Village was how staff and members created and advocated together.

I want to close this chapter with the story of the MHA bell that infused the culture of the Village throughout the years I worked there: Richard Van Horn, the longtime MHALA CEO and arguably the most important mental health advocate in California, would always tell this story from our MHA history of an unlikely group of courageous people who got over their fears and made a real difference, to new and old employees, to remind us of who we were and what our mission really was:

> In World War II, there were conscientious objectors to the military draft, mostly highly principled religious people, Mennonites, Quakers, and other pacifists who were willing to be spit at, cursed, and even beaten because of their pacifist principles. (I didn't know this. I thought conscientious

objectors began in the Vietnam War.) The government set up a system where they were required to give public service, instead of military service. One of the public service jobs they were given was to work in the most undesirable mental hospitals in the country. They were astounded by the squalor, the violence, the fear, and especially, the abuse in these neglected wards. Never good places, with almost all of the staff gone to the war, there were wards of hundreds of people, mostly hungry and nearly naked, watched over by a lone attendant who locked them all in when he went off on his lunch break. They applied their nonviolent principles to bring humanity to these wards—both for the patients and the staff. Using a Life magazine exposé, support from Eleanor Roosevelt, the first Mental Health Week, political advocacy including the governor in Minnesota, and even an educational newsletter for the newly created psychiatric technicians, they transformed the world of mental health.

One of the striking things that they did was to make the MHA bell. The MHA bell is a large iron bell weighing about 300 pounds. It was made in 1956 by melting down the chains that had been used to chain the patients in state hospitals, chaining them to their beds, to the walls, and to iron balls. The inscription on the bell reads, "Cast from shackles which bound them, this bell shall ring out hope for the mentally ill and victory over mental illness." Pause and think about that for a minute: We're not talking ancient history here. Relatively recently, we were literally chaining the people we were treating.

One year, while I was listening to the bell's story again, I realized that for us to be able to ring that bell in triumph now there must have been a moment in the past, actually there must have been a lot of moments, when somebody must have physically unchained someone to get the iron. I could almost see that moment, with a staff member and a patient facing each other, both uncomfortable, both far *outside their comfort zone. The staff is scared that if he unchains the patient, they'll attack them, but reluctantly dares to trust the patient. The patient wonders if the staff is really going to help them, or if they should take the opportunity to lash out in anger "at the person who led me by a leash to the toilet the day before," but reluctantly dares to trust the staff. They both work together, believing some new partnership is possible, and remove the chains.*

Chapter 17

Bon Voyage

We've come to the end of my guidebook. It's time for you—whether you're a person experiencing psychosis or other extraordinary experiences, a family member or friend, a community member, a mental health staff or student—to head out into your own adventures. I suppose I've written the book that I wish I'd had when I was first captivated by psychosis and other extraordinary experiences. I hope that I've helped you see how if you can free yourself from the oversimplification of *DSM*, the reductionism of the prevailing medical model, and the dehumanization of much of our current practices and beliefs, you can have very rich, diverse, humane, and healing journeys. Don't forget your compass!

These journeys require heart, minds, and hands. I've tried to give you stories to touch and inspire your heart, experience and knowledge to focus your mind, and practical tools and strategies to direct your hands. You can use this book as a reference book if you get stuck along the way. You can look up the people, programs, and research that I've included along the way, and maybe they'll influence you as they have me. But mostly, you must travel to learn and grow from your own experiences as they emerge.

You might still feel somewhat overwhelmed by the complexity and the challenges in these journeys, and you're probably right to be unsure of yourself. After all, these journeys are beyond our comfort zones and our frontiers. They can be very difficult and even tragic at times. Even after all these years, I have to continuously be open to what's new and unfamiliar about the individual I'm currently journeying with, or I'll be humbled and a poor companion.

At bottom, however, you can do this if you have three traits: curiosity, commitment, and acceptance.

About a decade ago, one of my son's classmates at medical school asked if I'd be a guest lecturer for his series on international psychiatry, sharing what I'd learned on my world trip. I naturally agreed, but he contacted me again a couple weeks later, saying that his faculty advisor had recognized me from Steve Lopez's book, "The Soloist," and since the movie had just come out, could I include something about that experience in my lecture even though it wasn't related to international psychiatry? I again agreed, but this time I had a condition:

"I need you to get a copy of the movie and set up your computer to play three scenes for me."

"Sure, what scenes?"

"The first scene is early in the movie when Steve is driving to work at the LA Times building in downtown LA, when he happens to see under an underpass a homeless man playing a cello with two strings, seemingly lost in the music. Everyone else drives right by Nathaniel, too busy or maybe too unconcerned to notice him, to even acknowledge his existence. Steve pulls his car over and walks up to Nathaniel to find out who he is and what his story is. He approaches him with genuine curiosity. He engages him and finds out that he was one of the first Black students at Julliard. He really wants to know more about him. How did he end up on the streets? How could this happen? What can he do to help?

"The second scene is later on when Steve decides to spend the night sleeping on the street with Nathaniel on Skid Row to see what it's really like. Nathaniel shows him tricks he's learned to survive on those streets, including having two wooden paddles to hit rats to keep them away, one that has Mozart and one that has Beethoven written on it. It's not that we have to sleep in Skid Row. In fact, I, and everyone else Steve asked, urged him not to. It just seemed too dangerous. After all, I'd heard that they were removing two

dead bodies a day from Skid Row. But Steve was committed to leave his comfort zone and his world to experience Nathaniel's world. We're unlikely to actually help people if we always expect them to come to our offices, at our hours, following our expectations and rules for them. We should be committed to being on this journey with them, wherever it may take us.

"The third scene is when Steve has spent an enormous amount of effort and finally arranged for a supported apartment with LAMP for Nathaniel to move in. He's incredibly pleased with what he's been able to do for Nathaniel, but Nathaniel is hesitant, and refuses to move to the apartment. Steve is now incredibly frustrated, in disbelief of how things could be going so wrong. Why wouldn't Nathaniel accept his help? This moment, when the helper has arranged everything only to be refused since he's not really seeing it from the other person's perspective, will occur multiple times in any journey like this. Steve does two things to get Nathaniel to at least look at the apartment. He tells him he can use it as a studio where he can play his cello and store it safely protected from the weather and thieves, and when Nathaniel tells him that he thinks that Steve is God in an airplane flying above them, he accepts his reality saying that if he's God, God wants him to see the room. Both strategies are unconventional and risky, but they're also accepting Nathaniel's reality, instead of acting out of frustration, demanding or even forcing Nathaniel to do what Steve believes is best for him. Nathaniel takes the first step to getting his own apartment."

I wanted those students to see those three traits—curiosity, commitment, and acceptance—at work, and see how they, too, are qualified to help people like Nathaniel.

I've had limited contact with Steve since then, but I've read many of his newspaper columns as he continues to share Nathaniel's life and advocate for people who are homeless. One of his recent columns, "A homeless musician changed my life. I wish I could do more to change his," on September 15, 2019 shared in an honest and heartfelt way how challenging and oftentimes frustrating both of these journeys had been. Here's an excerpt:

"When we met in 2005, I wouldn't have guessed we'd still be in each other's lives this far down the road.... Another thing I wouldn't have guessed is that all these years later, Los Angeles would still have thousands of people living under the stars, many of them reeling from mental illnesses as severe as his.... Nathaniel showed me a world I knew little about.... Early on, when I wanted to help Nathaniel but had no idea what I was doing, I'd call a psychiatrist for guidance [that was me], naïvely hoping that someone more knowledgeable would have an easy answer. I still have moments when I'm lost and frustrated as I try to help Nathaniel. And I still seek advice. But I no longer expect quick fixes.... Along the way Nathaniel became a part of my family, and he delivered on his part of the bargain. I still struggle to deliver on my end."

Beginning with curiosity, commitment, and acceptance, Steve has become a lifelong traveler beyond the frontier, and so can you.

Last story

Later this week, you may go to a grocery store and you might see a guy in a wheelchair working there, putting the pickles and the chips on the shelf and posting the prices. You might think, "Look at that guy working hard, being productive, even in his condition." You might even go over to him and shake his hand and say, "Congratulations. I think that's great that you're working here making something of yourself."

Or you might see a guy who is obviously developmentally disabled, who has Down's Syndrome, working there, putting the pickles and the chips on the shelf and posting the prices. You might think, "Look at that guy working hard, being productive, even in his condition." You might even go over to him and shake his hand and say, "Congratulations. I think that's great that you're working here making something of yourself."

But, if you see a guy who is obviously psychotic, talking to himself, wearing a tinfoil hat to keep the voices away, working there, putting the pickles and the chips on the shelf and posting the prices, you do not think, "Look at that guy working hare, being productive, even in his condition." You think, "I wonder if it's safe here. Where are my kids at?" (And mental illnesses aren't even that dangerous!) You don't go up to him and shake his hand. You'll decide, "I don't need anything in that aisle today anyway. I'll go another way. (And mental illnesses aren't even that contagious!)

When you can go up to him and shake his hand and say, "Congratulations. I think that's great that you're working here making something of yourself." or better yet, as one consumer advocate told me, when you don't really notice that someone psychotic is working in your grocery store and living in your neighborhood because that's just the normal way things are, just like people in wheelchairs have become, then we'd be living in the kind of world where almost everyone with psychosis could recover.

And wouldn't we all be very proud to be living and working in that world?

Bon voyage!

About the Author:

Mark Ragins, MD was the Medical Director for 27 years at the Mental Health America Village in Long Beach, California, an award-winning model of recovery based mental health services, before leaving to become the only campus psychiatrist at CSULB. His new book, *Journeys Beyond the Frontier: A Rebellious Guide to Psychosis and Other Extraordinary Experiences*, is based on the true stories of more than 30 years of clinical work with some of the most underserved and difficult to engage people in our community. Countless numbers of people came to experience the work being done at the Village firsthand and Mark has given hundreds of presentations and lectures to wide ranging audiences nationally and internationally. He is one of the true pioneers and leaders of person-centered, recovery-based psychiatry.

Many of his writings are posted online, including his short book *A Road to Recovery*, which has been translated into Japanese, Korean, and Czech. He was featured in Steve Lopez's book *The Soloist*. Over the years, Mark has won a number of awards including the American Psychiatric Association's Arnold Van Amerigan Award in Psychiatric Rehabilitation, the Psychiatric Rehabilitation Association's John Beard award for his outstanding lifetime contribution to psychiatric rehabilitation, National Alliance on Mental Illness (NAMI) California's recovery practitioner of the year, as well as being honored by Mental Health Advocacy Services for his lifetime of advocacy efforts on behalf of people with severe mental illnesses and selected as a distinguished fellow by the American Psychiatric Association.

Printed in Great Britain
by Amazon